THE MODERN MIDDLE EAST

The Modern Middle East

A Political History since the First World War

SECOND EDITION

MEHRAN KAMRAVA

UNIVERSITY OF CALIFORNIA PRESS

Berkeley   Los Angeles   London

University of California Press, one of the most distinguished
university presses in the United States, enriches lives around the
world by advancing scholarship in the humanities, social sciences,
and natural sciences. Its activities are supported by the UC Press
Foundation and by philanthropic contributions from individuals
and institutions. For more information, visit www.ucpress.edu.

University of California Press
Berkeley and Los Angeles, California

University of California Press, Ltd.
London, England

Library of Congress Cataloging-in-Publication Data

Kamrava, Mehran, 1964–.
    The modern Middle East : a political history since the First World
War / Mehran Kamrava. —2nd ed.
        p.   cm.
    Includes bibliographical references and index.
    ISBN 978-0-520-26774-9 (cloth : alk. paper)
    ISBN 978-0-520-26775-6 (pbk. : alk. paper)
    1. Middle East—History—20th century.   2. Middle East—
History—21st century.   3. Middle East—Politics and government—
20th century.   4. Middle East—Politics and government—21st
century.   I. Title.
    DS62.8.K365   2011
    956.04—dc22   2010023250

Manufactured in the United States of America

19 18 17 16 15 14 13 12 11
10 9 8 7 6 5 4 3 2 1

This book is printed on Cascades Enviro 100, a 100% postconsumer
waste, recycled, de-inked fiber. FSC recycled certified and processed
chlorine free. It is acid free, Ecologo certified, and manufactured by
BioGas energy.

To Melisa,
Dilara, and Kendra

Contents

Illustrations

MAPS

Tables

Acknowledgments to the First Edition

The research and writing of this book would not have been possible without the kindness and generosity of a number of individuals. I greatly benefited from the research assistance of Annmarie Hunter and Emily Smurthwaite. I am most grateful for their diligence and their enthusiasm for this project from start to finish. Terrence Thorpe, another outstanding student, also read several chapters and gave valuable suggestions. Bradford Dillman, Manochehr Dorraj, Nader Entessar, Mark Gasiorowski, Nikki Keddie, and Mahmood Monshipouri kindly read all or some of the chapters and gave invaluable and insightful advice. Of course, any omissions or shortcomings remain entirely my fault. Work on Chapter 8 was partly funded by a generous grant from the College of Social and Behavioral Sciences at California State University, Northridge.

This book is the outgrowth of more than a decade of teaching and lecturing on the politics and history of the Middle East. In the process, I have learned a great deal from the innumerable students who have shared with me their insights, experiences, criticisms, and comments. Both directly and indirectly, their input is no doubt reflected here. For that, I am grateful.

Chapter 9 is an expanded, much revised version of an article that originally appeared in *Third World Quarterly*, vol. 19, no. 1, 1998, pp. 63–85. I am grateful to *TWQ*'s editor, Shahid Qadir, for permission to quote extensively from the article here.

My wife, Melisa Çanli, deserves special thanks. Over the nearly five years that it took to write this book, she put up with my many solitary hours behind the computer, my frequent mood swings, and my far-too-often frowns. All along, she never wavered in her loving support for my work. As I was in the final stages of preparing the book, she gave birth to our beautiful daughter, Dilara. As a meager token of my love and gratitude, I dedicate this book to them both.

Acknowledgments to the Second Edition

Some five years after its original publication, the book continues to benefit from the input and advice of many colleagues and research assistants who helped with its original inception and its subsequent publication back in 2005. In the intervening years, countless friends and associates, and at times anonymous readers, have pointed out various ways in which the first edition could be improved upon. I am thankful for their input, their constructive criticisms, and their suggestions for improvement. I have been extremely fortunate to work with Naomi Schneider, my editor at the University of California Press, whose guidance, encouragement, and patience with delays in completing this edition were tremendously helpful in shaping the book. Grateful acknowledgment also goes to Simone Popperl, my superb research assistant on this book, especially for her help with updates to many of the tables appearing throughout the manuscript.

Any project of this magnitude is a product of love, and I have been extremely fortunate to be surrounded by a most loving family who selflessly gave me the time and the peace and quiet needed to complete work on this edition. My wife, Melisa, and our daughters, Dilara and Kendra, always provided the loving support and the emotional nourishment that I needed to work on the book's second edition. For that, and for much more that cannot be adequately expressed in words, I dedicate this book to them.

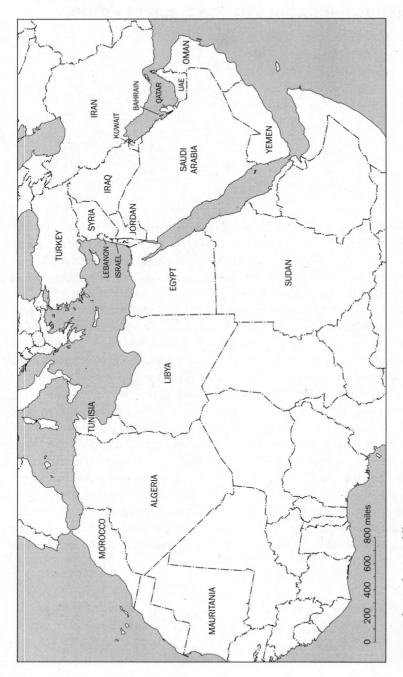

Map 1. The modern Middle East.

Introduction

This book examines the political history of the contemporary Middle East. Although it focuses primarily on the period since the demise of the Ottoman Empire, shortly after World War I, it includes some discussion of pre-Ottoman and Ottoman histories to better clarify the background and the context in which modern Middle Eastern political history has taken shape. The book uses a broad conception of the "Middle East" as a geographic area that extends from Iran in the east to Turkey, Iraq, the Arabian peninsula, the Levant (Lebanon and Syria), and North Africa, including the Maghreb, in the west. *Maghreb* is the Arabic word for "Occident" and has historically been used to describe areas west of Egypt. In modern times it has come to refer to Tunisia, Algeria, and Morocco. Libya is also sometimes included as part of the Maghreb, but it is more commonly grouped with Egypt as belonging to North Africa.

Although there are vast differences between and within the histories, cultures, traditions, and politics of each of these regions within the Middle East, equally important and compelling shared characteristics unify the region. By far the most important of these are language, ethnicity, and religion. Much of Middle Eastern identity is wrapped around the Arabic language. Poetry and storytelling have historically been viewed as elevated art forms. As Fouad Ajami has observed, "[P]oetry, it has been said, was (and is) to the Arabs what philosophy was to the Greeks, law to the Romans, and art to the Persians: the repository and purest expression of their distinctive spirit."[1] Even in places where it is not the national language and is not widely spoken, as in Iran and in Turkey, Arabic, the language of the Quran, permeates life with its many expressions and phrases.

Another common bond in the Middle East is Arab ethnic identity. From Iraq in the north down to the Arabian peninsula and west all the way to

1

Morocco, ethnic Arabs predominate. There are, of course, significant clusters of other ethnic groups. A majority of Iranians are Persians, and Turks are predominant in Turkey. Apart from the so-called "Arab-Israelis"— Palestinians who found themselves in Israel's borders when the country was born in 1948—Jews are the dominant group in Israel. As Chapter 7 discusses, however, there is a debate as to whether Jews are members of an ethnic group or believers in a religious faith. Additionally, there are several "stateless" ethnic groups, by far the largest being the Kurds, who are mostly in southeastern Turkey, western Iran, northern Iraq, and northeastern Syria. There are also sizable Berber communities throughout the Maghreb. But despite these diverse ethnic communities, much of the Arab world remains ethnically homogenous and strongly identifies with its ethnicity.

An even stronger bond uniting the region is religion, with some 97 percent of Middle Easterners identifying themselves as Muslim. That Islam is a whole way of life and not just a religion is a cliché. But regardless of their ethnicity, where they live, and what language they speak, the faithful share a compelling set of beliefs and rituals that transcend national boundaries with remarkable ease. At its strictest, Islam is austere and exacting. But even in its most liberal settings and interpretations, it permeates the life of the Middle East in ways few other phenomena do. Its relentless emphasis on community, its injunctions on the one billion faithful to all face Mecca in prayer and to fast together in the same month, its deep penetration of languages far removed from Arabic, its reverence for the Prophet Muhammad, who called for submission *(Islam)* to God *(Allah)*— all of these reinforce the sense of belonging to a whole far bigger than its individual, national components. Since the early decades of the twentieth century, Islam as a source of cross-national unity has steadily lost ground to state-specific nationalism, but it continues to be a powerful and compelling source of common identification among fellow Muslims around the world, especially in the Middle East.

In addition to the important, uniting phenomena of ethnicity, language, and religion are the curse and the blessings of a common historical heritage. Much of the Middle East, with the exceptions of Iran and Morocco, experienced centuries of Ottoman rule, generally from the mid–sixteenth century up until the waning years of the nineteenth century. The Ottomans' hold on the Middle East was often tenuous and frequently interrupted. Over the centuries, however, for better or for worse, from their capital in Istanbul they managed to leave their imprint on such far-off places as Cairo, Tripoli, and Tunis. Once the Ottomans were gone, the British and the French took their place, leaving on their colonial possessions their own distinctive marks. Perhaps the biggest relic of British rule, aside from the drawing of artificial national borders, was the institution of monarchy, which they secured in almost all the lands they ruled, from Egypt to Jordan, Iraq, and the Arabian peninsula. The French colonial inheritance was less political and more cultural, although in the Levant they left behind republican systems that mimicked their own. For the French what mattered most was the superiority of their civilization, and they ensured its posterity by making French the lingua franca of the Maghreb. Today, urban Moroccans, Algerians, and Tunisians speak and study in French with as much ease as they converse in Arabic. This, of course, is the case with millions of others in Francophone Africa as well.

Nevertheless, the powerful forces uniting the Middle East—religion, ethnicity, and language—have at times also been sources of division and conflict. In many historical episodes subtle differences in dialect or ethnic identity have served as powerful catalysts for the articulation of national or subnational loyalties and even political mobilization. The Middle East, it must be remembered, is far from monolithic and homogenous. Its differences have been a source of both strength and inspiration and, at times, violent bloodletting; witness the tragedy of Lebanon or the torment meted out to the Kurds.

In studying the Middle East, it is often tempting to overlook the region's rich diversity in geography, politics, and culture. Any book purporting to examine the political history of the modern Middle East is bound to remain at a certain level of generalization and not pay the necessary attention to the many, multifaceted differences within the various Middle Eastern countries and communities. This book, I am afraid, is no exception. I have taken care throughout to highlight the existence of differences, both between and within the countries and the peoples discussed, and I hope that the reader remains mindful of them as well. Nevertheless, I feel compelled to apologize to those groups whose identities or destinies may not be as thoroughly covered here as they should have been.

When the "modern" era of the Middle East begins is a matter of some debate. For our purposes here, I have taken it to be in the 1920s, after the collapse of the Ottoman Empire, when state systems as we have come to know them today began to be established throughout the region. But the political and historic phenomena that the Ottomans represented had roots far deeper in Middle Eastern and Islamic history than the early decades of the twentieth century. I decided, therefore, to go further back, much further back, and briefly retell the story of the Middle East since the appearance of Islam and how it shaped subsequent historical events in the region. Islam dramatically altered the life and historic evolution of the Middle East, but its appearance by no means marks the beginning of Middle Eastern history. As Chapter 1 makes clear, this was an arbitrary starting date, for I had to draw the line somewhere, and I chose to do so with Islam's beginning. Had this been a work on the *complete* political history of the Middle East, it would have had to start with the earliest days of human civilization, along the banks of the Tigris and the Euphrates in modern-day Iraq.

In addition to simple convenience and an arbitrary starting date, a deeper logic guides the choice of the chapters that follow and the topics they discuss. Politics and history are both dynamic and changeable *processes*. Thus the examination of either one in a snapshot is incomplete without attention to successive past developments. Contemporary political issues in the Middle East are deeply rooted in past historic and political events: consider, for example, three of the most central issues, the Palestinian-Israeli conflict, economic development, and the nature of prevailing state-society relations within each country. The present manifestation of the Palestinian-Israeli conflict resulted from the outcome of the Arab-Israeli wars, which were a product of competing varieties of nationalism, shaped by the machinations of Western colonial powers, who had gone to the Middle East once the Ottomans collapsed, and so on. The same line of inquiry could be applied to current state-society relations in the Middle East or to each country's level of economic development.

On the basis of this logic, the book is divided into two parts, one focusing on political history and the other on some key issues that resonate throughout the region. Part I lays out the historical context for the Middle East. It begins with a sweeping chapter on the history of the Middle East from the earliest days, when geographic considerations and military conquests led to the establishment first of cities and then of civilizations around them, up until the demise of the region's last major imperial power, the Ottomans. Chapter 2 continues the historical narrative, concentrating on the period between the two world wars and looking at the nature and trials of independence and state building. The emergence and rapid spread of nationalism throughout the Middle East is discussed in Chapter 3, and the two resulting Arab-Israeli wars in 1967 and 1973, each spectacular in its own way, are examined in Chapter 4. Nationalism, state building, and political consolidation (or lack thereof) led to one of the most dramatic developments in the contemporary Middle East, the Iranian revolution of 1978–79, which is discussed in Chapter 5. Revolutions and wars are seldom far apart, and both the 1980–88 Iran-Iraq War and the so-called Second Gulf War in 1990–91 and its aftermath are covered in Chapter 6. This chapter ends with a discussion of the causes and consequences of the terrorist attacks on the United States on September 11, 2001, and the subsequent U.S. invasion of Iraq in April 2003.

The historical processes discussed in Chapters 1 through 6 have had profound consequences for the contemporary politics of the Middle East, especially with regard to the overall nature of state-society relations in each country and the relationships between states. Part II discusses four of the most important current political manifestations of longer-term historical processes: the Palestinian-Israeli conflict; the challenges of economic development; the nature and makeup of states and their opponents in the Middle East; and the question of democracy. This is by no means an exhaustive list of the defining features of the region's contemporary politics. But it represents some of the most salient phenomena whose scope and consequences go beyond mere diplomacy, economics, or politics. These are the core issues that have shaped and defined contemporary Middle Eastern politics. They have had ramifications not only for the countries involved but for the region and the world as well.

Chapter 7 looks at the Palestinian-Israeli conflict. It begins with a discussion of how the two competing national identities have given resonance and force to the conflict through a mutual negation of "the Other." The chapter then looks at the situation on the ground, examining how the two sides' denial of each other's rights affects their daily lives and circumstances. There has been, especially of late, a glimmer of hope in this long and bloody conflict, as figures from both sides have embarked on the difficult task of reconciliation and peace. The chapter ends with a discussion of some of the maneuvers and the progress made so far in the elusive "peace process."

Chapter 8, on economic development, examines three features of the political economy of the Middle East: the pervasive role of the state; its pursuit of economic policies designed to minimize its extractive role in relation to social actors; and its limited abilities to control or even regulate many economic activities. Chapter 9 shifts the focus of attention to domestic politics. It looks at the current typology of Middle East states as they have been constituted and shaped through the historical processes discussed in the previous chapters. Also, the chapter examines the reasons for and manifestations of the different types of opposition that these states are likely to elicit, including groups like Al-Qaeda and the larger phenomenon of Islamic fundamentalism. This brings up the question of the autonomy and power of social groups in relation to the state and thus the prospects for democratization. These topics are explored in Chapter 10, which examines the varieties of democratic transitions, the prevailing patterns of state-society relations, and the possibilities and prospects for democratization.

The book ends with a brief discussion of some of the more important challenges the Middle East is currently facing or is likely to face in the coming decades. The last century has brought to the Middle East progress and change on multiple fronts, from the creation of impressive edifices of the state to the transformation of arid desert lands to massive urban areas and even agricultural lands (in Saudi Arabia). But problems also abound—from economically unsustainable rates of population growth to hazardous levels of pollution of environmental resources, to name only two—and their magnitude is amplified by official neglect or mismanagement. Sooner or later, state or private agencies need to substantively address the many challenges facing the Middle East, or the future will be more troublesome than the past.

PART I

A Political History of the Middle East

AS HOME TO SOME OF THE WORLD'S earliest civilizations and the birth-place of three great religions, the Middle East offers a rich tapestry of human life and deeply ingrained traditions. At the same time, the region's political history, both classic and modern, has been punctuated by the rise and fall of great powers, colonial domination, the birth or creation of new countries, and uneven marches toward political and economic development. The multiple consequences of these developments for the Middle East have been particularly pronounced since the early decades of the twentieth century. In reality, however, they can be traced as far back as the second half of the 1500s, when the Ottoman Empire began expanding its domain, and, in many ways, even before that, all the way back to the early development of Islam in the seventh century A.D.

From its inception, Islam has shaped politics and society in the regions where it is dominant, especially the Middle East. Even in those historical periods when political authority in the Muslim lands was fragmented or nonexistent, Islam continued to be a powerful social bond and a potential source of communal solidarity. The Ottomans united much of the Middle East under their own imperial banner, but their control over their far-flung territories was often tenuous and indirect at best. Despite the existence of the institution of *beyliks* (provincial governorships appointed by the Ottoman court), in much of the Middle East meaningful local political institutions never had the opportunity to emerge. The Ottoman "state" operated most manifestly in Istanbul and in the Anatolian heartland and seldom reached deep into the societies of the vast territories over which it ruled.

The collapse of the Ottomans in the early twentieth century resulted in the large-scale introduction of European colonialism into the Middle East beginning in the 1920s and officially lasting until the late 1940s, although in some cases British domination of local politics did not really end until the early 1970s. European colonialism took place under historical circumstances radically different from those that had existed during Ottoman rule. Nevertheless, the basic pattern of relationship between the colonial states and their subject societies—one of detachment, minimal contact, and top-down flow of power—remained largely the same.

The emergence of sovereign, independent states in the Middle East in the 1940s and 1950s dramatically altered domestic power equations and the traditional foundations for state-society relations in each Middle Eastern country. These ostensibly modern states were thrust unprepared into a competitive international environment in which they had to foster rapid economic and industrial development and, most importantly, satisfy the growing nationalist aspirations of their populations. These nationalist yearnings emerged in response to domestic social and political developments and as a result of the Palestinian-Israeli conflict, the latter itself serving as a catalyst for much regional conflict and instability. Not surprisingly, the political history of the modern Middle East as it unfolded in the twentieth century was one of wars, conquests, political turmoil, and extremism. Whether the current century will hold a different future for the region remains to be seen.

1 From Islam to the Great War

Since the Middle East is home to some of the world's earliest civilizations, it is difficult to choose a starting point for examining its political history, for no matter how far back the investigator searches, there still seem to be deeper layers of historical and political developments that influenced the course of later events. For convenience, and admittedly somewhat arbitrarily, I have chosen the dawn of Islam as the starting point of this book. This has some justification: Islam as both a system of beliefs and a historical-political phenomenon has distinctively marked the Middle East, and its rise and evolution created dynamics that continue to shape the destiny of nations today.

The rise, evolution, and spread of Islam in the seventh century A.D. were greatly influenced by the geography of the region in which it was born. Islam is not unique in this respect, for any religious or political phenomenon is shaped and influenced by its geographic circumstances. Thus the chapter begins with a brief survey of that larger context. It then traces Middle Eastern history from the birth and expansion of Islam to the rise of the Ottomans and, after nearly five centuries, their ultimate collapse and replacement by European colonial powers. Islam was born in the Arabian peninsula, a place nearly as harsh and inaccessible today as it was in the seventh century. The area was linked to the outside world primarily by the merchant caravans that left the Hijaz region (in western Arabia) for trading posts in Damascus and further north along the Silk Road. By the time of the rise of Islam, many civilizations just north of the Arabian peninsula had already gone through cycles of birth, death, and regeneration—the Akkadians, Babylonians, and Hittites chief among them—although two formidable dynasties continued to exist and, in fact, thrive. The Sassanids, concentrated to the northeast of the Arabian penin-

sula along the two sides of what is now the Iran-Iraq border, were gradually
restoring to the ancient Iranians some of the glory they had lost with the
collapse of the Achemenid dynasty at the hands of Alexander the Great.
The other great civilization was the Byzantine Empire, whose size and
powers were as impressive as the great city that bore its name. Between
the Sassanids and the Byzantines lay the ruins of a few other ancient
civilizations, by then long abandoned, the most notable of which were
the Babylonians. With these potential intermediaries long gone, frequent
quarrels erupted between the two regional giants, steadily weakening both
in the process. In 330 A.D., Constantine the Great made Byzantium the
capital of the Roman Empire and changed its name to Constantinople, the
City of Constantine. Islam appeared in 610 A.D. and expanded dramatically
after the Prophet's death nearly twenty-three years later. This expansion
was greatly influenced by the conditions in which Islam found itself and
the heritage of the peoples and the regions it conquered along the way.

THE SETTING

By the time Islam appeared in the Arabian peninsula, the two other civilizations in the region, the Byzantines in the north and the Sassanids in
the east, had come to adopt variations of two monotheistic religions, Christianity and Zoroastrianism, respectively. Several forms of Christianity
prevailed elsewhere in the Middle East: the Coptic Church in Egypt, the
Jacobite Church in Syria, and the Nestorian Church in Iraq. Parts of eastern
Iraq were also Zoroastrian, as was almost all of Iran, where the tradition of
divine kingship did not die out until after the Arab conquest, and even then
not very thoroughly.[1] Jewish and pagan communities were also scattered
throughout the area, including in the Arabian peninsula, where a majority
worshipped local deities.[2]

The religious makeup of the Middle East at the time of Islam's appearance tells us much about other aspects of life in the region. With religion
came the increasing differentiation of authority and the development of
religious and administrative hierarchies. Depending on local circumstances and conditions, local priests (*mobads* for Zoroastrians), bishops,
and popes could become tremendously influential in the day-to-day lives of
ordinary people, some even influencing the fates of entire dynasties. Places
of worship and congregation also assumed importance not only for articulating and perpetuating religious values but as sources of local organization and mobilization. Equally important was the use and manipulation of
religion by existing or aspiring political leaders, whether at the level of the

local community or the empire, the most brilliant manifestation of which could be found in Constantinople.[3]

Life was organized, and still is today, into three distinct but at times interrelated communities. First were urban communities, cities where markets and money economies had been firmly established, elaborate political and administrative apparatuses had been set up, and religious power and authority, as well as liturgy and customs, had evolved.[4] In broad, historical terms, cities in the Middle East can be divided into pre-Islamic and Islamic ones. With the rise and expansion of Islam, a few cities gradually died out as they ceased being centers of economic and political power. The Sassanid capital of Ctesiphon, near present-day Baghdad, is a case in point. Many more cities were established anew or grew out of military encampments. Kufa and Basra in southern Mesopotamia, Fustat in Egypt, Qayrawan in Tunisia, and, somewhat later, Marv in northeastern Iran were among the more notable in this group of cities.[5] Still others were changed not just in name but also in their political and historical significance. For example, Yathrib, a town north of Mecca, became Medina and the capital of Prophet Muhammad's new Islamic state. Some eight centuries later and under very different circumstances, Constantinople became Istanbul and the capital of an expanding Ottoman Empire.

While Islam has essentially been an urban religion, in both its genesis and its later evolution, there have been two other types of Middle Eastern communities as well: relatively small and often isolated villages; and tribes of nomads, many of whom were called bedouins (literally, "desert dwellers"). Both developed as a result of the "Neolithic Revolution," which began around 6000 B.C. and involved the development of agriculture and the domestication of new types of animals.[6] The proportion of villages and nomadic tribes appears to have oscillated depending on political currents and the rise and fall of local dynasties.[7] On the whole, strong central authority, and the concomitant security of the subject population from banditry and lawlessness, favored urbanization and the growth of cities. Political authority and urbanization assumed a mutually reinforcing relationship. With the decline of central authority and increasing levels of physical and economic insecurity, some of the less firmly settled urban groups or those in smaller towns and villages found it beneficial to migrate.[8] The reliance of many of these groups on camels and horses, and thus the search for pastures and oases, made migration for many nomads a seasonal or a semipermanent necessity. Dynastic declines did not directly give rise to nomadic and other tribal groups. But they certainly appear to have added to their numbers. Throughout the centuries, the center of political and imperial power shifted from one city and region to another several times—from Medina to Damascus, then to Baghdad, and eventually to Istanbul, with Cairo, Cordoba, and Esfahan experiencing their own power fluctuations. Each time the center of political power shifted, the fortunes of the populations in the nearby areas changed as well.

As with other parts of the world, particular patterns of population dispersion and settlements in the Middle East have been greatly influenced by the region's geography. As is well known, the great river systems of the Nile, the Tigris, and the Euphrates became cradles of civilizations. Along their banks grew two of the most magnificent cities, Cairo and Baghdad. Wealth and power here depended on the ability to dig and manage canals and other irrigation systems, thus giving rise to "hydraulic" states whose administrative powers and popular legitimacy rested on their ability to organize large numbers of workers successfully, maintain canals and other sources of irrigation, and manage and distribute the resulting agricultural yields.[9] But such river systems are few and far between in the Middle East, and the region, known for its aridity, is mostly filled with large expanses of desert and jagged mountains.[10] At the foot of these low-lying mountains grew some of the Middle East's other major cities: Mecca and Medina in the Hijaz, Sanaa in Yemen, Esfahan and Shiraz in Iran, Konya and Bursa in Turkey, and Marrakesh and Rabat in Morocco, to name a few. Inhospitable to similarly large urban settlements, the desert did not become home to larger cities save for a few, such as Yazd and Kerman in Iran, Riyadh and Buraydah in Saudi Arabia, Waddan in Libya, and Adrar in Algeria. Rather, the desert saw the proliferation of numerous isolated village and rural communities, existing alongside migratory nomadic tribes. Middle Eastern cities nevertheless experienced a decline in size, number, and importance beginning in the sixteenth century and did not regain their preeminence until some four centuries later.[11] Up until the 1950s, an overwhelming majority of people in the Middle East lived in villages, and to this day there are estimates of some fifty-five thousand villages in Iran and approximately forty thousand in Turkey, to name only two examples.[12] Despite annual rates of urbanization of 4.5 to 5 percent in the 1980s and the 1990s, some 40 percent of the peoples of the Middle East still live in village or tribal communities.[13] To this day, the urban populations of Egypt, Morocco, Sudan, and Yemen are less than 50 percent, and some 20 to 50 percent of the populations of Algeria, Iraq, Jordan, Syria, and Tunisia live outside the cities.[14]

This aspect of Middle Eastern geography—the development of one or two primary cities in each country and the widespread prevalence of village and other rural forms of life—has had a dual effect on the region's political history. On the one hand, population concentration in large cities has helped facilitate the establishment of central authority in the city because of social needs for order, physical and economic security, and, in cities close to bodies of water, maintenance of canals and irrigation facilities. On the other hand, the dispersion of populations outside the walls of the city and in remote and mostly inaccessible areas has often resulted in the state's inability to effectively establish its authority over the areas it has claimed to control. This was especially the case in places where river valleys were uncommon—that is, most of the Middle East—where, instead of centralized, hydraulic states, confederations made up of different local rulers emerged.[15] With the diffusion of power and lack of central authority came problems of state penetration and control, exacerbated during the rule of the Ottomans, who sought to govern the multiple provinces of their vast empire through a carefully devised system of loose control. The outcome, as we shall see later, was national entities that at best came into only partial contact with political institutions, whether indigenous or imposed from Istanbul. The dismemberment of the Ottoman Empire at the end of the Great War by victorious European powers, namely France and Britain, and the mandatory system through which they ruled, only compounded the problem.

Religion, political administration, economic activities, place of residence, and other forms of shared experiences provide a sense of cultural identity. A discussion of the complex, evolving cultural identities in the Middle East is beyond the scope of this book. But despite the universalism of Islam and those of the dynasties that claimed its mantle at one point or another, distinct if somewhat related cultural identities were formed relatively early on, whereby the Other was distinguished from the collective self. Naturally, with the progression of history and the changing nuances of empires and dynasties, cultural identities—wrapped in symbols and folklore, flags, oral traditions, and ways of life—were transformed and muted but never quite universalized. Many, in fact, later became rallying cries around which dormant animosities erupted and led to cross-national or even intranational conflicts and war. The Iran-Iraq War of the 1980s, for example, had cultural and historical roots that were deeper than mere disagreements over boundaries, as did the sectarian strife that tore Lebanon apart for some fifteen years beginning in 1975.

It is within this larger context that the political history of the Middle East has taken place. Retelling the narrative of this history is beyond the scope of this book, and it has been masterfully told by many others.[16] What follows are some of the more important highlights that have shaped the region's history and its current social, political, and economic landscapes.

THE RISE AND EXPANSION OF ISLAM

Muhammad ibn-Abdullah, Muhammad the son of Abdullah, was born in the city of Mecca in the Hijaz in 570 A.D.[17] Mecca had emerged as an affluent and powerful caravan city for two principal reasons. First, it housed the shrine of Ka'ba, where Abraham was said to have offered his sacrifice to God, and it had thus become an important destination for pagan worshippers whose belief systems included paying homage to that holy site. Mecca was also the halfway point along the lucrative incense-trading route between Yemen in the south and Syria in the north, making it a potentially attractive resting place for passing traders. One of the more intriguing theses about the preeminence of Mecca is presented by the historian Richard Bulliet, who attributes it to the city's ability to control the surrounding camel-breeding tribes. These tribes could both supply transportation and, more importantly, raid caravans. Gradually, the thesis holds, the Meccans organized the tribes so that they would manage trade rather than raid caravans, leading to a rise in the city's importance.[18]

Muhammad belonged to the Quraysh tribe, who had settled in and eventually dominated the city approximately a century earlier. Nevertheless, since its very founding Mecca had lacked central authority. Muhammad was not born into the most influential clan of the Quraysh. He lost both parents at an early age and was raised by his uncle, Abu Talib. As a young man, Muhammad worked for a caravan owner named Khadija, a woman twice widowed and with some wealth. She proposed to him, and the two married. Fifteen years his senior, Khadija bore Muhammad six children, four daughters and two sons, although only the daughters survived into adulthood. Khadija later became the first convert to Muhammad's religion, and he remained devoted to her throughout her life. Despite sanctioning multiple marriages and later practicing them himself, he did not marry anyone else until after Khadija's passing.

Disenchanted with the paganism of fellow Meccans, in 610 A.D., during one of his frequent visits to the nearby Mount Hira, Muhammad was visited by the archangel Gabriel and given the command to recite (*iqra* in Arabic) what was to become verse 1 of chapter (*surah*) 96 of the Quran (recitations): "Recite in the name of your Lord who created." God (Lah), Muhammad was told, was one (Al-Lah, the God), and man must submit to his will. Life was to be reordered on the basis of submission (*islam*) to God.

Besides Khadija, the earliest converts to Islam included some of Muhammad's closest relatives and friends, and among this group of companions (Sahabah) the new religion was practiced in secret for approximately three years. This secrecy was deemed necessary because of the revolutionary nature of Muhammad's message. The core principles of the new religion challenged the social and economic balance on which the life of Meccans had come to rely. In a setting where kinship and tribal affiliation determined everything from physical security to social and economic status, the call to replace tribal loyalties with submission to a single divine being shook the foundations of Arabian society. The Prophet's divine message caused the Meccan elites both practical and doctrinal problems. From a practical point of view, Islam upset the prevailing social and cultural balance of forces within Mecca. Doctrinally, it challenged deeply held beliefs about the sanctity of the city's three main goddesses.[19] Among other things, Meccans worried that the spread of a monotheistic heresy would damage their reputation before the three primary idol gods—Lat, Manat, and Uzza—and, more importantly, would discourage fellow pagan traders from passing through Mecca and paying homage to the shrine of Ka'ba.

Sometime around 613 A.D., Muhammad began to openly call on people to join his religion and to observe its evolving rites and principles. The anger of the Meccan elite was swift and intense. Some interpretations of Islam see the mention of the goddesses Lat, Manat, and Uzza in the Quran as an attempt by the Prophet to compromise with the Meccan elites, who during much of his life vehemently opposed his prophecy.[20] But not until around September 622 A.D. did Muhammad and his followers leave Mecca for the northern town of Yathrib, at the invitation of the city's notables, where they established a city par excellence, the City, Al Medina. During this flight *(hijrah)* the Prophet affirmed his support among the believers and declared the beginning of a new (lunar) calendar.[21] The year 622 A.D., therefore, is 1 A.H. (After Hijrah) in the Islamic calendar.

Here in Medina the first Islamic state was established and attained significant political and military power. The Prophet's entry into the city was facilitated by the signing of a series of treaties whereby the emigrant Meccans (Muhajerun) and the citizens of Medina would live in peace, act as one community *(umma)* while keeping their customs and laws, and bring their disputes to be solved by Muhammad.[22] In a sense, these agreements constituted one of the earliest written constitutions in the Middle East, spelling out the details of operation for what was to become an emerging empire's nerve center.[23] Chief among these agreements was the Compact of Medina, as the Prophet's main treaty with residents of Medina came to be known. Also referred to as a "constitution" of sorts, the compact included thirty articles, which, among other provisions, assured the protection and equality of the city's Jewish tribes. The Jews "who attached themselves to our Commonwealth," it said, "shall be protected from all insult and vexation. . . . [T]hey shall have an equal right with our own people to our assistance and good offices."[24]

Initially, Medina included some enemies of the Prophet: both pagans and the so-called Hypocrites (Munafiqun, also called the Doubters), whose allegiance to the Prophet was suspect at best. Despite the signing of the Compact of Medina, the Muslims also found themselves in frequent conflict with the city's Jewish populations. The Jewish tribes were eventually subdued, and the Prophet's other enemies were also steadily neutralized. Some were even killed. The Prophet became the leader of a thriving community of believers, the *umma*. Over time, he instituted detailed social and cultural reforms, economic principles, and political practices designed to run the city.

Steadily, the legal foundations of the evolving *umma* were laid out in the Quran. The Quran is not a "legislative document" in that it does not outline the features of an incipient Islamic political order. Instead, it includes various detailed pronouncements on proper conduct and social relations, including inheritance laws, marital relations, relations with non-Muslims, and punishments for crimes such as theft and adultery.[25] Gradually, especially after the Prophet's death, there developed three additional sources of Islamic jurisprudence: the Sunna (collections of accounts of the deeds and actions of the Prophet, regarded as "the perfect model of behavior"); *ijma* (consensus); and *qiyas* (analogical reasoning).[26] Together, these became the four foundations of *sharia*, commonly referred to as "Islamic law" but more correctly meaning "comprehensive principle of *total way of life*"—spiritual, mental, and physical.[27]

Of a total of 114 *surahs* contained in the Quran, 88 were revealed in Mecca and only 26 in Medina. However, the Meccan verses tend to be less elaborate and were designed primarily to lay down the foundations of the nascent religion. The Medinian *surahs* tend to be more elaborate and their subjects more specific.[28] The present form in which the Quran appears is based, not on the chronological order in which its contents were revealed to the Prophet, but on the order in which the Prophet is said to have arranged and recited the verses by heart during the month of Ramadan. This version was adopted and standardized during the reign of the third caliph, Uthman, from 644 to 655 A.D.[29]

Many of the principles of Islam were enunciated in Medina, some in response to existing or evolving predicaments. There are important connections between some of these religious principles and the nature and operations of the emerging Islamic state. Divisiveness and bitter rivalries marked the polities first of Mecca and then, to much greater extent, of Medina and its environs. It is not coincidental that one of the most powerful features of Islam is its emphasis on the community and the importance of its cohesion. The five pillars of Islam—prayer, fasting, tithing, pilgrimage to Mecca, and proclaiming belief in the religion—demonstrate the importance placed on communal solidarity. Although there is no evidence to suggest that any of the pillars were devised by the Prophet specifically for political purposes, once he was in Medina they did help strengthen the solidarity and cohesion of the Muslim community. Each pillar has a strong communal aspect: communal prayers in mosques on Fridays, a day whose Arabic translation, *jum'ah*, means "community" or "congregation"; the rituals attached to fasting in the month of Ramadan; the economic and financial obligation to support the community through tithes; the ritual pilgrimage to Mecca, the *hajj*, in conjunction with other believers; and the profession of faith by reciting the same, brief Quranic verse.

The Muslims of Medina at first supported themselves by raiding caravans, a common practice at the time, but gradually gained enough confidence to turn their attention toward Mecca. The Muslims and the Meccans fought a series of battles—in 624, 625, and 627—with inconclusive results. Finally, in 628, Muhammad signed a truce with the Meccan elite, whereby he and his followers were allowed to perform the *hajj* the following year. The treaty also allowed Muhammad to subdue some of the northerly tribes allied with the Meccans. In 630, Mecca itself submitted to the Prophet of Islam virtually without resistance. In less than two years, in 632, Muhammad died in his house in Medina. The city's central mosque, which he had also used as his administrative headquarters, became his last resting place.

Almost immediately, the Prophet's death unleashed two contradictory yet reinforcing developments. On the one hand, under the rule of his successors, the territories under the control of Islamic armies grew rapidly and dramatically. The early expansion was on two fronts, against the Byzantine Empire in Syria and from there on to North Africa, and against the Sassanids in Iraq and Iran. Damascus capitulated in 635, and Jerusalem was occupied in 638. A military encampment named Fustat was built on the Nile in 641, from which the fall of Alexandria was secured the following year. By 661 most of Byzantine Africa (Libya and Tunisia) was in Muslim hands, and Muslim domination over all of North Africa was complete by 700. The armies of Islam crossed into Spain via the Strait of Gibraltar beginning in 710, and Cordoba was captured in 712. The campaign against the Sassanids was similarly swift and decisive: the Persian armies suffered defeat in 637 and then again in 642. By 653, Muslim control over Iran was complete, and by the early decades of the eighth century it reached as far as western China.[30]

These expansions only magnified the multiple divisions within the Muslim community that the Prophet's death had brought to the surface. Geographic and ethnolinguistic divisions proliferated as the abode of Islam expanded. But there were initially far more serious divisions over the question of the *umma*'s leadership and the legitimacy of the Prophet's successors (caliphs).[31] Upon the Prophet's death, the leadership of the Muslim community passed on to four caliphs, collectively referred to as the Rashidun, or Rightly Guided Ones, because of their close companionship with the Prophet and their early conversion to Islam: Abu Bakr (632–34), Umar (634–44), Uthman (644–56), and Ali (656–61). However, as the empire grew and the economic and territorial stakes became higher, policy disagreements arose, and opposition, both from within and from the outside, grew. Uthman's policies aimed at centralizing tax collection, along with his preferential treatment of Meccan notables, provoked his murder by a group of disenchanted Arabs. His successor, Ali, suffered a similar fate at the hands of a man belonging to a group of zealots called the Kharajis (secessionists), who faulted him for agreeing to a council hearing on the murder of Uthman.[32]

Two civil wars would soon erupt, largely but not solely over the festering issue of succession, from 656 to 661 and again from 680 to 692. The cumulative result of these two wars was the emergence of an unbridgeable chasm between a minority of "partisans," the Shi'ites, and the majority of "traditionalists," the Sunnis. Ali was the Prophet's cousin and son-in-law, as well as one of the earliest converts to Islam. His caliphate caused a major conflict between two approaches to the question of succession, one "devoid of notions of hereditary sanctity" based on lineage ties to the Prophet and the other emphasizing these notions. Along with practical political and economic considerations, the notion of succession based on blood ties was later to become the most divisive issue separating Shi'ites and Sunnis.[33] At the core of the conflict was the question of who should succeed Ali and what his proper functions ought to be: the Shi'ites maintained that Ali was the only rightful caliph and that only his descendants should follow him; the Sunnis, on the other hand, accepted the caliphate rule of Mu'awiya, Uthman's cousin and the governor of Damascus, who had declared himself caliph.

Upon Ali's death in 661, Mu'awiya prevailed and moved the seat of the Islamic state from Medina to Damascus. Hailing from the Umayyad clan within the Quraysh, he established the Umayyad caliphate, which lasted for nearly a century until 750. Thanks in large measure to the efforts of the dynasty's founder, the Umayyads established a centralized, de facto dynasty, initiated administrative measures for running their expanding domain, issued gold and silver coins (the *dinar* and the *dirham*, respectively), introduced fiscal reforms and institutionalized tax collection, and significantly added to the size of the territory under their control. This is not to suggest that the Umayyads were able to establish a stable caliphate or ruled over quiescent populations. In fact, many of their development projects, which enriched members of the political elite and raised the tax burden on ordinary people, were so deeply resented that Yezid III (r. 744) promised not to undertake the construction of new buildings or canals.[34]

With the gradual routinization of the dynasty came new challenges, many of which the later Umayyad caliphs were ill prepared to handle. One of these challenges revolved around the treatment, and in turn the loyalty, of the growing population of non-Muslim and recent converts to Islam *(mawali)* under Umayyad suzerainty.[35] Although some individuals from these groups could reach very high offices in the Umayyad court, they were still subject to discrimination and at times even maltreatment. Adam Mez, the German scholar of Islam, has made the following observation about the status of religious minorities during the Umayyad and Abbasid caliphates: "The most amazing feature of the Islamic Government is the number of non-Muslim officers in state service. In his own Empire the Muslim was ruled by Christians. Old is the complaint that the decision over the life and property of Muslims lay in the hand of protected subjects. . . . Twice in the 3/9 century even the war Ministers were non-Muslims with the result that the 'defenders of the faith' had to kiss their hands and obey their commands."[36] In fact, it was from among the *mawali* in eastern Iran that a movement to unseat the Umayyads was set in motion, leading to the eventual establishment of the Abbasid dynasty in 750, this time in a newly built city, the magnificent Baghdad. The Umayyads, however, did not completely disappear. Abd al-Rahman I, a member of the extended Umayyad family, found his way to North Africa and then Spain, where he established a rival Islamic state.

THE HIGH CALIPHATE

Historians have generally referred to the reigns of the Umayyads and the Abbasids as the era of the high caliphate, a designation based on the scope of their rule; the unity they fostered among their subjects, albeit not always successfully; the magnificence of their capital cities; and, especially for the Abbasids, their patronage of the arts and the sciences. With the rise of the Abbasids came significant changes in the social and political life of the empire and, consequently, new challenges. With the caliphate's encouragement, Baghdad became an important intellectual center, and the imperial court patronized many artistic and scientific endeavors. By the same token, differing religious opinions and trends, a relic of Umayyad rule, proliferated, and the differences among them deepened. As a dynasty heavily reliant on religion as its primary source of legitimacy, the Abbasids grew increasingly sensitive to such ongoing debates and found themselves having to take sides among the different theoreticians to protect their reign.[37] As a general rule, the Abbasid caliphs went to great lengths to portray themselves as pious Muslims. The legendary caliph Harun al-Rashid once even walked from Medina to Mecca to earn divine merit.[38] But the royal court also became infamous for its pursuit of worldly pleasures, including wine and women.[39] Equally detrimental to the power and popularity of the Abbasids was the deliberate distance they cultivated between themselves and the populace. In many ways, the Abbasid caliph came to view himself in the same light as the old Persian kings: the King of Kings, or, alternatively, the Shadow of God on Earth. In either case, the Abbasids became distant, regal elites ruling over subject populations. The historian Von Grunebaum writes of them: "The court, the family of the caliph, his household servants, guards and administrators were the center of the empire; the standing with the ruler determines rank and influence. His favour raises the menial from nothing, his disfavour plunges him back into nothing."[40]

Before long, these developments had combined to weaken the Abbasids from within. As their rule was racked by rebellions and secessionist movements, as well as doctrinal and intellectual disputes, their power, prestige, and influence declined markedly after 945. First, the powerful Buyid family of northwestern Iran established itself as the "protector" of the Abbasid caliph from 945 to 1055, essentially turning the caliphal clan into mere figureheads. The Turkish Saljuqs similarly dominated Baghdad from 1055 until the middle of the twelfth century. The Abbasids, or what remained of them, were finally overrun in 1258 by the invading Mongols. By then, the Abbasid Empire had already started coming apart. Ruling clans within the different territories had begun to exercise considerable local autonomy. A revived Umayyad dynasty ruled Spain. Abbasid hegemony was also challenged in North Africa, where a Shi'ite group eventually conquered Egypt in 969, established the Fatimid dynasty, and built a new capital city called

Cairo (al Qahirah, the conqueror) along the Nile. The conquerors of Egypt were soon caught up by what may be called the "Pharaoh syndrome," which appears to have plagued many of Egypt's rulers, both ancient and contemporary. Their court was replete with splendor and ritual, the center of a city victorious and grand.[41]

Meanwhile, the first wave of Crusaders was sent from Europe to Jerusalem to protect the Christian Byzantine emperor in Constantinople from the menacing Muslims, further weakening the Abbasids and even the Fatimids. Here a Kurdish general by the name of Salah al-Din (Saladin) distinguished himself in bravery and eventually became the sultan of Egypt after the death of the last Fatimid caliph in 1171. Saladin's control of Egypt was initially in the name of the Abbasid caliph. In 1175, Baghdad recognized his sultanate over Egypt, Yemen, Palestine, and Syria, areas where Saladin was already in de facto control. On October 2, 1178, he also occupied Jerusalem and wrested its control from the Crusaders. But the Ayyubid dynasty that he established did not last long, having to rely on ex-slave soldiers, called Mamluks, to defend itself against the invading Mongols. The Mongol conquest had started in earnest in Asia Minor in 1219, overrunning Iran and in turn establishing the Ilkhanid dynasty there from 1256 to 1336. The Mamluks, meanwhile, established a dynasty of their own in Egypt in 1250, not to be overthrown until the advent of the Ottomans in 1517.

The Mongol conquests simply facilitated the release throughout the Middle East of centrifugal forces that had made their presence felt as early as the middle of the tenth century. In fact, many of these tendencies had never quite disappeared but had simply been obscured as peoples rallied around the common banner of Islam. The Mongol invasion of Iran was intense, bloody, and devastating. When the Mongols captured the city of Marv, for example, they reportedly killed some seven hundred thousand inhabitants, laying farmlands and entire cities to waste and carrying off thousands of Muslim artisans to Mongolia as slaves.[42] But in larger historical terms the invasion was relatively brief. Before long, the Mongols had established an increasingly Persianized dynasty of their own in Iran, the Ilkhanids, which tried to reverse some of the devastation of the earlier decades by encouraging public works and patronizing the arts. Under their patronage, painting and manuscript illustration, the recording of history, and the building of monuments, especially tombs, flourished.[43] The Ilkhanids collapsed by 1336, and a succession of smaller states emerged in areas previously under their control. A similar fate had befallen the earlier Saljuqs, who in the middle of the eleventh century had taken control of most of Anatolia, Armenia, and Azerbaijan, only to be broken up into smaller states soon afterward. Geographic circumstances and other administrative and bureaucratic limitations had forced both the Saljuqs and the Ilkhanids to rely on local, mostly landed elites to maintain their suzerainty.[44] This very decentralization and diffusion of power would not only germinate their own collapse but also facilitate conditions for the rise of their eventual successors, the Ottomans in Anatolia and the Safavids in Iran.

THE OTTOMANS

One of the more significant side effects of the radical political shifts in the Middle East was the steady ascent to power of a small Turkic tribe known by the name of one of its earliest leaders. The Ottomans originated in northwestern Anatolia, not far from the city that most rulers had dreamt of conquering one day, the magnificent Constantinople. The Ottomans were the beneficiaries of the declining powers of the Saljuqs in Anatolia, where in 1281 a chieftain's son named Osman conquered new territories and set out to defeat the Byzantine Empire. The Ottomans expanded quickly throughout Anatolia and by 1345 had crossed over the narrow Bosphorus Straits into Europe. In 1389 they scored a decisive victory in the Battle of Kosovo and established control over the western Balkans. Historical record indicates that the Ottoman advances into Europe, reinforced by the frequent settlement in major Balkan cities of Anatolians accompanying the troops, were not always deeply resented by the local populations. In fact, "The Balkan peasant soon came to appreciate that conquest by the Moslem invader spelled for him liberation from Christian feudal power, whose manifold exactions and abuses had worsened with the increase of monastic lands. Ottomanization was now conferring upon him unforeseen benefits. Not the least of them were law and order. As a French traveller was to write, 'The country is safe, and there are no reports of brigands or highwaymen'—more than could be said, at that time, of other realms in Christendom."[45] The grand prize remained elusive, however. Only in 1453, after a harrowing two-month siege, was Constantinople finally captured by the twenty-two-year-old Sultan Mehmet II, the Conqueror (Fatih), who declared it his new capital. The city gradually came to be called Istanbul. The new name was a corruption of the original "Constantinople," which was later pronounced Stinopol, Stinpol, Estanbul, and, eventually, Istanbul.

Had they not been separated in time from the Abbasids by some four centuries, the Ottomans, at least in their first century, would surely have deserved the esteemed designation of high caliphate as well. From the plains of Anatolia the Ottomans rose to become a world empire, uniting the Middle East under their rule from the Balkans in the northwest to the Hijaz in the south, going as far in North Africa as Egypt, Libya, Tunisia, and Algeria. The official government in Istanbul became known to Europeans as the Sublime Porte (first the Bab-i Homayun and then the Bab-i Ali in Ottoman Turkish, after one of the gates in the Grand Vizier's residence), from where much of the Middle East and North Africa was administered. Only Iran remained outside the Ottomans' control. There, in 1501, a militant Shi'ite Sufi named Ismail, at the time only thirteen years old, rose to prominence and established the Safavid dynasty.

The Ottoman centuries can generally be divided into three periods. The first period, from the early establishment of the dynasty around 1280 to the end of the reign of Suleyman I (r. 1520–66), was one of unprecedented growth in the power, prestige, and territorial size of the empire. This era coincides with the reign of the dynasty's first ten sultans, all of whom were, on the whole, capable administrators, successful military commanders, and wise rulers. Also during this period the Ottomans emerged as a "gunpowder empire" par excellence because of their military tactics and their technology, conquering lands in Europe and in the Middle East.[46] This military prowess was buttressed by a highly disciplined, well-trained corps of infantrymen called the janissaries, many of whom were drafted into the service of the empire at childhood and were raised as either future administrators or soldiers. The janissaries were provided with firearms and "used phalanx tactics to combine massed musket firepower with artillery."[47]

The second period, beginning approximately after 1566 and lasting until the early 1800s, was in many ways the beginning of the end. This was a time of frequent military defeats, territorial retreat and retrenchment, administrative decay, and industrial underdevelopment. Most of the territorial and military reversals occurred in Europe: the failure to capture Vienna in 1683; the surrender of Hungary to the Hapsburgs and the Aegean coast to the Venetians in 1699; another massive territorial concession in a 1718 treaty; the loss of the Crimea to Russia in 1774; and the loss of Egypt to Napoleon in 1798.[48] When Egypt was reclaimed in 1801, its military governor, the modernizing Muhammad Ali, grew so strong as to challenge Ottoman suzerainty over Egypt and Syria. Only with European help were the Ottomans able to regain Syria, but their loss of Egypt was permanent. Muhammad Ali was to establish an Egyptian dynasty that lasted until 1952.

There were, to be certain, occasional victories. In 1711, the Ottomans forced the surrender of the Russians at the river Pruth, and in 1715 the Greek provinces were recovered from Venice. But, in the words of the historian Andrew Wheatcroft, "whenever an Ottoman army met a European army on roughly equal terms the result was invariably a defeat for the Turks."[49] This was not a product of the Ottoman soldiers' lack of bravery or, on occasion, the ingenuity of their commanders. More often, it was a product of the innate conservatism and lack of adaptability that permeated the whole Ottoman system of rule, including warfare and conquest. "By the end of the eighteenth century," Wheatcroft continues, "the sultan's soldiers had not varied their equipment or method of war for more than two hundred years."[50]

There were multiple causes for the steady decline of the once mighty empire. Principally, however, decay began at the top, with the royal court and the janissaries. The janissaries increasingly lost their strict discipline, and the quality of their training deteriorated as many began using their positions for other, often personal pursuits. At one point they grew so powerful that they massacred most male members of the dynasty for fear of being disbanded, and it was not until 1826 that they were successfully attacked by the sultan and neutralized. The end came after the janissaries mutinied a second time against proposed reforms, when in a surprise move Sultan Mahmud ordered palace troops to open fire on the advancing janissary corps and then bombarded the barracks to which they had retreated. In the coming months, thousands of janissaries were killed, and the sultan proclaimed the formation of a new army, to be called "the Victorious Muhammaden Soldiery."[51]

There was also an unfortunate string of incompetent sultans who ascended to the throne beginning in the second half of the sixteenth century, many often far more interested in the pursuit of worldly pleasures than in attending to the affairs of the state. There were, of course, exceptions. Mahmud II (r. 1808–39), for example, implemented major reforms in the latter part of his reign. A number of reforming grand viziers also made their mark on the royal court, especially in the 1840s to the 1860s, and brought about significant improvements to the functions of the caliphate state. Nevertheless, on the whole, the overall quality of government saw a precipitous decline over time.[52]

Equally important was the gradual ascendancy of Russian imperial power, and, to a lesser extent, that of Hapsburg Austria and later Britain. In relation to Europe, the pattern of declining Ottoman power is unmistakable: superiority in the fifteenth and sixteenth centuries, parity in the seventeenth and early eighteenth centuries, and steady decline thereafter,

Figure 1. Turkish women in a late nineteenth-century harem.

so that the Ottoman Empire eventually became the "sick man of Europe."[53] This growing imbalance of power between the Ottomans and the West was partly military and diplomatic and partly historical. Equally culpable was "the soft embrace of Ottoman traditionalism," with military commanders and also rulers, including the few "modernizing sultans," ultimately preferring the old ways.[54] For whatever reasons, the Ottomans did not experience the profound, historic changes that were sweeping across western Europe from the sixteenth through the eighteenth centuries—the Renaissance, the Reformation, the Enlightenment, the Industrial Revolution. Consequently, they entered into the eighteenth century economically, technologically, and militarily far weaker than most of their traditional European adversaries.

The third period began in the nineteenth century, when it became increasingly clear that the empire as a whole and the dynasty in particular were inflicted with a systemic malaise, one whose cure necessitated fundamental reforms. This was the era of reforms and, eventually, demise. Increasingly aware of the empire's industrial and technological backwardness in relation to Europe, a succession of Ottoman sultans and their viziers, or chief ministers, sought to revamp the empire's central administration, reinvigorate the army, give order to the chaotic and inefficient tax collection system, and introduce modern industrial machinery (such as printing presses). This was the gist of the *Nizam-i Jedid* (New Order) as instituted by Sultan Selim III (r. 1789–1807), the inspiration for which was a similar set of reforms implemented in France after the French Revolution.[55] A second attempt at reforming the empire occurred during the reign of Sultan Abdulmejid from 1839 to 1876, the era of Tanzimat, or reorganization. Among other changes, the Tanzimat saw the introduction of a postal system (1834), telegraph (1855), steamships, and the beginning of railway construction in 1866.[56]

Not surprisingly, such changes were often viewed with suspicion and angst by the established political and economic hierarchy, not the least of whom were courtiers and the *ulama* (Muslim clerics). In fact, it was the *ulama* that instigated Selim's deposition in 1807 and the end of his New Order. The sentiments underlying these fears were articulated in an unattributed text circulating in Istanbul that is estimated to have been written sometime between 1880 and 1900. The anonymous author lamented the fact that because of inventions such the steam engine and the telegraph, "one's soul becomes conceited, . . . one relies upon created beings and ceases to put one's trust anymore in the Powerful, the Creator, and . . . ignores him. . . . One's recompense is diminished. [And] one's soul becomes insolent, because the soul is inclined to wicked deeds and most wicked deeds are generally [committed] for money and valuables."[57]

Such sentiments notwithstanding, those changes that had crept into Ottoman society had slowly engendered the rise of new classes of articulate modernists. By far the most important of these were two generations of Ottoman subjects, the so-called "Young Ottomans," who came to prominence around 1867, and the "Young Turks," who in July 1908 spearheaded a revolution of sorts by forcing the sultan to reinstate the long-suspended constitution of 1876. Inspired by the political ideals prevalent in Europe and dazzled by the industrial accomplishments of Britain, yet remaining committed to their Islamic religion and Ottoman heritage, both groups sought to reform the system from within. With their attempts at turning the dynasty into a constitutional parliamentary system, presumably along the Westminster model, they gave rise to a number of different, competing factions. By the early years of the twentieth century, the idea of a multinational, multireligious empire had become increasingly untenable, and the birth of local national identities and loyalties was tearing the empire apart. This problem was not unique to the Ottoman Empire. At about roughly the same time, the two other dynasties bordering the Ottomans, the Hapsburgs to the west and the Qajars to the east, also faced crises that threatened their very survival, eventually leading to their collapse. Though the specific causes of the crises facing the imperial households were different in each case, the Ottomans and the Hapsburgs shared similar challenges in ruling over vast, multinational territories.[58]

Within less than two decades, those who still hoped to retain the empire in its sixteenth- and seventeenth-century form had all hopes dashed by the advent of the Great War in 1914. The Young Turk movement, meanwhile, had given rise to the Committee for Union and Progress (CUP), which was resolutely secular and a firm believer in the idea of "Turkish nationalism" as compared to "Ottomanism." Backed by modernist elements within the military, the CUP assumed power in 1912, keeping the sultan as a titular head. Until the end of its rule in 1918, the CUP governed by decree, embarking, among other things, on a rapid program of secularizing schools and the judicial system, repressing Christian minorities and the Muslim *ulama*, and seeking to Turkify the various (Arab) provinces.[59] Millions of Armenians were expelled, and one and a half million of them were massacred because they were suspected of collaboration with the Russians and because their large-scale, historic presence in the Turkish heartland was now seen as inimical to the project of Turkish state building.[60] The powers and responsibilities of the *ulama* were also severely curtailed, and the idea

of Turkish nationalism was constantly propagated. Despite their tumultuous involvement in politics, however, by 1918 the Young Turks' ideal of a
constitutional government was no closer to reality than when they had
first come into power.[61]

The death of the Ottomans took a few painful years. The empire reluc-
tantly entered the war on Germany's side at the beginning of the Great
War. Britain and its allies in turn decided to chip away at the Ottomans'
Middle Eastern provinces. Russian advances in Anatolia were halted only
after the 1917 communist revolution. That same year Britain captured
Baghdad, and Jerusalem fell a year later. A rebellion calling for indepen-
dence also broke out among the Arab population of the Hijaz. The Ottoman
Empire was being systematically dismembered.

Amid the steady decay of a collapsing empire, the war did raise the fortunes of one Ottoman general, a certain Mustafa Kemal, whose strategic
genius had spared his forces from defeat in all the military campaigns in
which they were involved.[62] As the war was drawing to a close in 1918, the
Young Turk government in Istanbul went into hiding and Kemal took over
the reins of power. For the next three years he fought a series of successful
military campaigns against the Armenian republic in the Caucasus, the
French in Cilicia, and the Greeks in central Anatolia, as well as Ottoman
troops remaining loyal to the sultan. Emerging victorious, in 1921 he
established a Grand National Assembly in the interior city of Ankara
and promulgated a new, republican constitution the following year. The
Turkish republic was proclaimed on October 29, 1923. That same year the
independence of Turkey and its present boundaries were recognized by the
Treaty of Lausanne. Mustafa Kemal was declared president for life. In the
coming decades, Kemal (d. 1938) and his successors methodically set out
to dismantle the political, sociocultural, and religious vestiges of Ottoman
rule. The era of the Ottomans and everything they stood for—the caliphate, Turko-Islamic tradition, social and cultural conservatism, rule over
disparate *millets* (religious communities)—came to a dramatic end, and a
new era of Kemalist republicanism began.

THE SAFAVIDS AND THE QAJARS

To the east of the Ottomans was another important dynasty, the Safavids,
and their successors, the Qajars. Though originally from a Turkic tribe
based in northwestern Iran, the Safavids differed from the Ottomans in
several fundamental ways. To begin with, their reign never extended far
beyond the boundaries of modern-day Iran, and even in their territories

they often had to rely on semiautonomous tribal chieftains *(uymaqs)* scattered throughout the interior of the country. Equally important were the different religious characters of the two dynasties and their respective sources of popular legitimacy. By definition, the Ottoman sultans saw themselves as the successors to the Rashidun and, as caliphs, the protectors of the Sunni *umma*. The Safavids, on the other hand, traced their genesis to religious mystics (Sufis) who were militantly Shi'ite.[63] In fact, under the Safavids Shi'ism became the state religion of Iran, and the royal court was modeled after that of ancient Persian kings *(shahs)* rather than anything resembling the Ottoman sultanate.

The Safavid conquest of Iran began with Ismail in 1500 (d. 1524). For the next ten years, he consolidated his rule over the country and launched a thorough and at times brutal campaign to convert the majority Sunni population to Shi'ism. The conversion campaign lasted for nearly a century and succeeded in creating a core of Shi'ite co-religionists—eventually up to 90 percent—in much of the central part of the country. It is no accident that today Iran's Sunni minorities are concentrated among the country's non-Persian ethnic groups that are scattered along the country's borders: the Arabs along the southwestern border with Iraq; the Kurds along the western borders with Iraq and Turkey; the Turkmans along the northeastern border with Turkmenistan; and the Baluchis along the southeastern border with Pakistan. The Safavids belonged to the numerically more dominant Twelver (or Imami) branch of Shi'ism, which, as its name implies, believes in the sanctity of twelve imams (leaders of religious communities), the last of whom, the Mahdi, is in occultation and will return at the End of Time. The Safavids' own knowledge of Shi'ite theology and jurisprudence appears to have been scant, so the conversion process was reported to be quick and rather superficial, in some instances consisting merely of reciting a slogan.[64]

Within a few decades, during the reign of Shah Abbas (r. 1588–1629), the Safavids reached the zenith of their rule. Abbas moved the capital from the northwestern city of Tabriz to Esfahan, located in central Iran and a safe distance from the Ottomans. There he embarked on a concerted campaign to build a magnificent city with ornate palaces, mosques, a bazaar, and a grand central square.[65] For his own and his subjects' viewing pleasure, he also built a polo grounds and a carnival arena.[66] Shi'ite scholars were brought in from Syria, Iraq, and Arabia to help teach and propagate the new religion, and great mosques and religious schools *(madresahs)* were built in the major cities.

Despite the zeal and determination of the dynasty's founder, Ismail, and the splendor of the royal court and the capital under Shah Abbas, the Safavids were never quite able to consolidate their rule throughout much of the country. Much of the problem revolved around the dynasty's inability, and perhaps unwillingness, to develop viable institutions through which its rule could be enforced meaningfully across Iranian territory. Unlike the Ottoman system of rule, Safavid political institutions remained highly underdeveloped and far too dependent on the person of the shah to function effectively. Willem Floor's description of Safavid govern-ment institutions is revealing. "The shah was the sole source of political power," he writes. "His will was executed through a civil bureaucracy and, if need be, by an army. Both were loyal to the shah rather than to the political system. Hence, political rule, relations, and responsibilities were highly personalized. Put another way, the inner circle (civil, religious, and military) surrounding the shah derived their influence and power from their proximity to the shah. Thus, it was not so much their functions and responsibilities that gave them power but the knowledge for those lower on the social ladder that they held that function for the shah."[67]

Before long, the institutional deficiencies inherent in the Safavid sys-tem of rule made it exceedingly difficult for the dynasty to counter the strong resistance facing it from various nomadic tribes and from other local rulers. More importantly, the Safavids were challenged in their Shi'ite legitimacy and interpretation by an increasingly independent and vocal class of clerics.[68] Significantly weakened, by the late 1600s and early 1700s Safavid rule was being threatened nearly everywhere outside the capital city of Esfahan. According to the historian Ira Lapidus, "[T]he Safavid state remained a court regime in a fluid society in which power was widely dis-persed among competing tribal forces. These forces would in the end over-throw the dynasty."[69] The end came in the 1720s. Esfahan was captured in 1722 by one of the *uymaqs*, the Ghalzai Afghans, who then overthrew the dynasty in 1726.

A period of competing local dynasties followed, none quite capable of achieving meaningful territorial hegemony beyond its immediate areas of control. Nevertheless, one of these competing groups, the Qajars, was able to establish a precarious suzerainty over significant parts of Iran beginning in 1779, giving rise to a dynasty by the same name. Although their hold on power remained tenuous throughout, the Qajars did manage to last until 1925.

The dynasty was established by one of the Qajar tribal chieftains, Agha Muhammad Khan (d. 1797), whose depression is said to have been partly behind his choice as capital of an unremarkable small town named Tehran in 1785. Later Qajar kings—especially Fath Ali Shah (r. 1797–1834) and Naser al-Din Shah (r. 1848–96)—steadily nationalized the dynasty and neutralized many of the competing tribes and local rulers.[70] But neither they nor their successors could effectively counter the rising powers of the Shi'ite *ulama* or the commercial and territorial designs on Iran of the British and the Russians. Two disastrous wars with Russia, in 1804–5 and 1828, resulted in the loss of much of Iran's territory in the Caucasus to its northern neighbor. Not to be outdone, Britain encouraged British entrepreneurs to acquire monopoly export rights known as "concessions," and the Iranian government granted major concessions to British interests in 1863 (for telegraph lines), 1872 (for mining), and 1889 (for tobacco).[71] Both Britain and Russia also discovered loans—necessary to fund infrequent development projects or the far more costly royal visits to Europe—as a guaranteed way of securing the dependence of the fledgling Qajar state on their respective governments. In 1900, for example, the Iranian government secured a loan of £2,000,000 from Russia so that Muzaffar al-Din Shah (r. 1896–1907) and his entourage could go on an eight-month tour of Europe.[72] Before long, the combination of foreign dominance, institutional decay, and royal despotism sparked the Constitutional Revolution.

Iran's Constitutional Revolution is generally dated from 1905 to 1911. It involved three principal elements in Iranian society: the *ulama*, some of whom were procourt but many of whom favored limitations on the arbitrary powers of the monarch; the merchants, whose opposition was inspired by their organic links with the *ulama* and their resentment toward foreign concessions; and a small cadre of educated intellectuals, who were heartened by the success of the constitutionalists in Istanbul and the European phenomenon of limited, parliamentary monarchy. Also important were local notables *('ayan)*, many of whom were closely allied with, and were at times members of, the *ulama* or the merchant classes. Often divided and bitterly fractious, the emergence of revolutionary circumstances in the early 1900s brought these groups together, uniting them in the common purpose of a brewing revolutionary movement.[73] But their growing demands for a "House of Justice" (Edalat Khaneh) and eventually a parliament (Majles) were met by the recalcitrance of Muzaffar al-Din Shah, who agreed to decree a constitution only on his deathbed. Even then, his successor, Muhammad Ali (r. 1907–9), tried to quell the Majles by bombarding it. When he was forced to abdicate, power passed to the twelve-year-old Ahmad Shah, but by then neither domestic control nor control of the country's borders was in government hands, the former being controlled by tribal chieftains and the latter by Britain and Russia.

The Constitutional Revolution had a mixed legacy for Iran. To begin with, it is unclear whether the participants in the movement to impose constitutional restrictions on the monarchy—the clergy, members of the intelligentsia, local notables, and bazaar merchants—ever considered themselves "revolutionaries" per se. They neither sought to nor were able to overthrow the existing political order and replace it with a fundamentally different one. Instead, insofar as the movement's principal actors were concerned, they had embarked on a quest to bring about a government that would be in compliance with traditional notions of justice (*'edalat*) and freedom from tyranny (*zulm*).[74] In the long run, they failed. In the process, the movement gave rise to a number of local associations (*anjomans*), especially in Tehran and the northern city of Tabriz. Inspired by and modeled after the communist soviets, the associations were meant to choose local deputies for the Majles and to take an active role in local government. However, they had the unintended consequence of deepening existing factional divisions and greatly contributing to the country's administrative paralysis. And, as if to add insult to injury, the two great powers, Britain and Russia, only found Iran's chaotic circumstances more conducive to their larger imperial goals and expanded their presence and hold over the country.

Despite its multiple setbacks and negative consequences, the Constitutional Revolution turned out to be one of the most important events in Iranian history. Later generations of Iranians pointed to the "revolutionary" years of 1905–11 as the beginning of a long and protracted struggle to curtail the arbitrary powers of absolutist monarchy. Also, both the constitution (Qanun Asasi, or Basic Law) and the Majles were important political innovations for Iran, their foreign and imported nature notwithstanding. While in the early decades the Majles was politically emasculated and ceased to function as a meaningful parliamentary body, in the aftermath of the Second World War, when the Iranian monarchy was once again weakened, it did make its imprint on Iranian history. Finally, the same set of actors involved in the Constitutional Revolution went on to bring about a different sort of revolution some seven decades later—the Islamic revolution of 1978–79—this time with significant help from the urban middle classes.

In the short run, however, the Constitutional Revolution plunged Iran into chaos. With an ineffectual monarchy and the Majles torn by factional rivalries, the country drifted through the Great War at the mercy of foreign powers. Finally, in 1921, an army officer named Reza and a well-known journalist by the name of Seyyed Zia-alddin Tabatabai launched a military coup, becoming the commander of the army and the prime minister, respectively. Zia was eased out of power in 1923, and Reza deposed the monarchy two years later, thus bringing the Qajar era to an end. Having earlier adopted the last name Pahlavi, he declared himself shah and established the Pahlavi dynasty.

Habitation patterns, geography, commerce, and prevailing sociocultural norms often directly influence the life of human communities. In relation to the Middle East, great civilizations rose along major riverbanks and died out when they could no longer manage the canals and irrigation works around which their hydraulic states and societies had emerged. Related to this was the importance of cities and the resulting connection of their economic wealth and well-being with the structures and institutions of political power. Vast expanses of desert elsewhere led to the emergence of cities with significant population concentrations alongside remote, small villages and mobile nomadic tribes. Geographic distance, reinforced by a preponderance of mountainous and inaccessible desert areas, made centralized state building more arduous, often resulting in the extremes of either royal despotism or political dysfunction. In either case, political institutions became impermanent, often rising fast and falling hard, isolated from the larger social arena they sought to govern. Society, whether in Iran in the east or in Morocco in the west, went about its own life, largely impervious to the competition of tribes that aspired to become ruling dynasties. Territorial conquests and mass conversions did influence the daily lives of the masses, but the overall level of contact between the people, or their collectivity of "society," and the various apparatuses of political power, what we today call the "state," was minimal.

A survey of Middle Eastern political history highlights another important conclusion, namely the significance of Islam, from the very beginning, as both a moral order and a source of social organization and political mobilization. Repeated dynasties, the most notable and resilient of which were the Umayyads, the Abbasids, the Ottomans, and the Safavids, were inspired by the ideals and teachings of Islam and used their political power to spread it. A more cynical but equally valid interpretation would be to see Islam as a tool for political legitimation from the earliest times, manipulated, often mutilated, to suit specific political purposes. As the events of our own times demonstrate, the convenience of such use has not been lost on more recent generations of Middle Eastern politicians.

Finally, colonialism has a long history in the Middle East. The rhetoric of the Ottomans and what they stood for in real life, the caliphate, makes it easy to forget that their rule, especially outside their Anatolian heartland, was essentially colonial. The provinces were mostly considered backwaters, members of the *umma* good for the military protection of the Istanbul-based dynasty and the raising of revenues. Whatever economic development occurred there was not so much for the sake of the local population as for the greater good of the empire. Mosques were built, roads and waterworks repaired, and forts erected only insofar as they served the purposes of the royal court in Istanbul. In fact, many previously prosperous regions and provinces were bled dry by tax farming. Compounding matters, many of the conservative *ulama* identified science and technology with Europe, the abode of Christianity and the crusading nemesis of Islam. Sacrificed in the process were industrial development and the emergence of local political institutions and practices. The ensuing problems of economic underdevelopment and skewed political institutionalization would only become magnified in the twentieth century.

2 From Territories to Independent States

The end of the Ottoman dynasty marked the termination of caliphal rule as the Middle East had come to know it since the earliest years of Islam. The dramatic changes that were to come had actually started a few years before the death of the Ottomans, with Europe's growing economic and military interests in the region and an incipient Arab revolt having expedited the sultanate's demise. The more things change, goes the popular wisdom, the faster they change. This certainly applies to the political history of the Middle East after the end of the Great War, as the order of many things changed greatly and often did so with extraordinary speed. Though change was not new to the Middle East, the metamorphoses that occurred after the First World War took place faster and at a more fundamental level than those at almost any time in the past. More importantly, from our perspective, these were the changes whose effects and consequences the Middle East is still grappling with today.

In the chapters to come, I highlight three defining periods in the life of the contemporary Middle East: the interwar period, lasting approximately from the termination of the Ottoman Empire to the end of the Second World War; the 1940s and 1950s, when the state of Israel and its nemesis, Nasserism, were born; and the 1960s, 1970s, and 1980s, during which the Arab world witnessed a shameful military defeat in 1967, a confidence-inspiring victory of sorts in 1973, and the rise and fall of oil prices. This brings us to the Iranian revolution of 1978–79, discussed in Chapter 5. The 1967 and 1973 Wars also deserve separate treatment of their own, given in Chapter 4.

STATE FORMATION IN THE 1920S

The period between the end of the Great War in 1918 and the beginning of the Second World War in 1939 was an era of tremendous importance for the Middle East, one whose consequences still reverberate today, more than half a century later. What occurred in these fateful decades transformed the destiny of entire nations, created new countries, brought overt European rule to the region, resulted in the drawing and redrawing of national boundaries, and gave rise to new dynasties. Middle Eastern history has so many highlights that it is hard to settle on one as the start of the region's "modern" era. But the interwar period is perhaps the strongest contender. History, of course, is not an event but a process, and the unfolding of this process at this critical juncture, from the late 1910s to the mid- to late 1940s, gave rise to the contemporary Middle East we have come to know. Historical processes neither occur in a vacuum nor are irrelevant to or disconnected from the past and the present, and many of the processes set in motion at the conclusion of World War I continue to unfold today. The legacy of European rule still affects domestic and foreign policies; the state building that started in the 1920s was only intensified in the 1950s and 1960s and in some ways continues today; and even borders remain contested and are the cause of conflicts large and small. The ghosts of the past still roam the Middle East.

In the early twentieth century, three primary sets of players emerged in the politics and diplomacy of the Middle East: the two main European powers at the time, namely Britain and France, and local political actors and individuals who went on to assume historic importance. The slow death of the Ottoman Empire left a power vacuum, with the result that all these players sought to enhance and augment their own interests in the region. In so doing, they engaged in competition and rivalry, but at times they also cooperated and colluded with each other, covertly as well as overtly.

Britain's diplomacy in the Middle East at this time was based on three main interrelated and reinforcing objectives. Britain's biggest concern by far was the security of its hold over the "crown jewel," India, especially against possible encroachments by Russia and France. This meant ensuring not only that India's neighbors complied with British interests, thus necessitating active British attention to Iran, but also that the shortest maritime route to India for the British navy, through the Suez Canal, remained under British control. By one estimate, at the time of the canal's opening, a British ship would take only forty days to sail from England to India through the Suez Canal as compared to five months around the Cape.[1]

For the next three decades or so, until the strategic waterway was finally nationalized by a new, revolutionary government in Cairo in 1956, much of British policy in the Middle East revolved around the defense of the Suez Canal. In large measure, given that on a couple of occasions the British had faced military difficulties in confronting the Ottoman forces—most notably in the famous battle of Gallipoli and briefly in Palestine—it was the security of the Suez that prompted Britain to ensure that Palestine and Transjordan were in friendly hands. In Palestine they intervened directly, although, as we shall see below, their policies there were often confused and contradictory. In Transjordan, they oversaw the creation of a nominally independent country over whose foreign policy, economy, and military they retained control.

Second, especially given the expanding British navy's insatiable fuel requirements, Britain was keen on maintaining secure and free access to newly discovered oil along the northern tier of the Persian Gulf. Consequently, as the historian Roger Adelson put it, the Persian Gulf was turned into a "British lake."[2] Third, and perhaps most important, was the concern of what to do with the territories soon to be partitioned from the Ottoman Empire. The Ottomans were seen by the Europeans as sick and dying, and the fate of their vast empire, including their prized capital of Istanbul, formed the heart of the so-called "Eastern Question."[3] To safeguard its interests and expand its influence in the aftermath of the Ottomans' death, Britain, as we shall see presently, embarked on a series of historic diplomatic initiatives, the most important of which were the Hussein-McMahon Correspondence, the Sykes-Picot Agreement, and the Balfour Declaration.

French objectives in the Middle East were similar, if less clear. Not having a crown jewel like India to protect, French policy toward the Middle East was less coherent. France appears to have had two primary motivations: competition with other European powers, namely Britain and Germany, for acquiring more influence in the Ottoman territories; and the protection of the region's Christians, many of whom were historically concentrated in the Levant. As far as competition with its European neighbors was concerned, France was alarmed—as was Britain—by the German construction of the Baghdad Railway beginning in 1903. The attempt to finance and build a competing railway from Syria to Baghdad was representative of this competition.

Like Britain's, most of France's interests in the Middle East at this time revolved around commercial investments. On the eve of World War I, the French held fully 60 percent of all Ottoman loans, compared with Germany's 21 percent share and Britain's 14 percent.[4] French private investors were active throughout the Ottoman lands, as shown by their initial financing of the construction of the Suez Canal, along with some Egyptian financiers, under the auspices of La Compagnie Universelle du

Canal Maritime de Suez. In this regard, toward the beginning of the twentieth century, France and Britain decided to cooperate rather than compete. In 1904, they signed an agreement commonly referred to as the Entente Cordial. According to the terms of the agreement, France would retain a free hand in the Ottoman colony of Morocco in exchange for giving Britain free rein in Egypt. "His Britannic Majesty's Government," the treaty stipulated, "recognise that it appertains to France, more particularly as a Power whose dominion is coterminous for a great distance with those [sic] of Morocco, to preserve order in that country, and to provide assistance for the purpose of all administrative, economic, financial, and military reforms which it may require."[5] Nevertheless, despite what the agreement claimed, for France control over the Ottoman territories in the Maghreb—most notably in Algeria, which it had invaded in 1830, and Morocco and Tunisia—was not an economic or demographic necessity. It was, rather, a consequence of the desire to restore France's waning imperial glory.

The Levant, where France's extensive and long-standing presence was motivated by its desire to protect the region's Christian population, was somewhat of an exception. The European powers and even the Sublime Porte had come to recognize France's special role as the protector of the Levantine Christians, especially the Maronites. French charity organizations and schools were founded throughout Syria. In 1875, French Jesuits established the University of St. Joseph in Beirut. Before World War I, some fifty thousand Syrian students were attending French schools, as compared to only twenty-three thousand pupils in schools of all other nationalities.[6] Not surprisingly, when the French and British carved up the Asiatic Ottoman territories in the Sykes-Picot Agreement, Mesopotamia (Iraq), Arabia, and Palestine became British protectorates, while the Syrian and Lebanese protectorates went to the French. As for the Maghreb, which the French had generally come to consider not as colonies but rather as provinces linked to the mother country, independence had to come through warfare.

This is where the third set of actors, the local nation builders, came in. Some of these men—most notably Kemal Atatürk in Turkey, Reza Pahlavi in Iran, Muhammad V in Morocco, and Habib Bourguiba in Tunisia—were determined to end the backwardness of their peoples and the domination of European powers. Others, such as members of the Hashemite and Ibn Saud clans, realized that they could not acquire power without the support of the outsiders dominating their land at the time and therefore entered into strategic alliances with the British, or, in a few instances, with the French, or with both.

The Middle East of the early twentieth century also saw the unfolding of three interrelated and reinforcing developments. One was the Arab Revolt launched against Ottoman rule in June 1916. The revolt began in the Hijaz, led to the establishment of a short-lived dynasty in Syria, and eventually resulted in a longer-lasting (though still impermanent) monarchy in Iraq. The revolt was the product of a series of ten communications between its chief protagonist, a certain Sharif Hussein in Mecca, and the British high commissioner in the newly declared protectorate of Egypt, Sir Henry McMahon. The Hussein-McMahon Correspondence was part of a second phenomenon that characterized the larger Middle East at the time, namely the allocation of colonial territories called mandates and the drawing of maps through a series of bilateral and multilateral treaties. All treaties that affect borders and national designations are of historic importance, but some of the more important ones signed or issued around this time were the Sykes-Picot Agreement (May 1916), the Balfour Declaration (November 1917), the Conference of San Remo (April 1920), and the Treaty of Sèvres (August 1920). A third, related feature was the birth of countries carved out of former Ottoman territories: Turkey, Palestine, Syria, Lebanon, Transjordan, Iraq, and Saudi Arabia. Of these, Palestine had the shortest life span, ceasing to exist in 1948 and being replaced by Israel.

The Arab Revolt is important in two respects. First, it marked the beginning of the dismemberment of the Ottoman Empire in the twentieth century.[7] Second, it ushered in an era of extremely close relationships between Britain and those who came to eventually rule Transjordan and parts of Arabia, including Iraq. British policy in the Middle East during and immediately after World War I was largely determined by its concern for the protection of two of its strategic possessions—India and Egypt— whose importance was magnified thanks to the opening of the Suez Canal.[8] During the war, after much internal policy debate and in order to deflate the potential ferocity of a holy war (*jihad*) declared by the Ottoman sultan on the Allied Powers, Britain searched for an ally to check the Ottoman threat from within. From the Islamic heart of the empire came Mecca's ambitious local ruler, Hussein ibn Ali, whose title of Sharif, denoting descent from the Prophet's family, had earned him a certain amount of prestige throughout the Hijaz.[9]

Beginning in 1914, Hussein had started seeking British support for an uprising that he hoped would lead to the establishment of an independent Arab state, one whose boundaries stretched from the Iranian border in the east to the Mediterranean Sea in the west. The ensuing correspondence between McMahon and Hussein has since become the subject of great historical controversy due to different interpretations of exactly what territorial promises were conveyed to the aspiring rebels.[10] But in any case Hussein started his rebellion on June 5, 1916, declaring himself the ruler of the newly independent Hijaz. A protracted desert war ensued for the next two years, one of the effects of which was the rise of an adventurous British military advisor named T. E. Lawrence.[11] More important were the revolt's actual consequences for the political geography of the Middle East. In September 1918, as British forces marched toward Damascus, one of Hussein's sons, Faisal, declared himself the ruler of Syria. The dismemberment of the Ottoman Empire had thus begun, and so, it seemed, had Arab independence.

But the latter was not to be. By October 1916, Britain and France had finalized the Sykes-Picot Agreement, in the form of eleven letters exchanged between the two sides, through which they divided the Ottoman provinces into different spheres of influence (map 2). Under the agreement, upon partitioning the Ottoman Empire, Britain and France were "to recognize and protect an Arab State or a Confederation of Arab States . . . under the suzerainty of an Arab Chief." For those parts of the empire excluded from the Arab state, the two European powers were "allowed to establish such direct and indirect administration or control as they desire and as they may think fit to arrange with the Arab State or Confederation of Arab States."[12] Consequently, Greater Syria, which included southwestern Turkey in the north and Lebanon in the west, along with parts of northern Iraq, was to become the sphere of influence of France. Britain was to gain control over Iraq, the Arabian peninsula, and Transjordan. Palestine was subject to an international regime. To ensure their support for the Allied cause, Italy was promised southern Anatolia, and Russia was to obtain control over Istanbul, the strategically important Bosphorus Straits, and parts of eastern Anatolia.

The Sykes-Picot Agreement was later revised and in many ways substantially changed. Among the major changes to the agreement was the exclusion of Russia and Italy from its provisions, that of the former being due to the October 1917 revolution. The Balfour Declaration also seemed to undermine the status that the agreement accorded to Palestine. Moreover, the agreement did not delineate the precise boundaries of the territories in question, and only through later treaties did the current shape of many Middle Eastern countries emerge. But the ultimate importance of the Sykes-Picot Agreement lay in its allocation of spheres of influence to Europe's two remaining paramount powers. Awarded control over Syria through the agreement, French troops marched on Damascus on July 25, 1920, having defeated Faisal's army two days earlier.

The deposed king, whose reign had officially lasted for only a few

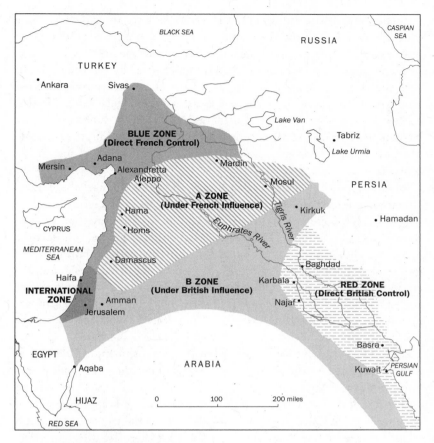

Map 2. The Sykes-Picot Agreement.

months, was not to be countryless for long. To quell an insurrection in Iraq in 1920, the British brought in Faisal, where, after a plebescite generally agreed to have been rigged, he was proclaimed king in 1921. His brother Abdullah, meanwhile, was persuaded by the British colonial secretary, Winston Churchill, to accept temporary control over the newly declared Emirate of Transjordan. No one, it appears, expected Transjordan to last, including Churchill himself. This is indicated by Abdullah's own account of a conversation with Churchill during which the British colonial secretary said he "hoped that in six months he would be able to congratulate us [i.e., Abdullah] on the return of Syria to our hands."[13] As history would have it, Transjordan did last, changing its name, in 1946, to Jordan.[14] For a time, under British tutelage, the Hashemites were in control of three countries: Hussein in the Hijaz and his two sons, Faisal and Abdullah, in Iraq and Jordan, respectively. The father's reign was the first to go, in 1924, swept away by a band of puritanical warriors headed by the Saud clan. In 1958 the Hashemites lost Iraq also, this time to a military coup inspired by the Arab revolutionary of the day, Egypt's Gamal Abdel Nasser. Jordan was a different story, however, for there the Hashemite dynasty not only has remained in firm control to this day but, especially in the last decade or so, has become the possessor of a political asset rather rare in the Middle East—popular legitimacy.

Mention must be made of what history has come to label the Balfour Declaration, issued on November 2, 1917, in the form of a letter from the British foreign secretary, Arthur James Balfour, to a leading Zionist, Lord Rothschild. The Balfour Declaration was neither a product of wartime humanitarianism nor a hasty improvisation in the face of mounting crises in Palestine. Rather, it was the result of months of calculations and deliberations, with numerous drafts of it being prepared beginning in summer 1917. The final version was released only after receiving the private approval of U.S. President Woodrow Wilson.[15] The released text, which has since assumed immense historical importance in the Middle East, read, "His Majesty's Government view with favour the establishment in Palestine of a National Home for the Jewish People, and will use their best endeavours to facilitate the achievement of this object, it being clearly understood that nothing shall be done which may prejudice the civil and religious rights of existing non-Jewish communities in Palestine, or the rights and political status enjoyed by Jews in any other country."[16] There are different interpretations as to why Britain issued such a declaration, to which a majority of British Jews and the only Jew in the ruling cabinet at the time were opposed. Two main reasons seem to underlie the declaration, one personal, the other political.[17] Politically, Britain appears to have hoped that the declaration would please American Jewry, who would in turn pressure the U.S. government to be more forthcoming in its assistance to the Allied war effort. It was also hoped that Russian Jews would apply pressure to Russia's revolutionary government to once again return to the war theater. "From a purely diplomatic and political view," Balfour is reported to have told the rest of the British cabinet, by making "a declaration favourable to such an idea, we should be able to carry on extremely useful propaganda both in Russia and America."[18] As it turned out, at the time of its publication, the declaration was hardly noticed by the British press and the public at large, and Russia left the war shortly afterward anyway.

Complementing these political considerations underlying the Balfour Declaration were several personal concerns by the various actors involved, especially close connections between leading advocates of the Zionist cause and members of the British cabinet. The famous Zionist Chaim Weizmann, later to become the president of Israel, was a close friend of Prime Minister Lloyd George and an influential figure in British political circles. Sir Mark Sykes, of Sykes-Picot fame, was also a strong believer in Zionism, though he himself was not a Jew.[19] Balfour and Rothschild had had a long personal and professional acquaintance as well. These and other British policy makers saw the declaration as a great historical opportunity, not only to leave yet another of their own marks on global politics but, more importantly, to right some of the wrongs that history had committed against the Jews.

From a larger historical perspective, it is hard to miss glimpses of Britain's imperial temptation. Here was Britain, standing increasingly alone. The Ottomans were mortally wounded, Germany was soon to be saddled with the Versailles Treaty, Russia was in the midst of a revolution and a civil war, and France had found itself a less equal partner in sharing the spoils of victory. British policy makers appear to have genuinely thought that they could solve the historic problems of the Jews once and for all and attend to the ensuing problems of the Arabs as well, while at the same time furthering Britain's imperial interests. The solution was thought to involve nothing more than a series of mandates. Before long, however, the force of circumstances had imposed increasing sobriety on the British. The Pandora's box they had opened was not to be closed anytime soon, in fact not until long after their imperial glory had faded.

The end of World War I brought to a head tensions between high-minded Wilsonian idealism emanating from the United States and the reality of colonial control over the Middle East by France and Britain. The outcome was the concept of mandatory rule, a polite disguise for what a couple of decades earlier had been unabashedly called colonialism. The actual carving up occurred at the Conference of San Remo in April 1920 and was soon adopted by the League of Nations. The Ottomans, on their deathbed and in no position to influence the course of events dictated to them, signed off on the region's new geopolitical realities the following August in the Treaty of Sèvres.

According to Article 22 of the Covenant of the League of Nations, "certain communities formerly belonging to the Turkish empire" had not yet reached a stage needed to become fully independent and to foster development. Therefore, "their existence as independent nations can be provisionally recognized subject to the rendering of administrative advice and assistance by a mandatory unit until such time as they are able to stand alone."[20] The mandatory powers were designated as "trustees" of their mandates, and one of their tasks was to administer "within such boundaries as may be fixed by them."[21] With slight modifications, the allocation of mandates occurred along the lines of the Sykes-Picot Agreement: Britain acquired the mandates of Iraq and Palestine (including Transjordan), and France the mandate of Greater Syria (including Lebanon) (map 3).

The introduction of the mandate system was challenged by many of the peoples it affected. The French mandate in Syria, for example, was imposed after King Faisal was first threatened and then ousted by French forces advancing on Damascus. There were also major uprisings in Iraq following the awarding of the Iraqi mandate to Britain, the causes of which have been attributed to a mixture of nationalist, sectarian (Shi'ite), and tribal sentiments.[22] Only the Zionists appear to have greeted with genuine excitement the idea of a Palestinian mandate going to Britain, which, in light of the Balfour Declaration, had already endorsed the idea of a Jewish homeland in Palestine. In fact, the British officials who drafted the Palestinian mandate, mostly junior in rank, did so on the basis of a Zionist draft and incorporated the Zionist program. The upper echelons of the Foreign Office, though not quite happy with the original draft, amended it only slightly.[23]

A word should also be said about the shape of the international boundaries that emerged from the San Remo Conference. With rulers in hand, French and British negotiators drew national boundaries and gave shape to the Middle East of today. What constrained or concerned them were not the wishes and aspirations of the peoples whose lives they were influencing but rather their own diplomatic maneuvers and agendas.[24] The creation of Lebanon is a case in point. For the sake of convenience, the French divided Syria into six administrative units based, in part, on the preponderance of religious groups in each area. The Sunni majority had never been enthusiastic about the idea of French rule, and administrative divisions were seen as an effective way of undermining the potential for anti-French solidarity on religious grounds.[25] To make some of the smaller areas economically more viable, in August 1920 several adjacent regions were attached to Lebanon, which had been one of the units, and the Greater State of Lebanon was subsequently created. Although separation from Syria and the creation of Lebanon were greeted with considerable excitement on the part of the new country's Maronite community, ensuring economic viability had come at the expense of social and religious homogeneity.[26] This was to have tragic consequences later. As for Syria, the remaining

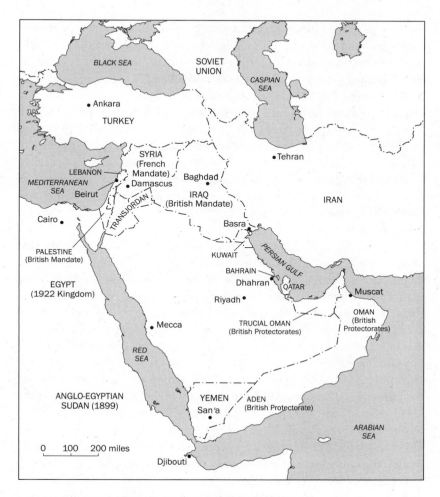

Map 3. French and British mandates after World War I.

administrative units *(velayats)* were also amalgamated into one, and in 1924 Syria as we know it today was formed.

The creation of Transjordan was also a thoroughly colonial endeavor, this time by Britain. Under Ottoman rule, the historic boundaries of Palestine had never been clearly delineated, and the area was at times viewed as part of "southern Syria." More commonly, Palestine was seen as the area bordering the Mediterranean on the west, Syria on the north, and the Hijaz on the east. But under British mandatory rule after 1920, the sparsely populated desert area east of the Jordan River gained increasing autonomy, and it was here that Churchill convinced Abdullah, Faisal's older brother, to abandon his Syrian campaign and become the ruler of the newly created Transjordan. By the time the League of Nations formally recognized the British mandate of Palestine in 1922, the area in question had already been partitioned into two, with Palestine west of the Jordan River and Transjordan on the east, and the Hashemites were in control of the latter.[27] A 1928 agreement between the British government and Abdullah, who had now adopted the royal title of emir, gave Transjordan its own government, with British tutelage over foreign policy and finance. A succession of British military officers, the most famous of whom was Glubb Pasha, were put in charge of organizing and commanding the new country's army, the Arab Legion.

Egypt's story at this juncture is somewhat different, although, like that of its neighbors, it is still replete with colonial intervention. In July 1882 Britain had invaded Egypt, which had long been an autonomous province within the Ottoman Empire, to protect its access to the Suez Canal, whose construction had lasted from 1854 to 1869. Throughout the First World War and for decades thereafter, safe and ready access to the Suez remained Britain's paramount goal.[28] This concern prompted British control over Egypt to be near-complete. While retaining the autonomous Ottoman governor (the khedive) in office, Britain controlled the Egyptian army and the ministries. The dominant political figure in Egypt, in fact, was not the khedive but rather the British consul-general.[29] By the war's end, however, rebellions in the Sudan (then part of Egypt) and serious anti-British riots in Egypt in 1919 had made overt British control of Egyptian affairs extremely costly. Weighing options that ranged from more extensive domination to conditional independence, Britain finally opted for the latter and, on February 28, 1921, unilaterally declared Egypt independent. But neither the control of the Suez nor the larger imperial interests of Britain were totally abandoned. Thus independence came with four conditions: control of the Suez and other British interests; control over Egyptian foreign policy and defense; control over the Sudan; and the right to protect foreign interests and religious minorities. Of all the former Ottoman provinces, Egypt was one of the first to become independent. But the extent and essence of this independence were far from complete.

In the Maghreb, meanwhile, the French remained firmly entrenched, having invaded and conquered Algeria in 1830, Tunisia in 1881, and Morocco in 1912. For some time, French merchants in Marseilles had retained commercial ties with the Maghreb, even after Libya, Tunisia, and

Algeria had fallen under Ottoman suzerainty in the mid- to late 1500s. Initially, in all three of its Maghrebi provinces, Ottoman rule followed the pattern practiced elsewhere in the empire: an Istanbul-appointed governor, assisted by a corps of professional janissaries, a religious judge *(qadi)*, and a navy, used primarily for privateering and harassment of commercial European ships in the Mediterranean.[30] But this was not to last long, as local governors soon started paying only lip service to Istanbul and exercising considerable autonomy and independence. Given the geographic distance from the Ottomans' Anatolian heartland and the Porte's own internal difficulties, Istanbul was hardly in a position to impose its imperial authority on its Maghrebi possessions. By the middle of the seventeenth century, with their local rulers enriched by the revenues accrued through piracy and the sale of captured ship crews as slaves, Tunisia, Algeria, and Libya had become all but independent from Istanbul.

Morocco, for its part, was geographically too remote and isolated to have become subject to Ottoman rule. Despite the Porte's initial efforts at conquest, Morocco developed an indigenous, tradition-bound system of religio-political rule of its own. From the 1550s until the 1830s, the country was ruled by a series of sherifian monarchs claiming to be descendants of the Prophet Muhammad (i.e., sherifs), belonging first to the Saadian and then to the Alawite dynasties. The sherifians made impressive headway in uniting the country and imposing central government authority throughout the territories. Nevertheless, on entering the twentieth century, in some respects Morocco remained divided into two parts. The Bilad al-Makhzan (the "government's place") was located along the north and northwest coast, was populated by Arabic speakers, and eventually became subject to the official jurisdiction of the central government. The Bilad al-Siba, in the interior mountains and desert areas, was populated mostly by Berbers and remained largely outside central government control.[31] The significance of Morocco's division into the Bilad al-Makhzan and the Bilad al-Siba is a matter of some debate, with some scholars considering it a defining feature of the country's colonial period and others seeing it as more of a divide deliberately perpetuated for purposes of colonial administrative convenience.[32] But there is no doubt that the sultan's power was geographically circumscribed and often contested.

Lack of preexisting central authority made it harder for the French to dominate the Maghreb. It took them nearly twenty years, for example, to pacify Morocco, and from 1921 to 1926 they were forced to fight a protracted war in the northern mountains of Rif. At its peak, some seven hundred thousand French and Spanish troops took part in what came to be known as the Rif War. Eventually, however, French colonial designs brought the whole of the Maghreb under direct French rule, with the exception of Libya, which fell prey to an Italian invasion in 1911. Unlike the British, who went into the Middle East to defend their imperial interests in the Indian subcontinent, the French went into North Africa with less clear strategic goals and interests. The French invasion of Algeria in 1830 appears to have been motivated primarily by domestic political considerations; competition with Britain seems to have been only a secondary concern. And when the French did conquer the Maghreb, they were initially and briefly undecided about what to do with their new acquisitions. Then Algeria was targeted for assimilation and treated as yet another French province—assuming, of course, that the Bureau of Native Affairs could make civilized Frenchmen out of the natives. Thus the colonial authorities actively promoted Algeria's rapid colonization, and before long an expanding and relatively affluent community of *colons*, with significant landholdings, emerged. Tunisia and later Morocco became protectorates, both used for their rich minerals and their farms, and, most importantly, for the protection of the newly acquired province. Consequently, French colonial rule was less direct than British rule, and some of the preexisting local institutions of judicial administration were allowed to exist side by side with colonial administrative organs.

Both British and French colonial authorities often contemptuously viewed the native population over whom they ruled as uncivilized. The French, additionally, frequently used violence and systematic mistreatment of the locals as part of their colonial policy, especially in Algeria. An 1833 report by a French parliamentary commission looking into the fall of Algeria is revealing:

> We have sent to their deaths on simple suspicion and without trial people whose guilt was always doubtful and then despoiled their heirs. We massacred people carrying [our] safe conduct, slaughtered on suspicion entire populations subsequently found to be innocent; we have put on trial men considered saints by the country, men revered because they had enough courage to expose themselves to our fury so that they could intervene on behalf of their unfortunate compatriots; judges were found to condemn them and civilized men to execute them. We have thrown into prison chiefs of tribes for offering hospitality to our deserters; we have rewarded treason in the name of negotiation, and termed diplomatic action odious acts of entrapment.[33]

Despite its chilling findings, the report led to few changes in the conduct of French policy in Algeria and even fewer changes in Tunisia and Morocco.

Figure 2. Women in Algiers in the 1880s.

Gradually, the political violence unleashed on the local populations was institutionalized, and all threats to colonial rule or the privileged position of the *colons* were harshly suppressed.[34] This was to have important consequences later for the manner and processes through which Maghrebi independence was won.

Not to be left behind in the Anglo-French grab for territories in the Middle East and North Africa, in October 1911, Italian military forces invaded the Ottomans' other province in the Maghreb, Libya. Italian colonialism was motivated by two primary concerns: maintaining the appearance of a great-power status and alleviating some of the demographic pressures stemming from the country's burgeoning population.[35] The Ottoman hold on Libya, like that on Algeria and Tunisia, had never been very firm, and, like Morocco, Libya entered the twentieth century ridden with tribal conflicts and lacking strong central authority. There was also an increasingly powerful Sufi order called the Sanusi, after its original founder, Muhammad al-Sanusi, who advocated reforming Islam, modeling it after the Islam practiced by the Prophet in Medina, and strongly opposed European colonialism. Libya's colonization by Italians had started as early as the late 1880s and was strongly supported by Italian industrialists, nationalists, and the Catholic Church.[36] When colonization met unexpectedly stiff resistance by the Sanusi and the local tribes, the Italian government was forced to agree to limited self-rule and autonomy between 1914 and 1922. The policy was soon reversed by Rome's fascist government, which viewed Libya as the "fourth shore" of fascist ideology and its conquest as an important step in resurrecting the Roman Empire in Africa. But Italy's conquest of Libya was not completed until 1932. Large agricultural companies supervised the large-scale immigration of poor Italian peasants from the south into Libya. By the early 1940s, out of a population of one million Libyans, some one hundred thousand were Italians. As fortune would have it, the outbreak of World War II brought Italy's imperial ambitions to an end.

Such was the shape of the Middle East and North Africa at the end of World War I. The Ottomans were destroyed and were succeeded by a republican system in Turkey. Britain and France became the region's dominant powers, each having mandates of its own: Palestine and Iraq for Britain, Syria and Lebanon for France. Egypt and the Emirate of Transjordan existed in a state of precarious independence, with Britain remaining the true master of their destinies. The Maghreb had already fallen to the French in the closing decades of the 1800s, and Libya was under Italian control in 1911. Finally, Iran and the Kingdom of Hijaz clung to an independence of sorts. Like Egypt, however, neither could assert complete sovereignty over its territory without British support. Whatever independence had come to the Middle East had done so haltingly, and it was yet to be fully played out in the chaotic decades of the 1930s and 1940s.

THE TURBULENT 1930S AND 1940S

The 1910s and 1920s were periods of profound international change, with new countries being born and old empires dying. The Middle East emerged from the postwar settlements of the 1920s with a new map, one almost unrecognizable compared to the map of the prewar era. Concurrently, it saw the participation of a host of new international actors—Britain, France, the League of Nations, and, to a much lesser extent, the United States— that previously had been only marginally interested in the region. By the time the 1920s drew to a close, the dust had almost all settled. Most of the outstanding border issues—for example, the question of whether the oil-rich, predominantly Kurdish city of Mosul would be part of Turkey or Iraq—were settled by 1925 (the British saw to it that Mosul remained in Iraq). Only one territorial swap occurred later, when Alexandretta was transferred from Syria to Turkey in 1939.

The 1930s, by contrast, were marked less by international changes, at least in the Middle East, than by a consolidation of the domestic political dynamics set in motion in the 1920s. Of the countries of the Middle East, Transjordan, Syria, and Lebanon did not necessarily experience significant changes, remaining mandatory territories and becoming independent only in the 1940s. Egypt also remained in a state of semicolonial submission to Britain, and the Egyptian world would not be turned upside down by Nasserism until after 1952. But far-reaching changes were fundamentally altering the social and political landscape of Turkey, Iran, Palestine, and the Arabian peninsula. Turkey and Iran became dominated by men who strongly advocated what may be labeled statist modernism: using the apparatus of the state, at times repressively, to impose modernization on their countries. Palestine was overcome by Zionism, and any doubts as to whether European Jews needed a distant Zion were settled by the madness of Nazi fascism. Arabia, finally, was taken over by the Saudis, a puritanical clan of warriors from the central Najd region. The Kingdom of Hijaz ceased to exist. In its place was born the Kingdom of Saudi Arabia.

Atatürk and the New Turkey

One of the most profound processes of change in the Middle East was set in motion in Turkey by Mustafa Kemal Atatürk and his fellow nationalist reformers. The changes Atatürk instituted in Turkey were so far-reaching that they are often considered to have been a national revolution.[37] How much of a "revolution" these changes constituted is open to debate.[38] But few can deny that the cumulative effects of what occurred in Turkey were revolutionary. The greatest change occurred in four areas. First was the transformation of subjects of the Ottoman Empire into Turkish citizens with a new, national identity. Linked to this issue of nationalism was the construction, after five centuries of caliphal rule, of a new state apparatus. Third was the state's engineering of far-reaching social changes to remedy a number of perceived ills. Fourth was the promotion of economic development, and hence state efforts to foster industrial modernization.

It would be unfair to the Young Turks and to the members and sympathizers of the Committee for Union and Progress (CUP) to call Mustafa Kemal the father of Turkish nationalism, for these earlier activists were the first to formulate and express ideas of national and popular sovereignty. The beginnings of Turkish nationalism can actually be traced to linguistic and literary innovations in Istanbul and elsewhere in the empire in the 1860s and 1870s.[39] But Kemal gave Turkish nationalism its most articulate expression, one that continues to have deep resonance in Turkey today. This was not an easy task at first, for Ottomanism not only stood for a political entity of sorts but, more importantly for those subject to it, also signified the caliphate (succession) and the guardianship of the larger Islamic community *(umma)*. Even some of Kemal's closest associates remained loyal to the notion of the caliphate. "I am bound by conscience to the Sultanate and the Caliphate," one is reported to have confessed. "It is my duty to remain loyal to the sovereign: my attachment to the Caliphate is imposed on me by my education. . . . To abolish this office and to try and set up an entity of a different character in its place, would lead to failure and disaster. It is quite inadmissible."[40]

Determined to create a new Turkey and a Turkish national identity, Kemal went about his task in incremental steps. First, in 1922, he abolished the Ottoman Sultanate (literally "family dynasty"), thus wresting political power from the Ottomans. But he allowed one of the Ottoman princes to remain as the caliph, thus appeasing the religious sensibilities of his associates and the masses at large. In 1924, when his powers had become more secure, he abolished the caliphate as well.

National identities are not created out of thin air, and Kemal and his like-minded colleagues had many materials to work with. Nevertheless, the task facing them was difficult. As a remedy, repression was applied liberally whenever the new stewards of the state deemed it necessary. The Ottoman Empire had long been multinational in character, and only in the early 1900s, as the empire was dying, did the idea of a distinctively Turkish nation gain currency among some of the younger generation. Even then, the idea of a Turkish nation was so new and tenuous that it lacked a name in the Turkish language. Only during the Young Turk movement, especially from 1908 to 1918, did the name *Türkiye* come into common usage.[41] But the nationalities problem persisted. That many nationalities under Ottoman rule started agitating for independence did not make matters easier. In 1915, the Armenians, who had for centuries lived in peace in Anatolia along with the rest of the population, were forcibly removed to Russian Armenia, with the tragic consequence that some 1.5 million of them perished. An untold number of Turks also lost their lives in the ensuing carnage as the Young Turk government forcibly resettled populations wherever it saw fit. Still, the emerging Turkish nation was by no means ethnoreligiously cohesive. Not only the Kurds in the southeast but a significant Greek population remained within the young country's borders. Consequently a massive population resettlement was undertaken in the 1920s, much like what was happening elsewhere in eastern and central Europe. Between 1923 and 1930, as a result of an agreement between Greece and Turkey, about 1.25 million Greeks were sent from Turkey to Greece, and a smaller number of Turks moved from Greece to Turkey.[42]

The ideals of nationalism were articulated by the political party Kemal came to head shortly after assuming power, the Republican People's Party (RPP). In its Third Congress in May 1931, the party officially adopted six principles as the pillars of what by then had come to be known as Kemalism (Kemalizm) or Atatürkism (Atatürkçülük): populism, nationalism, statism, republicanism, secularism, and reformism/revolutionism.[43] Interrelated, all of these principles were meant to support the larger project of state building facing the new rulers of Turkey. Nationalism was deeply imbued with militarism; the very idea of a Turkish nation had been born out of and sustained by a war of national liberation. That Kemal faced rebellions from the Kurds and from a Sufi mystic *(dervish)* named Şeyh Said within Turkey up until the mid-1920s, *after* he had secured Turkish independence from foreign powers, only served to heighten the military character of Turkish nationalism. Although theoretically he kept the military separated from the civilian apparatus of the state, militarism and nationalism went hand in hand and were seen as inseparable in Kemalism. This was to have lasting consequences for the life of the Turkish republic long after Kemal's death in 1938. Repeatedly, in 1960, 1971, 1980, and 1997, the Turkish military assumed the role of the savior of the republic and protector of the legacy of Kemalism, taking matters into its own hands—the last time from behind the scenes—to ensure that Kemalism remained the nation's guiding light.

The republican state that Kemal created allowed for no dissent. In 1924, an opposition party called the Progressive Republican Party was formed by some of the disenchanted members of the RPP, but it was crushed the following year and its leaders were arrested. Some five hundred political activists were put to death in 1926 and 1927 alone, many hanged publicly.[44] Another brief experiment with party politics in 1930, this time in the form of a loyal opposition named the Free Democratic Party, lasted for only a few months. From then on until 1946, the RPP remained the only venue for political activity. For the remainder of his life, Kemal ruled as an enlightened, modernizing despot. In the words of the historian Bernard Lewis, "Kemal's re-elections by the Assembly were no more than a matter of form. In fact, he enjoyed life tenure, with powers as great as those of any Sultan, appointing and dismissing Prime Ministers and other ministers at will."[45] Despite the continuity of despotism, however, the new system was markedly different from the one it had replaced. New ministries were formed, the civil service was reorganized, and the state assumed a plethora of economic and social functions in its attempts to reshape Turkish society and culture.

Engineering social change was one of the new state's highest priorities, and it was in this arena that the average Turk felt the impact of Kemalism most profoundly. Like the Young Turks and the CUP, Kemal ardently believed that Turkey's salvation lay in making itself European. Unlike the CUP, however, Kemal was virulently antireligious and saw Islam as the primary source of his country's backwardness. "I have no religion, and at times I wish all religions at the bottom of the sea," he is reported to have said once. "He is a weak ruler who needs religion to uphold his government; it is as if he would catch his people in a trap."[46]

Systematically, therefore, he set out to dismantle Islam's grip on Turkish society. He succeeded only partially, but his efforts and initiatives were revolutionary. In 1924, with only slight modifications, the Swiss Civil Code was adopted and replaced the *sharia* (Islamic law). The fez, traditionally worn by Turkish men as a sign of piety, was banned in 1925, and all men were mandated by law to wear Western-style bowler hats instead. Traditional clothing for women was also ridiculed, but, fearing too much of a backlash, Atatürk did not ban the veil outright.[47] There were municipal orders against the veil in some places, and Kemal's female relatives broke with Islamic tradition by appearing in public unveiled. One of his daughters went so far as to become a pilot in the Turkish air force.

An even more revolutionary step was taken in 1928, when Kemal introduced a new, Latin alphabet, abandoning the Arabic script in which Ottoman Turkish had been written. In an address to the nation on August 9, 1928, Kemal told his countrymen that "our rich and harmonious language will now be able to display itself with new Turkish letters. We must free ourselves from these incomprehensible signs, that for centuries have held our minds in an iron vice. You must learn the new Turkish letters quickly."[48] In 1934, all Turks were also ordered to adopt surnames, and their old titles were abolished. The National Assembly gave Kemal the last name Atatürk (Father Turk). At the same time he dropped the excessively Arabic Mustafa, thus becoming Kemal Atatürk.[49]

In the economic arena, the state embarked on a major industrialization program, symbolized by a much celebrated railway line from the new capital, Ankara, to the central city of Sivas. In the absence of a vibrant class of industrial capitalists, the republican state saw itself with little alternative but to actively intervene in the economy, in the process helping the private sector grow and mature.[50] Corporatism became the hallmark of the state's economic pursuits. To foster cooperation with the incipient business community and to finance various development projects, a Business Bank was set up in 1924, and in 1927 the Law of Encouragement of Industry was enacted. Burdened with high debt and a woefully inadequate infrastructure, the state entered into a number of joint ventures with foreign capital, inaugurating, with Soviet help, a massive textile mill in 1935.[51] Protectionist measures, meanwhile, were enacted in the hope of promoting domestic industries.

Such was the state of Turkey in the 1920s and 1930s. The six principles of the Republican People's Party—statism, republicanism, secularism, nationalism, populism, and reformism/revolutionism—were more than mere slogans; they informed the policies of the new republic both during and after the life of its founder. Turkey had forever been changed, not only in name and designation, but in far more profound ways than even the most imaginative scenarios could have predicted.

The last years of Atatürk's life saw a rapid decline in his health and vigor and an accompanying degeneration of what had once been measured and careful rule. As Lord Kinross, one of Atatürk's most celebrated biographers, describes, "A rationalist without a rationalist philosophy, he fell into a mood of disillusion and despondency. A man of action with no actions left to perform, he fell back on the familiar substitute, alcohol; and this began to undermine his physical and mental condition. . . . His nerves were no longer under control. He lost his temper more easily, the tiger now forever caged, snarling abruptly at friends and enemies alike."[52]

Atatürk's legacy, of course, did not go uncontested, and after the tenure of his onetime lieutenant Ismet Inönü ended in 1950, there were modifications to the one-party system over which he had presided. But the bulk of his policies remained in effect, and his larger legacy continues to reign supreme in Turkey today. In many ways, these policies served as models for the modernizing efforts of another contemporary Middle Eastern leader, Iran's Reza Pahlavi, although here the depth of reforms was significantly less than in Turkey.

Reza Pahlavi's Iran

Like Atatürk, Reza Khan was a soldier who had a distinguished record in the army and had risen rapidly through its ranks.[53] He had served in the Cossack brigade, a separate military unit set up and administered by Russia though technically under the control and supervision of the Iranian government. Throughout the Great War, Reza and others like him had seen the de facto dismantling of Iran into spheres of influence by the Allied powers and the steady disintegration of internal order and politics at the hands of a fractious Majles.[54] The Constitutional Revolution and his own lust for worldly pleasures had left the Qajar shah weak and ineffective, and it was within the context of a badly decaying polity that Reza Khan launched a military coup in February 1921. His co-conspirator in the coup was a thirty-four-year-old journalist named Seyyed Zia-alddin Tabatabai, who initially assumed the office of prime minister, with Reza becoming the commander of the army. This arrangement lasted only three months, however, and in May Seyyed Zia was forced to resign from his post and leave Iran.

Initially, the coup makers did not have enough power of their own or enough of a support base to assume total control. For some time, Reza Khan exerted power from behind the scenes while remaining in command of the army, although the Majles, the prime minister, and to a lesser extent the Qajar king, Ahmad Shah, managed on occasion to influence the course of events. Throughout this time, Reza Khan concentrated on establishing domestic order and security. Consequently, he became very popular not only among elements in the military but also among the civilian population and even many politicians.[55] By 1923 he had emerged as the dominant figure in the political establishment, eclipsing individuals in both the Majles and the royal court. In October of the same year, the shah was left with no alternative but to name the army commander as the new prime minister and to leave on a tour of Europe. Within less than two years, Reza Khan would overthrow the Qajars and replace them with a dynasty of his own.

The establishment of a republic in Turkey on October 29, 1923, had served as an inspiration to political modernizers in much of the Middle East, and soon talk circulated in Iran of establishing a similar system in preference over the archaic monarchy of the Qajars. The idea was celebrated by the small but growing cadre of intellectuals who equated republicanism with modernity. Poets, whose elevated art form had long been used to convey social and political messages, composed stirring poetry in praise of the new concept.[56] Reza Khan appears to have initially supported the idea as well, although he soon changed his mind after consulting with members of the Shi'ite clergy *(ulama)*, whose ranks in the central city of Qom had grown following the establishment of the British mandate in Iraq. Weakened central authority had also enhanced the influence of the clerical establishment. Seeing the systemic destruction of Islam's influence in republican Turkey, which had been the seat of the caliphate not too long ago, Iranian clerics feared a similar fate in a republican Iran. Reza Khan's personal ambitions for power dictated against active antagonism of the *ulama* and their possible alliance with Ahmad Shah.[57]

While the notion of republicanism was soon dropped, moves to change the dynasty continued. In fact, the idea of replacing Ahmad Shah with Reza Khan suddenly gained increasing currency, propagated most vocally by some of the regional army commanders and by members of the Majles, many of whom by now owed their positions to the country's strongman.[58] Finally, on December 12, 1925, by a margin of 257 to 3, the Majles voted to abolish the Qajar dynasty and to recognize Reza Khan as the new monarch, Reza Shah. A few months earlier, he had started using the last name Pahlavi, the name of an ancient Iranian script.[59] Thus was established the Pahlavi dynasty, first by a military coup and then by a legal, constitutional one.

Reza Shah and Atatürk were in many ways similar, and the two men are said to have struck up a personal friendship near the beginning of Reza's reign.[60] Both men sought to establish modernizing political systems that radically altered the traditional cultural landscape of their societies. But the two differed in the predicaments they faced and the extent to which they were willing or able to implement change in their countries. For Atatürk, the weakness of the Ottomans meant that the empire was losing its grip on the provinces but not necessarily on the Anatolian heartland, which was, instead, occupied by a number of foreign powers, the Italians and the Greeks chief among them. Once these areas were liberated, the project of state building was facilitated by the existence of previous mechanisms of centralized political control emanating from Istanbul.

This was not the case in Iran, however, where the Qajar dynasty had long lost its effectiveness and maintained only nominal control over the country's territories. Since the early 1900s, Russia and Britain had carved Iran up into respective spheres of influence—Russia in the north and Britain in the south—where their own agents and Iranian proxies operated with complete immunity from government forces. Weakened central authority had also given rise to a number of powerful tribal confederacies; the Bakhtiaris in central Iran and the Lurs in the west and northwest were especially defiant of government efforts to impose taxation and conscription. On the whole, as compared to Turkey, Iran was ethnically and tribally more divided, was economically and industrially less developed, and had a more powerful, conservative clerical establishment with which the modernizing state had to contend. For much of his fifteen-year reign, therefore, Reza Shah was busy extending government authority over contested areas, at times personally commanding the army. More frequent were his extensive trips throughout the country in an effort to personally supervise state building and economic development. While at times brutal, he was often forced to compromise with the *ulama.*

As stated earlier, Atatürk's self-ascribed mission in Turkey had four components: popularizing a new, Turkish national identity; constructing a new state apparatus; fostering economic development; and engineering social and cultural change. Reza Shah's goals in Iran were similar, although his nationalist aspirations were somewhat different in his ethnically and tribally diverse country than in Turkey, where by Atatürk's time the only remaining significant minority were the Kurds. Three aspects of Reza Shah's reign deserve special attention. First was the attempt to make the Pahlavi dynasty national in scope and nature. Second was the desire to bring about economic and infrastructural development. Last was the new shah's campaign to institute social change and to make Iran "modern." By the time his reign ended in 1941, tangible progress had been made in each arena, although the apex of Pahlavi political and military power would be reached during the reign of his son and successor, Muhammad Reza Shah. Muhammad Reza's rule would come to an abrupt and bloody end in 1979.

In an effort to make the Pahlavi dynasty national in scope, Reza Shah pursued a two-pronged policy. First, he sought to break the strength of the tribes and turn them into settled and increasingly "modern" subjects of the state. In the words of one historian, "[F]or Reza Shah, as for many urban Middle Easterners, the tribes are uncouth, unproductive, unruly, and uneducated savages who have been left behind in the primitive state of nature."[61] To accomplish his goal of neutralizing the tribes, he used the military and entered into a series of temporary alliances with competing tribes, sowing dissent among them and using each to reduce the powers of the others. Gradually he disarmed their warriors, undermined their chiefs, conscripted their youths into the army, and forced many to settle into villages. Forced settlement, he thought, was the first step toward progress. Along the same lines, he repeatedly urged the rural population to engage in agricultural activity, which he saw as the key to economic self-sufficiency. Government authority over the different regions and the roads linking them was guaranteed with the establishment of remote military garrisons and the founding of a road police. To facilitate communication and transportation throughout the country, the state also built an estimated thirteen thousand kilometers of roads.[62]

The shah also engaged in a series of political and institutional maneuvers designed to enhance the strength and longevity of his young dynasty. Most of these initiatives were calculated political moves designed to reduce

Figure 3. Mustafa Kemal Atatürk and Reza Shah Pahlavi confer.

the powers of the regime's opponents and entrench those of the monarchy. Steadily, Reza Shah undermined the independence and authority of the Majles. For example, he often personally determined who would or would not be elected to the body.[63] Political parties, once a vibrant feature of the political landscape, were either banned or forced to curtail their independence if they wanted to survive. Several newspapers were banned, and editors who dared to be unflattering to the ruler were frequently arrested and beaten. A rash of "heart attacks" struck the regime's famous opponents in the Majles, in the cabinet, and among other notables. At the same time, the army, from which the monarch's rise to power had become possible, emerged as one of the most powerful institutions in the new system, with the shah personally in command of the forces until the end of his reign in 1941. A Conscription Law, enacted in 1925, led to a significant increase in the size of the armed forces. The number of men in uniform grew from 40,000 in 1926 to 127,000 in 1941, and the country acquired numerous tanks, military planes, and navy ships. The new king always appeared in an undecorated military uniform, and the political system over which he ruled in many ways came to resemble a military dictatorship. Between 1928 and 1933, the War Ministry reportedly consumed nearly 42 percent of the national budget.[64] Complementing all of this was a burgeoning bureaucratic apparatus, which in time came to comprise some ninety thousand civil servants, ten cabinet ministries, and a host of administrators and functionaries at the provincial, municipal, and rural levels.[65] Thus Reza Shah's reign has been designated as the birth of the modern Iranian state.

Besides efforts to institutionalize and consolidate political control, Reza Shah sought to implement social and cultural changes designed to weaken the clerical establishment and modernize the country. These included judicial reforms in 1926, which led to the replacement of the *sharia* with a secular civil code, and the banning of traditional ethnic clothes in 1928 in preference for European-style clothing and Pahlavi caps (later replaced by so-called "international hats").[66] The same year a law was passed regarding the examination and licensing of religious students and teachers, and the authority of the Ministry of Education was expanded in 1934. The University of Tehran was also established in 1934, complete with a Theology Faculty designed to further undermine the influence of the Qom clerics.[67] Finally, beginning in January 1936, women were forbidden to publicly wear the veil *(chador)*, and they risked assault and arrest by the police if they were caught in public with their veils on.[68]

The state also undertook a series of economic and industrial projects in its efforts to modernize the economy, especially in later years, when political consolidation was at hand. In August 1938, the Trans-Iranian Railway, linking the Caspian Sea to the Persian Gulf, was completed at a cost of $154,708,000.[69] Several large-scale enterprises were established, mostly owned by the state, and manufacturing output and employment rose steadily. Agricultural output grew, although few deliberate efforts were made to increase the sector's productivity.[70] Determined not to resort to foreign loans to finance its various development projects, the government imposed heavy taxes and paid low wages to workers, prompting wildcat strikes in 1929 and 1931 in the oil and textile sectors, both of which were brutally suppressed.[71] But there was always a fear that the government might spend beyond its means, and an innate sense of conservatism, born out of war-induced austerity, characterized the state's finances. Reza Shah's personal finances were a different story, however, as love of real estate holdings made him one of Iran's richest men—if not *the* richest man—by 1941. By one account, by the time he was forced to abdicate in 1941, his assets included £3,000,000 in bank holdings and three million acres of land.[72]

The end for Reza Shah came in early September 1941, by which time the Second World War was reaching into the Middle East. Throughout the 1930s, Iran had looked toward Germany and the United States as welcome Western powers who could help it modernize and, at the same time, could check the traditional imperial designs of Britain and Russia. For the isolationist United States, however, Iran was too remote and geopolitically insignificant to warrant sending more than a few financial and technical advisors.[73] Germany, in contrast, flooded Iran with its advisors and technical experts in an effort to undermine British and Soviet influence there and, eventually, make inroads into India.[74] Most of the German advisors held sensitive positions in the telephone and telegraph offices. Despite repeated assertions of neutrality by Iran at the beginning of the Second World War, a combined force of British and Soviet forces invaded the country on August 25, 1941, the ground having been prepared earlier by virulent anti-shah propaganda beamed into the country by the British Broadcasting Corporation. An attempt to resist the invaders quickly proved farcical. On September 16, the shah announced his abdication in favor of his twenty-two-year-old son. The British government exiled him first to the island of Mauritius and then to Johannesburg in South Africa, where he died on July 26, 1944. The Pahlavi dynasty he founded was to last for another thirty-five years.

Reza Shah left behind a legacy of absolutist, personalist rule. When he had taken power in 1921, Iran was just emerging from the chaos of the Constitutional Revolution (1905–11) and the crippling effects of the Great War. The country did have a somewhat functioning parliament and the embryonic beginnings of party politics. But political life was at a standstill, economic progress a distant dream, and the influence of foreign powers paramount. Reza Shah's efforts, while not as revolutionary as those of Atatürk, brought some order to Iranian affairs, fostered a measure of economic growth, and changed the social landscape, albeit superficially and in many cases only temporarily. But his tenure saw little in the way of "political development," however the concept may be defined, with Iranian politics no less arbitrary and chaotic when he left office than when he took it. By the time of his forced exile, only three political institutions were left standing—the royal court, the bureaucracy, and the army. And, as the fateful summer days of 1941 bore witness, none could stem the tide of foreign invasion and imposition. At its core, the system was decayed and brittle, bound to fall with the slightest tilt in the balance of power. The son's reign, it might be noted, fared no better historically than the father's, ending unceremoniously thirty-five years later.

Ibn Saud's Arabia

While Iran and Turkey were going through profound changes in their social and political landscapes, in the 1920s and 1930s, the Kingdom of Saudi Arabia was just beginning to take shape. Here in the deserts of the Arabian peninsula, neglected by outsiders after the seat of the caliphate was moved from Medina, some of the most dramatic battles for national unification and political consolidation were fought in the late 1800s and early to mid-1900s. Although technically an Ottoman possession, the Arabian peninsula's geography and climate had long buffered it from Istanbul's penetrative reach, and the region had existed in a state of de facto semiautonomy. More important, by the late 1800s, Istanbul neither cared for nor was in a position to do much in Arabia; its concerns were limited to checking the incipient British presence there and, on occasion, arbitrarily imposing taxes on the local populace.[75] The eruption of the Arab Revolt and the establishment of the Kingdom of Hijaz, however brief, highlighted the increasingly fragile hold of the Ottomans on the region. Within this context, in 1902 a young desert warrior named Abdel Aziz ibn Abd el-Rahman, later to be called Ibn Saud, rose from the Saud clan and, under the banner of his family, eventually established a unified kingdom in Arabia, the Kingdom of Saudi Arabia.

The Sauds were one of the prominent families in the Najd (central) region of Arabia who had long lived in the vicinity of Riyadh. Officially, the Saud "dynasty" dates back to 1726, when a certain Muhammad ibn Saud settled in and started ruling over the city of Dara'iyah, northwest of Riyadh. In 1745 he met and was won over by the puritanical ideas of a traveling sheikh (literally, teacher) named Muhammad ibn Abdel Wahhab. Thus ensued a powerful alliance between the two Muhammads, with one in charge of military command and the other motivating the religioideological zeal of the Wahhabi movement. The Wahhabis were, more accurately, unitarians (Muwwahidun, from *wahid*, "one") who sought to reverse what they perceived to be the corruption of Islam's rigid monotheism by the increasing tendency among believers, particularly Shi'ites and Sufis, to deify certain individuals. The Muwwahidun's spread was fast and ferocious—resulting in the sacking of Karbala in 1802 and the occupation of Mecca and Medina in 1803 and 1805, respectively—but it was not irreversible. By the 1880s, the Saud clan was being eclipsed by another rising family, the Al Rashids, who in turn ran the Sauds out of the Riyadh area in 1890. Not until 1902 did a twenty-one-year-old member of the Saud family, Abdel Aziz ibn Abd el-Rahman, recapture Riyadh in a daring raid and from there go on to become the king of Arabia.

A detailed discussion of Abdel Aziz's conquest of Arabia and his rise to power, while fascinating and rich in melodrama, is beyond the scope of this chapter.[76] By all accounts, however, Abdel Aziz was a brave warrior who, through a series of military conquests, the spread of Wahhabi doctrine, and countless marriages, gradually brought all of Arabia under his control.[77] Throughout, he was aided in his endeavors by the British, who provided him with a monthly stipend plus arms and ammunition, finding him a convenient and willing thorn on the side of the Ottoman sultan.[78] Abdel Aziz encouraged Wahhabi nomads (bedouins) to settle into village communities and to farm. Calling themselves the Akhwan (brothers), they in turn became fanatical warriors for his cause. But before long the Akhwan had become too powerful and unruly, as well as opposed to such modern and supposedly corrupting innovations as the radio. More damaging to Abdel Aziz were their frequent raids on caravans and attacks on British interests in Iraq. In 1932, in one of his last battles, Abdel Aziz finally subdued and disbanded them.

Although most of Abdel Aziz's early conquests were in the Najd region, by the early 1920s his long-awaited dream of dominance over the Hijaz became a reality as British support for the Hashemite Kingdom of Hijaz began wavering. In 1924 the city of Ta'if fell to his forces, and within a few months he was in control of Mecca. Medina and Jedda fell the following year. By 1926, Abdel Aziz had grown confident enough to declare himself the king of Hijaz and sultan of Najd, a title he formally changed on September 27, 1932, to King of Saudi Arabia. His kingdom was now complete.

While Ibn Saud was renowned for his generosity—often giving visitors gold, Arabian horses, or cars (at a time when cars were a rarity)—the late 1920s and early 1930s witnessed a dwindling of his resources, to the point that at times he could not even pay his staff's salaries.[79] In May 1933, however, the Saudi government signed an oil concession agreement with the Standard Oil of California Company, which changed its name first to the California Arabian Standard Oil Company and then to the Arabian American Oil Company, Aramco. In many ways, the terms of this agreement, like those signed earlier between Western companies and other emerging Middle Eastern oil countries, laid the foundations for the later development of rentier economies (see Chapter 8). On the basis of the agreement, after an initial loan of £50,000 in gold, the company would pay Saudi Arabia an annual rent of £5,000 in gold and a further loan of £15,000 in gold as soon as oil was discovered in commercial quantities.[80]

The discovery was made in 1935 in Dhahran, and commercial exploitation began in 1938. By 1939, the once-impoverished kingdom was receiving an annual royalty of about £200,000 in gold.[81] British, Italian, German, and Japanese oil companies soon began jostling for the favor of Ibn Saud as well. But the old desert warrior was no modern statesman and knew little about state finances and budgetary matters. By the time of his death in 1953, the country was once again on the verge of bankruptcy. Saud, his successor, was hardly more successful in his endeavors, and not until the appointment of his brother, Crown Prince Faisal, as the finance minister did the country's finances assume a semblance of order.

The importance of oil in shaping the contemporary political history of Saudi Arabia cannot be overemphasized. Throughout the 1940s and 1950s, Aramco's influence inside the kingdom continued to grow, to the extent that in 1948 the U.S. Department of State became concerned about the company's assumption of extraordinary powers in dealing with the Saudi monarch and his ministers.[82] Dhahran, with its ever-increasing population of American oil workers, was also beginning to look more and more like an American city—the Bakersfield of Arabia—containing two townships that each housed about five thousand Americans and had almost everything American. But the company's Arab workers, mostly having only recently been introduced to machinery of any sort, lived in a different world, underpaid and often maltreated by their American foremen.[83] By one estimate, this resulted in their turnover rate of some 75 percent between 1945 to 1960.[84] Nevertheless, their purchasing power increased, as did that of Ibn Saud.

By the time of Ibn Saud's death in 1953, Saudi Arabia had finally attained internal security and political stability. Politically, however, little development occurred, as absolute power resided first with the kingdom's founder and then with his less able son, Saud. In fact, the once austere and frugal reign of the dynasty's founder had degenerated into corruption and vice near the end, with broken-down Cadillacs strewn across the desert by princes who didn't know how to or didn't care to have them repaired.

Saud's reign brought few changes to the ways of the royal court. His rule coincided with a time of profound disquiet in the Middle East— the Nasserite interlude of the 1950s and 1960s—and through much of that period he effectively entrusted the running of the country to his brother, Crown Prince Faisal. The royal family eventually deposed Saud in November 1964. In the reign of Faisal (r. 1964–82) a concerted effort was made to bring about political institutionalization by creating a modern bureaucracy and introducing procedural formality into the affairs of the state. As the finance minister during his brother's reign, Faisal had also put the dynasty's financial house in order earlier. Only then, by the mid-1960s, could Saudi rule be considered to have become consolidated.[85]

The Saudi Arabia of today is unrecognizable compared to the one Ibn Saud left behind, for it has made economic and industrial leaps and bounds that even the most optimistic assessments could not have imagined. But Ibn Saud's political legacy continues to loom large in the system he left behind. That the country's very name reflects the family's last name represents the degree to which the Saud family permeates the life of the country not only politically but also economically, culturally, and socially. Despite the increasing differentiation of political roles within the Saudi system and the steady involvement of professional technocrats and other qualified non-royals at the higher levels of the bureaucracy, politics in Saudi Arabia remains essentially a family venture. The state that once belonged to one man, Abdel Aziz, now belongs to a whole family, the Saudis. Absolute family rule and all that goes with it—internal conflicts, palace intrigues, patrimonial politics, potential narrowing of the political base—are still very much features of Saudi Arabian politics.

The end of the Ottoman era brought with it a fundamental redrawing of the map of the Middle East, resulting in the creation of a host of new national entities. But the termination of Istanbul's imperial control did not necessarily mean that indigenous, national forces could now assert themselves, at least not for another twenty years or so. Even before the Ottomans had died, Britain and France had begun a contest for the spoils of the Middle East, carving it up into respective protectorates with little understanding of or regard for what the locals wanted. Thus began the era of European imperialism in the Middle East. France established protectorates in the Levant and the Maghreb, going so far as to declare Algeria an integral part of its territory and seeking to assimilate its population into its culture. British protectorates were established in Palestine and Transjordan, and Britain maintained effective suzerainty over Egypt, Iraq, and the countries of the Arabian peninsula. Under the direction and protection of Britain and France, new countries were given shape and new political systems were engineered. Eventually, again under the watchful eyes of the British, Palestine and the Kingdom of Hijaz ceased to exist. National identities and nationalist sentiments were not long to follow, as were sharp reactions to European machinations and dominance.

This chapter highlighted developments in Turkey, Iran, and Saudi Arabia in the formative decades of the 1920s, 1930s, and 1940s. In each, the dismantling of the old order brought with it a new, radically different political system. In Iran and Turkey, the new order was composed of self-declared promoters of modernity and industrialization. In each country, the modernizers sought to destroy archaic social and cultural forces that they saw as inimical to progress toward modernity. In Turkey the changes went the furthest, with the state embarking on a concerted campaign to secularize society that included the introduction of a new alphabet and a new calendar. In Iran, however, somewhat because of the limits of his own agendas—some might say the limits of his intellectual horizon—and the continued powers of the conservative clergy, Reza Shah's "reforms" were not as far-reaching, though still substantial and significant.

In Saudi Arabia at the start of the 1920s, state building was at a far more embryonic stage than in Turkey or in Iran. In fact, while Abdel Aziz ibn Saud built a "state," he did not start its construction until *after* he had unified Arabia in the early 1930s, and even then he built only a skeletal one—a more urban and urbane version of what he had earlier ruled as a tribal warrior. What occurred in the Arabian deserts in the 1910s and 1920s was, more accurately, a process of "nation building," in which a series of conquests and alliances brought disparate tribes under one, increasingly national umbrella. Only after a measure of national cohesion had been accomplished could the construction of a state apparatus be started, a task that the first two Saudi monarchs undertook only haltingly.

Nevertheless, all three political systems discussed here had an important feature in common, and still do: they were created, maintained, and nurtured by one individual, someone who was not just a founding father but a personality larger than life, the embodiment of everything political. From the very beginning, each of these systems, like many others in the Middle East before and after them, was a personal creation, and, more importantly, a personal possession. Individuals came to personify systems; politics was relegated to the domain of personal relations; and institutions assumed only a secondary importance, to be bent and shaped in whatever way the nation's father willed. Such was Middle East politics from the 1920s to the 1940s, and its essence, as will be seen later, would change little for more than a half century afterward.

Just as the Great War fundamentally altered the political geography of the Middle East, so did the Second World War. Beginning in the second half of the 1940s, mandatory protectorates were given their formal independence, and a new country, the state of Israel, was born. Thus ensued one of the most traumatic phases in the life of the contemporary Middle East. The next chapter turns to that era.

3 The Age of Nationalism

In the Middle East, as elsewhere, nationalism has been a powerful force shaping the destiny and character of peoples and countries. Although most conventional accounts of nationalism in the Middle East trace its genesis back to the mid–nineteenth century, it was in the 1940s and the 1950s that nationalism became what it has been ever since, one of the most dominant forces—if not *the* most dominant force—in the region's politics.

Enormous scholarly energy has been spent on defining nationalism and exploring the causes of its birth, and what follows here is of necessity brief and general.[1] For the purposes of this chapter, I take *nationalism* to mean simply attachment on a national scale to a piece of territory, reinforced by common bonds of identity such as shared symbols, historical experiences, language, folklore, and whatever else creates a sense of commonality. At times, these common bonds include religion. This conception of nationalism has two important elements. First, there must be a definite territorial frame of reference, a piece of geography toward which a sense of attachment and loyalty is directed. This may be a result of economic ties to the land, its products having served as a source of livelihood for successive generations, or it may be more immediate and primordial, resulting from the need for shelter, personal security, and the sanctity of one's private household. Second, this territorial attachment needs to become national in scope, a transformation often achieved only through active ideological, political, and at times even military agitation on the part of political leaders and states.

The first element of nationalism, identification with a piece of territory for economic and/or personal reasons, has been a feature of human societies from the beginning of settled life, when the ability to own or at least to live and work on land became a central feature of daily living. By itself, however, this sense of attachment to land, rooted in necessity, is parochial and localized, limited in scope to units that can conceivably be as few as one or two families. What is essential is for such an attachment to become national in scope, embodying individuals not only in isolated pieces of territory but in an organically and emotionally linked territorial entity that contains various towns and cities. The organic and emotional links are reinforced by shared symbols and experiences and by other similar bonds of commonality. In other words, a *nation* needs to have been formed, or to at least be in the process of formation, for attachment to territory to be enhanced in scope and transformed into nationalism.

This sense of nationhood, or "becoming national," emerges out of a variety of developments.[2] Benedict Anderson traces it to the birth of "print-capitalism" in Europe, first in Latin and then in more local vernaculars, and the emerging "possibility of a new imagined community, which in its basic morphology set the stage for the modern nation."[3] Similarly, Ernest Gellner maintains that the spread of industrial social organization creates a certain level of homogeneity throughout society and in cultural norms, thus resulting in the emergence of the phenomenon of nationhood and, consequently, nationalism.[4] Similar material and cultural developments facilitated the social construction of nationality in the non-Western world as well, although here the deliberate role of individual personalities, whose resistance to colonial domination was often inspired in the name of a *nation*, was also important. Often either explicitly or in less conscious ways, these individuals mobilized people in the various cities and regions who already shared certain historical experiences and sociocultural characteristics.

In doing so, these emergent national leaders needed forums and institutions to spread their unifying messages more effectively, at times coercively. The forums often served as embryonic components of a state, through which the national project was formulated among an elite, then articulated for the masses and upheld against challenges from within and from the outside. The phenomenon of the state, therefore—or for stateless nations protostate organizations such as national liberation parties—is central to the development and spread of nationalist sentiments. Centrality of the state became all the more crucial in the early twentieth century, when several multinational empires—most notably the Russian, German, Austro-Hungarian, and Ottoman Empires—collapsed and gave rise to new national entities. In each of these newly independent or "successor" states, the idea of national independence had been a largely elite invention up until that point. Take, for example, the challenges facing the stewards of

Turkish independence upon the death of the Ottomans. As Bernard Lewis observes, "This new idea of the territorial state of Turkey, the fatherland of a nation called the Turks, was by no means easy to inculcate in a people so long accustomed to religious and dynastic royalties. The frontiers of the new state were themselves new and unfamiliar, entirely devoid of the emotional impact made by the beloved outlines of their country on generations of schoolboys in the West; even the name of the country, *Türkiye*, was new in conception and alien in form, so much so that the Turkish authorities hesitated for a while between variant spellings of it."[5] Slightly to the west of Turkey, leaders of the newly independent countries of Poland, Czechoslovakia, and Hungary grappled with nearly identical dilemmas. A few decades later, so did the champions of African independence.

The popular inculcation of the idea of the new nation, and the defense of its largely artificial boundaries, is the task of the state. In fact, the state, and frequently the primary actors within it, the "leaders," emerge as the chief protectors and embodiment of national independence. It is no accident that at certain points in history, depending on the prevailing conditions within the nation and the agendas and capabilities of the state and its leaders, nationalism can boil over into jingoist militarism. At the opposite extreme, nationalism may remain dormant and untapped.

Nationalist sentiments may also be awakened by developments elsewhere. Nationalism can at times assume an *antithetical* nature, being formed and expressed in opposition to something. That something is often the expressed identity of another nation—another nationalism—or an external development that awakens, or reawakens, a sense of national pride and self-assertion. This is precisely what occurred in relation to both Zionist and Palestinian national identities. Zionism, it will be seen shortly, originated in the wake of and in reaction to growing anti-Semitism in Europe in the mid- to late 1800s. In the early decades of the 1900s, this new sense of national identity, by then affixed to geographic Palestine, jolted and awakened a Palestinian identity that had lain dormant for some time.[6] In a sense, "Arabness and Jewishness were formulated as nationalist concepts in historically unprecedented ways."[7]

In the larger Middle East, several different nationalist sentiments emerged, some sequentially, some concurrently in different countries of the region, and still others in an overlapping manner among different peoples within the same geographic territory. This latter form of nationalism developed within the Palestinian and Zionist communities in relation to the same piece of land. Earlier, from approximately the mid-1500s to the mid-1800s, Ottoman nationalism—or, more accurately, Ottomanism—

held sway throughout Ottoman territories, articulated in and dictated from Istanbul. By most accounts, Ottomanism was successful in instilling a communal sense of belonging to an expansive *umma* (Muslim community) and in maintaining loyalty to the Ottoman state and to the sultan. But by the mid–nineteenth century, as the influence and intrigue of European powers in Ottoman territories gradually increased, especially in the Balkans, the sense of national belonging as articulated from Istanbul—of belonging to an imperial, caliphal, Ottoman nation—began to decline. In its place, more localized forms of nationalism, revolving around locally more resonant symbols and less expansive territories, emerged. At this stage Ottomanism was gradually supplanted by Turkish nationalism in Anatolia and by Arabism elsewhere in the empire. The rise and nature of Arabism, or Arab nationalism, differed from region to region in intensity, origin, and precise character.[8] The earliest forms of Arab nationalism, as envisaged politically by the likes of King Hussein of Hijaz and his sons, included the Arab territories of the Ottoman Empire from the boundaries of Iran in the east to Turkey in the north, the Red Sea in the west, and Egypt in the southwest.[9] Hussein's two sons, Faisal and Abdullah, who ruled over Syria (briefly) and eventually Iraq and Transjordan, had still more narrow conceptions of national identity and nationhood, though less out of ideological convictions than as a result of European mapmaking. Although the Ottomans allowed for considerable local autonomy, these territorially more specific versions of nationalism were more steeped in local, Arab (non-Turkic) social dynamics and cultural lore and symbolism.[10]

Political manifestations of Arab nationalism were eclipsed for a few years by the more powerful forces of European colonialism, which, among other things, redrew the map of the Middle East for their own administrative and political convenience. Nevertheless, during the period of European political and military domination, and largely in reaction to it, a number of Arab intellectuals began articulating nationalist ideals and sentiments through the publication of books and journals.[11] Once European colonialism started retreating in the 1940s, Arab nationalism regained the opportunity to assert itself politically, this time in a much more vocal and virulent manner. The Europeans had created new Arab countries, leaving behind new states for each country, and now the stewards of these new states called on their respective nations to awaken to their full national potential. By the mid–twentieth century, there were such brands of nationalism as Egyptian, Iraqi, Syrian, Lebanese, Jordanian, and Libyan. Turkish and Iranian nationalisms had emerged a few decades earlier, articulated by the Kemalist and Pahlavi states, respectively. Hopes

Figure 4. Female members of the Iraqi Home Guard march in Baghdad, 1959.

of resurrecting earlier, territorially more expansive conceptions of Arab nationalism—what came to be known as "Pan-Arabism"—lingered, at times motivated by more immediate political considerations. They led to territorial and political unions of Egypt and Syria (1958–61), as well as an ambitious proposed federation of Egypt, Libya, Syria, and the Sudan in 1971 and another proposed union of Syria and Iraq in 1979, neither of which materialized. These supranational creations were unrealistic and at

best impermanent. Their failure points to the powers of the more localized manifestations of Arab *nations* and the corresponding force of more
locally focused nationalisms.

This chapter examines the emergence and main features of four nationalisms in the Middle East: Zionism and early Israeli nationalism; early
Palestinian nationalism; Egyptian nationalism under Nasser; and Maghrebi
nationalism, as manifested in Morocco, Tunisia, Algeria, and, to a lesser
extent, Libya. These were not, by any means, the only forms of nationalism
in the Middle East in the early and mid–twentieth century. But they had
the most profound influence, affecting the lives of millions not just in the
countries where they flourished but in the whole region. In fact, Israeli and
Palestinian nationalisms unleashed forces and led to developments that to
this day continue to shape Middle Eastern and global political history. The
rest of the chapter concerns the genesis and nature of these two contending
national identities and their more immediate regional impact on Egypt and
the rest of the Middle East. The subtle nuances and complexities of each of
these national identities, and their contribution to the Palestinian-Israeli
conflict, are discussed further in Chapter 7.

ZIONISM AND THE BIRTH OF ISRAEL

The birth of the state of Israel was predicated on three key principles:
(1) the constitution of the Jews as a distinct people with a unique identity,
a nation; (2) the placing of this nation on a specific territory, the biblical
Eretz Israel; and (3) the territorial and juridical independence of this nation
in the form of a modern country. Since the late 1800s, and especially
beginning in the early 1900s and culminating in 1947–48, these principles
have formed the very core of Israel. The formation of a Jewish nation was
facilitated by Zionism: the nation's precise nature and character, and even
its language (Hebrew), were deliberately articulated by individuals who
set out to resurrect an ancient kingdom and its people in a new, modern
form. Every nation needs a territorial reference point, however abstract
in definition and reality, and for the Jewish nation that reference point
was in Palestine. And for the Zionist project to be successfully completed,
the Jewish nation needed political and territorial independence, so Israeli
statehood was declared on May 14, 1948.

The early history of Zionism reads like the determined crusade of a
handful of individuals, among whom Theodor Herzl, David Ben-Gurion,
and Chaim Weizmann stand out. Within a matter of years, however, what
had started as individual and at times highly criticized initiatives had snow-

balled into a large-scale migration of European Jewry into the Promised Land. This migration was reinforced by growing, barbaric anti-Semitism and Jewish persecution, first in Russia, then in eastern and central Europe, and eventually in Germany. Although Zionism reached its most articulate and organized manifestation in nineteenth-century Europe, earlier versions of it, in the form of a belief in the chosenness of the Jewish people and their return to the land the Bible identifies as Eretz Israel, existed among Jews scattered throughout the world. This classical Zionism did not, however, provide much incentive for a return of the Jews to Palestine, as one of its central precepts was that the Jews would return to Zion only at the coming of the Messiah.[12] Nevertheless, the Jewish diaspora had some religious ties with the existing, though very small, community of Jews in Palestine. Estimates put the total number of Jews in the early 1800s at around 2.5 to 3 million, of whom some 90 percent lived in Europe and only about 5,000 lived in Palestine. Palestine itself had an approximate population of between 250,000 to 300,000, of whom an overwhelming majority were Sunni Muslim, some 25,000 to 30,000 were Christian, and an undetermined number, perhaps several thousand, were Druze.[13]

Ironically, Zionism developed in a larger intellectual context that was initially opposed to the project of Jewish national assertion and uniqueness. Throughout the early 1800s, the dominant intellectual trend among the minority of learned European Jews who had not been consigned to the ghettos was the *haskala*. The *haskala* was a literary and cultural "Enlightenment" calling for greater integration into the European cultural mainstream and reform of some of Judaism's archaic rituals.[14] It was, in fact, a notable assimilationist, a prominent Austrian journalist named Theodor Herzl, who, upon witnessing the anti-Semitism of the Dreyfus affair firsthand, decided that the Jews' salvation lay in a hastened return to a territory of their own, a Zion free of prejudice and discrimination.[15] In 1896, Herzl published a pamphlet called *The Jewish State*, in which he deplored the futility of assimilation, pointed to the pervasiveness of European anti-Semitism, and called for the establishment of a separate Jewish state based on Jewish identity and self-determination. The following year, in August 1897, he organized the First Zionist Congress in Basel, Switzerland, which some two hundred delegates attended.

If *The Jewish State* was an attempt to articulate the characteristics of a nation, the First Zionist Congress, and the ones after it, represented that nation's emerging state. Herzl's book is concise, and its message, though simple, must have been compelling to its intended audience. "We are a people," he wrote, "one people."

We have honestly endeavored everywhere to merge ourselves in the social life of surrounding communities and to preserve the faith of our fathers. We are not permitted to do so. . . .

Let the sovereignty be granted us over a portion of the globe large enough to satisfy the rightful requirements of a nation; the rest we shall manage for ourselves. . . .

Let all who are willing to join us, fall in behind our banner and fight for our cause with voice and pen and deed.[16]

Herzl did not create Jewish national identity; no one person creates a national identity from scratch. What he did was awaken what had lain dormant by pointing out, with contagious passion, that a separate, unique, identifiable Jewish nation did exist. "This pamphlet will open a general discussion on the Jewish Question," he proclaimed.[17] And indeed *The Jewish State* did spark debate, in essence becoming, for the early generation of Zionists, a political and national manifesto.

The Basel conference gave organizational shape to Herzl's utopia. Its declaration stated simply that "the aim of Zionism is to create for the Jewish people a home in Palestine secured by public law." Herzl had already advocated as much. What the conference did was to initiate the necessary, concrete steps aimed at making the Zionist dream a reality. In this endeavor, it called for the implementation of four measures: promoting "the colonization of Palestine by Jewish agricultural and industrial workers"; organizing and uniting world Jewry through the creation of appropriate institutions; heightening "Jewish national sentiments and consciousness"; and securing international diplomatic support for the Zionist cause.[18] Implementing these goals was entrusted to a newly created World Zionist Organization, which became the seed of the future Jewish state. By the time the Second Zionist Conference was held in 1898, attended by about 350 delegates, the Zionist movement had grown significantly larger. Whereas only 117 local Zionist groups had been identified a year earlier, by 1898 their numbers had grown to over 900.[19]

Other statelike institutions were quick to follow: a Zionist bank, the Jewish Colonial Trust, in 1899; a Jewish National Fund to finance land purchases in Palestine; and even internal divisions between Herzl's largely secular, "political" Zionism and an emerging "cultural" Zionism calling for greater attention to the essence of Jewish identity and character.[20] The Jewish Agency, established in 1929 to manage the affairs of the Jewish community in Palestine, became something of a "state within a state." Before long, a Zionist Federation of Labor, the Histadrut, a labor party called the Mapai, and a defense force, the Haganah, were established as well.[21] Within this context successive waves of immigration to Palestine, called the *aliya,* were launched. The Jewish nation and the Jewish state were forming in a symbiotic, mutually reinforcing manner.

By the time the Basel conference ended in 1896, the first of five *aliya* was already slowly coming to an end (table 1). It had started in about 1881, and it lasted until 1900, during which time approximately twenty-five thousand mostly young, idealist Zionists immigrated to the Promised Land. But the experiences of this early group were less than successful, as many were new to farming and most were unfamiliar with actual living conditions in their new country. So unpleasant was the experience of the early arrivals that many returned to their countries of origin or emigrated to the United States.[22] Further, many early Zionists discovered, much to their surprise, that Palestine was actually densely populated and intensively cultivated and that available land was consequently expensive.[23] Nevertheless, by the end of the nineteenth century, the Jewish community in Palestine, the Yishuv, grew to approximately fifty thousand individuals. During the second *aliya,* from 1904 to 1913, the Yishuv grew considerably, this time with significant support from the expanding network of Zionist organizations and with financial assistance from wealthy European philanthropists, chief among whom were members of Britain's Rothschild family. The second wave of immigrants were mostly farmers and laborers. Since they had had little or nothing in their original countries to return to, they were determined to succeed in their new land. Thus the Yishuv increasingly assumed the characteristics of an integrated polity, more realistic and attuned to the conditions of its environment, and there to stay. Significantly, most of the leaders of the new state of Israel in 1948 would emerge from this *aliya.*[24] The third *aliya,* generally dated from 1919 to 1923, brought thirty-seven thousand new immigrants to Palestine, expanding the Yishuv to about eighty-four thousand. Another seventy thousand Jews immigrated to Palestine between 1924 and 1928, during the fourth *aliya,* this time mostly urban and mercantile in orientation. With them came the rise of Jewish urban settlements and an increase in the organizational strength of industrial laborers.[25] The fifth and last *aliya,* coming at the rise of fascism and the onslaught of the Second World War in Europe, occurred between 1932 and 1939, by the end of which the Yishuv's population had grown to some 445,000, or about 30 percent of the total population of Palestine.[26]

So far, there has been no mention of the Palestinians, the indigenous population of Palestine, who by 1947 numbered approximately 1.3 million. This omission is by design, for it was largely within a context of

Table 1. Jewish Immigration in Each *Aliya*

First *aliya*, 1881–1900	25,000
Second *aliya*, 1904–13	35,000
Third *aliya*, 1919–23	37,000
Fourth *aliya*, 1924–28	70,000
Fifth *aliya*, 1932–39	200,000[a]

SOURCE: Data from Mark Tessler, *A History of the Israeli-Palestinian Conflict* (Bloomington: Indiana University Press, 1994), pp. 60–61, 185, 208.
[a]Does not include illegal immigration.

Palestinian nonexistence—a perception that the Promised Land was empty of a people with an identity or rights—that the European immigrants set out on their successive waves of colonization of Palestine. Zionism, it should be remembered, was a product of the intellectual and political environment of nineteenth-century Europe, one in which an industrially advanced, "civilized" Europe was almost universally assumed to have the right and indeed the responsibility to dominate and colonize the rest of the world.[27] The Zionists were a product of this intellectual milieu, although, as more time passed, for them colonization increasingly became a matter of life or death. This was a sentiment shared not only by Zionists but by notable non-Jewish Zionist sympathizers as well. "Zionism, be it right or wrong, good or bad," wrote Lord Balfour, whose famous declaration paved the way for the official establishment of the state of Israel, "is rooted in age-long tradition, in present needs, in future hopes, of far profounder import than the desires and prejudices of the 700,000 Arabs who now inhabit this ancient land."[28]

Others denied the existence of a Palestinian people altogether. Golda Meir, one of Israel's most celebrated prime ministers, stated this position most emphatically: "There was no such thing as Palestinians. . . . They did not exist."[29] Similarly, the *Personal History* of David Ben-Gurion, one of the central figures of the Zionist movement and the Jewish state's first prime minister, is striking in its lack of mention of a previously existing Palestinian population.[30] In his memoirs he wrote: "I believed then, as I do today, that we had a clear title to this country. Not the right to take it away from others (there were no others), but the right and the duty to fill its emptiness, restore life to its barrenness, to re-create a modern version of our own nation. And I felt we owed this effort not only to ourselves but to

Figure 5. David Ben-Gurion, the first prime minister of the state of Israel.

the land as well."[31] This viewpoint was most pointedly summed up in the slogan "A land without a people for a people without a land."[32] The central assumptions of Zionism were that only God's chosen people should be in the Promised Land, that the backward trespassers who were there had no rights to it, and that the problems posed by their existence on the land could be easily dispensed with. A passage on the Palestinians from Herzl's diary, written in 1895, is instructive: "We shall have to spirit the penniless population across the border by procuring employment for it in transit countries, while denying it any employment in our own country. Both the process of expropriation and the removal of the poor must be carried out discreetly and circumspectly."[33] Some of Herzl's disciples were not as discreet, nor were they always willing to pay for Palestinian land. By most accounts, by 1948 only 6 percent of the land belonging to Palestinians had been bought by Zionists.[34] Most houses were either simply destroyed or appropriated. One Israeli researcher has estimated that nearly four hundred Palestinian villages were "completely destroyed, with their houses, garden-walls, and even cemeteries and tombstones, so that literally a stone does not remain standing, and visitors are passing and being told 'it was all desert.'"[35]

Many of the demolitions and other similar military operations in the Yishuv were carried out by one of the three active military organizations: the Haganah, the Irgun, and the so-called Stern Gang. The Haganah (literally, self-defense) was established in 1920 with a broad-based mandate to defend the burgeoning Jewish community in Palestine. Initially under the control of the Histadrut labor federation, the Haganah had ready access to a pool of eager volunteers and, under the command of former officers from the USSR and elsewhere, soon acquired an increasingly professional character. From the 1920s to the 1940s, the Haganah maintained an uneasy relationship with the British mandatory authorities: sometimes it was aided by a Bible-wielding, pro-Zionist British commander, Captain Orde Wingate, who collaborated with it against Vichy-dominated Syria; at other times it was declared illegal and its members were arrested.[36] Nevertheless, throughout, the Haganah secretly registered men and women volunteers and continued to grow. It was eventually amalgamated into the Israeli Defense Forces (IDF) once that organization became the new state's army.

A splinter military organization called the Irgun Zvai Leumi (National Military Organization), alternately referred to as the Etzel or the Irgun, was established in 1937 as a result of the withdrawal of an extremist group known as the Revisionists from the World Zionist Organization. Even more extreme was the group commonly known as the Stern Gang after the name of its founder, Avraham Stern, or, more officially, Fighters for the Freedom of Israel (Lehi for short). Both the Irgun and the Stern Gang rejected the Haganah's concept of "active defense." Instead, they launched an intensive campaign of shooting opponents and bombing both British and Palestinian targets. One of the Irgun's more infamous operations was the bombing of the King David Hotel in Jerusalem on July 22, 1946, in which ninety-one Britons, Palestinians, and Jews were killed and another forty-five were injured.

By the late 1940s, exhausted by the war in Europe, Britain was des-

Figure 6. Israeli women take an oath to join the Haganah, Tel Aviv, 1948.

perately searching for a way to end its mandatory rule over Palestine and simply leave. Earlier, from 1936 to 1939, it had also been forced to contend with an "Arab Revolt," the fallout from which had only heightened Zionist extremism and terrorist attacks on British as well as Arab targets. The years 1947 and 1948 turned out to be fateful, for the British withdrawal from one town and region after another set off a frantic race between Zionist and Palestinian forces to gain control of the installations and command structures the British were leaving behind. Britain decided to turn over the responsibility for the mandate to the United Nations, which on November 29, 1947, adopted Resolution 181, calling for the partition of Palestine into a separate Arab and a Jewish state, with Bethlehem and Jerusalem retaining international status (map 4). The UN Partition Plan, as the resolution came to be known, was highly favorable to the Zionists, who quickly accepted it, but was rejected by the outraged Palestinians.[37] Although at the time Jews made up only about 33 percent of the inhabitants of Palestine and owned between 6 to 7 percent of the land, the plan awarded the Jewish state 55 percent of historic Palestine, most of it fertile. The area under Jewish control was also to include some 45 percent of the Palestinian population. The proposed Arab state, however, was given only

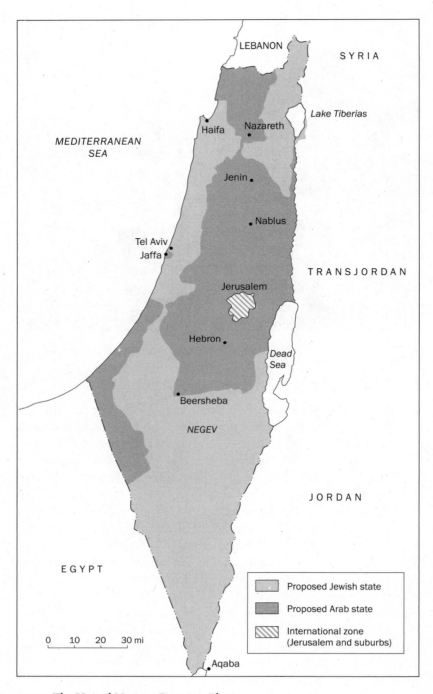

LEBANON

SYRIA

Lake Tiberias

Haifa • Nazareth

MEDITERRANEAN SEA

Jenin •

• Nablus

Tel Aviv •
Jaffa •

TRANSJORDAN

Jerusalem

Hebron •

Dead Sea

Beersheba •

NEGEV

JORDAN

EGYPT

0   10   20   30 mi

Proposed Jewish state

Proposed Arab state

International zone
(Jerusalem and suburbs)

• Aqaba

Map 4. The United Nations Partition Plan.

45 percent of the total land in dispute, much of it not fit for agriculture, and was to include a negligible Jewish minority. Jerusalem and Bethlehem were to remain under UN jurisdiction, and Jaffa, though geographically separated from the rest of the Arab state, was to be a part of it.

The Jewish acceptance and Arab rejection of the UN Partition Plan became the subject of great historical controversy, often cited by subsequent Israeli sources as an example of the Zionists' desire for peaceful diplomacy and the Arabs' determination to wage war on the Jews.[38] But more recently there emerged in Israel a group of so-called "new historians" whose documentary and interpretative analysis of the events leading up to and following the creation of the state of Israel fundamentally challenged many of the "myths" of what had actually happened in 1947 and 1948.[39] Among them was the intellectual and longtime political activist Simha Flapan (d. 1987), who had the following interpretation of the Zionists' acceptance of the plan: "[T]he acceptance of the UN Partition resolution was an example of Zionist pragmatism par excellence. It was a tactical acceptance, a vital step in the right direction—a springboard for expansion when circumstances proved more judicious. And, indeed, in the period between the UN vote on November 29, 1947, and the declaration of the state of Israel on May 14, 1948, a number of developments helped to produce the judicious circumstances that would enable the embryonic Jewish state to expand its border."[40]

Soon after the announcement of the Partition Plan and its aftermath, between December 1947 and May 1948, Palestine was systematically extinguished and a new country, the state of Israel, was created in its place. The death of a country and the birth of a new one are momentous, historic events. The fact that the country being born then was Israel, whose people had lived through the barbarity of the Final Solution and the Holocaust, made the birth all the more momentous. Numerous historians have participated in the celebratory retelling of this birth story, and accounts for Western audiences often highlight joyous tears, hard work, perseverance, and triumph.[41] True as they may be, these accounts are often woefully incomplete, for they say nothing of the other, concurrent development, a country's death, or of how that death occurred. But the historical record cannot be ignored.

According to one estimate, by 1948, Palestinian forces totaled around seven thousand fighters, including two separate volunteer forces, local rural militias, and various youth defense groups. Zionist forces, meanwhile, including the Haganah, the Irgun, the Stern Gang, and alleged professional volunteers from abroad, swelled from fifteen thousand to sixty thousand.[42] A protracted conflict started soon after the UN vote on the Partition Plan—

more sporadic Zionist-Palestinian conflicts had in fact been going on for some time—and a major Jewish military assault was launched in April 1948. One of the darker episodes of Israeli history occurred on April 9, when more than two hundred inhabitants of the Palestinian village of Deir Yassin were massacred, their bodies subsequently mutilated and dumped in wells.[43] Other cities and villages were quick to fall: Haifa, Jaffa, West Jerusalem, and eastern Galilee all in less than a week in late April, followed by equally decisive victories in the first two weeks of May. "The attacks were brutal," write two scholars. "Through terror, psychological warfare, and direct conquests, Palestine was dismembered, many of its villages purposefully destroyed and much of its people expelled as refugees."[44]

A massive Palestinian exodus out of Palestine was thus set in motion. Israeli sources put the number of refugees at 520,000, while Arab sources estimate the number to be anywhere between 750,000 and 1,000,000.[45] Like so much else in the Palestinian-Israeli conflict, the exact causes of the exodus are still debated and discussed.[46] Contrary to the long-accepted proposition that Arab radio broadcasts encouraged Palestinians to leave, it is now almost uniformly accepted that such broadcasts did not exist and that most Palestinians were in fact urged not to abandon their homes and communities.[47] Instead, the exodus appears to have been the result of two primary factors. Sheer terror appears to have been most compelling, with many Palestinians fearing a fate similar to that of Deir Yassin's inhabitants. Psychological warfare only fueled Palestinian fears, as pamphlets dropped from the air warned Palestinians of the risks they faced if they stayed behind.[48] Researchers later found that rumors of rape of women by Israeli soldiers and other "Jewish whispering operations" accounted for the movement of a significant percentage of Palestinians.[49] Equally instrumental were a variety of military actions. Notable was the Haganah's systematic depopulation campaign, aimed at clearing out clusters of Palestinians in the areas it considered to be territorially and strategically important. This campaign was officially adopted in May and June 1948 under the auspices of Plan Dalet, the basic premise of which was "the expulsion over the borders of the local Arab population in the event of opposition to our attacks."[50] According to the Israeli historian Ilan Pappe,

> Plan Dalet was a blueprint for the ethnic cleansing of Palestine. Had the Palestinians refrained from attacking Jewish targets after the partition resolution was adopted, and had the Palestinian elites not left the towns, it would have been difficult for the Zionist movement to implement its vision of an ethnically cleansed Palestine. . . . Plan Dalet was not created in a vacuum. It emerged as the ultimate scheme in response to the

way events gradually unfolded on the ground, through a kind of ad-hoc policy that crystalised with time. But that response was always inexorably grounded in the Zionist ideology and the purely Jewish state was its goal. Thus, the main objective was clear from the beginning—the de-Arabisation of Palestine—whereas the means to achieve this most effectively evolved in tandem with the military occupation of the Palestinian territories that were to become the new Jewish state of Israel.[51]

The plan officially went into effect on May 14, when the state was declared, by which time the exodus was well under way. Nevertheless, under the aegis of the plan, in July, in a ten-day period, over 100,000 Palestinians were driven into areas controlled by Egypt, Jordan, and Lebanon. Another 100,000 to 150,000 refugees were expelled the following October. The "decimation of Palestinian Arab society" was now complete.[52]

Within hours after the state of Israel was declared, shortly after midnight on May 15, 1948, five Arab armies crossed over Israeli borders in what was to become the first of many abortive attempts to "liberate" Palestine. These included the armies of Egypt, Lebanon, Syria, and Jordan and the (Palestinian) Liberation Army. Transjordan's King Abdullah was less concerned with Palestinian liberation than with his own territorial ambitions in Palestine and, especially, Jerusalem. His "flirtations" with members of the Jewish Agency just weeks before the invasion are generally thought to have been responsible for his army's relatively scant contribution to the conflict.[53] Nevertheless, a protracted and bloody war ensued, killing thousands of Arabs and Israelis in the process. Despite some initial successes, the Arab armies soon suffered humiliating losses, losing more territories than had been allotted to the Arab state under the UN Partition Plan. By the time an armistice agreement was signed in February 1949, Jordan occupied only the Arab sections of Jerusalem and the area that came to be known as the West Bank (of the Jordan River). Egypt held on to a narrow piece of Palestinian land along the northeastern border of the Sinai, the Gaza Strip. These were all that remained of a non-Jewish Palestine, and even they were at the mercy of non-Palestinian rulers now. Palestine was gone, its name erased from the world's maps, its people exiled to refugee camps across the region. The map of the Middle East was forever changed.

PALESTINIAN NATIONALISM

The geographic entity Palestine may have died in 1948, but Palestinian identity did not. In fact, as mentioned earlier, the sense of being Palestinian, along with Palestinian nationalism, had been alive for some time. Much has already been said about Palestinian nationalism, but in light of subsequent Israeli denials of its existence and validity, it is important to briefly highlight some of its features and evolving phases. Much of this denial by Israelis, although lately no longer the norm given changing political circumstances, was no doubt motivated by the need to depopulate Palestine and make room for the incoming immigrants. But equally important for both Israeli and Western social scientists has been the lack of recognition of the fundamentally different nature of Arab and Palestinian nationalism from nationalism in the West and among Zionists, who were, after all, the West's cultural and historical product. In the West, nationalism has historically been unidimensional and singular in focus and orientation. There has been only one series of objects, all organically related, toward which loyalty has been directed: one nation, one leader, one well-defined piece of territory, and one set of national symbols such as flags, anthems, and heroes. But Arab nationalism and its derivative of Palestinian nationalism have been multidimensional, layered, more diffuse in focus and orientation. Thus a Palestinian living in Jaffa or Haifa in the late 1800s could have simultaneously had loyalties and attachments to geographic Palestine, to the caliph in Istanbul, and to Islam and other symbols of caliphal rule. Over time, historical nuances prompted changes to popular conceptions of what constituted a nation. With the demise of Ottomanism and the Ottoman nation, focus shifted to Arabism and the Arab nation, the death of which in turn ushered in still more focused, more localized nationalist variations: Egyptian, Iraqi, Syrian, Jordanian, Palestinian, and so on. Each current overlapped with its succeeding one, never quite disappearing altogether but retaining some, albeit diminished, salience.[54] Such was the path taken by Palestinian nationalism into the middle years of mandatory rule.

Insofar as the distinctively Palestinian phase of Palestinian nationalism is concerned, we can detect five clearly identifiable periods (table 2). The first started in the early 1900s and lasted throughout the mandate up until 1948. This was a time of formation and initial expression of a uniquely Palestinian identity, which was shaped and hardened by a gradual awakening to the threat and the permanence of Zionism, the "Arab Revolt" of 1936–39, and the eventual *nakba* (catastrophe) of 1948. The second period was one of eclipse, the so-called "lost years" of Palestinian nationalism, marked initially by the shock and trauma of dispossession and then by the influence of Palestine's self-appointed liberator, the Egyptian Gamal Abdel Nasser. Palestine's "lost years" continued until 1967, when the liberator was himself defeated and his own territory was occupied by a victorious Israel. What followed was a third phase of Palestinian nationalism, marked

Table 2. Phases in Palestinian Nationalism

Phase	Characteristic	Time Period
Mandatory period	Formation and initial expression	1914–28 Peaceful resistance 1928–36 Radicalization 1936–39 Arab Revolt 1939–48 Continued resistance by local notables
"Lost years"	Eclipse	1948–52 Shock and silence 1952–67 Overshadowed by Nasser
PLO years	Organizational self-assertion	1967–82 Militarism and PLO diplomacy 1982–87 PLO retreat and decline
Intifada	Local, indigenous uprising	1987–93 Populist nationalism
Palestinian National Authority	Institutionalization of national identity	1993–present Protostate Palestinian organizations in the West Bank and Gaza

at first by institutional reorganization and military self-assertion—the rise of the Palestine Liberation Organization (PLO)—and then a second dispersion, this time of the PLO to locations even further away from the homeland. For the sake of convenience, these may be called "the PLO years," lasting from about 1967 to 1987, although the PLO was officially established in 1964. Palestinian nationalist sentiments once again assumed their local, indigenous character beginning in late 1987. This time they took the form of a spontaneous uprising, the *intifada*, that took the West Bank and the Gaza Strip by storm, lasting into the early 1990s. This prompted the signing between Israeli authorities and PLO officials of the Declaration of Principles, commonly referred to as the Oslo Accords, in 1993, which led to the emergence of a set of protostate institutions with the name "Palestinian National Authority." Each of these phases, shaped and influenced by the one before it, witnessed a different facet of Palestinian nationalism, conditioned often by circumstances beyond the Palestinians' own control.[55]

Three broad, interrelated developments were responsible for the gradual emergence of Palestinian nationalism and its supplanting of Ottomanism.

The first was the steady dismantling of Ottoman rule in Istanbul, in turn facilitating the rise of so-called "Westphalian sovereignty" and more locally based nationalist sentiments in the various provinces (velayats). In fact, in the decades before the collapse of the dynasty, the Ottoman sultan had been forced to acquiesce to the convening of a parliament. Although the phenomenon was short-lived, the presence of local representatives in the parliament heightened locally based nationalist sentiments throughout the Arab provinces.[56] A second development was the advent of "print capitalism," the spread of the printed press and books, especially the publication of many influential newspapers such as *Filastin*, *Al-Karmil*, and *Al-Mufid*.[57] A number of highly celebrated "cultural leaders" also emerged—writers, poets, journalists, and other public intellectuals—and their influence was felt in such areas as Palestinian literature, the arts, historical awareness, and education. In the words of one observer, "Palestinian Arab writers during the British Mandate . . . did not produce literature that was only of abstract historical interest. On the contrary, by influencing the nationalism of the upper sectors of the population, they played an integral part of the historical process by which national consciousness spread through the various classes of Palestinian Arabs until it reached the masses of the population."[58] These two developments occurred within the context of, and largely in reaction to, the massive influx of Zionists into Palestine and the increasing entrenchment and institutionalization of the powers of the Zionist community. Together, these three developments combined to produce the earliest manifestations of Palestinian nationalism.

During the time of the British mandate, Palestinian nationalism itself can be divided into three phases. The first phase, which actually started just before Britain's mandatory rule, somewhere around 1914 to 1917, was one of peaceful resistance. Apart from the flourishing of Palestinian literary and cultural nationalism, this period witnessed notable Palestinians' employment of various methods of persuasion aimed at getting the British to abandon their pro-Zionist policies and to grant the Arabs a measure of self-rule.[59] But these notables were bitterly divided among themselves; they could not meaningfully organize and coordinate their efforts, and their repeated petitions to British authorities fell on deaf ears. A second phase thus gradually emerged, one of increasing radicalization of Palestinian identity, beginning in July 1928. By this time the Zionists were well on their way to creating a separate, Zionist economy in Palestine, one from which the indigenous population was largely excluded. Palestinian anger and resentment were reaching a boiling point. Attempts were made to shore up the organizational aspects of Palestinian efforts, although they were short-circuited by the eruption of violent riots in August 1929. Not until 1936, however, did a revolutionary, third phase come into being, a three-year rebellion known as the Arab Revolt.

The Arab Revolt started out as a general, nationwide strike in April 1936. While the strike itself was in specific response to the Haganah's retaliatory murder of two Palestinians, it occurred in a highly volatile atmosphere built up over the preceding years. The strike lasted for six months, during which Palestinian unions, chambers of commerce, virtually all businesses, and transportation ceased to operate. Initiated at the height of the fifth *aliya*, when an unprecedented number of Zionists were entering Palestine, the economic and long-term consequences of the strike were disastrous for the Arabs. The revolt only encouraged the deepening and exclusivist nature of the emerging Zionist economy; desperate Jewish laborers were only too happy to fill the void left by striking Palestinians. But before the strike ended, a spontaneous, violent rebellion had started and by 1938 had swept up almost all the Arab population of Palestine. Historian Benny Morris estimates that the number of active participants in the revolt grew from between 1,000 and 3,000 in 1936 to between 2,500 and 7,500 in 1937 and another 6,000 to 15,000 in 1938.[60] The intensity of the violence grew accordingly. In 1937 alone, the rebels launched 438 attacks, of which 109 were against the British police and military, 143 were against Jewish settlements, and another 109 were against "Arab houses."[61] In 1937, in retaliation, British authorities deported most leaders of the Arab Revolt to the Seychelles. Only after a massive commitment of force by the British was order restored and the rebellion put down in 1939.

In response to the rebellion, the British promised to limit immigration into Palestine and to grant the country its independence in ten years. But British repression had also increased significantly during the rebellion years, and the Palestinians emerged from the revolt weaker and more defeated than when they had started it.[62] By the time the rebellion was over, some five thousand Palestinians were dead and another ten thousand wounded. Scores were arrested and fined, and many of the revolt's leaders were deported. Palestinians became even more marginalized in the country's economic life after the rebellion. Zionists were now more determined than ever to secure their independence from Arab labor and Arab markets.[63]

As devastating as it was, the Arab Revolt only foretold a bigger "catastrophe" that was to befall Palestinian nationalism in less than a decade. The Palestinians never fully recovered from the revolt, and their efforts both then and later to see glory in defeat could only go so far, and then

Table 3. Palestinian Refugees of the 1948 War

Total Arab population of Palestine in 1948	1,400,000
Arab inhabitants under Israeli control in 1948	900,000
Total displaced from Israel	846,000
Prewar population of West Bank	425,000
Postwar population of West Bank	785,000
Prewar population of Gaza	80,000
Postwar population of Gaza	280,000
Refugees' distribution:	
West Bank	360,000
Gaza	200,000
Jordan	100,000
Syria	82,000
Lebanon	104,000

SOURCE: Samih K. Farsoun and Christina E. Zacharia, *Palestine and the Palestinians* (Boulder, CO: Westview Press, 1997), p. 137.

only psychologically rather than in reality.[64] By the time 1948 and 1949 came around, there were no leaders, only refugees. And no real leaders, at least Palestinian ones, would emerge for another two decades. For the Palestinians, the interlude from 1948 to 1967 thus became one of shock and silence, introspection, and, near the end, mounting frustration to do something, anything. By then the Palestinian problem had become a full-blown Arab problem, with hundreds of thousands of Palestinian refugees scattered throughout the Arab world (table 3).

Because of the geographic dispersion of the Palestinian nation and the birth of a Palestinian diaspora, its leaderless and organizationless character, and the larger geopolitical predicament in which it found itself, from 1948 until about 1967 Palestinian nationalism lost its geographic focus and gave way to a more encompassing, seemingly more powerful, Arab nationalism. This broader nationalism also came to be known as Pan-Arabism. That the primary rallying cry of Pan-Arabism was the liberation of Palestine is itself indicative of the resonance of Palestinian nationalism. But for a variety of reasons, many of which revolved around political considerations at home, the Palestinian cause was now picked up by non-Palestinian political aspirants near and far, large and small. Of these, by far the most influential and history making, and the one on whom not only the Palestinians but millions of other Arabs pinned their hopes, was Gamal Abdel Nasser. Nasser had been a volunteer from Egypt in the 1948 war and later became a lieutenant colonel in the Egyptian army. After 1952, he became Egypt's strongman. For nearly two decades, "Nasserism" would sweep across Egypt and the rest of the Middle East.

THE NASSERIST PHENOMENON

The 1948 war and the ease with which the Arab armies were defeated exposed the malaise of the Arab political order. In that war, an emergent, fundamentally European and colonial society struggling for its life and survival was pitted against an array of feudal monarchies with fragile domestic roots and little popular legitimacy. For the Arab side, the war was not so much a matter of life or death as a sideshow, an adventure, a chance to entertain illusions of grandeur and revive memories of old conquests. But, as it turned out, 1948 did become a matter of life or death for many of the Arab leaders involved, as their defeated armies, one after another, avenged their loss by turning against leaders seen as incompetent and corrupt, belonging to an era whose time had long passed.

Arab nationalism now assumed a new manifestation, articulated by young, restless Arabs yearning to emerge out of the shadows of their defeated leaders. This generation of Arabs was motivated not only by the shame of military defeat but also by a sense of solidarity with their Palestinian brethren, now scattered in refugee camps throughout the region. This post-1948 nationalism had three principal features. First, it was closely equated with "modernity," seeking to rid itself of archaic, feudal traditions. Second, it was militaristic, seeing military might and discipline as immediate remedies for the defeat. Third, it saw strength in numbers, assuming that with unity the Arabs would become a force hard to defeat. Each of these strands was personified in Gamal Abdel Nasser, who from the mid-1950s until he was himself defeated by Israel in 1967 came to embody much of Arab nationalism.

At around the same time that Nasser was reaching the pinnacle of his popularity, a rich literature was beginning to emerge from various Arab nationalist intellectuals, some of the more notable of whom were the Egyptian Taha Hussein, the Yemeni Sati al-Husri, and the Syrian Michel Aflaq.[65] Nasser's nationalism, of course, was practical and political, not literary or intellectual. He was a soldier, a politician, a political animal in every sense of the word. His astounding appeal among the masses—his success in presenting himself to the peoples of Egypt and other Arab states as their hope and their savior—came from tapping into nationalist forces that had long been dormant and were desperate to be released. Increasingly, for a time at least, the question of Palestine, the catalyst for the emergence of this latest phase of Arab nationalism, was pushed into the background. It became fodder for the rhetoric of nationalism, but the actual focus and substance of that nationalism was Egypt and its president, Nasser.

Gamal Abdel Nasser was born in Alexandria on January 15, 1918. His generation came of age at a time of profound political instability, corresponding with historic developments occurring not only in Palestine but also much closer to home, in Egypt itself. The Egyptian monarchy, under the incompetent and corrupt leadership of King Farouq, presided over a country that was only nominally independent, with Britain maintaining a heavy-handed presence in Egypt's economic and political life. Political chaos was the order of the day, with various groups often agitating against the monarch, the British, or, more commonly, both. Perhaps the most important was the Wafd Party, formed after World War I by a group of wealthy Egyptian landowners and industrialists. The Wafd emerged as an especially important player in Egyptian politics in the final years of the monarchy, but after 1952 it withered away and did not re-emerge until the late 1970s. Even more instrumental in the collapse of the monarchy was the Muslim Brotherhood (Ikhwan Muslimeen), established in 1928, an ardent advocate of the need for greater social morality and full independence from Britain. Beginning in 1933, a group calling itself the Young Egypt Society (Misr al-Fatat) was also formed. Made up mostly of students at Cairo University's Law Faculty and seeking to imitate the example of European fascists, the society's adherents called themselves the Greenshirts and often clashed with Wafdist Blueshirts. Organizations such as the Muslim Brotherhood and the Young Egypt Society were essentially nationalist and populist, and although they seldom had a coherent platform or ideology of their own they were united in disliking the ruling elite, deploring its military and political incompetence, and wishing to reverse the general malaise that gripped Egyptian and the larger Arab social and political life. By the mid-1930s, both groups had penetrated the Egyptian army and were beginning to attract followers among the officer corps.[66] More importantly, their efforts had helped create a political atmosphere highly charged against both the monarchy and the British. It was in this context that Nasser entered the Military Academy in 1937 and, from there, rose relatively quickly through the ranks of the army. By 1952, he had become a lieutenant colonel.[67]

It did not take long for Nasser to become politically active. The early to mid-1940s were especially traumatic for Egyptians and for the larger Arab world in general, culminating in the 1948 war. In 1942, for example, the British had humiliated King Farouq by surrounding his palace with tanks and ordering him to appoint as prime minister a politician of their choosing. Soon after returning from the Palestine war, in late 1949 Nasser organized a secret military cell, called the Free Officers, with the specific aim of capturing political power. Nasser's own words are revealing: "We were fighting in Palestine but our dreams were in Egypt. Our bullets were aimed at the enemy lurking in the trenches in front of us, but our hearts were hovering around our distant Mother Country, which was then prey to the wolves that ravaged it."[68]

The group, which by the early 1950s numbered into the hundreds, was made up mostly of younger, junior officers, many drawn from the Military Academy itself, where Nasser had become an instructor. Although void of a "philosophy" per se, the cabal was united around certain key principles: getting rid of the king and his clique, putting an end to British imperialism, and using the armed forces to achieve national objectives. The years 1950 through 1952 were especially tense, characterized by frequent assassinations of political figures and sporadic violence. Finally, in the early morning hours of July 23, 1952, the Free Officers staged a relatively bloodless and swift takeover of the state. The government was overthrown and replaced by a Revolutionary Command Council (RCC), made up of the nucleus of the Free Officers movement. Within days, King Farouq was forced to abdicate. A new order was proclaimed; the revolution had begun.

Too young to be assured of their own credibility before the Egyptian people, in September members of the RCC asked an older, popular army general, Muhammad Naguib, to serve as the prime minister. The following January all political parties were outlawed and a three-year "transition period" was declared, during which the RCC was to rule and to facilitate the country's revolution. Nasser wrote that year (1953) that "[p]olitical revolution demands, for its success, the unity of all national elements, their fusion and mutual support, as well as self-denial for the sake of the country as a whole."[69] In June Egypt was proclaimed a republic and Naguib became its first president, still retaining the office of the prime minister. But the president's star did not shine for long, and he soon fell victim to Nasser's machinations in the RCC. In February 1954, the RCC branded Naguib a traitor and ousted him. A month earlier, the RCC had banned the Muslim Brotherhood and had suppressed pro-Naguib elements within the army and among street demonstrators. Naguib was brought back temporarily, now only as president and with much reduced powers, but within a few months he was accused of complicity in a plot to assassinate Nasser and was removed from office again, this time for good. By 1956, Nasser had clearly emerged as the dominant figure within the RCC, having a year earlier represented Egypt at the Non-Aligned Summit in Bandung, Indonesia, where he had been hailed as the leader of Egypt and the Arab world. In a referendum held in June 1956, a new constitution was inaugurated, based on which the RCC was formally abolished and Nasser was elected to the presidency. Within months, the president was to reach the pinnacle of his power and popularity because of the Suez Canal crisis.

Before discussing the Suez Canal crisis and its consequences, a word needs to be said about Nasser's march from relative obscurity in the late 1940s to the height of power by the mid-1950s. In *The Philosophy of the Revolution*, which he wrote in 1953 and published the following year, Nasser admitted that the transformation of his military coup to a full-blown revolution was a matter more of necessity than of advanced planning. "After July 23rd I was shocked by the reality. The vanguard had performed its task," he wrote, referring to the military. "It stormed the walls of the fort of tyranny; it forced Farouk to abdicate and stood by expecting the mass formations to arrive at their ultimate object. . . . A dismal picture, horrible and threatening, then presented itself. I felt my heart charged with sorrow and dripping with bitterness. The mission of the vanguard had not ended. In fact it was just beginning at that very hour. We needed discipline but found chaos behind our lines. We needed unity but found dissensions. We needed action but found nothing but surrender and idleness."[70] For all his efforts behind the scenes, first among the Free Officers and then within the RCC, initially Nasser was neither generally liked by the Egyptians nor trusted very much. In fact, many feared him, and, as the brutal crackdown on the Muslim Brotherhood and other dissidents showed, they did so for good reason.[71] But once the popular Naguib was out of the picture, it was Nasser's turn to shine, and this he did by two primary means: his foreign policy, and his populist domestic social and political programs.

In domestic politics, Nasser knew the language of the street, having himself risen from a modest middle-class background. His rhetoric was electrifying, his charismatic personality magnetic, his message simple and compelling. Following an alleged attempt on his life by members of the Muslim Brotherhood in Alexandria on October 26, 1954, Nasser, unscathed, climbed to the podium and delivered a rousing speech: "My countrymen, my blood spills for you and for Egypt. I will live for your sake, die for the sake of your freedom and honor. Let them kill me; it does not concern me so long as I have instilled pride, honor, and freedom in

Figure 7. Egyptian women celebrate Nasser's announcement of women's right to vote, 1956.

you. If Gamal Abdel Nasser should die, each of you shall be Gamal Abdel Nasser."[72] This was a far cry from the image the average Egyptian had come to have of King Farouq or, especially, British officials. Nasser's charisma was backed by a series of highly popular social policies, chief among which was the Agrarian Reform Law, enacted by the RCC in September

1952 within weeks of coming to power.[73] Another project in which Nasser was personally involved from the earliest days, the construction of the High Aswan Dam, was also a matter of national pride and a highly emotional issue for all Egyptians. To present a forum for the participation of the masses, in 1953 a Liberation Rally organization was formed, with Nasser as its secretary-general. All other parties were banned shortly thereafter. In 1956 a new constitution was promulgated, and the Liberation Rally changed to a new party, the National Union (NU). In 1962, when under the aegis of a Socialist Charter the regime formally adopted socialism as the most desirable path for social transformation, the NU was changed to the Arab Socialist Union (ASU).

While the ASU's elaborate organizational structure ensured mass participation in the political process, the repressive apparatus of the state was never far from sight. The army and the security services, the dreaded *mukhaberat*, became omnipresent. They struck fear into the hearts of Nasser's potential opponents and helped keep intact the mystiques of total power and popular adulation.

All these domestic accomplishments aside, it was in the foreign policy domain, and largely because of it, that Nasser emerged as a larger-than-life figure. Like his contemporaries, Nasser's leadership was crystallizing at a time of intense military and diplomatic competition between the communist bloc and the West. To survive against domestic adversaries and potential challenges from abroad, all Middle Eastern leaders at the time— from the shah of Iran to the generals ruling in Turkey and King Hussein of Jordan, as well as the fledgling monarchies of the Arabian peninsula—had cast their lot with the West. This was represented initially by Britain's extensive involvement in the region, and, later, beginning in the 1950s, by that of the United States. Whatever the actual wisdom of such alliances, the peoples of the Middle East often saw their leaders as Western puppets, lackeys installed by imperialism to do its dirty work. Partly out of conviction and partly to cement his populist image, Nasser became one of the main figures within the Non-Aligned Movement (NAM), espousing a policy of "positive neutralism" that, in theory at least, was meant to favor neither the Eastern bloc nor the West.[74] In the 1955 NAM Summit Nasser was seen as the spokesman of the Arab world and, in league with the likes of Jawaharlal Nehru and Josip Tito, its primary advocate and protector against the global forces of colonial domination.

Nasser's actual confrontation with the West was not long in coming. For some time, Egypt's foreign policy had featured four specific goals: securing financial support for building the Aswan Dam; acquiring military hardware for its army; wresting control of the Suez Canal from British and French commercial interests; and clarifying the status of the Sudan regarding its independence or unification with Egypt. Of these, the Sudan issue was resolved the earliest, in 1953, when the country was given the option of deciding its fate on its own through a referendum. In 1954, the Sudan unilaterally declared independence.

The three remaining objectives became points of contention and, soon thereafter, conflict. In summer 1956, the United States offered Egypt financial aid for the Aswan Dam project. In an apparent move to humiliate Nasser, however, once the Egyptian president accepted the aid offer, it was withdrawn. In retaliation, Nasser nationalized the British-owned Suez Canal Company in July and proceeded to secure massive economic and military assistance from the Soviet bloc. With tensions at an all-time high, Israel invaded Egypt on October 29, 1956, ostensibly in retaliation for frequent raids into Israel from Egyptian territory by Palestinian fighters called the Fedayeen. The following day Britain and France warned the belligerents to cease fire; Egypt's refusal to do so was followed by British bombing of Port Said at the mouth of the Suez and the landing of French and British troops in the Canal Zone on October 31.

For different reasons, each of the invading countries wanted to see Nasser toppled. For Britain and France, Nasser's incendiary advocacy of Third World liberation had to be stopped before independence struggles like the ones in India and Algeria had a chance to spread elsewhere. France was especially troubled by Nasser's generous support for the National Liberation Front in Algeria, which was directing the fight against French rule from Cairo. Israel, of course, had its own reasons to see Nasser overthrown, as his seemed the most credible and immediate threat to Israeli national security.

Ironically, it was the United States that came to Nasser's rescue, pressing the invaders both directly and through the United Nations to withdraw from Egyptian territory. This was, of course, motivated less by the American policy makers' love for Nasser than by their concerns over the reemergence of British and French military ascendancy in the region. A UN Emergency Force (UNEF) was set up to supervise the evacuation of foreign troops from Egypt and, once the evacuation was complete, to stand guard at the Egyptian-Israeli border. By late December 1956, the last of British and French troops left Egyptian territory, and, with great reluctance, Israel finally withdrew on March 9, 1957.

The Suez invasion was a military disaster for Egypt, exposing the shocking ease with which Israeli forces overran Egypt's defenses and

Figure 8. Egyptian boys and girls receive military training during the Suez Canal crisis, 1956.

occupied much of the Sinai and the Egyptian-administered Gaza Strip.[75] In fact, fearing further losses, Nasser had ordered his forces to retreat to save them from further British and French attacks. The Egyptian air force nevertheless inflicted some casualties on Israeli forces, and the invaders met with surprisingly heavy resistance in Port Said and other towns in the Sinai.

Once the dust of the invasion settled and the invaders were forced to withdraw under international condemnation and pressure, Nasser turned his military defeat into a great diplomatic and moral victory. Such a victory, however imaginary, was just what an increasingly dictatorial, charismatic leader like Nasser needed. "I have declared in your name that we shall fight and not surrender," he told masses of adoring Egyptians after the crisis, "that we shall not live a dishonorable life however long they persist in their aggressive plans."[76] With his domestic enemies and potential rivals eliminated, Nasser could now delay delivering the promises of the 1952 revolution by pointing to his struggle against "Western imperialism." Not surprisingly, after 1956 the regime turned its attention increasingly to foreign affairs, and, consequently, Nasser directed his rhetoric to an audience beyond Egypt's borders. It was then that the phenomenon of

Pan-Arabism—the process whereby the Arab nation sought to transcend artificial, colonially drawn borders and to become one—moved beyond the realm of academia and intellectual fancy and into the realm of diplomacy and practice. And Nasser, the one Arab leader who had stared down imperialism until the latter blinked, became its chief articulator and protagonist.

For a people defeated and humiliated, for those receptive to the idea of a liberator, for the peoples of the Middle East whose leaders seemed remote and uncaring, Nasser was a hero. His fiery speeches, broadcast by Egypt's *Voice of the Arabs*, were listened to as far away as Lebanon, Jordan, Syria, and Iraq. Like most other populist leaders, his popularity was at times greater outside Egypt than in his own country. The Egyptians feared and admired him; elsewhere in the Arab world, for the most part, he was lionized and idolized. He soon became the liberator the Palestinians never had, the voice the Arabs had yearned for, the military strongman that the times seemed to call for. Before long, in 1958, one of the most concrete steps toward Pan-Arab unity was taken when Syria and Egypt joined to form the United Arab Republic, with Nasser as its president. Arab intellectuals celebrated the birth of the UAR as a powerful synthesis of Pan-Arab ideals, and other leaders elsewhere—in Yemen, the Sudan, and Libya especially—sought to forge similar alliances so as not to be left behind. By the late 1950s and early 1960s, Pan-Arabism was in full swing.

NATIONALISM IN THE MAGHREB

Nasser's Egyptian nationalism, and before that Zionism and Palestinian nationalism, were not being articulated in a historical and geographic vacuum. In fact, they were part of a continuum of nationalisms that thrived in the Arab east as far as Iraq and in the Maghreb as far west as Morocco. Despite fundamental differences in the genesis and evolution of the nationalisms that swept across the Middle East in the early twentieth century, there were striking similarities in both their causes and their effects. In the case of Zionism, the emergence of nationalism owed much to the mobilizational efforts of early Zionist leaders and their success, over time, in combining a collective, distinct sense of Jewish identity with a viable set of statelike organizations. Once these organizations and the collective identity out of which they had arisen were transplanted onto a piece of territory, that of historic Palestine, Zionist (or Israeli) nationalism was complete. This transplantation in turn created—or re-created—a Palestinian nationalism. Egyptian nationalism was nothing new, but only after the defeat of 1948, the "catastrophe" *(nakba)*, were some Egyptians prompted to take matters into their own hands and, as they saw it, redeem the honor of the Egyptian and the larger Arab nation. Nasserism was Egyptian nationalism writ large, a reaction to military incompetence, national disgrace, and industrial and economic backwardness.

These were also the targets of Maghrebi nationalism, although here the culprit was not a domestic despot but an outside colonizer. And in this region, unlike the Arab east, it was not Britain that dominated but rather France. In each country of the Maghreb, the nature, extent, and duration of French colonialism directly influenced the emergence of nationalist sentiments and, eventually, national independence movements. This was also the case with Libya, the only country in the Maghreb, and in the entire Middle East for that matter, that was occupied by Italy. In turn, the nature of the nationalist forces leading the movement for independence, and the way independence was achieved, had direct consequences for the politics of each of the newly independent countries.

In broad terms, Algeria's colonial domination by France was the longest lasting and most extensive. It started in 1830, lasted for 132 years, and resulted in the transfer of 1.7 million French *colons* to Algeria, or 11 percent of Algeria's total population. It also featured the annexation of geographic Algeria as yet another provincial administrative unit of France. By contrast, French colonial rule in Tunisia started in 1881, lasted seventy-five years, and resulted in less than 7 percent of the Tunisian population being made up of the *colons*. Morocco's colonial domination was even less extensive. Begun in 1912, it lasted for only forty-four years and resulted in a *colon* population of only about 5 percent.[77] Most important, in both Tunisia and Morocco, especially in the latter, existing political institutions—the *beylik* in Tunisia (a relic of Ottoman rule) and the monarchy in Morocco—were not destroyed. In fact, the "protection" of these indigenous institutions theoretically formed the raison d'être of the French protectorate. Precolonial Algerian institutions were not as fortunate. The French effectively eradicated all of them and sought to make Algeria as thorough a French possession as possible.

The Italians tried to do the same thing in Libya, but in a much shorter time span. Italian conquest of Libya started in 1911, lasted for slightly more than thirty years, and resulted in a settler population of one hundred thousand out of a total of about a million, approximately 10 percent. Only in 1951, long after the Italians were defeated in World War II and Libya's control had been turned over to a joint British-French administration, did the country's geographic boundaries and political structures take form under the aegis of the United Nations. Still, Libyan nationalism took nearly another two decades to emerge and make its presence felt on both the domestic and the international stages.

Morocco and Tunisia both became independent in March 1956. As we shall see presently, in each of these cases the causes and consequences of nationalism were different, although the two countries did, naturally, maintain a symbiotic relationship. In large measure, however, the French acquiesced in giving independence to Tunisia and Morocco in 1956 because they were being threatened with the loss of their much larger, older possession, Algeria. This is not to imply that Tunisian and Moroccan independence came easily. As compared to the Algerian case, however, the struggles involved very little violence. The independence movements in Morocco and Tunisia were headed by individuals and organizations that came to symbolize and articulate nationalist aspirations, thereby giving added ferocity and direction to nationalist sentiments in each country. In Morocco, the monarch, Muhammad V, emerged in this role when he opposed the French protectorate. In Tunisia, the role fell to the Neo-Destour Party and one of its most capable leaders, Habib Bourguiba. When independence eventually arrived, both the Moroccan monarch and the Tunisian Bourguiba became, in their own way, the Nassers of their respective countries.

As in Morocco and Tunisia, Algerian nationalist sentiments were strengthened by American President Woodrow Wilson's advocacy of the right of national self-determination and, later, by the French defeat in World War II. Nevertheless, the outbreak of the Algerian war of "national liberation" on November 1, 1954, appears to have come as a total surprise to the French, and they resisted its success to the bitter end. Before the war of independence, Algerian nationalists had been divided into three groups: some called for greater assimilation with the French; others advocated cultural nationalism; and still others called for outright independence. Despite a seven-year, bloody war with the French, the Algerian revolutionaries did not develop a united, corporate sense of identity and a common vision of the future. In large measure, this was because the Algerian nationalists did not have a single, dominant figure like Nasser, Muhammad V, or Bourguiba. The Evian Agreements, signed in March 1962, finally brought the bloody war to an end and resulted in Algeria's formal independence the following July. The Front de Libération Nationale (FLN), which had led the revolution from abroad, assumed power but failed to develop unity. By 1965, the FLN's leader, Ahmed Ben Bella, had been overthrown and replaced by one of his lieutenants and former comrades, Houari Boumedienne.

In his seminal study of North African politics, Clement Henry Moore argues that in the face of colonial domination, three modes or "moments" of nationalist consciousness are possible, and that one or a combination of these three modes was found in Morocco, Tunisia, and Algeria. The first mode of nationalist consciousness is "liberal assimilation," in which "sons of the old shocked elite admire and imitate the new rulers, assimilate some of their styles and values, accept their rules of the game, and attempt to engage in dialogue."[78] A second mode of nationalist consciousness is "traditionalist anti-colonialism," "entailing a reassertion of traditional values against the alien presence."[79] Third and last is the "radical outlook," rejecting both assimilation and traditionalism and being the "only mode of consciousness that can sustain a coherent modernizing elite and generate a new political design."[80]

Moroccan nationalism featured a preponderance of the second mode of consciousness, traditionalist anticolonialism. As mentioned earlier, the French protectorate of Tunisia and Morocco was technically meant to protect the sovereigns of each country. In Morocco, the sixteen-year-old Moulay Muhammad had acceded to the throne in 1927. Gradually, the new king emerged as a vital mediator among Morocco's competing nationalist forces, a moderating influence whom the French found next to impossible to silence.[81] Because of his "dual capacity as the temporal leader of the entire country and . . . spiritual leader, [the king] could serve as an excellent unifying force."[82] He was thus able not only to rally elements of the urban society but also to unite the country's Arabs and Berbers in the cause of independence.

The king, of course, was not the only one giving expression to the nationalist aspirations of Moroccans. In January 1944, a group of educated Moroccans formed a political party called the Independence (Istiqlal). The party went on to play an important role in popularizing the ideals of independence among the tiny but influential class of Moroccan intelligentsia. More importantly, the tactical alliance of the king and the Istiqlal—the Makhzan and the urban elite—proved ultimately more powerful than that between the intransigent *colons* and successive French resident generals. In the process, the king rather than Istiqlal emerged as the symbolic embodiment of Moroccan nationalism. Istiqlal's founders had a "fundamentally legalistic and religious frame of mind" and were "better versed in public oratory than in mass organization."[83] But in the popular eye, the king already had religious legitimacy; he was both a sherif (descendant of the Prophet) and the commander of the faithful (Amir al-Mu'minin). He was even considered to have been endowed with *baraka*, an indefinable divine blessing akin to charisma.[84]

Any doubts about Muhammad V's nationalist credentials were erased in

August 1953, when the French authorities, having gone to Morocco to "protect" the king, forcibly deposed him and installed one of his little-known grandsons as the new sultan. By November 1955, with Muhammad V more popular than ever before, a Liberation Army demanded the restoration of his throne. The French, by now eager for a political settlement, returned the deposed king to power. He promptly demanded an end to the protectorate and "the beginning of an era of full independence."[85] France had little option but to grant the wish of a monarch who now openly rejected their protection. On March 2, 1956, French Morocco became formally independent. Within a month, the Spanish government, which still held on to parts of northern Morocco, followed suit. Generalissimo Franco had long supported Moroccan nationalist efforts in order to undermine French interests in the region. Now that the French were gone, the Moroccans wanted full independence. Spanish Morocco became independent on April 7, 1956.

Moroccan nationalism as articulated by Muhammad V and, in his shadow, various Moroccan political parties was qualitatively different from the nationalism of Nasser and his Arab Socialist Union. Nasser was a self-proclaimed revolutionary and, at least into the early 1960s, was seen as such by a majority of Egyptians and others. His conception of nationalism was informed by a "progressive" socialism that would fundamentally change the domestic socioeconomic order as well as the international balance of power. But Muhammad V, though he wanted the French and the Spanish out of Morocco, was a monarch whose legitimacy rested on centuries of tradition, and he by no means welcomed radical domestic changes to the structure of Moroccan society. Nor did he necessarily favor large shifts in regional or global international relations. From the start, therefore, Moroccan nationalism as officially articulated was in the "traditionalist anticolonialist" mode alluded to earlier.

This tradition, and a salient historical memory on which to build a nationalist consciousness, was precisely what the Algerian nationalist revolutionaries lacked. The French conquest of Algeria was rapacious and thorough. Although it occurred in stages, it involved considerable violence directed at the native population. The historical context within which the Algerian colonial conquest began in the 1830s was markedly different from the contexts in which the Tunisian and later the Moroccan protectorates began in the 1880s and 1910s, respectively. French colonial officials saw the native Algerians as barbaric savages, uncivilized and in need of redemption.[86] The aim here was assimilation, not protection. For the French colonial authorities and the often violent *colons*, this meant forcible subjugation of native Algerians. "Indiscriminate search-and-destroy tactics, the routine burning of crops of 'disloyal' tribes, and occasional incinerations, in villages or even caves, of hundreds of men, women, and children, terrorized populations into submission."[87] By the beginning of the twentieth century, all local centers of power had been either vanquished or eliminated altogether, and local revolts were brutally suppressed. The French domination of Algeria was total and complete.

Within the context of French domination, the three modes of nationalist consciousness emerged side by side, undermining nationalist efficacy and hampering elite cohesion. Some Algerian intellectuals called for greater assimilation with the French, while others advocated cultural authentication, and still others proposed a radical break with France. For a handful of Algerian nationalists frustrated by these internal divisions and the resulting political impotence of the nationalist movement, the launching of an armed struggle seemed like the most promising way to achieve internal unity and dislodge the French.[88] Thus began the FLN's campaign in November 1954 to achieve Algerian independence. But France was in no mood to be ousted from its old colony, and in 1956 it gave Morocco and Tunisia independence so that all its efforts could be focused on keeping Algeria French. Shortly after the first attacks on French colonial interests on November 1, 1945, the French prime minister, Pierre Mendès-France, assured the world that Algeria would forever remain irrevocably French.

For the next eight years, the French and the FLN battled each other violently. By the time the conflict ended in 1962, some one million French soldiers had been mobilized (up from an original eighty thousand in 1954), one million Algerians were dead, and another two million Algerians were imprisoned in concentration camps. Out of its inability to deal with the Algerian crisis, in 1958 the Fourth French Republic collapsed and the Fifth Republic was born. Charles de Gaulle, the new republic's founder, combined the French military campaign with a much-touted Algerian charm offensive, promising to redistribute 250,000 hectares of state land to the Algerian Muslims, encourage industrial development in the colony, and create four hundred thousand new jobs there.[89] After relentless pressure by the French forces, by 1959 the Algerian revolution seemed on the verge of collapse. On the defensive, the FLN took its activities to the international level, mounting a campaign to vilify and isolate France in the global community.

Had the conflict ended earlier, perhaps the FLN would have stayed more unified. But as the war dragged on, and as the political landscape in Algeria and in France itself changed, the internal dynamics of the FLN changed a great deal as well. Structurally, the FLN became divided along two fundamental axes: one separating "internal" from "external" resisters and another separating the organization's military operatives from its political activists. An additional split proved to be especially disruptive: that between the more moderate and the radical elements within the organization. Largely because of the difficult, underground circumstances within which it operated and the organizational deficiencies of many of its key figures, the FLN never developed an effective means of internal conflict resolution. While the Algerian nation became increasingly unified in the goal of attaining independence, the FLN—and thus the Algerian elite—did not. The project of national independence had rallied the elite against the common French enemy. But once French resolve weakened and the Evian Agreement ending the war was signed in 1962, whatever bonds still held the elite together soon began to disappear. The nationalist aspirations of the Algerian masses might have been achieved at that point, but there was no single articulator—no Nasser, or Bourguiba, or Muhammad V—to give the movement official direction from that point on. The victorious FLN, riven by internal discord and coups, turned out to be ill equipped for such a task. Only by the early 1970s was the Algerian government stable enough to present a cohesive conception of Algerian nationalism to the people.

As compared to the other cases in the Maghreb, Tunisian nationalism had a much longer gestation period. Moreover, because of Tunisia's social structure and the nature of its colonial experience, Tunisian nationalism evolved in gradual stages. With the emergence and then the passage of each stage, nationalist sentiments became more salient, assumed greater ideological sophistication, and developed corresponding organizational abilities. Perhaps most significantly, the manner and context in which this nationalism evolved helped solidify rather than erode the cohesion of the Tunisian elite. Tunisia's independence in 1956, and its transformation into a republic the next year, allowed the elite the opportunity to give official sanction to a conception of nationalism that had already become quite popular.

Unlike Algeria but like Morocco, Tunisia had become a French protectorate in 1881, the justification having been France's desire to protect the largely autonomous Ottoman bey who governed Tunisia at the time. Largely bereft of the historic legitimacy that the Moroccan sultanate enjoyed, the Tunisian *beylik* had neither the opportunity nor the wherewithal to emerge as the symbolic embodiment of Tunisian independence. Instead, the small but influential circle of young intellectuals was the first group among whom nationalist sentiments circulated. Initially, their goal was to secure a constitution (*destour* in Arabic), leading to the establishment of the Destour Party in 1920. The granting of a constitution was seen as perfectly compatible with the framework of the protectorate. In fact, the party's founders appear not to have favored a radical break with the status quo. For them, Tunisian nationalism meant working to gradually enhance Tunisia's internal autonomy within the confines of the protectorate.

It was this innate conservatism that prompted a group of younger intellectuals to break from the party in 1934 and form the Neo-Destour Party. Neo-Destour quickly tapped into the nationalist aspirations of the Tunisians that the older party had ignored. Its leadership was composed of more professionals, it was more dynamic, it remained flexible in its tactics, and it was more able to achieve results in its confrontations and negotiations with the French authorities.[90] More importantly, many party leaders had achieved social mobility through the educational system, not through family prestige, and most, having graduated from the same academic institution, developed a strong esprit de corps.[91] Complementing the cohesion of the party's leadership was the rapid rise in its mass popularity. Whereas the old Destour leaders had been mostly elitist in their outlook, the Neo-Destourist leaders came from the masses. Many had personally traveled throughout the country to see the people's plight firsthand. They had forged organic and organizational ties to trade unions, while avoiding ideological labels so as not to get distracted from the practical task of independence.

Of the party's leaders, none had the popularity of Habib Bourguiba, a tireless orator, a consummate politician, and the party's most recognizable face. His revolutionary credentials were backed by a total of ten years in French prisons on charges of anticolonial agitation. Genuinely adored by the Tunisians, he was soon called the people's Supreme Combatant (Mujahid al-Akbar).[92]

Bourguiba wanted not just independence from France but also the forging of a new Tunisian nation. By the time independence came in March 1956, Bourguiba's paramount position within the nationalist movement was unchallenged. In the new government, he became the premier, as well as the defense and the foreign minister. In July 1957, when the *beylik* was set aside, Bourguiba became the new republic's president. Even before that, he had set about shaping Tunisia's modern national identity, and, by implication, defining Tunisian nationalism. Gradually, with neither the bombastic rhetoric of Nasser nor the ruthlessness of Atatürk, he implemented various social reforms: he changed personal status laws to enhance the position of women, banned polygamy, reformed the educational system, and, on the grounds that it impeded administrative and economic efficiency, even sought to undermine the hallowed tradition of fasting in the month of Ramadan.[93]

Bourguiba's conception and articulation of nationalism fell somewhere between those of Muhammad V and the FLN. Like the Moroccan monarch, he had a more domestic focus. And like the FLN, he wanted to remake the society that he had inherited from the colonial master. But beyond that, he shared little with the FLN, especially insofar as the latter's attention to Pan-Arabism was concerned. Nasser had actively supported the FLN, and Algeria's postrevolutionary state became one of the central players in the Pan-Arab phenomenon of the 1960s. For both regimes, the projection of nationalist identity into transnational realities was as much a question of domestic political necessity as a matter of ideological principle. Soon Nasser, at the head of a self-created Arab union of sorts, would pay dearly for his ambitions.

Nationalism has been one of the most compelling and powerful forces of the nineteenth, twentieth, and now twenty-first centuries. For the countless millions in the Middle East who have been subjected to its manifestations and consequences, the experience of nationalism has been dramatic and indeed traumatic. Here we see the emergence of several nationalist movements, at times overlapping and complementing one another, at other times opposing and feeding off each other's antagonism. In the recent history of the Middle East, one of the earliest forms of nationalism was Ottomanism, a loose sense of loyalty and commonality centered on the Ottoman Empire. After Ottomanism ended in the early 1920s, there emerged Turkish nationalism and a variety of Arab nationalisms defined, again loosely, by emerging state boundaries and unique national symbols. At this time a distinctly Palestinian identity also began to develop, its seeds having been sown some time earlier in reaction to yet another emerging nationalist phenomenon, Zionism.

Both Israelis' and Palestinians' sense of national identity was largely formulated in the context of a denial of the other: for Zionists and Israelis, Palestine and Palestinians never existed, and for Palestinians, Zionism was never a national movement and Israel never a nation. Thus from the very beginning, the two groups had no dialogue with each other; instead, each took the stance of a frantic, violent rejection of all things affiliated with "the enemy." The ensuing struggle, of course, was never equal, for it pitted a leaderless, largely rural society, riven by internal divisions, against a far more organized and determined, largely urban and modern one. There was also a larger imperative at work. For Zionists, failure was not an option; the Europe of the Second World War did not welcome Jews even into its ghettos. The Zionist project had no alternative but to succeed. But the

Palestinians had not tasted refugee life yet, did not and could not compre-
hend what awaited them, and thought of their predicament as temporary.
Life, they figured, would soon return to normal. Liberation was right
around the corner. More than sixty years later, three million Palestinians
still live in refugee camps in Lebanon, Jordan, Syria, the West Bank, and
the Gaza Strip.[94]

While Ottomanism died along with the dynasty that had sought to
inculcate it throughout the region, there remained in the Arab world a
strong current of thought that defined the Arab nation in much broader
terms, composed of all of those who spoke the Arabic language, shared the
same Arab culture, had been the victims of the same historical injustices,
and needed to overcome the same set of obstacles. For many of the earliest idealists of the Arab nation, Islam was only incidental, if for no other
reason than that many Arabs, Michel Aflaq chief among them, happened
to be Christian. Significantly, the constitution of the United Arab Republic
made no mention of Islam as the official state religion, a glaring omission
in light of its mention in revolutionary Egypt's constitution a few years
earlier. These were resolutely secular nationalists, and the role ascribed
to Islam by Nasser, Bourguiba, and many of the other leaders at the time
never went beyond mere lip service.

Arab nationalism, of course, did not begin or end in the 1950s and
1960s. As we shall see in the next chapter, Pan-Arabism, for all its excitement and intensity, turned out to be quite ephemeral, attractive in rhetoric
but unworkable in practice. The devil, after all, is in the details. Before
long, more localized, state-centered versions of nationalism, like the ones
in Tunisia and Morocco, made their presence felt in more countries of the
Middle East. As much as revolutionary leaders and intellectuals tried to
transcend the borders that had been artificially drawn for them, in the end
they remained their victims, circumscribed in the scope of their interests
and in the articulation of the nation by more immediate surroundings—
those that were shaped and influenced by geography, state leaders, and
symbols such as flags, anthems, heroes, and holidays. By the late 1960s and
1970s, Nasser's Pan-Arabism was a distant dream.

4 The Arab-Israeli Wars

After the Suez Canal crisis of 1956, Nasser's popularity underwent a gradual but steady decline. As it turned out, 1956 was the apex of his popularity, both domestically and internationally. Almost immediately afterward, the Egyptian president started suffering one setback after another. Throughout the 1950s and into the late 1960s, he remained the hero of the Arab masses, the main protector of "the Arab nation." But he became increasingly a victim of his own successes, intoxicated by a make-believe victory over "global imperialism." Soon thereafter, with delusions of grandeur and power, he lost touch with his own people and with reality. Admittedly, most of the predicaments that led to Nasser's decline were thrust upon him by others or by circumstances beyond his control. This was especially the case with Syria's proposal for union with Egypt in early 1958, and with the plea for military and other forms of assistance by revolutionary Yemenis in 1962. As the self-proclaimed leader of Pan-Arabism, Nasser could not possibly reject either of these requests. Both undertakings turned out to be costly misadventures with disastrous consequences. This same self-constructed trap put a reluctant Nasser on a collision course with Israel in 1967, resulting in his devastating military defeat and humiliation in the Six Days' War in June. By the time the 1960s drew to a close, Nasser was a shadow of his former self, an empty and spent force. He died a broken man in September 1970. Not until a full three years later, in October 1973, could Nasser's successor, Anwar Sadat, avenge his loss to Israel in yet another military conflict with the Jewish state. Sadat emerged out of the 1973 War victorious. But the victory was more psychological than actual.

By the time the dust of the 1973 War had settled, the whole political geography of the region had changed. Nasser, the hero of the 1950s and 1960s, was a distant memory. The hero of the hour was now Sadat, the liberator of nothing but the smasher of Israeli invincibility. However, the new president's penchant for solo diplomacy and his peace with Israel soon alienated him from international allies and darkened his image before the Egyptians and other Arab masses. By the end of the 1970s and the early 1980s, Sadat was almost universally vilified in Egypt and elsewhere. It was self-proclaimed heroes from elsewhere—from Libya and, a few years later, Iraq—who sought to resurrect the ghost of Nasserism. As history would have it, their success was as ephemeral and elusive as Nasser's.

This chapter begins by tracing the tormented history of Nasser's steady decline, starting with the ill-advised union with Syria from 1958 to 1961. Nasser's commitment of troops and resources to the Yemeni civil war from 1962 to 1967 only expedited his downward spiral, sealed by his total and utter defeat by Israel. What occurred in those fateful six days in June 1967 profoundly and permanently changed the history of the Middle East, not to mention its political geography, its balance of power, the fate of the Palestinians, and the status of Israel as a regional and global military powerhouse. These very consequences, as well as the need for the defeated Arabs to redeem themselves, led to the 1973 War. Once again, there were profound ramifications not only for the belligerents but for the region as a whole.

NASSER'S QUAGMIRE

The beginning of the end for Nasser can be traced back to 1958, when he agreed to a hastily arranged union between Egypt and Syria. The unification process had actually begun in the closing weeks of 1957 at the behest of a group of young Syrian military officers enamored with Nasser's progressive social policies and fervent Pan-Arabism. Most were members or supporters of an exciting new political party called the Ba'th (Renaissance), whose ideals and platform closely mirrored Nasser's domestic and foreign policies. Since independence, Syria had had a functioning, albeit coup-ridden, presidential political system. There were also a variety of political parties, although most reflected larger inter-Arab divisions and rivalries rather than substantive doctrinal differences.[1] Unable to find a workable professional or political medium, the Syrian army, which itself had failed to develop a unifying sense of corporate identity, had repeatedly intervened in the political process. Meanwhile, the country's civilian politicians, an array of whom alternated between the presidency and other high offices, had proven to be equally incapable of governing. Amidst chronic turmoil and political instability within the system, elements from the armed forces sought to foster a union with Egypt.

There were four interrelated and reinforcing causes for the union between Egypt and Syria. First, of great importance was the larger global context of the Cold War, within which domestic political agendas in the Middle East and elsewhere were being formed. Second was the replication of superpower rivalries among Middle Eastern actors and the ensuing division of the Arab states into two camps, "progressive" (i.e., nonaligned) and "conservative" (i.e., pro-Western). Third was a steady growth and ascendancy within the Syrian polity of elements advocating ever-closer ties or actual unification with Egypt. Last was Nasser's predicament, in many ways self-made, that left him with little alternative to spreading his protective wings over Syria, especially as Cold War and inter-Arab divisions grew more and more polarized.

Throughout the 1950s, Britain and the United States searched for ways of containing what they perceived as the threat of Soviet and communist expansion in the Middle East. Such efforts had actually begun soon after the end of the Second World War, when in 1946 the Soviet Union had temporarily occupied Iran's northern province of Azerbaijan and set up a puppet republic there. Western efforts to combat the potential for increased Soviet influence in the Middle East had crystallized in Turkey's admission into NATO in 1952, a CIA-sponsored coup in Iran in 1953, and the abortive invasion of the Suez Canal in 1956. A year earlier, in February 1955, Washington had sponsored the establishment of the Baghdad Pact, which was intended to serve as a diplomatic and military alliance of pro-Western states against the Soviet Union and its regional allies. The pact was originally composed of Turkey and Iraq, joined a year later by Iran, Pakistan, and Britain. Soon after its establishment, the United States also joined the pact's Military Committee. Although in the long run largely ineffective, especially after Iraq's withdrawal in 1958 following the country's Ba'thist coup, at the time the alliance was seen as a serious threat to Nasser's populist regime and as inimical to the interests of the peoples of the Middle East.[2] Britain had also sponsored the establishment of the Arab League in 1944, intended largely as an instrument of its Middle East policy, although by the late 1950s Nasser had effectively turned the league into a forum for his own agendas.[3]

Following the outcome of the Suez Canal invasion, the United States sought to fill the vacuum left in the Middle East as a result of France and Britain's diplomatic retreat from the region. In January 1957, President Eisenhower launched a major Middle East foreign policy initiative that came to be known as the Eisenhower Doctrine. Its main goal was to foster close economic and military cooperation between the United States and any Middle Eastern country threatened by communist infiltration.[4] Toward this end, the U.S. president proposed a two-year aid package of some $400 million earmarked for America's Middle Eastern allies. In a not-too-subtle reference to Nasser, Eisenhower justified his policy initiative by arguing that "in the situation now existing, the greatest risk . . . is that ambitious despots may miscalculate. [If they] estimate that the Middle East is inadequately defended, they might be tempted to use open measures of armed attack . . . [and] that would start a chain of circumstances which would almost surely involve the United States in great military action."[5]

Like the Baghdad Pact and its successor, the Central Treaty Organization (CENTO), the Eisenhower Doctrine proved to be largely a failure, embraced in the Arab world only by Lebanon. The doctrine focused exclusively on Cold War dynamics and ignored the real concerns of Middle Eastern leaders, the most pressing of which was not the threat of communist infiltration but the existence and the policies of the state of Israel.[6] Nevertheless, the initiative and subsequent American efforts to gain Middle Eastern support for it added to the region's existing diplomatic tensions. For a country like Syria, with its chronic political instability, such an international environment was quite unsettling.

Syria's fears about regional tensions turned out to be more real than imagined. At the time of the announcement of the Eisenhower Doctrine, Syria happened to have a ruling elite closer in orientation to Nasser than to the conservative camp. By 1957, the war of words that had erupted between Damascus and Washington following the announcement of the Eisenhower Doctrine had inched closer to a crisis, culminating in the discovery, on August 12, of a CIA plot to overthrow the Syrian government.[7] In September, in an alleged attempt to stem communist infiltration into the country, NATO member Turkey amassed troops along its southern border with Syria, only to back off when threatened with Soviet reprisal.

All of this was happening at a time of profound political instability in Syria. The country had experienced three separate military coups in 1949 alone, followed by further episodes of military intervention in 1952 and 1954. Despite its history of repeated takeovers of the state, or perhaps because of it, up until the early 1970s the Syrian armed forces had never really developed a cohesive organizational hierarchy or a corporate sense of identity. Factions within the military competed with each other for power and influence and, in turn, with civilian politicians, most of whom belonged to the country's wealthy, old-school oligarchy. Syria thus drifted from one domestic and international crisis to another, headed by leaders generally seen as incompetent and self-serving. Enter Nasserism and the force of all it stood for. When in late 1957 Ba'thist officers of the Syrian army approached Nasser about unification, he had no alternative but to agree. After all, ever since 1955, and especially after the tripartite invasion of his country, Nasser had positioned himself as the protector of the interests of the Arab "nation," the region's chief guardian against imperialism. With Syria threatened from all sides and with the plea for unity coming from within Syria itself, Nasser could not possibly reject the proposal. On February 1, 1958, Nasser and Syrian President Shukri Quwatli announced in Cairo the unification of their two countries under the new name United Arab Republic. Nasser became the UAR's president. His position was approved in a popular plebiscite held three weeks later, as was a new, "presidential democratic" constitution.

The unity project was doomed from the very beginning because of the haste with which it had been put together and because of the way Nasser set out to govern. Before the actual unification, the two countries had taken few concrete steps to facilitate the process. They had signed a series of trade and economic agreements only the previous September, and Egypt had dispatched a few troops to Aleppo in October during Syria's border conflict with Turkey. But the details of how a postunification state would operate and what it would be like had not received the treatment they deserved. It was up to the new republic's executive branch, dominated by Nasser and the rest of the Egyptian leadership, to work out the details of the new state. Nasser, in keeping with the tenor of the times, devised a highly central-ized, presidential system. The UAR was to have an Egyptian and a Syrian region, each with an executive council whose powers would be determined by the president. There would also be a four-hundred-member legisla-tive assembly appointed by the president, half from each country's sitting legislature. Finally, an independent judiciary was supposed to administer Egyptian and Syrian laws separately in each region.[8] Cairo would be the UAR's capital.

It soon became apparent that unification had in effect meant Nasser's takeover of Syria. Although his cabinet featured two Syrian vice presidents along with two Egyptians, almost all of the UAR's key ministries were placed in Egyptian hands, and many well-known Syrians, including former President Quwatli, were either demoted or dropped from the cabinet alto-gether.[9] Field Marshal Abdel Hakim Amer, one of the UAR's vice presidents and a longtime personal friend of Nasser, was put in charge of the Syrian region and given a mandate to implement sweeping economic, industrial, and land reforms. As a precondition for unification, Nasser had demanded that all Syrian parties, including the Ba'th, disband. Instead, political activists could join the National Union, another populist, mass-based party set up in Egypt in the same mold as the now-defunct Liberation Rally (see below). When the Syrian Communist Party failed to dissolve itself, scores of its members and sympathizers were arrested and its assets were seized by the government.

Though never fully articulated, the vision that Ba'thist officers had had for the UAR was hardly consistent with what Nasser was implementing in the Syrian "region." The Ba'thists were ideologues and visionaries, believing that in the postunification era they could implement their ideals in a federally governed Syria. But whatever ideals Nasser might have started with as a former revolutionary, by the late 1950s he had become a hardened pragmatist, eager not so much to put his experimental ideas into practice as to solidify his grip on power both domestically and internationally.[10] Ba'th members were also disenchanted with the union because of their increasing political marginalization. The heavy hand of the Egyptian bureaucracy, Nasser's penchant for personal political control, and his ill-advised plans to implement statist economic policies in Syria as he had done in Egypt only heightened popular Syrian anger against the unification process.[11] Syrian military officers also resented the preferential treatment that their Egyptian counterparts were receiving in postings and promotions.

Sensing tensions, by the summer of 1961 Nasser made some adjustments aimed at placating the brewing opposition in Syria. He ordered the transfer of an unpopular Syrian military commander (Abdel Hamid Sarraj) from Damascus to Cairo, promised to spend four months a year in Damascus, and gave Syrians more visible positions in his administration. But these efforts proved to be too little and too late. On September 21, Syrian army units marched on Damascus and, in yet another of the country's many coups, proclaimed Syria's independence from the UAR.

The coup and Syria's separation from the UAR were a crushing blow to Nasser. In many ways, he was defeated at his own game and by his own actions. This time, unlike 1956, Nasser could not blame Western imperialism or Zionist conspiracy for his troubles. And he could not, even if he wanted to, turn this defeat into some sort of imagined victory. This was a defeat through and through—political, diplomatic, economic. As if to underscore the futility of the whole endeavor, Nasser made a half-hearted attempt to reverse the coup but then acknowledged the irreversibility of the secession in a radio broadcast the next day. Perhaps to hang on to some vestige of the unity experience, Nasser retained the name United Arab Republic for Egypt. In fact, in April 1963, following military coups in both Iraq and Syria, the three countries entered into negotiations over another proposed union, this time far less centralized and based on what one joint declaration characterized as "studied and clear foundations."[12] Before it got off the ground, however, this venture was also doomed, with Nasser declaring that "we cannot . . . have any link, any alliance, any unity or objective with a Fascist state in Syria."[13]

No sooner was the unification fiasco with Syria over than Nasser found himself in yet another quandary, this time in Yemen. Nasser needed a diplomatic victory and needed it fast. Syria's secession from the UAR had occurred within the context of—and had in turn heightened—an Arab "cold war" of sorts.[14] With Syria taking its case against Egypt before the Arab League, supported this time by Iraq and by the Saudi and Jordanian monarchies, Nasser the Pan-Arabist was finding himself increasingly isolated from the rest of the Arab world. He had also long been at odds with Tunisia's strongman, President Habib Bourguiba. In fact, by the early 1960s, Nasser's circle of Arab allies had largely been reduced to one, Algeria's Ahmed Ben Bella, a fellow revolutionary. Nevertheless, his anti-imperialist rhetoric and his charisma still resonated with the Arab masses, and it was because of this continued popularity among aspiring Arab revolutionaries that he and his country were drawn into the Yemeni civil war.

Yemen had remained one of the world's most isolated and conservative countries for more than a thousand years, ruled as a theocracy by a successive string of absolutist imams who governed under Ottoman suzerainty. In 1893, Britain occupied the southern dry port of Aden and established what came to be known as the Protectorate of Aden. Once the British withdrew in 1967, the leftist National Liberation Front seized power and, in 1970, renamed the country the People's Democratic Republic of Yemen. The north, meanwhile, had won its independence from Ottoman rule in 1918 but had remained isolated and deeply steeped in tradition. Palace coups had occurred in 1948 and again in 1955, but the overall nature of state-society relations and the absence of social progress had not changed.[15] Imam Ahmad, the kingdom's ruler, had been initially attracted to the ideals expounded by Nasser, to the extent that on the day the UAR was established, Yemen also joined the two countries in a loose confederation called the United Arab States. But there was little substance to the confederation beyond the exchange of diplomatic pleasantries, and, along with Syria, Yemen terminated its association with the UAR in 1961. On September 26, 1962, a group of Yemeni officers launched a military takeover in the hope of ending their country's conservative monarchy and replacing it with a progressive, republican regime. Despite declaring the establishment of a Yemen Arab Republic, the coup makers did not immediately succeed in overthrowing the monarchy. The day after the coup, Nasser rushed Egyptian troops to Yemen to help republican officers fight against royalist forces. But Nasser had miscalculated. Yemen was about to plunge into a protracted civil war that would last for five years—a nightmare for the people of Yemen and an intractable dilemma for Nasser. Yemen became "Nasser's Vietnam."[16]

Nasser's dispatch of troops to prop up the fledgling Yemen Arab Republic was a product of his efforts to reclaim his position as the undisputed leader of the Arab world.[17] For revolutionaries revolutions never end, and Nasser had to keep on fighting, even if thousands of miles away from Egypt. Yemen had originally offered Nasser the perfect opportunity to carry out the various facets of his revolution. It had all the right ingredients: a "revolutionary" military leadership willing to follow his lead; a chance to create state structures from scratch based on the Nasserist model; and, perhaps most important of all, a foothold deep inside the Arabian peninsula, long a bastion of monarchical conservatism as epitomized by the Saudis. But if Nasser saw Yemen as his golden opportunity, the Saudis saw it as a mortal threat, fearing that a republican victory in Yemen might inspire their own subjects to challenge the Saudi monarchy. Before long, therefore, the Yemeni civil war became a war by proxy between Egypt on the one side and Saudi Arabia and some of its allies—such as Jordan, Iran, and Pakistan—on the other. At their peak, Egyptian forces in Yemen numbered some seventy thousand.[18] As it turned out, such a massive commitment of troops and resources only deepened what soon became Nasser's Yemeni quagmire.

For Nasser, involvement in Yemen turned out to be far from the quick military and hence political victory he had hoped. Initial estimates of the extent of the republicans' success turned out to be exaggerated, and in less than a year it became obvious that a more sizable commitment of Egyptian troops was needed than originally thought.[19] However, the numerical weight of the additional Egyptian troops was offset by their lack of preparedness to fight in Yemen and by the Saudis' proportionate increase in their support for the royalists. The Egyptian army, trained and equipped for conventional warfare, found itself in an unfamiliar terrain and facing an enemy adept at using guerrilla tactics. Moreover, Yemen's porous northern borders with Saudi Arabia enabled the Saudis to send additional supplies to their royalist allies with relative ease. The balance of power was made all the more complicated by the tendency of many Yemeni tribes, with which the country was replete, to change sides on the basis of practical considerations.[20] By the summer of 1963, the civil war had degenerated into a stalemate that would last for nearly three more years.

The longer it dragged on, the more of an obsession the Yemen war became for Nasser. By 1966, he was locked into a series of increasingly dangerous cat-and-mouse games with the Israelis, but he stubbornly refused to waver on his commitment to Yemen's republicans. A series of diplomatic initiatives sponsored by the United Nations, the Arab League, and other regional actors all failed to bring a peaceful end to the Yemeni conflict. Only because of mounting expenses and increasing resentment at home did Egypt slowly begin reducing the number of its troops in Yemen in late 1966. But even after Egypt's humiliating loss to Israel in June 1967 and the occupation of its territory, Nasser remained obsessed with his Yemeni venture, refusing to back down.[21] In the end, however, he had no option but to withdraw his forces. He finally accepted the implementation of a 1965 agreement with Saudi Arabia for the joint withdrawal of all foreign forces from Yemen. By late summer 1967, Egypt's military presence in Yemen had been significantly reduced. By October, with the last vestiges of the monarchy gone, Yemeni republican leaders finally assumed control over the country. Incidentally, they also resumed their own internal squabbles.[22]

THE 1967 WAR

Nasser's Yemeni misadventure presented him with yet another imperative to salvage his international prestige and his faltering leadership of the Arab cause. Far from unifying the Arabs, the civil war in Yemen had significantly heightened inter-Arab rivalries, with Saudi Arabia and Jordan on one side and Nasser's UAR on another. The ruling Ba'thists in Damascus also remained mistrustful of Nasser and his designs on Syria. Moreover, while by this time Ba'thist officers had also taken over the reins of power in Baghdad, relations between Iraq and Syria remained cool and often tense. Elsewhere in North Africa, only revolutionary Algeria remained resolutely supportive of Nasser, having finally defeated the French in 1962 after a long, bloody war of liberation, and then having experienced a military coup of its own in 1965. Libya remained under the control of an archaic monarchy and, for now, was militarily and diplomatically marginal to the rest of the Middle East. Morocco had its own border conflict with Algeria, and Nasser's support of the Algerian position did not endear him to the Moroccans. And Tunisia's President Habib Bourguiba had repeatedly criticized Nasser and other Arab "radicals" for their lack of realism and moderation.[23]

By 1966, however, these divisions were temporarily masked because of heightened tensions between Israel and three of the frontline Arab states: Jordan, Syria, and the UAR. After Syria's secession from the UAR in 1961, Palestinians were becoming increasingly suspicious of the commitments of the various Arab states to their cause; many feared that the state of Israel would become a permanent reality unless the entire political geography of the region was changed. The only way to bring about such a change, many reasoned, was to encourage the Arab countries to wage another war on Israel. Toward this end, to increase the potential for conflict, Palestinian commandos called the Fedayeen launched a low-intensity campaign of infiltrations and hit-and-run attacks against Israeli targets beginning in the early 1960s. In May 1964, the Arab League, and especially Egypt, had taken the lead in creating the PLO for the specific purpose of curtailing Fedayeen attacks on Israeli targets, thereby reducing the potential for war. These efforts were of little consequence, however. By 1966, because of Fedayeen raids as well as a number of other factors, Israel and its Arab neighbors were on a collision course, one that culminated in the Six Days' War in June 1967.

The immediate causes of the 1967 War can be divided into three general categories: the highly volatile atmosphere of the region throughout 1966 and 1967, made all the more explosive by a series of bellicose statements coming out of Damascus and Cairo; the regional and international predicaments of Nasser; and the domestic political predicament of the Israeli prime minister at the time, Levi Eshkol. To begin with, there were the provocative activities of the Fedayeen. These commando raids had intensified after yet another coup in Syria in February 1966, when the new crop of ruling officers in Damascus were more sympathetic to the PLO's main guerrilla unit, the Fatah. Adding to the tension between Israel and Syria were disputes over water resources and cultivation activities in their border areas, which had resulted in massive aerial bombardment of Syrian villages by Israeli jets on several occasions.[24] Toward the end of 1966, the Soviet Union, which by now had started supplying a limited number of arms to Syria, announced that Israel was amassing troops along the Syrian border in preparation for an all-out invasion.

Nasser once again found himself in a quandary. As the self-proclaimed leader of the Arab world and the liberator of the Palestinians, the Egyptian leader could not remain on the sidelines for long. On November 4, 1966, the UAR and Syria signed a mutual defense pact, set up a joint military command, and agreed to place their forces under the command of the Egyptian chief of staff in the event of war. Nasser hoped that this show of unity and force would deter Israel from further attacks on Arab targets.[25] But this was not to be, for shortly thereafter Israel mounted a serious attack on a Jordanian village, resulting in many casualties and the demolition of a mosque.

Throughout these months and into 1967, Nasser was keenly aware that the Arab armies were not prepared for war against Israel.[26] His strategy appears to have been one of trying to buy time until the Arab armies would be more united and stronger. "I am not in a position to go to war," Nasser is quoted as having said around this time. "I tell you this frankly, and it is not shameful to say it publicly. To go to war without having the sufficient means would be to lead the country and the people to disaster."[27] The bulk of his own forces were bogged down in Yemen, and those in Egypt had not had sufficient time yet to train and familiarize themselves with the advanced Soviet weaponry they were receiving. But Nasser had once again become a victim of his own rhetoric. When on April 7, 1967, the Israeli Defense Forces (IDF) shot down six Syrian jet fighters over Syrian territory, Syria and Jordan both criticized Nasser for not having done anything in Syria's defense. At this time the Egyptian president embarked on a campaign of intimidation against Israel, one over which he was soon to lose control.

Events now began unfolding far more rapidly than Nasser had anticipated. On May 15, amid maximum publicity, Egyptian troops started marching toward the country's borders with Israel in the Sinai desert. Nasser also asked for the formal removal of the United Nations Emergency Forces (UNEF), which had been stationed along the Egyptian-Israeli border following the 1956 conflict. The UN secretary-general, U Thant, quickly agreed. Nasser then closed the Strait of Tiran, located at the southern tip of the Sinai, to Israeli shipping, an act Israel had vowed not to tolerate. Nasser's fiery rhetoric continued unabated, however, and, in a dramatic gesture of unity, Jordan and the UAR announced the signing of a joint defense agreement and the placing of Jordanian troops under the command of an Egyptian general. Iraq and Saudi Arabia also announced their readiness to send troops in support of the Arab armies.

Throughout, Nasser had hoped to avoid a military confrontation with Israel and had at times moderated his rhetoric with proclamations to that effect. His primary goal was to score a political victory at Israel's expense by forcing the Israelis to stop their massive retaliatory attacks on Jordan and Syria.[28] But the more he pursued this goal the more intractable and inflexible his position became, to the point that he could not go back on his statements. Ironically, this was the same predicament in which the

Israeli prime minister found himself in relation to other Israeli political actors. Levi Eshkol had often been accused of being weak and indecisive by the opposition Rafi Party and by members of his own Mapai Party.[29] Like Nasser, Eshkol was reluctant to wage war, fearing, among other things, that it might provoke retaliatory measures by the Soviet Union.[30] But once Egypt closed the Strait of Tiran, Eshkol had no option but to act. He brought in the popular retired general Moshe Dayan as the country's new defense minister, and, in the early hours of June 4, the Israeli cabinet voted in favor of war. At 7:30 A.M. on June 5, Israel commenced a relentless campaign of aerial assault against Egypt.

The Israeli campaign was brilliantly planned and executed. Because of Israel's small size and population, its military doctrine had long been based on massive, surprise, offensive attacks that concentrated the greatest firepower on the biggest foe.[31] Accordingly, within the first few hours of the war, the Israeli air force managed to destroy almost all of the Egyptian airplanes that were parked in air bases within range of its jet fighters. These included seventeen airfields and approximately three hundred aircraft.[32] By the end of the second day, the IDF claimed to have destroyed a total of 418 aircraft from Arab countries, including 309 from Egypt, 60 from Syria, 29 from Jordan, 17 from Iraq, and 1 from Lebanon.[33] Left with no support from the air, Egyptian forces in the Gaza Strip were overwhelmed by the end of the second day, and by the end of the third day the entire Sinai, extending as far west as the Suez Canal, was in Israeli hands (map 5). Highways leading out of the peninsula were littered with bombed-out cars and buses carrying fleeing Egyptians.

On the morning of the third day, June 7, Israeli forces turned their attention toward the Jordanian-controlled West Bank and, once again in complete control of the skies, overran Jordanian forces by that evening. The city of Jerusalem, with all its religious and historical significance for the Jews, was now in Israeli hands. For the first few days, the Syrian front had been relatively quiet, and activity there had been limited to isolated runs over Israeli territory by the remaining Syrian jets. On the fifth day of fighting, however, Israel initiated a massive attack on Syria, by the end of which it had captured the strategic Golan Heights. The Golan had housed Syria's strategic missile batteries, whose positions had earlier been revealed to the IDF by an Israeli undercover spy named Elie Cohen.[34] The Syrians initially put up a stiff resistance, but by early afternoon of the next day their defenses collapsed and they retreated. Earlier, on June 7 and 8, Jordan and Egypt, respectively, had agreed to a UN-sponsored cease-fire. Syria had also agreed to a cease-fire on June 9. Only after its

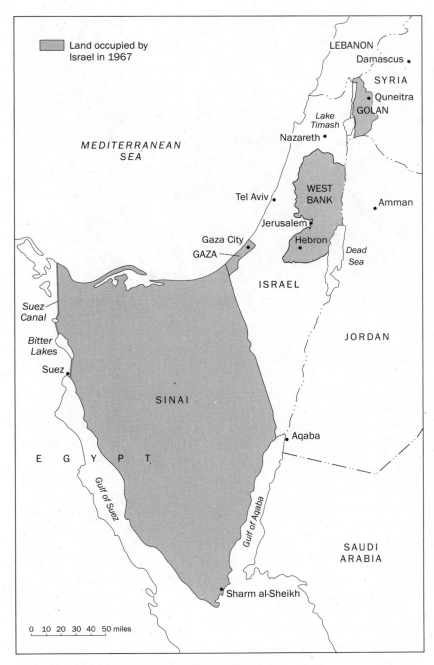

Map 5. Territories captured by Israel in 1967.

Figure 9. Israeli soldiers celebrate capturing Jerusalem in the 1967 War.

capture of the Golan was complete, on June 11, would Israel agree to stop all hostilities.

After six days of relentless attacks, Israel's war against its Arab neighbors was over. In a brilliant series of military maneuvers and tactics, Israel had started, directed, and concluded a war all on its own terms. Within six days it had managed to wipe out the Arab air forces, rout the Arab armies, and capture the Sinai, the West Bank, and the Golan Heights. All in all, it was estimated that fewer than a thousand Israelis, both civilians and soldiers, lost their lives in the conflict. The casualties and losses on the Arab side were staggering: twenty thousand dead soldiers; twenty-six thousand square miles of lost territory; and thousands of prisoners of war, including, if the IDF is to be believed, nine generals, ten colonels, and three hundred officers.[35] There were now also over 500,000 new Arab refugees (in addition to the Palestinian refugees from 1948), including 120,000 Syrians and 250,000 Egyptians.[36]

The war had other profound consequences for the actors involved in it, both Arab and Israeli. For the Arabs, defeat, complete as it was, came to symbolize the fallacies of an entire era, of a style of politics and more generally a perspective incapable of coping with the realities of the surrounding world. A wave of recrimination and self-criticism was set in motion, and the defeat brought on a deep psychological reevaluation of what Arab intellectuals saw as the chief culprits: incompetent leaders and their hollow regimes and, more importantly, the cultural milieu that had given rise to them. Even such sacred aspects of life as Islam and the Arabic language, with the latter's penchant for hyperbole, were not spared from criticism.[37] A wave of Arab literary works appeared, including al-Sadiq al-Azm's *Self-Criticism after the Defeat*, which has been called "one of the most impressive and controversial pieces of Arabic political writing in recent times."[38] The revolutionary regimes of the day now came to be seen as "regimes of defeat" *(anzimat al-hazima)*.[39] In the words of the noted Arab scholar Fouad Ajami, "What the defeat did was to show that the Arab revolution was neither socialist nor revolutionary: The Arab world had merely mimicked the noise of revolutionary change and adopted the outside trappings of socialism; deep down, under the skin, it had not changed."[40]

For Egypt, the 1967 War meant the end of Nasserism. This was not an event that the Egyptian president could somehow turn into a victory. It was a defeat through and through. The Egyptian air force had been wiped out, the army soundly beaten, and Egyptian territory occupied. To add insult to injury, in the first couple days of the war, radio broadcasts from Cairo had boasted about spectacular victories by the Egyptian forces.[41] For the people of Egypt, the defeat was a monumental psychological shock, a *naksa*, "step backward," or yet another *nakba* (catastrophe) (the first one having occurred in 1948). As one observer noted, "[I]n just one week, a system that had begun to evoke feelings of trust, confidence, and a certain degree of commitment from broad sectors of the public became either suspect or despised."[42] In disgrace, Nasser announced his resignation from the presidency on June 9, while the war was still raging at the Syrian front.[43] Following mass demonstrations and pleas not to resign, some of which appear to have been orchestrated, he withdrew his resignation the next day. Instead, Nasser expanded his own powers and initiated a major purge of the armed forces, including some of his closest friends, most notably army commander Field Marshal Abdel Hakim Amer and Defense Minister Shamseddin Badran. With rumors of a coup in the air, Amer was arrested some time near the end of the summer, and on September 14 it was announced that he had committed suicide.

Nasser must have known that he was not fully exonerated by the Egyptian public. Soon after the war ended, the Soviet Union rushed massive amounts of arms to Egypt to prevent the total collapse of Nasser's armed forces or, more plausibly, the possibility of a pro-American coup. By

1971, a year after Nasser died, Egypt's Soviet-made arsenal is reported to have included 450 MiG planes, 100 warships, 1,350 tanks, and an undetermined number of SAM missiles, overseen by some fifteen to twenty thousand Soviet military instructors.[44] But Nasser and Nasserism were never quite the same again. Different ideological currents made their presence felt in "street politics," and on February 20, 1968, the regime was jolted by massive protests by an estimated forty thousand to fifty thousand workers and students.[45] The old lion seemed to know that he had now been reduced to a shadow of his former self. The propaganda machine of the Voice of the Arabs was shut down; Egyptian troops were withdrawn from Yemen; and the Arab League ceased to be an instrument of Nasser's diplomacy. Even his "War of Attrition" against Israel, designed to increase the cost of occupying the Sinai, backfired, as Israel, now equipped with the latest American jet fighters, retaliated with ever-greater ferocity. His health, meanwhile, rapidly deteriorated. On September 28, 1970, just as he had finished negotiating a cease-fire agreement between warring Palestinian commandos and Jordan's King Hussein, the fifty-two-year-old Nasser suffered a fatal heart attack. Despite several attempts by others to resurrect the Nasserism that he personified, it died with him.

The 1967 War also marked a watershed for the Palestinians. The Palestinian movement became more militant, as represented by the ascendancy of the Fedayeen and growing intensity of their attacks on Israel. There was also a realization that the old set of Arab actors—Nasser, PLO leader Ahmad Shuqairi, King Hussein—were unwilling or unable to do much for the Palestinian cause. The Fedayeen, now concentrated mostly in Jordan since Israel had captured the West Bank, became more daring and effective in their attacks on Israeli targets, their resolve hardened by Israel's imposition of draconian measures in Gaza and the West Bank, demolition of more Palestinian homes to make room for Israeli settlers, and annexation of East Jerusalem. An additional four hundred thousand Palestinians became refugees and fled from their homes in Gaza and the West Bank.[46] Many of the younger refugees joined the ranks of the PLO's guerrilla fighters in the Fatah. The Fatah, in the meanwhile, had scored an impressive military victory of sorts over Israel, when early in 1968 it had managed to down six Israeli jets and destroy twelve tanks in one of the frequent border skirmishes.

From its establishment in 1964 up until the 1967 War, the PLO had been largely used as an instrument of inter-Arab and especially Egyptian diplomacy. But by the late 1960s, especially after Nasser's defeat in 1967, a new generation of younger, professional Palestinians, who had long been viewed with suspicion by other Arab leaders, were beginning to assume a more active role within the organization. The steady growth within the PLO of the National Liberation Movement (Fatah), and its young leader, Yasser Arafat, represented this trend. Fatah was originally established in 1957, began armed action in 1965, and started being led by Yasser Arafat in 1968. Other similar Palestinian organizations that appeared in the late 1960s and became influential within the PLO included the Popular Front for the Liberation of Palestine (PFLP), established in 1967, and the Democratic Front for the Liberation of Palestine (DFLP), established in 1969. Some of the other, smaller organizations within the PLO were the PFLP-General Command (est. 1968), the pro-Syrian Vanguard for the Popular Liberation War (est. 1968), the pro-Iraqi Arab Liberation Front (est. 1968), the Palestinian Liberation Front (est. 1967), and the Democratic Union, known as FIDA (est. 1990). In addition to its legislative organ, the Palestine National Council (PNC), and its military wing, the Palestine Liberation Army (PLA), the PLO included a host of smaller organizations, many of them formed by various splinter groups. In the 1968 meeting of the Palestine National Council, the Fatah emerged as the dominant group within the PLO, and its leader, Yasser Arafat, became the PLO's chairman.

The Palestinian Fedayeen's military and thus political ascendancy in Jordan was not to last long. By 1970, the Fedayeen had become so powerful as to openly defy the authority of the Jordanian state. They set up unauthorized roadblocks and conducted their own military operations, and some even called for the establishment of a "progressive regime" in Jordan. To call international attention to the plight of the Palestinians, the PFLP, one of the PLO's more radical groups, hijacked three international jetliners on September 6, 1970, and forced them to land in the Jordanian city of Zarqa. Once the PFLP blew up the (empty) planes and the crisis was over, Jordanian forces decided to move against the Fedayeen, who a few months earlier had been implicated in an attempt on the king's life. An intense battle erupted between the Jordanian army and the Fedayeen between September 17 and 27, featuring house-to-house battles in Amman and Irbid. The situation became even more volatile after a brief invasion by Syria into Jordan in support of the Fedayeen. In a speech broadcast to the Arab leaders gathered in Cairo to deal with the Jordanian crisis, Arafat, speaking from his hideout in Amman, said, "There is a sea of blood. Some twenty thousand of our people are killed or wounded. . . . From amidst the dead, the debris and our patient people . . . I appeal to you to move your conference to Amman immediately so that you can see for yourselves the magnitude of the crime and the ugliness of the massacre."[47]

The Palestinian leader's appeals were ignored, however. Syrian forces soon withdrew, and on September 27 a cease-fire agreement was signed in Cairo between King Hussein and Arafat (the day before Nasser's death). The agreement failed to ease tensions, however, and by the following July open warfare between the two sides erupted once again, this time resulting in a crushing defeat of the Fedayeen. Scores were killed, many escaped to Syria (and from there to Lebanon), and many, ironically, sought refuge in Israel in preference to being captured by the Jordanians. Arafat set up his headquarters in Beirut. A new chapter in the Palestinian movement had started.

As a transnational conflict with multiple dimensions and actors, the 1967 War was also bound to have a profound impact on the larger international community and, more specifically, on its perceptions of means of resolving it. Significantly, in the aftermath of the 1967 War the notion of "land for peace" first became popular internationally, and it was subsequently enunciated in the United Nation's landmark Resolution 242, passed unanimously by the UN Security Council on November 22, 1967. A product of intense diplomacy, especially on the part of its chief author, the British ambassador to the United Nations, Lord Caradon, the resolution declared "the inadmissibility of the acquisition of territory by war and the need to work for a just and lasting peace in which every state in the area can live in peace." Moreover, the resolution called for:

(i)   Withdrawal of Israeli forces from territories occupied in the recent conflict; [and]

(ii) Termination of all claims or state of belligerency and respect for the acknowledgment of the sovereignty, territorial integrity and political independence of every state in the area to live in peace within secure and recognized boundaries free from threats or acts of force.[48]

The historic importance of Resolution 242 cannot be overstated. Given the language of the resolution, its acceptance by the Arab states meant their implicit recognition of the right of the state of Israel to exist. Egypt and Jordan accepted the resolution almost immediately. Syria, however, did not accept it until after the 1973 War, and the PLO also initially rejected it. At the Arab summit conference in Fez in 1982, all Arab states except Libya voted to accept the resolution. The PLO did not formally endorse Resolution 242 until 1988, as the basis of a comprehensive peace settlement in the Middle East. Israel accepted the resolution early on, although it has since refused to unilaterally withdraw from the territories it occupied in

1967. Instead, Israel's position has been one of preferring bilateral agreements, beginning with the Camp David Accords with Egypt, based on which it withdrew from the Sinai in 1982, and eventually leading up to treaties with Jordan and with the PLO itself (the 1993 Oslo Accords). As if to compensate for the return of the Sinai to Egypt, however, in 1981 the Israeli Knesset voted to formally annex the Golan Heights. The map of the region was forever changed.

THE 1973 WAR

The Arab world entered the 1970s in a deep malaise. The *nakba* of 1948—the loss of Palestine—had been compounded by another catastrophe, made all the more humiliating by its boastful prelude and the endless, loud promises of liberation and victory that preceded it. The psychological wounds were deep both in the frontline states and elsewhere. A whole generation of public intellectuals emerged whose essays and stories gave popular expression to the collective anguish of their societies.[49] Among them was the prolific and highly successful Egyptian author Naguib Mahfouz, whose bitter condemnation of Nasser's repressive police state and its military and economic failures now reached a new crescendo.[50] Nasser's death had done little to assuage defeatism and shattered spirits. In the Egypt he left behind, the economy barely functioned, and the War of Attrition (more on which below) was far from a resounding success. Not only had the Israelis captured the Sinai, they had now built a settlement on it and were claiming the peninsula as part of biblical Eretz Israel. Syria's predicament was not much better, its ruling revolutionary generals having lost the Golan and nearly Damascus itself. Jordan's loss of the West Bank was equally humiliating, but its war with the Fedayeen had served to strengthen the king's hand among the East Bankers and the conservative Arab states.

The Arabs needed to vindicate themselves and to escape from under the heavy burden of so thorough a defeat. There was no other option. The psychology of the masses would not tolerate the defeat indefinitely, and neither, the leaders reasoned, would the judgment of history. By now, there was an even more urgent need to back up the obligatory rhetoric of Arab prowess and solidarity with actions. For the Egyptians and the Syrians especially, what was at stake was no longer the liberation of the Palestinians and the abstract righting of a historical wrong but the reclaiming of their own territories, the instinctive desire to avenge loss and to strike back. They therefore saw another war as inevitable and in fact necessary as the only way their pre-1967 borders would be restored.

Once again, the mantle of Arab leadership fell on Egypt. Egypt's leaders and army had lost the most, and its new president, Anwar Sadat, had the most politically urgent need for a military victory. Sadat had long been a friend and confidant of Nasser, having come up through the ranks of the Nasserist political machinery as one of the original Free Officers, then as the secretary-general of the Arab Socialist Union, as the Speaker of the parliament, and, eventually, following the purges of 1968, as Nasser's vice president. But he had always remained in the shadow of Nasser's magnetic personality and was generally considered to be a political lightweight. In fact, Nasser is said to have picked Sadat as his designated successor precisely because of the latter's limited involvement in the regime's internal political rivalries.[51]

Without a solid base of his own, Sadat had to contend with powerful adversaries almost from the beginning of his presidency. This climaxed in an attempted coup by Nasser's former associates in May 1971. But the purges and the arrests that ensued did not go far in making the president feel secure in his position. A much publicized "corrective revolution" followed, ostensibly designed to dismantle the Nasserist police state but in reality intended to consolidate Sadat's position within the regime. But Sadat's powers remained tenuous well into 1973. The president might have neutralized his political enemies, but he still lacked the popularity and stature that Nasser had once enjoyed among the masses. More importantly, Egyptian territory still remained occupied, and Sadat had to find a way to put an end to the country's festering national humiliation. The continued occupation of the Sinai and the closure of the Suez Canal eroded more than political capital. "The cost of maintaining a huge mobilized army in the desert was becoming an impossible burden on the economy," and without a solution to the Sinai's occupation there were few prospects for economic and political revitalization.[52] Getting the Sinai back was now more than a matter of political or even national vindication. Increasingly, it was a matter of economic survival.

These domestic political considerations had prompted Sadat to embark on an ambitious diplomatic campaign almost immediately after taking office. His principal aim was to secure some territorial concessions in the Sinai from Israel. Most of these efforts occurred first through the United Nations and then through the United States, whose active diplomacy had finally brought an end to the 1969–70 War of Attrition. The War of Attrition had started in March 1969, when the Egyptian army launched a large-scale assault on Israeli forces occupying the Suez Canal. Nasser's intent was to prevent Israel from turning the canal into a de facto border with Egypt, to increase for Israel the costs of Sinai's occupation by making it suffer steady losses in soldiers and equipment, and, eventually, to force it to withdraw to the pre-1967 border. To achieve these goals, with his armed forces gradually rebuilt by the Soviets, he resorted to the heavy bombardment of Israeli defenses, accompanied by occasional air strikes and mobile commando raids. The war dragged on through the spring and summer months inconclusively, interrupted only by an unsuccessful attempt by the United States to broker a cease-fire. The American initiative was rejected by the Israeli government, which in early 1970 decided to take the war to the Egyptian hinterland by starting aerial bombardments of Cairo's suburbs. Finally, in August 1970, following extensive military and economic assurances by the Nixon administration, the Israeli prime minister, Golda Meir, agreed to end the war that Nasser had started.

The War of Attrition formed the backdrop against which Sadat's diplomacy in the early years took shape. Despite its inconclusiveness, many in the Israeli cabinet considered Israel to have been the real victor in the latest military conflict with Egypt. From a strategic standpoint, although Soviet help to Egypt had reduced Israel's near-dominance of the skies, Egyptian forces had made little or no tangible progress in their costly, eighteen-month confrontation with the IDF. Considering the Jordanian civil war and Nasser's subsequent death in September 1970, Golda Meir viewed the Arab bargaining position as too weak to merit negotiations. More could be achieved, she reasoned, by a "diplomacy of attrition," in which Israeli intransigence would eventually lead to the signing of a comprehensive peace treaty with Egypt.[53] So early in his career, and with the Sinai still occupied, Sadat was in no position to sign a comprehensive peace treaty with Israel. For now, his immediate goals were to see the Suez Canal opened, thereby restoring to Egypt one of its most vital economic lifelines, and, if only as a symbolic gesture, to station some Egyptian troops on the canal's east bank. Mistrustful of Sadat's real motives, Meir and other hard-liners in her cabinet opted instead to strengthen Israel's hold over the West Bank and Gaza by encouraging the building of more settlements and factories in Palestinian areas.

Sadat declared in a broadcast to the nation, "1971 will be the Year of Decision, toward war or peace. This is a problem that cannot be postponed any longer. We have prepared ourselves from within, and we ought to be ready for the task lying ahead. . . . Everything depends on us. This is neither America's nor the Soviets' war, but our war, deriving from our will and determination."[54] But the "year of decision" came and went with no tangible results. Always with a flair for the dramatic, Sadat had to make good on his rhetoric sooner or later, either through diplomacy or on the battlefront. True to form, the Egyptian president did not disappoint. In July 1972, he abruptly expelled the estimated fifteen thousand Soviet advisors who were helping Egypt rebuild its armed forces after their destruction in 1967. He also broke off relations with Jordan over a relatively minor pretext—a proposal by King Hussein to form a Jordanian federation with sovereignty over Palestinians. Golda Meir and many of the hard-liners in her cabinet interpreted these developments as further signs of the Egyptian president's weakened strategic and military position. Surely the Egyptians, who had been so decisively routed back in 1967, could not pose a serious threat to Israel now that they had lost their Soviet patrons and Jordanian allies! The reality was quite different, however. Sadat's expulsion of Soviet military advisors and diplomatic row with Jordan were actually intended to give him a freer hand in waging war on Israel.

The war came on October 6, 1973, in the middle of the Muslim holy month of Ramadan and the Jewish Yom Kippur.[55] In a brilliantly coordinated and executed blitz, at 2:00 P.M. Syrian and Egyptian forces attacked and in a few hours overran Israeli defensive positions in the Golan and the east bank of the Suez, respectively. On the Sinai front, the attack featured some seven hundred Egyptian tanks. By nightfall, under a barrage of artillery fire, the Israeli defensive fortification known as the Bar-Lev Line—named after its creator, Lt. Gen. Chaim Bar-Lev—was breached. Helped by the latest bridge-building technology from the Soviet Union and their own ingenuity and drive, Egyptian personnel and artillery units were ferried over to the east bank of the Suez by the hundreds, and Egyptian commandos were airlifted deep into the Sinai to attack and destroy Israeli command and communications facilities. Israel's losses on the Syrian front were even more dramatic: by the end of the first day's fighting, the entire Golan Heights had been recaptured by Syrian forces. In its initial efforts to prevent the Syrians from gaining further ground, the Israeli air force lost some forty aircraft in the first few days of the conflict. An Israeli counterattack in the Sinai, which resulted in one of the biggest tank battles since World War II, also failed to dislodge the Egyptians from the Suez. For the first three days, up until October 9, it appeared as if the Syrian and Egyptian forces were assured of victory.

The course of the war shifted dramatically in Israel's favor thereafter. Before the remainder of the war is examined, a few words need to be said about the reasons behind the Arab armies' initial stunning victories. Broadly, these can be divided into three sets of developments. By far the most significant was the increasing professionalization of the Egyptian and

Figure 10. Egyptian soldiers celebrate crossing the Suez Canal in the 1973 War.

Syrian armies in the years following the June 1967 War, resulting from the purging of incompetent commanders, a strengthening of discipline through the ranks, and greater familiarity with the available Soviet weaponry.[56] Equally important was the overconfidence of the Israelis, who, continuing to perceive Arab military capabilities in 1967 terms, saw the Arabs as overly boastful, incompetent, incapable of handling their sophisticated Soviet weaponry, and easily frightened.[57] The chronic political instability in Syria and Sadat's image problems at home and abroad did little to change the general Israeli view of the Arabs' predicament. Last were a number of strategic and tactical considerations. The Israelis did not think the Arabs would attack during Ramadan, when observant Muslims fast, and certainly not in broad daylight. Therefore, only a skeletal force was defending the Bar-Lev Line, most others being on leave to celebrate Yom Kippur.[58] The Israelis were also unfamiliar with the Egyptians' new equipment, such as rocket launchers carried in small suitcases, high-powered water pumps to puncture holes in defensive walls, and light ladders for scaling walls. This was an entirely different war from the one seven years earlier.

The tide of the war turned for two primary reasons. The first concerned war psychology and its tactical consequences. Apparently both the Syrian and Egyptian forces were stunned by the ease with which they had overrun Israeli forces and had not really planned on what to do once they had recaptured lost territory. Conversely, the Israelis soon overcame the shock of the collapse of their forces and regrouped. One of the most spectacular episodes of the war occurred on the night of October 15, when the IDF's Major General Ariel Sharon led a small force of Israeli commandos across the Suez and inflicted heavy casualties on Egyptian forces.

But such daring tactical moves would not have been possible had it not been for a second factor, the massive airlift of military equipment and supplies to Israel by the United States. Everything from tanks to aircraft was rushed to Israel from aircraft carriers belonging to the U.S. Sixth and Seventh Fleets, some directly from military bases in the United States, and the equipment was put to use within hours of delivery.[59] According to one military analyst, "[I]n replacing Israel's downed aircraft, the United States literally stripped some of its own active air force units," sending forty F-4 jet fighters to Israel and leaving its own air defense system vulnerable for six months.[60]

By the third week of October, the Arab position had become untenable. The Syrians had been evicted from the Golan again, and Israel's campaign to destroy the Syrian economy was having devastating consequences. Syria's only oil refinery, in Homs, was set ablaze by Israeli jets, and the ports of Banisa, Tartus, and Latakia were heavily damaged. Damascus itself was being threatened by Israeli forces. In the Sinai, meanwhile, Israel's counterattack was beginning to bear fruit, to the point that by October 17 the Egyptian Third Army was encircled and in serious danger of annihilation. Meanwhile, U.S. Secretary of State Henry Kissinger had embarked on his famous "shuttle diplomacy," flying from one capital to another in search of a cease-fire agreement. On October 22, the UN Security Council adopted Resolution 338, calling for an immediate cessation of hostilities, the implementation of Resolution 242 of 1967, and the start of peace negotiations under international auspices. Egypt and Syria readily agreed to the resolution; Israel did not cease hostilities until a further resolution was passed on October 23.

Conspicuously absent from the October 1973 War was Jordan. By some accounts, Sadat and Syrian President Hafiz al-Assad had deliberately kept King Hussein in the dark regarding the details of their plans to jointly attack Israel.[61] Jordan's small army and its long border with Israel made the country's participation in the war very risky for the king. Sadat had informed King Hussein of his military plans as early as spring 1973, but the Jordanian monarch remained skeptical of the chances of success of even a limited attack on Israel. "It is clear today that the Arab nations are preparing for a new war," the king wrote to his generals in May. "The battle would be premature."[62] Nevertheless, as a token of his support for the Arab cause, the king dispatched an armored brigade to Syria, although there was no military significance to such a move. Iraq's contribution to the war was somewhat more meaningful, at least in theory, with the participation of a squadron of twelve Iraqi MiG fighters beginning on October 8. Of the twelve fighters, half were mistakenly shot down by Syrian gunners and the other half were destroyed by the Israelis.[63]

In military and territorial terms, the 1973 War, unlike the 1967 conflict, did not result in a transfer of large parcels of land or the decisive victory of one side over the other. But the war had deep and lasting consequences for all the parties involved in the Arab-Israeli conflict. The fallout from the war not only influenced the domestic politics of each of the actors in the conflict but had wider regional and international ramifications. Egypt and Israel were the most profoundly affected, but so were the PLO and the larger Arab world. Also, a new factor entered the international political economy of the Middle East and that of the entire world: oil.

The consequences of the 1973 War appear to have been greatest for the life and politics of Egypt. "The Ramadan War" was Sadat's war, conceived, coordinated, and carried out under his leadership. By bringing the IDF to the verge of defeat, Sadat had done what Nasser had tried but had miserably failed to accomplish. Sadat had now quieted the skeptics, and had done so with authority. Standing tall shortly after the war, Sadat declared, "The Arab armed forces performed a miracle in the Ramadan War as judged by any military measure. The Arab world can rest assured that it has now both a shield and a sword."[64] Indeed, as three Egyptian generals later wrote triumphantly in *The Ramadan War,* the twin myths of Israeli invincibility and Arab incompetence were both shattered.[65] After all, Israel, which had so decisively obliterated the Arab air forces on the ground in 1967, had now lost a total of 115 aircraft.[66] Israel might not have been defeated, but as far as the Egyptians were concerned victory was theirs. A new pharaoh had emerged, a man who had finally ended the Arabs' collective shame and humiliation. Sadat could now add a new moniker to his name: "The Hero of the Crossing."

On the diplomatic front, the war influenced Sadat in two ways. On the one hand, inebriated with his victory and assuming himself to be the new spokesperson of the Arab world, Sadat now felt powerful enough to pursue solo diplomacy based on what he considered to be prudent for Egypt and for other Arab states. But the conduct of what he proudly called "electric-shock diplomacy" only served to alienate him from his fellow leaders and soon resulted in the isolation of Egypt from the rest of the Arab world.[67] The break started in 1974, shortly after Kissinger negotiated a disengagement agreement first between Egypt and Israel and then between Israel and Syria (on January 17 and May 29, respectively). The first Egyptian-Israeli disengagement agreement became known as Sinai I. This was followed by the signing of Sinai II in 1975, in which Egypt opted to settle on a separate agreement with Israel instead of holding out for a comprehensive peace settlement involving the other Arab parties as well—including the Palestinians—to which Israel was opposed.[68]

Sadat's penchant for "going it alone" was reinforced by a second realization. As the war had dramatically shown, Israel could not be defeated on the battlefront. Even if the Arabs could mount effective attacks on Israel, they could not overcome Israel's American patronage. The most effective way to reclaim the Sinai, in fact the only way, would be to negotiate with Israel and to do so with American support. On November 19, 1977, to everyone's shock and surprise, Sadat flew to Jerusalem. His reason, as he wrote in his autobiography, was to prove to the Israelis unequivocally that he was serious about a lasting peace.[69] It was only a matter of time before Egypt's breach with the rest of the Arab world would become complete.

To his dismay, Sadat's dramatic gesture failed to yield tangible results.

Israel's invasion of Lebanon in March 1978, lasting into the summer, did not help Sadat's position domestically or in the larger Arab world. In September 1978, U.S. President Jimmy Carter invited Sadat and Israeli Prime Minister Begin to the Camp David retreat to work on the peace process. The Camp David Accords resulted in an agreement over the phased withdrawal of Israeli forces from the Sinai, but it also led to the near-complete isolation of Egypt from the rest of the Arab world. In March 1979, when the final provisions of the accord were signed, Arab leaders met in Baghdad and agreed on the imposition of economic, diplomatic, and political sanctions on Egypt.[70] Egypt, the self-ascribed leader of the Arab world, was now more isolated from its Arab brethren than ever before.

In addition to diplomatic initiatives, after the 1973 War Sadat embarked on a major economic reform program that came to be known as the *infitah*, or open door policy. The main premise of the *infitah* was to liberalize the economy by attracting foreign investments and rolling back some of the state's functions in relation to the economy. Talk of such economic reforms had circulated among the ruling elite since the beginning of Sadat's presidency, but only after 1973 did the regime feel secure enough to actually enact laws aimed at reforming the economy.[71] Moreover, the statist policies of the Nasser era had failed to turn the Egyptian economy around, and the diplomacy of détente that in the mid-1970s informed Egypt's foreign policy further supported the liberalization thrust. Increasingly confident in his domestic base, Sadat further dismantled the Nasserist state by fostering the demise of the Arab Socialist Union in 1976–77. After briefly flirting with limited political liberalization, in 1978 Sadat oversaw the re-establishment of another corporatist party, this time called the National Democratic Party.[72]

In the end, neither the "victory" of the 1973 War nor the *infitah*, nor even the corporatism of the National Democratic Party, could save Sadat from his own vanity and the wrath of his people. By the end of the 1970s he had become increasingly authoritarian and intolerant of dissent. In 1979, residents of Cairo staged a number of demonstrations protesting the country's deteriorating economy. Tensions rose throughout 1980 as the peace process went nowhere and Egypt's isolation from the rest of the Arab world grew deeper. In the opening weeks of 1981, following bloody sectarian violence between Muslims and Copts, some 1,500 Islamic activists were rounded up and arrested. Finally, on October 6, 1981, while reviewing a military march celebrating the anniversary of the 1973 War, Sadat was assassinated. The "Hero of the Crossing," Nasser's triumphant heir, was dead.

The war had equally profound consequences for Israeli politics. It demonstrated to the Israelis that they had succumbed to the same type of complacency that had characterized the Arabs before 1967. The "pulverizing Syrian offensive" and the ease with which the Bar-Lev Line had fallen drove home for many Israelis the inherent vulnerability of Israel as a sovereign state. Moreover, just as had occurred in Egypt and Syria after 1967, the 1973 War set in motion a nationwide process of soul-searching.[73] Many Israelis started to rethink their priorities, in relation to both their political leaders and the Palestinians in the Occupied Territories. Insofar as political leaders were concerned, the old generation of founding fathers—that of Ben-Gurion, Levi Eshkol, and Golda Meir—was increasingly pushed to the sidelines, and a younger generation of leaders, best represented by Prime Minister Yitzhak Rabin and Defense Minister Shimon Peres, came to the fore.[74] Not surprisingly, the average age of ministers in Rabin's cabinet was lower than that of any previous cabinets, and only seven of the nineteen ministers had served in previous administrations.[75]

The shock of the war did not bring about a meeting of the minds among the Israeli public over the questions of Palestine and the Occupied Territories. In fact, the previous rift between Israel's "hawks" and "doves" became a chasm, and a new center-right political party, named the Likud (Unity), was formed. At the same time, many Israelis (three-fourths of those surveyed) thought that the idea of peaceful coexistence with the Arabs and the exchange of land for peace should at least be discussed publicly.[76]

Israel's signing of the Sinai I and II treaties with Egypt was part of a larger formula aimed at strengthening the Israeli government's hand in dealing with Syria. Prime Minister Rabin calculated that peace with Egypt would militarily neutralize Syria's most powerful ally. Israel could then deal with Syria on its own terms, through either negotiations or confrontation.[77] Rabin also firmly believed that Israel's long-term security would be best served by relinquishing control over the Occupied Territories. But he was unwilling to engage in the necessary negotiations in the shadow of the 1973 War, since, he reasoned, the Arabs might take this as a sign of Israeli weakness.[78] Not until 1993, exactly two decades after the 1973 War, did Rabin finally negotiate with the PLO over the status of the West Bank and the Gaza Strip. By then, Israel's position within the Occupied Territories and throughout the Middle East had become supremely powerful.

Ironically, the war also led to a hardening of the attitudes of Palestinians living under Israeli occupation in the Gaza Strip and the West Bank. The post-1967 mood of resignation and despair was replaced by a newfound confidence and sense of the self. There was a gradual rise in passive, and at times even active, resistance to the authorities following the war, and the local atmosphere in the Occupied Territories changed noticeably.[79] These trends culminated in and were reinforced by the establishment of a Palestine National Front in August 1973, intended to act as a liaison between the PLO and the "national forces" in the West Bank and Gaza.[80] The Israeli response was decisive and draconian, in turn fueling the vicious cycle of violence and bloodshed that by the mid-1970s had become a feature of the Palestinian movement.

Israel's heavy-handed treatment of the Palestinians in the Occupied Territories notwithstanding, the 1973 War appears to have greatly benefited the PLO, even though the PLO did not itself participate in the conflict. The post-1967 generation of Palestinians who had become active and dominant within the PLO were now gaining steady international recognition for the Palestinian cause and for their own leadership role within it. In October 1974, the Arab League's summit meeting in Rabat, Morocco, endorsed a resolution that recognized the PLO as "the sole legitimate representative of the Palestinian people." This was a significant victory for the PLO and a major setback for Jordan's King Hussein, who did not officially relinquish his hopes of one day ruling over the West Bank until the late 1980s. In November 1974, the Palestine question was once again taken up by the United Nations, and Arafat was invited to speak to the General Assembly. "I appeal to you," he implored the delegates, "to enable our people to establish national independent sovereignty over its own land."[81] Two weeks later, the UN granted the PLO observer status. The previous July, Moscow had invited Arafat for an official visit to the Soviet Union. Both the Palestinian cause and the Palestinian leadership were now beginning to gain widespread recognition and, more than ever before, respectability.

Another significant consequence of the 1973 War was the emergence of oil as a highly effective economic and diplomatic weapon. Even before the war, Arab oil producers had discussed the possibility of an oil embargo as a way of helping the Palestinian cause. In October 1973, they announced that they would cut their oil production by 5 percent a month until Israel withdrew from the Occupied Territories. In retaliation for the West's support for Israel during the war, they instituted a further 25 percent production cut across the board.[82] The embargo, which succeeded in bringing much of the industrial machinery of the West to a standstill, lasted until March 1974, by the end of which the price of oil had risen threefold. Crude oil, for example, was approximately $3.01 per barrel (pb) before the outbreak of hostilities. By the time the war ended, it was trading at about $11.65 pb, having at some point reached as high as $17 pb.[83]

Through a careful analysis of oil production data for the Middle East before and after the oil embargo, the political economist Giacomo Luciani has argued that "the embargo was fictional" and that the Arab oil producers' *threat* to cut oil production was never actually put into practice.[84] "Middle East oil production increased rapidly and steadily until 1974," he claims. It declined the following year because of the recession and the decrease in oil demand triggered by the increase in prices. In fact, *oil was never used as a weapon.*"[85]

The international (as well as domestic) implications of such enormous, sudden wealth were astounding. The Arab states, working through the Organization of Petroleum Exporting Countries (OPEC), had now acquired the ability to dramatically influence the economies of the advanced capitalist countries. Luciani questions the degree to which the fictitious oil embargo actually helped the long-term interests of Middle Eastern oil producers as reliable suppliers of a much needed energy resource and trustworthy trading partners.[86] Nevertheless, for a time in the late 1970s there did develop at least the appearance that the more conservative states of the Middle East, of which the shah's Iran and Saudi Arabia were prime examples, were beginning to get the upper hand in influencing the course of regional politics. Ironically, the embargo signaled the ascendancy of America's allies in the Middle East, joined by Sadat's *infitah* Egypt, and the eclipse or at the least the checking of the new progressive, revolutionary states (Libya, Algeria, and Iraq). In the mid-1970s, the United States, still recuperating from the dual fiascos of the Vietnam War and the Nixon presidency, eagerly looked forward to a new era of international stability and global détente. But, as the Iranians would have it, that hope would not be fulfilled.

By the end of the 1970s, the political landscape of the Middle East had shifted dramatically. The idea of Arab unity, once so compelling to millions of Arabs, was now all but dead, a mirage dispelled first by the unhappy marriage of Syria and Egypt and then by the unfolding of events after 1973. Even in those years when the chief proponent of the idea, Nasser, was alive, the whole project had been exposed as primarily a means for him to expand his influence over Syria, Yemen, and elsewhere. There had hardly been a genuine attempt to unite the Arabs toward some progressive, revolutionary set of goals. Despite the appeal of Arab unity as an abstract idea among the Arab masses, in practice it had come to mean the personal and political aggrandizement of Nasser. Consequently, when Nasser died, the main impetus for Pan-Arabism died with him. Nasser did leave behind much younger protégés who sought to complete his unfinished unity project—first Libya's Mummar Qaddafi and later Iraq's Saddam Hussein—but none succeeded even to the limited extent that Nasser had. For all the noise they made, Qaddafi and Saddam, like Nasser, were motivated more by their own immediate circumstances than by a genuine belief in the cause of Pan-Arabism. Spouting some rhetoric and putting that rhetoric into practice are quite different things.

There was a change in the collective psychology of the Middle East, especially among the Israelis and among the Arabs with whom they had fought. The 1967 War had instilled an attitude of defeat among the Arabs and of victory among the Israelis. But this had been no ordinary war. For the Arabs it was a defeat of historic proportions, a big "step backward" *(naksa)* that shook their belief in themselves and their abilities. For the Israelis, the conquest of so much additional territory could only mean the further validation of the Zionist cause and what Israel and its people stood for. The contrast could not have been more stark. On one side stood a righteous conqueror, claiming support from history and the Old Testament, while on the other side stood a defeated, bewildered force, its energies sapped by false promises and structural atrophy.

The 1973 War changed all this. The war itself was inconclusive and without any clear winners or losers. But it resulted in an important psychological victory for the Arabs by reversing the defeatism that had become so rampant after June 1967. In the immediate aftermath of the October War, the prevailing psychology of the Arab-Israeli conflict was one of mutual fear and mistrust, a begrudging respect for the opponent on both sides based on the realization that the enemy was indeed capable of inflicting serious wounds in any future conflicts. The ensuing military stalemate gave rise to a war of nerves, with the Israelis tightening their grip on the Occupied Territories, the Syrians refusing to recognize Israel as long as the Golan Heights were occupied, and the Egyptians going it alone and getting the Sinai back through negotiations. The Palestinians, desperate and alone, sought solace in violence. And Lebanon, under the weight of its own fragile political system and the added stress of Fedayeen attacks, imploded into civil war. In these precarious circumstances the 1970s were ending, but not before the eruption of yet another drama of historic proportions, this time the Iranian revolution of 1978–79.

5 The Iranian Revolution

Few words in the language of politics are as overused and abused as *revolution*. The Third Worldism of the 1950s and the national liberation movements of the 1960s gave special currency to the word, with self-declared revolutionaries promising liberation from the forces of global oppression and evil at home and abroad. In many ways, the historic developments in China, in Cuba, and throughout Africa in the 1950s and 1960s were indeed revolutionary. Old political orders were destroyed, new ones were built in their place, and existing relationships between the state and society were profoundly altered. But the use of the term broadened and gained potency as more and more politicians discovered the domestic and international benefits of calling themselves "revolutionaries," especially before jubilant followers.

Despite what the Nassers and the Qaddafis of the world want their followers to believe, a revolution is more than delivering moving speeches. It is more than clenching fists or wagging fingers at more powerful and dominant adversaries. Theatrics, of course, are as much a part of revolutions as they are of other political forms; indeed, revolutions tend to be theatrical and require careful attention to imagery, symbols, and rhetoric. But as historical developments—monumental political explosions set off by the hopes and actions of the masses that extend to the social, cultural, and economic domains as well—revolutions are relatively rare occurrences. They involve ingredients not always easy to come by: millions of people for whom pursuing a cause has become more pressing than the chores of daily life; the collapse of state institutions and their replacement by other, new ones; and the reconstitution of a political order radically different from the old order. These changes resonate not only domestically but also regionally and globally, affecting balance-of-power equations, alliances, and international economics. For these reasons, the Iranian revolution of 1978–79 merits detailed analysis.

First, however, a few conceptual points regarding revolutions and revolutionary movements need to be clarified. Let us begin with a definition of revolutions. As a phenomenon, a revolution entails a fundamental change in the institutions, agendas, and overall nature of the state and its relations with society.[1] Revolutions, therefore, are more profoundly transformative than coups and other forms of state takeover. Coups often consist merely of changes in officeholders and, at most, their policies. A revolution, however, entails structural changes in the basic composition and operations of the state and thus in the way the state relates to society.

At the broadest level, it is possible to distinguish four ideal types of revolutions: planned, spontaneous, negotiated, and instigated from above. Planned revolutions, which have historically taken the form of successful guerrilla movements, start out as premeditated, preplanned movements by a select group of self-declared "revolutionaries" whose specific purpose is to capture political power. The Chinese and Cuban revolutions were perhaps the best examples of planned revolutions, although the revolutions of Algeria, Vietnam, and Nicaragua also involved considerable advanced planning by revolutionary fighters. By contrast, spontaneous revolutions, of which the French and Iranian revolutions are prime examples, entail little advance planning and start out as haphazard, largely unorganized acts of protest. Encouraged by the steady weakening of the state, the rebellions soon snowball into a full-blown revolution. In the process, the movement becomes increasingly more radical, valorizes the protesting masses, and gives rise to an emerging cadre of leaders, some of whom are themselves caught by surprise and are later pushed aside in the unfolding drama.

Negotiated revolutions ensue when the state has become weak and is vulnerable to pressure from society but is not weak enough to be overthrown, and when society has become politically emboldened and empowered but is not powerful enough to take over the state. The only solution to the political stalemate is for representatives of the state and society to negotiate, as they did in much of eastern Europe in the late 1980s, resulting in a largely peaceful, often democratic, transfer of power. Finally, some revolutions come from above, led by the new inheritors of the state, often its former army commanders who have now assumed political control and wish to mold society to their own liking. Atatürk and Nasser viewed their missions in such a vein, and so did Qaddafi for much of his reign. Despite their greater frequency as compared to other types of revolutions, revolutions from above tend to have fewer lasting effects in the long run, since they are dictated by state leaders rather than being a product of impulses from within society.

The Iranian revolution was a product of a series of spontaneous, largely unorganized strikes and demonstrations that erupted throughout the country beginning in late 1976 and early 1977. Mounting frustration with rising unemployment and the bursting of the oil bubble beginning in 1975 only heightened the country's general feelings of anxiety. The middle classes directed their economic frustrations at political targets and demanded government accountability, an end to corruption, and, increasingly, deeper and deeper political changes. The state, long isolated from society and buffered by sycophants and "yes-men," was incapable of responding to what was rapidly becoming a crisis and instead drifted from one panicked reaction to another. Within the opposition, the clergy, whose religious position brought them popular respect and influence, had the upper hand. Among them, a certain Ayatollah Khomeini was best positioned to become the movement's—soon the "revolution's"—leader. Panic only expedited the monarchy's collapse. The end came in January 1979, and shortly thereafter Khomeini triumphantly returned from exile. The task of postrevolutionary consolidation was facilitated by a long hostage drama involving American diplomats, and an even longer, bloody war with Iraq for eight years.[2] Both suited Khomeini's purposes in ensuring his hold on power. With the death of the ayatollah in 1989 a Second Republic was inaugurated, quite unofficially, and then the Third Republic started in 1997 with the surprise election of a dark horse, reformist candidate to the presidency.

Thirty years after the revolution's success, the Pahlavi state is for most Iranians—a majority of whom were born after the revolution—an abstract historical footnote.[3] But the revolution would not have even begun, and would not have had a chance to succeed, had it not been for the internal decay and inherent fragility of the Pahlavi state. After all, a revolution's occurrence depends primarily on the incumbent state's susceptibility to pressures from below. It is, therefore, important to look at Iran's prerevolutionary state to better understand the seeds of its demise.

THE PAHLAVI STATE

The history of the Pahlavi state can be divided into four general phases. The first phase began with the formal establishment of the Pahlavi dynasty in 1925 by Reza Shah and lasted until his forced abdication in 1941. As Chapter 2 demonstrated, during this period the Iranian monarchy laid the foundations of a new state, one that was heavily dependent on the person of the king. The monarch was in turn supported by an expanding army and a small, though steadily growing, bureaucracy. There was also a theoretically functioning parliament (the Majles), and therefore a prime minister, though neither the Majles nor the prime minister was allowed to play a meaningful role in the country's political process. Throughout Reza Shah's rule, the parliament remained a rubber stamp, set up to provide the appearance of democracy, and the prime minister's tenure in office depended solely on the whim of the shah.

Despite some chronic weaknesses, the state managed to institute an unprecedented level of political centralization. Tribal challenges to the central government were quashed, although occasional instances of banditry and scattered armed opposition to government soldiers continued to occur.[4] Additionally, the clergy, whose cultural influence had long pervaded all layers of society, were effectively suppressed, and their opposition to the state's modernizing agendas was largely neutralized.[5]

By the end of his reign, the state that Reza Shah had established had acquired a number of pronounced features. The shah's primary goal was to turn Iran into a "modern" country, an endeavor he saw as synonymous with secularization. The state was not only authoritarian but highly personalist, with the person of the shah dominating all of the state's other institutions (e.g., the Majles, the bureaucracy, political parties). Personal dominance and control should not be confused with legitimacy and staying power. The personalization of the system undermined its long-term consolidation in relation to society, and the regime continued to be relatively fragile. When the British removed Reza Shah from his throne in 1941, it was only under their initial protection that his twenty-two-year-old son could stay in power.

The second phase in the history of the Pahlavi state began with the reign of Muhammad Reza Shah in 1941 and lasted until 1953. This was a time of profound political instability, with none of the country's political institutions or actors able to deal effectively with the various crises that at the time engulfed Iran. Reza Shah's removal unleashed the various centrifugal forces that he had once suppressed. The British justified their removal of Reza Shah on the grounds of his pro-German sympathies. While the charge was to some extent true, the real reason for the shah's removal had more to do with Britain's desire to move war supplies to its ally, the Soviet Union, through Iran with little or no Iranian resistance. In August 1941, Britain and the Soviet Union divided Iran into two spheres of influence, as they had done once earlier during the time of the Constitutional Revolutions (1905–11). The country, beset by famine, drought, and plague, drifted through the war years. Tribes now reasserted their autonomy, in some parts of the country even forcing government soldiers out of the areas they had previously lost.

After World War II, the British relinquished their sphere of influence in the south, but the Soviets refused to follow suit in the north. Instead, they supported two popular uprisings that had erupted in the Kurdish- and Azeri-speaking areas of the northeast. They refused to let central government forces quell the rebellions and instead set up two puppet Soviet republics in Iranian Kurdistan and Azerbaijan, respectively. The Soviets finally departed as a result of what turned out to be the first success of the newly established United Nations, and the two rebellions collapsed.[6] Nevertheless, the central government remained generally incapable of asserting full control or effecting meaningful changes in the country.

A primary reason for the state's weakness in relation to society was its internal divisions into various contending centers of power. These included the person of the shah, the bureaucratic-military establishment, and the Majles. The British, Soviet, and, increasingly, American embassies in Tehran were also highly influential, but they never functioned as quasi-state institutions in Iran, as they did in several other developing countries at the time. Reza Shah's abdication proved especially beneficial for parliamentary politics, as it led to the increasing ascendancy of the Majles. Throughout the 1940s, a string of elections to the Majles brought in different cabinets and resulted in what for many Iranians resembled a democratic political process. But the Majles was riddled with factionalism and filled with careerist politicians. Moreover, with a constitutionally mandated term of only two years, it could not embark on long-term planning or foster political stability. The young shah's deep-seated hostility toward the Majles and his constant attempts to manipulate and undermine it did not help the cause of political stability. Cabinet turnovers and reshuffles were one indicator of the extent of Iran's political instability at the time. From 1941 to 1953, the country had twelve prime ministers, who formed seventeen cabinets, which underwent twenty-three major reshuffles. The average age of each cabinet was eight months, only three months if the reshuffles are taken into account.[7]

There was tremendous tension between the crown and the Majles. The shah had long had a distaste for parliamentary democracy. According to the U.S. ambassador to Iran at the time, the shah had sought American advice on ways to amend the constitution in order to restrict the powers of the parliament.[8] The constitutional powers granted to the monarchy were already extensive, and the Majles was weak and fractured. Nevertheless, to strengthen his hand against the Majles, the shah forged close ties with the military and with those in the upper echelons of the bureaucracy. In some ways, his privileged position in handing out patronage and cementing clientalistic ties made such an alliance inevitable, and the powers of the Majles steadily eroded as those of the monarchy increased. When in February 1949 the shah was slightly wounded in an unsuccessful attempt on his life, he seized the initiative by sponsoring legislation that further augmented his constitutional powers and limited those of the Majles. Also, new elections were called for a senate, which had been stipulated in the constitution of 1907 but had never convened.[9] The senate, half of whose members were to be appointed by the shah, significantly strengthened the powers of the monarchy in relation to the Majles.

The second phase in the history of the Pahlavi state ended when the shah overcame what was perhaps the most serious challenge to his rule. One of his most vocal opponents in the Majles had been an old-time politician named Dr. Muhammad Musaddiq. Over the years, Musaddiq had emerged as one of the main champions of Iranian nationalism, especially with regard to British control over the country's oil resources. Despite the steady erosion of the powers of the parliament beginning in 1949, in March 1951 Musaddiq managed to get an oil nationalization bill passed in both the Majles and the senate, following which the shah was left with no alternative but to appoint his old foe as the new prime minister. Protracted and bitter negotiations followed with Britain over the fate of the Anglo-Iranian Oil Company (AIOC), which Musaddiq now replaced with the National Iranian Oil Company (NIOC). In the end, the negotiations were to no avail. In retaliation for the nationalization, Britain imposed a blockade on the export and sale of Iranian oil, resulting in a drastic deterioration of the country's economy. Musaddiq's two requests to the United States for financial assistance were, meanwhile, both rejected. The prime minister's popularity, once unassailable, began to decline as the initial euphoria of the nationalization gave way to worsening economic realities and the conservative clergy's reluctance to openly side with him.

On February 28, 1953, the shah made his first serious move against Musaddiq by organizing a paid mob to attack the prime minister. The plot failed. A second attempt, set into motion August 15, also failed, and the shah hurriedly left Iran, first for Baghdad and then for Rome. Musaddiq, meanwhile, had further undermined his own popularity and position by holding an unconstitutional referendum for the closure of the Majles and the election of new deputies.[10] By now, the U.S. government had identified Musaddiq as a potential communist sympathizer whose initiatives were inimical to the interests of the United States and its allies, most notably Britain. The third attempt to overthrow Musaddiq, this time organized by the CIA, did not fail.[11] On August 19, hired mobs started demonstrating against the prime minister and in support of the shah.[12] By evening, Musaddiq's house was captured and looted, although the prime minister had earlier escaped to a safe location. A royal decree was issued dismissing Musaddiq from the prime minister's post and appointing a loyal general, Fazlollah Zahedi, in his place. The next day, Musaddiq and some of his associates surrendered themselves to the police, and a new era, one of near-complete monarchical absolutism, dawned in Iranian politics.

The whole coup took no more than nine hours. The move against Musaddiq had involved several retired and active military commanders, both hired and spontaneous demonstrators, and a few clerics who were worried about the possibilities of a rise in anticlericalism. Many of the *ulama* also saw threats of republicanism and communism arising from the Musaddiq movement.[13] As soon as the coup succeeded, many of the prime minister's former associates were tried and imprisoned. Some were sentenced to death. Musaddiq, frail and still too popular to be executed, was tried and sentenced to three years' solitary confinement.[14] After his release, he spent the rest of his days under virtual house arrest in a village on the outskirts of Tehran, where he died in 1967.

Musaddiq's overthrow ushered in a third phase in the history of the Pahlavi state, the era of royal absolutism, which lasted from 1953 until about 1975. The 1953 coup put an effective end to the independence and powers of the Majles and practically every other institution in the state other than the crown. Parliamentary elections became charades that no one, even members of the political establishment, took seriously. For example, provincial governors were authorized to use the rural gendarmeries and the city police to ensure that only the government's candidates were elected to office.[15] Parliament again became the rubber stamp it had been under Reza Shah. If, on rare occasions, an unapproved candidate somehow slipped into office, he was duly disqualified and arrested.[16] The crown, and more specifically the person of the shah, became the state.

In addition to his successful destruction of the parliament's political autonomy, the shah ensured his ascendancy over the system by a combination of structural changes to the state machinery. One of the most important was the construction of an elaborate and highly efficient police apparatus that permeated, or at least was thought to permeate, every aspect of life in Iran. With the CIA's help, in 1957 the shah established an intelligence organization under the name SAVAK (acronym for Sazman-e

Ettela'at va Amniyat-e Keshvar). SAVAK soon developed a reputation for ruthlessness and omnipotence, and the mere mention of its name evoked fear among average Iranians. There was also a massive buildup of the armed forces, a goal whose fulfillment was always one of the shah's top priorities. Locked in a Cold War struggle with the Soviet Union, the United States was only too happy to satisfy the shah's insatiable appetite for advanced weapons. By the mid-1970s, when the dramatic rise in oil prices was enriching the Iranian treasury to unprecedented amounts, the shah was purchasing weaponry from the United States faster than his armed forces could effectively absorb.[17]

These and other structural changes were complemented by initiatives designed to enhance the stature and credibility of the royal household. As a counterbalance to Musaddiq's highly popular policy of "negative equilibrium," whose main premise had been diplomatic nonalignment, the shah touted what he called "positive nationalism" and promised to expedite Iran's march toward a "Great Civilization." In one of his books, the shah defined his concept of "positive nationalism" as "a policy of maximum political and economic independence consistent with the interests of one's country. On the other hand, it does not mean non-alignment or sitting on the fence. It means that we make any agreement which is in our own interests, regardless of the wishes or policies of others."[18] In another book, this one published after his overthrow, he offered a definition of his vision of the Great Civilization: "an effort toward understanding and peace which creates the perfect environment in which everyone can work. I believe each nation has the right, the duty to reach or to return to a Great Civilization."[19] The regime also made a concerted effort to co-opt members of the intelligentsia into its own ranks, an endeavor in which it had considerable success. As a result, the higher echelons of the bureaucracy and many university faculties were staffed mostly by loyal technocrats and academics.

Perhaps most significant of all these initiatives was the highly publicized Land Reform Law of 1962, which the following year grew into a larger campaign that the shah called the White Revolution (Inqilab-e Sefeed). He later changed the name of his campaign to the politically loaded "Revolution of the Shah and the People." In hindsight, the whole endeavor can be seen as a clever royal move designed to void the term revolution (inqilab) of any politically oppositional substance by making it part of the parlance of the state. Banners praising the virtues of the White Revolution were hoisted in streets and boulevards throughout the country, and the revolution's anniversary and the genius of its chief architect, the shah, were annually celebrated. "The real strength of our Revolution," the shah wrote confidently shortly after its inception, "will easily address the needs of all classes of Iranian society and in the process bring us in line with the world's greatest scientific, technical, and social advances."[20] At least temporarily, the state's make-belief "revolution" succeeded in preempting a real one.

Along with land reform, the White Revolution originally called for the nationalization of forests; the sale of state-owned enterprises to the public; workers' profit sharing in 20 percent of net corporate earnings; the extension of voting rights to women; and the formation of a Literacy Corps, composed of fifty thousand high school graduates to be sent to villages to teach. Initially these reforms met with considerable enthusiasm among some secular intellectuals, who were especially attracted to its land reform and women's franchise provisions. But the opposition to these two provisions was far stronger than the support they generated. This opposition was spearheaded by a cleric named Rouhollah Khomeini.

The conservative clergy saw the White Revolution as evidence of yet another frontal assault on their position and prestige. Most, however, refrained from open opposition to the crown, probably because of their innate conservatism and divisions and disagreements within their ranks.[21] But Khomeini was unrelenting in his attacks, and this quickly won him respect and popularity. His popularity was reinforced by his unique radicalism within the clerical establishment and by his esteemed position as an ayatollah.[22] The disturbances were eventually quelled, though not until some fifty people were killed in the mayhem. Khomeini was exiled to Turkey. From there he found his way to the Iraqi Shi'ite holy city of Najaf.

The shah, emerging from the 1963 riots more confident than before, went on to add a few more principles to his People's Revolution every other year or so. By late 1975, his revolutionary principles had grown to a total of nineteen, by now including such empty slogans as "fight against corruption" and "campaign against profiteering."[23] Even the regime's most loyal supporters began to see the White Revolution as merely a (mostly failed) political gimmick.

But who dared oppose the shah? The secret police, SAVAK, were thought to be everywhere. By the mid-1960s, even the prime ministers with a modicum of independent thought were a thing of the past. Gone were such relatively able men as Ahmad Qavam (1941–43 and 1946–48), Muhammad Musaddiq (1951–53), and Ali Amini (1961–63). In 1965, the shah appointed as his premier a nonthreatening political lightweight named Amir Abbas Hoveida. Hoveida and his twelve-year tenure in office to this day remain subjects of debate and disagreement, with some accusing him of causing "more harm to Iranian society than any single individual" and others seeing him as a conscientious and honest administrator.[24] But all agree that he was "the champion of the line of least resistance" and that his long premiership was both a symptom of and a catalyst for the shah's royal absolutism.[25]

Mention must also be made of the Rastakhiz Party, established in 1975 by the shah as the country's sole legal political party. All Iranians over the age of eighteen were supposed to join the party. As a political party the Rastakhiz was a complete farce, failing either to enhance the regime's legitimacy or to foster meaningful political participation among the urban classes. The shah, however, was completely oblivious to the harm he was causing his own reign and failed to grasp the depth of popular resentment against his hollow "revolutionary" innovations. To the contrary, he believed that he enjoyed genuine and widespread popularity among the Iranian masses.[26]

As far as the shah was concerned, there was no reason not to like him. Even late into his reign, when the whole facade of royal power was beginning to crumble, he and other courtiers were convinced of the people's love and affection for him.[27] Those who opposed his reign, he thought, were a small minority of communists who were collaborating with reactionary clerics—"the unholy alliance of red and black," as he called them.[28] The bulk of the population was thought to be basking in the benefit of the country's unprecedented economic growth. Indeed, the rate of economic growth in the early 1970s was phenomenal, not so much because of His Majesty's astute leadership as because of the dramatic rise in oil revenues following the 1973 Arab-Israeli War. Iran's oil revenues shot up from $2.4 billion in 1972 to $18.5 billion in 1974, and government spending multiplied accordingly.[29] The Fifth Development Plan was revised to account for an increase of some 156 percent for expenditures on the oil industry, 112.5 percent for the gas sector, and 95 percent for other industries (only 2.4 percent for education and 0 percent for provincial development).[30] As long as the going was good and money flowed in, the wheels of the state were sufficiently oiled to run smoothly, if undemocratically. As fate would have it, however, the oil bubble burst within only a year or two. The monarchy was soon to start a rapid and fatal descent.

The fourth and last phase in the history of the Pahlavi state started in 1975 and lasted until its formal collapse in January 1979. In many ways, the year 1975 marked the beginning of the end of the Pahlavi dynasty in Iran. Instead of an anticipated surplus, the government's 1975 budget featured a deficit of $1.7 billion (a deterioration of nearly $6 billion over the previous year), and the 1976 budget had a deficit of $2.4 billion.[31] Mismanagement, poor planning, and rampant corruption at all levels of the state were beginning to take their toll. After nearly thirteen years in office, Hoveida was asked to step aside, and his finance minister, Jamshid Amuzegar, became the new prime minister. The regime's sense of panic was palpable. The shah's words to his court minister in January 1977 reveal his paralyzing anxiety: "We're broke. Everything seems doomed to grind to a standstill, and meanwhile many of the programs we had planned must be postponed. Oil exports have fallen by as much as 30 percent, and the recent price rise will do little to compensate."[32] The minister's own words, recorded the following June, were more ominous: "It terrifies me that one day everything will simply cave in around us. Please God that we may be spared this."[33]

By now, the Pahlavi state was headed for total collapse, and only a miracle could save it or reverse the course that Iranian history was about to take. A revolution, not of "the shah and the people" but of the people against the shah, was brewing and would succeed in about a year. The dynasty's collapse was now certain.

THE REVOLUTIONARY MOVEMENT

The steady atrophy and implosion of the state was expedited by, and in turn reinforced, a popular movement that was increasingly assuming revolutionary dimensions. When faced with internal discord and political opposition, authoritarian states often either clamp down and suppress their opponents or, to preempt the possibility of further opposition, try to placate their opponents by introducing some token reforms. The Iranian state tried a combination of the two tactics, allowing some very controlled expressions of political discontent by a select group of individuals while reacting violently to riots and strikes that did not have official sanction.

As he had done back in 1963, the shah initially appears to have thought that he could make the brewing revolution his own: allow the masses to express their frustrations; convene commissions and parliamentary debates that would place the blame on cabinet ministers and other government officials; create an aura of responsiveness and empathy; and then emerge as the people's chief defender against unscrupulous officials. This is a charitable interpretation of the state's overall intent. More likely, the state's growing incapacitation, symbolized and reinforced by the shah's spreading cancer, robbed it of the ability to respond to the brewing crisis decisively. At a time when the state needed to respond to the deepening crisis quickly and with foresight, the shah's legendary political instinct turned out to be more legend than reality. At the same time, the shah was becoming a prisoner of his fixation with his image abroad. His image problem was becoming all the more pronounced by President Jimmy Carter's injection of human rights concerns into U.S. foreign policy, coupled with the growing attention paid to Iran by Amnesty International and the International Association of Jurists.[34] The shah himself complained bitterly about U.S. foreign policy in the crucial final months of his rule. "The fact that no one contacted me during the crisis in any official way," he wrote later, "explains everything about the American attitude. I did not know it then—perhaps I did not want to know—but it is clear to me now that the Americans wanted me out."[35]

The regime's inept responses to the crisis only polarized the situation by helping fan the flames of political discontent that had long been suppressed, making heroes and martyrs out of ordinary demonstrators, and further demonizing the shah and the whole Pahlavi establishment before the court of public opinion. Steadily, the once-scattered riots and strikes became more frequent and organized. Meanwhile, the more permissive political environment began to give more voice to individuals and groups that had been silenced by the SAVAK or by fear. What initially started as the implosion of a state, which in turn set off haphazard strikes and demonstrations, was becoming a full-fledged "movement," and a revolutionary one at that. And, slowly, the movement was beginning to acquire "leaders." Naturally, these "leaders" came mainly from the ranks of the regime's opponents, whose voices had long been silenced by the state's authoritarianism.

Broadly, the regime's opponents and thus the leaders of the revolution could be divided into four groups. The first group was made up of the two nonregime political parties that had been banned in the mid-1950s but had continued to exist clandestinely, the National Front and the communist Tudeh Party. The National Front was organized by Musaddiq out of a coalition of smaller parties that were mostly to the left and/or center of the political spectrum.[36] By the time of the 1978–79 revolution, only a few of the original leaders of the National Front remained, most others having either retired or passed away. Nevertheless, the memory of Musaddiq and what the National Front stood for made it popular among a significant group of middle-class Iranians. The same was true of the Tudeh (literally, masses), although the party's overtly pro-Soviet posture did not sit well with the nationalist sensibilities of many urban Iranians. The Tudeh had fared worse than the National Front after the 1953 coup, with many of its members rounded up and executed and others in self-imposed exile abroad. As an astute observer of the party has noted, by the late 1950s the Tudeh was a shadow of its former self.[37] By the late 1970s, even the impending death of the Pahlavi state did not go a long way toward reviving the once impressive party.

A second group of the regime's opponents was made up of two guerrilla organizations, the Mujahedeen-e Khalq, whose ideology was a blend of Islam and socialism, and the Fedayeen-e Khalq, who were Maoist in doctrine and orientation. Both of these organizations were set up by younger individuals from middle-class backgrounds—primarily university students—who were disenchanted with the inactivity of the Tudeh and the National Front, and wanted, in their separate ways, to spark a revolutionary movement. The Mujahedeen were formed in 1965 and the Fedayeen in 1971. At different times and independently of each other, both groups had come to the conclusion that the Land Reform Program had effectively neutralized the "revolutionary potential" of the peasantry. As a result, they needed to concentrate their efforts in the cities in order to "dispel the police atmosphere" pervading the country's urban centers.[38] From there, it was thought, the revolution would spread to the countryside and would eventually engulf the entire country.

Despite their theoretical aspirations, before the late 1970s neither guerrilla group was able to foster the revolutionary conditions it had hoped for. The efficiency and brutality of the SAVAK had proved a major hindrance; at one point the Mujahedeen had even been penetrated by agents of the secret police.[39] Each party also had the serious problem of getting its message heard by a wider audience. Not only did the regime's repressiveness make this all but impossible, but the parties' muddled and alien ideologies—with subtle or overt references to socialism (read, atheism)—did not sit well with a majority of Iranians. Devoid of any popular ideological resonance among the people, the most the two organizations could do was to engage in hit-and-run attacks on targets associated with the Pahlavis. On occasion they would rob a bank, attack an American military advisor, or throw Molotov cocktails at the offices of the Israeli Cultural Center.[40] But these attacks did little to spark a people's revolution. The revolution that did come arrived on its own, the result of a people acting at their own behest and not inspired by the heroics of the guerilla activists.

The third group opposing the Pahlavi state was made up of independent intellectuals who did not necessarily belong to any of the political parties or the guerrilla organizations. A majority of these individuals came from academia or were writers, poets, and journalists. These were men like Jalal

Al-e Ahmad, a writer whose celebrated work *Westoxication (Gharbzadegi)* poignantly exposed middle-class Iranians' fascination with all things Western.[41] Another intellectual in the same mould was Ali Shariati, a sociology professor whose occasional public lectures on Islamic modernism riveted and excited those who could hear him.[42] Also notable was Mehdi Bazargan, another academic and an old Musaddiq collaborator, who wrote critically on the general state of Iranian society.

The direct contributions of these and other independent intellectuals to the revolutionary cause, like those of the guerrilla organizations, were minimal. Both Al-e Ahmad and Shariati had passed away long before the disturbances, and most of the other intellectuals who actively opposed the Pahlavi state did so from abroad. Also, again like the guerrillas, the intellectuals had the simple problem of communication. How to communicate with a mass of people suspicious of and unreceptive to grand theories, and to do so in an atmosphere of stifling police repression? Nevertheless, the main contribution of these and other intellectuals of the time was to give currency to a trend of thought best described as political Islam. Through a general revitalization and reformulation of Islamic and Shi'ite precepts, these intellectuals hoped to better equip religion to address the problems of modern society and politics. In sum, most Iranian intellectuals contributed to the revolution indirectly by helping articulate and spread what turned out to be a "theology of discontent."[43]

The fourth group of regime opponents consisted of the clerics, or at least those of them who had not opted for ascetic quietism or been co-opted by the regime. The clergy, of course, were far from a monolithic group and included men with a variety of political dispositions. But clerics who opposed the regime enjoyed some unique advantages. The pulpit of the mosque gave them relative immunity from the wrath of the SAVAK and bestowed on them a measure of popular authority. Many filled their sermons with double-talk that could be interpreted as either purely religious or highly political. Most important, the central role of mosques as popular social institutions and gathering places afforded clerics a ready and highly receptive audience with whom they could communicate in a language both easily understandable and emotionally compelling. The number of mosque-goers swelled especially after 1975, when the slump in the construction industry prompted more and more unemployed construction workers and other recent arrivals from the countryside to attend religious services with greater frequency. This resulted in the establishment of a crucial and highly effective nexus between the oppositional clerics and a mass of disenchanted, easily mobilizable Iranians. As riots and strikes became more and more frequent, the clerics were in a perfect position to emerge on top and ride the crest of the revolutionary movement.

Meanwhile, Rouhollah Khomeini, the old ayatollah who back in 1963 had opposed the shah's White Revolution and had been expelled to Iraq, again started to call for the Pahlavis' overthrow. This time, however, he was not speaking to an isolated group of individuals. By now the whole nation was in turmoil, and Khomeini's revolutionary rhetoric suited the tenor of the times. Other clerics inside the country started echoing his sermons, and those unable to attend mosques could hear recordings of his speeches on cassette tapes. The "revolution" was not only gathering steam but, more ominously for the Pahlavi state, also acquiring a symbol in the person of Ayatollah Khomeini. Before long, even average Iranians started to refer to Khomeini as "the imam," a title of tremendous symbolic value for the Shi'ite masses. In a desperate attempt to discredit Khomeini by exposing his archaic views to the world, the shah asked the Iraqi government to expel him from the southern Iraqi city of Najaf, and the ayatollah and his expanding entourage relocated to a suburb of Paris. Ironically, when the Western media and expatriate Iranians flocked to the cleric's modest home, they were disarmed by the simplicity and appeal of his revolutionary message and the firmness of his resolve. A number of Western-educated Iranians became his spokespersons and his collaborators, and together they set out to lead what had by now become a revolution of historic proportions. The shah could now do little but frantically react to circumstances outside his control. His reactions, in hindsight, helped him little.

The end for the Pahlavis came in the early weeks of 1979. In a desperate attempt to keep his state and his whole dynasty from collapsing, from 1977 on the shah appointed and fired a series of prime ministers with unprecedented frequency. As a final move, he turned to an old figure in the National Front, Shapour Bakhtiar, a man with impeccable oppositional credentials who was still loyal to the monarchical system. He then hurriedly left Iran on January 18, 1979, for "medical" reasons. By now, millions of Iranians were pouring into the streets on a daily basis, demanding the abolition of the monarchy, the death of the shah, and the return of Khomeini. Bakhtiar could do little. The army, once among the most powerful in the world, was disintegrating at a rate of one thousand to twelve hundred desertions a day.[44] Khomeini returned to Iran on February 1, greeted by an estimated one million jubilant people who lined the streets of Tehran to welcome him back. On February 11, a group of technicians in an air base located at the heart of the capital mutinied against the Pahlavi regime, and Bakhtiar's orders to military commanders the following day to bombard

Figure 11. Ayatollah Khomeini, leader of Iran's Islamic revolution.

the air base were ignored. Instead, the commanders went into hiding. The shah's massive army had collapsed. Bakhtiar also went into hiding. The revolution had succeeded. Power now was in the hands of the people, and their leader was Imam Khomeini.

IRAN'S THREE REPUBLICS

Following the collapse of the monarchy, it was natural for Iranian revolutionaries to want to establish a republic, which, in the popular psyche at least, was seen as synonymous with democracy. That the new system would be republican was certain; the controversy revolved around the precise type of republic to be adopted. The emergence of Islam as the primary vehicle for the revolution made it almost inevitable that religion would play a role in the postrevolutionary system. The heightened religious sensibilities of Iranians because of the revolutionary odyssey also made the postrevolutionary marriage of religion and politics not only palatable but desirable. But the revolution had not started out as singularly religious, and it did have early inheritors who wanted to reap its benefits in a secular environment. In the event, Ayatollah Khomeini, who had now emerged as the undisputed "imam" of millions of Iranians, prevailed, seeing to it that the incoming republic was in every way "Islamic." On March 30 and 31, 1979, a historic referendum was held in which Iranians were asked to answer a simple question: "Should Iran be an Islamic republic?" Some 98.2 percent of the more than twenty million ballots cast answered in the affirmative. The Islamic Republic of Iran was therefore established.

The Islamic Republic has had three phases, or, more aptly, it has really been three republics. The First, Second, and Third Republics roughly correspond, respectively, to the eras of postrevolutionary consolidation, construction, and factional infighting. The First Republic lasted from its inception in 1979 until the conclusion of Iran's war with its neighbor Iraq in July 1988. This was by far the most radical phase in the evolution of the postrevolutionary system. Domestically, the First Republic witnessed the steady and often ruthless narrowing of political space brought on by the elimination of the "revolution's enemies," many of whom had once been Khomeini's close collaborators. Internationally, the Islamic Republic shocked the world and incurred isolation and condemnation by holding U.S. diplomats hostage for 444 days and refusing to accept repeated ceasefire offers from Baghdad until 1988.

The Second Republic, by contrast, was one of reconstruction and relative moderation. Ayatollah Khomeini's death in June 1989 gave greater maneuverability to revolutionaries who were eager to open Iran to the outside world and to give substance to their vision of a modern Islamic state. The Second Republic lasted only eight years, however, and in 1997 was replaced by the Third Republic, one in which deep fissures within the ruling elite became apparent. By its very nature the Third Republic is bound to be impermanent as it features profound disagreements at the highest levels of the system over the ideological underpinnings of the Islamic Republic state and its relations with society. Only time will tell what ultimate shape the state will take, and what the outcome will be of the evolution of Iran's revolution.

The First Republic got off to a rocky start. During this time, the post-revolutionary leadership consolidated itself forcefully and brutally, eliminating rivals one by one and, in the process, giving shape to its vision of the new social, political, and economic orders. In this phase, the revolution's victors set out to institutionalize their powers, a task in which they succeeded on a variety of fronts, ranging from creating a political party to dominating the Majles, then the presidency, and eventually, through extensive purges, the bureaucracy and the military. Whoever disagreed or refused to toe the "imam's line" was accused of being a "counter-revolutionary," a "monarchist," a lackey of "the Great Satan," or, worse yet, a "hypocrite" (munafiq). The regime that emerged was highly authoritarian, a self-appointed guardian of Islam and public morality, and, as it turned out, highly resilient. Initially, most of its opponents were not easily brushed aside or suppressed, and the regime suffered some truly devastating blows resulting from the assassination of some of its highest-ranking leaders. But Khomeini and his increasingly small inner circle persevered through it all and, at the expense of many former comrades, eventually prevailed. The First Republic was clearly built on and sustained by a reign of terror.

The postrevolutionary experience had started out very differently in the days and weeks immediately following the monarchy's collapse. The demise of Pahlavi authoritarianism unleashed popular energies that had been pent up since the early 1950s. The initial absence of effective central authority ushered in a temporary era of anarchy and lawlessness. Most institutions of the state had already collapsed or were about to collapse, and new ones had not yet emerged to replace them. Thus many people took the law into their own hands, emboldened by the estimated three hundred thousand weapons they had acquired in the monarchy's final days.[45] The revolutionary government's repeated pleas to people to turn in their weapons met with little success. In the Revolutionary Committees, called the Komiteh, that sprang up in all neighborhoods and districts, young men with little previous experience gave themselves responsibilities for traffic control, policing, arresting monarchists, fighting other "counter-revolutionaries," and enforcing the revolution's new morality. The provisional government, to which Khomeini had appointed the longtime National Front activist Mehdi Bazargan, was too moderate in temperament and disposition to cope with the revolutionary tempo of the times. Bazargan's cabinet could not even stop the summary justice being meted out by the Revolutionary Courts, as a result of which some sixty-eight people were executed after speedy "revolutionary trials."[46]

The fate of Bazargan's cabinet ended up being decided in the streets. Daily street demonstrations had become a fact of life, with each faction in the revolutionary struggle taking its cause to the streets to express itself and to impress others with its show of strength. Real power lay in the streets, and increasingly, thanks to the efforts of club-wielding ruffians calling themselves members of the Party of God, the Hezbollahis, the street listened only to Khomeini. Passions remained too inflamed and the excitement of the revolution too fresh for the country's political rhythm to assume any semblance of normalcy. But the stakes were too high for Khomeini to let control slip away now, and he had to ensure that he remained the revolution's undisputed leader.

Meanwhile, the deposed shah and his royal entourage were flying from one host country to another in a desperate effort to find a suitable place of exile. Upon leaving Iran, the royals spent some time in Morocco but were encouraged to move on when King Hassan, who had his own domestic difficulties, grew concerned about hosting a deposed monarch. There had always been influential Americans who thought it shameful for the United States not to stand by its old friend in difficult times. Many, in fact, started pressing the Carter administration to allow the shah into the United States to receive medical treatment for his recently disclosed cancer. But the Carter administration had viewed the ensuing diplomatic fallout and the potential dangers to American citizens in Iran as too great to allow the shah's entry into the United States.[47] Nevertheless, the shah's friends, chief among them former Secretary of State Henry Kissinger and the influential David Rockefeller, were relentless. From Morocco the shah moved to the Bahamas but eventually had to relocate when his security and privacy there could no longer be guaranteed.[48] Next came Mexico, where the shah spent most of summer 1979, as his friends pressured Washington to let the dying ex-king receive medical care in a New York hospital. They finally succeeded, and on October 23 the shah was allowed to travel to New York, where he was operated on at New York Hospital the next day. All along, the Carter administration was worried about the reaction of both the revolutionary government and the excited masses in Tehran. These fears turned out to be justified.

Two weeks after the shah's arrival in New York, on November 4, one of the street demonstrations in Tehran took an unexpected turn. Mindful of the CIA's role in installing the shah back in power in 1953, some of the demonstrators scaled the walls of the U.S. embassy and took its staff hostage. Everyone—from U.S. policy makers in Washington to members of Bazargan's cabinet, the hostages, and even the attackers themselves—expected the whole episode to last no more than a day or two. A similar event had occurred the preceding February, and the Iranian authorities had quickly reined in the demonstrators and given assurances of increased security for the U.S. embassy and its staff. This time, however, the takeover was to last 444 days.

Following the embassy takeover, the shah left New York for a military base in Texas, where he recuperated, and from there went to Panama, where rumors circulated about his impending arrest and extradition to Iran. He found himself on the move again in March 1980, this time to Egypt, as guest of his old friend President Sadat. He died there on July 27.

Two days after the embassy takeover started, on November 6, Bazargan's frustration with the course the revolution was taking and his anger at the imprisonment of American diplomats prompted him to resign from office. Several political dynamics were now set in motion that fundamentally influenced later events. Bazargan's resignation turned out to be the beginning of a long process whereby Khomeini steadily eliminated one "moderate" revolutionary after another. With the cabinet having resigned, Khomeini transferred power to the secretive Revolutionary Council, one of whose responsibilities was to prepare for elections to an Assembly of Experts. It was up to the assembly to draft a constitution. Not surprisingly, it was packed with members of the Islamic Republic Party (IRP), a cleric-dominated party supportive of Khomeini and claiming allegiance to "the imam's line." The constitution that the assembly produced sanctified Khomeini's position as the Supreme Leader *(velayat faqih)*. As its Article 5 stipulated, "[T]he governance of the nation devolves upon the just and pious Faqih who is acquainted with the circumstances of his age; courageous, resourceful, and possessed of administrative ability; and recognized and accepted as leader by the majority of the people."[49] Presidential elections were held in January 1980, resulting in the landslide victory of Abol Hassan Bani-Sadr, who had been popular in the heady days since the monarchy's collapse and was a close associate of Khomeini. But Bani-Sadr's presidency was also ill-fated. His eventual break with Khomeini came on June 21, 1981, when he went into hiding to avoid arrest and eventually escaped to France.

Khomeini's handling of what evolved into the "hostage crisis" was representative of his modus operandi as a shrewd, populist political animal. Every time events of this nature happened—and in revolutionary Iran they happened a lot—he would initially sit back and gauge the popular response, then opt for the most "revolutionary" (i.e., radical) option. This is precisely what he did in response to the takeover of the U.S. embassy in Tehran by "Students Following the Imam's Path." His role in the progressive purging of his once-close revolutionary collaborators followed a similar pattern, as did his response to Iran's invasion by Iraq, his *fatwa* on the British author Salman Rushdie, and countless other political maneuvers unknown to outside observers. There are some indications that the takeover of the U.S. embassy might not have been as spontaneous as it initially appeared, although no one suspected that it would drag on as long as it did.[50] But it did serve an important political function for Khomeini and his supporters in the IRP. It helped consolidate the ayatollah's near-absolute hold over the postrevolutionary polity and enabled him to eliminate more of his rivals.

Meanwhile, the hostage drama inside the embassy compound had given rise to a flurry of frantic efforts by officials in both Washington and Tehran to bring the saga to an early end. As the days turned into weeks and the weeks turned into months, the United States on several occasions discovered that the Iranians did not speak with one voice. The moderate elements were being cast aside one after another, and those who remained, such as Bani-Sadr, could not deliver on the promises they kept making. The Soviet Union's invasion of Afghanistan in late December 1979 only complicated an already volatile regional climate. The United States pursued multiple tracks and explored a variety of options, some of which were outside normal diplomatic channels.[51] Several times it appeared that a deal was imminent and that the hostages would be released soon, but then the delicate negotiations would be denounced by Khomeini and things would fall apart. But President Carter was doggedly determined to secure the hostages' release, and toward this goal he was willing to explore all options, including military ones. In fact, on April 24, 1980, an elite American commando unit made up of eight helicopters set out from the warship USS *Nimitz* in the Persian Gulf on a daring and complex mission to attack the embassy compound in Tehran and release the hostages. The mission had been secretly planned for months. But two of the helicopters soon developed mechanical problems in the Iranian desert, and, in the process of abandoning the mission and returning to base, a U.S. transport plane and a helicopter collided on the ground and eight American servicemen were killed.[52] The failed rescue mission gave Khomeini cause for keeping the hostages even longer.

The hostage crisis was to drag on for another eight months. Protracted negotiations, always through third-party intermediaries, continued intermittently, and some in the U.S. administration favored the execution of yet another rescue mission.[53] Finally, in September 1980, the Majles passed a resolution that spelled out the conditions under which the hostages would be released. These included the United States' release of Iranian assets (estimated at around $12 billion) that had been frozen in retaliation for holding the hostages; a commitment by the United States not to interfere in Iranian affairs militarily or politically; and the confiscation of the shah's assets in the United States and their return to Iran.[54] With an eye toward the upcoming presidential elections, the Carter administration found these clear conditions a hopeful beginning and used them as the basis of its negotiations with Iran, with the government of Algeria acting as go-between. Long and arduous negotiations were set into motion, many times coming to the brink of collapse. No doubt, the hostages' release before the November general elections would have strengthened President Carter's chances of reelection. But such was not to be, and Carter was to lose in a landslide to his Republican opponent, Ronald Reagan. The negotiations with Iran continued up until and into the day of the U.S. presidential inauguration, January 20, when a number of last-minute details were still being worked out. Finally, on that day, all the complex details of the massive transfer of funds and other legal considerations were worked out, and, as Ronald Reagan took the oath of office, the U.S. diplomats were ferried to two Algerian planes standing by at Tehran's airport and flown out of Iran.

The long ordeal was finally over. Everyone involved had suffered a great deal: the hostage diplomats, their families, the Carter administration, and the Iranian people. The only victor, it seemed, was Khomeini—and, of course, Ronald Reagan.

It appears that the benefits of the hostage crisis to the Reagan campaign and the timing of the hostages' release were not all that coincidental. There had long been rumors of clandestine contacts between the Reagan campaign and the Iranian hostage takers. While the truth is still murky and may never be entirely known, years later great substance was added to these rumors by the investigative works of Gary Sick, a former White House insider, and a number of journalists.[55] In broad terms, Sick has constructed the following scenario. After several clandestine meetings in Madrid between Iranians close to Khomeini and Reagan's campaign manager, William Casey, an old spymaster and later the head of the CIA, an agreement was reached whereby the hostages would not be released until after the November 1980 U.S. presidential elections. Casey is said to have preferred that the hostages be released during the Reagan presidency (they were released about twenty minutes after Reagan took the oath of office, following an unexplained four-hour delay in Tehran as they sat on board a plane waiting to take off). In return, the United States sanctioned Israel's sale of American military equipment to Iran, which it badly needed in its war against Iraq.[56] This explains why, in negotiating the hostages' release, the Iranian side was willing to settle for financial terms far less advantageous than they could have demanded. Later the Reagan White House repeated the same idea—swapping hostages for military equipment through Israel—in what came to be known as the Iran-Contra Affair.[57]

The repressive campaigns of Iran's First Republic did not end with the conclusion of the hostage crisis. In fact, they were heightened as Ayatollah Khomeini's efforts at consolidating clerical rule kicked into high gear. As the war with Iraq raged along the country's western borders, the regime unleashed a reign of terror on its domestic political opponents, the most active of whom by now were the Mujahedeen guerrillas. In a spectacular explosion in June 1980, the Mujahedeen managed to kill some of the IRP's most influential figures, including the party's leader, four cabinet ministers, ten deputy ministers, and twenty-seven Majles deputies. In retaliation, within three months, the regime had executed over one thousand people by hanging or firing squads.[58] Other political parties, such as the communist Tudeh, were banned, and the authorities began exercising almost total and direct control over all electronic and printed media. The war with Iraq helped facilitate the mobilization for the war effort of countless volunteer militias, the Basijis, thus expediting the process of political consolidation under the auspices of a dictatorial, populist regime. Even notable clerics were not immune to Khomeini's wrath if they disagreed with him. When in 1986 Grand Ayatollah Kazem Shariatmadari, highly respected and a renowned revolutionary in his own right, challenged Khomeini's absolutist interpretation of the *velayat faqih*, Khomeini had him defrocked.

Accordingly, the revolutionary state's social and cultural agendas reflected Khomeini's very conservative, narrow interpretation of Islam. Women had to observe the Islamic dress code in the strictest sense, and many were encouraged to leave the workforce and to resume duties at home.[59] A cultural revolution kept the universities closed for a number of years to ensure their purification and their observance of the regime's Islam. By the mid- to late 1980s, the chaos of the earlier years had subsided, and the Islamic Republic, with regular elections to the presidency and the Majles, had reached a fairly stable level of institutional consolidation.

In the late 1980s, two significant developments occurred that signaled the end of postrevolutionary Iran's First Republic and the beginning of the Second Republic: the end of the war with Iraq in July 1988, and the passing of Ayatollah Khomeini in June 1989. By now, after years of revolutionary rhetoric, war mobilization, postrevolutionary terror, and emotional volatility, the people had grown weary. Literally every family had lost a member or knew of someone who had been lost in the revolutionary struggle, or had perished at the war front, or had been killed or imprisoned in the terror of the early years. Added to this general exhaustion was a deep sense of injured pride. Iran had become the pariah of the world, criticized at every opportunity, isolated, and besieged. The urban middle classes had also seen a steady erosion of their living standards and a concomitant loss not only of their purchasing power but also of their social clout and affluence.[60] The revolutionaries might have been adept at capturing power, but their managerial skills and their ability to efficiently and effectively run a modern economy left much to be desired. Declining oil revenues and the strains of eight years of war on hardware, infrastructure, and manpower—not to mention the sheer agony of the personal strains of war—did not help matters.

In many ways, by the late 1980s the Iranian revolution had reached a milestone. For nearly a decade the Iranians had received promises and had sacrificed for them. They had marched and demonstrated, fought in the trenches and mourned their dead, rationed their food, and earned and spent less. Now that the war was over and the "imam" was gone, they wanted results. All of their sacrifices somehow had to be justified. A generation later, the inheritors of the revolution were keenly aware of the popular pulse, of the need to change the performance of the revolutionary system if not its essence.

Whereas the First Republic was one of terror and destruction, the Second Republic featured relative moderation and reconstruction. In fact, the word *construction (sazandegi)* came up frequently in the speeches and statements of policy makers and in many ways became the new mantra of the state. The change in the priorities and even the composition of the state's highest-ranking officials was apparent. To begin with, nomination to the cabinet and confirmation by the Majles became increasingly based on merit and qualifications rather than revolutionary conviction. Revolutionary radicals were gradually, though not totally, pushed out of policy-making positions and replaced by largely nonideological technocrats. In fact, many regime insiders called President Ali Akbar Hashemi Rafsenjani's 1989 cabinet "the Cabinet of Reconstruction."[61] The president himself was blunt in signaling the beginning of a new era of state politics and in welcoming the contributions of those who had once been cast aside: "For the sake of the reconstruction of this vast country and for renovation of war damages, we are prepared to accept the participation of friends and governments who will deal with us . . . without any expansionist and colonialist motives."[62]

Elections to the Fourth Majles, held in 1992, confirmed the trend. The "antiradicals" scored a landslide victory. Members of the new Majles tended to be less doctrinaire and younger. There was also a much larger percentage of MPs with doctorates or master's degrees, and, more importantly, more women were elected from Tehran and the provinces.[63] Pragmatism, it seemed—as much as the revolution's legacy allowed—became the order of the day.

In addition to a relative liberalization of the political arena and a general relaxation of revolutionary zeal, the Second Republic featured two important developments, one institutional and the other economic. Institutionally, in late 1988, the state undertook a major revision of the 1979 constitution, designed to make the system more efficient and less unwieldy. The original constitution, written when the postrevolutionary state had not yet been fully institutionalized, had embodied several fundamental contradictions.[64] Most notably, it had allowed for a split executive—both a prime minister and a president—without clearly delineating the division of labor between the two. Also, the precise nature of the position and powers of the Faqih needed to be clarified. These were two of the most important areas in which changes were made, although the total number of amendments to the constitution was around fifty. Along with other changes, the amended constitution eliminated the office of the prime minister and created an "executive presidency." Equally important, it streamlined the powers of the Supreme Leader by removing the provision allowing for his replacement by a three- to five-member committee. The primary goal of these changes appears to have been the reduction of possibilities for factional infighting at the regime's highest levels.

More difficult to implement were the state's efforts to liberalize the economy and, presumably, improve its performance. There had long been many "bottlenecks" in the postrevolutionary economy. Such structural problems included a lack of adequate managerial skills within the various developmental institutions of the state, incessant and counterproductive statist intervention in economic affairs and the work of enterprises, and the existence of several parallel, often competing, state organizations charged with similar tasks.[65] The costs associated with the war with Iraq and the slump in the oil market only exacerbated the economy's difficulties.

Without adequate infrastructure, and with the needs arising from the dislocating effects of the war and inadequate resources, the state's economic liberalization drive encountered severe difficulties. Many of the larger economic problems could not be simply remedied by state disinvestment. Also, some within the regime, especially Majles deputies, strongly resisted the implementation of neoliberal economic policies. The lack of a comprehensive economic reform program and the absence of resources and the political will to carry it out continue to plague postrevolutionary Iran's economy to this day. In the words of one observer, "[T]he crisis continues. . . . The theocracy that claimed to be the government of the oppressed has no way other than to crown itself a 'run of the mill' capitalist state."[66] And, it might be added, not a very successful one at that.

As scheduled, presidential elections were held in May 1997, and to everyone's surprise a dark horse candidate named Muhammad Khatami was elected president. Khatami's presidency has ushered in a Third Republic. In the early 1990s, Khatami had briefly served as the minister of culture, but his tenure had been cut short after he was impeached by the Majles for his overt advocacy of reforms. While having name recognition, therefore, he was generally seen as a political outsider. Moreover, his clerical background and rank of *hojjatoleslam* gave him additional credibility with the masses and made him a safe compromise candidate between the moderates and the more radical elements of the regime. All expectations were that Khatami's candidacy would be just that, a candidacy, and that the hard-line Speaker of the Majles, Ali Akbar Nateq-Nuri, would be elected president. But with more than 70 percent of the votes cast in his favor, Khatami's victory was decisive.

Khatami's election turned out to be a turning point of sorts for the Islamic Republic. Having been reelected in 2001, for eight years the president relentlessly pursued a policy of openness and reforms domestically and confidence-building and reconciliation internationally. In the international arena, he oversaw steady improvements in Iran's relations with the outside world, especially insofar as Iran's immediate neighbors and the West were concerned. His foreign policy objectives in relation to the Arab world were meant to build trust and confidence between the two sides and to put behind the tensions and the mistrust that still lingered in the aftermath of the Iran-Iraq War.[67] With regard to the West, Khatami also greatly improved Iran's relations with the European Union and, somewhat halfheartedly, especially during the tenure in office of President Clinton, also sought ways of mending the acrimonious state of affairs between Iran and the United States. All of this was done under the auspices of a "Dialogue of Civilizations," through which Khatami tried to narrow the gap in cultural understanding and respect dividing Iran and Muslim world from the West.

Some of the most significant accomplishments of the Khatami presidency were in changing the tone and tenor of domestic Iranian politics. As president, he sought to give substance to his campaign promises of encouraging the spread of civil society and observing the rule of law. As much as he could, and within limits, he relaxed social strictures concerning the youth in general and women in particular. Restrictions on the printed media were also relaxed, and, in a departure from the past, the Ministry of Culture and Islamic Guidance, one of whose responsibilities it was to grant licenses for books to be published and movies to be made, loosened its previous guidelines of what were and were not permissible forms of academic and artistic expression. It is no exaggeration to maintain that under Khatami Iran underwent an intellectual revolution of sorts.[68]

Despite initiating seismic shifts in Iran's international relations and its domestic politics, by the time Khatami left office in June 2005 his popularity among Iran's urban middle classes had dwindled. This was largely because of his multiple failures to overcome trenchant opposition within the system to his reform programs. Khatami had been reelected back in 2001 with the assumption by most urban Iranians that he would give added substance and weight to his reforms. But it soon became evident that the president was either unwilling or unable to do so, and his star steadily dimmed among those who had vested so much of their hopes in him. Part of this halted approach to reforms was a product of Khatami's own fears that he would become the Mikhail Gorbachev of Iran, inadvertently initiating reforms that would bring about the collapse of the entire system. But even more significant was the fact that in the larger scheme of Iranian politics Khatami was a relatively powerless president. The president and some of his allies controlled the offices of the presidency and the cabinet. But the Majles and the judiciary, and far more significantly the office of the Supreme Leader, remained firmly under the control of conservatives and radicals. In fact, it was not so much Khatami's reforms but rather factionalism—at times bitter internal divisions—that appeared to be emerging as the defining feature of Iran's Third Republic.

Precisely these internal divisions resulted in the election of the hard-line mayor of Tehran to the presidency in 2005. Dr. Mahmoud Ahmadinejad's career closely mirrors those of countless others who actively took part in the revolution and the war against Iraq. Once the war was over, many of these individuals, deeply committed to the ideals of the revolution and to Ayatollah Khomeini, went on to assume increasingly influential positions in the state bureaucracy, at the same time enhancing their academic and professional credentials. In the process, they developed diverging views about the proper interpretations of Khomeini's legacy and the next stage in the evolution of the revolution. Khatami and the "reformists" *(eslahta-laban)* had to contend with the "conservatives" *(mohafezehkaran)*, who cared less about political reforms than about economic development. Both camps were in turn opposed by the radical "principlists" *(osulgarayan)*, who rejected as revisionist and deviant any digression from what they saw as the revolution's true principles. Reversing many of Khatami's domestic reforms and international initiatives, Ahmadinejad's presidency was not just a reaction to the openness and reformism of the Khatami period. It was, in fact, a throwback to the earliest days of the revolution. The president's rhetoric, his populist domestic policies, his confrontational and uncompromising foreign policy objectives, and even his persona—down to his choice of clothing—all harked back to the early days of the Islamic Republic, when ideological politics and rousing speeches ruled the day.

Ahmadinejad's presidency polarized the factional alignments and tensions inherent within the system, resulting in its near-implosion during the June 2009 presidential elections. In his attempt to secure reelection, the incumbent president based his campaign on promises of destroying Iran's "power mafia." For his part, Ahmadinejad's main opponent, Mirhossein Mousavi, prime minister from 1981 to 1989 and long a member of the regime's inner circle, openly and repeatedly accused the president of corruption and incompetence. The electorate, which had not seen anything quite like this in the thirty-year life of the Islamic Republic, took to the streets in the millions, generating an election euphoria that shook the very foundations of the regime.

When election results determined that Mousavi had suffered a resounding defeat, demonstrations in Tehran and in other major cities, made up of millions decrying electoral fraud, became even more threatening to the establishment. A brutal campaign of suppression followed, with the Basij forces, often in plainclothes, unleashing indiscriminate violence on the protesters. When people took their protests indoors and started shouting *Allah-o Akbar* (God is Great) from rooftops at night, the security forces began breaking into homes, beating up women and hauling men to jail.

The suppression campaign bore fruit. Mousavi, the insider turned reluctant revolutionary, was quieted down, and many of his vocal supporters were jailed; the street demonstrators, fearful of being discovered, retreated into their homes and kept their heads down; families whose loved ones were killed by the Basij mourned in quiet; and Ahmadinejad remained as the president. But what also remained, and remain to this day, are the deep fissures that run along stark factional and ideological lines across the Islamic Republic system. Also persisting has been the remarkably resilient and adaptable Green Movement—green having been the color of Mousavi's campaign—which emerged spontaneously and is made up of supporters of the former prime minister. Members of the Green Movement, who are mostly students and other young Iranians, often use holidays and other notable dates on the regime's own revolutionary calendar to gather in city squares and streets across the country and to protest what has become a dictatorship bereft of any popular legitimacy. As the regime's indiscriminate campaign of suppression against the Green Movement and other scattered acts of civil disobedience continues, so does the popular yearning to finally give meaning to the slogans of a revolution that was originally fought three decades ago.

Like most other revolutions, especially the French, with which it shared a number of parallels, Iran's "Islamic" revolution was accompanied in its early years by a repressive reign of terror that brutally eliminated enemies, rejected the outside world, and went about creating the institutions that it needed to consolidate itself. Ayatollah Khomeini, the revolutionary zealot, was determined, shrewd, and brilliant at gauging popular sentiments and manipulating them. Within a year of coming to power, he had constitutionally sanctified his position and had officially ensured his personal role as Iran's supreme leader.

But even imams die, and the ayatollah's death in June 1989, less than a year after the end of the war with Iraq, ushered in a new era and a new emphasis for Iranian politics. The emphasis on revolutionary purity was replaced by one on the urgent need for national reconstruction. Economic limitations hampered the extent to which such a "construction crusade" would be fruitful, but the state's shift in focus and priorities was undeniable. The postrevolutionary state, it seemed, by now felt secure in its hold on power and the resilience of its institutions to take on the daunting challenge of economic reform. Evidence, nonetheless, does not reflect too kindly on the state's accomplishments in the economic arena.

The third and current phase in the life of postrevolutionary Iran started with the surprise election of Hojjatoleslam Muhammad Khatami in May 1997. Since then, we have seen the bitter rivalry of deeply entrenched factions along the three axes of reformism, conservatism, and radicalism. In unprecedented ways, the bitterly fought presidential election of June 2009, which controversially returned President Ahmadinejad to office, showed the alarming degree to which the Islamic Republic state is internally divided. To what extent the Iranian masses, especially those in the major cities, remain bystanders in this factional state conflict, or become participants in social movements energized by the state's ideological divisions, remains to be seen. What is clear for now is that the last act of the Iranian revolution is yet to be written.

Of course, Iran's 1978–79 revolution did not alter the life of Iran and Iranians alone. It set into motion events whose repercussions were felt both in the immediate vicinity and in places as far away as the United States and western Europe. The fears that the Iranian revolution inspired among its immediate neighbors, and the regional vacuum that the shah's sudden demise left behind, prompted Iraq to invade Iran in September 1980. The duration and outcome of this war in turn prompted Iraq to undertake further, and in hindsight riskier, international ventures. The next chapter turns to these international conflicts.

6 The Gulf Wars and Beyond

By nature, the consequences of revolutions go far beyond domestic boundaries. They influence, often with great ferocity, prevailing international
power relations and the diplomatic status quo. They create power vacuums
and opportunities to be exploited, look for allies and enemies on the other
side of the border, give rise to those who seek to export the revolution's
message and ideals, and, quite often, culminate in a war involving two or
even more belligerents.

The Iranian revolution was no exception. The overthrow of the shah had
left a power vacuum in a region of great significance to western Europe
and the superpowers, especially the United States. Beginning in the mid-
1960s and especially the 1970s, the Persian Gulf had been lined from one
end to the other by overtly pro-Western leaders, the 1973 oil boycott and
Iraq's occasional rhetoric to the contrary notwithstanding. By the late
1970s, the states of the Persian Gulf had firmly placed themselves in the
Western camp in the Cold War competition, and, despite repeated efforts
and considerable investments in diplomacy and hardware, Soviet policy
in the region had suffered one setback after another.[1] However, by early
1980, the fall of the shah, the capture of the U.S. embassy in Tehran, and
the Soviet invasion of Afghanistan (in December 1979) had thrown the
policies of the United States and other Western powers toward the Persian
Gulf into serious confusion.[2] The revolutionary rhetoric emanating from
Tehran, promising export of the revolution to the nearby countries ruled
by conservative monarchies, aggravated the regional instability and chaos
that was beginning to engulf not just the immediate vicinity but much of
the Middle East. Within this volatile and charged international atmosphere
Iraq invaded Iran in September 1980, setting in motion an eight-year war
between the two countries.

The Iran-Iraq War was a bloody and devastating conflict, with an estimated one million dead and tens of thousands of prisoners of war captured by both sides. But as wrenching as the conflict was for Iranians and Iraqis, it had ramifications far beyond the two warring countries and their respective allies. The direction in which the war evolved and the circumstances under which it was concluded directly led to another war, this time resulting in Iraq's invasion of its neighbor to the south, Kuwait. The "liberation" of Kuwait was carried out by a U.S.-led force of international allies under the banners of defending national sovereignty, upholding international law, and defeating aggression. Had the Iranians not violated international law themselves so blatantly by taking American diplomats hostage, perhaps the same level of moral outrage would have been directed at Iraq's earlier invasion and occupation of Iranian territories. That Kuwait was very much pro-Western and a major producer of oil added force to the immorality of its occupation by Iraq. Ultimately, Iraq itself was invaded and the country was occupied, this time by an American-led "Coalition of the Willing" searching for weapons of mass destruction and promising to root out terrorism.

In some ways, the Iran-Iraq War appears to have been the last gasp of the dying phenomenon of Arab unity. A credible argument can even be made that such a phenomenon never existed beyond the tired and hollow rhetoric of leaders such as Nasser and Qaddafi. Empty as it might have been, the rhetoric served as a rallying cry for some, and, if nothing else, at times it succeeded in provoking panicked reactions by Israel and the West. Given the history of flimsy political institutions in the Middle East and the greater importance of personalities, rhetoric was a powerful political tool for both domestic constituents and international audiences. But with the death of Nasser and the dismantling of Nasserism at home and abroad, even the rhetoric of Arab unity started to die out, only occasionally sounding from the Libyan desert or from isolated and desperate Palestinian "revolutionaries." Ironically, the religious character of the Iranian revolution did nothing to promote unity with the Iranians' co-religionists in the Arab world. In fact, although the radical and radicalizing rhetoric of the revolution led to a brief episode of Arab unity, it only widened the rift between the Iranians and much of the Arab world.

As we have seen so far, much of the modern history of the Middle East has been shaped by the two seemingly contradictory forces of nationalism and Arab unity. In reality, these forces have been one and the same, differing only in the definition and scope they attach to the concept of nation. Is the Arab nation defined by virtue of its common language and literary tradition, its common culture and religion, or its common ethnic bonds? Or is it fragmented into smaller units that are separated by borders drawn up in the period of colonialism? Whatever the depth and breadth of the Arab nation, for more than fifty years it has had to contend with diverse states, and the resulting entities have come to assume different characters, proud identities, and widely differing priorities. Emotional appeals to an overarching Arab nation have resurfaced only when they have suited the interests of specific Arab leaders at particular times: Nasser in the late 1950s and early 1960s, Qaddafi in the 1970s and 1980s, and Saddam Hussein in the 1980s. For many years, a genuine sense of commitment to the Palestinians, coupled with a need to blame domestic shortcomings on outside evils, made Israel the common enemy of many Arab states, thus keeping the ideal of unity alive in the collective memory of the Arab masses. But ideal and reality are two different things. As Israel proved again and again to be undefeatable, hopes for Arab unity grew increasingly dimmer and its promises more empty. When in the 1980s Iran emerged as a new common enemy, menacing Arab states near and far, the old ideal regained some life. Saddam, declaring himself the defender of the Arab nation, promised to slay the new enemy and to defend the honor and interests of all Arabs against Iranian ambitions. But as it turned out, he assumed that the Arab nation would be only a passive audience, viewing with admiration his state's countless victories. Soon the Iraqi state would itself rampage through the Arab nation with the banner of Arab unity. What started as a tragic farce—the Iran-Iraq War—soon led to another wrenching charade, the Second Gulf War.

The cumulative effects of the two bloody Gulf Wars was a serious weakening of the regional state system in the Middle East. By the early 1990s, any measure of unity that had once grouped the Arab states in a "focused system" with a single goal was all but gone, and potential hegemonic powers like Egypt or Iraq had been weakened or isolated both within the region and internationally. The ensuing power vacuum was filled by the United States, now emboldened by the demise of the Soviet Union and the dawning of an American-dominated "New World Order."

Power has its privileges, but it also attracts anger and resentment. A decade after the Gulf War ended, that anger manifested itself in a horrific attack on the American mainland by fanatics from the Middle East. September 11, 2001, marks a watershed in American diplomacy around the globe and especially in relation to the Middle East. This chapter examines the causes, consequences, and aftermath of the 9/11 attacks, especially the U.S. invasion and occupation of Iraq, as well as those of the two major military conflicts in the Middle East before that—the Iran-Iraq War and Iraq's invasion of Kuwait.

THE IRAN-IRAQ WAR

On September 22, 1980, Iraqi forces invaded Iran at eight points on land and bombarded Iranian airfields, military installations, and economic targets.[3] Tensions had been building along the two countries' shared border for some time, and there had been sporadic exchanges of fire since the previous February. These border clashes had come at a time of profound political uncertainty and chaos in both countries, especially in Iran, which was still boiling with revolutionary fervor. Tensions between the two countries continued rising throughout 1979 and 1980. On September 17 of that year, Saddam Hussein declared the abrogation of the 1975 treaty with Iran, which had marked the halfway point of the Shatt al-Arab waterway as the two countries' common border, and claimed complete Iraqi sovereignty over the river. Shortly thereafter, on September 22, his forces invaded Iran.

The Iraqi invasion of Iran was a result of the interplay of four broad dynamics: (1) the domestic political predicament of the Iraqi president, Saddam Hussein; (2) the power vacuum in the new Islamic Republic; (3) the intensive propaganda of Iranian revolutionaries calling on the Arab masses to overthrow their leaders and to follow the lead of the Islamic Republic; and (4) Saddam's regional ambitions as he sought to emerge as the new guardian of the Arab cause and the Nasser of his day. Each of these factors merits a closer look.

Saddam (1937–2006) had originally entered politics at the age of twenty, when he had joined the Iraqi Ba'th Party. The Ba'th Party, which saw itself as one of the primary vehicles for fostering Arab unity, was originally established in Syria, the birthplace of its main theoretician and founder, Michel Aflaq. In the late 1950s, a group of middle-class Iraqis set up a separate Ba'th Party in Iraq. Although the two parties never formally merged, in the late 1950s and early 1960s they did, to some extent, coordinate their political and theoretical positions. By the late 1960s, Aflaq was finding himself increasingly at odds with the ideological officers running Syria, eventually leaving for Iraq in 1968. In many ways this was a result of the increasing factionalization of the Syrian Ba'th in the late 1960s and its division into various competing groups before Hafiz al-Assad effectively dominated the party and imposed on it a measure of unity. Tensions between the Iraqi and the Syrian Ba'th Parties were soon to develop, and by the early and mid-1970s each party accused the other of undue interference.

The 1958 coup that overthrew Iraq's monarchy did little to improve the fortunes of the Iraqi Ba'th. In 1959, after mounting repression, a group of Ba'thists, including Saddam, was assigned to assassinate the dictator Abd al-Karim Qassem. Despite later glorifications of his role in the unsuccessful attempt, it appears that Saddam actually botched the operation.[4] To avoid capture, he escaped to Syria, where he was warmly received by the Syrian Ba'th leadership, and from there to Egypt, where he received a high school diploma and briefly studied law at the University of Cairo. Egypt at this time was in the midst of the Nasserist phenomenon, and Nasser's penchant for political theater and quest for Arab leadership appear to have left lasting impressions on the young Saddam.[5] In 1963, when Qassem was finally overthrown and the Ba'th briefly captured power, Saddam returned home, only to find himself on the margins of political life because of his long absence. After a short stint in prison for attempted murder, Saddam managed to rise quickly within the Ba'th hierarchy and was put in charge of its military organization. His rise through the ranks of the Ba'th owed much to his family ties to the party's leader, Ahmad Hassan al-Bakr. When the Ba'th returned to power in 1968 and al-Bakr became president, Saddam's political ascent picked up speed. He was made deputy chairman of the Revolutionary Command Council (RCC), at the time the country's most important decision-making body. A series of ruthless purges of the Ba'th soon followed, whereby potential opponents of al-Bakr and Saddam were eliminated one after another. By the early 1970s, Saddam had emerged as the second most powerful man in Iraq, in fact beginning to overshadow his older patron. He also meticulously cultivated a presidential image among the political elites and the larger masses by touring the country, signing international treaties on behalf of Iraq, and exerting his power both overtly and from behind the scenes. As two of his biographers write, "The voice was Bakr's—but the hands were Saddam's."[6] On July 16, 1979, al-Bakr notified the nation of his retirement due to "health reasons" and gave his blessing to the succession of his deputy. Saddam "reluctantly" accepted the presidency. Few people bought the staged theatrics. A bloodless coup had occurred.

The conditions that allowed Saddam's ascent to power, coupled with the political predicaments he faced as Iraq's new president, were the primary reasons for his invasion of Iran the following year. The fact that Saddam Hussein had never formally served in the armed forces was symptomatic of a deeper divide between the Ba'th and the Iraqi military establishment. Throughout the late 1960s and 1970s, the Ba'th had increasingly asserted its dominance over the army, and in January 1976 al-Bakr appointed Saddam to the rank of lieutenant general (retroactive from July 1973).[7] Saddam's assumption of power saw a concomitant rise in the size and powers of the Popular Militia, set up by the Ba'th as an ideological army and, in many ways, a rival to the regular armed forces. The ruthless purges of the 1970s also picked up pace with the new president's inauguration, and some of the regime's most recognizable figures were accused of treason or other antistate crimes and were eliminated. The purges within the RCC and the Ba'th were the most extensive, with some five hundred high-ranking party members said to have been executed within weeks of Saddam's assumption of the presidency.[8]

Authoritarian leaders seldom rule by repression alone. Depending on the larger circumstances in which they govern, they also try to gain some measure of popular legitimacy, however banal and fruitless such efforts might be. In Iraq, as in many other Middle Eastern countries, political leaders have often cultivated a sense of historic mission—an exaggerated account of the importance of their rule in relation to the country's larger history—in order to enhance a supposedly popular mandate to govern and to "protect" the nation. Saddam's image as such a "protector," not just of the Iraqis but of the whole Arab nation, was bound to significantly broaden his mandate and, consequently, to expedite his determined quest for total political control. He made full use of the symbolisms involved, referring to the war with Iran as Saddam's Qadisiyya, after the famous battle in which Muslim Arab forces conquered ancient Persia in 637 A.D.[9] All observers agree that at the time of its invasion of Iran, the Iraqi state was "brimming over with self-confidence and a sense of its own achievements."[10] A quick and decisive victory over a historic enemy, now crippled by its own internal squabbles, offered political rewards too tempting for Saddam to resist.

That the enemy was busy decimating its armed forces through revolutionary trials and speedy executions only helped expedite Saddam's decision to attack. The political upheavals in Iran and the ensuing power vacuum were a second leading cause of the Iran-Iraq War. Soon after the revolution's success, Iran's new rulers launched a frenzied campaign to purge the ranks of the state of all nonrevolutionary elements. Within months, some twenty thousand teachers, eight hundred foreign ministry employees (out of a total of two thousand), and four thousand civil servants had been dismissed. The hardest hit were the armed forces, suspected of deep loyalties to the deposed shah; as many as two thousand to four thousand officers were quickly dismissed.[11] At the same time, some Iranian tribes, located mostly along the country's northern, eastern, and western borders, began pressing for greater regional autonomy. The Kurdish challenge to the fledgling revolutionary government was especially serious, and armed clashes began to occur throughout Iran's northwestern and western Kurdish regions. By late 1979, Iran's continued detention of U.S. diplomats and the prolonged hostage crisis were quickly turning the country into a regional and indeed global arch-villain. Internal bickering among the revolutionaries, the youthful exuberance that publicly betrayed their inexperience, and the multiple domestic and international challenges they faced all made Iran's new masters seem like easy prey to the seasoned, calculating Saddam Hussein.

Iran's revolutionaries might have seemed weak and vulnerable to the outside world, but they also seemed threatening. The rhetoric of the Iranian revolution, and the stated goals of Khomeini and his associates to export their Islamic revolution beyond Iran's boundaries, constituted a third cause of the Iran-Iraq War. Among Khomeini's many statements to this effect, the following is representative: "We should try to export our revolution to the world. We should set aside the thought that we do not export our revolution, because Islam does not regard the various Islamic countries differently and is the supporter of all the oppressed peoples of the world. On the other hand, all the superpowers and the [great] powers have risen to destroy us. If we remain in an enclosed environment we shall definitely face defeat."[12]

Already, by virtue of its geographic size and location, its population, and its resources, Iran posed a formidable strategic challenge to its Arab neighbors to the west and south of the Persian Gulf. Adding an ideological crusade to the challenge was perceived by the adjacent Arab states as a mortal threat. The fear that domestic instability might prompt the Iranian revolutionaries to attack their neighbors only added force to the threat. At this critical juncture, Saddam reasoned, only he could effectively defend the Arab nation against Tehran's revolutionaries.

Saddam's regional ambitions and his desire to emerge as the new, powerful leader of the Arab world were a fourth reason for his initiation of the Iran-Iraq War. With one brilliant, quick attack, he would occupy Iran's oil-rich southwestern region—an area Iraqi maps refer to as "Arabistan"—establish Iraqi supremacy over the Shatt al-Arab River, replace the deposed shah as the new "gendarme" of the Persian Gulf, and become the Nasser of his day. By 1979–80, the Arab world desperately needed a new hero, a new leader who would inspire confidence, project power, personify the Arabs' resurgence, and dispel their collective malaise. Nasser was long gone; Sadat had betrayed the Arab cause by negotiating with the Zionist enemy; and the bombastic Qaddafi was too removed from the heart of the Arab world.

Saddam saw himself as the only natural standard-bearer of the Arab world, the only one capable of restoring to the Arabs the glory they deserved, defending the honor and territory of the Arab peoples, and giving hope to the millions let down by Nasser and betrayed by Sadat. Cairo, Damascus, and even Beirut had had their day in the sun. Now it was Baghdad's turn.

On July 17, 1980, on the first anniversary of Saddam's ascension to the presidency and shortly before the war with Iran, the Iraqi government ran a two-page ad in the London *Times* that read, in part, "Iraq was more than once the springboard of a new civilization in the Middle East, and the question is now pertinently asked, with a leader like this man, the wealth of oil resources and the forceful people like the Iraqis, will she repeat her former glories and the name of Saddam Hussein link up with that of Hammurabi, Ashurbanipal, al-Mansur and Harun al-Rashid? To be sure, they have not really achieved half of what he has already done at the helm of the Ba'th Arab Socialist Party, [and] he is still only 44."[13] Clearly, the Iraqi invasion of Iran fit into Saddam's attempts to consolidate his rule and establish a cult of personality. And, it seems, he intended for his audiences to extend far beyond Iraq and its immediate neighbors.

The Iraqi invasion of Iran started in earnest on September 22, 1980. Broadly, the Iran-Iraq War can be divided into three phases. The first phase lasted just under a year and was marked by dramatic Iraqi successes and the capture of sizable Iranian territory in the oil-rich southwestern parts of the country. The second phase, which started in late September 1981 and lasted until late July 1982, saw a steady and almost complete reversal of the first. It was marked by a series of successful Iranian counteroffensives that recaptured significant portions of lost Iranian territory and put the Iraqi forces on the defensive. But the Iranian drive eventually lost steam because of a series of tactical and strategic errors that were compounded by the limitations of the Iranian forces. The third phase of the war was the longest, lasting almost exactly six years, from July 1982 to July 1988. In this third and final phase, the war settled into a seemingly endless stalemate, with neither side able to score a decisive victory. Finally, after the combined loss of hundreds of thousands of men by both sides, on July 18, 1988, Iran accepted a UN-brokered cease-fire agreement, and after a few weeks of additional skirmishes the war ended.

Iraq's invasion was quick and initially very successful. Iraqi military planners had hoped to capture the four principal Iranian cities in the southwest: Khorramshahr, Abadan, Ahvaz, and Dezful. Toward this end, before crossing into Iran, Iraq forces pounded Khorramshahr and Abadan with heavy artillery for nearly a week. Given that an estimated 30 to

40 percent of the Iranians who live in the region are Arabic speakers, the Iraqis had counted on the support and sympathy of the local Iranian population. At the very least, they had hoped to demoralize the Iranians by their unrelenting artillery barrage. But this was far from the case, and Khorramshahr's defenders, who were geographically closer to the Iraqi border, put up a spirited defense. Khorramshahr fell to the advancing Iraqi forces on November 10, but only after bloody, hand-to-hand combat in the city's streets. In the battle, each side lost an estimated seven thousand men. Iraqi losses alone included about one hundred tanks and armored vehicles.[14]

The battle of Khorramshahr proved unexpectedly costly and difficult for the Iraqis.[15] Realizing he had underestimated the Iranians' resolve to fight back and the battle-readiness of their forces, and determined to keep Iraqi casualties to a minimum, Saddam decided not to try to enter the other main Iranian cities but instead to encircle each and to pursue tactical advantage by capturing key highways and strategic positions. This shift in tactics proved highly successful. Within three months of the invasion, Iraq was holding onto an estimated ten thousand square miles of Iranian territory.[16] Before long, southwestern Iran had turned into an occupied, battered land, littered with human corpses and broken-down military equipment.

Contrary to Saddam Hussein's anticipation, the war did not weaken but rather strengthened the Tehran regime by focusing nationalist sentiments on the common objective of defending the country and, by implication, supporting Ayatollah Khomeini. The Iranians, who had just been through a bloody mass revolution, had a relatively easy time channeling their still-furious anti-shah sentiments toward the new villain to their west. Moreover, with the onset of the war, Tehran's revolutionaries initially halted their purge of the military and rushed troops and equipment to the front. Even more determined, if somewhat less effective, were irregular militia volunteers called the Basij (literally, volunteers, more on which later), who were under the command of the Revolutionary Guards. In fact, Tehran's populist revolutionaries had a much easier time mobilizing resources and volunteers for the war than did Baghdad's ruling elite, many of whose soldiers were Shi'ite and thus had suspect loyalties. At the start of the war, each country had about 240,000 men in uniform. By the time the war ended in 1988, Iran's forces had grown to include some 250,000 men in the Revolutionary Guards Corps and another 350,000 in the Basij.[17] Khomeini, masterful at winning popular support through manipulating nationalist and religious symbols, now began elevating the virtues of martyrdom. His rich repertoire of revolutionary utterances soon came to include statements such as "We regard martyrdom as a great blessing, and our nation also welcomes martyrdom with open arms."[18]

After some initial setbacks, Iran scored a series of military victories beginning in the summer of 1981 and culminating in the recapture of Khorramshahr nearly a year later, in May 1982. By now, the ongoing political struggle in Tehran had led to the impeachment and removal of President Bani-Sadr (for alleged military incompetence) and greater cohesion in the Iranian military's command structure.[19] As Iran's conditions improved somewhat, for a time it seemed as if nothing was going right for the Iraqis. On June 7, 1981, Israeli warplanes bombed and destroyed a nuclear installation near Baghdad.[20] Iraqi forces were further demoralized by a terrifying tactic the Iranians first put to use in November 1981: the use of human wave attacks to clear mines, cut through barbed wires under fire, and overrun the enemy in hand-to-hand combat. These human wave attacks have been largely misconstrued in the West. "The Iranians did not merely assemble masses of individuals, point them at the enemy, and order a charge. The waves were made up of . . . twenty-two-man squads. . . . Each squad was assigned a specific objective. In battle, they would surge forward to accomplish their mission, and thus gave the impression of a human wave pouring against the enemy lines."[21] Despite the loss of untold numbers of civilian volunteers, the tactic proved highly effective in unnerving Iraqi commanders and spreading panic among their troops.[22] By the spring and summer of 1982, the momentum had clearly shifted in Iran's favor.

Iran's success at retaking Khorramshahr marked the end of the war's second phase and, in many ways, the end of Iran's brief military momentum. Buoyed by their success in the southwest, Iranian commanders mistakenly assumed that they could march into Basra, whose predominantly Shi'ite population had risen up against Saddam. But liberating one's own territory is quite different from capturing someone else's, especially if the intended target is the country's second largest city. Iraqi Shi'ites showed just about as much pro-Iranian sympathy as Iran's Arabs had demonstrated pro-Iraqi leanings. For both peoples, irrespective of ethnic or sectarian affiliations, nationalism was the overriding force. Iran's offensive proved of little value, and before long the war settled into an agonizingly long stalemate.

The third phase of the Iran-Iraq War was characterized by repeated massive Iranian assaults aimed at dislodging the Iraqis and Iraqi successes in holding onto their defensive positions. Throughout 1983 and 1984, the Iranians launched a series of attacks all along the border in hopes of at least demoralizing the Iraqi armed forces. But these had the exact opposite effect, with the Iraqis gaining in resolve and confidence as Iranian advances were either very limited or were reversed.[23] Throughout, Iran's attacks on ships carrying Iraqi oil in the Persian Gulf, and Iraq's bombardment of Iran's largest cities with its notoriously inaccurate but deadly missiles, failed to change the course of the conflict decisively.

Back in 1980, Saddam Hussein had counted on a speedy, decisive victory over Iran in no more than three weeks. As mentioned earlier, his intent had been to consolidate his position domestically and internationally and to establish complete Iraqi control over the Shatt al-Arab River. But he quickly realized he had miscalculated Iran's strength and its resolve to fight back. Within weeks of the invasion, therefore, the Iraqis asked for a cease-fire, especially as the casualties of the war, both in human life and in economic terms, began mounting. Tehran's ayatollahs had quite a different perspective on the war. They found it a convenient tool for the continued mobilization of the masses, the extension of clerical rule over the remaining organs of the state, and the elimination of their opponents. Iran, therefore, continued rejecting Iraq's demands for a cease-fire, ostensibly on the grounds that Iraq first needed to withdraw from all Iranian territories before negotiations could commence. In fact, beginning in 1983 the Iranian army appears to have devised an attrition strategy, counting on its numerical superiority to eventually wear down the Iraqis.[24] Consequently, throughout the mid-1980s the Iranians launched massive infantry assaults on Iraqi positions, often with little conclusive result. Beginning in early 1984, Iraq also used chemical weapons, specifically mustard gas and nerve agents. According to Iranian health officials, over the course of the war some sixty thousand Iranians were exposed to Iraqi chemical weapons.[25] Over fifteen thousand Iranian veterans were said to have died from illnesses related to chemical weapons in the twelve years following the end of the war with Iraq.[26]

Iran's attrition strategy did not work in the long run, and by late 1987 Iranian forces began suffering repeated military setbacks. By now, the United States and Iraq's Arab allies, especially Saudi Arabia and Kuwait, had succeeded in making Iran's regional and international position untenable. Early in 1988, Iran lost the strategic Fao peninsula, which it had captured earlier, and then lost several naval vessels in one of its frequent engagements with the U.S. Navy. In February, Iraq also unleashed chemical weapons on its own Kurdish population in the north, especially in the city of Halabje, resulting in the massacre of thousands of Kurdish civilians. Beginning with the Halabje attack, Iraqi forces used chemical weapons with unprecedented frequency, and from then on they became a regular feature of Iraq's battle order. Iranian forces were highly demoralized and, for the first time since 1982, on the defensive. The tide of the war had clearly turned in Iraq's favor. Then on July 3, an American naval cruiser operating in the Persian Gulf shot down an Iranian jetliner with 290 passengers on board. Khomeini decried that the "Great Satan" had massacred innocent Iranians on purpose. The United States called the shooting an unfortunate accident, claiming to have mistakenly identified the civilian airliner as a hostile Iranian jet fighter.[27] Two weeks later, on July 15, in order to "avoid further loss of innocent life," the Iranian leadership accepted UN Resolution 598 calling for a cessation of the hostilities and negotiations with Iraq. Now that the war had outlived its usefulness and begun to spiral out of control, Khomeini brought it to an end.

There were, of course, no winners in this bloody and devastating conflict. Not even Saddam or Khomeini could claim to have come out of the war as victors. The best each side could do was to exaggerate the damage it had inflicted on the enemy and deemphasize its own problems. Estimates put the total number of dead at 205,000 to 310,000 Iranians and 105,000 Iraqis.[28] Altogether, nearly a million people were either injured or killed. Tens of thousands of soldiers on both sides were missing in action, and untold numbers were taken prisoner of war. Tehran is estimated to have had between fifty thousand and seventy thousand Iraqi captives. Iraq's stock of Iranian POWs, believed to be smaller, was never fully determined. The war also had incalculable economic costs, running into hundreds of billions of dollars. Excluding weapons imports, Iran is estimated to have spent between $74 and $91 billion to conduct the war, and Iraq between $94 and $112 billion.[29] Iraq's economy was especially hard hit, as it was saddled with a crushing debt burden of around $89 billion, about $50 to $55 billion of which was owed to Iraq's allied neighbors to the south: Saudi Arabia, Kuwait, and the United Arab Emirates. The cost of the necessary economic reconstruction in Iraq alone was estimated at around $230 billion.[30]

Saddam Hussein, who had initially tried to insulate Iraq's general population from the effects of the war by pouring money into the economy and promising a quick victory, was now faced with one of the gravest threats to his rule. Far from consolidating his hold on power, the war had spun out of control and had left his economy crippled. Early on, Iran's ruling clerics had imposed rations on basic foodstuffs and banned the import of luxury goods, and they were thus better positioned to deal with the war's adverse economic consequences. Far from undermining them, the war had strengthened their hold on the various levers of power, and its conclusion brought no credible threat to the clerical dominance of the state or to the overall legitimacy of the Islamic Republic. The predicament of Field Marshal Saddam Hussein was quite different. His three-week victory had turned into an eight-year nightmare, and he had nothing to show for it, only hundreds of thousands of dead and injured, billions of dollars in debt, and an economy scarcely able to absorb a demobilizing army of a million men. Saddam, the wily politician with a legendary survival instinct, needed to do something and do it quickly. Within two years, he undertook yet another international adventure. This time, he invaded Kuwait.

THE SECOND GULF WAR

In the early morning hours of August 2, 1990, approximately one hundred thousand Iraqi troops stationed near the Kuwait border marched south and, in a matter of hours, occupied the small sheikhdom and its capital city, Kuwait City. Almost all members of the Kuwait ruling family, including the emir, Sheikh Jaber al-Sabah, fled to Saudi Arabia. In a few hours, Saddam once again stood at the apex of power. He had handed his generals the quick and easy victory that had eluded them for eight years in the war with Iran, and this time the rewards—the looting and plunder of one of the world's richest countries—were far more handsome and immediate. In less than a week, on August 6, Baghdad formally annexed Kuwait and declared it to be Iraq's nineteenth province. While apprehensive about the ominous consequences of such an adventure, the people of Iraq celebrated Saddam's seemingly awesome military prowess and his expansion of Iraqi territory. As foolhardy as the invasion might have seemed to the people of Iraq, few of them felt sorrow at the annexation of Kuwait, which many considered an artificial, colonial creation anyway. Kuwait now belonged to Iraq, and both firmly belonged to Saddam Hussein.

The Iraqi invasion of Kuwait followed months of mounting tensions between Iraq on the one hand and its southern neighbors and the United States on the other. Saddam apparently had started preparing for his southward invasion shortly after the formal conclusion of the war with Iran. By the time the Iran-Iraq War finally ended, the peoples of the two countries were both worn down and eager to get on with their lives. As Chapter 5 demonstrated, the Iranian state, in response to a general desire for social and political relaxation, undertook an extensive program of economic reconstruction and ushered in what amounted to a Second Republic. Such was not the case in Iraq, however, for Saddam Hussein's increasing political desperation ruled out domestic or diplomatic normalcy. For a few weeks in the spring of 1990, he floated talk of instituting democratic institutions,

Figure 12. Iraqi female police officers stand to attention during their graduation ceremony at the Baghdad Police College. Photo courtesy of Getty Images.

even going through the formalities of holding new elections to the National Assembly and inaugurating a new constitution. But democracy cramped Saddam's style, and before long the new constitution was suspended and even the pretence of acting democratically was set aside. Instead, Saddam decided to divert domestic attention by pointing to a host of international conspiracies against Iraq, this time hatched not by the Iranians but by the United States, Israel, and their Persian Gulf allies—Saudi Arabia, Kuwait, and the United Arab Emirates.

Early in 1990, several foreign banks are said to have estimated that Iraq would finish the year bankrupt, owing some $8 to $10 billion to foreign creditors.[31] Not surprisingly, Saddam demanded that Kuwait pay Iraq $10 billion and cancel the debt it had accumulated during the war with Iran. At the meeting of the Arab Cooperation Council in February, he is reported to have said, "I need $30 billion in fresh money, and if they don't give it to me, I will know how to get it."[32] While the saber rattling against Kuwait continued, Saddam turned his attention to Iraq's other new enemies. He intensified his verbal attacks on Israel; charged an Iranian-born British journalist with spying and executed him; and accused the UAE and Kuwait of conspiring to harm Iraqi interests. Saddam shortly added territorial encroachments by Kuwait to his list of complaints.

Both the UAE and Kuwait undertook a number of conciliatory gestures—Kuwait, for example, announced cutting its oil output by some 25 percent—but to no avail. The Egyptian president, Hosni Mubarak, sought to act as a mediator and for a while appeared to have succeeded in easing Iraqi-Kuwait tensions. But Saddam had already made up his mind. By the time the sun rose over the hot sands of Kuwait on the morning of August 2, Iraq's army was in control of most parts of the small country. By two o'clock that afternoon, Kuwait City had fallen.

What ensued can best be described as a "war of miscalculations." Every party in the unfolding conflict misread the situation and miscalculated the intentions, the resolve, and the strength of its opponent. The Iraqi leadership completely miscalculated the international community's reaction to its occupation of Kuwait and its resolve to restore to the Kuwaitis their sovereignty. Baghdad also miscalculated its own strength, believing that it could inflict serious damage on the American-led military alliance. Moreover, Iraqi leaders misread the public mood in the United States, thinking that the memory of the Vietnam War would erode popular support for another open-ended military engagement. What Baghdad did not realize was that after some twenty years the memory of the Vietnam War had grown faint among the younger generation of Americans, for whom the Reagan-Bush years—punctuated by the release of the hostages in Tehran and military victories in Grenada and Panama—had resulted in a resurgence of patriotism and renewed national self-confidence. For an American public yearning for a victory that would decisively erase the painful memory of Vietnam, and for a Pentagon eager to display its new hardware and smart weapons, the prospect of fighting a distant, evil dictator was too tempting to pass up. Saddam, as he himself soon discovered, was barking up the wrong tree. That Kuwait was one of the world's largest producers of oil only added to the resolve of the hastily assembled "Allied Forces" to press for the small sheikhdom's liberation.

As it turned out, the Iraqi armed forces were suffering from three basic, mortal flaws. First, throughout the war with Iran, the Iraqi military had exhibited weaknesses in planning, coordination, and strategy. By and large, these difficulties had arisen out of Saddam Hussein's personal involvement in military decision making and his penchant for micromanaging his field commanders.[33] Second, the Iraqi army was far more battle-fatigued than battle-tested. The eight-year war with Iran, for which the Iraqis were neither economically nor psychologically prepared, had been a bigger drain on Iraq than either Saddam or his adversaries initially realized. When it came time to fight, Iraqi soldiers showed little actual resolve to stand firm, and many started surrendering en masse. Some even surrendered themselves to Western journalists whom they mistook for military personnel. The sustained and highly effective carpet bombing of Iraqi defenses in the first few days of the conflict quickly impressed upon the Iraqis that their new adversaries were far more deadly than the beleaguered, undersupplied Iranians they had faced earlier. Fighting the new enemy meant almost certain death and very little chance of survival, never mind victory.

A third, even more fundamental problem faced the Iraqis. Because Iraq was a developing country, its military capabilities and ensuing military doctrine were largely defined by, and limited to, its overall position within the world system. For the Iraqis, it was one thing to take on another Third World country next door but quite another to pick a fight with a super-power. The Iran-Iraq War had featured heavy reliance on the infantry and on trench warfare. It had even seen many vicious hand-to-hand combats. But the new adversary relied not on infantry troops but on smart bombs released from hundreds of miles away. Trenches, troop concentrations, fortified bunkers, and other usual features of conventional warfare were now either obsolete or, in many instances, liabilities. In addition to heavy reliance on chemical weapons, many of Iraq's battle successes against Iran had become possible only after the United States had shared satellite intelligence with the Iraqi military.[34] Now the former patron was itself the enemy. Saddam's archaic military thinking did little to compensate for the comparative technological inferiority of his armed forces.

The lopsided nature of the conflict became apparent from its earliest days, when Iraqi defenses began collapsing like a house of cards. By the time the war was over, 142,000 tons of bombs had been dropped on Iraq and Kuwait. More than one hundred thousand Iraqi soldiers were reported to have been killed, and another sixty thousand surrendered. Fully 3,700 Iraqi tanks were destroyed, as were 2,400 armored vehicles and 2,600 artillery pieces. The only way the Iraqi air force was able to escape widespread destruction was by flying the bulk of its jet fighters, as many as 135, to neighboring Iran after a hastily arranged cooperation agreement. By contrast, American casualties numbered no more than 148 dead, 35 of them by "friendly fire." Fifty-seven American jet fighters and helicopters were also shot down, but not a single American tank was lost.[35]

Eventually, the U.S.-led coalition grew to include some thirty-six countries, although its principal contributors remained the United States, Great Britain, and Saudi Arabia.[36] In theory, the United States and Saudi Arabia were in joint command of the operation. In reality, however, the whole affair was an American endeavor. An important aspect of the operation was that it featured the contributions of Arab states outside the Persian Gulf area, most notably Egypt, Syria, and Morocco. Saddam's invasion of Kuwait placed Arab leaders in the unenviable position of having to either join the military coalition against Iraq or, by staying away, appear to support its occupation of Kuwait. The invasion of Kuwait, it must be remembered, was not all that unpopular among Arabs outside the Arabian peninsula. The invasion and the tensions leading up to it happened to coincide with the daily death of a number of Palestinians in street clashes with Israeli soldiers and a flaring up of the *intifada* movement. In light of America's unwavering support for Israeli statehood and territorial expansion, the mounting of Operation Desert Shield seemed to most Arabs utterly hypocritical. The United States, many reasoned, had done nothing to stop or to reverse Israel's invasion of Lebanon in 1982 or its continued expansion of settlements in Palestinian territories. But it was now rushing to the aid of a corrupt ruling family with vast oil resources. Throughout the region, from Jordan to Egypt and Morocco, anti-American, pro-Iraqi rallies were held, and political leaders had no choice but to let the people vent their anger. Popular passions were further inflamed when Saddam made his withdrawal from Kuwait contingent on Israel's withdrawal from occupied Palestinian territories. Jordan's King Hussein, sensing the depth of his people's anger, declared his neutrality and offered to mediate between Saddam and the Kuwaiti ruling family. The PLO openly sided with Iraq. Most others, however, cast their lot with the United States, suppressed serious dissent at home, and, lured by the prospects of American economic assistance and subsidized oil from the Persian Gulf, sent troops to Saudi Arabia. In a contentious meeting held in Cairo a week after the invasion, the Arab League voted twelve to three, with two abstentions, to join the Desert Shield alliance.[37]

Operation Desert Storm was launched on January 16, 1991, with a massive aerial bombardment of Iraqi troop fortifications in Kuwait and throughout Iraq itself. Within a week, the Iraqi ground forces were decimated; the lucky ones who had the chance surrendered. Civilians were also hit, and the tragic bombing of a civilian shelter in Baghdad on February 13 led to the deaths of more than one thousand individuals. Washington claimed that the shelter had actually been a command and control facility.[38] To expand the war and to give credence to his anti-Israeli credentials, two days after the war started, on January 18, Saddam ordered the firing of twelve SCUD missiles at Tel Aviv. Four days later, another three were fired, this time killing three Israeli civilians and injuring scores of others. Uncharacteristically, Israel refrained from retaliating, impressed upon by the Americans that to do so would play into the Iraqi leader's hands.[39]

Five weeks after the aerial bombardment commenced, by which time little fighting spirit or capacity was left in the Iraqi forces, on February 24,

Figure 13. Iraqi forces on the "highway of death."

the allied forces launched a multipronged ground offensive to dislodge what was left of Saddam's forces. The road from Kuwait back into Iraq was cut off, and thousands of fleeing Iraqi troops were strafed and carpet bombed. For forty hours, Highway 80, the main link between Basra and Kuwait, became the "highway of death" as orders were given, in the words of one U.S. officer, "to find anything that was moving and take it out."[40] Finally, on February 27, Iraq accepted UN Resolutions 660, 662, and 674, which declared the Iraqi annexation of Kuwait null and void and deemed it responsible for war reparations. The following day, both sides agreed to a cease-fire and hostilities ceased. The ground war had lasted only one hundred hours.

The end of the war brought Saddam one of the most serious challenges to his rule, not from his military commanders but from Iraq's two main religious and ethnic minorities, the Shi'ites in the south and the Kurds in the north. Iraq is one of the Middle East's most ethnically and religiously heterogeneous countries. Approximately 15 percent of Iraqis are ethnic Kurds. Moreover, Shi'ites constitute some 50 percent of the total population (the rest are about 40 percent Sunnis and 10 percent members of various Christian sects). Saddam's relations with these two long-suppressed minorities had long been marked by friction and frequent bouts of violence.[41] As soon as the war ended and Baghdad's central authority was at its nadir, they found the opportunity to rebel against Saddam and his state.

Two major uprisings started in the northern and southern parts of the country, where the Kurds and the Shi'ites predominated, respectively. The close proximity of the Shi'ite regions to Iran made their control more pressing for the government. Beginning in early March, Iraq's regrouped forces, or what remained of them, launched a massive, brutal campaign to regain the south. Without the foreign assistance they had believed would be forthcoming, the Shi'ite rebels, with little military training and poorly equipped, quickly succumbed to Saddam's forces. The Iraqi leader then turned his attention to the north, where, within weeks of the cease-fire, Kurdish rebels had gained control over twelve major towns and cities. By the month's end, most of the north was also recaptured, but not before an estimated one hundred thousand Kurds had been killed.[42]

The international community's condemnation of the massacre of Iraqi Kurds and their mass expulsion to Iran and Turkey was slow in coming, but it eventually did come. Soon the United States and Britain declared the establishment of a "safe haven" for the Kurds in northern Iraq and prohibited Iraq from flying fixed-wing aircraft, presumably jet fighters, in a southern and northern "no fly zone." A de facto partition of Iraq went into effect, with the Kurdish north outside the government's reach. Elsewhere in Iraq, however, Saddam's rule remained unshakable. After years of bickering and finger-pointing, even the UN inspection teams, which had been sent to supervise the dismantling of Iraq's chemical weapons program, left the country because of the United Nations' frustration in dealing with Baghdad.

Once it was all over, Saddam Hussein was still standing, unfazed by the torment he had caused millions of people. Kanan Makiya, an Iraqi human rights activist, eloquently described the situation of Iraq after the Kuwait invasion:

> The state that the Ba'th built in Iraq is far worse than one purely built on confessional or ethnic criteria. It is worse because it is consistently egalitarian in its hostility to everything that is not itself. The Ba'th demand from all Iraqis absolute conformity with their violence-filled, conspiratorial view of a world permanently at war with itself. Saddam Hussein invents and reinvents his enemies from the entire mass of human material that is at his disposal; he thrives on the distrust, suspicion, and conspiratorialism which his regime actively inculcates in everyone; he positively expects to breed hate and a thirst for revenge in Sunni and Shi'i alike. As a consequence civil society, attacked from every direction, has virtually collapsed in Iraq.[43]

Figure 14. Shi'ite Iraqi women mourn after the Gulf War in 1991.

Saddam's "republic of fear" was not to last indefinitely, however. In 2003, the Iraqi regime succumbed to an all-out invasion and occupation of the country by the United States. Under the banner of "war on terror," President George W. Bush vowed to effect "regime change" in a country he had branded as a member of an "axis of evil." By mid-2003, Saddam's regime was a thing of the past, and Iraq was being run by American occupying forces.

THE POST–GULF WAR MIDDLE EAST

The Second Gulf War turned out to be a major watershed in the international relations of the Middle East. The Gulf War put a definitive end to any doubts concerning the death of Arab unity that had remained after Sadat's defection from the "Arab cause" in the mid- to late 1970s. Pan-Arabism had suffered its first serious blow as far back as 1967, when the hollow rhetoric of Arab prowess cost each of the Arab participants large pieces of strategic territory. In hindsight, the wounds of 1967 turned out to be mortal, but their lethal effects took decades to materialize. Propaganda aside, the 1973 War was not really designed either to liberate the Palestinians or to vindicate the larger Arab nation. Its main goal was to enhance the position from which Egypt could negotiate the return of the Sinai and Syria could reclaim the Golan. By the time the 1970s were ending, the "focused system" that Nasser had so meticulously crafted had begun fragmenting along multiple axes.[44] Egypt was isolated; the oil monarchies sought shelter under the protective umbrella of the United States; Syria, Iraq, and Libya, with their own internal discords, clung to an increasingly irrelevant rejectionist position in relation to Israel; Jordan was mastering its perennial balancing act; and Algeria and Morocco were grappling with their own mounting political and economic difficulties. Even the interlude of the 1980s, featuring the menace of the common Iranian enemy, failed to rekindle the once vibrant united Arab alliance. Syria remained supportive of Iran throughout, lured by generous Iranian oil, and Libya and Oman also remained on friendly terms with Tehran's radical clerics.[45] A measure of unity did develop in the cause of defending against Iran's revolutionary Shi'ism, but that too dissipated within a couple of years. By 1990, the Arab world was arrayed against one of its own members. Iraq's brutal "rape of a sister country" had to be stopped, no matter what the costs.[46]

For the following decade, from 1991 until the fateful day of September 11, 2001, the Middle East was utterly fragmented, with each state motivated by self-interest and realpolitik. Even the alliance against Iraq during and immediately after the invasion of Kuwait, hailed by the few remaining Pan-Arabist apologists and hopefuls as a manifestation of Arab unity, came together out of individual national-interest calculations rather than lofty ideals of defending Kuwait sovereignty, let alone saving the larger Arab family from a wayward son.[47] The Arab world of the 1990s suffered from internal discord, deepening dependence on international aid providers (Egypt and Morocco) and Western trading partners (the oil monarchies of the Arabian peninsula), and the sudden loss of the Soviet backing with which it could once balance out American influence (Syria). The United States was now the only game in town, and the American president, with his own domestic concerns, was determined to teach Saddam a lesson. Even Jordan's refusal to join the international coalition against Iraq was motivated by self-interest. King Hussein, always one step ahead of his domestic and foreign opponents, knew well that he could not risk further antagonizing his subjects, who had only recently taken part in troubling "bread riots." Among Americans, Jordan's image was tarnished only temporarily, but among Arab peoples it was enhanced. President Bush's much heralded New World Order, for the Middle East at least, meant furthering national self-interest under the auspices of American hegemony.

The 1990s featured several significant events, each of which directly influenced Middle East diplomacy: the start of Iran's Second Republic; Iraq's de facto truncation; the Palestinian-Israeli signing of the Oslo Accords in 1993; Jordan's 1994 peace treaty with Israel; the Algerian and Sudanese civil wars; and increasing competition over oil production and pricing within OPEC, and between OPEC and nonmember oil producers such as Norway and Mexico. At the global level, meanwhile, the young Russian republic had its own economic and political growing pains, being preoccupied with a dysfunctional economy and an uncontrollable breakaway movement in Chechnya. The United States had neither a coherent vision nor a mean-ingfully articulated policy toward the Middle East. At best, Washington's Middle East policy was geographically limited. Under the rubric of "dual containment," the Clinton administration sought to narrow the options open to Iraq and Iran, America's most vocal adversaries, in order to ulti-mately bring about a regime change in Baghdad and policy shifts in Tehran (especially toward the Palestinian-Israeli peace process).[48] Nevertheless, as Chapter 7 demonstrates, the Clinton administration did become deeply involved in Palestinian-Israeli negotiations near the end of the decade.

There was, quite simply, no common cause around which to rally, no common enemies to unite against, no liberating hero to follow in unison. There were other, more substantial reasons for Arab unity's demise. Three stand out. First, the Arab world of the 1990s lacked a hegemonic core under whose auspices notions of Pan-Arabism could be reinvigorated and made accessible for the Arab masses at large. Since the 1950s, this historical role had been Egypt's, as was almost natural given that country's history, size, population, and heritage. But who would claim Arab leadership once Egypt was gone? And this was not just any ordinary departure. Sadat had *betrayed* the Arab cause; consequently the Arab League, the very symbol of Arab unity, was moved from Cairo to Tunis, and Egypt was expelled from it. Qaddafi did try to succeed Nasser, but he turned out to be too far from the Arab heartland, too erratic, and, once attacked by an American air raid in 1986, quickly silenced. Iraq would have been a far more likely can-didate than Libya by virtue of its geographic position and its history, but its leader was too rapacious of the Arab family to be trusted. As for Saudi Arabia and its conservative Persian Gulf allies, whose economic power and closeness to the United States after the Gulf War were second only to Israel's, they were in no position to initiate such a regionally hegemonic bid: besides money, they had almost none of the other necessary ingredi-ents for such an endeavor—not enough manpower, no popularity outside their small countries, no salient heritage outside the Arabian peninsula (besides Islam), and no ideological tools.[49]

A second, equally important reason for the near-complete eclipse of Arab unity in the 1990s was the disappearance of a common Arab *identity* as a viable source of trans-state unity. We saw in Chapter 3 how nationalism in the Middle East has developed different historical layers that sometimes complement and sometimes compete with one another—from Ottomanism to Pan-Arabism to territorially defined nationalisms. Political elites, whether based in imperial Istanbul or in the capitals of sovereign and independent states, have always played a pivotal role in articulating and popularizing each of these different layers of nationalism. By the waning decades of the twentieth century, the exigencies of political institutionalization and legitimacy prompted more and more state elites to articulate nationalism in terms of territorially specific, state patriotism. As the political scientist Michael Barnett observes, "Arab states have had strikingly different views of the desired [regional order]. . . . Although such differences might be attributed to principled beliefs, the more prominent reasons were regime interests, beginning with but not exhausted by survival and domestic stability. As a consequence, over the years Arab leaders have vied to draw a line between the regimes' interests, the norms of Arabism, and the events of the day."[50] Arab identity, with its own multiple layers of complexity, has not completely dissipated as a factor in foreign policy making.[51] But it is only *one* of the factors, and today it is evoked almost always only when it serves regime purposes.

A third and final reason for the precipitous decline of Pan-Arabism after the Second Gulf War has to do with the absence of viable institutions that could sustain and nurture such a trans-state phenomenon in the face of increasingly narrow, state-centered loyalties. In other words, once Pan-Arabist champions like Nasser were gone or exposed as false prophets (Sadat and Saddam Hussein), there were no institutions to fill the vacuum. For several decades, two overlapping institutions had operated to reinforce Pan-Arabism. One was the official institution of the League of Arab States (the Arab League), originally established in 1945, and the other was the summit system, which Nasser inaugurated in 1964. By the 1980s, the popular excitement and sense of solidarity that both the Arab League and various summits once generated had all but dissipated, victim to the many broken lofty promises and frequent boycotts by the more radical leaders. The league itself was paralyzed. From 1990 to 1996, at a time when momentous developments like the Oslo Accords were taking place, the Arab League did not hold a single summit.[52]

Amid the disunity of the 1990s, there nevertheless did appear one proposal for region-wide unity in the Middle East. It came, of all places, from Israel. The proposal, under the label "New Middle East," came from one of Israel's professional politicians, Shimon Peres. In 1993, fresh from signing the historic Oslo Accords with the Palestinians, Peres outlined his vision of a peaceful, economically integrated Middle East: "Maintaining the present situation is pointless, and . . . the status quo cannot continue in any case. Recognizing the hard truth is a criterion for the success of the peace process—without victors, without victims. War does not solve any problems; peace is the solution. As the results of our accord with Egypt have shown, we can have a peaceful relationship with our neighbors. By compromising—minimum concessions and maximum justice on both sides—we will live to see the day when nations are free of the sorrow of war, including our own nation as well."[53]

Before long, however, Peres, who was Israel's foreign minister at the time, was out of office, and the Oslo Accords were set adrift by the larger vagaries of the Palestinian-Israeli conflict. When in November 1997 Israel attended the fourth annual Middle East and North Africa Economic Conference in Doha, Qatar—an event that could have given substance to Peres's vision—most Arab countries boycotted the conference in protest over Israeli Prime Minister Netanyahu's actions in the Occupied Territories. By the end of the year 2000, the Al-Aqsa *intifada*—the second bloody uprising in the Palestinian territories against Israeli occupation—had all but erased any hopes for peaceful coexistence and regional economic cooperation.

The decline in the salience of Pan-Arabism has had two profound consequences for the Middle East. To begin with, the "Arab system," which had become "centerless" in the 1980s, shattered into pieces in the 1990s.[54] Instead, from a balance-of-power perspective, two non-Arab state actors gained increasing military and hence diplomatic dominance over the region: Israel and Turkey.[55] The region's emerging international architecture has turned the Arab-Israeli conflict steadily into the Palestinian-Israeli conflict. As a result, Israel's policies in relation to the Palestinians since the 1990s have lacked some of the constraints they would have had if the Egyptians, the Jordanians, the Syrians, or others had been involved. As for Turkey, Iraq's northern neighbor and a regional powerhouse among the Central Asian republics, the Gulf War allowed it to regain the position of strategic importance that it was beginning to lose by the Cold War's end. As if to make a deliberate point of their growing ascendancy, in the late 1990s and early years of the new century Turkey and Israel entered into a series of unprecedented military and economic alliances. They held joint military maneuvers, expanded economic trade, and further cemented their diplomatic friendship. Meanwhile, in the Arab world, we saw the emergence of what one scholar has called a "balance of weakness." "Mutual recriminations of 'stoogism,' 'treason,' and 'adventurism' as well as vendettas still linger on [all] sides. In a word, Arab society is seriously bruised, with the marks likely to remain for a long time. This is not a political or psychological context conducive to partnership."[56]

A second, related consequence of the decline of Pan-Arabism has been the increasing rate at which political Islam as an alternative has grown over the last decade or so. Political Islam did not emerge in the aftermath of the Gulf War; its roots are much deeper, and its genealogy is much older. Neither are its causes and consequences found only in international developments; every Middle Eastern country has had its own, home-brewed Islamic movement.[57] But with the steady decline of Arab unity as a salient form of collective identity, there has been an inverse rise in the popularity of political Islam in all its manifestations—reformist, fundamentalist, populist, domestic, and transnational. It was no accident that political Islam—and, more precisely, Islamic fundamentalism—instigated the next political convulsion involving the Middle East: the attacks of September 11, 2001.

SEPTEMBER 11 AND ITS AFTERMATH

On a clear and balmy Tuesday morning in late summer 2001, life in New York City was changed forever when at 8:45 A.M. a jetliner full of passengers flew into one of the two main towers of the giant World Trade Center. Twenty minutes later, a second plane flew into the Trade Center's other tower. Within an hour, the two 110-story skyscrapers collapsed, burying nearly three thousand civilians working there and the hundreds of police and firefighters who had rushed to their rescue. Less than an hour later, another passenger plane crashed into the Pentagon building in Washington, D.C., killing all aboard and some 190 employees of the U.S. Defense Department. A fourth jetliner crashed in a field in Somerset County, Pennsylvania, again with no survivors.

It was quickly learned that all four planes had been hijacked and used as flying bombs. The Pennsylvania plane had apparently been intended for the White House, but its passengers had struggled with the hijackers and had forced the plane to crash far from its intended target. America was shocked and bewildered, attacked out of nowhere, for no apparent reason. For the first time in living memory, what seemed like a coordinated attack on American civilians had taken place on the American mainland—on

America's heartland in Pennsylvania, on its military might in the capital, and on its economy in New York City.

All fingers pointed to the Middle East, this time with justification. A few years earlier, in 1995, when the Murrah Federal Building in Oklahoma City had been bombed, many Americans had suspected a Middle East connection, only to discover that the attack had been the work of domestic terrorists. But this was no Oklahoma City. The September 11 events had all the hallmarks of earlier attacks on the World Trade Center in 1993 (this one with very limited success) and on other American targets abroad—in Somalia in 1993, in Saudi Arabia in 1995 and 1996, in Kenya and Tanzania in 1998, and in Yemen in 2000—which had all been linked to a wealthy Saudi national named Osama bin Laden. Attacked so callously, the American public demanded retribution and revenge. Whoever the culprits were behind the attacks—whether bin Laden or the people who gave him shelter and refuge, or anyone else directly or indirectly involved—had to be brought to justice.

With American patriotism at an all-time high, the new administration in Washington had to act quickly and decisively. President George W. Bush had come to office following a questionable election the previous November. The "accidental president," for whom some 75 percent of the American electorate had either actively or passively not voted, could now ill afford to be seen as weak.[58] Almost immediately, the president declared that the United States was engaged in a "war on terrorism." Within a month, American military forces and equipment had been deployed in their efforts to defeat the network of terror that had wreaked such havoc in September. The primary targets were bin Laden, his organization, called Al-Qaeda, and his hosts in Afghanistan, the Taliban. The war in Afghanistan, code-named Operation Enduring Freedom by the U.S. Central Command, was to start a new chapter in the political history of the Middle East.

The shape of the world order to emerge in the aftermath of September 11, and more specifically the roles of the United States and the Middle East within that order, are still not fully clear, at least as of this writing. Nevertheless, some of the more noticeable trends that point to an emerging global order in relation to the Middle East are highlighted below. For now, it is important to ask *why* the attacks of September 11 occurred. In particular, why was the United States the target? To blame the attacks on Islamic fundamentalism is, at best, simplistic. The culprits were, of course, Islamic fundamentalists. In Chapter 9 we examine why and how Islamic fundamentalism has spread in the Middle East over the past couple of decades. But why did the fundamentalist disciples of bin Laden choose to attack the United States?

The answer is found in the exercise of American foreign policy in relation to the Middle East, both historically and especially after the Gulf War. By virtue of its position as a global superpower, and after the end of the Cold War the *only* superpower, the United States provoked the anger and resentment of many Middle Easterners by its policies and agendas throughout the world, especially in the strategically important Middle East. Following the Gulf War, American involvement in the Middle East became more pervasive than at almost any other time in the past, with the U.S. Navy maintaining a seemingly permanent presence in the Persian Gulf and American troops stationed in Kuwait, Saudi Arabia, and Bahrain. This new "pax Americana" was sure to inflame the simmering anger of the economically frustrated, politically repressed Middle Easterners. They channeled this anger toward local rulers and their powerful patron, the United States. Throughout the 1980s and 1990s, the deepening penetration of the Middle East by the United States provoked increasing anti-Americanism. As the scholar Fouad Ajami has keenly observed, "From one end of the Arab world to the other, the drumbeats of anti-Americanism had been steady. But the drummers could have hardly known what was to come. The magnitude of the horror that befell the United States on Tuesday, September 11, 2001, appeared for a moment to embarrass and silence them. The American imperium in the Arab-Muslim world hatched a monster."[59]

America's role in the Middle East after the Gulf War was an outgrowth of its pursuits in the region as far back as the late 1940s. American policy toward the Middle East since World War II has all too often been incoherent, reactive, and inconsistent. Nevertheless, it is possible to discern three primary objectives or guidelines that have generally informed U.S. policy toward the Middle East: maintaining the region's territorial status quo in terms of the post-1948 boundaries; securing relatively easy access to the region's vast oil resources; and containing the threat posed to U.S. interests by regional or global rivals, whether that threat came from the former Soviet Union during the Cold War or from Iran and Iraq afterward. The degree to which successive administrations in Washington have succeeded in defending U.S. interests in the Middle East has varied greatly from president to president or, in volatile Middle Eastern politics, from year to year. The Carter administration, for example, started off on a high note in terms of its Middle East policy thanks to the Camp David Accords, but it ended with (and because of) the Iran hostage crisis. The one factor that has remained almost always consistent throughout each of the U.S. presidencies, however, has been the resentment that American policies have caused among many average Arab and Muslim Middle Easterners. These individuals by no means have been a majority of the population, but they often have been vocal, determined, and at times violently radical.

To better understand the causal relationship between American foreign policy and the prevalence of anti-American sentiments in the Middle East, we should look more closely at the consequences of each American policy objective in the region. Let us begin with the goal of maintaining the Middle East's territorial status quo. For American policy makers, this has basically meant unqualified support for Israel, whose international boundaries have been subject to the most recent changes. To be certain, some American presidents and policy makers have adopted a more balanced, less lopsided policy toward the Palestinian-Israeli question.[60] Presidents Franklin D. Roosevelt, Eisenhower, Nixon, Carter, and George H. Bush at one point or another in their presidencies tried to initiate policies that were sensitive to Palestinian and Arab aspirations. By and large, however, attention to the predicament of the Palestinians has paled in comparison to the amount and nature of support the United States has provided to Israel, which by some accounts hovers around $3 to $4 billion a year in assistance.[61]

The "special relationship" between the United States and Israel arises from the "general familiarity with the Jews that exists in America."[62] More specifically, Jewish and non-Jewish Americans who support Israel have been quite successful in lobbying U.S. policy makers in the executive and legislative branches to ensure their sustained support for Israel. The power of the American Israel Public Affairs Committee (AIPAC) is said to be unsurpassed by that of any other lobby group in Washington. According to a former U.S. congressman, "It is no overstatement to say that AIPAC has effectively gained control of virtually all of Capitol Hill's actions on Middle East policy. Almost without exception, House and Senate members do its bidding, because most of them consider AIPAC to be the direct Capitol Hill representative that can make or break their chances at election time."[63]

The Palestinian cause might have been repeatedly exploited by Middle Eastern politicians for their own narrow political purposes, but it remains popular among the peoples of the Middle East at large. There is a widespread perception that the Palestinians have been wronged, that their rights and aspirations have been constantly trampled on by Israel, and that the United States directly contributes to the injustice meted out to them on a routine basis. With the spread to more of the Middle East of conventional and new media—the Internet and satellite television stations such as Al-Jazeera—more and more Middle Easterners see wrenching images of the conflict: Palestinian homes demolished, Israeli tanks and troops "mopping up" in the West Bank, Palestinians arrested en masse. According to recent public opinion polls, a consistently large percentage of Arabs believe that the United States and Israel have mutual interests in the region (from 2006 to 2009, on average 38 percent) or that Israel is a tool of U.S. foreign policy (25 percent).[64]

Worse yet, many Middle Easterners see the United States as directly responsible for the frustration of their own political aspirations. America's other strategic objectives—checking the influence of adversaries and ensuring the open flow of oil to the West—have meant close support for and alliance with Middle Eastern leaders who have not always been terribly popular at home. The realpolitik calculations on which U.S. foreign and security policies have been based have seldom found congruence with the ideals and aspirations of the peoples of the Middle East. In fact, in the 2006 Annual Arab Public Opinion Survey, conducted in six countries (Egypt, Jordan, Lebanon, Morocco, Saudi Arabia, and the UAE), fully 72 percent of those surveyed saw the United States as the biggest threat to them, second only to Israel, seen by 85 percent as the biggest threat.[65]

Ensuring the open flow of oil, for example, has meant supporting the corrupt and repressive royal family of Saudi Arabia and turning a blind eye to its blatant disregard of human rights. Up until the late 1970s, it also meant supporting the equally corrupt and repressive shah of Iran. Anwar Sadat, America's "man of peace" in the Middle East, was hardly thought of in such terms in his own country. Most Egyptians feared and despised him.

The patron-client relationships between the United States and pro-Western Middle Eastern leaders have cost the United States. When it works, patronage has its advantages. But when it fails, those who feel wronged by the client may turn on the patron. American political patronage in the Middle East has been additional fuel for anti-Americanism. In 2008, for example, 83 percent of those polled in the Annual Arab Public Opinion Survey expressed unfavorable attitudes toward the United States, though that percentage was lowered to 77 percent in 2009 with the coming to office of President Barack Obama.[66]

U.S. foreign policy objectives toward the Middle East did not change in the aftermath of the Gulf War. In fact, they remained very much the same. What did change was the way the United States carried them out. With intraregional relations characterized by a "balance of weakness," with the Soviet Union dead, and with the unpredictable Saddam Hussein still in power, U.S. involvement in the Middle East became far more direct and substantively more in depth. In 1990, the United States secured access to naval and air bases in several of the Gulf Cooperation Council (GCC) countries, acquired the right to preposition war matériel there, started frequent combined military exercises with GCC members, and was guaranteed access to Persian Gulf oil at "acceptable" prices.[67] Also, as part of the "dual containment" policy, the United States spearheaded the imposition of economic sanctions on Iraq under the auspices of the United Nations. The sanctions did little to weaken Saddam's hold on power but made life for ordinary Iraqis even harsher. Again, pictures of suffering Iraqis and the American armada "patrolling" the waters of the Persian Gulf were beamed into Middle Eastern living rooms. The expansive pax Americana only added to the already deepening feelings of anti-Americanism. Osama bin Laden was the most radical and monstrous face of a pervasive, far less violent wave of resentment against the United States in the Middle East.

Bin Laden's journey to violent fundamentalism started back in 1980, when, at twenty-three, he joined the Mujahedeen Afghan guerrillas who were fighting against occupying Soviet troops. Soon after the Soviet Union invaded Afghanistan in December 1979, many young Arabs volunteered to join the Afghan Mujahedeen in their struggle against the "Godless communists." Initially, President Sadat encouraged Egyptian militants to go join the fight in Afghanistan, hoping to appear as a champion of Islam and at the same time get rid of potential troublemakers at home.[68] In the mid-1980s, the CIA and the Pakistani intelligence service, the ISI, also started to actively encourage Islamic militants from throughout the region to join the Afghan fighters in their increasingly bloody campaign against the Soviet occupation. By the time the Soviets withdrew in 1989, an estimated one hundred thousand militant Muslims from forty-three countries in the Middle East, North and East Africa, Central Asia, and the Far East had somehow been involved in the Afghan fight against Soviet forces.[69]

Bin Laden was one of the so-called Afghan Arabs. Born to wealthy parents in Saudi Arabia, in the 1980s he settled in the Pakistani city of Peshawar near the Afghan border, from where, with CIA blessing, he oversaw the financing and construction of roads and tunnel complexes inside Afghanistan used for storage and as bases for military operations. He also established a shadowy group called Al-Qaeda (the Base). Initially, Al-Qaeda served as a service center and clearinghouse for many of the Arab fighters who found their way from Pakistan to Afghanistan. Soon, however, the organization became a military and guerrilla training camp and a base of support for bin Laden.

Following the Gulf War, bin Laden was incensed by the stationing of U.S. troops on Saudi soil, offering the royal family to guard the kingdom with his own militia instead. His proposal was rejected, and, fearing his increasing militancy, the Saudi government forced him to leave the country in 1992 and stripped him of his citizenship in 1994.[70] Bin Laden lived in the Sudan from 1992 to 1996, when, after pressure from the Khartoum government, he left for Afghanistan. There he allied himself with one of the more fanatical factions of the Mujahedeen called the Taliban. This happened to coincide with the Taliban's steady advances in the Afghan civil war, which had erupted among the various Mujahedeen factions shortly after the Soviet departure. Hence was fostered the Al-Qaeda alliance with the Taliban. Meanwhile, having identified the United States as the primary enemy of the Muslim people everywhere, bin Laden embarked on his deadly terrorist campaign against American interests and targets around the world: the suicide bombing of the Khobar military tower in Riyadh, Saudi Arabia, in 1996; the attacks on U.S. embassies in Tanzania and Kenya in 1998; the bombing of the *USS Cole* in Aden, Yemen, in 2000; and the September 11 attacks in 2001.

The American response to the attacks of September 11 gave shape and direction to an emerging "Bush Doctrine." Since President Bush had been in office for only eight months before the attacks, before September 2001 the main principles of the Bush Doctrine had been only loosely articulated: unabashed American unilateralism in global affairs; reliance on tactical nuclear weapons; and the creation of a national missile defense system.[71] Following the attacks, U.S. national security strategy became much sharper and more focused on the interrelated concepts of "prevention" and "preemption."[72] Accordingly, the U.S. administration gave the international community a simple choice: "In the war on terrorism, you're either with us or against us." The following January, delivering his annual State of the Union address, President Bush outlined his vision in greater detail: "Many nations are acting forcefully [to combat terrorism]. . . . But some governments are timid in the face of terror. And make no mistake about it: if they do not act, America will." Branding Iran, Iraq, and North Korea as members of an "axis of evil" that threatened American interests around the world, the president issued a clear warning: "All nations should know: America will do what is necessary to ensure our nation's security."[73]

If Osama bin Laden thought that by attacking the United States he would force the Americans to withdraw their bases from Saudi Arabia, he was mistaken. In fact, the exact opposite took place. The pax Americana of the post–Gulf War era was geographically expanded and militarily deepened. The American-led war in Afghanistan did not take long to topple the Taliban regime in Kabul and to send Al-Qaeda running for cover in caves

Figure 15. Osama bin Laden's videotaped messages were broadcast on Al-Jazeera.

and mountains. But the American military presence has now expanded not only into Pakistan and Afghanistan but also across the Persian Gulf and Central Asia. A 2008 report by the U.S. Defense Department puts the total number of overseas U.S. military facilities at 761, making it, according to the report, "one of the world's largest 'landlords' with a physical plant consisting of more than 545,700 facilities (buildings, structures and linear structures) located on more than 5,400 sites, on approximately 30 million acres."[74]

Of more immediate consequence for the Middle East has been the U.S. attack on Saddam Hussein's regime and its occupation of Iraq beginning in March 2003. The war in Afghanistan, President Bush repeatedly told the American public, was only "the first phase" of the much larger "war on terrorism." Iraq, the Americans were told, was next. The U.S. drive against Saddam Hussein was motivated by both ideology and practical considerations. Ideologically, the removal of Saddam was in keeping with the Bush Doctrine's division of the globe into the binary worlds of good and evil. Saddam, President Bush repeatedly said, was an "evildoer." From a more pragmatic standpoint, the policy of dual containment was taking too long to show tangible results. Meanwhile, Iraq's alleged possession and continued production of chemical weapons were seen as a serious threat to U.S. strategic interests and to Israel. Closer to home, with American patriotism at an all-time high after September 11, President Bush's popularity had reached levels unprecedented in American presidential history—as high as 84 percent.[75] Only one other president had come close to reaching such a milestone before, the older President Bush, at the height of another patriotic time, the 1990–91 Gulf War. But his son did not forget that the older Bush had gone on to lose the 1992 election.

THE U.S. INVASION AND OCCUPATION OF IRAQ

The American invasion of Iraq in 2003 appears to have been caused by three primary, interrelated factors. The first was President George W. Bush's strategic vision of America's global role. Equally significant was the geostrategic importance of Iraq, in terms of both its location and its oil resources. Last, the dynamics at work in domestic American politics were highly influential in shaping U.S. foreign policy objectives before, during, and after the war.

The attacks of September 11 gave the "accidental presidency" of George W. Bush the opportunity to articulate a grand vision of America's role in the world at large and in the Middle East specifically. A presidency that was at first largely oblivious to international developments now suddenly began defining itself by its defense of the United States against the real threat of terrorism from the Middle East. It is unclear whether this "grand vision" had already been articulated before 9/11 or whether it came about somewhat haphazardly in response to emerging threats and opportunities in the aftermath of the attacks. There is credible evidence that suggests the plans for attacking Iraq had been made some time before 9/11.[76] But whatever its genesis, the grand vision was one of unabashed unilateralism and preemption. "You're either with us," President Bush said again and again, "or you're against us." When the United Nations and others expressed doubts about the wisdom of American action, they were brushed aside and their relevance was questioned. The president's State of the Union speech before Congress in January 2003 is revealing: "All free nations have a stake in preventing sudden and catastrophic attacks. And we're asking them to join us, and many are doing so. Yet the course of this nation does not depend on the decision of others. Whatever action is required, whenever action is necessary, I will defend the freedom and security of the American people."[77]

By pointing to Iraq's stockpiling of weapons of mass destruction, and by alleging that Saddam Hussein harbored terrorists and was linked to

Al-Qaeda, the Bush administration began to openly declare its objective to bring about a "regime change" in Baghdad. The United States was duty-bound, the president argued, to defend itself and its allies in the region from the menace of Saddam's regime. By the time Saddam let UN weapons inspectors return and promised to disarm, the United States maintained that these measures were too little, too late. The Iraqi president was said to have sealed his own fate.

The geostrategic position of Iraq in the Persian Gulf and in the larger Middle East played a central role in its invasion and occupation by the United States. Since Iraq was located at the mouth of the Persian Gulf and, as the Second Gulf War had demonstrated, within striking distance of Israel, U.S. military presence there was considered to have manifold military and diplomatic advantages. It removed a viable threat to Israel, extended the presence of American military forces north of the Arabian peninsula, and allowed the United States to keep both the Iranian and Syrian regimes in check. For a time it even seemed that the United States might use Iraq as a base to effect additional regime changes in Syria or Iran, or both.

Most important, the occupation of Iraq allowed the United States easy access to Iraqi oil. According to U.S. government estimates, Iraq has the world's second largest proven reserves of oil (112 billion barrels), behind Saudi Arabia. Meanwhile, Iraq's oil production costs are among the lowest in the world. The country also contains 110 trillion cubic feet of natural gas, one of the highest levels in the world.[78] Members of the Bush administration gave numerous assurances that oil played no role in the decision to invade Iraq. Nevertheless, it is hard to imagine that the United States would have initiated such a massive and costly military campaign had Iraq been a resource-poor country. That both the American president and his vice president came from oil backgrounds themselves only reinforces such a suspicion.

Last, the Bush administration gave prominence to several highly in-fluential pundits and policy makers, both inside and outside the formal structures of government, with pronounced conservative, often pro-Israeli views. President George W. Bush's own ideological conservatism was remi-niscent of Ronald Reagan and the 1980s, except that it was deeply imbued with religion. Not surprisingly, many of the more influential figures in the Bush administration had earlier served in the Reagan White House and injected the new cabinet with a degree of conservatism not found in either the Clinton or the first Bush presidency. Some of these "neoconservative" figures were Douglas Feith, undersecretary of defense, a vocal opponent of the Arab-Israeli peace process and closely allied with Israel's Likud Party; Richard Perle, with the advisory Defense Policy Board, who urged Prime Minister Netanyahu to cancel the Oslo Accords and opposed further negotiations with the Palestinians; and Paul Wolfowitz, deputy secretary of defense, who urged military action against Iraq only a few weeks after the September 11 attacks.[79] Together, these and other key administration figures—such as National Security Advisor Condoleezza Rice, Secretary of Defense Donald Rumsfeld, and Vice President Dick Cheney—moved American foreign policy in a highly ideological direction. The invasion of Iraq was the crystallization of a vision of America's role as a unilateral guardian of international peace and security.[80]

The United States and its principal ally, Britain, at first decided to effect regime change in Iraq through diplomatic means. In early November 2002, the UN Security Council adopted Resolution 1441, offered jointly by the United States and the United Kingdom, in which Iraq was given thirty days to prove that it was not "in material breach" of previous UN resolutions concerning disarmament and its chemical weapons program. Iraq was required to give a new UN inspection team "immediate, unimpeded, unconditional, and unrestricted access" to its weapons facilities. Otherwise, it would "face serious consequences as a result of its continued violations of its obligations."[81] In his formal report to the United Nations the following February, the head of the inspection team, Hans Blix, reported that inspectors had found no "smoking guns" and that Iraq was in fact in compliance with UN 1441.[82] France and Germany, meanwhile, launched an intense diplomatic campaign to prevent U.S. and British unilateral military action against Iraq without UN approval. Joined by Russia, in early March France and Germany released a joint declaration promising to block another UN resolution authorizing military action against Iraq. When it became clear that a second UN resolution on the issue was unlikely, the United States and Britain decided to bypass the United Nations altogether. The invasion of Iraq commenced on March 20, 2003.

Once the invasion got under way, the collapse of the Saddam Hussein regime took only days. In the buildup to the invasion, some 170,000 U.S. troops had been amassed near the Iraqi border in Kuwait, and once the war commenced the number of American military personnel rose to approximately 300,000. Britain, meanwhile, had a force of less than 30,000. British forces were given the charge of capturing the southern city of Basra while American troops made a dash through the desert for Baghdad. By April 3, the Americans were in control of the Baghdad Airport, and within a week they had captured most of the city. On April 9, 2003, in a historic

Figure 16. Saddam Hussein's statue is toppled in Baghdad.

scene, U.S. troops helped residents of Baghdad bring down a giant statue of Saddam located in one of the city's main squares. The city of Tikrit, Saddam's birthplace and one of his main bases of support, fell to U.S. troops on April 14. By about the same time, British troops, who had encountered unexpectedly heavy resistance in the south, gained full control of Basra and the nearby town of Umm Qasr.

The disintegration of central authority plunged Iraq, especially Baghdad, into chaos as looting and lawlessness became routine. The United States appointed its own administrators to run the country on an interim basis, but it would be some time before law and order could be restored to a country with the size and predicament of Iraq. Saddam's "republic of fear" might have collapsed, but its immediate aftermath was a nightmarish republic of anarchy, death, and destruction. Many Iraqis took the law into their own hands as they tried to settle old scores with former Ba'thist officials. Clean water and electricity became scarce as elements loyal to the Saddam regime blew up power generators, water mains, and major oil pipelines. Before long, the country was said to have also been infiltrated by Al-Qaeda fighters bent on harming American interests wherever and however possible. Although within weeks of Saddam's overthrow President Bush triumphantly declared that major combat in Iraq was over, American

Figure 17. President Saddam Hussein.

commanders on the ground soon admitted to having a full-blown urban guerrilla war on their hands.

It soon became apparent that the careful American planning for the invasion had not been extended to include the occupation period. Interagency squabbles and policy inconsistencies only added to the bewilderment of the U.S. policy makers in the postinvasion period.[83] Ordinary Iraqis, meanwhile, suffered from lack of security and a near-total absence of most basic necessities. Before long the country plunged into civil war, with pro-Saddam, Shi'ite, and Al-Qaeda militia groups fighting the American forces, the weak central government, and each other. The fighting continued to rage even after Saddam Hussein was discovered to be hiding in a spider hole and was captured in December 2003, and, more ominously, even after the alleged leader of Al-Qaeda in Iraq, Abu Musab al-Zarqawi, was killed by the U.S. forces in June 2006. Saddam's trial and subsequent execution in December 2006 also did little to calm Iraq's tumultuous life. According to a study published in the British medical journal *The Lancet*, from the start of the invasion until July 2006, some 654,965 Iraqis, or an estimated 2.5 percent of the country's total population, had lost their lives as a consequence of the war.[84] By mid-2007, international aid agencies were estimating that 2 million Iraqis had fled the country and had become international refu-

Figure 18. British occupation forces search Iraqi women for weapons.

gees, principally in Jordan and Syria, while another 2.2 million had become internally displaced inside the country's borders.[85]

The U.S. occupation forces also suffered significant losses, with an estimated 31,300 American soldiers injured as a result of the fighting and another 4,300 dead between the start of the war in March 2003 and May 2009.[86] Not surprisingly, the occupation of Iraq emerged as one of the major issues in the American presidential elections of 2008, and the incoming administration of President Barack Obama made good on his campaign promise of pulling U.S. combat troops out of Iraq by the start of 2010. By then, the government of Prime Minister Nouri Al-Maliki in Baghdad had proven itself surprisingly resilient, and, although the country's security situation had improved little, Iraq, in tatters, was left to fend for itself.

What does the future hold in store for the Middle East? Predicting Middle East politics is always risky. But a few trends are hard to miss. We have seen that over the last two decades the style and delivery of Middle East politics and policies may have changed, but their essence and substance have not. Mutual distrust and tensions still govern the relationship of many of the region's supposed allies; few if any Middle Eastern states have done enough to address popular grievances arising from economic and political limitations; and U.S. policy toward the region essentially continues to be what it was at the height of the Cold War, only modified to fit today's realities. U.S. military action in Afghanistan and invasion and occupation of Iraq have done little to strengthen the states of the region, undermine the appeal of Islamic fundamentalism, or reduce the levels of anti-Americanism. If anything, as public opinion polls indicate, they have had quite the opposite effects. In fact, given the institutional weaknesses inherent in Middle Eastern states (discussed in Chapter 9), and given the decline in the likelihood of future interstate wars as viable means of conflict resolution, the types of attacks perpetuated by multinational terror networks such as Al-Qaeda are likely to continue.[87] Neither the underlying reasons for becoming a terrorist—or a "martyr"—nor the destructive means available to carry out future attacks have been eliminated. Barring extraordinary developments, the prospects for radical changes in the near future seem remote.

The 1980s and 1990s saw two bloody and devastating wars in the Middle East, the first between Iran and Iraq and the second between Iraq and an international coalition assembled to eject it from Kuwait. Saddam Hussein initiated both wars, hoping in the first instance to exploit the weaknesses and self-inflicted wounds of Iran's ruling ayatollahs and, later on, to finally give his army a victory to cheer about. Whereas Iraq's invasion of Iran in 1980 was motivated by Saddam's overconfidence, the invasion of Kuwait a decade later was a product of his desperation and panic. Saddam had originally counted on a quick and easy victory over the Iranians, and his campaign to bring Tehran's revolutionaries to their knees won him the diplomatic and material support of most other Arab states in the Persian Gulf and elsewhere. However, this partial Arab unity did not outlast the Iran-Iraq War. Almost as soon as the war was over, former friends turned on each other, sobered now by the loss of a common enemy and the difficult realities of political normalcy. Saddam, the self-described Nasser of his age, needed another enemy and, more than ever before, a quick and decisive victory. That the new enemy was a former ally was only a minor inconvenience. The benefits, Saddam calculated, far outweighed the risks.

The Second Gulf War brought destruction first to Kuwait by the invading Iraqis and then to Iraq by the allied coalition. In the course of the two wars, hundreds of thousands of lives were lost in successive tragedies of epic proportions: first in Iran and Iraq, then in Kuwait, then among the Iraqi Shi'ites, Kurds, and ordinary citizens. By the time his regime was toppled in 2003, Saddam had left behind a trail of ruin and shattered lives, of broken spirits and destroyed homes. Iraq, once a cradle of civilization,

Figure 19. Iraqi women inspect the site of a car bomb explosion in Bayaa district. Photo courtesy of Corbis.

was plunged into darkness, and its capital, once proud and magnificent, had been looted and plundered.

In many ways, the tragedy of Iraq has come to symbolize the larger predicament of the whole region. Institutional decay and atrophy, despotism, cross-border conflicts, ethnic and sectarian tensions, foreign invasions—all relics of the past—continue to haunt much of the Middle East to this day. In some ways, the Middle East appears to be trapped in a vicious circle from which it cannot escape. But there are also profound changes. After more than a century of denying the right of the other to exist, *some* Israelis and Palestinians are finally talking to each other. The whole region has seen levels of economic growth and development that would have been unimaginable only a few decades ago. While different shades of authoritarianism continue to remain pervasive throughout the Middle East, halting steps toward democratization are being taken in a number of Middle Eastern countries. These are all signs of change—change amid continuity. The next section of this book examines these developments.

PART II

Issues in Middle Eastern Politics

CURRENTLY, THREE PRINCIPAL ISSUES SHAPE the politics of the contemporary Middle East. The first is the ongoing inability of the Palestinians and the Israelis to come to terms with each other's legitimate national rights and to peacefully coexist. For more than a century now, the intertwined histories of Israel and Palestine have been written in blood and tears. On rare occasions it has seemed as if peace were on the horizon, as in the early 1990s. So far, however, the drumbeats of war and mutual recrimination have drowned out the voices of dialogue and peace. Chapter 7 examines the makeup and perspectives of the two sides and the history of the conflict between them.

Another defining feature of Middle Eastern politics is the issue of economic development. As the coming chapters demonstrate, one of the pillars of politics in the Middle East has been an implicit "ruling bargain" between the state and society. This bargain has been predicated on certain key assumptions: the state's guarantee of physical and national security; the provision of economic goods and services by the state as a trade-off for lack of elite accountability; and, when necessary, the state's resort to repression to maintain power. For some decades, the question of Palestine was often also part of the ruling bargain, as heroes near and far promised to bring about the liberation that many others had failed to provide. Increasingly, however, the *Arab*-Israeli conflict has turned into a *Palestinian*-Israeli struggle once again, and the deinternationalization of the Palestinian cause is removing it from one Middle Eastern national agenda after another.

Nevertheless, economic performance—such simple questions as "What do I have?" and "What has the state done for me?"—remains at the core of the ruling bargain. And as technology and circumstances change in the twenty-first century from what they were in the 1960s and 1970s—as alternative energy sources become more widespread, single-commodity economies experience more stress, and the forces of globalization intrude—there is increasing need to renegotiate some of the basic premises of the ruling bargain. Again, how the challenges of economic performance are resolved and in what direction the ruling bargain changes remain to be seen. No doubt, however, economic challenges will be central to the politics of the Middle East in both the near and the distant futures. The topic of economic development will be explored in Chapter 8.

Equally important in shaping Middle Eastern politics has been the struggle between the popular forces that have long yearned for democracy and the entrenched autocracy of the ruling elite. No one can deny that over the last few years some of the illiberal states of the Middle East have taken steps to liberalize their rule: public officials have become more accountable, the ruling elites have been expanded to become more representative, and in some instances such democratic institutions as parliaments and elections have been introduced. But political elites in the Middle East have often shown a great flair for public presentations, and democratic utterances and displays ought not be confused with democratic substance. For the time being, the substance and spirit of democracy—contrary to public declarations and superficial appearances—are generally absent from the Middle East. There is, indeed, a genuine struggle under way today in Iran over the scope and depth of popular representation, curtailing arbitrariness, and defining a clear set of political rules. But what is happening in Iran is unique to its revolution, and, so far at least, it has been characterized by setbacks, factional infighting, and violent reactions by trenchant undemocratic forces within the state. Chapters 9 and 10 explore domestic political dynamics and the prospects for democracy in the Middle East, respectively.

7 The Palestinian-Israeli Conflict

One of the most vexing problems in the political history of the modern Middle East, and indeed of the larger global community, has been the conflict between Israelis and Palestinians. Through the vicissitudes of history and the vagaries of power politics, both international and domestic, these two peoples have come to inhabit the same piece of territory. We have, essentially, as the late political scientist Deborah Gerner put it, "one land, two peoples."[1] Over the years, they have fought, cajoled, killed, and harassed one another. And they have been unwilling or unable to find ways of "sharing the promised land."[2] An overwhelming majority of peoples on both sides have come to view the other as "the enemy," dehumanized and devoid of rights or legitimacy. In defending a cause they view as singularly righteous and just, each side has inflicted pain and misery on the other. Today, neither side has a monopoly over fear of violence from the other.

History has been kind to neither the Zionists nor the Palestinians. Both communities have been scattered throughout the world at different times and forced to live in exile. In the diaspora, the Jews faced persecution and the threat of annihilation. The Palestinians, many of whom still live outside Palestine, are frequently used by Middle Eastern despots who claim the cause of Palestinian liberation for their own narrow, domestic political purposes. Since 1948, when the state of Israel was created and geographic Palestine ceased to exist, Israel has had the upper hand politically and militarily. Successive Israeli governments have deepened their dominance over former Palestine with every war they have fought, every policy initiative they have enacted, every new house or road they have built and every old one they have demolished, and every "settler" they have geographically placed in the land of Eretz Israel. But as Chapter 3 demonstrated, the death and dismemberment of geographic Palestine have not destroyed the iden-

Figure 20. Emuna Zvi Yona bathes her son at the unauthorized outpost of Maoz Esther, which was demolished for the seventh time in August of 2009. Photo courtesy of New York Times Co.

tity of the Palestinians. Rather, these events have continued to shape not only their identity—or, rather, evolving identities—but also their attachment to Palestine and their sense of nationalism. Zionist territorial and military conquest of Palestine is now more than a century old. It started with the first *aliya* in 1881, achieved spectacular successes in the wars of 1948, 1967, and 1973, and continues to this day through the construction of settlement colonies in the remaining areas with large Palestinian populations. However, seldom in history have military conquests led to the total annihilation of indigenous identities. For the Palestinians, their sense of identity continues to define and distinguish them from those they consider to be occupiers and colonizers. Battles may have been won and lost, but the conflict continues.

Any examination of the political history of the Middle East would be incomplete without an account of the conflict between Palestinians and Israelis. But any treatment of the Palestinian-Israeli conflict in one chapter is also bound to be incomplete. Consequently, the scope and purpose of the present chapter are modest. I seek to highlight the competing notions of identity among the Palestinians and Israelis, an integral part of which for both peoples is a connection to the same piece of land. Both Israelis' and Palestinians' sense of identity has been shaped by and has in turn shaped their actions and their contemporary history. Their identity-based actions have led to the emergence of conditions on the ground with which most outside observers are not adequately familiar but that are, for people on both sides, the reality in which they have to live. I will, therefore, as much as possible present a picture of the circumstances on the ground, especially those created and perpetuated by each side to further its national agenda. Finally, the chapter will turn to the search for peace, undertaken by some but not all Palestinians and Israelis, and the difficulties that have, for the time being, made such a possibility distant and elusive.

COMPETING NATIONAL IDENTITIES

At the core of the conflict between Palestinians and Israelis has been a persistent negation of the identity of the other side. From the very beginning, both sides felt that the other side had no right to exist. When the first of the five *aliyas* began in the early 1880s, this negation of identities intensified, and it gradually but steadily reached the crescendo of open conflict and warfare. As time went by, and as the irreconcilability of the two sides' identities became starkly clear, the religious aspects of each side's identity became more pronounced. In its earliest manifestations, Zionism was assertively secular, strongly influenced by a pervasive yearning for social justice and egalitarianism among European intellectuals of the time. While Judaism formed the larger cause and the context within which the Zionist project was articulated, the origins of Zionism lay in secular nationalism and a desire to escape the growing anti-Semitism of European Gentiles. As the Zionists' conflict with non-Jewish Palestinians intensified, however, their claim to be the rightful inheritors of the land increasingly assumed biblical justifications. By the 1930s and 1940s, the failure of the Zionist project was not an option for those in European Jewry who were lucky to have escaped Hitler's concentration camps. This only deepened the biblical conviction that the artificially created territory called Palestine had no right to exist. No less of an authority than the Bible had promised Eretz Israel to the Jews. There was no such thing as Palestine or a Palestinian. Thus, for purposes of cohesion and self-validation, the evolving identity of Israelis drew more and more on the religious roots of Zionism.

The route that Palestinian identity took to assert its validity and vitality was somewhat different, at least up until relatively recent times. As Chapter 3 demonstrated, Palestinian nationalism was sparked in the 1920s in reaction to the increasing physical presence and economic dominance within Palestine of incoming Zionist immigrants. Whereas the overall premise of early Zionism was vaguely religious, from the very beginning Palestinian nationalism was primarily territorial and secular. This is not to say that religious personalities and institutions were insignificant in the formation and direction of a Palestinian sense of identity. The full-scale Palestinian rebellion of 1936–39, in fact, was led by the grand mufti of Jerusalem, Hajj Amin al-Husseini. However, during the formative years of Palestinian identity, from about 1948 to the beginning of the *intifada* in late 1987, when a sense of identity was about all that the stateless Palestinians had, religion's role was only secondary. The idea of Palestine as an actual territory and a historic memory shaped what it meant to be Palestinian. That the Palestinians themselves are divided into Christians and Muslims, very unequally but still divided, had much to do with the general deemphasis of religion as a source of Palestinian identity during much of this period. Only later, in the *intifada* years of 1987–93 and afterward, did the perceived failures of the secularly led PLO prompt many Palestinians in the Occupied Territories to look for other alternatives. At that point, religion, and more specifically Islam, once again asserted a role in the formation of Palestinian identity.

Thus both Palestinian and Israeli identities have demonstrated that they are changeable and dynamic. In a roughly parallel pattern, both have evolved from being predominantly secular to becoming heavily (but not entirely) religious. Perhaps more important has been their symbiotic relationship, each having influenced the other by its own nuances and changes over time. In some ways, as the conflict has unfolded, the two identities have fed off each other. The ever-present danger posed by the very existence of "the Other" has given both identities a degree of cohesion that they might not otherwise have had. Multiple divisions run through both the Palestinian and the Israeli communities. The Palestinians are primarily divided along the lines of class standing, religious affiliation, and place of residence; the Israelis, along the lines of ethnicity and degrees of religiosity. The gravity of the conflict and the fear of defeat—or, for the Palestinians, even more defeat—have blunted the potential of each of these sources of division. Nonetheless, beneath the surface the divisions do exist and in profound ways affect the collective identity of each of the two communities. Consequently, they merit further exploration.

The most pronounced source of division within Israeli identity concerns the ethnic background of Israel's Jewish inhabitants. Jews are likely to consider themselves as belonging to one of two groups, the Ashkenazim, or those with a European background, and the Sephardim, broadly considered to be of Spanish or "Eastern" origin. Although all non-European Jews are generally considered to belong to the Sephardim, the correct use of the label actually applies only to the descendants of the Jews who were expelled from Spain in 1492.[3] Other non-European Jews from the Middle East and North Africa are called the Mizrachim (also pronounced Mizrahim). Nevertheless, the two terms *Sephardim* and *Mizrachim* are today used interchangeably in Israel, and people belonging to the two groups are considered as one. In 2007, of Israel's Jewish population of approximately 5.5 million, some 28 percent had been (or their fathers had been) born in Asia and Africa, 36 percent in Europe and America, and the rest, about 28 percent, in Israel.[4] Of those who immigrated to Israel from 1990 to 2007, just under one million people, 11 percent were from Asia and Africa and 89 percent were from Europe and America.[5] An overwhelming majority of immigrants to Israel during this period had been born in the former Soviet Union, former Soviet republics, and other former communist states in eastern and central Europe, notably Poland, Romania, Bulgaria, and Hungary.

As these numbers indicate, whether Ashkenazi or Mizrachim, Israel's Jewish immigrants often bring with them specific cultural practices, social norms, and even religious observances and rituals from the countries they left behind. In many ways, the adoption of the Hebrew language as the primary medium of communication in Israel serves an important unifying role among culturally and linguistically disparate groups.[6] However, differences in physical appearance, dialect, accent, food, customs, and even ritual observances often persist for several generations, sometimes even permanently.

The Ashkenazi-Mizrachim ethnic divide is the larger context for several other divisions that run through Israel's Jewish community, including those of economic and class status, Jewish doctrine, and political affiliation. At the most general level, the Mizrachim tend to be concentrated in the lower socioeconomic levels of Israeli society, complain of discriminatory treatment by the politically and economically dominant Ashkenazim, and, as a result, generally side with the nonestablishment parties of the Right. The Ashkenazim, many of whom trace their origins back to the early days of Labor Zionism in the late 1800s, have long held most of the economic and political power in Israel. For example, the Ashkenazi-dominated Labor Party ruled uninterruptedly from 1948 until the 1977 elections.

There are also doctrinal differences between the two ethnic groups dating back to the earliest days of European Zionist settlements in Palestine. The Mizrachim do not have different doctrinal movements within them. The Ashkenazim, on the other hand, are divided into an Orthodox (mainly Hasidic) and a more numerous non-Orthodox category, and the latter are themselves divided into the Reform and the Conservative movements.[7] Early in the history of the Zionist movement, as the Mizrachim living in Palestine found themselves increasingly outnumbered because of successive *aliyas* from Europe, they challenged the Jewishness of the Ashkenazim, claiming that only Mizrachim rituals and observances represented the true Jewish faith.[8] They were unsuccessful; in fact, "the Euro-Israeli establishment attempted to repress the 'Middle Easternness' of Mizrahim as part of an effort to Westernize the Israeli nation and to mark clear borders of identity between Jews as Westerners and Arabs as Easterners."[9] Today, the ethnic divide—the sense of "otherness"—has not changed much, having in recent years assumed added potency with the birth and successes of a Mizrachim-dominated political party, the Shas.

The socioeconomic differences between the Ashkenazim and the Mizrachim are especially glaring. The Mizrachim constitute what one Israeli scholar has called a "semi-peripheral" group in Israeli society, located between the "peripheral" Palestinians, whether Israeli citizens or non-citizens, and the dominant Ashkenazim.[10] Although precise data on levels of income and standards of living for the two communities are not available, the per capita income of the Mizrachim is estimated to be about two-thirds the figure for the Ashkenazim.[11] The Mizrachim tend to be concentrated in lower-income neighborhoods, attend poorer schools, and are overrepresented in the ranks of the poor and the working classes. The Mizrachim also form the bulk of Israel's Jewish prisoner population and constitute a high percentage of Israelis convicted of crimes. Although nearly a quarter of all Jewish marriages are now mixed, the social and cultural gaps between the two communities remain considerable. Only about 25 percent of Mizrachim high school students graduate, compared to 46 percent of Ashkenazi. Primarily because of poorer schooling, the Mizrachim make up only about 20 percent of Israel's university student population, whereas the figure for the Ashkenazim is over 70 percent. Throughout the country, there are only a few Mizrachim university professors. Although since the mid-1970s the Mizrachim have made noticeable socioeconomic advances in Israeli society, these gains either have been outstripped by those of the Ashkenazim—in areas such as education, occupational status, and income—or have been in fields whose social significance has declined—such as careers in the military and ownership of small shops and businesses.[12] In fact, as compared to first-generation Jewish immigrants from various Middle Eastern countries, the income gap between second-generation Mizrachim and Ashkenazim has increased, and the percentage of second-generation Mizrachim who hold blue-collar jobs is more than twice that of first-generation Mizrachim.[13]

Differences in levels of education, purchasing power, places of residence, and living standards have had other social and cultural consequences as well. The Mizrachim complain about having their heritage and their contributions to Jewish thought and life marginalized in school textbooks, in the popular media, and even in the writings of Ashkenazim intellectuals.[14] For some time now, for example, many respected Israeli intellectuals (all of Ashkenazim background) have openly wondered what it means to be an Israeli and have written about an Israeli "identity crisis" (more of which below). Often conspicuously absent from their discussions, however, has been attention to the predicaments and identities of the Mizrachim, implying that the Mizrachim are at best marginal to the formation of a collective Israeli identity and at worst irrelevant.[15] The massive influx of new Ashkenazi Jews in the early 1990s following the collapse of the former Soviet Union has only exacerbated the Mizrachim's sense of marginalization.

All this has influenced the Mizrachim's political proclivities. Most of the Mizrachim immigrated to Israel beginning in the 1950s, by which time the Ashkenazim had already solidified their control over the institutions of the state and the economy, including the bureaucracy and the Israeli Defense Forces (IDF). Upon arrival, most Mizrachim were subjected to indignities by Ashkenazi officials—including being sprayed with DDT before being allowed into the country—and found themselves on the economic, political, and social margins of Israeli life.[16] They blamed their predicament on the Ashkenazi-dominated Labor Party, which happened to be social-democratic in its ideological orientation. Some two decades later, by which time the Mizrachim immigrants had learned the rules of Israel's political game, they felt confident enough to exert themselves politically, casting their votes in opposition to Labor and in favor of the Right.[17] Thus began the ascendancy of the Likud beginning in 1977 and, later, the religious Shas Party in 1984 (the party itself was formed in late 1983).[18]

As a political party founded by and largely representing the interests of the Mizrachim community, the Shas is a relatively recent phenomenon in Israeli politics. For a group that found itself increasingly on the margins of Israel's political, cultural, and economic life, the Shas has represented a powerful tool for self-actualization and social integration. Since its entry into Israeli politics in 1984 after winning four seats in the Knesset (the parliament), the party's rise has been both steady and impressive, at one point in the mid- to the late 1990s emerging as the country's third largest party.[19] This rise was further facilitated by the party's populist appeal to lower-income Mizrachim, especially in the smaller towns and cities, where the larger political parties, notably the Likud and the Labor, have not had as strong a foothold as they do in places like Tel Aviv and Jerusalem. Through control over such key cabinet offices as the Ministries of Labor, Interior, and Religious Affairs, Shas leaders were able to funnel government funds to many of their constituencies, thus enhancing their own chances for reelection. They even sought to strengthen their relations with Israel's Arab bedouins, whose traditional values they to some degree share.[20] Moreover, the Shas controls an extensive network of schools and religious seminaries, each offering a deep reservoir of volunteers in any given election, and throughout the year runs missionizing seminars to expand the circle of the "new returnees to Orthodoxy," the baalei tshuva.[21]

Clearly, the continued threat presented to both the Ashkenazim and the Mizrachim from a completely alien, even hostile ethnic group, the Arab Palestinians, has greatly blunted the potential for ethnic tensions among Israeli Jews. Despite their complaints, therefore, the Mizrachim have almost uniformly embraced the concept of mizug galuyot, the fusion of the exiles.[22] Located in an intermediary position between the peripheral Palestinians and the dominant Ashkenazi, they have allied themselves with the Ashkenazim and with the Israeli state apparatus, seeking greater integration into the "mainstream" of Israeli society rather than segregation from it.[23] According to one Israeli scholar, "By the early 2000s, more than 50% of Mizrahim belonged to the middle-class. Among this population, as shown by [previous] research, many were married to spouses of Ashkenazi origin and raised children hardly aware of any ethnic allegiance. This is widely accounted for by the broadly non-ethnic 'all-Israeli' mood prevailing in middle-class secular milieus and which, as such, cannot legitimately object to the acceptance of socially-mobile Mizrahi individuals. Mobility resulted in greater exposure to the dominant culture and rapprochement to secular patterns of life."[24] Many Mizrachim have not only assimilated but also reached impressive upward mobility in the political establishment, as demonstrated by the career of David Levy, a Moroccan-born former foreign minister. For its part, the (Ashkenazi-dominated) political establishment cannot afford to ignore this important "counterelite," especially with the political muscle of the Shas behind it, and has embarked on frequent, much-publicized campaigns designed to improve the living standards of the Mizrachim. These have included schemes such as job creation and training, subsidies and allowances, and, of course, inclusion in the highest echelons of the state, especially the cabinet.

Alongside the Ashkenazim-Mizrachim ethnic divide and its multiple social, economic, and political facets, a larger debate has emerged in Israel over the precise nature of Israeli national identity and particularly the proper role of religion—Judaism—in the constitution of Israeli identity.[25] The increasing powers of the political Right in recent decades, coupled with unprecedented increases in the pace of building new settlements in Palestinian territories, have led to intensified exploration of the relationship between Zionism as a nationalist movement and Judaism as a religion. Questions such as "What does it mean to be an Israeli?" and, more basically, "Who is a Jew?" have become part of the dominant intellectual discourse of the country.[26]

Such questions were a product of the profound soul-searching instigated by the psychological shock of the 1973 War. In the words of one Israeli scholar, "When the October 1973 War destroyed the image of material power upon which the feelings of security of most Israelis was based, a deep sense of anguish was bound to pervade the whole nation. The crisis was all the more profound because of the rapidity with which the whole nation passed from a situation of pseudo-normality to one of a total struggle for survival. . . . The Israeli had been brought face to face with himself, with his split identity and his cultural alienation, and for the first time had no possibility of avoiding a look into the mirror of realities."[27]

Equally important in sparking such debates has been the Israeli state's historical trajectory since its establishment. When the state was initially created, such thorny questions as Judaism's role in the political process and the precise definition of a Jew were put on the back burner so as not to upset the fragile coalition of various Zionist tendencies fighting for the state's creation. This is why Israel does not have a written constitution yet, although, at this point, after more than half a century of successful operation, it may never adopt one. Now, with all the wars fought and with Israel's physical and military security more firmly established, the profound questions of being and identity have come to the fore again. In many ways, the ongoing scholarly debates signify a maturing of the national project, such that Israelis feel confident enough to undertake a thorough self-examination of Zionism and Israeli identity. That such discussion has emerged at a time when there are still Palestinians who reject the whole notion of an Israeli identity—as there are Israelis who reject Palestinian identity—attests to the sense of security that the debate's protagonists feel.

For the Palestinians, becoming stateless has served as a particularly compelling source of cohesion. Internal divisions, derived from differences in religious affiliation, economic standing, and place of residence, tend to run deeper among Palestinians than Israelis. These divisions have remained constant, but other traditional characteristics of Palestinians, such as secularism and a weak middle class, have subtly but noticeably

shifted, to a large extent because of the increasing loss of popular legitimacy among the primary articulators of Palestinian identity: traditional
Palestinian notables and the Palestine Liberation Organization (PLO), both
of whom saw themselves, initially with some justification, as the legitimate
representatives of the Palestinian people.[28]

Institutions play defining roles in shaping all national identities. Such
institutions may be social (e.g., the family, the neighborhood community,
religious institutions, self-help groups) or political (e.g., the state or statelike institutions, political parties). Whatever their genesis and functions,
institutions and national identity often have a symbiotic, mutually reinforcing relationship, each influencing and being influenced by the other.[29]
For Palestinians—whose nation has been diminished and fragmented by
the birth of the state of Israel, by exodus and exile, and by life in seemingly
permanent refugee camps—social and political institutions play an especially pivotal role in the articulation of national identity. These institutions
are, after all, for many Palestinians the only tangible manifestations of
national existence and a sense of self.[30] In turn, the changes experienced
by Palestinian institutions—especially the rise or decline of their popularity—often reflect larger changes within Palestinian national identity. As
this chapter demonstrates, the sense of identity that had given rise to the
near-complete dominance of Palestinian politics by the PLO after 1967
underwent dramatic changes beginning in the late 1980s. The transforming effects of the *intifada* on Palestinian national identity gave rise first to
a non-PLO-affiliated "counterelite" and then to the Hamas organization.
By 1993, when the Oslo Accords were signed, the Palestinians' uncertainty
over their national identity was reflected in the chasm between the two
main Palestinian institutions, the Palestine National Authority and Hamas.
Several Palestinian civil society organizations were also established in the
mid- to late 1990s, although their long-term efficacy and the consequences
of their actions for Palestinian identity are so far unclear.[31] Meanwhile,
economic and cultural divisions began pulling the Gaza Strip and the West
Bank in different directions, a chasm accentuated by expansive ideological and political differences between the Palestinian National Authority
(PNA) and the Hamas, with the former in control of the West Bank and
the latter in control of Gaza. Intermittent armed clashes between the two
groups throughout 2007 and 2008 led to scores of casualties and arrests
by each side of supporters and sympathizers of the other, and the seemingly unbridgeable gap between the two territories took what remained of
Palestine to the brink of civil war. As of this writing, in mid-2010, a tense
and uneasy state of acrimony marks the relationship between the two.

Mention of the continued dispersion of Palestinians, both throughout the diaspora and within the Occupied Territories, must precede analysis of the causes and consequences of changes in Palestinian identity. Palestinians are divided by their place of residence into several different groups. According to the Palestinian Central Bureau of Statistics, run by the PNA, the total number of Palestinian population in the world in 2003 was estimated at around 8.5 million (not including an estimated 1.4 million Palestinians with Israeli citizenship), of whom 4.8 million live outside pre-1947 Palestine and 3.7 live in the Occupied Territories (approximately 2.3 million in the West Bank and 1.4 million in the Gaza Strip). By 2007, by far the largest number of Palestinians outside of the Occupied Territories lived in Jordan, some 2.6 million or 54 percent, with sizable Palestinian communities also found in Syria (401,000), Lebanon (385,000), the United States (272,000), Egypt (53,000), and other Arab countries (272,000).[32] Of these, many hold official refugee status; of the 8.5 million Palestinians who do not hold Israeli citizenship, 4.7 million, or 54 percent, are officially registered as refugees by the UN. According to the United Nations Relief and Works Agency for Palestine Refugees (UNRWA), as of December 2008, of a total of 4.67 million Palestinian refugees worldwide, some 1.37 million lived in registered refugee camps, with the highest concentrations being in the Gaza Strip (495,000), Jordan (338,000), and Lebanon (223,000).[33] Additionally, approximately 1.5 million Palestinians, or nearly 12 percent of the worldwide total, live in Israel and are considered Israeli citizens.[34]

It is only natural that prolonged residence in different regions and countries gives different perspectives, dispositions, and identities to members of the same larger group. Life in Amman or Beirut is radically different from life in Bethlehem, and both in turn are different from life in Gaza or West Bank refugee camps. At some level all Palestinians share the characteristics of a dispossessed people, no matter where in the diaspora they may be, and the refusal of most of the host Arab countries to grant them citizenship and other rights has inadvertently served to strengthen their own Palestinian identity.[35] Nevertheless, diaspora life is bound to have assimilating effects on the lives and identities of those experiencing it, especially in light of continued Israeli unwillingness to even discuss the possibility of Palestinian repatriation.[36] At the very least, a subtle and gradual disconnect develops between the member of the diaspora's *perceptions* of life in the home territory and the *reality* of that life as those remaining behind experience it. Following the news of back home with great interest, or even trying to *make* news at home from a distance, as the PLO tried to do during its exile years, is quite different from experiencing developments firsthand. Slowly but surely, the "outside" leadership of the Palestinians, especially the PLO, and by implication their local allies, especially the notables, lost touch with the reality of life in the Occupied Territories. Not surprisingly, they found themselves shunted aside by an emerging counterelite that was a product of local developments.

The increasing prominence of the Palestinian counterelite in the politics of the Occupied Territories reflected itself in two other aspects of Palestinian identity, the Palestinian community's general class composition and its orientations toward religion. Approximately 10 to 12 percent of Palestinians are Christians. The rest of the population, nearly 90 percent, are Sunni Muslims. Historically, most Palestinian Christians have resided in larger towns and cities, and therefore their ranks have been overrepresented among the middle classes and urban professionals. Palestinians living in the Gaza Strip, for example, where living standards are markedly lower than in the West Bank, are almost entirely Muslim. From the very beginning, Christians constituted a substantial minority in the PLO, and this in turn largely accounted for the organization's avowedly secularist ideology.[37] In recent years, with the rise of the more locally based counterelite within the Occupied Territories, Palestinian Islamists have found an especially receptive audience among the Gazans.[38]

During the last few decades, a somewhat deeper process of socioeconomic transformation has been at work in Palestinian society. Gradually, the more established class of notables, the *a'yan*, have been losing much of their traditional powers and social prestige to an emerging counterelite that is generally younger and less willing to tolerate Israeli occupation. Traditionally, Palestinian society was composed of a small class of landed elites and local notables and a large class of landless peasants, farmworkers, and residents of refugee camps. Throughout the twentieth century, several factors—chiefly Israeli occupation, involuntary exile or the voluntary departure of those who could afford it, and a general absence of economic opportunities and sources of mobility—combined to hinder the emergence and deepening of an indigenous Palestinian middle class. Whatever middle class did emerge or managed to retain its status did so primarily in the bigger urban areas of East Jerusalem and Bethlehem and, to a lesser extent, in Jericho and Gaza City.[39] By the early to mid-1970s, however, the emerging counterelite was rapidly acquiring the political dispositions and articulateness of the middle classes, if not necessarily their economic standing.

This transformation was largely the unintentional result of Israel's economic and political policies in the West Bank and the Gaza Strip after 1967, when it repeatedly confiscated Palestinian lands and opened its economy to migrant day laborers and farmworkers from the territories. Both practices undermined the patronage powers of the traditional Palestinian elites and their sources of influence in local communities, instead facilitating the emergence of a younger, increasingly more confident and articulate generation of dispossessed Palestinians.[40] The opening of various West Bank universities—namely Bir Zeit (1972), Bethlehem (1973–74), and al-Najah (1977) Universities—helped sharpen the younger Palestinians' organizational skills, mobilizational possibilities, and, most importantly, sense of the self.[41] By the mid-1980s, the Palestinian counterelite had started to eclipse not only the traditional notables but also the PLO, which by now had been run out of Lebanon and was in exile in distant Tunisia. Within this context the popular uprising known as the *intifada* began in late 1987.

The actual events that precipitated the *intifada* and its unfolding will be discussed in the next section. For now it is important to pay attention to the transforming effects of the uprising both for the structure of Palestinian society and for Palestinian identity. The *intifada* signified the start of a new phase of Palestinian nationalism, one in which the expression of Palestinian identity assumed a popular, grassroots form. The period from 1948 to 1967 had been the "lost years" of high-level but hopelessly inconsequential diplomatic-military negotiations by Arab leaders on behalf of the Palestinians. The "PLO years" of the late 1960s to the mid-1980s turned out to be equally frustrating for the Palestinians (table 2). The *intifada* signified a qualitative shift in the structure of Palestinian society and the expression of popular sentiments—or, more aptly, popular frustrations—by new groups that had now come to the fore. The PLO's geographic distance from the territories belied an even wider subjective and emotional chasm between its seemingly inconsequential leadership and an increasingly restive, steadily changing constituency. Even the notables who had been traditionally associated with the PLO saw a significant decline in their prestige and stature, with their traditional functions of patronage replaced by the thousands of local popular committees *(lijan sha'biya)* springing up throughout the West Bank and Gaza.

Insofar as contemporary Palestinian political history is concerned, the *intifada* turned out to be an incomplete revolution. As will be shown shortly, the PLO, in collusion with Israel, eventually hijacked the movement and used it to give legitimacy to its own efforts at establishing a statelike institution, the PNA. But neither the PLO nor the burgeoning apparatus of the PNA could easily contain the new popular structures and identities to which the *intifada* had given rise. The *intifada*, generally dated from late 1987 to 1993–94, was far from a monolithic, cohesive

Figure 21. Yasser Arafat, chairman of the Palestine Liberation Organization and president of the Palestinian National Authority.

movement. In fact, in its last year or two, the movement in many ways turned on itself, degenerating into a bloody hunt for suspected Israeli informants and collaborators. But it left behind an important imprint on the Palestinian mind that the PNA's emerging authoritarianism has not been able to erase. For one thing, the extensive participation of women and children in the uprising—their "contributions to the national struggle," as the Palestinians saw it—challenged the patriarchal nature of Palestinian society and, by implication, the influence and legitimacy of the chief patriarch, PLO leader Yasser Arafat.[42]

Equally important, the *intifada* reoriented Palestinian identity toward the actual conditions of the Occupied Territories. The reference points for Palestinians' identity—as inhabitants of historic Palestine, as victims first of Zionist colonialism, then Arab betrayal, and finally Israeli repression, as faithful soldiers of the PLO's struggle—underwent a subtle shift. The weight and repression of the occupation and the impotence of the PLO caused Palestinian identity to be defined more by immediate, existing circumstances. In addition to everything else that composed Palestinian identity, being Palestinian meant having your land confiscated, being at the mercy of an Israeli employer, experiencing prolonged water and electricity shutoffs, being harassed at local military checkpoints, being confined for weeks to the house or to specific areas as a result of frequent "closures" by Israeli authorities, being reminded daily of limited opportunities and inferior living standards as compared to those of Israeli settlers, struggling with bureaucracies to secure identity cards and other necessary documents, and enduring everything else that made daily life unbearably difficult. The *intifada* made Palestinian identity more realistic and sober, defined less by political institutions or historic events than by the actual circumstances that governed life from one day to the next. It also led to the steady emergence of local leaders with little or no affinity for the PLO who, especially in Gaza, would emerge as serious alternatives to the PNA's secular, PLO-affiliated leaders.

The Oslo Accords enabled the PLO, or, more specifically, the "outside" leadership of the Palestinians, to once again reassert its control over the Palestinian community, but only under very tight Israeli control and supervision. The establishment of the PNA in many ways signified, initially at least, the institutionalization of Palestinian identity, the birth of a set of actual and symbolic institutions that had risen from the collective struggles and aspirations of Palestinians. Now Palestinian national identity had a flag, an anthem, a president, a representative assembly (the Palestine National Council), a police force, and many of the other necessary accoutrements of a state.

It did not take long, however, for the Palestinians to realize that their initial euphoria had been misplaced. Apart from symbolic acts and empty promises, the PNA was no more capable of alleviating daily stresses and miseries than the PLO had been before the *intifada* started. The Oslo Accords did stop the *intifada*, but they could not put the genie back in the bottle unless, of course, they brought tangible improvements to the lives of Palestinians. And that they could not do. As we shall see shortly, before long, by the late 1990s, the Palestinian powder keg once again exploded. By late 2000, what came to be known as the Al-Aqsa *intifada* was under way.

Like the first *intifada*, the second uprising was a response to the frustration of rising expectations, increased repression by the Israeli occupation authorities, and the continued inability of the PNA leadership to meaningfully improve the harsh realities of daily life, or, for that matter, to contain the spiraling violence of Hamas and the Islamic Jihad (more of which below). By now, the manifold failures of the "outside" leadership had also led to the discrediting of its ideological stance of secular nationalism. For many in the ranks of the ever-more strident counterelite, political Islam became increasingly attractive.

Islam had long served as one of the pivotal elements of Palestinian national identity and a main source of mobilizing opposition to Israeli occupation. Not until the late 1970s and 1980s, however, was it able to emerge out of the shadows of the PLO's secular nationalism and, in many ways, to shape and dictate the events unfolding in the Occupied Territories. In fact, the rise in the popularity and spread of political Islam can be traced to the 1980s and even earlier, when a general trend in the politicization of Islam began sweeping across the Middle East following the Arab "victory" in the 1973 War and the success of the Iranian revolution. The harsh repression of Israeli occupation, the seeming impotence of the PLO, the social and cultural resonance of Islam, and the religion's actual and perceived abilities to deliver on the promises that the PLO had abandoned all combined to enhance Islam's legitimacy as a powerful political force. Not surprisingly, from 1967 to 1987—from the beginning of the occupation of the West Bank and Gaza until the eruption of the *intifada*—the number of mosques increased from 400 to 750 in the West Bank and from 200 to 600 in the Gaza Strip.[43] The Palestinian branch of the Muslim Brotherhood organization, which had started in Egypt in 1928, had also long been active in the Occupied Territories and, throughout the mid-1980s, had experienced a rise in its prestige and popularity concurrent with the PLO's mounting difficulties.[44]

Nevertheless, the outbreak of the *intifada* caught the Muslim Brotherhood by surprise as much as it did the PLO. Both organizations scrambled to establish their own institutional hegemony over the uprising. The PLO encouraged the establishment of a Unified Leadership of the Uprising (ULU), made up of secular individuals sympathetic to or loosely affiliated with the PLO. For its part, the Muslim Brotherhood created a parallel organization called Hamas (meaning "zeal" and constituting an acronym of Harakat al-Muqawama al-Islamiyya, the Islamic Resistance Movement). A smaller, slightly older organization, the Islamic Jihad, which had started as a more radical offshoot of the Muslim Brotherhood and become officially established in 1980, also saw in the *intifada* the opportunity to expand its social and political base. All three entities—the ULU, Hamas, and the Islamic Jihad—actively participated in organizing the demonstrations, strikes, and other events that collectively constituted the *intifada*. Of the three, the actions of the Islamic Jihad were by far the most violent. The organization saw the uprising as a perfect opportunity to carry out a *jihad* (in this sense, crusade) against Israel and its occupation. Most of its members came from modest backgrounds in Gaza, and many had spent time in Israeli prisons, having become even more radicalized by their experience.[45] But radicalism alone was hardly sufficient to maintain the Islamic Jihad's popularity during the course of the *intifada*, and, as time went by, the organization sought to compensate for its ideological limitations by launching spectacular attacks on Israeli targets. Grenade attacks and car bombs, along with other actions that risked the "glory of martyrdom," only served to further weaken the Islamic Jihad because of the severity of Israeli retaliations. Often Israel, having realized the radicalizing effects of prison sentences, retaliated by deporting the organization's leaders or assassinating them.[46]

Whereas the Islamic Jihad emerged from the *intifada* weakened by frequent and highly effective Israeli attacks, Hamas thrived and gradually subsumed its mother organization, the Muslim Brotherhood. One of the primary reasons for the increasing popularity of Hamas as compared to the Islamic Jihad, both throughout the *intifada* and afterward, has been the former's carefully calculated ideological flexibility and willingness to work with other Palestinian forces.[47] While opposed to the secularism of the PLO and subsequently the PNA, and while viewing the Oslo Accords as a betrayal of the Palestinian cause, Hamas was initially careful to avoid direct intra-Palestinian conflict. It also managed to acquiesce to the PNA's recognition of Israel without compromising its own rejectionist stance in relation to Israel, maintaining that a partial Palestinian state (in the West Bank and Gaza) is only a prelude to the establishment of an Islamic state in all of Palestine.[48] At the same time, Hamas's ability to carry out relatively successful violent attacks against Israeli targets during the *intifada*—thirty-two in 1989, including the kidnapping and murder of Israeli soldiers—helped enhance the organization's popular appeal among most Palestinians.[49] Israel's heightened repression in response to the *intifada*, including the deportation of 415 Islamic activists to Lebanon in December 1992, only made Hamas's intransigence and its violent rhetoric more popular.

Violent activities were not the only types of actions advocated by Hamas during the *intifada*. Like the ULU, through leaflets and announcements, Hamas encouraged Palestinians to engage in noncooperation and civil disobedience in relation to Israeli authorities. It also called on the Palestinians to sever their economic ties with the Jewish state. Again, being in tune with the popular pulse of the Palestinian community helped strengthen Hamas's appeal among Muslim Palestinians.

In sum, the 1990s witnessed a gradual shift within Palestinian identity, as manifested in the rise of a more indigenous, locally based counterelite and the growing popularity of Hamas. Through and because of the *intifada*, Palestinian identity was no longer predominantly secular but now contained a strong Islamic component. It centered not so much on the PLO or the Fatah (the PLO's largest and most popular component group) as on refugee camps, local mosques, and schools and universities. The *intifada* did not so much split Palestinian identity as give it additional layers of complexity and a richer texture. The unresolved, largely aborted nature of the *intifada* in many ways resembles and reflects the ambiguity and uncertainty that currently surround Palestinian identity. The Palestinians are the "citizens" or subjects of the PNA, an officially recognized and elected governing body, yet they mostly still live in refugee camps and in their day-to-day life are at the mercy of Israeli occupation authorities. The final shape of this identity—democratic or uncompromising, secular or religious, or a blend of everything—has yet to be determined. What is certain is that such an identity will continue to be shaped by the prevailing circumstances within the Occupied Territories.

THE SITUATION ON THE GROUND

Competing national identities form the backdrop against which the realities of everyday life take place. The term *Occupied Territories* is so frequently and regularly used that the essence of what it expresses—occupation— is often overlooked. Subjective, national identities apart, and irrespective of which group was there first and whose claims are valid, today, more than a century after it all began, the Palestinian-Israeli conflict has essentially become a contest between an overwhelmingly dominant power and a dispossessed, dispersed, subjugated community. No matter how they are presented or what justifications are given for them, the facts on the ground and their force in motivating certain actions cannot be ignored.[50] This section focuses on conditions in the Occupied Territories to better explain the predicaments of the Palestinians and how these predicaments led to the outbreak of the first *intifada* beginning in 1987. Also important to examine are the changes that have come about since the establishment of the PNA, reasons for the eruption of the Al-Aqsa *intifada* beginning in 2000, and, ultimately, the factors that have helped or hindered the prospects for a lasting solution to the conflict.

It was earlier mentioned that the Palestinian-Israeli conflict is essentially a contest between two national identities that refuse to accept the validity and the rights of the other to exist. But Israeli identity has emerged as victorious and dominant—politically, militarily, and economically. In victory, Israel's general assumption that the Palestinians do not have a right to exist on the land of biblical Israel has not changed.

Israel's denial of the Palestinians' rights to exist on Jewish Holy Land has manifested itself in three broad policy options pursued in relation to the Palestinians. The first has been depopulation: reducing, by as much as possible, the actual number of Palestinians living in areas under the military and political control of the state of Israel, first from 1948 to 1967, and then from 1967 until the present. A second, related policy option has been repopulation: encouraging, either actively or passively, the spread of Jewish residential settlements throughout the territories in which Palestinians (or, in the Golan Heights, Syrians) are concentrated. While the "unrightful" Palestinians are being encouraged to leave, their place is being taken by the "rightful" Israelis. Finally, the third policy option has been to control the remaining Palestinians through incapacitating them by whatever means possible, especially in their social and economic development. The cumulative effects of these policies, especially since 1967, when they were extended to the Occupied Territories, resulted in the eruption of the *intifada* from 1987 to 1993. When it became clear that the newly established PNA was incapable of qualitatively changing Israeli policies toward the Palestinians, the Al-Aqsa *intifada* erupted in September 2000.

The departure of Palestinians from the territories in which they have historically lived has occurred by three primary means: expulsion in times of war, encouragement to leave in ordinary times through fostering a repressive environment, and house demolitions. Perhaps the biggest mass exodus of Palestinians from Israel occurred at the outset of the formation of the state of Israel in 1948, when a total of 840,000 Palestinians were displaced from Israel (table 3). For some time, the general Israeli explanation for this "miracle" of "population transfer," that it was either voluntary or in response to encouragements by Arab leaders, was accepted as historical truth.[51] But a number of works by notable Israeli scholars, chief among them Benny Morris and Ilan Pappe, have conclusively demonstrated that most Palestinians reluctantly left their homes because of campaigns of psychological terror, false Israeli radio broadcasts, or the destruction of their villages.[52] A second major Palestinian exodus took place in the three months following the 1967 War, when over 300,000 Palestinians were forced out of the West Bank and the Gaza Strip. Of these, 120,000 were second-time refugees and had spent the previous twenty years in refugee camps.[53]

More prevalent has been Israel's general fostering of an environment in the Occupied Territories that is stifling and unbearable. The simplest and most mundane of everyday acts—driving, farming (which most Palestinians do), securing work permits (needed for travel from the territories to and from Israel)—require cumbersome, often frustratingly long procedures and paperwork. Life in the Occupied Territories is full of hazards and petty restrictions, and the dangers of being subjected to prolonged "administrative detention," collective punishment, or harassment or attack by Israeli settlers are both real and constant.[54] The treatment of Palestinians as second-class citizens goes beyond guaranteeing Israel's security needs. According to the U.S. Department of State's *Country Report on Human Rights Practices,* compared to the Palestinians who live under Israeli rule, Israeli Jews living in the Occupied Territories "receive preferential treatment from Israeli authorities in terms of protection of personal property rights and of legal redress."[55] Israeli legal procedures within the Occupied Territories, most of which are in contravention of the Hague Regulations of 1907 and the Fourth Geneva Convention of 1947 (concerning the "Protection of Civilian Persons in Times of War"), are designed to go beyond merely ensuring Israeli control over the Palestinians. They also help facilitate the expropriation of land held by Palestinians by deciding what "state land" is, effectively taking it out of indigenous control and turning it over to Israeli government agencies or to civilian settlers.[56] An Amnesty International report issued in 1999 found that some 35 percent of the land in East Jerusalem had been confiscated, at least 90 percent of which had been previously owned privately by Palestinians.[57] Life in the Occupied Territories holds few luxuries and many pitfalls for Palestinians. For many, the risks and uncertainties of migrating abroad count for less than the pains of staying behind.

One main danger of life in the Occupied Territories is that of having one's house demolished by Israeli military authorities. House demolitions are one of the most effective—and controversial—methods used by the Israeli authorities to depopulate parts of the Occupied Territories. According to Amnesty International,

> Since 1967, when Israel occupied the West Bank, including East Jerusalem, and the Gaza Strip, thousands of Palestinian homes have been demolished. Some had been built and inhabited for years; they are furnished, occupied often by more than one family with many children, who are often given only 15 minutes to gather their possessions and leave. A squad of workers may throw the furniture into the street; or the furniture may still be in the house when the family sees the bulldozers move in. Other houses are still uninhabited but have been built as the fruit of months of work and the expenditure, sometimes, of all the family's savings.[58]

A more recent Amnesty International report states that "[f]or years, the Israeli authorities have pursued a policy of discriminatory house demolition, on the one hand allowing scores of Israeli settlements to be built on occupied Palestinian land, in breach of international law, while simultaneously confiscating Palestinian lands, refusing building permits for Palestinians and destroying their homes. The land vacated has often been used to build illegal Israeli settlements. International law forbids occupying powers from settling their own citizens in the territories they occupy."[59]

Immediately following the annexation of East Jerusalem in 1967, Israeli authorities drove out an estimated five thousand Arab residents and destroyed their homes in order to guarantee security access to the Wailing Wall. From 1967 to 1974, in the West Bank alone (excluding East Jerusalem), some 4,425 Palestinian houses were demolished. Another 2,399 were demolished from 1987 to the first three months of 1999. An estimated 14,500 people, including at least 6,000 children, were rendered homeless as a result of these demolitions.[60] At the same time, permits for the construction of new houses in the Occupied Territories were so difficult to obtain that they totaled no more than 2,950 between 1967 and 1999.[61] By contrast, according to the *Statistical Abstract of Israel 2000*, between 1997 and 1999 alone, 7,350 buildings were constructed in the Occupied Territories by Israeli civilians and official agencies. In only one year, 1999, Israelis began work on the construction of an additional 2,510 buildings.[62] A report by the United Nations, issued in October 2000, also found that vandalism of Palestinian homes by Jewish settlers was widespread and that the IDF directed "random gunfire at water tanks on the roofs of homes."[63] According to the Israeli human rights group B'Tselem, over the past ten years Israeli authorities have demolished more than 2,200 Palestinian homes, leaving more than 13,000 Palestinians homeless.[64]

The depopulation of the Occupied Territories of their Palestinian residents is taking place at a time of their repopulation with Israelis.[65] This repopulation has taken the form of establishing Israeli settlements in the Occupied Territories from immediately after their capture in 1967 to the present, so that today nearly 480,000 Israeli settlers live in Palestinian areas (table 4). At first, the settlements were established according to the Allon Plan, named after then-Labor Minister Yigael Allon, who favored the establishment of civilian Jewish neighborhoods in the form of security belts in the Golan Heights and around East Jerusalem. The initial goal was to "create facts on the ground," with Israelis moving to sparsely populated Palestinian areas to show continuous Jewish residence.[66] Following its victory in 1977, the Likud cabinet drastically accelerated the pace of the settlements and changed their geographic focus. Instead of concentrating on areas with few Palestinians, settlements were now deliberately made in areas with large Palestinian populations, the goal being to consolidate Israel's control over

Table 4. Population Growth in Selected West Bank Settlements

Settlement	Population (1000s)			
	1983	1995	2006	2008
Gush Ezyion	2.6	6.5	13.0	14.4
Har Hevron	0.2	2.8	5.3	6.0
Megillot Dead Sea	0.4	0.7	0.9	1.0
Matte Benyamin	4.7	19.2	40.8	45.6
Avrot HaYarden	2.1	2.6	3.4	3.5
Shomeron	3.5	11.7	21.6	23.6
Total	13.7	43.6	85.1	94.1

SOURCE: "Localities and Population, by Municipal Status and District," *Statistical Abstract of Israel, 2009*, Table 2.13.

the areas and make territorial compromises difficult. Despite the frequent change of cabinets since, this policy still remains in effect today.

Settlements represent more than mere demographic colonization of the Occupied Territories by Israel. They signify a *deepening* of Israeli control over the territories and their Palestinian residents. In addition to expanding Israeli military control, settlements are designed to facilitate Israel's access to two additional strategic resources: land and water. An elaborate road system has been constructed to link Israel directly to the new settlements while bypassing major Arab towns in the West Bank such as Nablus and Ramallah. According to Israel's Central Bureau of Statistics, the number of new settlement dwellings sold in the West Bank jumped from 437 in 2006 to 733 in 2008.[67] New settlements and housing units bring with them additional Israeli infrastructures and military patrols—in addition, of course, to heavily armed settlers—thus solidifying the extent and nature of Israeli control. The Palestinian city of Hebron, while an extreme example, starkly demonstrates this point: "Because Hebron is the only city in all of the West Bank where Jews actually live among the Arabs—as opposed to living in self-contained settlements near Arab towns—the Israelis have retained control over 20 percent of the city so they can protect the 540 Jewish residents. However, 20,000 of Hebron's 125,000 Arabs . . . live or work in the area still under Israeli control."[68]

Hebron's settlers, it must be pointed out, are "ideological" or "political" settlers who have moved into predominantly Palestinian areas mainly

Figure 22. A settler tosses wine at a Palestinian woman on Shuhada Street in Hebron. Photo courtesy of New York Times Co.

to "establish facts on the ground." Initially all settlement activities were ideological and were orchestrated by a fundamentalist group calling itself the Gush Emunium (bloc of the faithful).[69] In recent years, relatively inexpensive property prices have drawn an increasing number of nonideological bargain hunters motivated by convenience, especially in light of the preferential treatment they receive from the government when it comes to "the provision of space, construction, water provision and grants."[70] Today, nearly 60 percent of all settlers are nonideological Israelis in search of hilltop properties at affordable prices.

In addition to depopulation and repopulation, Israel has sought to control the Occupied Territories by marginalizing and incapacitating them economically and politically. The political incapacitation of the territories, in the form of tight controls and the imposition of measures that are all too often draconian, was alluded to earlier. Complementing these political-military measures have been specific policies designed to ensure the continued economic underdevelopment of the West Bank and Gaza. Occupation policies, and restrictions on construction activities or the physical movement of people, have resulted in the underdevelopment or complete absence of industrial, construction, and service sectors throughout the territories, so that small-scale agriculture remains one of the most common forms of economic activity. The spread of Jewish settlements throughout the territories and the rapid development of the Israeli economy have instead created a number of job opportunities for Palestinians inside Israel. By 2000, an estimated 125,000 Palestinians were employed as day laborers inside Israel, some 60,000 of them having work permits and another 65,000 working without permits.[71]

The economic dependence of the territories on Israel is further deepened by Israel's ability to literally close off the territories to through traffic. The road system, as already mentioned, reinforces the segmentation of the Palestinian economy and impedes economic integration and development. Attempts at slowing the pace of Palestinian economic development can also take more direct and blatant forms. On many occasions, for example, Israeli authorities have prevented fishermen and agricultural producers from Gaza and the West Bank from harvesting their crops or exporting them in a timely manner as needed.[72]

As a result, both Gaza and the West Bank, especially the former, have consistently suffered from crushing poverty. According to the World Bank, the Palestinian per capita gross domestic product (GDP) in 2006 ($1,130) was 40 percent less than what it was in 1999. In late 2007, unemployment averaged around 19 percent in the West Bank and a staggering 33 percent in Gaza. The percentage of Gazans living in "deep poverty" increased from 21.6 percent in 1998 to nearly 35 percent in 2006. Meanwhile, because of closures and replacement with new arrivals from the former Soviet bloc, the number of Palestinians working in Israel or in settlements declined from 116,000 in 2000 (by UN estimates 125,000) to less than 64,000 in early 2007.[73]

Collectively, these are the conditions within which the two *intifadas* took place. For the thousands of young Palestinians who have taken part in the uprisings, life has held little promise. Their days have been defined by threats and intimidation, discrimination, poverty, and despair. Under conditions in which access to health care and garbage collection seem like unattainable luxuries, the Palestinians' frustrations turned them into stone throwers in the late 1980s and the early 1990s, and, as the violence has escalated, into suicide bombers in the late 1990s. Like all spontaneous revolutions, the two *intifadas* developed their own logic and momentum, their own symbols, martyrs, and leaders. They also gave ample opportunities to those bent on unleashing indiscriminate terror on the Israelis, and many innocent bystanders were killed as a result.[74] The Al-Aqsa *intifada* was especially violent. According to the U.S. Department of State, in 2002 an estimated 469 Israelis were killed and over 2,498 were injured as a result of more than sixty Palestinian suicide bombings.[75]

From the beginning, the *intifada*'s mass-based, popular nature made it virtually impossible for the Israeli army to contain. In desperation, in the late 1980s the Israeli government turned to its archenemy, the PLO, which had itself become greatly weakened and was desperate to reassert its control over the full-fledged rebellion. In the process, the PLO hoped also to reinvigorate its ties with its constituency. By now, the sheer scope of the uprising and the gravity of the Israeli government's response had made many ordinary Israelis question the wisdom of their country's continued hold on the Occupied Territories. The alternative to peace, it seemed, was too costly, too brutal, and too much at variance with the original goals of Zionism. Somehow the madness needed to be stopped. Peace appeared as the most viable and attractive solution to the quagmire that the Occupied Territories had become.

THE ELUSIVE SEARCH FOR PEACE

The conflict between the Israelis and the Palestinians had been raging for nearly a century. At least four wars had been fought, tens of thousands of people had been killed on both sides, and countless lives had been shattered. The accumulated human and emotional costs of the conflict could be fully grasped only by the Israelis and the Palestinians who bore them. One land, two peoples—that's how it all started. In the process, each side degenerated into "the enemy" of the other. Eager to defend their survival and right to exist, both sides all too often lost perspective and compromised their own humanity. Wars numb the senses, blur the distinction between right and wrong, and confuse means and ends. The conflict over Palestine/Israel was approaching the century mark, and it was only a matter of time before each side realized what it had become. Such was the realization of some, but by no means all, Israelis and Palestinians.

The imperative of peace making was not so much a sudden epiphany by the actors involved as the product of a larger historical evolution of the conflict. Over time, a group of Palestinians and Israelis had come to realize that they could not deny the existence of the other, no matter how hard they tried or what weapons they used. They were also troubled by the increasing inhumanity to which the conflict had given rise—not only the enemy's inhumanity but also their own. On each side of the divide there thus developed a group of "accommodationists" who gradually became convinced of the need to accommodate the other side and recognize its right to exist. Idealists willing to compromise with and accommodate the enemy had always existed on both sides. However, their voices had been drowned out by a majority righteously bent on the total destruction of the enemy. But the seven-year *intifada*, which had turned into the longest sustained battle between Palestinians and Israelis, drove home the costs of war for more Palestinians and Israelis. The 1967 War had lasted only six days and the 1973 War only a few weeks. But the *intifada* opened people's eyes to the sobering realities of war: home demolitions, suicide car bombs, mass deportations, abject poverty, despair, fear and paranoia, stabbings, and a host of other tragedies unfolding before the eye day after day. In the words of two Israeli scholars, "The violence also deeply affected Israel itself. Many Israelis perceived their country's occupation as morally indefensible, socially deleterious, economically ruinous, and politically and militarily harmful. Israel's political leadership faced mounting pressures from broad segments of the public to stop quelling the uprising by force and instead to propose political solutions."[76] A similar process was also occurring among Palestinians, for whom the costs of the *intifada* were even more immediate and devastating.

By 1992, the leaders of the state of Israel—notably Foreign Minister Shimon Peres and Prime Minister Yitzhak Rabin, who had done long service in the military—had become convinced of the necessity of peace. Earlier, when he had been the defense minister, Rabin had tried desperately to stop the *intifada* but to no avail. Peace, he must have reasoned, was the only viable alternative. With the larger "accommodationist" trend growing among many Israelis, he could now sell his vision of the future to a larger audience. This vision, incidentally, was articulated most idealistically by Shimon Peres.[77] The PLO, meanwhile, exiled in Tunis and despondent over its inability to fully control the *intifada* and the activities of those "inside," saw accommodation with Israel as the only way to salvage its continued political viability and its relevance for the Palestinians. The PLO's shift in strategy was welcomed by many Palestinians who were elated at the prospect of finally living in peace.

Palestinian and Israeli accommodationists have been opposed by equally determined "rejectionists." For many people on both sides, the wounds are too deep to let go, the stakes are too high to compromise, and the enemy is too untrustworthy to negotiate with. For whatever reason, they cannot move beyond the "familiar, comfortable wall of hostility."[78] And they see the accommodationists as sellouts and traitors. Rabin, the military man turned peace hero, paid for his vision with his life. On November 4, 1995, soon after addressing a peace rally, he was assassinated by an Israeli seminary *(yeshiva)* student. In his defense, the assassin, Yigal Amir, claimed that Rabin had failed the Jewish people and had therefore deserved to die.[79] In fact, as will be shown shortly, besides signing an agreement with them, by the time of his death Rabin had given the Palestinians very little.

A convergence of the interests of the accommodationists on both sides and a realistic assessment of how the interests of their peoples could be served brought about the Oslo Accords. In some ways, the Oslo Accords were a by-product of two major, previous Arab-Israeli peace initiatives, the 1978 Camp David Accords and the 1991 Madrid Peace Conference. The Camp David Accords initially held much promise for the Palestinians but ultimately ignored them altogether. The ensuing "absence of peace" paved the way for face-to-face Israeli-Palestinian talks beginning in 1991. As it turned out, these negotiations, first in Madrid and then in Washington, D.C., were a charade meant to conceal more meaningful, parallel negotiations under way in Oslo, Norway.

The Camp David Accords came about after a realization by Egyptian President Anwar Sadat that the United States simply would not allow anyone to defeat Israel in a military conflict. This point had been made most forcefully during the 1973 War. The only way to win the Sinai back for Egypt and gain autonomy for the Palestinians, Sadat reasoned, would be through negotiations with Israel, under the auspices of an American-sponsored agreement. With a flair for the dramatic, Sadat flew to Tel Aviv on November 19, 1977, and, the next day, addressed the Knesset, Israel's parliament, in Jerusalem.[80] In a long and flowery speech, he proposed a peace agreement based on five specific points:

> Ending the occupation of the Arab territories occupied in 1967.
>
> Achievement of the fundamental rights of the Palestinian people and their right to self-determination, including their right to establish their own state.
>
> The right of all states in the area to live in peace within their boundaries. . . .
>
> Commitment of all states in the region to administer the relations among them in accordance with the objectives and principles of the United Nations Charter. . . .
>
> Ending the state of belligerence in the region.[81]

The Israeli leadership, then composed of members of the Likud Party, was considerably less keen on including the issue of Palestinian rights in a peace agreement with Egypt. Prime Minister Menachem Begin simply mistrusted Sadat and his motives. According to Ezer Weizman, Israel's defense minister at the time, Israel "seemed to be finding every possible tactic to impede the peace process."[82] At the most, Begin was willing to offer the Palestinians limited autonomy in the West Bank and Gaza. U.S. president Jimmy Carter also vacillated on the issue. The PLO's own vehement, public rejection of Sadat's initiative did not help matters.[83] Nevertheless, despite numerous obstacles, from September 5 through 17, 1978, Israeli and Egyptian negotiators gathered in the U.S. presidential retreat at Camp David. After tense negotiations that several times came close to collapsing, they hammered out an agreement.

The Camp David negotiations resulted in signing a treaty that contained two major components (or negotiating tracks). The first component was called "A Framework for the Conclusion of a Peace Treaty between Israel and Egypt," based on which Israeli forces were to withdraw from the Sinai over a three-year period. Provisions were also made for establishing a demilitarized zone between the two countries, setting up a peacekeeping force, and making other security arrangements. Full diplomatic ties were also to be established between Egypt and Israel within nine months of signing a peace treaty.[84] The second component, labeled "A Framework for Peace in the Middle East," sought to make provisions for a comprehensive Arab-Israeli peace settlement. Some of the key points of the accord were acceptance by all parties of UN Resolution 242; resolution of the "Palestinian problem in all aspects"; the establishment of mechanisms for the conduct of "good neighborly relations"; and "full autonomy" for the residents of the West Bank and the Gaza Strip based on arrangements to be worked out between Egypt, Israel, and Jordan.[85]

While on paper impressive in its scope and breadth, the Camp David Accords' "Framework for Peace in the Middle East" immediately encountered problems. It assumed Jordan's participation without having consulted its leaders, thus undermining Jordanian sovereignty. Instead, throughout the 1980s, King Hussein carried out his own secret talks with Israel.[86] More consequential was the pressure put on Begin by the Israeli Right as a result of concessions the agreement made to both the Egyptians and the Palestinians. This in turn prompted the prime minister to interpret the provisions dealing with the Palestinians very differently than either the Egyptians or the Americans did. Gradually, those provisions were all but forgotten. By now, Sadat had invested too much of his prestige and personal legitimacy in the peace process with Israel to back out, and his position was made all the more unshakable by his increasing isolation within the Arab world.

Sadat did get the Sinai back for Egypt, but ultimately he could not deliver for the Palestinians. King Hussein, meanwhile, wanted the West Bank for himself, and only in July 1988, amid mounting economic difficulties at home and an uncontainable popular uprising among the West Bankers, did he renounce his claims to the West Bank.[87] Israeli-Palestinian peace, meanwhile, became more elusive and remote as the drama of Middle Eastern diplomacy took one tragic turn after another. From 1975 to 1991, Lebanon was engaged in a bloody civil war. In 1978 and again in 1982, Israel invaded Lebanon. Only in 2000 did Israel fully pull out of Lebanon, but even then the hostilities between the two countries continued. In 1980 Iraq invaded Iran, and the two countries fought each other to exhaustion until 1988. Then in 1990 Iraq invaded Kuwait. In 1991, a U.S.-led alliance fought and ejected the Iraqis from Kuwait. As the Middle East drifted from one crisis to another, the Palestinians felt forgotten and ignored. The *intifada* was a cry of anguish, and the Israelis soon realized that they simply could not suppress it. Thus ensued the Madrid Peace Conference in 1991 and, more meaningfully, secret negotiations between the PLO and the Israeli government in Norway in 1993.

In October 1991, the United States and the Soviet Union jointly invited Israel, Syria, Jordan, Egypt, and the Palestinians to a peace conference in Madrid. Since neither the United States nor Israel recognized the PLO, the Palestinians were to attend as part of a joint Jordanian-Palestinian delegation, and, theoretically at least, those attending could not be affiliated with the PLO. The Palestinian delegation was made up of respected and influential "insiders," many of whom had been hardened by nearly four years of the *intifada*. The talks soon degenerated into endless squabbles over procedures and mutual recriminations. Slowly but surely, the "internals" allowed the PLO to make the major decisions for them during the talks, which by then had moved from Madrid to Washington. Israel knew this but looked the other way. In the words of a senior Israeli diplomat, "[T]hough we would never admit this openly, we were engaged in a charade. In Washington, we were actually negotiating with Yasser Arafat by fax!"[88]

Israel's 1992 elections brought back to power the Labor Party, headed by the idealistic Shimon Peres and the more pragmatic Yitzhak Rabin. The former became the foreign minister and the latter the prime minister. Sensing the weakness of the PLO—its isolation, financial bankruptcy, and loss of control over both the *intifada* and a growing number of internals— Israel decided the time was ripe to hold direct talks with the PLO. Earlier, a Norwegian academic had facilitated informal contacts in Oslo between two Israeli academics and members of the PLO, and that in turn served as

Figure 23. Yitzhak Rabin and Yasser Arafat sign the Oslo Accords.

the conduit for in-depth, formal discussions between the two archenemies beginning in May 1993. In less than four months, the two sides signed a Declaration of Principles (DOP) that became the basis for a future peace agreement between them.[89]

The secret talks in Oslo were always tense and on several occasions came near the breaking point. Throughout, Arafat and his team negotiated from a position of increasing weakness, and in many ways Israeli negotiators were able to dictate the terms of the resulting agreement.[90] The agreement that was reached contained two parts. The first, which took the form of letters exchanged between the PLO and the Israeli government on September 9 and 10, 1993, dealt with mutual recognition, whereby each side recognized the right of the other to exist. The second was a Declaration of Principles (DOP), which the two sides signed in a face-to-face meeting at the White House between PLO leader Yasser Arafat and Shimon Peres and Yitzhak Rabin. After years of violent animosity, the former enemies sealed the agreement with a historic handshake.

The DOP outlined "interim self-government arrangements" for the Palestinian territories. For the Israelis, " 'gradual' was the key word describing the transition from occupation to self-rule, from violence to peaceful coexistence."[91] Israel was to withdraw its troops from the Gaza Strip and the West Bank city of Jericho within six months after the declaration went into effect. Within nine months, Israel would redeploy its troops in other areas of the West Bank and elections would be held for a Palestinian Council. Within two years, negotiations would begin on the "permanent status" of the West Bank and the Gaza Strip. These permanent status negotiations, which were to take no more than three years to complete, would settle all outstanding (and for both sides highly emotional) issues such as the status of Jerusalem, the "right of return" for Palestinian refugees, Israeli settlements, and control over borders.[92]

Historic as it was, the DOP contained major flaws. To begin with, it was highly ambiguous and dealt with important issues—such as the status of Jerusalem and Palestinian refugees—only in very broad terms.[93] More importantly, while each of the two sides came to the bargaining table with the general intent of putting an end to years of violence and bloodshed, for both, immediate political considerations appear to have been more important. For Arafat and other "outside" PLO leaders, progress on the negotiations with Israel meant being able to finally territorialize the quasi-state apparatus of the PLO, supplant the "inside" leadership that had become emboldened as a result of the *intifada*, and consolidate the PLO's rule throughout the Occupied Territories. All of these, in fact, the PLO did—now under the label Palestine National Authority—as soon as it was officially recognized as being in charge of parts of the Occupied Territories.

For Rabin and the rest of his cabinet, meanwhile, Israel's national and security interests—defined in the form of facts on the ground—far outweighed any other consideration. In the words of an Israeli observer, "Rabin's policies between 1992 and 1995 were disastrous for the Palestinians and very favourable to Israel. He had somehow succeeded in turning around Israel's isolation (caused by the *intifada*) while still holding on to virtually all of the West Bank and a wholly disproportionate slice of Gaza. Rabin's genius was in appearing to compromise whilst in fact securing all of Israel's objectives."[94] But the signing of the DOP unleashed a torrent of angry emotions among the "rejectionists." Before his assassination in November 1995, Rabin was maligned by many Israelis, some even likening him to Hitler or calling him "Arabin."

The reaction on the Palestinian side was not quite as violent, at least initially, but it was equally determined. Many "outsiders," most prominently Columbia University professor and longtime activist Edward Said (d. 2003), called the DOP "an instrument of Palestinian surrender, a Palestinian Versailles."[95] In its zeal to become "a kind of small-town government," Said charged, the PLO had negotiated away the rights of fourteen thousand Palestinian prisoners in Israeli jails, leaving Israel in control of "land, water, overall security, and foreign affairs in [the] 'autonomous' areas."[96] Instead, Arafat had concentrated on the centralization of power: the Palestinian police force was some eighteen thousand strong, and Arafat's personal bodyguards alone were said to number approximately 125.

The complaints voiced by Said were not just those of a frustrated outsider. By signing the peace agreement with Israel and establishing his Palestinian Authority, Arafat managed to end the *intifada* but failed to bring qualitative changes or improvements to the lives of ordinary Palestinians. In the process of consolidating power, during Arafat's presidency the PNA often resorted to highly autocratic and patrimonial methods, frequently stifling dissent, ensuring the political dependence of the once-burgeoning Palestinian civil society, and, whenever possible, undermining prospects for democratic opening.[97] The PNA's difficulties were compounded in May 1996 with the election to office of hard-line Likud leader Benjamin Netanyahu, who shared neither the vision of Rabin and Peres for Israel's future nor their enthusiasm for the DOP. Netanyahu's premiership set the Oslo Accords adrift. For three years, until he lost his bid for reelection to Labor's Ehud Barak in May 1999, Netanyahu did his best to derail the Oslo Accords, to the extent that Israel met few of its obligations outlined under the terms of the DOP. Ariel Sharon, at the time Netanyahu's foreign minister, went so far as to call the accords "national suicide." "Everybody," he is reported to have said, "has to move, run, and grab as many hilltops as they can and to enlarge the settlements because everything we take now will stay ours. . . . Everything we don't grab will go to them."[98]

Despite such attitudes, neither the Israeli nor the Palestinian leadership, nor for that matter the Clinton administration in Washington, could afford to be seen as indifferent to the "peace process" or, worse yet, to seem as if they were obstructing it. On October 23, 1998, therefore, after tense negotiations sponsored by the White House, Arafat and Netanyahu signed the Wye River Memorandum, named after the resort where the talks were held.

The Wye agreement broke no new ground but instead sought to facilitate the implementation of prior accords, in turn paving the way for the "final status negotiations" originally outlined in the Oslo Accords. In reality, the new agreement gave legitimacy to Prime Minister Netanyahu's highly peculiar interpretation of Oslo, outlining in great detail the steps that the Palestinian leadership needed to take—under the aegis of PNA cooperation with the American Central Intelligence Agency—in guaranteeing Israel's security and preventing future terrorist attacks on Israel.[99] Desperate to deliver something, anything, out of Oslo Accords that by now had all but collapsed, Arafat and the PNA were only too willing to buy for themselves some sorely needed international legitimacy through signing another agreement, even if it meant cracking down on Palestinian activism through cooperation with the CIA. As the scholar Norman Finkelstein observed, "[T]otally dependent, Palestinian elites will continue to do Israel's bidding, while enjoying the prerequisites of collaboration."[100]

"If Peres was a dreamer," writes one Israeli scholar, "Benjamin Netanyahu was the destroyer of dreams."[101] Ultimately, his foot-dragging on the Oslo Accords and his perceived "character flaws" before the Israeli electorate cost him his reelection in the May 1999 parliamentary elections. Instead, some 56 percent of the electorate voted for Ehud Barak, leader of the Labor Party and one of Israel's most decorated soldiers. Since the beginning of the *intifada,* a number of Israelis had warmed up to the idea of exchanging "land for peace" if in the process Israel's security could be guaranteed. In his campaign for office, Barak had promised to withdraw IDF forces from southern Lebanon, sign peace treaties with both the Palestinians and the Syrians, and, at the same time, maintain some of the so-called "red lines": Jerusalem would remain Israel's "eternal, united capital"; there would be no return to the pre-1967 borders; Jewish settlements would not be dismantled; and no Palestinian or foreign army would be allowed west of the Jordan River.[102]

Barak won the elections by a landslide, but insofar as the Palestinians were concerned, Israeli policy changed little. In fact, the construction of new settlements continued at a feverish pace. Palestinian homes continued to be demolished, and even more Palestinian land was annexed. According to one estimate, from the signing of the Oslo Accords in 1993 until September 2000, which saw the eruption of a new *intifada,* one hundred thousand new Israeli settlers moved into the West Bank and Gaza, doubling the settler population, and thirty new settlement or settler-related infrastructures were built. During the same time, the Israeli government confiscated over forty thousand acres of agriculturally viable Palestinian lands worth more than $1 billion.[103] The closure of Palestinian territories by the Israeli occupation authorities, and therefore their economic strangulation, became a regular feature of life in the West Bank and Gaza.

Despite his landslide victory, Prime Minister Barak was forced to rely on a highly diverse and fragmented coalition to put together a cabinet. Consequently, from the very beginning his domestic and foreign policy initiatives encountered significant resistance within the Knesset and even among his coalition partners. In the meanwhile, with the PNA increasingly relegated to oblivion and out of touch with the Palestinian "street," sporadic Palestinian attacks on Israeli targets continued, each time followed by massive Israeli reprisals. For the Israeli electorate, Barak's election promise of "peace and security" seemed more and more hollow. Within the context of the PNA's steady irrelevance and desperation, and the Barak cabinet's political fragmentation and increasing unpopularity, the two sides met once again in the United States in July 2000, this time to tackle the Oslo Accords' most difficult provisions, the so-called final status negotiations. They were hosted at the Camp David retreat by President Bill Clinton, himself in the final months of his presidency and eager to be remembered for fostering Palestinian-Israeli peace rather than for personal indiscretions while in office.

The final status negotiations included by far the most contentious aspects of the Palestinian-Israeli conflict, at the core of more than fifty years of bloodshed: control over Jerusalem; "the right of return" of Palestinian refugees; the issue of Jewish settlements and control over territory; and access to and control over natural resources, especially water. Arafat and other Palestinian negotiators felt that tackling these issues was premature without first negotiating over other outstanding matters. "Madam Secretary," Arafat is reported to have said to U.S. Secretary of State Madeleine Albright, "if you issue an invitation to a summit, and if it is held and fails, this will weaken the Palestinian people's hopes for achieving peace. Let us not weaken these hopes."[104] According to an American official involved at the summit, "Like Barak, the Palestinian leader felt that permanent status negotiations were long overdue; unlike Barak, he did not think that this justified doing away with the interim obligations."[105] But the summit was held anyway, this time at the site made famous by an earlier historic peace treaty between Israel and Egypt.

From the beginning, Camp David II was doomed to failure. Each side felt that it was making major concessions to the other, at great political cost to its standing with its own domestic constituents, yet each felt that the other was unwilling to come to a reasonable compromise. The issue of Jerusalem turned out to be the biggest obstacle. The city is home to the religious site that the Israelis call the Temple Mount and the Palestinians call Haram al-Sharif. For Muslims, the Haram, which houses the Dome of the Rock and the Al-Aqsa Mosque, is Islam's third holiest site after Mecca and Medina. The western flank of Haram al-Sharif forms the Western (or Wailing) Wall, the most important site of Jewish prayer and pilgrimage. Jews consider the Mount to have been the site of the First and the Second Temples and home to the future Third Temple. Since Israel's capture of East Jerusalem in 1967, the area has been under Israeli jurisdiction, but it is administered by the Council of Waqf (religious endowment) and Muslim Affairs.

Barak offered that the Palestinian leader could become the "custodian" of the Haram al-Sharif and fly the Palestinian flag over it but that the site would remain under Israeli sovereignty.[106] While the proposal represented a major departure from Israel's traditional stand toward Jerusalem and ignited intense debate in the Israeli press, it was not acceptable to Arafat, who felt that neither the Palestinian "street" nor the Muslim world at large would accept his negotiating away full control over the Haram. Various proposals for compensation, resettlement, and even "reunification" of a limited number of refugees with their families in Israel were also floated. Again, this represented a break with past Israeli approaches to the issue. But Prime Minister Barak was unwilling to recognize the principle of Palestinian "right of return."[107] This was also unacceptable to the Palestinian negotiators.

As for Israeli settlements, whose numbers had mushroomed since Barak's election, the prime minister offered to return to the Palestinians 90 percent of the West Bank in return for the annexation of three large Israeli settlements, whose total population was approximately 160,000. According to the terms of the proposal, between 80,000 and 100,000 Palestinians would have been disenfranchised; an encircled and divided East Jerusalem would have been cut off from its Palestinian hinterlands; and the West Bank would have been divided into four cantons, with passage between them under full Israeli control.[108] The Palestinians rejected this proposal as well. With regard to control over natural resources, the most precious of which in the area was water, the Israelis insisted on control over all aquifers in the West Bank.[109]

Before long, it became obvious that the summit was at an impasse; in fact, while some creative solutions were suggested, the summit had failed to resolve the core issues of the conflict. On July 25, 2000, the summit concluded without a final agreement. A frustrated President Clinton publicly expressed his anger at Arafat and his negotiating team for their unwillingness to accommodate Prime Minister Barak's visionary proposals. How much of this was out of genuine exasperation with the Palestinians and how much was a maneuver to stop Barak's steady decline in opinion polls in Israel is unclear. The Palestinians viewed Barak's "generous offers" as public relations stunts without any real value to their people. Their frame of reference at the start of the negotiations had been Israel's pre-1967 borders; it was these borders that were up for "negotiations," not the status quo borders from which Barak wanted to negotiate. In fact, the Palestinian negotiating team, not wanting to be accused of "giving away Palestine" again, as they had been after Oslo, had gone to Camp David "almost apologetically, determined that this time they would not be duped."[110] The PNA had already lost substantial ground to Hamas in the aftermath of Oslo's failure to change the daily lives of ordinary Palestinians. It could not lose any more. As luck would have it, both Barak and Arafat lost even more after Camp David II's failure.

On September 28, 2000, Knesset member and former foreign minister Ariel Sharon, who had by now become the leader of the Likud Party, visited the Haram al-Sharif in Jerusalem, flanked by more than a thousand Israeli soldiers. Campaigning for the office of the prime minister, Sharon meant the visit to signify Israel's control over the religious compound and Likud's unwillingness to negotiate it away. One of contemporary Israel's most controversial figures, Sharon had commanded Israel's ill-fated invasion of Lebanon in 1982. Subsequently, he had been condemned by an Israeli commission for failing to stop the massacre of 1,300 Palestinian civilians by Lebanese Christian Phalangists in the refugee camps of Sabra and Shatila outside Beirut.[111] Today he is one of the most reviled Israeli figures among the Palestinians.

The Palestinians saw Sharon's visit to the Haram al-Sharif not only as an affront to one of the most important symbols of their nationality but also as an insult to Islam. Even the United States asked Prime Minister Barak to prevent Sharon from visiting the compound, but to no avail. The day after the visit, on September 29, massive Palestinian demonstrations erupted. This was the tinder that set the Occupied Territories ablaze once again and precipitated the Al-Aqsa *intifada*. According to a report prepared by former U.S. Senator George Mitchell,

> What began as a series of confrontations between Palestinian demonstrators and Israeli security forces, which resulted in the Government of Israel's (GOI) initial restrictions on the movement of Palestinians in the West Bank and Gaza Strip (closures), has since evolved into a wider array of violent actions and responses. There have been exchanges of fire between built-up areas, sniping incidents and clashes between Israeli settlers and Palestinians. There have also been terrorist acts and Israeli reactions thereto (characterized by the GOI as counter-terrorism), including killings, further destruction of property and economic measures. More recently, there have been mortar attacks on Israeli locations and IDF ground incursions into Palestinian areas.

The report went on to conclude that "[t]he Sharon visit did not cause the 'Al-Aqsa intifada.' But it was poorly timed and the provocative effect

Figure 24. Women march in support of Hamas.

should have been foreseen; indeed it was foreseen by those who urged that the visit be prohibited. More significant were the events that followed: the decision of the Israeli police on September 29 to use lethal means against the Palestinian demonstrators; and the subsequent failure . . . of either party to exercise restraint."[112]

The scope and nature of the violence that ensued was astounding even by the standards of the Palestinian-Israeli conflict. Both sides unleashed violence on the other side—the Palestinians through suicide bombings, the Israelis by tanks and bulldozers. Countless innocent civilians died on both sides. As the cycle of violence became more and more vicious, and as the PNA became increasingly incapable of influencing the ebb and flow of events on the streets, a radicalized Hamas found itself with an expanding pool of young Palestinians willing and eager to find glory in martyrdom. According to the U.S. Department of State, in 2001, fifty-five Israeli civilians were killed in attacks by Palestinian suicide bombers, some of whom had strapped nails to their bodies in order to inflict maximum damage on their intended victims.[113] Altogether, in 2001 there were some 1,970 attacks against Israeli targets, including shootings, ambushes, mortar attacks, and stabbings.[114] Each attack was soon followed by ferocious retaliation by the IDF. Before long, the Al-Aqsa *intifada* had developed a violent logic of its own. Innocent civilians on both sides of the divide, some as young as two months old (a Palestinian boy) or four months old (an Israeli girl), became victims of the spiraling violence.

In late November 2001, as the Al-Aqsa *intifada* was picking up in intensity and violence, Prime Minister Barak surprised the Israeli political establishment by calling for early elections the following February. The choice for the Israeli electorate was simple: to reelect a man who had been willing to negotiate away so much and at the end had achieved nothing, or to vote for Ariel Sharon, the tough and uncompromising leader of the Likud, a man who was seen as capable of effectively quelling the *intifada*. A final attempt at reviving the Israeli-Palestinian negotiations before the elections proved futile.

In the February elections that followed, Ariel Sharon beat Barak handily. The resumption of negotiations with the PNA, Sharon declared, depended solely on the ability of the PNA to curb the violence against Israel. But neither Arafat's security and police apparatus nor even Israel's mighty IDF was able to contain the Al-Aqsa *intifada*. The prodding of the United States, so vital in bringing the Palestinians and the Israelis to the negotiating table time and again, was conspicuously absent in the bloody months of 2001, 2002, and early 2003, as U.S. leaders were preoccupied primarily with the "war on terror" at home and in Afghanistan and Iraq. Also absent, in stark contrast to the final months of the Clinton administration, was President George W. Bush's personal interest in and intimate knowledge of the conflict. Finally, in March 2003 President Bush announced his vision of Palestinian-Israeli peace under the rubric of a "road map" toward achieving comprehensive and lasting peace between the two sides.

The "road map for peace" would have three phases. In phase 1, the Palestinians would be required to "undertake an unconditional cessation of violence," while the Israelis would "immediately dismantle settlement outposts erected since March 2001."[115] This phase would entail a series of other confidence-building measures, such as a progressive withdrawal of Israeli forces from the Occupied Territories. This would lead to phase 2, which would come about sometime in December 2003, during which a Palestinian state would be established and an international conference would be convened to hammer out some of the most contentious issues dividing the two sides. In phase 3, during the year 2005, a comprehensive peace treaty would be signed that would finally resolve some of the most intractable points of contention, most notably the status of Jerusalem, the location of a Palestinian capital, and the issue of "right of return" for Palestinian refugees.

President Bush's "road map" for ending the Palestinian-Israeli conflict ended up sharing the fates of the Oslo Accords, Camp David II, and the many other stalled peace initiatives. Within weeks of toppling Saddam Hussein, Washington found itself in an Iraqi quagmire, bewildered and scrambling to contain an urban guerrilla war for which neither the Pentagon nor the military commanders had prepared themselves. By all accounts, the "road map" died before it had a chance to get started, and both the Palestinians and the Israelis did their best to ensure its demise.[116] Hamas and the Islamic Jihad refused to relent on their bloody campaign of suicide bombings directed against Israeli civilians—some one hundred bombings occurred between 2001 and 2003 alone. Each suicide bombing was followed by massive Israeli retaliatory strikes, in the course of which many Palestinian civilians have perished.

Sharon's government, meanwhile, embarked on the construction of a massive concrete wall intended to physically separate the West Bank from the rest of Israel. The thirty-foot-high wall, or "security fence," is complemented by electrified wires designed to prevent anyone from crossing it. When completed, the $2 billion project will be at least 625 miles long, although the so-called green line separating Israel and the West Bank is only 224 miles long. This is because the wall frequently veers off into Palestinian territory to keep Israeli settlements on the Israeli side, often cutting off Palestinians from their farmland, uprooting countless orchards and fruit trees belonging to Palestinians, and separating Palestinian families.[117] By the time the wall is completed, sizable portions of the West Bank will be separated from it.

The wall's stated purpose is to help keep suicide bombers out of Israel. Its real impact will be to create new facts on the ground. How it will influence the Palestinian-Israeli conflict and its outcome remains to be seen. Whether the wall, which most members of the Israeli Left denounce, will remain a permanent feature of the physical and psychological landscape of the region is also a question that only time will answer.

After a mysterious illness in late 2004, Arafat slipped into a coma and died on November 11. Long the symbol of Palestinian resistance, in the waning months of his life the old warrior had become a virtual prisoner in his presidential headquarters in Ramallah. For nearly two years he had been unable to leave his compound, which was surrounded, and repeatedly battered, by Israeli tanks and bulldozers. Death frequently vindicates fallen heroes, and Arafat was no exception. But the collective mourning of his passing by Palestinians was followed by the excitement of Mahmoud Abbas's election to the presidency of the PNA in January 2005. An old Fatah

Figure 25. A Jewish settler prays at sunrise from a former outpost near Nablus. Photo courtesy of New York Times Co.

insider and with impeccable nationalist credentials, he was admired even by many Israelis in the know for his commitment to the cause of peace and his reasoned, steady approach to the conflict's complexities and its solutions.

Earlier, in December 2003, Prime Minister Sharon had announced a unilateral "Disengagement Plan" from Gaza, one that would, he promised, "reduce terrorism as much as possible and grant Israeli citizens the maximum level of security." As subsequent events demonstrated, Israel's unilateral withdrawal from Gaza was driven less by the imperative to "minimize friction between Israelis and Palestinians," as Sharon claimed, than by a need to "relieve the pressure on the IDF and the security forces in fulfilling the difficult tasks they are faced with."[118] Approved by the cabinet, amid chaotic scenes of clashes between Israeli soldiers and settlers refusing to leave, the withdrawal occurred in August 2005.

The Palestinians' euphoria aimed at reclaiming the entirety of the Gaza Strip proved short-lived as the Israeli withdrawal did little to reverse Gaza's descent into political turmoil, lawlessness, and economic despondency. The PNA failed to capitalize on the opportunity to deepen its base of support and legitimacy across Gaza. That opportunity instead went to the

Figure 26. A Palestinian woman inspects the rubble of her destroyed house after Israeli missile strikes in the central Gaza Strip, December 30, 2009. Photo courtesy of Corbis.

Hamas, whose slogan "Islam is the answer" propelled it to victory in the first Palestinian legislative elections that were held for the first time in a decade in 2006. The elections signified an almost complete divorce of the Fatah-dominated West Bank, led by the PNA, and the Gaza Strip, now controlled by Hamas. Singularly lacking in charisma and content with being a manager rather than a leader, President Abbas was left with no option but to invite Hamas to form a cabinet in March 2006, thus forging a coalition administration destined to fail from the very beginning. In the meanwhile, the refusal of the United States and the European Union to recognize Hamas's victory, coupled with their punishing withholding of much-needed financial assistance to the PNA, further eroded the PNA's administrative capacities, which were already hampered by widespread corruption and ineptitude. The Hamas-PNA rupture was not long in coming, resulting in a brief civil war between the two in June 2007, with the United States and Israel allegedly instigating the clash and arming a pro-Fatah militia group.[119] The fighting ended, but the rift has not healed. Frequent and deadly clashes continued, meanwhile, between the Hamas and the IDF. Following repeated attacks by ineffective and inaccurate rockets fired

Figure 27. A Palestinian woman flashes the "V for victory" sign at Israeli soldiers as hundreds of women wait to cross the West Bank Israeli checkpoint of Qalandia into Jerusalem to attend the third Ramadan Friday prayers at Al-Aqsa mosque in the old city on September 11, 2009. Photo courtesy of Getty Images.

from Gaza into Israel, the IDF launched Operation Iron Cast, a massive and deadly assault on Gaza in December 2008–January 2009, which, according to a United Nations report issued shortly afterwards, left over 1,300 Palestinians dead, over 5,000 injured, and thousands more displaced and without food or shelter.[120] But even widespread allegations of Israeli war crimes in Gaza failed to bring the bickering Palestinians together.[121] The Hamas and the Fatah fragmented the Palestinian body politic in ways that even Israel could not have dreamed of. With friction and animosity characterizing intra-Palestinian relations, it is not surprising that meaningfully ending the Palestinian-Israeli conflict seems today like a distant dream.

As of this writing, the conflict between the Israelis and the Palestinians shows no signs of a resolution. Different solutions for a peaceful end to the conflict continue to be offered by old actors and even new ones, including Saudi King Abdullah and the Quartet on the Middle East (composed of the United States, the United Nations, the European Union, and Russia). For a region racked by more than a century of war and bloodshed, the need for a lasting peace has never been greater. For now, however, the prospects of such a peace seem painfully remote.

Despite repeated setbacks and the seeming futility of the never-ending "peace process," monumental progress has indeed been made over the years on several fronts in relation to certain specific aspects of the conflict. As we have seen so far, this is a conflict whose very essence has been shaped and reified by the blood, sweat, and tears of the antagonists on either side. The fault lines run too deep, the responses are too visceral, and the stakes are too high for there to be any easy solutions, or perhaps *any* lasting solutions at all. But to dismiss all efforts toward peace as hopeless and futile would be at best ignorant of what has been accomplished so far and at worst fatalistic and resigned to an absence of peace. Despite its flaws and go-it-alone character, the Camp David Accord did return the Sinai to Egypt and led to an Israeli-Egyptian peace that has lasted since 1978. The Oslo Accords, for their part, though maligned and ignored soon after their signing, brought about the institutional ingredients and an actual, albeit truncated, territorial frame of reference that are key elements in the eventual construction of a state. And the second Camp David summit, held in July 2000, crossed some of Israel's most firmly drawn red lines by having the Jewish state's prime minister offer to put up for negotiations the status of Jerusalem and the right of Palestinian refugees to return home and be reunited with their families. As the Israeli scholar Avi Shlaim has put it, "The mere fact that . . . the core issues of the Israeli-Palestinian conflict were discussed at all is significant. Jerusalem is no longer a sacred symbol but the subject of hard bargaining. The right of return of the Palestinian refugees is no longer just a slogan but a problem in need of a practical solution. A final status agreement eluded the negotiators, yet everything has changed."[122]

By the accidents of history and geography, the two peoples of Palestine and Israel found themselves on the same piece of land. Each side has tried to stake a claim for its right to control the land. The ensuing conflict has been not just a dialogue of the deaf but a brutal, violent struggle to destroy or at least dehumanize and demonize the enemy, to take away its spirit and its life. In some ways, the passage of time has forced the antagonists to face the sobering realities of the conflict. But the wounds of the past are too fresh and the memories of historic wrongs remain too deep to allow either side to trust the other. The oscillating preferences of the Israeli electorate in the last few elections reflect their unease and uncertainty over the wisdom of finally embracing the enemy. The same dilemma exists for the Palestinians, who are equally torn between the rejectionism of Hamas and the Islamic Jihad and the relative moderation of an increasingly beleaguered and ineffectual PNA. This popular anguish has manifested itself in the form of the *intifadas.*

For all their mutual hatred and distrust, the Arabs and Israelis in general and the Palestinians and Israelis in particular have managed to travel far on the road to peace. The Camp David Accords of 1978 resulted in a peace between Israel and Egypt that has so far lasted for more than two decades. Despite frequent frictions and disagreements, the Egyptian-Israeli peace shows no signs of collapse. In the same way, the 1993 Oslo Accords brought the historic adversaries together and, at the very least, made each party realize that "the enemy" does indeed have a face, a family, human emotions, and, most important, a right to exist. Many on both sides still deny this basic right, but their denials can no longer be backed by empirical data. Reality, the "facts on the ground," may be subject to different interpretations, but it cannot be denied. Israelis and Palestinians exist, and despite their best efforts at destroying each other, neither side shows signs of simply vanishing.

In one important respect, the tangible progress made so far on the issue of Palestinian-Israeli peace has made it harder for would-be Nassers or Khomeinis, and other self-declared liberators of Palestine, to claim the mantle of the Palestinian leadership. Alas, there has been no shortage of liberationists in the Middle East, and future Qaddafis and Saddams may still appear. Soon after it started, the struggle between Palestinians and Israelis became known as the "Arab-Israeli conflict," and now, after many decades and many wars, it has once again become more of a Palestinian-Israeli conflict. Ultimately, the two peoples need to resolve their conflict themselves, although, as with any other passionate arguments, third-party mediations often help.

History is both written and directed by victors, and how the Israeli-Palestinian question finally gets settled depends on who holds which trump cards. Edward Said warned of the permanent ghettoization of the Palestinians and the establishment of a two-tiered, apartheid-like state, whereby Israeli dominance would be ensured by the complicity of a self-serving PNA.[123] Aharon Klieman, a respected, liberal Israeli academic, envisions two peoples that are "separate but dependent" as a realistic (and desirable) outcome. Perhaps, he argues, there could even be some type of a confederation between the three, otherwise small entities of Palestine, Israel, and Jordan.[124] These are, at best, all conjectures. For now, the future is far from certain; but it is clear that the peoples of Israel and Palestine must learn to share the same piece of land.

8 The Challenge of Economic Development

In one form or another, and to one extent or another, all developing countries have faced formidable obstacles in their efforts to foster economic development. For a variety of reasons, the twists and turns of history have left developing countries in an inferior global position in relation to other, increasingly more powerful and advanced economies. Domestic political institutions and procedures have remained equally underdeveloped and have been subject to violent oscillations and even revolutions, so that making rational economic policy has been even more difficult. Economic and industrial infrastructures could not or have not been allowed to develop, and when they have developed they often have fallen victim to foreign economic domination, the greed or incompetence of domestic tyrants, or, as is often the case, a combination of both. It did not take long for the developing world to lag significantly behind in basic indices of development such as the availability of transportation and storage facilities (roads, ports, and warehouses), hydroelectric dams and power-generating plants, steel mills, and various other industrial complexes that manufacture consumer goods and provide employment opportunities.

By the 1950s and 1960s, the glaring underdevelopment of what by now had emerged as the "Third World" made the large-scale importation of Western industry an attractive and indeed necessary option. Import-substitution industrialization (ISI) policies were adopted in one developing country after another from East Asia to South America, including the countries of the Middle East. The hope was to eventually indigenize the imported industry and, once the industry had become "developed," to engage in the profitable export of manufactured goods such as appliances, automobiles, spare parts, and other technologically advanced products. For some time, the countries of East Asia—most notably South Korea and Taiwan—were the only developing countries that made the successful transition from the import phase of ISI to its more mature export phase. But the self-perpetuating dependence on imports did not dissuade most other developing countries, including those in the Middle East, from zealously following ISI as a viable path to industrial development.

This was the general economic predicament in which the countries of the Middle East found themselves by the mid–twentieth century. In many ways, the economic conditions of most Middle Eastern countries in the 1950s and 1960s were not that different from those in many other parts of the developing world at around the same time. The cumulative effects of the Great Depression of the 1930s and the Second World War had been ruinous for almost all countries of the Middle East. Before the 1950s, Middle Eastern economies had relied heavily on agriculture as their primary source of production and capital. The 1920s and 1930s had brought about a period of "deglobalization," in which previously significant levels of capital flows to and from Europe, derived from the export of primary goods—such as cotton, silk, pearls, and fruits—were greatly reduced.[1] Shrinking exports brought about deteriorating terms of trade and balance-of-payment difficulties, to which were added shortages and disruptions of various kinds during World War II. Although the consequences of World War II were not as devastating for the Middle East as had been the case with the First World War, the region's economies did suffer as a result of the conflict. Iran, for example, was occupied by British and Soviet troops during the war and experienced severe shortages of basic foodstuffs and disruptions to its economy. Turkey, while neutral, was forced to keep a standing army some five hundred thousand strong, which affected its agricultural output.[2] Egypt also experienced shortages and hardship during the war. Though it had a brief spurt of economic growth while it served as a base for British troops and was cut off from the rest of Europe, this limited economic progress was offset by its rapid population growth rate, so that per capita income showed no real signs of overall improvement from 1913 to the late 1940s. This appears to have been the case in Syria/Lebanon as well.[3]

Beginning in the 1950s, a new crop of state actors assumed power in various Middle Eastern countries. These nationalist leaders were painfully aware that their countries' low-income, agrarian economies needed fundamental structural changes if they were to develop. This chapter examines the challenges these state actors faced in their quest to bring about economic development. Development, of course, is a process shaped by past limitations and present possibilities, and as such it cannot be adequately studied in a historic vacuum. Therefore, the chapter begins with a brief historical account of what the states of the Middle East have done since the 1950s to foster economic development. In the 1950s and 1960s, "statism" became the order of the day; it became even more extensive because of the economic upturn of the 1970s and then was haltingly and gradually modified beginning in the 1980s. Economic policies are shaped not only by the agendas and capabilities of state actors but also by the availability and mobilization of different resources. The emerging political economy of the region became one based primarily on "rent seeking," with the intent of lessening the potential for economic grievances on the part of the populace. At the same time, few Middle Eastern states have been able to effectively manage or regulate the various sectors of the economy. Specifically, much economic activity remains either completely "informal" or, at best, "semi-formal." Increasing interaction with the global economy over the last few decades has not changed the dynamics underlying the region's political economy in any fundamental ways. Naturally, intentions and outcomes are not always the same, especially in the emerging economies of the developing world, and for much of the Middle East development has been highly uneven at best and elusive at worst.

STATISM AND ITS AFTERMATH

By the mid- to late 1950s, the state was almost universally assumed in the Middle East—and elsewhere in the developing world—to be the actor most capable of fostering the structural transformations deemed necessary to bring about economic development. The state was therefore assumed to have a national duty to play a "major role . . . in the direction of the economy both directly through the operation of state-owned enterprises and indirectly through the management of the overall economy."[4] Statism—also referred to by its French variant, *etatism*—thus became the dominant norm in the political economy of the Middle East. As Alan Richards and John Waterbury argue, "The Middle Eastern state took upon itself the challenge of moving the economy onto an industrial footing, shifting population to urban areas, educating and training its youth wherever they lived, raising agricultural productivity to feed the nonagricultural population, redistributing wealth, building a credible military force, and doing battle with international trade and financial regimes that held it in thrall. These were goals widely held by state elites but poorly understood by citizens at large. There were no impediments, then, to the expansion and affirmation of the interventionist state."[5]

These interventionist states ushered in what could best be described as state capitalism: a process of accumulation that gave rise to a state bourgeoisie, who in turn controlled but did not own the major means of production.[6] The state accepted the general premises and practices of capitalist competition as effective means of generating economic growth. But it still saw a need for regulating the economy and did so extensively.[7] "The economy, from the view point of state capitalists, is simply too important to be left to the 'invisible hand' of the marketplace. Individual capitalists, in their view, are too concerned with immediate profits to recognize either their own long-term interests or those of society as a whole."[8]

Statism in the Middle East is generally dated from the 1950s to the late 1980s, although in at least two countries of the region, Turkey and Iran, it dates back to the 1930s. By the late 1980s, the developmental policies of the state had generally been proven to be failures, thus compelling most states in the Middle East to embark on ambitious-sounding liberalization programs. Nevertheless, today, more than two decades after the start of liberalization programs, the extent to which statism has been dismantled is not at all clear. In many ways, as we will see later, statism remains the norm in the Middle East. Lately, however, many Middle Eastern states have been pretending to have more liberal, open economies.

In the Middle East and elsewhere, state actors opted for statist policies for three general, reinforcing reasons. First, in the absence of a preexisting industrial base and given the pervasiveness of economic and political underdevelopment, they saw the state as the primary agent capable of and responsible for effecting meaningful change, not only socially and politically but economically and industrially as well. Second, most nationalist leaders, especially the generation that came to power in the 1950s and 1960s, viewed the private sector with suspicion and skepticism, seeing it either as an agent of foreign capital or as economically parasitic, or both. This conviction was reinforced by a painful awareness of the state's disadvantaged position in relation to many multinational corporations and thus the need for greater centralization and policy coordination in dealing with them. Related to this was a third and final factor, namely the widespread adoption of ISI policies, with the state retaining for itself the role of a central actor. The hope was to satisfy the needs of the expanding domestic market for consumer goods and, at the same time, to eventually replace the export of raw materials with industrial and technological exports. As it turned out, it was in relation to this last goal that statism suffered perhaps its biggest setbacks.

Statism in the Middle East reached its peak in Algeria (1962–89), Egypt

(1957–74), Iran (1962–present), Iraq (1963–2003), Libya (1969–present), the Sudan (1969–72), Syria (1963–present), Tunisia (1962–69), and Turkey (1931–83). Compared to that in the rest of the developing world, Middle Eastern statism has tended to be more extensive and deeper. According to World Bank estimates, for example, worldwide, state-owned manufacturing enterprises accounted for 25 to 50 percent of value added in manufacturing around the year 1980. The comparable percentage for Egypt was 60 percent and for Syria it was 55 percent.[9] In Egypt in 1953, a year after Colonel Nasser's coup, the total output from the public sector was £E128.0 million and from the private sector was £E736.6 million. By 1973, the year before President Sadat officially announced the open door *(infitah)* policy and the start of his liberalization program, public sector output had grown by eleven times, to £E1409.8 million, while private sector output had grown by only 2.5 times, to £E1807.1 million.[10] By the 1980s, the Egyptian public sector included 391 companies, employed 1.2 million workers, and had assets with a market value of £E38 billion.[11]

The state's economic reach has been equally pervasive elsewhere in the Middle East. In Syria, between 1970 and the 1990s, there was a fivefold increase in the number of civilians employed by the state. By the early 1990s, the state employed some 700,000 civilians, of whom more than 420,000 were part of the state bureaucracy, and another 530,000 men and women served in the armed forces and the security apparatus, bringing the total number of individuals on the state's payroll to 1,215,000.[12] According to the state's own figures, by 2007, despite the repeated promises of economic liberalization, of a total labor force of 4,850,000, more than one million individuals were still in one way or another employed by the state.[13]

In Algeria, similarly, the state became the biggest employer and the primary agent of industrial development, setting up a network of forty-five national industrial corporations (the biggest one being the gas and petroleum giant SONATRACH), eight banks and financial organizations, and nineteen national offices, all designed to ensure the state's monopoly over virtually every facet of the economy.[14] By the late 1980s, the state employed 80 percent of the industrial workforce and accounted for 77 percent of total industrial production. A total of 45 percent of Algeria's non-agricultural labor force was on the state's payroll.[15]

Equally high percentages of public employment were found in Iraq prior to the U.S. invasion in 2003: government employment in the late 1970s (410,000 people) amounted to nearly half of the organized workforce. The state also owned some four hundred industrial enterprises, employing nearly one in every four Iraqi citizens.[16] Next door in Iran, the 1978–79 revolution ushered in a new wave of nationalization of banks and industry, and by the early 1980s the state owned some six hundred enterprises.[17] In the 1980s, some four-fifths of all new jobs created were in the public sector, and by 1986 public sector employment accounted for 31 percent of total employment.[18]

Similarly high levels of government involvement are found in the economies of ostensibly "liberal" monarchies. In Jordan, in the late 1990s it was estimated that as many as 40 percent of all gainfully employed Jordanians worked for the state, ensuring an elaborate welfare and job protection system meant to sustain the Hashemite monarchy in power.[19] In the oil monarchies of the Arabian peninsula, where the state owns and then distributes the revenues accrued from oil, the oil sector accounts for consistently high portions of the gross domestic products. According to 2009 estimates, revenues derived from oil constitute roughly 80 percent of total government income in both Saudi Arabia and Kuwait.[20] Similarly, export revenues accrued from oil sales account for some 90 percent of Saudi Arabia's total exports and 85 percent of Kuwait's.[21]

Despite the pervasiveness of statism, extensive state intervention in the economy has failed to have the desired developmental effects in the Middle East. While brisk in the 1960s and especially in the 1970s, thanks to dramatic rises in oil revenues, the overall rate of economic growth in the Middle East over the last few decades—as measured by annual growth rates in the gross domestic product—has not been outstanding compared to other regions of the developing world (tables 5 and 6), even though oil prices exploded in 1973–74 and then briefly rose again in the late 1970s. When oil prices collapsed and the region experienced a general recession from 1985 to 1995, most Middle Eastern countries witnessed severe economic reversals. Only after 2000, when oil prices rose steadily before their spectacular collapse in 2007, did most Middle Eastern countries experience impressive rates of growth. Overall, the annual growth rate of the gross domestic product (GDP) in the Middle East and North Africa was nearly halved from 6.9 percent in 1990 to 3.7 percent in 1998, before recovering to 5.9 percent in 2007. As table 6 demonstrates, the reversals were most acute in Iran, Israel, Lebanon, Saudi Arabia, Tunisia, Turkey, and the UAE. Overall, the percentage of GDP growth only inched up from 2.0 percent in 1980–90 to 3.0 percent in 1990–2001, and 4.5 percent in 2000–2007. Again, only significant increases in the price of oil helped the region's economies in the early to mid-2000s.

Statism brought with it largely stagnant economies. This stagnation resulted from a combination of factors. To begin with, these economies

Table 5. GNP and GDP Average Annual Growth Rate
in Developing Countries

	1970–95 (GNP)	1990–2000 (GDP)	2000–2007 (GDP)
South Korea	10.0	5.8	4.7
Botswana	7.3	6.0	5.3
China	6.9	10.6	10.3
Thailand	5.2	4.2	5.3
Indonesia	4.7	4.2	5.1
Malaysia	4.0	7.0	5.4
Egypt	3.7	4.4	4.3
Oman	3.3	4.5	4.7
Tunisia	2.3	4.7	4.8
Israel	2.0	5.4	3.2
Morocco	1.8	2.4	5.0
Syria	1.4	5.1	4.5
Iran	−2.4	3.1	5.9
Saudi Arabia	−2.9	2.1	4.1
Kuwait	−3.5	4.9	9.2
UAE	−4.0	4.8	7.7
Libya	−4.8	…	3.7
Qatar	−5.9	…	6.1 (2005)

SOURCES: World Bank, *World Development Indicators, 1997* (Washington, DC: World Bank, 1997); World Bank, *World Development Indicators, 2009* (Washington, DC: World Bank, 2009); World Bank Online Country Profiles (www.worldbank.org).

have been run by highly bloated and inefficient bureaucracies that continue to be mired in red tape, corruption, and nepotism. In every country in the Middle East, corruption was, and remains, a pervasive obstacle to substantive economic development.[22] The problem of "urban bias" and a preference for industrial development over agriculture has led to a near-total neglect of rural areas. This has resulted in increasing levels of dependence on agricultural imports and an exodus of rural migrants into the cities. The region's aridity and water scarcity have not helped agricultural development. Even in Egypt, where agricultural output has showed some modest increases— 2.9 percent annually in 1960–70, 3.0 percent in 1970–80, 2.6 percent in

Table 6. Growth of GDP in Selected Middle Eastern Countries, 1980–2008

	1980–1990	1990	1997	1998	1990–2001	2007	2008	2000–2007
Algeria	2.7	-1.3	1.1	5.1	2.0	3.1	3.0	4.5
Bahrain	—	1.3	3.1	2.1	—	7.8 (2005)	—	4.3
Egypt	5.4	5.7	5.5	5.6	4.5	7.1	7.2	4.3
Iran	1.7	11.2	3.0	1.7	3.6	7.8	5.0	5.9
Israel	3.5	6.8	2.0	3.3	4.7	5.4	—	3.2
Jordan	2.5	1.0	1.3	2.2	4.8	6.0	5.5	6.3
Kuwait	1.3	-1.7	6.3	—	3.4	6.3 (2005)	—	9.2
Lebanon	—	15.5	8.5	8.0	5.4	2.0	5.5	3.3
Morocco	4.2	4.0	-2.3	6.5	2.5	2.7	5.8	5.0
Saudi Arabia	0.0	8.6	1.9	2.3	1.5	3.4	—	4.1
Syria	1.5	7.6	4.0	5.0	4.8	6.6	5.1	4.5
Tunisia	3.3	8.0	5.4	5.0	4.7	6.3	5.0	4.8
Turkey	5.3	9.3	7.7	2.8	3.3	4.6	1.0	5.9
UAE	-2.1	17.5	2.1	-5.7	2.7	9.4 (2006)	—	7.7
Total Middle East/ North Africa	2.0	6.9	2.5	3.7	3.0	5.9	—	4.5

SOURCES: World Bank, *World Development Report, 1999/2000* (Washington, DC: World Bank, 2000); World Bank, *World Development Indicators, 2003* (Washington, DC: World Bank, 2003); World Bank, *World Development Indicators, 2009* (Washington, DC: World Bank, 2009); World Bank Online Country Profiles (www.worldbank.org).

1980–89, and 4.5 percent in 1991–2000—such gains can hardly keep pace with the growth of the population (see Chapter 11). Additionally, levels of agricultural production are kept in check by patterns of land owner-ship and land use that often resist technological improvements and effi-ciency.[23] In Saudi Arabia, the government has pumped millions of dollars into expanding agricultural output both through direct investments and through massive subsidies and other incentives given to private farmers. However, the country's harsh climate and inefficient farming practices have so far undermined the possibility of profitable yields.[24]

Besides bureaucratic red tape and neglect of agriculture, statism had other structural limitations that severely inhibited industrial development on a national scale. Consumer prices continuously rose, forcing many states to embark on extensive subsidization programs for basic foodstuffs and other essential items. Despite overwhelming attention to industrial development, domestic industry was hardly competitive internationally, and, if given a choice, consumers frequently preferred foreign products over domestic ones. Most industrial enterprises also operated at far below capacity. Industrial imports remained consistently high, therefore, as domestic industry lagged behind in quality and caliber of production.[25] The state's attention to heavy industries—steel mills, power plants, automobile assembly plants, and the oil sector—also impeded the emergence of nationwide industrial linkages, resulting in the underdevelopment and inefficiency of various other sectors of the economy, such as banking, insurance, construction, and transporta-tion. The state then had to either fill the ensuing gaps itself or turn to for-eign enterprises to do so, thus contradicting its own ideological justifications for economic intervention. Inadequate planning and lack of sufficient tech-nical and administrative resources only exacerbated the situation. The dif-ficulties experienced by Algeria in many ways mirrored those experienced by other states of the Middle East: "As pressures grew to meet unrealistic targets, the central planning office and the larger state corporations were frequently overwhelmed by the magnitude of their tasks. Programs were subject to long delays and escalating costs. State corporations let contracts to foreign companies to build complex turnkey enterprises, which greatly increased development costs and at the same time created new dependency on foreign suppliers and expertise. The avoidance of such dependency had been one of the primary goals of the national economic strategy. The pro-cess also stamped the emerging industrial infrastructure with a technologi-cal incoherence that inhibited integration."[26]

Pressures for economic reforms mounted throughout the 1980s. By the end of the decade, cost-of-living riots had occurred in Morocco in 1965,

1982, and 1984; in Tunisia in 1978 and 1984; in Egypt in 1977; in the Sudan in 1985, acting as a catalyst for a successful military coup; in Algeria in 1988; and in Jordan in 1989.[27] For countries such as Turkey, Algeria, Egypt, Jordan, Tunisia, and Morocco, additional pressures were exerted by international lenders such as the World Bank and the International Monetary Fund, which had helped finance various development projects and thus had some leverage over domestic state actors. For other countries, such as Syria and Iran, which either had largely avoided World Bank loans (Iran) or did not care about the pressure to repay them (Syria), much of the impetus for reforms came from within.[28] After decades of revolutionary promises, it was time for the state to start delivering. Even in Syria and Iran the population was getting restless.

By the late 1980s and 1990s, "structural adjustment programs" became the new buzzword among Middle Eastern economic policy makers. Turkey, Iran, Egypt, Jordan, Tunisia, Algeria, and Morocco promised to implement especially ambitious reform packages. So far, however, only Turkey, Tunisia, and Morocco have made significant strides toward implementing meaningful reforms aimed at disentangling the many tentacles of the state from the economy.[29] In most of the region's other countries, the need for extensive economic reforms has seldom moved from debate and deliberation to implementation. According to the World Bank, by 2001, in the Middle East and North Africa as a whole, investments in infrastructure projects with private participation—projects in telecommunications, energy, transport, and water and sanitation—remained largely negligible as compared to the rest of the world.[30] Throughout the region, private sector development still has a long way to go and is often victim to a state that is reluctant to relinquish any measure of control or ownership. Not surprisingly, the state continues to be the dominant actor in the economy.

The reasons for the slow pace of economic liberalization are both political and economic. Economically, private savings are often much too small to make the purchase of state-owned enterprises possible. Also, most governments are reluctant to sell off unprofitable enterprises at below-market prices, but neither do they have the resources necessary for making such enterprises profitable again. Moreover, the state is often reluctant to sell to foreign buyers and investors, especially since such sales may spark adverse nationalist reactions among the populace.[31]

Political considerations, however, are by far more important in explaining the timid—and at times nonexistent—course of economic liberalization in the Middle East over the last two decades or so. Statism, it must be remembered, has been more than just a pattern of economic development.

It was, and remains, one of the central means through which successive Middle Eastern regimes have sought to consolidate themselves in relation to their societies. Giant bureaucracies and state-owned enterprises have been seen as the means through which the state ties itself to the various social classes. By ensuring the continued dependence of social actors on its largesse, the state seeks to guarantee society's continued political compliance. With the possible exception of revolutionary Iran, by the late 1970s most Middle Eastern states had exhausted the ideological and symbolic sources of legitimacy on which they could rely. As a result, they were reluctant to relinquish the institutional mechanisms that made the urban classes beholden to them. Meaningful economic liberalization meant energizing society and enhancing its potential for (economic) autonomy, and this was a risk the state could ill afford. The widespread collapse of authoritarian states in South America and eastern Europe in the mid- to the late 1980s did little to allay the fears of Middle Eastern state actors.

Even in instances in which states have sought to foster genuine economic liberalization programs, the institutional infrastructures needed for the promotion of the private sector have tended to be highly underdeveloped. Across the Middle East and North Africa, privatization efforts have been hampered by the lack of political will on the part of state actors, the unavailability or underdevelopment of institutions meant to encourage investor confidence, and the inability or unwillingness of the state to promote the efforts of private domestic exporters abroad (in comparison, for example, to similar efforts by the South Korean and Brazilian states).[32] "Investor perception is that while change is occurring, it is at times reluctant. Since there are powerful social groups that still resist change, investors are concerned about the chance of backsliding."[33]

The political economy of the Middle East has in many ways always been more *political* than *economic*. In its reformation, therefore, political factors have taken great precedence over economic ones. In fact, the limited measures of economic liberalization that have taken place so far—and the even more circumscribed measures of political liberalization in the region—are essentially elaborate survival strategies, designed to enhance incumbent states' resilience and institutional capabilities in light of emerging difficulties. Appearances to the contrary, Middle Eastern states have done little to alter their basic economic relationship with society, a cornerstone of which is the substitution of rent revenues for various forms of direct taxation. Rent-seeking activities remain one of the primary economic concerns of the state, in turn buffering the state from extensive domestic pressures to disinvest from the economy. It is little surprise that today, some two decades into the era of structural adjustment, Middle Eastern economies remain largely statist.

RENTIERISM

Excessive state intervention in the economy, coupled with the imperative of pursuing economic policies that boost fragile political legitimacy, has resulted in the large-scale adoption of rent-seeking economic practices throughout the Middle East. The resulting rentierism has had two broad consequences for the region's political economy. First, it has curtailed the degree to which society has been able to obtain autonomy from the state, thus undermining the possibilities of democratization "from below." The paucity of such possibilities is discussed in Chapter 10. Second, rentierism has kept the potential for greater economic and industrial development in check, instead perpetuating the very unproductive practices that keep rentierism alive.

Rentierism is the result of earning high profits from economic activities that do not require proportionately high levels of productivity.[34] For example, the costs of extracting and exporting oil are far less than the profits accrued from its sale abroad. In the Middle East, in fact, petroleum products have become a primary source of rent for most of the region's governments, and the oil monarchies in particular have become rentier states par excellence.[35] But rent seeking is not limited to the export of primary products at highly profitable rates. "Rationing foreign exchange, restricting entry through licensing procedures, and instituting tariffs or quantitative restrictions on imports are all ways of creating rents."[36]

In sharp contrast to "extractive" economies, rentier economies can provide for the population by demanding little or nothing in return. Access to rents reduces the state's need to extract taxes or other sources of revenue from society.[37] Naturally, not all states have equal access to various sources of rents, and for some states rent income constitutes a lower percentage of the gross national product than for others. A useful distinction can be made here between rentier states and rentier economies. In a rentier state rent incomes are "quite substantial and accrue directly to the state," whereas in a rentier economy "the absolute and relative percentage of rent is lower" and "rent does not accrue directly to the central government."[38] In the Middle East, the oil monarchies plus Libya may be considered rentier states, whereas the region's other countries, including foreign aid–dependent Israel, may be said to have rentier economies.[39]

The emergence of rentierism in the Middle East can be traced back to the early 1950s, some two decades before the start of the so-called "petro-leum era." Since then, there have been steady increases in the royalties that the region's ruling elites receive from the oil companies that extract and export their oil. Initially, almost all these oil companies were foreign owned, although in later decades most were either nationalized or oth-erwise replaced by domestic, state-owned enterprises. The earliest and most direct beneficiaries of oil-based rentierism were the oil producers along the Persian Gulf, including Iran and Iraq, in addition to Libya and Algeria. But the oil boom helped foster "rentier economies" in the non-oil producers as well. In the oil monarchies, the oil boom led to the creation of vast employment opportunities in each country and opened the door to hundreds of thousands of expatriate workers from Jordan, Egypt, Syria, Lebanon, the Palestinian territories, and Yemen. The remittances these workers sent back became a major source of rent: "[T]he salaries of the expatriates abroad are higher than they would be had they remained at home and the differential constitutes a form of quasi-rent."[40] Since these non-oil producers simply could not afford the political costs of becoming extractive states, they resorted to three additional means to enhance their rentier features: they ran chronic trade deficits, importing more and more consumer goods for the consumption of the urban middle classes; they ran large budget deficits; and they permitted consumption and investment levels well above what the country's gross domestic product could sustain.[41]

By the 1960s and especially the early 1970s, virtually all Middle Eastern states were embarking on aggressive rent-seeking initiatives of one form or another in order to strengthen their clientalistic ties with the various social classes.[42] To ensure the active participation of the urban middle classes in maintaining the political status quo, or at least their passive compliance, the state engaged in rent-seeking activities and pumped the proceeds into the urban economy.[43] With varying degrees of success, depending on the larger context in which rent seeking occurred and corporatist and patron-client relations were forged, a self-perpetuating, implicit understanding emerged between a politically and economically omnipresent state and a deepening, increasingly dependent pool of societal clients.[44] These clients of the state were primarily urban-based labor groups and unions, industri-alists, and civil servants and other public employees (bureaucrats, teachers, physicians working in state-run hospitals, etc.). The essence of the ruling bargain was that the state provided social goods and services by renting out access to natural resources—often hydrocarbons or, for those not endowed with oil, migrant labor—in return for general societal acquiescence to a nonaccountable, undemocratic government.[45]

By the early to mid-1980s, however, drastic shortfalls in oil revenues, compounded with mismanagement and rampant corruption, threw established methods of rent seeking and the supporting corporatist system of patron-client bonds into serious crisis.[46] Oil output fell from a high of 31 million barrels per day in 1979 to 18 million in 1982, while the price of oil fell by 50 percent. Reluctant to revise the political bargains that had served them so well in the 1960s and early 1970s, Middle East leaders initially borrowed heavily from international lenders. According to one estimate, by 1985 the Arab countries had a cumulative debt of some $80 billion, a figure that rose to $144 billion by the end of 1986.[47] This represented an increase of 21 percent in only two years. Before long, the need for new survival strategies could no longer be masked by massive borrowing, and entrenched corporatist arrangements had to be altered accordingly.

Middle Eastern states responded by introducing austerity measures and liberalizing their economies—again, of course, to vastly differing degrees.[48] In confronting the crisis of rentierism, a vast majority of states in the Middle East changed their modus operandi only slightly and silenced their opponents with heightened repression and reinvigorated authoritarianism. Only a handful—notably Iran, Lebanon, and Morocco, and to a much lesser extent Jordan and Kuwait—instituted certain political reforms aimed at placating potential opponents (see Chapter 10). For the state, maintaining the status quo has meant finding new sources of rent (especially in the form of World Bank loans and grants); tightening the corporatist links between the state and its societal allies; and resorting to tactical or blanket repression to remind its opponents of the consequences of nonconformity.[49] To satisfy international creditors, several states have also embarked on a highly selective privatization campaign, conspicuously absent from which have been those institutions that generate rent incomes, such as heavy industries, banks, insurance companies, the oil and phosphate sectors, airlines, and railways.

Rentierism, in short, remains highly vibrant in today's Middle East, having modulated itself to respond to the crises of the 1980s and early 1990s. In fundamental ways, this pervasive rentierism has undermined the possibilities for further economic growth and development. In itself, rentierism is not necessarily a hindrance to economic development. Throughout the developing world, many states engage in rent seeking through subsidies, the logic being that price distortions will stimulate the economy. A select number of states, however, have been able to enforce tight discipline over the recipients of the subsidies, especially firms, demanding from them performance standards in return for favorable prices and terms of trade. This is what has occurred in East Asia's newly industrialized countries, such as Japan, Taiwan, and South Korea.[50] Most Middle Eastern states, however, have been unable to impose discipline on the recipients of rent benefits. As a result, they have inadvertently fostered the emergence of what may best be described as "unruly rentierism." The underlying causes of unruly rentierism are the precarious nature of the state's political and ideological legitimacy and the way state building and political consolidation were achieved. In Middle Eastern countries, unlike many East Asian countries, political consolidation was attained simultaneously with and through the incorporation of certain social and economic classes into the state-building project. The state, therefore, became beholden to such groups for its continued hold on power and was forced to embark on what one scholar has called "precocious Keynesianism" to keep its societal allies acquiescent.[51] But in most East Asian countries, especially Japan, Taiwan, and South Korea, attempts to bring the popular classes into the orbit of the state occurred only *after* state actors had secured and consolidated political power. These states were much better positioned, therefore, to place demands on various social groups.

The institutional context and historical evolution of rentierism in the Middle East have had several negative consequences for the developmental potentials of the region. To begin with, extensive state intervention in the economy has brought with it highly bloated and inefficient bureaucracies. Additionally, these bureaucracies are highly susceptible to corruption (more of which below). At the same time, unruly rentierism has resulted in the development of highly inefficient and uncompetitive industries. Ironically, although one of the original intentions of statism was to curtail the growth of a parasitic private sector, this is exactly what the state's rentier policies have helped foster. At the same time, particularly in the more oil-dependent rentier economies of Saudi Arabia, Iran, and Algeria, those segments of the private sector that happen to be productive tend to fall victim to the effects of the so-called Dutch disease, whereby steady attention to the profitable oil sector often occurs at the expense of non-oil sectors, not only making them less productive and less competitive but in fact increasing their vulnerability to fluctuations in the foreign exchange rate, inflation, and, ultimately less expensive imports. Equally detrimental, especially on the manufacturing sector, tend to be the effects of rising exchange rates, making it more expensive for domestic manufacturers to export their goods abroad.[52]

Similarly important is the direct dependence of rentier economies on factors over which they seldom have any control: international demand for their primary sources of rent income (such as oil); international developments that can drastically reduce their rent revenues (the Gulf War and the resulting expulsion of many Jordanian expatriate workers from Kuwait); and other market vagaries. The rentier economies of the Middle East tend to be particularly susceptible to fiscal uncertainty both because of the region's frequent international crises and because of the short-term concerns and considerations on which their national budgets are based. Especially in the oil monarchies of the Persian Gulf, where the state has devised elaborate, cradle-to-grave welfare states, fluctuations in levels of rent income can potentially have significant political repercussions.[53]

Despite the multiple negative side effects of the "resource curse," some rentier economies have managed to achieve high rates of economic growth while maximizing social welfare sustainably. The economies of Botswana and Costa Rica can be counted among the select few that have employed rentier practices rather successfully. The difference there has been the existence of democratic polities that have introduced a measure of transparency in public revenues, and, more importantly, relative state autonomy from vested societal interests, thus giving room to policy makers to pursue sound economic policy.[54] Equally instrumental, of course, have been more stable rent streams (especially diamonds for Botswana) that have not had the volatility of oil prices over time. In all Middle Eastern rentier economies, however, the underlying dynamics of rentierism have been different. Essentially, the rentierism of Middle Eastern economies has been *unruly*, trapping the state in a vicious cycle: the state must constantly strive to keep its societal clients quiescent, while at the same time staying mindful of domestic or international developments that could cut its rent revenues.

THE STATE AND ECONOMIC SECTORS

Despite state efforts to the contrary, statism and rentier practices have not helped the state establish its desired levels of control over the different sectors of the economy. In broad terms, Middle Eastern economies can be divided into three main sectors: formal, informal, and semiformal. The characteristics and agendas of the semiformal sector are especially instrumental in contributing to the basic "weakness" of Middle Eastern states in relation to their societies, as manifested by their inability to control or regulate many of the economic interactions of the more affluent social actors. Even the most extensive programs of statist development, of which there have been plenty in the Middle East, have failed to quell or even to penetrate the vibrant capitalism of the semiformal and the informal sectors of the economy. Countless other small business establishments are, at best, only seldom regulated by the state. However, the economically derived social autonomy that ensues as a result does not automatically undermine the authoritarianism of the state, as these sectors are more concerned with maintaining economic independence from the state than with pursuing political goals. Thus, despite crises of rentierism throughout the region and apparent moves toward economic liberalization, economic actors in the Middle East so far have not emerged as advocates or supporters of political change. When economic actors have put their economic clout to political use—as Iranian bazaar merchants did during Iran's 1978–79 revolution—they have failed to permanently curtail state power vis-à-vis society.

Much of the literature on the political economy of the Middle East focuses on the formal sector and its relations with the state.[55] A few other studies, equally rich in depth and insight, concentrate on the informal economy.[56] Although there have been some perceptive studies of the bazaar merchants and other economic "informal networks," none examine systemically the semiformal economy and the pivotal relationship between its actors and the state.[57] The core of the semiformal sector is made up of merchants who operate out of small, nondescript stalls often found in the commercial districts of cities large and small, especially in the bazaar area and other inner-city marketplaces. In relation to each of these sectors, the state faces a basic problem of penetration. Given that the formal sector is—theoretically at least—the most organized and is bound by procedures and official regulations, the state has the most influence and control over its activities and its growth in size and productivity. In contrast, the informal and semiformal sectors remain largely outside the state's purview, the former often because of the state's deliberate neglect but the latter despite the state's efforts to the contrary.

As in the rest of the developing world, the formal sector in the Middle East is made up of business establishments and enterprises that tend to be large, may be partly or wholly owned by the state or by private interests, and, despite occasional attempts at evading government regulations (e.g., labor laws, import-export fees), are by and large subject to the state's official policies and laws. Within the formal sector, economic endeavors range from those occurring within the state bureaucracy—which, at least technically, is subject to close government scrutiny and influence—to those of private enterprises, whose owners are eager to skirt government regulations whenever possible. While extensive programs of economic liberalization have been launched in the Middle East—as seen in Iraq before the Gulf War and in Egypt, Jordan, Tunisia, Turkey, and the Persian Gulf states—the state continues to own numerous enterprises and closely regulates many others. In fact, even in Egypt and Turkey, which have undergone some of the most extensive economic liberalization programs within the developing world, state-owned enterprises continue to be seen as "indispensable to accomplishing the productive and distributional goals of national policy."[58] The state bureaucracy, in which the bulk of the urban middle class finds employment, remains particularly massive and cumbersome despite occasional state promises of greater efficiency and streamlining.[59] It is often through the bureaucracy and state-owned enterprises that Middle Eastern states perpetuate the ruling bargain. They use the economy as a tool through which they reinforce patron-client relations with domestic and at times extranational actors and, eventually, enhance their standing in society.[60]

No matter how direct or extensive the state's influence within the formal sector may be, it can at best only indirectly affect the overall life and the internal dynamics of the informal sector. The informal sector itself may be divided into two economic groups. One—the *mobile* informal sector—is forced to move from place to place and from job to job in a constant struggle to make ends meet. It is primarily composed of what is traditionally referred to as the lumpenproletariat: recent, unskilled immigrants from the countryside whose inability to secure regular employment forces them to resort to creative ways of earning a living. Male immigrants usually work as day laborers on construction sites, although a more frequent source of employment for both males and females is domestic service in the houses of the upper middle classes and the wealthy. Countless others shine shoes on sidewalks or sell fruits, vegetables, bread, cassette tapes, lottery tickets, or other trinkets. Though not to the extent found in Latin America, children living in the streets are also becoming more and more prevalent in some of the Middle East's larger metropolitan centers such as Alexandria, Cairo, Istanbul, and Tehran. With little or nothing at stake in the village communities they left behind or the urban community in which they remain marginal and alienated, these members of the informal sector drift through life from one low-paying job to another, frequently at the mercy of wealthier shopkeepers, construction foremen, or others in the middle classes who can easily hire or fire them.

The second group within the informal sector is *stationary*. It is made up of rural immigrants who are slightly better off and whose resources or savings have enabled them to purchase small stalls or shops from which they sell goods and at times even certain services. Small shopkeepers and grocers—especially those in the inner cities, the slums, and small towns and villages—are the most common examples of such stationary entrepreneurs. In some of the larger fringe communities, however, such as Cairo's City of the Dead or Istanbul's Kasimpasha, one may also come across individuals with stalls or other settled spaces in which they practice dentistry and medicine (in addition to performing circumcisions), lend money, service the neighborhood's cars, serve tea and coffee, sell alcohol or other beverages, and perform a variety of other functions. Most of these family-run businesses remain small and, despite the hiring of neighborhood children for negligible wages, seldom enable their proprietors to build up substantial savings.

Because of mounting problems of underemployment and insufficient job opportunities in much of the Middle East in recent decades, especially outside the oil monarchies, the lines between members of the stationary informal sector and the urban lower middle class have become increasingly blurred. It is extremely difficult, for example, to pinpoint the socioeconomic background of the owner and employees of a small mechanic shop, a herbal store, or a fruit seller's. Making the distinctions even more muddled are the close personal, kinship, and neighborhood ties that pervade Middle Eastern societies: for example, friends, especially youngsters, from different economic backgrounds working together or for each other.[61]

In ordinary circumstances, both the mobile and the stationary members of the informal sector have minimal and sporadic contacts with the state and its agents. This holds true even for those who own small shops or stalls. For a minority of stall owners, their only contact with any state agency comes at the start of their operation, when they formally register themselves with the government. Many, however, continue to operate without officially registering. Subsequent contacts with the state or with its agents—building code inspectors or those from the Health Ministry, for example—are practically nonexistent. In fact, members of both of the categories in the informal sector tend to view the state, including those affiliated with it, in an adversarial light.[62] "Those in the government have done little to assist us," goes the conventional wisdom, "and not evading them can end up costing in fees, taxes, or bribes." The stationary informal sector, with its entrepreneurial, self-starter mentality, is especially keen on evading the intrusive reach of the state. For a low-budget, small-scale business that relies on its immediate physical and economic environments to survive, government regulations can be both prohibitively costly and unimaginably tedious to bear. The rural immigrant starting such a business, already wary of state institutions, has neither the time nor the resources to go through official licensing procedures or to abide by the endless array of rules and regulations the state imposes.

None of the states of the Middle East make concerted efforts to penetrate or drastically influence the stationary informal sector. The manpower and the institutional capabilities needed to extend the reach of the state that deep into urban society often simply do not exist.[63] From an economic and bureaucratic standpoint, state leaders and policy makers do not rank the regulation of small, largely informal businesses high on their list of priorities. Far more fundamental and pressing difficulties within the national economy—the price of oil on the world market, the rate of inflation, currency reserves and foreign loans, IMF-mandated austerity measures, the official and unofficial exchange rates, unemployment—demand more immediate attention from the state.[64] Few state leaders, in fact, are oblivious to the safety-valve function of the informal economy: informal traders and enterprises, especially so long as they refrain from dealing in contraband and smuggled goods, can serve as useful means through which an otherwise desperate segment of the population earns a living.[65] That continued economic marginalization is thus perpetuated and that a potentially lucrative tax base for the state remains outside its reach seem a small price to pay for keeping a potentially dangerous—easily mobilizable—fringe social class economically active.

Even if Middle Eastern states decide to bring the stationary informal sector under their regulatory supervision, as some have done on rare and brief occasions, they are likely to face numerous practical problems in implementing their policies. How would the state ensure that all of the businesses in operation were officially licensed or registered? One of the state's most feasible options is to hire inspectors—or to assign existing civil servants—to go through different neighborhoods and determine which business establishments are legally registered and which are not. To my knowledge, so far none of the states of the Middle East have adopted such a tactic, nor have they assigned their conscript soldiers with such a task.[66] Even if such a tactic were adopted, given the pervasiveness of social and personal bonds in Middle Eastern societies, it is unclear how many of the state's hired agents would actually initiate measures that might well result in the closure of a business that was someone else's main source of livelihood. Reducing the strength of interpersonal bonds by assigning employees to inspect businesses in cities other than their own also seems impossibly difficult for the state to coordinate and afford.

The state's approach to the mobile informal sector also tends to be one of unofficial tolerance. Much the same difficulties (or lack thereof) that hinder the state's relationship with the stationary informal sector also influence its conduct and posture toward the mobile informal sector. Nevertheless, the state's treatment of the mobile informal sector tends to differ from that of stall owners in two important respects. In the "inclusionary" polities of the Middle East—those of Libya, postrevolutionary Iran, and Saddam Hussein's Iraq—members of the lumpenproletariat frequently form an overwhelming majority of the state's foot soldiers.[67] As Chapter 9 demonstrates, all three of these states created paramilitary and quasi-political institutions whose primary purpose was to mobilize popular political support for state leaders and to carry forward the unending plethora of revolutionary projects—the Islamic Revolutionary Guard Corps in Iran, the Popular Army in Iraq before 2003 (also known as the Popular Militia), the Revolutionary Committees in Libya—that the state constantly embarked on. Membership in these and other similar organizations is by no means limited to recent rural immigrants. In fact, almost all influential positions within such organizations are filled with ideologically committed militia "commanders" who come from mostly urban, middle-class backgrounds. Nevertheless, becoming part of the burgeoning rank-and-file popular militia benefits not only the rural immigrants but the state as well. It enables the lumpenproletariat to become as much a part of the economic and political mainstreams as possible. These and other similar state-affiliated institutions provide rural immigrants with shelter, a meager but sufficient income, and, most important, a new purpose in life and prestige among co-immigrants and in the village communities left behind. The benefits to the state are just as compelling: a ready pool of recruits who are easily mobilizable and who do not come with preexisting ideological baggage often acquired in the cities.

In a second important respect the state treats the mobile informal sector somewhat differently. Although statistical evidence is not available, it often appears that the state is more eager to prosecute the lumpenproletariat who commit criminal acts than those with more economic resources and social or political connections.[68] The state, both in the Middle East and elsewhere, often uses the punishment of the poor and other marginal elements of society to demonstrate its determination to combat crime, to impress society with its powers, and to intimidate its opponents.[69] For example, according to Amnesty International, in Iran, the state routinely uses "force against marginalized segments of society to assert its power," frequently imposing harsher punishment on the poor as compared to the more wealthy.[70] Early on in the life of the revolution, recidivist thieves, an overwhelming majority of whom come from society's fringe elements, also routinely had their fingers amputated as other criminals were forced to watch. In Algeria, villages and other small towns, which are used as way stations to bigger cities by many rural immigrants, also bore the brunt of the country's bloody civil war of the 1990s. In 1997, government militias—known as the Groupes d'autodéfense (self-defense groups) or Patriotes (patriots)—allegedly massacred two thousand villagers in the Blida and Medea regions near the capital, another three hundred in the village of Rais, and some two hundred in Bentalha.

The approach of the Egyptian government to the less wealthy, from among whom most of the state's opponents come, is instructive. Egyptian security forces frequently use heavy-handed tactics in the poorer neighborhoods of Cairo, Alexandria, Asyut, and elsewhere to ferret out members and sympathizers of the opposition group Gama'a Islamiyya. These and other similar operations are not surprising given that Egypt is a security-conscious state that is suspicious of its citizens and fears, often for good reason, the violence of the Gama'a. However, since the launch of the *infitah* now more than three decades ago, the Egyptian government's economic policies have consistently aroused the ire of its opponents. For example, the 1996 repealing of the 1952 Land Reform Law, which had guaranteed farmers security on rented land, considerably heightened tensions between the state and those who were finally forced to abandon the countryside and now live on the fringes of urban areas. In many respects, the state's campaign against the Gama'a has acquired an economic, class character.

The same type of inequity in the state's punishment of the less wealthy occurs in the oil monarchies, where most of those on the fringes of urban life are expatriate workers from Yemen, Jordan, Egypt, and South and Southeast Asia. In the emirate of Ras al-Khaimeh (in the United Arab Emirates), begging is punishable by flogging. A consistently large percentage of individuals executed in Saudi Arabia, which has one of the highest execution rates in the world, are foreign nationals working in the country at menial jobs and earning minimal wages.[71] Also in Kuwait, nomadic bedouins have no citizenship rights and are frequently harassed and viewed with suspicion by government forces.

The third sector in Middle Eastern economies is semiformal, composed of an entrepreneurial class with substantial economic resources. Unlike the formal and informal sectors, whose economic activities are marked by extremes of procedural formality or complete informality, the semiformal sector operates out of formally established enterprises but conducts its business with little regard for formal procedures or regulations. Although the business establishments active in the semiformal sector are often officially registered and licensed, many of their transactions are conducted informally and unofficially, bound not by specific government regulations but by internal, complex dynamics that have evolved within and between the businesses. Usually operating out of small, rather nondescript shops and stores that give a misleading impression as to the high volume of capital they generate, these businesses generally fall into one of two categories. Many specialize in the sale of one specific type of item—fabrics, carpets, jewelry, leather, copper and brass, bridal and dowry goods, herbs and spices, nuts and dried fruits, patisseries. There is often only one owner, although some stores are owned by a partnership of two or more entrepreneurs. Many of these businesses are found in the bazaar—in fact, these are often the *only* businesses found in the bazaar, with each wing of the bazaar or section within each wing housing similar businesses. Nevertheless, there are too many of these establishments to all fit into the narrow alleys and limited spaces available in the bazaar. They can therefore be found throughout the business districts of most larger towns and cities as well.

Other businesses in the semiformal sector offer a variety of services, including but not limited to lending money, selling cars or real estate, operating as general contractors, and importing industrial or automobile spare parts. Because such businesses tend to be more capital intensive and to require some technical or bureaucratic know-how, many of these enterprises are partnerships of two or more investors and businesspeople. Often an individual has investments or other types of involvement in several such businesses. Unlike shops and stores that sell goods and products, service businesses tend not to be concentrated inside the bazaar. Instead, many line the streets and the neighboring areas around the bazaar and are also found in other hubs of economic activity throughout the city.

Despite their often unassuming storefronts, semiformal entrepreneurs tend to be affluent and have substantial capital at their disposal. In this they differ from the middle classes, which throughout the Middle East, except in the oil monarchies, have difficulties in making ends meet. The regional recession that started in 1986 and lasted into the 1990s did not help matters: many have to take second or even third jobs to be able to afford their rents or mortgages or the modern appliances that have become essential to middle-class living (washing machines, refrigerators, TVs and VCRs, and, more recently, computers, satellite television, and cellular telephones). More and more families find it necessary to have two incomes, and more wives have had to join the ranks of the formally employed.[72] Members of the semiformal sector also differ from the professional technocrats and other wealthy members of the upper classes—physicians, industrialists, high-ranking bureaucrats—in that they seldom engage in conspicuous consumption. Despite their wealth, their purchasing habits and lifestyle more closely resemble those of the middle classes. Most important, they do not owe their station in life to the state and are not directly or even indirectly dependent on the government for their continued economic well-being.

Like those in most developing states, Middle Eastern governments often see the private sector as weak, likely to engage in speculation and profiteering, and prone to selling out the national good through alliances with foreign capital.[73] The state tries to regulate what goes on in the semiformal sector as much as possible and to collect its share of tax revenues generated by the sector's economic activities. But it is inherently weak when it comes to pursuing its goals and agendas. Its contacts with the semiformal sector are irregular and sporadic. Its ability to collect taxes and other fees from members of the sector is highly limited and inconsistent, depending on factors such as the cleverness of entrepreneurs in evading state institutions and its personnel, the effectiveness of the state's own agents, the whims of policy makers, and the zealotry or apathy of bureaucrats charged with implementation.[74] Thus the state's penetration of the semiformal sector and its ability to extract resources from it are uneven and often minimal. In short, in the Middle East one finds what one scholar calls "limited states" both in general and in specific relationships to the semiformal sector.[75]

The state's inability to firmly establish its authority over the semiformal sectors is due to complex interactions and processes. Both in its stated policies and in actual practice, the state wants to bring the semiformal sector under its control, at least financially if not bureaucratically. It thus creates bureaucratic institutions and agencies for this purpose (e.g., the Ministry of Economy, the Chamber of Commerce). But midlevel merchants and entrepreneurs often simply ignore state agencies and their functionaries. Their successful snubbing of the state is partly due to the state's own inherent limitations: the state needs to preserve its available resources for the pursuit of larger economic goals, as it does not have, despite pretensions to the contrary, the omnipresence that its policies would require. Equally important are the dispositions and the capabilities of the merchants themselves. Members of the semiformal sector often perceive the state to be an obstacle to their desired economic goals, and this perception tends to be more accurate than not. Like the middle classes, they tend neither to trust the state's intentions nor to agree with its overall ideological, political, or economic agendas, and their relation to the bureaucracy is especially adversarial.[76] They have at best a utilitarian approach toward state institutions and officials: best avoided at all costs unless they somehow further one's own benefit, which happens only rarely. Consequently, although the state has often created highly elaborate procedures aimed at regulating the operations of businesses, the semiformal sector seldom binds itself by state regulations in such crucial matters as hiring or firing employees, lending or borrowing money, setting the price of goods and services, observing child labor laws, and remaining open or closed on certain days. Frequently, business proprietors in the semiformal sector consider government regulations in these and other similar matters intrusive and ill informed, tedious, and cumbersome, designed to maximize the benefits accrued to the state and thus ultimately harmful to business. In an attempt to derive revenues from society in forms other than what may appear as taxes or levies, many Middle Eastern states collect "fees" from businesses. To the merchants and businessmen who bear the brunt of these fees, they often appear as arbitrary and unfair, wasted at best on misguided state projects or at worst on corrupt officials. Even banks and other official lending agencies are viewed with suspicion: they enable the state to keep track of one's assets, to tax hard-earned savings, and, in times of crisis or instability, to seize one's assets. Unofficial moneylenders, especially those with a history of doing fair business, are often held in much higher esteem than formal banks and other institutions affiliated with the state. Thus evading the state and its multiple layers of institutions and officials is central to the economic vitality of the semiformal sector.

Sometimes a mutually beneficial relationship develops between the state and the semiformal sector that reinforces both the political and the economic status quo. This type of relationship appears to have developed in the mid- to late 1970s in Egypt, when many entrepreneurs benefited from, and in turn vigorously supported, President Sadat's *infitah* policies.[77] Throughout the oil monarchies also, there is a wealthy and influential class of merchants, often situated just below the royal family, with whom the royals maintain extensive familial, clientalistic, political, and economic ties.[78] And, in Iran, in the early years of the Islamic Republic at least, there appeared to be substantial support for the new regime and its policies in the bazaar and in other segments of the semiformal economy.[79] In these and in other countries of the Middle East, the pursuit of clientalist politics and rentier economics by the state has kept the semiformal sector content and politically quiescent for relatively lengthy periods of time. Clearly, favorable conditions for growth, prosperity, and high levels of consumer spending, as fostered and encouraged by the state, go a long way toward alleviating the potential irritations of the semiformal sector with the state and, over time, may even turn entrepreneurs into one of the state's main sources of financial support.

The political liberalizations of the 1980s and 1990s, and the economic difficulties that precipitated many of these changes, have chipped away at the powers of the Middle Eastern state. However, neither the semiformal sector nor others socially positioned to articulate popular demands—such as the educated elites, the clergy, and technocratic professionals—have seen a meaningful rise in their level of influence on state matters. The experiences of the past decade or so have left almost all Middle Eastern states weaker than before and in need of new justifications, new slogans, and even new institutional devices. But the substance of "new" political formulas seems little different from the old. If anything, preoccupation just with surviving and weathering internal political and economic contradictions has made the state even less meaningfully attentive to, and even more disconnected from, various social actors.

The informal and semiformal sectors have been divorced from and largely untouched by the political and economic machinations of the state. Neither of these sectors had much to do with the state's formal institutions or procedures to begin with, and the cosmetic institutional changes of the past decade have done little to change things. Even more substantive changes have not in any meaningful way involved either of these two sectors politically. The formal sector has received the bulk of the state's attention, and the state has tried the hardest to placate its members, especially the more wealthy and influential ones.[80] Factory owners and other industrialists, members of the bureaucracy, and professionals such as engineers and physicians, along with clerics and intellectuals, have been the main targets of the state's attempts at making itself more presentable. But the basic economic disconnection between the state and the informal and semiformal sectors of the economy persists. By and large, the economic lives of these two sectors go on as if the political dramas of the last few years had not occurred at all. The merchants of the *suq* (bazaar) still sell their wares or services free of most state regulations, and, as always, those in the informal sector simply struggle to make a living.

The semiformal and informal sectors' "exit" from interactions with the state can have consequences that go beyond economics. Not only do state agendas become harder to implement, but society's own abilities to mobilize around political goals become somewhat compromised. By virtue of their cultural dispositions and their social status, members of the semiformal sector are likely to harbor politically oppositional sentiments. By the same token, however, when the general political environment is conducive to earning high profits, they have no reason to engage in overtly oppositional activities. Thus the autonomy that the semiformal sector enjoys from the state does not automatically make it a natural agent for demands for political change or accountability. In the final analysis, the semiformal sector is a commercial class that is likely to put its economic interests above political ideals. Even more likely to do this are members of the informal sector, for whom earning a livelihood is a matter of survival. It is little wonder, then, that despite highly adverse economic conditions throughout the Middle East in recent years, political activism in both the semiformal and informal sectors has at best been episodic and rare.

THE RIDDLE OF GLOBALIZATION

On the basis of the analysis presented so far, it should come as no surprise that the Middle East and North Africa region lags behind most other parts of the world when it comes to globalization. "Globalization" itself is a contested phenomenon, and there is no universal agreement over its precise meaning or its consequences.[81] For the purposes of this discussion, I focus on the economic aspects of globalization. Globalization is seen here as the substantive integration of national economies into international and global economic forces, and the establishment of multidimensional linkages between them. Broadly, globalization entails the global expansion of capitalism, whereby capitalist economic dynamics traverse national political borders, thus creating institutional and financial linkages and interdependencies between national economies on the one hand and international economic forces on the other. One frequently used index for measuring economic globalization is the level of Foreign Direct Investment (FDI) into the national economy.[82] While attracting FDI might be a viable mechanism for fostering national economic development, by itself it is not a sufficient indication of levels of economic globalization. Globalization requires the existence of sufficient institutional and infrastructural depth (such as politically independent banks and other financial institutions, investment mechanisms, and manufactured exports) that would allow for a national economy's integration and active participation into the global markets, rather than its mere penetration by powerful and resource-rich multinational corporations. This distinction becomes particularly relevant in relation to the Middle East, where in specific sectors of the economy— the automobile or petroleum industries, for example—there may be high levels of FDI while overall levels of economic globalization continue to remain comparatively low.

Globalization's economically derived linkages do not develop in a vacuum and are bound to have manifold and often far-reaching politi-

Figure 28. Skyscrapers of Sheikh Zayed Road, Dubai, at night. Photo courtesy of Getty Images.

cal and cultural consequences. Given the pervasive patterns of political development and legitimacy across the Middle East, it is precisely these political and cultural dimensions of globalization that have proved most problematic for the region's states. Not surprisingly, most states of the Middle East have at best an uneasy and unsettled posture toward globalization, welcoming some of its fruits while fiercely seeking to fend off some of its òther aspects.

In the remaining pages of this chapter, I will focus on two specific aspects of globalization insofar as it relates to the Middle East. First, I will empirically demonstrate that compared to most other regions of the world, the Middle East has experienced relatively low, or at best uneven, levels of globalization. Although in certain instances FDI levels may be high by global standards, overall indices of economic globalization in the Middle East remain low. Second, I will explore the economic and political reasons that underlie the uneasy relationship between most states in the Middle East and globalization, analyzing the causes of why some states in the region are more welcoming toward globalization while others keep it at arm's length, and still others fiercely fight it on every front. Throughout, the analysis is informed by a theme introduced earlier, namely that insofar as the region's political economy is concerned, political forces and consider-

Table 7. Global Levels of Foreign Direct Investment

	FDI Net Flows (billions of US$)		High-Technology Exports (% of manufactured exports)	
	2000	2007	2000	2007
World	1519.7	2139.3	23	18
East Asia and Pacific	45.2	175.34	31	31
Latin America and Caribbean	79.3	107.27	16	12
Sub-Saharan Africa	6.8	29.93	4	8 (2006)
Middle East (and North Africa)	4.9	28.91	4	4
South Asia	4.4	28.73	4	5

SOURCES: Data collected from the World Bank Online Data Profiles from the World Development Indicators Database (www.worldbank.org); World Bank, *World Development Indicators, 2009* (Washington, DC: World Bank, 2009).

ations all too frequently trump the influence and significance of economic ones.

Insofar as net inflows of FDI are concerned, the Middle East has consistently ranked near to bottom in comparison to other regions of the world, followed only by South Asia (table 7).[83] Similarly, as table 8 further demonstrates, the countries of the Middle East rank at the bottom of the global scale when it comes to another key index of economic globalization, namely the volume of high-technology exports as a percentage of total manufactured exports.[84] In fact, the Middle East as a whole tends to be one of the world's top importers and bottom exporters of manufactured goods (table 8). Within the region, although trade in merchandise far outweighs trade in services almost everywhere except in Lebanon—whose small economic base and concentration of wealth among a narrow elite have hampered the growth of the services industry—only a small percentage of manufactured exports tend to be high-technology goods. Moreover, across the region FDI as a percentage of the gross domestic product remains very low (table 9). This is further supported by the available data for the region's Arab countries, for whom, unsurprisingly, petroleum is the biggest export while manufactured goods plus machinery and transportation equipment are the biggest imports (table 10).

Another key index of economic globalization is intraregional trade and

Table 8. Share of Manufactures in Total Merchandise Trade
by Region, 2007 (%)

	Exports	Imports
Asia	81.6	63.7
Europe	78.6	72.1
North America	72.2	72.8
South and Central America	30.9	69.1
Commonwealth of Independent States (CIS)	25.1	76.7
Middle East	21.0	75.7
Africa	18.8	68.0
World	69.8	69.8

SOURCE: World Trade Organization, *International Trade Statistics, 2008*
(Washington, DC: World Trade Organization, 2008), p. 45.

the establishment of economic linkages among regional trading partners.
In many ways, regional economic integration is both a by-product and
a smaller scale of globalization, expanding markets and transportation
networks, enhancing investment and trade opportunities, facilitating
labor mobility, and deepening linkages between local enterprises and
those abroad. The European Union and the North American Free Trade
Agreement (NAFTA) represent two of the world's largest regional trading partnerships, with the Association of Southeast Asian Nations and
the Mercado Comun del Sur (MERCOSUR) having also made significant
strides toward fostering regional economic linkages and integration in
Southeast Asia and South America respectively.[85] Insofar as the Middle
East or even only its Arab subregion are concerned, however, there are yet
to emerge discernible patterns of regional economic or trade linkages. In
fact, as table 11 demonstrates, overall, the Arab countries tend to trade less
with each other than with other regions of the world. From 2003 to 2007,
the latest year for which data are available, only 8.3 percent of exports and
12.1 percent of imports by Arab countries were the result of intra-Arab
trade. The Middle East has yet to witness meaningful regional economic
integration.

Such low levels of regional integration are not for lack of trying, nor,
in fact, have they always been the case. World War II, for example, saw
increased levels of intraregional trade, largely because the Middle East
was used so extensively by the United States and Britain as a supply route

Table 9. Trade Indicators in Selected Middle Eastern Countries, 2007

	Trade as % of GDP Merchandise	Services	High-Technology Exports (% of manufactured exports)	FDI Flows (% of GDP inflows)
Algeria	64.9	n/a	2	1.2
Egypt	33.2	26.3	0	8.9
Iran	46.1	n/a	6	0.3
Israel	69.0	23.8	8	5.9
Jordan	121.3	43.5	1	11.6
Lebanon	65.0	92.4	—	11.7
Morocco	61.7	23.4	9	3.7
Saudi Arabia	85.0	10.1	1	-2.1
Syria	69.4	16.3	1	1.8
Tunisia	97.1	22.0	5	4.6
Turkey	42.3	6.7	0	3.4

SOURCE: World Bank, *World Development Indicators, 2009* (Washington, DC: World Bank, 2009).

Table 10. Commodity Structure of Arab International Trade, 2003–7

	Arab Exports					Arab Imports				
	2003	2004	2005	2006	2007*	2003	2004	2005	2006	2007*
Food and drink	3.6	3.1	2.8	2.4	2.2	14.2	12.8	12.2	11.7	12.7
Raw materials	2.5	2.6	2.2	2.1	2.1	5.0	5.1	5.0	5.0	4.9
Petroleum	69.6	71.0	74.7	75.1	75.4	4.5	5.5	7.9	7.0	5.9
Chemical products	4.1	4.1	3.2	4.0	3.6	8.7	8.4	8.2	7.8	7.9
Machinery and transportation equipment	4.2	4.3	3.6	4.1	4.0	36.4	36.9	36.4	38.3	38.0
Manufactures	15.1	14.2	12.8	11.6	11.8	28.3	28.6	27.5	27.5	27.8
Miscellaneous	0.9	0.7	0.7	0.7	0.9	2.9	2.7	2.8	2.7	2.8
Total	100.0	100.0	100.0	100.0	100.0	100.0	100.0	100.0	100.0	100.0

SOURCE: Arab Monetary Fund, *The Joint Arab Economic Report, September 2008* (Abu Dhabi: Arab Monetary Fund, 2008), p. 146.
*Preliminary data.

Table 11. Arab World Trade Partners, 2003–7 (direction of foreign trade of Arab states)

	Total Exports from the Arab World					Total Imports to the Arab World				
	2003	2004	2005	2006	2007*	2003	2004	2005	2006	2007*
Arab world	8.2	8.7	7.7	8.5	8.3	10.7	10.8	12.4	13.3	12.1
European Union	24.5	23.8	23.5	22.1	18.3	44.2	40.0	39.2	35.7	36.0
United States	12.1	12.1	11.3	11.5	9.8	7.9	6.9	8.2	9.2	9.2
Asia	37.1	38.1	38.1	38.4	35.3	25.7	28.8	29.1	33.6	33.3
Japan	14.1	13.5	13.8	13.7	11.4	6.0	5.1	4.8	5.6	5.5
China	4.0	4.7	4.9	5.0	5.3	6.3	6.3	7.1	10.1	10.8
The rest of Asia	19.0	19.9	19.4	19.7	18.6	13.4	17.3	17.2	17.9	17.0
The rest of the world	18.1	17.3	19.3	19.5	28.3	11.5	13.5	11.0	8.2	9.4
World total	100.0	100.0	100.0	100.0	100.0	100.0	100.0	100.0	100.0	100.0

SOURCE: Arab Monetary Fund, *The Joint Arab Economic Report, September 2008* (Abu Dhabi: Arab Monetary Fund, 2008), p. 144.
*Preliminary data.

to the Soviet Union.[86] Beginning in the late 1950s there was an attempt to establish an Arab Common Market, although the effort was abandoned in the mid-1960s as a combined result of internal political bickering and the advent of the Nasserist state across the region. By the end of the 1980s, with the region more divided than before, rhetorical declarations and promises of increased intraregional trade flew in the face of mutual mistrust and bitter acrimonies.[87] Hopes for increased regional integration were once again rekindled in the 1990s with three major developments: the signing of the Oslo Accords and the promises of peace and economic trade with Israel that it entailed; the unveiling of the Euro-Mediterranean agreement to establish a free trade area in manufactured goods between a number of European and Arab countries by 2010; and, after much delay, substantive moves by the states of the Gulf Cooperation Council to give meaning to their promises of monetary and economic union.[88] As the statistical evidence presented above indicates, such hopes have not yet come to fruition.

There are several key reasons for the comparatively low levels of economic globalization—and, correspondingly, regionalization—in the Middle East. Mention has already been made of the stunted growth of institutional and structural mechanisms across the Middle East that would help facilitate the expansion of modern global capitalism into the region. Chief among these would be a politically independent and transparent banking system, which economists argue is central to fostering growth and development.[89] Central banks, one of whose main responsibilities is to set monetary and fiscal policy, play an especially elemental role in this regard. There are, however, literally no central banks across the Middle East that would qualify as politically independent, with the ineffectual central bank of the Palestinian National Authority, at least on paper, being an exception.[90]

Other structural factors that slow the pace of globalization in the Middle East include the continued presence of the state in the national economy, despite economic liberalization moves designed to curtail the intrusiveness of state institutions, as well as the state's own inability to create an attractive and transparent regulatory environment that would foster deeper linkages between the local and the international economies.[91] Related to structural constraints on globalization are political and diplomatic ones, with a number of Middle Eastern countries proving too unstable and inhospitable for foreign investments, or being subject to stringent international economic sanctions, or both. For much of the last thirty years or so, for example, Iran and Iraq have been either at war with one another or locked in a cold war with the West and under sanctions, the end result being their increasing isolation from the world economy. For different reasons and under different circumstances, Syria, Libya, and Sudan—also Algeria during its civil war in the 1990s—have also been under international trade sanctions or have otherwise been too unstable politically to meaningfully engage with the global economy.

Equally important is the political management of the cultural dimensions of economic globalization. By revolutionizing information technology and facilitating easier access to means of communication across the globe, globalization can be just as consequential—at times, in fact, far more consequential—in the spreading and diffusion of cultural values as it is in bringing about economic linkages and interactions. As Chapter 9 will demonstrate, a number of states in the Middle East take very deliberate, and often guarded, postures in relation to the diffusions into their societies of norms and values from abroad, frequently viewing them as inimical to the cultural milieu that they seek to create and on which their legitimacy is built. The culturally conservative states in Iran and Ṣaudi Arabia are two extreme examples of states fearing the cultural consequences of globalization. While perhaps not as directly frightened as state leaders in Tehran and Riyadh, most political elites elsewhere in the Middle East tend to be apprehensive about possible responses and reactions by the various groups in their societies to globalization's cultural dimensions. It should be remembered that "Westernization" is not the only side effect of globalization. With the spread of the Internet and the rise of multiple satellite television channels beaming out of many Middle Eastern capitals, a phenomenon pioneered by Al-Jazeera, "Islamization" and the appearance of "global muftis" can be considered just as much products of globalization.[92] The attempted cherry-picking by political leaders of which aspects of globalization to embrace and which ones to fend off, or how tightly to control a process that by nature does not lend itself to control, largely accounts for its uneven and halted spread across the Middle East.

Finally, perhaps the most important factor hindering the pace and depth of economic globalization in the Middle East has to do with the different conceptions of nationalism that state elites have adopted across the region as it pertains to their political legitimacy. As Chapters 3 and 4 demonstrated, nationalism remains a potent force throughout the region, and one that is frequently employed for purposes of political mobilization or legitimacy. How this nationalism is articulated and conceptualized by the political elite is key in shaping a larger national context that might prove hospitable or inimical to economic globalization. If nationalism is presented by the elite as ownership and control over national resources, and is in turn generally accepted by the public to have such a meaning, then the prospects for economic globalization, which entails investments by and interactions with foreign capital, are extremely bleak. This is the nationalism that was so loudly proclaimed by Nasser and that resonates to this day in the far corners of the Middle East. It is a nationalism at the center of which rests the notion that the nation's resources belong to none other than the nation itself, and that consequently their development and marketing cannot be realized through reliance on foreign capital and expertise.

If, however, nationalism is presented less as controlling the process for developing domestic resources than as ownership over the outcome of such development, then the larger national context is more amenable to economic globalization. Throughout the small, politically conservative oil monarchies of the Persian Gulf, as well as in Turkey and Israel, this is the perception of nationalism that has been articulated by the political elites and has been largely accepted by the public. In the oil monarchies, policy makers have been painfully aware of their societies' demographic and technological limitations. Even if they wanted to, they could not possibly manage the exploitation of their vast oil resources on their own, having instead to rely on Western multinational corporations to extract and export the very oil that brought them fabulous riches. With rentierism underwriting the political bargain, this emerging conception of nationalism quickly began revolving around the state's management of the oil wealth—creating cradle-to-grave welfare states—rather than its heroic struggle against the insidious devices of imperialism. Today, completely different conceptions of nationalism exist on the northern shores of the Persian Gulf, in Iran, as compared to its southern shores, where the gleaming cities of Manama, Doha, Abu Dhabi, and Dubai would not have existed in their current forms had it not been for the pervasive presence of multinational corporations.

Both on a regional scale and globally, economic integration with the outside world has largely eluded the countries of the Middle East, except perhaps the handful of small states in the Arabian peninsula. Across the Middle East, regional integration has lagged because of mutual mistrust and lack of commitment and political will by state leaders to foster meaningful means of economic linkage across national borders. At the same time, the overwhelming majority of Middle Eastern economies lack the institutional capacities and the expertise needed to partake in global economic activities on an equal footing with their European and Asian counterparts, thus being forced, almost by default, to be on the receiving end of globalization rather than active participants. The deep-seated skepticism of many local policy makers regarding the larger phenomenon of globalization has only reinforced its comparatively scant engagement with the Middle East. Not surprisingly, then, the region lags behind on most indices of economic globalization.

This chapter has highlighted three aspects of the political economy of the Middle East: pervasive statism; unruly rentierism; and the state's uneven control over and penetration of the different sectors of the economy. The combined consequence of these three phenomena has been a political economy that supports and sustains authoritarianism. Each phenomenon, in fact, has a self-perpetuating logic and has so far managed to resist serious changes or reforms. So long as the basis of the political economy remains unchanged in much of the Middle East, authoritarianism is likely to remain intact.

Beginning in the 1920s and 1930s in Turkey and Iran, respectively, and then in the 1950s in the rest of the region, the state in the Middle East assumed a direct role in owning and controlling, or at the very least extensively regulating, the various forces and means of production. The assumption was that the state was in the best position to decide on and implement the most prudent course of economic development. But the state's assumption of numerous developmental tasks, and its proportional growth in size in the process, masked a more fundamental institutional weakness. This weakness was derived from the state's need to consolidate its powers through incorporating the popular classes and catering to many of their demands. The state, in other words, secured its hold over power by placating the popular classes and subsequently found itself beholden to them. What ensued was an undisciplined, unruly rentierism, one that has kept the developmental potentials of the region in check.

At the same time, a negative equilibrium of sorts has developed between a state that is not quite able to implement many of its economic agendas and a society whose economically autonomous actors, in the form of the semiformal sector, are only partially able to evade the regulatory reach of the state. The state, of course, is far from irrelevant. Its orchestration of the national macroeconomy still influences the lives of all citizens, rich and poor, irrespective of the economic sector to which they belong. The noneconomic initiatives of the state—conscription, policies toward ethnic or religious minorities, state-sponsored gender equity or discrimination initiatives, and compulsory education laws, to mention only a few—can be just as profoundly consequential for the lives of the citizenry. But in terms of routine economic interactions between the state and those outside the formal sector, the prevailing pattern of relationship is one of disconnection. State control over social actors, their resources, and their activities is neither as direct nor as complete as state actors would like. Nevertheless, it is sufficient for state actors to continue holding onto power and, if they so choose, to maintain the status quo seemingly indefinitely.

On the whole, despite crises and changes, the political economy of the Middle East has not helped society become empowered and/or autonomous in relation to the state. We have in the Middle East states whose developmental potentials are curtailed by the tangled webs they themselves have woven, presiding over societies whose ability to mount autonomous action in relation to the state—whether in opposition to the state or even in its support—is severely curtailed by various bureaucratic and police institutions. This does not bode well for democracy, at least democracy "from below."

9 States and Their Opponents

Democracies, it is often assumed, do not wage war on each other, since they are made up of institutions through which international conflicts can be peacefully mediated and resolved.[1] The absence of "democratic peace" in the Middle East, as chronicled in the preceding chapters, results from the region's main political dilemma, namely the absence of democratic political institutions. In fact, as we have seen so far, in the Middle East the state and war have historically assumed a symbiotic relationship: war has been waged by Middle Eastern states, and these states have in turn been shaped by war. By the end of the twentieth century, state formations in the Middle East had come to reflect the imperatives of military security as safeguarded throughout the political arena. Various conceptions of "national security" became the overriding concern of state elites and the institutions they crafted for governing. Real or imagined threats to national security, and the near-constant drumbeats of one war or another, helped foster oversized states for whom notions of civil liberties and democracy became irritants, even outright threats, that diverted resources and attention from the far more urgent task of defending the motherland. With only a few exceptions, therefore, nondemocratic states in the Middle East have become the norm, and, as Chapter 10 explains, have so far kept the prospects for democracy at bay. The question of democracy and the prospects for and patterns of democratization in the Middle East are explored in that chapter. Here we examine the historical and political dynamics that have given rise to the varieties of nondemocratic, or at best quasi-democratic, political institutions found throughout the Middle East.

Middle Eastern states can be classified into four ideal types: exclusionary, inclusionary, sultanistic, and quasi-democratic.[2] Exclusionary states survive primarily by excluding the masses from the political process. They are "praetorian" dictatorships built on repression, relying on policies that stifle not only dissent but also other unauthorized expressions of political opinion by social actors.[3] Algeria, Egypt, Sudan, Syria, Yemen, and Tunisia belong in this category. Only two of these states, Algeria and the Sudan, rely solely on sheer repression to stay in power, and the Sudanese state does so only in the south. Most of the other authoritarian dictatorships have managed to manipulate enough social dynamics to reign over largely placated and effectively repressed societies. Inclusionary states, on the other hand, thrive on populism, perpetuating and then relying on a myth of popular participation in order to survive. But their populism varies greatly in nature and in degree, and they may in fact be more exclusionary in reality than in appearance. Forty years into his rule, Mummar Qaddafi has turned Libya into a far more exclusionary than inclusionary state. With wars subsiding and the list of enemies nearing exhaustion, it is becoming harder for the Libyan state to sell the myth of revolutionary democratic inclusion to the populace. From the very start, Saddam Hussein's rule in Iraq tended to be just as autocratic as it was populist, although to the bitter end he held on to the illusion of including the masses in the Iraqi body politic. During the First and to a lesser extent the Second Republic, Iran also had an inclusionary state, although the dynamics characterizing the country's Third Republic are decidedly different.

Sultanistic states are the monarchies of the region—Bahrain, Kuwait, Oman, Qatar, Saudi Arabia, the UAE, Jordan, and Morocco—although Jordan and Morocco differ fundamentally from the rest in that neither has a wealthy economy or the benefits of a political history that makes the state seem almost a "natural" corollary of social forces.[4] Thus they have to rely more on a deliberately propagated civic and political-historical myth. But this "civic myth" has been subject to a variety of challenges, especially from the emerging urban middle classes. As we will see later, in the late 1980s and early 1990s the correlation between structural characteristics and liberalization seemed the strongest in this category of Middle Eastern states. Having neither the vast riches enjoyed by the wealthy oil monarchies nor the historical reservoir of tribal and traditional legitimacy, when confronted with structural difficulties (such as economic downturns or international crises) the civic myth monarchies were more likely to resort to liberalization as an option, even if only as a survival strategy. Chapter 10 charts the halted liberalization processes of both states. For a variety of reasons, Jordan's liberalization became comparatively "frozen," while Morocco's continues to proceed, albeit slowly.

Finally, in three Middle Eastern countries the state has conventionally been given the label *democratic:* Israel, Lebanon, and Turkey. In all of these, democratic institutions and practices have been part of the political landscape, even if in the latter two on a sporadic and imperfect basis. Of the three states, Israel comes closest to approximating a liberal democracy, but even it places significant limitations on the scope and nature of its citizens' democratic liberties. For these and other reasons explored below, all three of the Middle East's democracies are best categorized as quasi-democratic.

Each group of states has a markedly different historical genesis. Most Middle Eastern monarchies are colonial constructions, although the connection with the colonial power was eventually severed by indigenous historical and political forces. Some of the monarchies fell to revolutions and became, at least initially, inclusionary. These included Nasser's Egypt after 1952, Qaddafi's Libya after 1969, the Islamic Republic of Iran from 1979 until about 1997, and "revolutionary" Iraq from 1958 into, with some interruptions, the 1990s. Other monarchies, notably in Morocco and Jordan and in the Arabian peninsula, have managed to stave off revolutions and have remained sultanistic. A number of other inclusionary states—post-independence Algeria, Habib Bourguiba's Tunisia, Hafiz al-Assad's Syria, the Egypt of Anwar Sadat and Hosni Mubarak, and the Sudan—steadily lost their populist zeal and, with their revolutions increasingly institutionalized, became more and more exclusionary. By itself, historical genesis does not guarantee the political longevity of autocracies. What appears to be key is the evolution of the institutions of repression and their ability to suppress or manipulate society.

Before each of the regime categories is examined in greater detail, a cautionary word is in order. The categories outlined here are ideal types. It is extremely rare to find a state that fits entirely within one category and has no characteristics in common with a state belonging to a different category. This holds especially true for the Middle East's nondemocratic states, which often employ a combination of political and economic formulas—such as charisma and repression, exclusion and patronage, or religiosity and modernity—to stay in power. For example, almost all the sultanistic states of the region are exclusionary also. While sultanistic states rely heavily on tradition as a source of political legitimacy, all have poor human rights records and will not hesitate to quell political opposition by whatever means necessary. Similarly, while the Tunisian state remains essentially exclusionary, since the late 1980s it has embarked on a number of highly successful populist campaigns aimed at boosting the popularity of the state in general and of President Ben Ali in particular.[5] Political repression and exclusion have long been staples of Bahraini and Saudi politics, especially since the polarizing Shi'ite-Sunni tensions following the Iranian revolution.[6] And Iran, with its unusual mix of open parliamentary politics, revolutionary flavor, and theocratic underpinnings, could just as validly be placed in the exclusionary category as in the inclusionary or even quasi-democratic categories. What is important is the *degree* to which a state exhibits the characteristics that predominate in one category as opposed to another: the Iranian state, especially during the First and Second Republics, was more inclusionary than anything else; President Ben Ali's Tunisia today is more exclusionary than populist; the states of Saudi Arabia, Bahrain, and Qatar are more sultanistic than exclusionary; and so on.

EXCLUSIONARY STATES

Middle Eastern praetorian dictatorships are comparatively benign. In other parts of the developing world, the scope of dictatorial regimes may range anywhere from weak kleptocracies (Mabuto's Zaire) to predatory regimes (Duvalier's Haiti) and highly repressive bureaucratic-authoritarian systems (in South America before the early to mid-1980s). By contrast, most exclusionary regimes in the Middle East simply try to exclude from the political process social actors who are not already part of or affiliated with the state. Of course, political exclusion is guaranteed through repressive means, with each state relying on an extensive network of intelligence agencies *(mukhaberat)* that, as in Syria, often also watch over one another.[7] But repression is only implicit in the political equation. In fact, a surprising number of dictatorial regimes in the Middle East often allow the expression of discontented opinion over nonstate matters. Most Middle Eastern states—especially Iran, Egypt, Tunisia, Algeria, Morocco, Kuwait, and to a lesser extent Saddam's Iraq—allow critical (even satirical) reporting by the media on local officials and local issues such as housing shortages, high prices, and mismanagement.[8] In Egypt, the judiciary enjoys considerable independence from the executive.[9] In Tunisia, despite significant constraints instituted by President Ben Ali since the late 1980s and 1990s, "opposition" parties (with the exception of the al-Nahda) still maintain a skeletal existence.[10] Furthermore, Middle Eastern exclusionary states do not tend to be radically transformative, as were the formerly communist states of eastern Europe or authoritarian South America. Instead, most are interested in fostering gradual, even controlled social and economic transformations that do not disrupt their monopoly on political power.

From a historical perspective, the exclusionary states of the Middle East are currently in the third stage of state formation. In the first stage, state institutions had to be built from scratch from the ruins of the Ottoman Empire. This task was undertaken under the direct supervision or indirect tutelage of Britain and France (Algeria in 1830; Tunisia in the 1880s; Sudan in the 1890s; Egypt beginning in 1914; Syria after 1920).[11] Once the foundations for a state were laid, a second stage started in the 1950s and 1960s, when what by then had become "traditional" states were overthrown and "modern," transformative ones were inaugurated. Colonel Nasser and the Free Officers in Egypt started the phenomenon in 1952, to be followed in 1956 by Tunisia's independence from France, the 1958 coup by Abd al-Karim Qassem and his Free Officers in Iraq, Algeria's independence from France in 1962, the Ba'thist coup in Syria in 1963, the so-called October Revolution in Sudan in 1964, and the coup in Libya by Mummar Qaddafi and his Free Officers in 1969.

In the second stage of formation, these states had several significant features. Most notably, all originated from the ranks of the military and continued to rely heavily on the armed forces to carry out their domestic as well as international agendas. Equally important was their initially inclusionary and populist nature, mobilizing citizens for a variety of state-sponsored projects that ranged from the nationalization of foreign and private industries to land reform, the sponsoring of ambitious economic development projects, and, of course, the liberation of Palestine. The coups that brought these states to power were invariably represented to the public as "revolutions," and in almost every state a Revolutionary Command Council became the fount of all power. A "ruling bargain" emerged in which the state promised to provide for the prosperity and security of citizens in return for their political quiescence.[12] Existing bureaucratic institutions were revamped and reorganized, and new ones were created and staffed by high school and university graduates and army officers. Thus the edifice of the state became pervasive, bloated, and omnipotent. The Egyptian bureaucracy, which had employed 250,000 individuals in 1952, had swelled to around 1,200,000 employees by 1970.[13] The number of state-owned corporations also jumped from one in 1957 to sixteen in 1970.[14] In the Sudan, the total number of state employees grew from 176,408 in 1955–56 to 408,716 in 1976–77.[15] In Algeria, the reign of President Houari Boumedienne, from 1965 to 1978, came to be known as the "bureaucratic dictatorship," during which statist policies similar to those of Nasser were carried out.[16]

The third stage in the formation of exclusionary states began in the mid- to late 1970s. This stage came about as a result of the necessity of employing economic and political survival strategies. Populist authoritarianism under the aegis of the military had failed, and significant structural changes were needed if the state were to remain in power.[17] Economically, state-led growth had resulted in the neglect of the agricultural sector and increasing dependence on food imports, the running up of budget deficits and inflation, and a failure to eliminate social and economic inequalities.[18] As we saw in Chapter 8, structural readjustments, known in the Arab world as *infitah*, started to form the main thrust of the economic policies of states considered "socialist" (e.g., Algeria and Syria) as well as "pro-Western" (e.g., Egypt and Tunisia, among many others). At the same time, the military found it more and more difficult to justify its highly visible presence in the state, especially considering its defeat in the 1967 War against Israel and its lack of a tangible victory in 1973. Reflecting on Egypt, Fouad Ajami writes: "In defeat, the socioeconomic ascendancy of the military became unbearable, and the dormant resentments of the civilian graduates toward their military counterparts came to the surface."[19] Similarly, state mobilization attempts began to wane, and the all-embracing political parties established for such purposes became sluggish and increasingly irrelevant. These included the Neo-Destour Party in Tunisia, the Arab Socialist Union in Egypt, the National Liberation Front in Algeria, and the Ba'th Party in Syria (and Iraq).

Also responsible for ushering in the third, formative stage of exclusionary states was the removal from office of the main architects of the second stage. Boumedienne died in office in 1978, paving the way for Chadli Benjadid to initiate economic reforms and end Algeria's international isolation. Nasser's death in 1970 gave Sadat a free hand to pursue radically different policies, highlighted by the new president's own flair for the dramatic. Sadat's death in 1981 pushed the Egyptian state even further away from its once pervasive Nasserism.[20] In Tunisia, Bourguiba was removed from office in 1987, and the new president, Ben Ali, initially introduced a series of political and economic liberalization measures. Even the Syrian Hafiz Al-Assad, in power from 1970 to 2000, substantially altered his regime's domestic and international postures in the late 1980s.

There was more to this phase than the rise of new personalities who governed through old political formulas. With each new personality came a new style, a new set of agendas, and, concurrent with evolving economic and international developments, a new outlook, domestically and internationally. Most importantly, the nature and functions of the military within some exclusionary states changed. In some states, the military has assumed an increasingly background role, and the state's authoritarian policies have been instead maintained through greater reliance on professional technocrats and the intelligence services. Egypt, Syria, and Tunisia belong to this category of "intelligence" or *mukhaberat* states. These states pursue a policy of political demobilization of their citizens, thus designing their institutions accordingly.[21] In a few other countries, however, in each case for very different reasons, the military has continued to dominate the state. This group includes Algeria during its civil war in the 1990s, where in 1992 the military decided to abort the democratization process and instead rule directly, and the Sudan, where a civil war along geographic and religious lines continues to ravage the country.

On the surface, *mukhaberat* states look civilian. The military's control over and presence within the state has become less erratic, more subtle, and, despite an apparent decrease in the number of army officers within the state, more pervasive. From a Weberian perspective, one might say that the military's rule has become routinized, having assumed a "pattern of normative rules" that have bestowed on it a new and seemingly permanent sense of "legality."[22] The state has retained its essential dependence on the military. But it has also increasingly civilianized itself, thereby enhancing its legitimacy among the population and ensuring its permanence. Virtually all heads of state in this category come from military backgrounds: Presidents Hafiz Al-Assad, Ben Ali, Zeroul (Algeria), and al-Bashir (Sudan) all held the rank of general within the army. Before becoming Sadat's vice president in 1975, Hosni Mubarak was the commander of the Egyptian air force. But apart from special occasions, hardly any of these leaders are seen or photographed in their military uniforms.[23] There has also been a notable decline in the number of other policy makers from military backgrounds. In the wake of the 1967 War, for example, 65.4 percent of President Nasser's cabinet members came from the military. By contrast, fewer than 13 percent of all Sadat's cabinet members had military backgrounds, and the figure for Mubarak's cabinets is only 10 percent.[24]

The once highly visible, active presence of the military in the higher echelons of the state has given way to pervasive reliance on the military in more subtle, often nonpolitical ways. Beyond weapons procurement and small-arms manufacturing, the armed forces of Syria, Iraq (before the U.S. invasion), Sudan, and Egypt are all involved in a variety of economic ventures, ranging from fruit processing to running outlet stores and construction.[25] The armed forces still receive the largest share of the national budget, retain a strong and visible presence in the country (on street corners, highways, and intercity roads), are generally viewed positively in society, and continue to enjoy special privileges (in the form of housing, special officers' clubs, and cooperative shops). The *mukhaberat* are everywhere, or at least thought to be everywhere, although the state goes to considerable pains to maintain a semblance of democracy. At times, even loyal opposition parties are allowed to function. The parliament meets regularly and discusses peripheral policy issues. And pro forma presidential elections are held according to the cycle mandated by the constitution.

Despite these states' pretence of being democratic, they all tend to be remarkably paranoid about the loyalty of their subjects, especially those in the middle classes. The state rules not so much by inducing fear among its subjects as by constantly fearing them, frequently worrying that what may pass as an innocent act is a cover for a sinister political plot. Thus state operatives and agents are everywhere—among university students and teachers, colleagues at work, bankers, industrialists, fellow soldiers, pharmacists, journalists, physicians, and even clergy—keeping an eye on potential troublemakers or anyone else who may disrupt the country's forced political tranquillity. This suspicion goes both ways: just as government agents look for troublemakers in every circle, every individual fears a government agent in his or her circle. Mutual mistrust and suspicion account for much of the relations between the state and society. Therefore, what keeps these *mukhaberat* states in power is the authoritarianism that lies just beneath the surface. Fear becomes the great political stabilizer at the disposal of the state. As one observer of Syrian politics has noted, even under normal circumstances, "the ordinary citizen feels virtually defenseless vis-à-vis the state. However prosperous a man might be, or however eminent in his profession, he could be summoned for interrogation by one or another of the security organs, and, in the worst case, he could lose everything overnight. The notion of citizens' rights is not well developed, nor does the judiciary provide any real safeguards."[26]

At different times, civil wars pushed political repression in Algeria and the Sudan to new extremes. In both countries, the military-led state battled armed enemies—the Islamic Salvation Front (FIS) in Algeria and the Sudanese Liberation Army in the Sudan. By 2000–2001, the Algerian state had effectively succeeded in eradicating the FIS, and gradually the state reverted to becoming once again a *mukhaberat* state. Political tensions and repression, or the threat of repression, remain ever-present. In these cases, most pretences of democracy are dispensed with, although there are promises of elections on the horizon. In Algeria, in fact, presidential elections were held in April 2009, in which the incumbent, Abdelaziz Bouteflika, was elected to a third term. A few months earlier, the president had overseen a change to the constitution that removed a two-term limit on the presidency.

Despite elections, in both Algeria and Sudan, the state, and along with it the military, considers itself locked in a struggle for survival. In November 1995, for example, Sudan's state-run radio announced that "the Armed Forces are courageously and heroically continuing to foil all attempts being made by the aggressive forces."[27] Whereas *mukhaberat* states seek only to depoliticize their subjects by breaking down their political spirit, military-based states actively try to find and eliminate their armed enemies. In *mukhaberat* states, the regime's active adversaries form only a small and often informal underground group. This is precisely the case with the Gama'a in Egypt and the Muslim Brotherhood (Ikhwan al-Muslimeen) in Syria.[28] In Tunisia, al-Nahda has for all practical purposes been eliminated by the state.[29] But in both Algeria and the Sudan, the armed opposition is (or was) far more extensive and organized, actively engaged in rebellion against the state and encouraging others to join its side.

In sum, the exclusionary states of the Middle East are invariably republican (i.e., they have presidents), and they hold regular but largely meaningless elections for the presidency and the legislature. They rely extensively on the military as the subtle foundation of the regime, and they have allowed their intelligence services to become pervasive in various government and social institutions (the civil service, schools, mosques, etc.). Repression and violence are implicit in the state's approach to society, all the while thinly veiled under a democratic guise. Consequently, when the exclusionary states have been faced with important political or economic crises, their impulse has been to tighten the reins of repression rather than to adopt liberalization as a survival strategy. In Tunisia, despite much initial excitement over the prospects for democracy in 1987 and 1988, by the 1990s there were widespread reports of arbitrary arrests, torture, and extrajudicial killings.[30] In Egypt, since the 1980s there have been violent clashes between government forces and the underground Gama'a, resulting in frequent mass arrests and executions. The Syrian state is by far the most repressive of the three mentioned here, as the residents of the city of Hama discovered in February 1982, when an estimated ten thousand to twenty-five thousand people were massacred by government forces.[31] Under these circumstances, the prospects for democratic openings in these countries are, to say the least, bleak.

INCLUSIONARY STATES

At the opposite end from exclusionary states are the states found in Khomeini's Iran, Saddam Hussein's Iraq, and Mummar Qaddafi's Libya. Up until the 1970s, before the steady depoliticization of public life throughout the country, Algeria also belonged to this category of ostensibly "revolutionary" states.[32] In one form or another, all these states consistently and over time strive to include "the masses" in the political process through the theater of the streets, neighborhood committees, youth groups, "councils," and other similar organs designed to give the larger population a sense of political inclusiveness. There are three crucial differences between the inclusionary and exclusionary states of the Middle East. These involve the institutional makeup and nature of state institutions; the way state institutions deal with various groups and segments in society; and the state's larger approach to and attitudes toward cultural norms and practices. But there is also one crucial similarity: when faced with crises—whether economic crises or those of political legitimacy, or both—inclusionary states, like exclusionary ones, are more likely to resort to repression than to liberalize. This is because of the pervasiveness of authoritarian institutions alongside populist ones, whereby popular inclusion into the political process is ensured through forceful repression. *Mukhaberat* agencies exist alongside a variety of "revolutionary" organizations. The leader—whether Saddam or Khomeini or Qaddafi—*must be loved,* and his directives must be carried out to the letter. Those showing insufficient devotion are dealt with harshly. Not surprisingly, many of the military-based states discussed in the previous section were "revolutionary" and inclusionary not too long ago. And it is likely that the former populism of the Iranian, Iraqi, and Libyan states was really a ploy to prolong the lives of repressive, authoritarian states.

The institutional makeup of inclusionary states differs from that of exclusionary ones in several important ways. In exclusionary states, an elaborate network of bureaucratic and intelligence agencies supports a presidency that tries to deemphasize its military roots and promote a civilian image instead. Consequently, while pictures of the president adorn most city squares, boulevards, and buildings, the state does not actively seek to promote a leader's cult of personality.[33] In inclusionary states, however, the leader *is* the state. He is "elevated into a demigod towering above the people and embodying their historical roots, future destiny, and revolutionary martyrs."[34] Not only does he personify the state, but he is portrayed as the central means by which the will of the masses is translated into the power of the state.

The leader's indispensability to the state is guaranteed both objectively, through institutions, and subjectively, through the representation of the state to the people. In Iran, the Islamic Constitution of 1979 was revised in

1989 to strengthen the already powerful position of the leader (*velayat-e faqih*—jurisconsult) at the expense of the powers of the presidency, the parliament (Majles), and even popular sovereignty.[35] That same year in Libya, Qaddafi declared that all institutions had been put directly under the control of the masses (*jamahir*), paving the way for a perfect *jamahiriya*, "a political system purportedly marked by popular rule but without political parties or their representatives."[36] The implications are clear: institutions mean little, but the masses express themselves through their leader (i.e., Qaddafi). In Iraq, although the 1970 constitution called for the creation of a National Assembly, the 250-member body did not meet until 1980. But within only a few months, soon after the invasion of Iran in September, the assembly once again became a meaningless appendage void of any real powers.[37] The devastating consequences of the Gulf War and the subsequent de facto partitioning of the country prompted Saddam Hussein to rule the country more single-handedly and repressively than ever before.

Whereas charismatic rule by nature involves few institutions, the inclusionary states of the Middle East are highly bureaucratized. Complementing the personal autocracy of the leader are three separate but reinforcing sets of institutions: the armed forces, the bureaucracy, and various mass mobilization organizations. In Iran, with the death of Ayatollah Khomeini and the emergence of the Second Republic, primacy was given to an increasingly professional and less doctrinaire and militarized bureaucracy.[38] Instead, a "general de-ideologization of the machinery of government" occurred from the late 1980s to the mid-1990s, with no military personnel being appointed to President Rafsanjani's 1989 cabinet.[39] However, after the 2005 election that brought Mahmoud Ahmadinejad to power, a steady remilitarization of the state got underway. In President Ahmadinejad's second term, in fact, the Islamic Revolutionary Guards Corps (IRGC) became a far more visible force in the affairs of the state than at any other time in the past.[40] Throughout, the persistence of numerous "revolutionary" organizations and individuals across the system has impeded a radical break with the populist past. Consistent with its efforts at expediting the revolutionary transformation of society—and after 1988 the reconstruction of war-ravaged areas— the Islamic state has established a number of gigantic institutions, many called *bonyad* (foundation), that replicate the functions of other, parallel organizations.[41]

Comparatively, the Iraqi state's classification as inclusionary before its overthrow by the United States in 2003 is somewhat problematic. With Saddam Hussein as its ruthless, paramount leader, this "Republic of Fear" was often likened to an Orwellian totalitarian state.[42] Exclusionary as far back as the 1960s, the Iraqi state reverted to populism only belatedly, when its war with Iran failed to bring in a quick victory and turned instead into a costly stalemate. Although its leadership was ostensibly civilian, the Iraqi state never abandoned its military base, instead expanding it constantly. From 1981 to 1988, the government spent an average of 22.7 percent of its gross domestic product (GDP) on the military, compared with an average of 10.5 percent for most other Arab countries.[43] By 1988, Iraq had almost one million men in uniform.[44] This was in addition to an undetermined number of individuals belonging to the "popular militia" (also called "people's army"), which was run by the state *mukhaberat*.[45] Equally pervasive was the Ba'th Party, which was estimated to have a membership of 25,000 and another 1.5 million "supporters."[46] Beginning with the first purges of 1979, shortly after Saddam's assumption of the presidency, the party lost some power and relevance in the decision-making process, but up until the very end it remained an essential venue for career advancement and security for civil servants and military personnel.[47]

In Libya, the personality of Mummar Qaddafi also overshadows all other institutions, both civilian and military. In contrast to Iraq, however, the Libyan state still considers itself to be embroiled in a revolutionary, transformative process that started with the 1969 coup. To this end, Colonel Qaddafi periodically engages in a new grand experiment to enhance and perpetuate the underlying populism of the body politic. Recent Libyan political history illustrates the point, with a variety of "people's" organizations—the General People's Congress, revolutionary committees, later replaced by the Ministry of Mass Mobilization and Revolutionary Leadership, and the like—created to take over such formal institutions of power as the cabinet and the legislature.[48] Given its economic structure and a much smaller population base, the Libyan state finds it easier to engage in populist experiments of various types as compared to either the Iranian or the Iraqi states. Nonetheless, in Libya as in the two other countries, repression is a frequently used option in the state's exercise of authority.

Equally pervasive in all three states is the leader's cult of personality. With political centralization in the person of the leader comes the cultivation of charismatic authority, in some cases more successfully than in others. The leader enjoys charismatic legitimacy during his rule (Khomeini), or is constantly trying to portray himself as charismatic (Saddam Hussein), or was at some point highly charismatic and now refuses to acknowledge his loss of charisma (Qaddafi). But by nature charisma is hard to come by, is impermanent when it does exist, and is insufficient by itself to run a modern state. Therefore, the inclusionary states of the Middle East have created personality cults instead, portraying the leader as larger than life in every possible way. Monuments, art, postage stamps, giant portraits, and national holidays commemorate the leader's accomplishments large and small.[49] In Iraq, "al-Hussein" missiles were used in the Iran-Iraq War, which the Iraqi government referred to as "Saddam's Qadisiyya" after the 637 A.D. battle in which Arab armies decimated Persian forces.[50]

But there is more to the cult of personality of inclusionary states than the mere glorification of repressive autocrats. Through the leader, in his image and in his name, the masses are pulled into the political system, forcibly if need be. The deeds, accomplishments, and agendas of the leader, and by implication of the larger state, are used to mobilize the masses in support of various state-led projects. Thus the people are given what they are told is a historically significant project in which to participate. People are made to feel indispensable to the political process. In this way, the inclusionary state hopes to reinforce the emotional ties that bind "the masses" to their leader (the state). Projects have included experiments in mass empowerment (the *jamahiriya* polity in Libya); "liberation" and "national" wars of various kinds (against historic enemies by both Iraq and Iran; against Kuwait by Iraq; against Israel by Iraq, Iran, and Libya); and the elimination of foreign and domestic enemies (the Munafiqin [regime code word for the Mujahedeen opposition group], the "Great Satan," and later the author Salman Rushdie by Iran).

Perhaps the most important feature distinguishing inclusionary from exclusionary states is the former's conscious and ceaseless efforts to manipulate cultural norms and symbols for political purposes. Of all three non-democratic state types in the Middle East, inclusionary states are the most actively involved in crafting and influencing cultural values that support their political agendas. They often reinvent tradition. Sultanistic states, by and large, do not craft cultural norms but selectively magnify existing ones and manipulate them for political purposes. Exclusionary states deal with culture at best only implicitly, playing by its rules and defying them only at great cost. The overt and deliberate manipulation of cultural values makes inclusionary states and most sultanistic regimes the least susceptible to liberalization pressures.

While unable to ignore the forces of culture completely, exclusionary states relate to prevailing cultural values only implicitly, capitalizing on such pervasive phenomena as personalism, patrimonialism, lack of formality, and familism.[51] Except for Atatürk and Iran's two twentieth-century monarchs, Reza and Muhammad Reza Pahlavi, no exclusionary leaders in the contemporary Middle East have tried systematically to alter the cultural basis of social relations or politics. Atatürk succeeded by coercion; Mohammad Reza Shah was overwhelmed by culturally rooted forces. Other exclusionary states have had at best an uneasy relationship with the entrenched cultural forces of their country. The Algerian state's neglect of "Arabist" students (giving preference to francophone ones) led to increasing political tensions beginning in the 1980s.[52] Sadat's refusal to acknowledge the pervasive social influence and powers of Islamists cost him his life. Hafiz Al-Assad relied extensively on an inner circle of fellow Alawis to guard against the ambitions of the predominantly Sunni Muslim Brotherhood.

In contrast, inclusionary states set out to create the individual and the whole society anew. The state actively promulgates its self-ascribed mission of safeguarding the nation's revolutionary heritage, even if that heritage has to be constructed overnight. Ideological indoctrination and cultural transformation take place through the theater of the street, where the individual sheds his previous identity and assumes a new, corporate one in common with his fellow countrymen. Culture becomes political, politics becomes collective, and the individual and his society are transformed. Qaddafi's nationwide experiments, designed to create a new Libya, have already been alluded to. In Iran, the Islamic Republic initially sought to create an ideal *homo Islamicus* from the state's all-encompassing program of religious and political transformation.[53] Like so many other phenomena related to culture, the degree of success of this transformation is impossible to measure. But it does take place, with some apparent success.

Incorporated into the political process, social groups are left with little autonomy to pursue agendas of their own, including pressing for liberalization measures. What appear as spontaneous eruptions of public support are often highly choreographed demonstrations organized by the state. "People power" may be glorified, but power emanates down from the leader and not up from the masses.[54] The state placates those who demand political participation with what looks like street democracy. Those who are not sold on the ideals of the regime are repressed. The manipulation of culture gives inclusionary states an added advantage over exclusionary states in terms of political stability. By actively promoting subjective, ideological, and emotional links with society in addition to the institutional bonds that already exist, inclusionary states are better able to deflect tension and to resist the emergence of pressures from within society. After all, rebellion is more easily justified against such modern-day pharaohs as Sadat and Mubarak than against imams, national saviors, and leaders.

SULTANISTIC REGIMES

Somewhere between exclusionary and inclusionary systems are the Middle Eastern sultanistic states. Invariably authoritarian, these monarchies rely on a combination of coercive and administrative institutions (e.g., the National Guard and the bureaucracy) to maintain power. Also key to the political formula is the traditional legitimacy of the ruling family, which is deeply rooted in the history, cultural heritage, and lore of the country. Not only does this traditional legitimacy distinguish sultanistic states from exclusionary and inclusionary ones, but, in the Middle East, its resonance and strength differentiate one group of monarchies from another. For the oil monarchies of the Arabian peninsula—Bahrain, Kuwait, Oman, Qatar, Saudi Arabia, and the UAE—historical tradition is an important source of legitimacy. This legitimacy is further reinforced by the state's access to vast oil riches and the resulting royal benevolence toward society. Consequently, the state has by and large been able to placate societal demands for major political changes. Only in Kuwait have there been periodic demands for and episodes of political participation, especially in times of acute economic stress (in the 1930s and 1980s) or political crisis (after the Iraqi invasion of 1990–91).[55] Nevertheless, free and meaningful political participation has not been sustained over a long period, and authoritarian policies have been reinstated soon after the end of the crisis.

The two remaining Middle Eastern monarchies outside the Arabian peninsula, Jordan and Morocco, have neither the huge petrodollars nor the long historical tradition of the oil monarchies. While Jordan and Morocco both rely on rentier economies, their access to rent revenues is not through oil but mostly through worker remittances from abroad for Jordan and the exploitation of mineral resources for Morocco.[56] Compounding the economic difficulties of relatively small rent revenues are the lack of a historically resonant tradition of monarchy, especially in Jordan, and the problems of crafting a popular lore of monarchical legitimacy based on local tradition and heritage. This problem is not as acute in Morocco, where, as we saw in Chapter 2, dynastic rulers from as far back as the sixteenth century justified their position on grounds of being descendants of the Prophet *(sherifs).*[57] To this day, both the Moroccan and the Jordanian monarchs claim to be *sherifs,* and the king of Morocco has the additional title of Commander of the Faithful (Amir al-Mu'minin).[58] Still, institutionally, both monarchies appear to be on more tenuous ground than their counterparts in the Arabian peninsula. Since the 1960s, Moroccan politics has been characterized by serious internal challenges to the state, in the form of assassination and coup attempts against the king (in 1971 and

1972) and occasional riots and mass unrest (in 1973, 1981, 1984, 1989, and 1991). In Jordan, the foundations of the monarchy have been threatened time and again: in 1955 by widespread demonstrations; in 1956 and 1968 by attempted coups; in 1958 by the overthrow of King Hussein's cousin, King Faisal, in Iraq; in 1970 by the Black September civil war; throughout the 1970s by tensions with the PLO; in the late 1980s by extensive "bread riots"; and in the early 2000s, by the rise of religious radicals.

Apart from obvious economic differences, two important dynamics account for the different levels of political stability in the oil monarchies versus Jordan and Morocco. The first dynamic is historical, dealing with the radically different patterns of state formation in the two groups of monarchies. The second dynamic, which is political, is directly linked to the first. In oil monarchies, state formation resulted in the evolution of three power sources through which the state rules: a corporate royal family, which relies on traditional authority; the civil service, through which a welfare state is maintained; and the *mukhaberat* and the armed forces, which ensure the security of the state against internal and external threats and are personally controlled by the royal family.

The same three power centers also emerged in the civic myth monarchies, but with substantially different characters. Especially in Jordan, the royal family relies not on traditional authority but on an "imagined" tradition, a myth based more on the state's reinterpretation of history than on factual heritage and reality. Also, the civil service does not act as an agent of the welfare state. It simply provides employment for the middle classes and facilitates the penetration of the *mukhaberat* into opposition groups. Finally, the royal family's personal control over the armed forces is not as extensive and complete as is the case in the oil monarchies. The state, therefore, is far more sensitive and vulnerable to potential challenges from within and without. When faced with such challenges, the state's traditional response has been either to clamp down on the opposition or to liberalize. Given the global political and economic context of the 1980s and 1990s—a time when a powerful Middle Eastern monarchy was swept away by revolution, military juntas in South America abandoned the presidential palace and returned to the barracks, East European communist states collapsed one after another, and the "wave" of democracy seemed unstoppable—the civic myth monarchies of the Middle East have felt compelled to opt for liberalization as a survival strategy. Unlike the other nondemocratic states of the region, they do not have the institutional capabilities to continually resort to repression. Liberalization, limited and controlled as it may be, has become structurally necessary.

The oil monarchies have been better equipped than the civic myth monarchies to deal with potential challenges arising from within. The historical process of state formation in the oil monarchies has been decisive in giving them their current institutional characteristics and determining their patterns of rule. By the time independence came to the Persian Gulf states—beginning in the late 1880s in what later became Saudi Arabia but not until 1971 for the UAE—most of the ruling families had already established their supremacy over the tribal areas that later became independent states.[59] British support was a critical factor in transforming ruling clans into royal families. With independence came the institutionalization of the tribal chieftaincy and its simultaneous transformation into the leadership of an increasingly modern and differentiated state. Up until the 1950s and 1960s, the ruling families governed through a combination of British material and diplomatic protection, traditional, tribal legitimacy, and a reservoir of tribal recruits who could be relied upon if a domestic military challenge arose. The discovery and later sale of oil in the 1950s and 1960s changed the political equation considerably, resulting, among other things, in a steady bureaucratization of the monarchy and the development of a modern civil service. A modern armed forces was created almost overnight, providing for yet another official institution through which tribal support could be channeled and maintained. A pyramidal power structure emerged, with the royal family at the top, supported by the civil service and the armed forces.

Key to the relative stability of the oil monarchies has been the successful cultivation of a sense of legitimacy among the larger population in general and among tribes in particular. This is not to suggest that these states enjoy unsurpassed and unchallenged legitimacy, as recent, repeated episodes of terrorism in Saudi Arabia, Bahrain, Kuwait, and elsewhere demonstrate. Nevertheless, the oil monarchies have developed institutions and patterns of rule that have considerably cushioned their vulnerability against popular uprisings or other similar domestic threats. Their rule is largely considered legitimate on grounds of what Max Weber labeled traditional authority: "an established belief in the sanctity of immemorial traditions and the legitimacy of the status of those exercising authority under them."[60] In such polities, "obedience is owed to the *person* of the chief who occupies the traditionally sanctioned position of authority and who is (within its sphere) bound by tradition. The obligation of obedience is a matter of personal loyalty."[61] In the oil monarchies of the Middle East, this type of traditional authority would not have been possible without the pervasive social and political influence of tribalism.

Despite growing sedentarization and modernization of tribes in recent decades, tribal and clan identity and values continue to figure prominently in politics. At the level of political institutions, tribalism is epitomized by the royal family, even though the monarchy has become highly institutionalized and has far less direct contact with the tribes than ever before. Nevertheless, tribal practices such as *shura* (consultation) and institutions such as the *majlis* (an informal advisory council) remain important symbolic elements in the state's modus operandi. Even more significant is the way "tribal corporations" have been formally or informally integrated into the political structure. In Kuwait, tribal corporations operate unofficially and through existing political institutions such as the National Assembly, the Municipal Council, and some of the loosely organized political clubs and voluntary associations. In Saudi Arabia, Oman, and Bahrain, tribal corporations are semiofficial and are heavily represented in the police force and the National Guard. In the UAE, meanwhile, they are considered one of the institutions of the state itself, their status having been codified through legislation.[62] Finally, as if incorporation were not enough, all oil monarchies use the offerings and patronage of the state—education, medical treatment, subsidized food, housing, and employment—to establish and reinforce direct clientalistic ties with social actors and to strengthen existing bonds with their own and with other tribes.[63] Patronage enables the ruler to court the support of other tribal leaders (sheikhs) and to maintain his own position as the paramount sheikh *(sheikh al-masha'ikh).*[64]

Further reinforcing the strength of the royal family is its essentially corporate nature. A product of its genesis as a tribal chieftaincy, the corporate character of each of the royal families differs on the basis of the overall characteristics of the family itself and the specific personality and capabilities of the *amir* (king) in power. The al-Sabah of Kuwait, for example, have such a strong corporate identity and interests that they have evolved an intricate set of organizations, epitomized by a Family Council specifically designed to run the affairs of the royal family.[65] In contrast, the al-Thani in Qatar have at times shown disregard for the ruler's authority and have often demonstrated little corporate identity.[66] Saudi Arabia's unusually large ruling family is estimated to number between fifteen thousand and twenty-five thousand individuals, although it is controlled by only about two hundred senior princes.[67] This large size presents challenges as well as advantages. On the one hand, it increases the possibilities of court intrigue and personal rivalries among members of the royal family, as the six-year public feud between King Saud, his half-brother Faisal, and Prince Talal demonstrated from 1958 to 1964. On the other hand, it allows the royal family to monopolize all important bureaucratic, military, and provincial institutions. These include cabinet ministries and other high-level positions within the civil service, command of the various branches of the armed forces, and the governorate of the different provinces.

This is not unique to Saudi Arabia.[68] In Bahrain, Kuwait, Oman, Qatar, and the UAE, the offices of the prime minister, foreign minister, interior minister, and defense minister are all occupied by members of the royal family, in some cases by the king himself. Moreover, in all the monarchies, including Bahrain, where the royal family is not as wealthy as in the other states, princes and princesses are deeply involved in a variety of commercial and business activities.[69] This strengthens their ability to maintain clientalistic ties with wealthy merchants and consequently with the larger society. Further reinforcing the royal family's dominant position in relation to various social groups is the state's central role in the real estate market. "Land gifts" have long been a regular policy of the Saudi state, and the governments of Kuwait, Qatar, and the UAE have systematically manipulated the real estate market to benefit wealthy merchants and other important personalities.[70] Patronage offers the state yet another means of maintaining its hegemony and legitimacy in relation to society.

Despite declining oil revenues beginning in the 1980s and the shock of the Gulf War in 1990–91, oil monarchies continue to placate domestic pressures for liberalization. Even in Kuwait, where the resumption of parliamentary politics after the end of the Gulf War has not translated into a curtailment of the al-Sabahs' arbitrary powers, there has so far been little apparent backlash from the population. Admittedly, the impact of declining rent revenues is far more pronounced on the economies of civic myth monarchies. Nevertheless, the near-complete absence of demands for liberalization in the oil monarchies is as much a product of the state's continued institutional strength as it is a result of the comparatively robust nature of the economy. The royal family is synonymous with the state, not just in terms of the government's representation of the royals to their subjects, but in terms of the very real ways in which royal personages control powerful state institutions.

More important, the royal family relies on the profoundly salient and resonant tradition of tribalism, portraying itself as the embodiment of tribal values, practices, and heritage. The bureaucratization of the monarchy and its transplantation into opulent palaces have not destroyed its ability to manipulate social and cultural norms that are valued—often romanticized—by society. In Saudi Arabia, the royal family has the added advantage of claiming the guardianship of Islam and its two holiest sites.[71]

With its survival not seeming threatened by forces that can easily be subdued through repression, the monarchy has little reason or incentive to
liberalize or even to make a pretence of liberalizing.

The structural differences between the oil monarchies and the civic
myth monarchies are striking. Neither Jordan nor Morocco has the institutional characteristics that would enable it to easily ride out economic
or political crises. Both, especially Jordan, lack the resonant tribal tradition that has expedited the state-building process in the oil monarchies.
Monarchy has, in a sense, seemed less "natural" to these states than it has
in the Arabian peninsula. Therefore, Jordanian and Moroccan claims to
legitimacy based on traditional authority come into even sharper contradic-
tion with the realities of modernity than is the case in the oil monarchies.
To this category also belonged Iran's Pahlavi dynasty, which ultimately
collapsed despite its best efforts at balancing traditional politics with modern economic and sociocultural development. Moreover, the monopoly
over state institutions by the Jordanian and Moroccan royal families has
been incomplete because of their comparatively small size.

While fragile, the ensuing civic myth monarchies have generally shown
staying power so long as rent revenues continue flowing into the economy.
In recent years, however, declining rents have exacerbated the structural
limitations of the two states. Within this context, in the mid-1990s the
Jordanian and Moroccan monarchies initiated some liberalization efforts.
These moves were designed to transform the monarchies' legitimacy from
one based on anachronistic claims to traditional authority into one that is
increasingly democratic.

For Jordan, the problem of creating a civic myth supportive of the monarchy has been particularly acute. In the oil monarchies, state building
occurred concurrently with the formation of a national identity. In fact,
the two processes complemented and reinforced one another. Even the
existence of many foreign nationals throughout the Persian Gulf countries,
countered by some of the most stringent citizenship laws in the world, has
not hampered the evolution of, say, Saudi, Bahraini, or Qatari identity. In
Jordan, however, the process of state formation, from the 1920s until full
independence from Britain in 1948, took place during the steady dissolution
of Palestine and the growth of a sizable Palestinian community in Jordan.
By and large, the Jordanian state is still trying to carve out a distinct sense
of Jordanian national identity and nationalism. Only in July 1988 did King
Hussein renounce any claims to Palestine and decide to end the subsidies
he had paid to the West Bank for years. Time and again, the security of
King Hussein's reign was threatened because of the Palestinian-Israeli

conflict. Given that Jordan has a population that is at least 60 to 70 percent Palestinian in origin, geographic proximity to Palestinian territories, and a history of clashes with Palestinian (and Israeli) forces, the question of its national identity and the ultimate legitimacy of the monarchy before the citizenry is not yet settled.

This problem is compounded by two additional developments. First, in Jordan the state and the ruling family have no tangible tribal and/or religious reference points to serve as sources of traditional legitimacy and support. The Jordanian state tries actively to perpetuate national and historic symbols that are meant to enhance the legitimacy of the regime. For example, the colors of the Jordanian flag represent Hashemite rule as part of a much longer historic tradition. King Hussein often appeared in public and in photographs wearing the bedouin headgear *(kaffiya)*. Other forms of creating and reinforcing nationalist symbols—naming public buildings and monuments after the king, celebrating national holidays, manipulating school textbooks for political purposes—abound. But these and other efforts are mostly symbolic, often grounded in the state's interpretation of reality rather than in reality itself. In the past, bedouin tribes in the southern parts of the country have shown loyalty to the king. However, as their extensive participation in the riots of 1989 demonstrated, this loyalty is based more on the strength of economic patronage than on blood ties and kinship. In the oil monarchies, clientalistic bonds play an important role in linking the tribes to the royal family. The royal family itself has extensive tribal connections, maintained by *'asabiyya* (blood ties and relations of mutual support). The Jordanian monarchy, however, does not have access to vast oil revenues. Instead, to ensure the loyalty of the country's southern tribes, it must make a greater effort to emphasize the royal family's tribal and religious roots.

Second, there is the interrelated problem of a ruling family that is too small either to dominate state institutions or to form a pervasive corporate identity of its own. Named after the monarchy, the country's official designation is, indeed, the *Hashemite* Kingdom of Jordan. Nevertheless, the actual significance of this is nothing like the naming of Saudi Arabia after the Ibn Saud. More important, the ruling family's small size has from the beginning forced it to rely on loyalists, professional technocrats, and even Palestinians to staff key state institutions such as the Foreign Ministry, the Defense Ministry, and the Prime Ministry. Before Crown Prince Hassan was removed as the designated heir and replaced by Prince Abdullah, he was somewhat active in state affairs. However, he did not hold any formal cabinet portfolios or command positions within the armed forces.[72]

Ironically, Prince (now King) Abdullah, King Hussein's son, who was not the heir apparent until two weeks before his father's death in February 1999, commanded his own unit in the army. In fact, the constitution of 1952, which is technically still in effect, stipulates that authority be jointly exercised by the king and a bicameral legislature (Majlis al-'Umma). While this provision of the constitution was virtually ignored until the early 1990s and the king's powers remained paramount, the loyalty of those in sensitive state positions could not always be counted on, as represented by attempted coups by some military officers in the 1950s and 1960s.

The predicament of the Moroccan monarchy is only slightly different. As we saw in Chapter 3, Morocco, unlike Jordan, has had a long dynastic tradition, steeped in and justified by the Kharajite branch of Islam. Monarchy was restored after the end of protectorate rule by France and Spain from 1919 to 1956, but with powers far surpassing those of pre-protectorate days. The monarchy's supreme political and religious positions were enshrined in the 1962 constitution, and the three subsequent constitutions written since then—in 1970, 1972, and 1992—have altered the political balance only marginally.[73] In theory as well as in practice, the king considers himself the supreme religious and temporal authority of the land, "above other institutions and above any juridical order, including that of the Constitution itself."[74] In this respect, the monarchy relies on an invented political tradition, as the pre-1912 sultanate was ruled in tandem with the *ulama*. In fact, power sharing between the ruler and others survived well into the 1940s and 1950s, when, during the independence movement, Mohammed V cooperated with and endorsed the nationalist Istiqlal Party's manifesto calling for the establishment of a democratic monarchy upon independence. Today, however, few Moroccans are reminded of this aspect of the independence movement.

Nevertheless, given the long religio-political tradition of sultanistic rule in the country, the Moroccan monarchy has had an easier task of crafting legitimacy on traditional grounds than the Hashemites in Jordan. The problem has been the monarchy's inability to count on the absolute loyalty of some of the key institutions in the state. Like the Jordanian monarchy, the Moroccan royal family is too small to enable it to place princes in control of the armed forces and other important state institutions. Instead, the country's two most recent monarchs, Kings Hassan and Mohammed VI, have used favoritism and patronage to ensure the loyalty of senior figures and the armed forces. During the "state of emergency" that lasted from 1965 to 1971, the army emerged as the bulwark of the regime, repressing the Istiqlal and other parties with considerable efficiency. But this did not prevent attempted military coups from taking place in 1971 and 1972. At this time the king felt compelled to initiate a rapprochement with the political parties, thus inaugurating what he called Hassanian democracy.

Hassanian democracy soon proved to be little more than a political ploy, as evident from this description of the role the king envisioned for opposition parties in his new, democratic order: "[I]f we were in opposition, we would say, 'We are before anything else servants of the king, who is the king of all Moroccans.'"[75] In 1985, Istiqlal left the government and, with other parties, demanded that real reforms be implemented. By the early 1990s the monarchy could no longer ignore the demands of the "opposition" political parties inside and outside the parliament. The old political formula that placed the king and his legitimacy above and beyond everything but God no longer worked. Despite his best efforts at keeping the parties from developing a life of their own, King Hassan had failed to create a docile "loyal opposition." New parliamentary elections were held in July 1993 amid much popular excitement. The results were far from a landslide victory for the opposition but were sobering enough that the monarchy realized the necessity of sharing power with the opposition.[76]

In 1999, the Middle East's two remaining civic myth monarchies (along with Bahrain) weathered their most serious challenge in recent years when the long-reigning monarchs who had come to personify the political system passed away and were succeeded by their sons in orderly and smooth transitions. In February 1999, Jordan's sixty-four-year-old King Hussein died after a long battle with cancer and was succeeded by his son, King Abdullah II (b. 1962). Morocco's King Hassan II (b. 1929), who had reigned since 1961, died of a heart attack the following July and was succeeded by his oldest son, Mohammed VI (b. 1963). A similar transition occurred in Bahrain, where Sheikh Isa ibn-Sulman al-Khalifa (b. 1934), who had ruled the island nation since 1961—Bahrain gained its independence from Britain in 1971—died in March and was succeeded by his son, Sheikh Hamad (b. 1950). In all three cases, the institutional viability and strength of the monarchy were tested, and then proven, during the transition. Perhaps the biggest potential threat to the monarchy arose in Jordan, where, because of an apparent family feud, King Hussein abruptly replaced his brother with his son as the crown prince only two weeks before he died. Nevertheless, as subsequent events have shown, the Jordanian monarchy remains on solid institutional grounds, and the deposed Prince Hassan has not challenged Abdullah II's rule.

QUASI-DEMOCRACIES

It is a given that not all democracies are equally democratic, some being more true to the essence and spirit of democracy than others. For a variety of reasons, some democratic systems place institutional limitations on the scope and nature of the political rights and liberties they grant to their citizens. The degree to which civil liberties are curtailed and the reasons for their curtailment differ from case to case and depend on specific historical and political circumstances. However, these democracies often feature a plethora of official or unofficial political "red lines" that the electorate cannot cross. These red lines might be drawn around certain broad issues, such as the overall ideological character of the state, or around the participation of specific groups in the political process, such as various ethnic or religious minorities. Seldom are these restrictions outlined in the constitution or in any of the other legal frameworks on which the state relies. They are, nevertheless, widely observed and guarded by state actors and by other self-ascribed guardians of the state, whether the armed forces or specific elite groups. By and large, the electorate is also mindful of the boundaries beyond which it should not step, although at times it is willing to risk pushing the boundaries to see what happens. Despite the existence of the institutions and practices of democracy, therefore, such democracies often place obvious political restrictions around certain issues or specific groups. For this reason, they might be best classified as "quasi-democracies."

There is a subtle but important distinction between quasi-democracies and democracies that are "partial" or "incomplete." As Chapter 10 discusses, processes of democratic transition are often fraught with tension and conflict among state leaders, whose loss of institutional or ideological cohesion, or both, paves the way for competing groups to press their demands on the state. While the state is in the process of transition, its nondemocratic elements and features continue to resist giving up power. The ensuing political system is full of contradictions, at least temporarily, until its precarious "negative balance" is tipped one way or another. Some aspects of the state, such as elections to the parliament, are very democratic, while others, such as nonelected figures' continued hold on power, are highly undemocratic. This makes the system at best a partial democracy. In Chapter 10, we examine the emergence of such a political system in contemporary Iran. In these partial democracies, the contradictions are institutional; some of the institutions of the state are democratic, others are not. This is not the case in quasi-democracies, in which existing political institutions tend to be uniformly democratic, except, of course, for the armed forces. Here the system's contradictions are not institutional.

Instead, they revolve around the larger political culture that informs and guides the broader understanding of the permissible forms and limits of political participation. Democracy exists for some but not for others. Some political issues are open for discussion; others are not. As we will see below, these quasi-democratic systems are the sort found in the Middle East, especially in Israel, Lebanon, and Turkey.

Several interrelated and reinforcing dynamics result in a political system developing into a quasi-democracy as opposed to a more "viable" democratic polity.[77] Three factors stand out: age, institutional design, and the political role of the middle classes. To begin with, quasi-democracies all tend to be rather young political systems in relative historical terms, with their establishment traceable to no more than one or at most two generations of political leaders. By itself, age is not a determinant of the nature of a political system. However, especially in democracies, where the deliberately crafted institutions of the political system need time to settle into their mutually dependent, countervailing relationships, age and experience can be highly stabilizing, maturing factors. With time, imperfect democracies can—though not all will—work out their internal contradictions. In the American democracy, for example, with time, a serious secessionist movement was suppressed (the Civil War of 1860–63), slavery was outlawed (Thirteenth Amendment, in 1865), voting rights were extended to blacks (Fifteenth Amendment, in 1870) and then to women (Nineteenth Amendment, in 1920), and racial inequities were targeted for change (the civil rights movement of the 1960s).

The Middle East's three existing democratic systems are all relatively recent in historical terms. Israel has the oldest uninterrupted democracy, dating back to 1948. Lebanon's fragile democracy, which took shape after the country's independence in 1943, was shattered in 1975, not to be reconstituted until the civil war ended in 1990. Turkey's first democratic elections were held in 1950, but there were military coups in 1960, 1971, and 1980. Another "silent coup" occurred in 1997, when, from behind the scenes, the military forced the resignation of the sitting prime minister.

Age is only one factor pushing an emerging democratic system in the direction of limited democracy. Many West European democracies are equally young but are quite vibrant and are free of the built-in institutional limitations that saddle quasi-democracies. The circumstances that give rise to a democratic system, and the larger sociopolitical and diplomatic context within which that system is established, are even more important. Viable democracies tend to have their genesis in society and are often initiated "from below." A relatively wide coalition of social actors puts pressure on the state and, if successful, forces it to democratize. As we shall see in Chapter 10, the depth of civil society is a crucial determinant of the viability and vitality of a democratic political system. Quasi-democracies, in contrast, tend to come "from above." They are often initiated either by state actors themselves for the specific purpose of protecting their privileges, as in Turkey, or by social elites, for whom the protection of privilege also emerges as an important priority, as in Lebanon. The political system thus crafted, democratic as it may be, also reflects an institutional imperative to protect the privileged position of certain elements in society, such as the armed forces (in Turkey and Israel), prominent social elites (in Lebanon), or dominant ethnic groups (the Jews in Israel and the Turks in Turkey).

Crucial to any democracy is the role of the middle classes, without whose sustained participation in the political process a democracy becomes hollow and meaningless. This is especially the case in younger democracies, where initially the electorate comes to play a deliberate, guardian role in ensuring the system's integrity. In many of the more recent democratic transitions in the developing world, the middle classes have played a most vital role, at least in the initial phases of the struggle to bring about a democratic political system. Before long, however, economic pressures and circumstances force much of their attention away from political activities and toward economics, thus giving state elites a freer hand in pursuing their own agendas. The confidence of the middle classes in the stability of their economic position—not having to work multiple jobs to keep their middle-class standing—and their economic independence from the state—not having to rely on direct state salaries or indirect state largesse—determines the extent and nature of their role as watchdogs over political elites. In other words, what "the people" let their elected officials get away with has a lot to do with how confident they feel about their economic standing. As we shall see, in Lebanon and Turkey, and to a lesser extent in Israel among the country's Arab citizens, there are large segments of society for whom sustained, routine attention to politics is a luxury they cannot afford.

In all three of the democratic systems in the Middle East, built-in features make the systems more quasi-democratic than viably democratic. In one way or another, and to one extent or another, especially when compared to the liberal democracies of the West, they restrict the scope of political participation or civil liberties by certain groups (e.g., the Kurds in Turkey and the Palestinians in Israel) or ensure the continued hold on power by specific oligarchies (e.g., in Lebanon). Also, in both Turkey and Israel, concern with national security, broadly defined, has led to far more influence by the armed forces in civilian policy making than is the case in almost all other democracies. In fact, one ironic label that has been used to refer to both systems is *military democracy*.[78]

Let us begin by examining the Turkish political system. As we saw in Chapter 2, the modern state that Atatürk founded involved two primary projects: the forcible secularization and modernization of Turkish culture and society, and the institutionalization and propagation of a distinctly Turkish as opposed to Ottoman national identity. Both tasks, coupled with the other projects of Atatürk's "revolution from above," involved significant state coercion. Having all come from military backgrounds, Atatürk and his associates liberally used the armed forces to achieve their political ends. In practical terms, this meant the significant presence of the army in civilian life, at least behind the scenes, and the military's heavy-handed suppression of non-Turkish minorities, such as the Kurds. Kurds who did not accept the state's efforts at forced ethnocultural assimilation into the "higher" Turkish identity were brutally repressed.[79]

Once Atatürk was gone from the scene, the Turkish military assumed for itself the mission of safeguarding his legacy and ensuring that civilian politicians did not deviate from the path which he had started. From 1950 on, an imperfect but functioning multiparty democracy governed Turkey. But the system was beset by political infighting and tension and by chronic economic crises. The first direct military intervention occurred in 1960, after some ten years of rule by the Democratic Party had brought the country to the verge of chaos and civil war. Viewing its mission as temporary and its goal as the restoration of the Kemalist republic, the ruling military junta drafted a new constitution and, after new elections in 1961, retreated to the barracks. Before doing so, however, it ensured its own institutional oversight of the civilian power structure through the establishment of the National Security Council (NSC). According to the 1961 constitution, the NSC was set up to assist the cabinet "in making decisions related to national security and coordination."[80]

The 1960 coup was carried out by junior officers of the Turkish military. Throughout the 1960s, however, the military's sense of corporate identity, its internal discipline and cohesion, and the political and economic privileges of its high command grew significantly. With vested economic and political interests in maintaining social peace and stability, in 1971 the military stepped in again, this time to stop the increasingly rampant terrorism of left- and right-wing extremists. Unlike the 1960 coup, the 1971 intervention was at the behest of senior army officers, who, once again, used the 1971–73 interlude to enhance their own institutional autonomy within the ostensibly civilian body politic. A new constitution was drawn up and the NSC's powers were expanded. However, once the military withdrew again, a succession of weak governments followed, none of which were able to deal with the mounting, often violent tensions and disturbances that ensued. By September 1980, the military once again felt the need to intervene. In a radio-television broadcast to the nation, the coup makers announced that they were only after "ensuring the prevalence of law and order . . . [and] restoring the state authority in an impartial manner."[81] This time, the coup was spearheaded by the NSC itself, which remained the principal ruling body for the coup's three-year duration. Martial law was imposed, most of the political parties were banned, many politicians were banished or imprisoned, and scores of ordinary Turks were rounded up and arrested. As before, a new constitution was drafted, again guaranteeing the NSC's dominance within the system.

Even after new elections in October 1983, the military's hold on public life did not change significantly. The NSC remained one of the most pivotal institutions of the state, and, despite civilian rule, the military's presence in the public sphere remained extensive. Nevertheless, the 1980s witnessed a gradual demilitarization of the Turkish political system, promoted by several different factors, such as Turkey's need to secure loans from the World Bank and the International Monetary Fund, its desire to be seen more as part of Europe, and the general global trend of the 1980s toward the depoliticization of many Third World militaries. By early 1984, martial law was lifted province by province. By the middle of the decade, state elites were floating civilian notions such as "civil society" and even showing signs of real autonomy vis-à-vis the military.[82] The military, it seemed, had left Turkish politics for good.

The appearance that the Turkish democracy was being consolidated was shattered in June 1997, when the military once again flexed its muscle and forced the sitting prime minister, Necmettin Erbakan, out of office. This episode is often referred to as the "silent coup," since the military, through the NSC, summoned the prime minister to a meeting and demanded his resignation. Erbakan, a perennial political activist with Islamist tendencies, had become prime minister at the head of the vaguely religious Refah Party in June 1996. This in itself had sent shock waves through the system. In his short few months in office, the prime minister also embarked on a series of highly controversial measures, many of which were deemed threatening to Atatürk's secularist legacy. He improved Turkey's relations with Iran and Libya, adopted a populist rhetoric with vague references to Islam, and advocated the establishment of a Just Order, the underpinnings for which appeared nonsecular.[83] It took only a year before the military removed him from office.

Today's Turkish military may have become "depoliticized" in the conventional sense of not directly launching a coup. But as its move against Erbakan and the Refah Party showed, it still views itself as the vanguard of a reinvigorated Kemalist legacy. Although there is a democratic system of sorts in Ankara, the continued dominance of the military and its ability to force its preferences on civilian state actors seriously erode the system's democratic legitimacy. And as if that were not enough, Turkish Kurds by and large remain a repressed minority.

The general refusal of state elites to acknowledge the existence of alternative, non-Turkish national identities within their borders resulted in the eruption of an armed insurrection in the Kurdish-dominated southeast regions of the country in 1984. Headed by the Kurdish Workers' Party, the PKK, the Kurdish national movement has elicited sharp and violent reactions from the Turkish army, which has often been heavy-handed in its dealings with Kurdish insurgency. There have been numerous accusations of mass arrests, torture, destruction of property, and forced assimilation by Turkish forces against the Kurds and PKK fighters. Even Kurdish members of the Turkish parliament have been arrested and expelled from it. In the mid-1990s, the Turkish government was said to have amassed some 220,000 troops in the southeast to defeat the PKK and to have launched operations involving as many as thirty-five thousand to fifty thousand soldiers.[84] In May 1999, Turkish commandos captured the PKK's leader, Abdullah Öcalan, and the movement appears to have seriously weakened or even collapsed after that. Nevertheless, even if Turkey's Kurdish movement has faltered for now, the essentially restricted nature of the Turkish democracy remains the same. A viable, liberal democratic polity is still some ways off.

Compared to the Lebanese and Turkish political systems, Israel more closely approximates a liberal democracy. It has one of the most vibrant parliamentary systems in the world, it has had regular elections since November 1949, within a few months of independence the previous May, and since 1977 it has seen regular rotations in the party in power and in the parliamentary majority in the Knesset. In fact, a generally valid perception that the electoral system was too diffuse resulted in its overhaul in 1992, whereby Israeli voters cast separate ballots for the prime minister and for the party list to be elected to the Knesset.[85] Moreover, despite occasional wavering, the judiciary has largely maintained its independence from the country's dominant political currents. As one observer has noted, "[O]n the whole . . . the Israeli judicial system is professional and unpolitical, and, in that sense, very un-Israeli. This is what makes it such an important bastion of Israeli democracy in a sea of forces that would hasten the erosion of its foundations."[86]

Nevertheless, two features of Israeli democracy point to its illiberal nature: the treatment of the Arab citizens of Israel, and the prevailing pattern of civil-military relations. In different ways, each of these factors undermines the integrity of the Israeli democracy, or, at the very least, relegates it to a category separate from the liberal democracies of the West. Israeli civil-military relations are heavily tilted in favor of the military, so much so that civilian oversight of the military is at times more fiction than fact. And although Arab Israelis are technically Israeli citizens with rights equal to those of Jewish Israelis, they frequently face official discrimination and bias.

In 1948, when the state of Israel was founded, according to official Israeli sources, 160,000 Arabs—mostly Muslims with some Christians and Druze—were living within the boundaries of the newly independent state. Today (as of 2007) they number more than 1,450,000, or 20 percent of the total population of 7,240,000.[87] From the start, the Arabs in Israel were given Israeli citizenship and many of the rights that accompanied it: they vote, have representation in the Knesset (seven out of the 120 seats after the 2009 elections, or approximately 6 percent), and have their own political parties (the largest being the United Arab List, with four MKs). These statistics, while demonstrating impressive quantitative achievements by Arab Israelis within the Knesset, mask more important qualitative facts. For nearly twenty years, from 1948 to 1966, official mistrust of Arab Israelis led the government to place them under military administration. "Most Arab towns, villages, farms, and property in Israel were destroyed or taken over by the new Jewish government."[88] The existing farming economy was destroyed. Many Arabs also found themselves victims of arbitrary arrests, expulsions from the country, and forced exile to other villages within Israel.

While the treatment and living standards of the Arab Israelis have improved in recent years, most avenues of upward economic and political mobility remain closed to them. For average Israelis, service in the Israeli Defense Forces (IDF) is often key for obtaining access to social prestige, political influence, and a secure pension. But out of mistrust and for security reasons, Arab Muslim citizens of Israel are barred from military service, although Christians and the Druze can serve. In a country where religion—Judaism—defines the official essence of nationality, non-Jews face formal restrictions of various kinds. The state treats them with suspicion. Only 2 percent of the budget of the Ministry of Religious Affairs is devoted to the needs of their community. Yet with less than 20 percent of the population, they form 50 percent of those living below the poverty line.[89] As two longtime observers of Israeli politics have noted, "The Arabs . . . are excluded from many basic institutions of the state, from the state's collective memory, and from most national symbols. No Arab citizen of Israel has ever held a leading position in any state political institution. The highest ranks obtained by an Arab have been deputy minister, mayor, or district court judge."[90]

Equally problematic for Israeli democracy has been the prevailing nature of civil-military relations in the country. Given that the Israeli state was born into war, from the very beginning the armed forces were seen as indispensable to its survival and security. To ensure personal control over military matters, and by some accounts to prevent the possibility of a coup, Ben-Gurion decided to hold onto the Defense Ministry in addition to the Prime Ministry. He did this all three times that he became the prime minister, and his example was later followed by Prime Minister Levi Eshkol (1963–67). The unintended consequence of this dual control by the prime minister, especially in the formative years of the young republic's life, was the lack of development of viable civilian institutions for effective oversight of the military. Repeated military conflicts in 1956, 1967, and 1973 drove home the importance of security matters, in turn giving military planners increasing freedom to do what was deemed necessary to defend the country. In the process, the Defense Ministry became "the civilian aide for the military," often acting as a sort of Ministry of Military Procurements in peacetime.[91]

Since Israel does not yet have a written constitution, the constitutional limits of the military's influence and the nature of its oversight by civilian institutions remain unclear.[92] Consequently, many high-ranking IDF officials have become very influential in policy-making circles. In fact, Israeli military officials were highly active in the 1993 Oslo Accords negotiations and others that followed with the Palestinians and later the Syrians. Since the mid-1970s, especially after the Likud Party came to power in 1977, many high-ranking IDF officials have engaged in what has come to be known as "parachuting": they wait out the obligatory hundred days of retirement and then assume influential positions in one of the political parties, usually the one in power.[93] None of this, of course, brings the IDF anywhere close to the levels of power enjoyed by the Turkish military, where the Turkish NSC and the military high command can effectively dictate the policies that the prime minister must follow. Nevertheless, the IDF's influence throughout the Israeli polity remains enormous by almost all democratic standards. "The Middle East's only democracy," as Israel is often called, still has some ways to go to become fully democratic.

Of the quasi-democracies, Turkey and Israel are at the opposite extremes of most and least restrictive, respectively, and Lebanon falls somewhere in the middle. Lebanon's 1926 constitution was meant to accommodate the country's fragmented sectarian mosaic, divided into no less than seventeen official religious communities. According to the 1932 census, the largest religious community was Christian, with 51.2 percent of the population (nearly 30 percent of them Maronites and the rest Greek Orthodox, Greek Catholic, and Armenians), while the Muslims were about 48.8 percent of the population, most of them Sunnis (22.4 percent) and Shi'ites (19.6 percent) and the rest Druze (6.8 percent).[94] Within such a highly fragmented society, local notables *(zu'ama)* assumed crucial importance as the articulators and defenders of communal interests and power. In times of instability and crisis, the *zu'ama* and other primordial sources of loyalty, such as family and kinship, became particularly instrumental for those feeling threatened by others or by circumstances. The developments in postindependence Lebanon only served to strengthen primordial and sectarian loyalties, at the expense, as it turned out, of a cohesive sense of national identity.

Shortly after independence in 1943, a notable Sunni delivered a talk in which he outlined a Muslim-Christian understanding regarding the overall nature and the character of the Lebanese state. The National Pact (Al-Mithaq al-Watani), as the talk came to be known, reaffirmed Lebanon's independence from France, its separateness from Syria, and its Arab identity. It also outlined an institutional arrangement for power sharing among the various sects. According to this "informal" provision, the presidency was reserved for the Maronites, the office of the prime minister for the Sunnis, and the speakership of the parliament for the Shi'ites. These same distribution patterns came to be replicated among other echelons of power as well, from the command of the army (going to a Maronite), to the various ministries (Justice Ministry for the Greek Orthodox and Defense Ministry for the Druze), and on to the state bureaucracy.[95] Although unwritten, the National Pact essentially became the constitutional foundation of the Lebanese state. For the few happy years that followed, Lebanon became something of a "consociational" or "consensus" democracy—that is, a "government by elite cartel designed to turn a democracy with a fragmented political culture into a stable democracy."[96]

By 1975, the precarious arrangements on which the Lebanese state had come to rely could no longer withstand the multiple stresses that confronted them. The political system had turned out to be largely unworkable, with the parliament too weak and the president too powerful. The country's demography had changed significantly since the 1932 census, with high Muslim birthrates and an influx of Palestinians after 1970. Pressures also arose from Lebanon's frontline status in relation to Israel, since Palestinian guerrillas attacked northern Israel and Israel retaliated against Lebanese targets. Many of the country's Shi'ites, especially in the south and in the Biqa valley, experienced abject poverty and discrimination and felt alienated from the politically and economically dominant Christians. Elite infighting and the increasing balkanization of state institutions only exacerbated the state's inability to effectively contain its own disintegration. Civil war erupted, and, as it dragged on, members of each of the various confessions sought deeper and deeper shelters in their primordial identities. "Lebanese" identity was thus subsumed by Maronite versus Sunni versus Shi'ite versus Druze identities.

Not until October 1989, by which time most of the warring factions had fought each other into near-exhaustion, was a serious attempt made to end the civil war in Ta'if, Saudi Arabia. Under Saudi, Syrian, and American sponsorship, thirty-one Christian and thirty-one Muslim deputies from the 1972 parliament—the last one to have been convened before civil war broke out—met and agreed to reform the system. Two of the provisions of the Ta'if Accord stand out: (1) the powers of the presidency, still informally in Maronite hands, were reduced, while the powers of the prime minister, under Sunni control, were increased; and (2) the number of MPs for a new parliament was set at 108, to be divided equally between Christians and Muslims.[97] Syria, which had maintained troops in Lebanon since 1976, promised to withdraw them in the near future when circumstances allowed. A new president was also elected. The Lebanese civil war itself continued into 1990. By that time almost all Lebanese factions had given up fighting except the followers of the Maronite General Michel Aoun, who insisted on the withdrawal of Syrian forces before surrendering. He was not as concerned about Israel's continued military presence in southern Lebanon, where, following the 1982–85 invasion of the country, Israeli forces had declared a "safety zone" in which they had stationed troops. At the invitation of the Lebanese government, Syrian forces crushed Aoun's well-equipped militia in October 1990, and the long and bloody civil war finally came to an end.

To the surprise of most observers, the Ta'if Accord, which did not differ a great deal from the other unsuccessful agreements that preceded it, has managed to hold up so far despite the state's frequent political paralysis and continuing hostilities with Israel. Amid jubilant scenes of celebration by the Lebanese, Syrian forces withdrew from the country in April 2005. Earlier, in 2000, Israeli troops had pulled out of most of the "security zone" areas in the south. In many ways, the Shi'ite Hezbollah still defies the central authority of the state and represents something of a state-within-a-state in Lebanon. Up until their collapse and surrender in 2000, the South Lebanese Army, made up of Christian fighters and supported by Israel, also operated with little regard for the central authority of the state. In July and August 2006, Israel launched a massive military assault on Lebanon following a Hezbollah attack on an Israeli patrol, leading to the death of more than a thousand Lebanese civilians and the widespread destruction of property and infrastructure.[98] Hezbollah, with alleged Iranian support, proved itself to be a worthy opponent to Israel, but only at great human and infrastructural cost. The Lebanese polity eventually recovered from this shock, but only after the state once again moved to the brink of implosion as a result of internal bickering and paralysis by the country's multiple factions in 2007–8. Only after persistent mediation efforts by the Saudi and especially the Qatari governments in the summer of 2008 did Lebanon's fractious political parties agree to once again work together in a coalition cabinet.

In essence, the Lebanese polity is being reconstituted, yet again, and state authority is once again becoming the paramount political force in the country. In many ways, the reconstituted system is a somewhat reformed and apparently more workable version of consociational democracy. The reasons the reconstituted polity is once again democratic are explored in Chapter 10. For now, it must be noted that the democratic system has yet to shed its highly elitist character, which is a product of the larger phenomenon of the *zu'ama* system. The final shape of the Lebanese democracy has yet to emerge. For the time being, the larger sociocultural and political circumstances in which it was born lend it the features of a quasi-democracy as opposed to a viable democracy.

POLITICAL OPPOSITION

Given the types of institutional arrangements that Middle Eastern states are likely to assume, it is worth asking what forms of political opposition they allow or provoke. As events in the political history of the modern Middle East have demonstrated, even the most repressive and dictatorial states of the region have encountered severe political crises at one point or another. Some regimes that once seemed politically invincible have succumbed to popular revolutionary movements, as in Iran, while others have faced violent opposition from actors within society, as in Algeria and Egypt. To deflate the potential for popular uprisings, some states, such as the Jordanian, Moroccan, and Kuwaiti monarchies, have allowed limited forms of "loyal opposition" while still retaining tight restrictions on the scope of political activity. Whatever their form might be, Middle Eastern states encounter various types of political opposition, and the nature of this opposition directly influences the state's agendas and capabilities, as well as its broader relationship with society.

Political opposition in the Middle East tends to be divided along two principal axes: officially recognized versus clandestine (or formal versus informal), and secular versus religious. Except for the more conservative kingdoms of the Arabian peninsula—notably Saudi Arabia, Qatar, and Oman—states in the Middle East allow for the existence of one or more political parties and their participation in a parliament. From about the 1950s to the mid-1970s, most countries had one all-encompassing political party. The primary function of the sole official party was to foster controlled popular political participation and to channel the ensuing mass energy into support for various state agendas. Examples of these state parties—in each country acting as the "Ministry of Mobilization"—included the National Liberation Front in Algeria, the Arab Socialist Union and its future incarnations in Egypt, the Neo-Destour in Tunisia, the Ba'th in both Syria and Iraq, and, though hardly successful, the Rastakhiz in Iran.[99]

Since the mid-1970s, and especially since the late 1980s, most states have allowed limited, highly controlled activities by a few officially approved political parties. In fact, beginning especially in the late 1980s, in countries such as Jordan, Morocco, Tunisia, Egypt, and Kuwait, nonstate parties have been allowed to recruit members, hold meetings, and even field candidates in parliamentary elections. Some of these parties have had relatively long traditions of activism, although the state has often banned them and then lifted the ban depending on changing political conditions: the Wafd, the Muslim Brotherhood, and the National Progressive Unionist Party in Egypt; the Istiqlal in Morocco; and the Muslim Brotherhood in Jordan. Other parties emerged in the late 1980s and early 1990s specifically as a result of the more open political atmosphere of the time. Some had been established earlier but were not transformed from paper parties into actual organizations until the late 1980s. Examples include the Islamic Salvation Front (FIS) in Algeria, the Democratic Unionist Party (al-Wa'ad) and the Islamic Action

Front (IAF) in Jordan, the al-Nahda and the Social Democratic Movement Parties in Tunisia, the National Entente in Morocco, and the Islah (Reform) Party in Yemen.

Official recognition by the state, or even parliamentary representation, has not necessarily led to the increased popularity of these parties among the urban middle classes. Many, in fact, have turned into little more than obscure, semiofficial, elite clubs. For example, the Islamic Action Front, established in 1992, initially caused much excitement among the Jordanian electorate and was able to get sixteen of its candidates elected to the Jordanian parliament in the 1993 elections. In municipal elections two years later, however, by which time some of the luster of the new party had worn off, the IAF did relatively poorly and lost much ground to procourt candidates from the tribal, southern parts of the country. By 1997, the party, whose fortunes had significantly declined by now, thought it best to boycott parliamentary elections. Tunisia's officially recognized "opposition" parties are in even worse shape, to the extent that in the run-up to the 1994 elections the Tunisian state decided to subsidize them to ensure their viability, at least as long as they remained politically docile. When they failed to do so, the government arrested and imprisoned their leaders. Today they have been marginalized to the point of near-oblivion. As one observer has noted, "None of the Tunisian parties present any credible alternative to the [state party]. At best, they are gadflies, consciences, safety valves; at worst, they are salon clubs, ego trips, window dressing. Most ironic, the government need do nothing repressive to keep them in that ambiguous status."[100]

There are several reasons for the chronic obscurity and lack of meaningful popular support for the majority of officially recognized political parties in the Middle East. First, to secure recognition from the state and to operate openly, most parties have had to tone down their ideologies considerably and have greatly modified their political agendas. Legal status has necessitated tacit cooperation with the state and the explicit recognition of the legitimacy of the existing political system. Worse, it is seen as recognizing the legitimacy of the current ruling establishment—an establishment that to the popular eye often looks highly authoritarian and corrupt. Although most of these parties go to extraordinary lengths to distance themselves from the ruling elite and reject the political hegemony of those they see as politically incompetent, they are often seen as "guilty by association" by most ordinary citizens, for whom participating in the system even as an "opposition party" is tantamount to complicity with autocrats.

There is also the perception, accurate or not, that these political parties are elitist in their social composition and their ideological disposition. High-level parliamentary politics do little to alleviate the economic difficulties saddling the middle classes or the pervasive poverty plaguing the cities and their slums. This perception is reinforced by two characteristics found in most Middle Eastern parties. Very few political parties in the region have developed—or have been given the opportunity to develop—viable means of organizational networking with an intended constituency. At best, "party organization" has often meant little more than an office in the capital city, sometimes in the provincial capitals as well, and a periodic "congress" attended by party loyalists and sympathizers. At worst, the party resembles a social club in which like-minded elites gather and discuss politics. Some viable political parties have succeeded in such essential functions as interest articulation and electoral mobilization. The former Refah Party in Turkey, discussed above, had some initial success because it developed an elaborate organizational structure for the mobilization of potential voters extending all the way down to city districts and neighborhoods. Similarly, the initial success of the Islamic Action Front in Jordan was largely a product of its extensive ties with the country's Engineers' Association, thereby presenting the party with an existing organizational apparatus.

In addition to the lack of organizational means for meaningful contacts with voters, many political parties in the Middle East suffer from leadership squabbles and a lack of internal cohesion. Given the restrictive political environment in which they operate, and an absence of a tradition of organizational evolution and maturity, many political parties continue to suffer from personalism and lack of institutional depth. This makes them vulnerable to splintering and frequent disagreements among the leadership. In the mid-1990s, the rapid descent into oblivion of the Jordanian al-Wa'ad was largely due to bickering among its leaders. In the late 1980s in Morocco, the Mouvement Populaire (MP) ousted its founder, Mahjoub Aherdane, who then formed the Mouvement National Populaire (MNP). In 1996, a number of MNP members broke away and formed another party, called the Mouvement Democratique et Social (MDS). This pattern of switching offices and acronyms without meaningfully altering ideological disposition or mobilizational efforts can be seen in several other countries in the Middle East and North Africa as well. Naturally, this erodes the potential for voter mobilization and interest articulation.

There have been two important consequences to the general oblivion of officially recognized, nonstate political parties in the Middle East. First, given that traditional political institutions such as parliaments and political parties have turned out to be highly circumscribed in their scope of activities and their efficacy, alternative, nonstate institutions in which urban professionals are involved have instead become quite significant. Institutions such as chambers of commerce, trade unions, professional associations, think tanks, and even nongovernmental journals and magazines have assumed many of the functions usually performed by political parties. Through articulating their views and exerting indirect, subtle pressure on the state, such organizations are able to influence the nature and tenor of ongoing debates, put forward ideas on economic and social policies, and influence the state's larger agendas in relation to society.[101] Labor unions, for example, have become influential players in domestic politics in Morocco, Algeria, Tunisia, Egypt, Turkey, and Bahrain. Professional and/or business associations have become especially important in Jordan and Tunisia. Nongovernmental journals and newspapers have emerged as powerful voices of dissent in Iran's Third Republic, frequently banned and then relicensed under a different name.

A second important consequence of the decline in the significance of officially recognized political parties has been the radicalization of political opposition in the Middle East and the growth in the number and activism of clandestine organizations. Over the last three decades or so, this trend has corresponded with the steady emergence of political Islam as a powerful medium for political expression. The increasing radicalization of political opposition and the concurrent Islamization of political discourse have led to the growth of "radical Islam," or what is commonly called "Islamic fundamentalism." This broad label is somewhat misleading and overly simplistic, for it obscures vast differences among the trends that have appeared under the larger rubric of political Islam. Before analyzing each of these trends, it is important to get a better understanding of the underlying reasons for the spread of Islam as a powerful forum for political expression.

Growth in the popularity of political Islam over the last few decades is part of a broader historical trend in which other competing, secular ideologies have experienced an inverse decline in fortune after having first seen their own growth and popularity. As we have already seen, up until the 1960s and early 1970s, one of the most compelling ideologies among both state actors and the popular classes was secular nationalism, which contained few or no religious ingredients. Ba'thism, Bourguibaism, Nasserism, Arab Socialism, Qaddafi's Third Way—all of these were essentially secular ideologies in which the dominant ingredients were the state and its articulation of the national interest. If religion had any role to play, it was ancillary in relation to the expression of the national identity. Buttressed by the charismatic leadership of real or would-be liberators, these ideologies enjoyed a genuine popularity among the urban classes.

By the early 1970s, however, there was widespread realization throughout the Middle East that the state's articulation of secular nationalism was not all it was cracked up to be. Most significantly, as the fateful events of June 1967 demonstrated, the states were woefully incapable of defending the national interest, let alone liberating the Palestinians. Far beyond the borders of the defeated states, the Arab public was shocked and in disbelief at the secular states' near-complete impotence. And, psychologically comforting as it might have been, the states' search for scapegoats and blaming of incompetent military commanders only partially reversed their loss of ideological legitimacy.

Compounding matters was an increase in state repression, which had actually been a part of the state's modus operandi from the very beginning, and the steadily more blatant corruption of its officials at all levels of power. To hold on to the reins of power, virtually all the states of the Middle East and North Africa resorted to higher levels of repression as a substitute for declining ideological popularity. Repression was complemented by expansive networks of clientalism and patronage, thus widening the chasm between the haves and the have-nots. By the early to mid-1970s, few, if any, of the promises of the revolutionary, "progressive" era of the preceding decade had been fulfilled. The events of 1967 exposed regimes such as the ones in Egypt, Syria, Iraq, and Jordan as inherently weak and corrupt, headed by incompetent officers or officer-kings with little understanding of their own limitations or what it meant to run a modern state. Rhetoric made secular nationalism popular; reality made it crash and burn.

Starting in the mid-1970s, throughout the Middle East and North Africa, the popular appeal of secular, nationalist ideologies declined precipitously among the urban classes. These urban classes were going through other experiences as well. The oil boom of the 1970s was fostering unprecedented economic and industrial growth and consequently dizzying social change. Rural-urban immigration, uncontrolled urbanization, new industries and modes of employment, increasing diffusion and contact with other cultures—all of these developments had consequences for Middle Eastern societies' perceptions of themselves and their state leaders. In the face of hostile and incompetent states, and a pervasive sense of social and cultural alienation among segments of the urban population, shelter was sought in the familiar and the comfortable, in Islam. Once Islam had proved itself to be a viable and powerful force for political mobilization in Iran in 1978–79, its popularity among politically minded Middle Easterners grew rapidly throughout the region. For state actors everywhere, this was a serious threat. Islam had been used as a vehicle for political expression for centuries, and in the twentieth century its politicization went as far back as 1928, when a schoolteacher named Hassan al-Banna established the Muslim Brotherhood group in Egypt. But now, beginning in the late 1970s and early 1980s, Islam was establishing itself as a political force to be reckoned with. Fouad Ajami captures it best: "In the simplified interpretation we have of that civilization, the young had taken to theocratic politics; they had broken with the secular politics of their elders."[102]

Throughout the Middle East, Islamist opposition to the state is likely to come from four groups, although the boundaries between them are not clearly defined: the conservative clerical class (ulama), lay intellectuals, populist organizations, and fundamentalist groups and organizations. These groups are far from monolithic, and all of them feature significant intragroup diversity. They also often have a symbiotic and reinforcing relationship with one another: a conservative cleric issues a fatwa (religious opinion) sanctioning a specific act, which is in turn carried out by a group of fundamentalists, or a secular intellectual becomes one of the main ideological inspirations of a populist organization. Despite these overlapping relationships, it is possible to place many individuals or organizations in a specific category.

As a social group, the ulama have been an integral feature of Middle Eastern societies ever since the spread of Islam beyond Mecca and Medina, even though Islam does not formally recognize a distinct class of religious specialists. Over time, many of these interpreters of religion became powerful possessors of religious knowledge, educators, guardians of the hadith (the Prophet's tradition), trustees of religious endowments (owqaf), and arbiters of social conflict. The inevitable clash between the ulama's desire to maintain their vast privileges and responsibilities and the modern state's attempts to mold society on the basis of its own agendas was, to varying degrees, settled in favor of the state. Some state leaders (e.g., Atatürk) tried to destroy the ulama as a social force, while others (Reza Shah, Muhammad V, Nasser, King Hassan) sought a partial accommodation with them. Still others, such as the Saudi royal family, tried to neutralize the clergy by incorporating them into the state apparatus and making them a part of the power equation. Nevertheless, in one form or another, by the late twentieth century, most Middle Eastern states were able to force their political and institutional hegemony on the ulama and to ensure the clerical establishment's political marginalization, if not total subordination.

The period from the 1950s through the 1970s did not go well for the *ulama*. Modern state institutions were created and took over many of the functions that had long been the preserve of the clergy. State-run schools and universities supplanted the many seminaries that had monopolized education for the bulk of the masses. "Family protection" laws were introduced, and women in most places were given the right to sue for divorce. *Waqf* land was taken over by the state, and in every country a Ministry of Religious Affairs or something similar to it was established to "supervise" the clergy. In 1961, the Al-Azhar, Egypt's cradle of Islamic learning and one of the oldest universities in the world, was nationalized, and its *ulama* became employees of the Nasserist state. This same pattern was repeated in practically every other country of the Middle East. The *ulamas'* position as judges and arbitrators was steadily eroded, their economic power was weakened, they lost students, and their political and institutional autonomy was curtailed.

It was no accident that most clergy around this time became politically "quietist." Faced with increased repression and other acts of manipulation by the state, many retreated to their seminaries and mosques, immersing themselves in their religious studies and teachings. Some cooperated with the state and became mouthpieces of the "official Islam" *(al-Islam al-rasmi)* to which even the most secular leaders paid lip service. But by and large the mainstream *ulama* resented (and still resent) the state and most of what it stands for. They quietly decry the state's moral corruption, its political mismanagement, its seemingly total submission to the Western powers, and its ceaseless efforts to "Westernize" society.

By themselves, the *ulama* have not been a powerful social force for spearheading political opposition or change. Even in Iran, as we saw in Chapter 5, they succeeded only when they entered into strategic alliances with secular parties and intellectuals. They have, nevertheless, been highly influential sources of inspiration and general religious guides for various secular intellectuals who see in religion remedies for many social and political maladies of their societies. A generation earlier intellectuals had been rabidly secularist. They had included the Lebanese poet and educator Khalil Hawi (1920–82), the Iraqi-born poet Buland Heidari (1926–96), the Iranian writer Sadeq Hedayat (1903–51), the Syrian poet and literary critic Adonis, the pen name for Ali Ahmad Said (b. 1930), and the legendary Egyptian writer and novelist Naguib Mahfouz (b. 1911), to name only a few.[103] But the new crop of Middle Eastern intellectuals, almost all younger, invariably saw the political world through the lenses of Islam. Whether "progressive" or "reactionary" in the conventional sense, they identified themselves as Muslim thinkers who happened also to be Middle Easterners, not Middle Eastern thinkers who happened to be Muslim.

There was, in fact, an inverse relationship between the decline of the *ulama* as a social force and the rise of a new breed of Muslim intellectuals. "The ineffectiveness of the traditional ulama meant that the way was open for the emergence of a new style of Muslim intellectual who would work to create a modern but not secularist alternative to both the conservative ulama and the secular intellectuals. To a remarkable degree, the new intellectual perspectives peripherized the old secular intellectuals and converted the traditional ulama into more activist Islamic advocates and reformers."[104] This Islamist generation includes figures such as the Egyptian thinker Hasan Hanafi (b. 1935), the Tunisian activist Rachid al-Ghannouchi (b. 1941), Sudan's Hasan al-Turabi (b. 1932), Iranian ideologues Ali Shariati (1933–77) and Abdolkarim Soroush (b. 1945), Malaysia's Anwar Ibrahim (b. 1947), and Indonesia's Abdurrahman Wahid (b. 1941). Operating within the socioeconomic contexts and the intellectual traditions of their own countries, all these thinkers in their own ways have sought to reconcile Islam and modernity through contemporary interpretations of Islam and to propose viable Islamic solutions to problems of contemporary society.

Given their intellectual concerns and larger political environment, many of these Muslim thinkers have become politically active within their own countries.[105] Hasan Hanafi was active in the Egyptian Muslim Brotherhood as a young man, although he has gone on to become a highly respected professor at Cairo University and has held visiting appointments in numerous other institutions around the world. In the 1990s, his unorthodox views earned him the ire of Egypt's conservative religious establishment, and some figures at Al-Azhar even went so far as to brand him an apostate. Iran's Abdolkarim Soroush has found himself in a similarly precarious position, although most of the opposition to him comes from the conservative *ulama* within the state—or within the state's orbit—rather than from nonstate clergy. Rachid al-Ghannouchi was the head of the Tunisian party called the Islamic Tendency Movement until he was forced into exile in the early 1990s. A former law professor at Khartoum University and a central figure in Sudanese politics since 1964, al-Turabi was believed to be the major ideologue of the regime that came to power in Sudan in 1989 and, ever since, has sought to establish an "authentic Islamic state." By 1999, however, he had apparently fallen out of favor with the state's leading figure, President Umar Hasan al-Bashir, and was dismissed.

Similar developments also occurred in two non–Middle Eastern countries that are among the largest Muslim countries in the world, Malaysia and Indonesia. In Malaysia, Anwar Ibrahim had long been active in the country's legal opposition, but as part of the general Islamization of Malaysian politics in recent decades he had gradually risen within the state apparatus and by the early 1990s had held several different cabinet positions. Eventually, in 1993, he was named deputy prime minister and was assumed to be the successor to Prime Minister Mohathir Mohammad. By 1998, however, he, like al-Turabi in Sudan, was out of office. In a sensational trial in 1999, he was convicted of corruption and sexual misconduct and was sentenced to prison. In Indonesia, meanwhile, Abdurrahman Wahid, who had been one of the country's most prominent Islamic figures, rose to even greater heights in Indonesian politics, becoming the country's first democratically elected president in October 1999. However, he was unable to effectively deal with the country's mounting economic crises, and after sustained mass demonstrations he was forced to resign in 2001.

Despite their occasional forays into politics and the innately political nature of their undertaking, the primary concerns of most Muslim intellectuals remain theoretical and epistemological. Most are academics, men and women of letters whose main vocations are writing, lecturing, and, on occasion, political activism. While many of these intellectuals at times have been involved with various political parties both directly and indirectly, they form a category of their own insofar as the Islamist opposition is concerned.

Another category is composed primarily of Islamist political parties. Found in every Middle Eastern country, these parties vary greatly in the degree to which Islam informs the ideologies of their overall platforms and in the precise role that they ascribe to Islam in relation to political and socioeconomic questions. For example, Turkey has had a series of ostensibly "Islamic" political parties, almost all of which have a common leadership genealogy: the National Salvation Party, the Refah, the Fazilet, and the Saadet. But although each party has been successively banned by the highly secularist political establishment, each, in order to operate, has downplayed its Islamist character and has instead played up its adherence to Atatürk's (secular) legacy. At the opposite end of the scale have been parties such as the Egyptian and Jordanian Muslim Brotherhood and the Islamic Action Front in Jordan, which have been unabashedly Islamist in every aspect, from their ideological platform to their base of support in mosques and among seminary students. The Tunisian Al-Nahda (Awakening) was another Islamist party. Although it was comparatively moderate, it too was banned by the Tunisian state.

Despite the differences in their specific ideological platforms and their tactics, these Islamist parties share certain characteristics. To begin with, their relationship with the state has been tense and inconsistent. The Muslim Brotherhood in Jordan and especially in Egypt has often been banned by the state, only to be allowed to operate later. In Turkey, the state frequently bans the existing Islamist party, but the same party leaders establish a new one shortly thereafter. In Tunisia, Al-Nahda was banned altogether and not allowed to resurrect since the government was highly sensitive to the events unfolding in neighboring Algeria.

More important, the Islamist parties share largely populist ideologies that appeal especially to the middle and lower middle classes, such as attention to the economic plight of the lower classes, emphasis on economic nationalism, greater respect for tenets of Islam in public life, and an end to government corruption. Although generally critical of the state and its leadership, these Islamist parties tend to endorse the overall legitimacy of the existing political order by agreeing to participate in it. They may boycott specific elections in protest over the government's unfair advantage (or their own electoral weakness), but they generally endorse the existing institutional framework of the state and do not call for its overthrow. At most, they advocate changes through legislation and state directives.

This is in stark contrast with the extremist ideologies and strategies of Islamist parties and/or individuals that are commonly called "fundamentalist." Islamic fundamentalists differ from other Islamists—conservative clerics, intellectuals, and relatively moderate parties—in degree. A product of the zero-sum political cultures that often pervade Middle Eastern polities, Islamic fundamentalists generally reject the legitimacy of the existing political order on the grounds of its essentially un-Islamic character. All state laws and regulations, they argue, must be based on Islamic law, the *sharia*. Some, such as the Islamic Liberation Party in Jordan, also advocate the resurrection of the caliphate system of rule.[106] Others, such as Egypt's Gama'a, argue that sovereignty belongs only to God and that believers are called upon to engage in *jihad* (in this sense, battle) against leaders who are unbelievers *(kafir)*.[107] Other examples of fundamentalist parties are Hamas and the Islamic Jihad in the Palestinian Occupied Territories, the Muslim Brotherhood in Syria, the former Islamic Salvation Front (FIS) in Algeria, and the Justice and Welfare Party (Adl wal-Ihsan) in Morocco, and Al-Qaeda.

Again, the various Islamic fundamentalist groups have important differences. The Lebanese Hezbollah, for example, is in some respects more concerned about the plight of the Lebanese Shi'ites than it is about the immorality of the Lebanese state. Hamas and the Islamic Jihad have emerged in specific national and historical contexts that are unique to Palestine. Nevertheless, the shared features of these and other fundamentalist organizations tend to outnumber their differences. Practically all these organizations and the individuals who belong to them have a literalist interpretation of Islam and its precepts. Their world is one of simple divisions: good versus evil; the oppressed versus the oppressors; the abode of Islam *(dar al-Islam)* versus the abode of war *(dar al-harb)*. For them, the best way to achieve their goals is through *jihad,* which they take to mean "holy war" rather than, as more sophisticated interpretations of Islam would have it, "striving" for betterment. Since they reject the legitimacy of the political order, they view *jihad* against the state as one of their fundamental obligations.[108]

All of this has often translated into violent attacks on state leaders and institutions, and, on occasion, on the state's perceived foreign patrons. The FIS, for example, tried, largely without success, to take its struggle against the Algerian state to France, which it saw as the main supporter of the Algiers government. Osama bin Laden's attacks on American targets were similarly inspired by a belief that the United States was the biggest patron of the Saudi royal family. Also, throughout the 1990s, the Gama'a attacked tourists visiting Egypt's historic monuments, hoping both to embarrass the Egyptian state internationally and to deprive it of tourist revenues. Such terrorist activities have elicited equally violent and brutal reactions from many Middle Eastern states, thus perpetuating a vicious cycle of political violence that has become all too familiar.

The events of September 11, 2001, put the global spotlight on Islamic fundamentalism. Although its most archaic (and brutal) manifestation was practiced by the Taliban in Afghanistan, fundamentalist Islam has pervasive roots in every country of the Middle East, from the highly "Europeanized" Turkey to the ultraconservative Saudi Arabia. Fundamentalism breeds in a vacuum of intellectual political discourse, when the authoritarianism of the state makes it impossible to discuss and examine complex social and political problems in a reasoned manner. State terror elicits terror of a different kind, the terror of the young and the restless who want answers and solutions but find most avenues of expression blocked by an intransigent elite.

The precarious lives of the middle classes make them all the more receptive to extremist alternatives. As we saw in Chapter 8, almost all Middle

Eastern states launched ambitious economic liberalization programs in the late 1970s and the 1980s. Invariably, this meant inviting foreign investors, encouraging joint venture enterprises, and giving tax and other investment incentives to domestic entrepreneurs. A few small and medium-sized state-owned enterprises were also privatized and sold off. Apart from multinational corporations, the prime beneficiaries of these privatization efforts were the domestic upper classes, who were well positioned to take advantage of the state's slow retreat from the economy. They were the ones who had the necessary contacts to secure state contracts, acquire foreign partners, and invest in the newly privatized areas. Many opened up hotels and restaurants, bought and managed buildings, founded factories for food processing and other lucrative businesses, or imported the many foreign consumer items that the middle and upper classes craved—everything from cereals to auto parts, appliances, candy, and the like. Those who could afford it, the rich, were getting richer.

When the recession of the 1980s and 1990s came, the middle and lower classes who by now worked for these businesses were hit hard. Even the multinational corporations scaled back, frightened by the ever-present threat of terrorist attacks (especially in Algeria and Egypt) or disenchanted by the continued inefficiency and corruption of the government. Recession meant unemployment; privatization meant fewer secure government jobs. Even the civil servants who enjoyed job security found it difficult to make ends meet on their government salaries as the price of basic commodities continued to rise and inflation spiraled. Many in the upper classes could ride the wave, but the less wealthy were not as lucky. Today, throughout the Middle East, the middle classes are barely hanging on, many having to work two or three jobs to maintain their middle-class status. Extremism offers the middle and lower classes—disillusioned and frustrated, living in fear of losing even more economic ground, and powerless to protest the state's policies—a way to strike hard at the state. And given the steady demise of other ideological alternatives, that extremism has taken on an Islamic character.

Some important conclusions can be drawn here. It should be obvious that Islam is not inherently prone to extremism or violence. In fact, as we have seen, there is a rich array of interpretations and differences between and within the conservative, intellectual, and fundamentalist varieties of Islam. Over the last few decades, there has been a steady politicization of Islam as secular ideologies have either been repressed by state elites (as in the case of socialist ideologies) or have lost popular credibility among the masses on their own (as in the case of Pan-Arabism and secular nationalism). Islam was first politicized and then steadily radicalized. Hence Islamic fundamentalism was born. Of the varieties of political Islam, Islamic fundamentalism has attracted by far the most attention because of its violence and its transnational character. The primary fuel for this Islamic fundamentalism has been poverty, both economic poverty and a poverty of political discourse imposed by the state. As long as poverty and political repression remain basic facts of life in the Middle East, there is little reason to believe that Islamic fundamentalism will subside.

As the preceding discussion reveals, the prevailing patterns of political rule by various types of states in the Middle East have impeded the emergence of meaningful and viable forms of political opposition in the region. Except for the democracies in Israel and Turkey, and even there in imperfect forms, the underlying authoritarianism of Middle Eastern political systems has rendered organized, institutional opposition to state leaders literally impossible. As oppositional political parties have declined in relevance, unorganized forms of political protest have become more popular and commonplace. Secular intellectuals spearheaded the oppositional tendencies of the earlier, postindependence decades, the 1950s to the 1970s. Steadily, however, Islam emerged as a far more viable medium for political opposition and, especially beginning in the mid-1970s, informed the discourse of the state's opponents. This opposition was likely to come from the conservative *ulama*, activist intellectuals, or, most commonly, relatively moderate Islamist parties or fundamentalist organizations. In any case, the institutional, ideological, and emotional chasms between the state and society remained unbridged and in many instances widened.

Today nondemocratic political systems continue to dominate the political landscape of the Middle East. These states are likely to be either inclusionary, exclusionary, or sultanistic. The region's three democracies, Lebanon, Turkey, and Israel, are more aptly classified as quasi-democratic, although in recent years Israel has moved more and more in a liberal democratic direction. These are, of course, ideal type classifications, and significant differences mark the states within each of the categories. From a comparative perspective, for example, both the Turkish and Israeli political systems are here labeled quasi-democratic because of the excessive influence of the military in politics and the state's treatment of ethnic minorities living within its borders—the Kurds in Turkey and the Arabs in Israel. Nevertheless, the degree to which the Turkish military is involved in civilian politics is far more extensive and the Turkish state's treatment of the Kurds much harsher than is the case in Israel with respect to the IDF or the

Arabs. Similarly, vast differences separate the two civic myth monarchies of Jordan and Morocco.

These categories are not fixed, and states can and at times do slip back and forth between categories. Of the various categories, inclusionary states are perhaps the most prone to becoming exclusionary as, with age, they begin to rely more and more frequently on sheer intimidation and exclusion of the masses from the political process instead of their inclusion. Iran's case has been somewhat different, since the Islamic republican state has lost its elite and ideological cohesion in recent years and has ushered in a system that oscillates between allowing extensive participation and resorting to indiscriminate repression.

Similar difficulties arise when one tries to categorize the types of political opposition in the Middle East. That some groups or organizations are allowed to openly operate one year but are banned the next year makes their classification especially difficult. Also, individual thinkers and political parties are not always distinguishable, since they may cooperate with one another. At times, it is also difficult to differentiate between "secular" and "religious" intellectuals. These difficulties notwithstanding, political opposition in the Middle East has historically come from organized political parties, Islamist thinkers, conservative clerics, Islamist political parties, or extremist groups espousing Islamic fundamentalism.

Given this state of affairs, it is important to ask what the consequences are for the overall nature of the state-society relationship, and, more important, for the prospects of democracy in the Middle East. The next chapter considers these questions.

10 The Question of Democracy

The "third wave" of democratization that swept through southern Europe, South America, and much of eastern Europe in the 1970s and 1980s was conspicuous for its exclusion of the Middle East.[1] Initially, with the collapse of the Soviet Union and the dawn of a supposedly "new world order," some observers of the Middle East viewed the advent of democracy in the region as inevitable, arguing that such basic ingredients of democracy as civil society, elections, and parliamentary politics were beginning to foster conditions for democratic transitions in a number of Middle Eastern countries.[2] To this day, however, authoritarian systems of various types are pervasive in the region, and many of the Middle Eastern countries that once held the greatest promise of democratization—most notably Algeria, Egypt, Jordan, Kuwait, Tunisia, and Yemen—have taken significant steps away from greater political accountability and representativeness. Of course, democracies do not appear overnight, and democratic transitions are often the product of complex interactions between state and societal dynamics that take a long time to bear results. Seldom is the process of democratization clear-cut and unidirectional. All too often it is a protracted struggle between entrenched political elites and an emerging group of social actors demanding greater political accountability and representation. In fact, "gradual improvements, with periodic setbacks, are to be expected in transitions that result from lengthy bargaining between elites and oppositions."[3] But only the most optimistic interpretations of the Middle East would argue that even such embryonic moves toward democratization are under way in the region on any meaningful scale.

This chapter argues that in the Middle East there generally continue to be formidable obstacles on the path of transition to democracy. Changing political circumstances and declining economic fortunes have prompted a number of Middle Eastern leaders to modify their political rhetoric and some of the traditional practices through which they have historically governed. Buoyed by the example of the Iranian revolution and the collapse of authoritarian regimes in South America and eastern Europe, political aspirants in the Middle East have also been more vocal in their expressions of opposition to state elites, their policies, and their many failures. At the same time, a general rediscovery of the potency of the phenomenon of civil society and its contribution to democratization by Western academics has prompted many observers to see similar dynamics at work in various Middle Eastern countries.[4] I maintain, however, that prospects for democratic transitions in the Middle East depend overwhelmingly, if not exclusively, on the agendas and goals of actors and leaders *within* the state.

For some time now, state-society relations in the Middle East have been predicated on a "ruling bargain," an implicit understanding that has evolved over time between state elites on the one hand and social strata and actors on the other, based on which the state has catered to the economic, physical, and emotional needs of the populace in return for general political compliance and consent. The emerging state-society consensus has had its share of frictions, and periodic episodes of economic slowdown or outright political incapacity—as in Iran in the late 1970s, Egypt in the early 1980s, and Jordan and Morocco in the late 1980s—have resulted in at times violent bouts of political instability. By and large, however, with the exception of the prerevolutionary Iran, Middle Eastern states have been able to effectively respond to the various crises that have cropped up since the 1980s and, backed by a fair amount of coercion, to reestablish the old ruling bargains, albeit often with slightly modified formats. These modified formats have invariably taken the shape of institutional devices aimed at broadening the scope of state inclusiveness, such as the *majlis* in the Arabian peninsula or the parliament in Morocco, Jordan, and Kuwait. But they serve primarily as safety valves, institutional modifications designed to make entrenched authoritarianism appear more palatable. In the long run, they undermine the prospects of democratization by strengthening authoritarian elites and enhancing the institutional mechanism by which the state can respond to emerging crises and threats. Social actors, meanwhile, remain largely on the sidelines, threatened with arrests, imprisonment, and even death if they openly and directly call on state leaders to abide by the principles of democracy. The evolving "national dialogue" among activists and the literati—as carried on in journals, newspapers, and books—becomes constantly preoccupied with evading government censorship and harassment. "Civil society," in its full sense, faces even greater difficulties. If a process of democratization is indeed in the offing in the Middle East, for the time being its necessary ingredients are strangely and conspicuously absent.

This is not to maintain that future prospects for democratization in the Middle East are virtually nonexistent. As mentioned, some cosmetic changes have already been made to portray the state as more responsive to social demands for greater representation. It is conceivable that these institutional changes will assume more meaningful substance in the future and gradually change some of the foundations on which state-society relations are currently based. Also, there is nothing to prevent the current or future slates of the state's political opponents from forcing state leaders to yield to some democratic demands. But these remain hypothetical possibilities and, for ·the time being at least, have little bearing on the realities of Middle Eastern political life. Only in Iran, where after two decades of war and revolutionary upheavals a set of postrevolutionary "rules of the game" appeared to be emerging, was there a discernible process of bargaining under way among state elites and between the state and society. As the violent clampdown on the protesting thousands demonstrated after the June 2009 elections, even Iran's seemingly promising progress toward democratization has been fraught with setbacks, factionalism, and violence. And the uniqueness of Iran's experience—featuring revolutionary mass mobilization, an eight-year war with Iraq, the death of a charismatic leader, and the imperative of postwar reconstruction—makes it unlikely that the halted changes to Iranian authoritarianism can serve as a model for the rest of the region.[5]

This chapter looks first at the larger dynamics that make transitions to democracy possible, focusing on changes and developments within the state, within society, and in the interaction between the two. It then examines some characteristics of Middle Eastern states and societies, respectively, and the ways in which the two interact in the context of the region's politics. The chapter argues that the prevailing "political bargains" have only been modified slightly so as to preempt or deflate pressures for democratization. Most social actors, meanwhile, have "exited" from the political process, have been repressed, or have had their message rendered irrelevant because of the machinations of the state. Democracy from below remains, for now at least, largely absent from the Middle East.[6] Nevertheless, the state itself remains an effective and viable source for potential opening of the political process. In fact, important state-originated (not necessarily state-sponsored) changes in traditional patterns of state-society relations are occurring in three Middle Eastern countries—Iran, Morocco, and Lebanon. The chapter ends with an examination of these three specific

Figure 29. Iranian president Mahmoud Ahmadinejad. Photo courtesy of Corbis.

cases, demonstrating how in Iran and Morocco the state experimented but ultimately decided against opening up, whereas in Lebanon it continues to struggle to viably constitute itself under democratic auspices. In all three cases, as elsewhere in the Middle East, the state remains the final arbitrator of the ultimate course of state-society relations.

VARIETIES OF DEMOCRATIC TRANSITIONS

There are three general, ideal patterns of transition from authoritarianism to democracy: those in which civil society takes a prominent role, those initiated by the state "from above," and those resulting from a protracted process of give-and-take between competing political groups and actors that previously used the state's own procedures to gain access to its institutions and resources. From a comparative perspective, the first type of transition occurred primarily in eastern Europe in the late 1980s, most notably in Poland, Hungary, and former Czechoslovakia. "Democracy from above," in which state elites give up power in a preemptive move to protect themselves from a revolutionary tidal wave, was responsible for most of the transitions in Latin America in the 1980s and early 1990s, especially in Argentina, Brazil, Uruguay, and Chile.[7] In the Middle East, Turkey also witnessed such a transition in 1983. The third type of transition, resulting from internal competition within state-affiliated elites, gave rise to the democracies of the Philippines and Nicaragua, among others.

Civil society–driven democratizations come about basically as a result of the increasing empowerment of society and an inverse erosion of state power. In this pattern, for a variety of reasons, the state either cannot or will not perform many of the functions that society expects of it. In addition to simple administration and political management, the state's social responsibilities range from the economic to the sociocultural and even emotional. Social actors and classes expect the state to provide a reasonably safe environment in which to live, officially regulate or allocate the resources needed for making a living (e.g., salaries, a reliable banking system, regulations for commerce), foster policies that promote economic development, and uphold the national, historic, and cultural symbols that a majority of the people hold dear. If a nondemocratic state fails in its basic task of delivering on these and other similar expectations of social actors, then over time it becomes bereft of legitimacy. Before long, its stock of legitimacy—whether based on a resonant ideology, economic performance, or both—will be depleted. Operating in a subjective vacuum created by society's increasing political alienation and disenchantment, the state has to rely more and more on coercion or its threat in order to stay in power and ensure societal compliance.

Under certain conditions—which prevailed in parts of eastern Europe in the late 1980s and, to a somewhat lesser extent, in parts of South America a few years earlier—society's political alienation and the real or apparent incapacity of the state to properly perform its functions lead groups within society to take matters into their own hands and start addressing their needs themselves. Most of these groups are small and highly localized: neighborhood watch groups, communal kitchens, self-help groups that sponsor literacy or sewing classes, and the like.[8] As these examples indicate, most are also nonpolitical and arise in response to the specific needs of members of a community or a small group of individuals. Their primary purpose is "social self-management."[9] But one or two similarly organized gatherings may also emerge that have more direct political consequences and a sharper political message. An unofficial workers' group that functions like a trade union is a case in point, as was the case with the Solidarity organization in Poland in the 1980s. Various "discussion groups" and "forums" that sprang up in Hungary, Czechoslovakia, and East Germany had a similar significance, as did the Base Ecclesiastical Communities that appeared in Brazil and to a lesser extent in Chile and Argentina.[10] These and other similar groupings are considered to be "civil society organizations" (CSOs). Such organizations are not necessarily political in activity and orientation—they do not necessarily have ideological platforms and overt political agendas—but their overall message and their larger consequences for society help erode the legitimacy and efficacy of the state. At a time when the state's legitimacy in relation to society is at its nadir, civil society organizations can increase the gap between the two by bestowing on society a sense of empowerment and independence from the state.

CSOs are self-organized, are politically independent of the state, and, because of their focus on issues of local import, can generate considerable enthusiasm and commitment among their members. They can have two important consequences for democratization. First, as organizations with specific focuses, CSOs must have a leader, and these leaders can, through their grassroots efforts and social activism, achieve great renown and popularity. They may even be elevated to the status of a folk hero— as Lech Walesa was in Poland—or, if articulate and prone to theorizing, may be seen as highly respected public intellectuals, as was the case with Václav Havel in Czechoslovakia. In either case, these CSO leaders can rise to positions of social prominence, and if they are branded by the state as its opponents, their popularity is heightened by the state's panicked reaction. If the state were to collapse, or if the elite somehow left the scene, these CSO leaders would be well positioned to ride the popular wave to power.

CSOs can have a second consequence for democratization. On their own, they may be nothing more than local groups that meet on occasion and, at most, debate some issues. But if there is a proliferation of CSOs, and if they either formally or informally reinforce one another—if nothing else, giving each other moral support—then their collective potency is all the more magnified, and eventually they lead to the emergence of civil society. CSOs are the smaller components of civil society. Civil society is born when CSOs proliferate to such an extent that they bestow on society a general sense of political empowerment—what Juan Linz and Alfred Stepan call "political society"—and replace its feelings of powerlessness with confidence and political assertiveness.[11]

Of course, none of these developments has any serious consequences for democratization if the state somehow does not feel the need to respond to civil society. Developments in society can have tangible political results only if they can meaningfully alter either the functions of the state or overall state-society relations. In addition to the state's general alienation from society, which gives rise to CSOs to begin with, for democratization to occur the state needs to have become weak and vulnerable to pressures from society.[12] Precisely what causes this vulnerability varies, but factors such as economic paralysis (hyperinflation), political misadventures, or the loss of a powerful patron (in the form of the Soviet Union) all can have drastic consequences. Pressures from the outside by other governments or multinational agencies, whether overt or subtle, can also limit the scope of the state's response.

State incapacitation and civil society–driven social empowerment bring about a condition between state and society that may best be described as "negative equilibrium." Neither has enough power to effectively overwhelm the other, yet neither is so weak as to implode or become irrelevant. The state's crisis of penetration deepens, and, its legitimacy practically nonexistent, the most it can do is rely more on its coercive institutions. Governance becomes increasingly untenable, and the ensuing friction between state and society only emboldens civil society and further valorizes CSO leaders. The only way for the state to get out of the quagmire is to negotiate some sort of a pact with society—more specifically with CSO leaders—and, as a last resort and a face-saving gesture, to "let the people decide"—that is, to sponsor elections.[13] Such was the process through which the new democracies of eastern Europe—most notably Poland, Hungary, and Czechoslovakia—were born.

In civil society–driven democratic transitions, state leaders are forced into a reactive role and often find themselves at the mercy of unfolding events over which they have little or no control. At most they may try to manipulate the results of the elections, and even that is made difficult by the vigilance of the newly invigorated civil society. But in some instances state leaders see the writing on the wall and assess their long-term chances of survival as best served by actually giving up power instead of being forced out. They therefore make a calculated decision to sponsor democratic elections, viewing possible electoral defeat as less disadvantageous to their own interests than the probable alternative. These types of democratic transitions occurred primarily in Greece, Portugal, and Spain beginning in the 1970s and, a few years later, in Turkey (1983), Argentina (1983), Uruguay (1985), Brazil (1986), and Chile (1989).[14]

In each of these instances, although there were some pressures from below, from groups within society, the causes that prompted state leaders to embark on the transition process were often indigenous to the state itself. Most frequently, state leaders perceived that their long-term institutional interests lay not necessarily in holding onto the institution of, say, the presidency at all costs but rather in giving up power on their own terms at a time when they could still dictate the terms of their exit agreement. In all the cases cited above, the state leaders who set in motion processes for their own exit had come from the armed forces. All had declared early on that their control of the state machinery was only temporary and would last only as long as dictated by the needs and imperatives of national security. The military's political control had been predicated and legitimized on the grounds of setting the country's messy political house in order, eliminating the enemy within (e.g., communist activists), and fostering rapid economic and industrial development. But by the early years of the 1980s, the armed forces had failed in most or all of these self-articulated sources of legitimacy: the costs of political repression could not simply be explained away on grounds of national security; political stability was as problematic as ever; and the economic consequences of import-substitution industrialization were disastrous.[15] The choice confronting the state's military leaders was simple: hang onto power and risk being overthrown and made to answer for past mistakes, or give up power but do so with guarantees of immunity from future prosecution. Additionally, state elites could set the pace for the devolution of power to elected, civilian authorities, as was the case in southern Europe and Brazil, and greatly influence the shape and limits of the incoming democratic polity.

The important role of international developments in prompting authoritarian leaders to embark on transitions from above cannot be overlooked. Especially in southern Europe, and also in South America, the desire to be considered as part of the Western community of democratic nations was highly influential in compelling state elites to represent themselves as advocates of a controlled transition to a more open political system.[16] Whereas in the 1950s and 1960s both academics and diplomats could more easily explain away military-based states, by the 1970s and 1980s such political systems were beginning to be seen as archaic and unseemly. These were relics of an underdeveloped, premodern past, no longer suited to the world of the late twentieth century. For both the southern European and the South American leaders who slowly and voluntarily gave up power, democratization was a question of national political identity.

A third pattern of democratization is the result less of the efforts of civil society or the calculated decisions of nondemocratic state elites than of a protracted, often unwieldy, process of give-and-take within the state among old-time "hard-liners" and up-and-coming "soft-liners."[17] As in cases of democratization from above, in these instances the role of civil society is also minimal in bringing about the initial impulse to democratize, although later on, at the stage of consolidation, societal dynamics assume great importance in giving popular currency to the norms of democracy. The key development at work here is the state elite's increasing lack of cohesion and the emergence within it of differences of opinion over the proper nature of state-society relations. Such a chasm is likely to occur in states in which a cause or a charismatic leader once served as a rallying point for an otherwise diverse coalition of politically minded individuals. The charismatic leader's departure from the scene (by death as was the case in Iran or by self-humiliation as in the Philippines) or the gradual waning of the unifying cause (as in both Iran and Nicaragua) makes it less risky over time to advocate visions of politics slightly different from what has hitherto been dominant.[18] A subtle, very protracted internal competition is set in motion, whereby—through statements and initiatives that are sometimes highly guarded and circumspect—the public comes to distinguish between hard-line purists and advocates of change.

The competition between these two groups is often complicated by the provision of electoral politics at the local, legislative, and even presidential levels, through which each side tries to enhance its control over the various institutions of the state. Although to some extent these electoral competitions enhance the democratic legitimacy of the state, few would argue that the political system in its current incarnation is genuinely democratic. It is not the elections per se that make the system democratic but the larger consequences of these elections for the composition of state elites and the outcome of the tension between their competing political visions. Will the new state elites, who share with existing elites some common ideological and political dispositions, use the institutions of the state to make it more democratic, or will they be co-opted and keep things basically the same? As this question implies, if the outcome of the elite's internal jockeying makes the system more democratic, the basic institutional features of the state are preserved but are modified slightly so as to make them more responsive to societal demands. There is seldom need for writing a new constitution, as is often the case in the two other varieties of democratization, nor is there considerable popular drama associated with the ongoing changes in the state. The public, of course, follows the unfolding political competition with great interest, and, as the factional infighting intensifies, election turnouts also increase. But by and large the unfolding drama is a political one fought within the state, with resort to official procedures and through state institutions. Apart from its attentiveness to the news of the day and its active participation in elections, the public tends to be largely sidelined in the state's potential transition to a more democratic one.

Of the three varieties of democratization outlined here, the first and second have been conspicuously absent from the Middle East, with the exception of Turkey, where in 1983 the military-led state inaugurated an imperfect democratic system. As mentioned earlier, democracies from above are often brought about by the return to the barracks of military juntas who had previously taken over the state. In the Middle East, the 1950s and 1960s did see a host of military takeovers of the state in much of the Arab world, but a corresponding retreat into the barracks did not take place. Instead, military leaders increasingly presented themselves to the public as civilian authorities while keeping old patterns of civil-military relations basically intact.[19] Generals and colonels traded their uniforms for suits but did not sever their institutional ties with the military and, under the title of president, continued to rule largely by fiat. Meanwhile, both these presidents and the remaining monarchs—in Jordan, Morocco, and the Arabian peninsula—ensured that the state retained enough social relevance and semblance of legitimacy so that societal alternatives would not thrive and proliferate.[20] The fate of the shah of Iran—and before him Farouq of Egypt and Faisal of Iraq—was not something that the Middle East's other monarchs easily forgot. Any politically autonomous, self-organized group, therefore, was viewed with great suspicion and, if the state learned of its existence, was likely to be closely watched by the state police. That in recent decades many of these groups have been made up of religious activists with highly pronounced political agendas has only added to the ferocity with which the state has gone after many of their organizers.[21]

The third pattern of democratization, by contrast, appears to be unfolding in a number of Middle Eastern countries, most notably in Iran and Lebanon and, according to some observations, in Morocco. In each case, processes appear to be under way in the state through which the parameters of politics are being redefined slowly. Even if the states in question are not becoming more democratic, they are making themselves more susceptible to democratic pressures. Through an arduous and, in Iran at least, highly contentious process of remodulation, the state is modifying some of its basic assumptions about its proper role and scope in relation to society. The process, of course, is by no means uniform across the three cases, or even within each. Two steps forward, one step back; a democratic opening here, a retrenchment there. But all indications are that centrifugal dynamics are pulling the state in a generally democratic direction.

STATE-SOCIETY RELATIONS IN THE MIDDLE EAST

The question then becomes, what is it about the Middle East that so far has kept it out of the "third wave" of democratization? The answer lies in the evolution of a modus vivendi between the state and society, an implicit "ruling bargain," based on which the governed have acceded certain rights and privileges to the government in return for the provision of most or some of the goods and services they need. Of course, the emerging ruling bargain is stronger in some countries of the Middle East and weaker in others, as its precise terms and its resilience depend on the resources, capabilities, and agendas of the state on the one hand and the malleability, dispositions, and goals of social groups and actors on the other. In the "oil monarchies" of the Arabian peninsula, for example, the state has been blessed with extensive economic wealth, with which it has bought a fair amount of social compliance, and an ability to generally present itself as the guardian of the highly resonant and pervasive social forces of Islam and tribalism.[22] Most tribes and members of the traditional *ulama* (clerics), meanwhile, have been incorporated into the political establishment and have therefore generally accepted the legitimacy of the state. As a result, this part of the Middle East has enjoyed an unusually high degree of political conservatism and, except for occasional extremist acts, an absence of sustained societal pressures on the state.[23] By and large, those challenging the state's legitimacy are either the local Shi'ite minority who feel like second-class citizens, as in Bahrain, or religious fundamentalists who view state leaders as apostates, as in Saudi Arabia.[24] Overall, however, state-society relations here tend to be harmonious and lack prolonged periods of friction. It remains to be seen whether the increasing pervasiveness of American military presence in the region following the U.S. occupations of Afghanistan and Iraq, and the negative reactions it evokes, coupled with the continued identification of local elites with the United States, will lead to a significant erosion of the legitimacy of rulers throughout the Arabian peninsula.

Elsewhere in the Middle East, where state capabilities and resources are not as extensive as in the oil monarchies, and where political tensions are more pervasive and not confined to marginalized minorities, the prevailing ruling bargains have experienced far more strain. In fact, most states have been forced to revise and rewrite some of the basic premises of the ruling bargain in recent years. The devising of "national charters" in the early 1990s in such diverse countries as Jordan, Tunisia, Algeria, and Morocco reveals the scope of the need to refine prevailing ruling bargains. Even in countries like Kuwait and Saudi Arabia the state has found itself on the defensive since the 1990s and been compelled to change some of the privileges to which it had become accustomed. But as the next section shows in greater depth, *revising* the ruling bargain has not generally meant altering its basic premises.[25] As it turns out, the revisions made to the ruling bargains have been sufficient so far to placate and/or subdue society while keeping the state and its modus operandi basically intact.

The answer to the question raised earlier—Why has there been no democratization in the Middle East so far?—lies here. Over the last few decades imperfect but generally resilient ruling bargains have emerged between Middle Eastern states and societies. In the 1990s, declining state capabilities throughout the region and increasing demands for political responsiveness by social actors necessitated the bargains' modification, not only in the Maghreb (Morocco, Algeria, and Tunisia) and the Mashreq (Jordan, Saudi Arabia, and Kuwait), but also in the non-Arab Middle East (Iran). These were only superficial revisions; many did not even deserve the much-heralded label of liberalization but were part of "survival strategies" of one kind or another.[26] But, backed by a good bit of coercion, they have served their intended purpose for the ruling elites: preserving the essentially nondemocratic nature of the state-society relationship.

Specific national variations notwithstanding, throughout the Middle East the ruling bargain is predicated on four primary, mutually reinforcing features. The first is the state's presentation of itself as the sole and ultimate guarantor of the "national interest." The second is patrimonialism, through which the state's "protection" of the national interest assumes a personal character and extends down through successive, overlapping layers of patrons and clients. Closely related to patrimonialism is a third feature of the ruling bargain, the existence of a corporatist political economy through which the private sector's cooperation with the state and the state's ultimate superiority are guaranteed. The fourth and last feature is state authoritarianism, whereby the compliance of those who question the merits of the three other aspects of the bargain is guaranteed.

The state asserts its nationalist legitimacy by presenting itself as the historic extension, and therefore the rightful protector, of nationalism. In the aftermath of the 1973 War and the sobering realities of global economics and diplomacy, nationalism in the Middle East lost some of its raw ideological edge, especially now that Nasserism was but a distant memory, and became more of an implicit phenomenon than an explicit guiding force. It did not lose its compelling qualities, and everywhere in the Middle East it continued to be part of the implied understanding on which the state's larger legitimacy rested. But only in three countries—Iran, Iraq, and Libya—where its blatant political manipulation was deemed necessary to carry on the state's "revolutionary" agendas in the 1980s and 1990s, did it continue to be one of the defining features of state ideology and propaganda. Elsewhere, the state's reliance on and manipulation of nationalism has tended to be more subtle and implicit.

But the nationalism that the state has been subtly propagating as a support of legitimacy is not always the same as popular perceptions of nationalism and national interest. In fact, only in one area do the "official nationalism" of the state and the "unofficial nationalism" of the populace correspond and overlap. Official nationalism is defined in terms of domestic political stability (even if imposed); statist economic development in conjunction with foreign investors; regional supremacy and a clear articulation of international and strategic interests; and a subtle but carefully calculated promotion of conspiracy theories that blame outside elements for domestic problems or acts of terrorism. This is often done through the popular media, with official sanction, of course, in which everything from economic shortages to acts of sabotage is frequently linked to groups financed by an adversary. Tehran's revolutionaries, their credentials riding on their rhetoric, have been favorites of the Arab media. They are alleged to have financed the terrorism of the Shi'ites in Lebanon, Bahrain, and Saudi Arabia, and Islamic radicals stretching from Turkey to Egypt and Morocco. The Sudanese are alleged to have done the same in Egypt, and the Libyans all over the Middle East. For Middle Eastern leaders, domestic shortcomings and problems are seldom a product of failed policies or misguided agendas. They must, invariably, be the works of outsiders.

Unofficial nationalism, whether articulated by the literati or generally perceived by the urban middle classes, differs in three key respects. It sees state leaders not as protectors of the national interest but as impediments to it. In terms of economic development, it deplores what it considers to be the plunder of national resources by international capitalists and their local agents. It also sees the state's international alliances and strategic calculations—close relations with the United States, implicit or explicit recognition of Israel, perceived abandonment of the Palestinian cause, support for or lack of meaningful opposition to the U.S. invasion of Iraq—as wrong and downright immoral. But in one key respect, unofficial nationalism overlaps and agrees with the official version articulated by the state: right or wrong, a sizable portion of the middle classes generally buys into the state's explanation of the threats posed by foreign (neighborly) conspiracies. While most middle-class Middle Easterners tend to be highly suspicious of government explanations and policies in general, their national identities, proud to the point of defensiveness, make most of them receptive to theories of foreign conspiracies. Accurate public opinion data in this regard are not available. But if the sensationalism caused by frequent revelations of foreign bank accounts and secret shipments of arms and cash is any indication, such theories hold much sway in most Middle Eastern capitals.

Compared to the 1950s and early 1960s, most Middle Eastern states today have exhausted their once extensive popular legitimacy. They promised victory but lost war after war, talked of liberating Palestinians but abandoned them in short order, promised economic riches but brought the middle classes declining living standards and the rest abject poverty, and advocated moral purity while drowning themselves in worldly pleasures and material possessions. Nevertheless, though now hanging by a thread, the state retains some nationalist legitimacy. It remains the only viable defender of the nation's sovereignty, not necessarily against the possibility of wars, which are today rather unlikely, but against the constant machinations of more elusive, less obvious foreign adversaries.

A second, more compelling aspect of the ruling bargain is patrimonialism. While traditionally associated with monarchies that cultivate and rule through a series of highly personalized relationships, in the Middle East patrimonialism is equally pervasive in monarchical and presidential political systems. Most republican political systems in the region, after all, are in reality "presidential monarchies" in which the president is routinely reelected in elections that can hardly be considered democratic. The election of President Bashar al-Assad in Syria by the country's parliament following the death of his father, President Hafiz al-Assad, gives the term *presidential monarchy* new meaning. In Iraq, there were rumors that President Saddam Hussein had designated his son Uday to be his heir apparent.

Patrimonial leadership features the pervasiveness of personal ties that directly bind the sovereign to successive layers of subordinates and in turn bind those subordinates to officials beneath them. These personal ties between the leader, who is the ultimate patron, and progressively lesser patrons beneath him are replicated throughout the system. James Bill and Robert Springborg explain the phenomenon best:

> In the patrimonial Middle East, the sovereign is located at the center of the political system. He is surrounded by advisors, ministers, military leaders, personal secretaries, and confidants. The one thing that all members of this inner circle share is unquestioned personal loyalty to the leader. This is best indicated by their continual reflection of the will and personality of that leader. These individuals may relate submissively and passively to the leader, but they do not relate in this way to their own peers and followers. Here, they are caught up in intense manipulations and machinations. . . . Although the vertical relationships tend to be one-sided, the horizontal patterns are characterized by balanced rivalry. . . . The traditional politics of patrimonial leadership in the Middle East, therefore, tends to consist of a chain of vertical manipulation and horizontal competition that cuts through the sociopolitical fabric.[27]

Reinforcing patrimonial ties are those fostered through corporatist political economies, which, in one form or another, are found throughout the Middle East.[28] Just as the leader is the ultimate dispenser of sociopolitical privileges and favors in a patrimonial political system, so is the state the ultimate arbiter of various economic privileges in a corporatist political economy. By definition, corporatism divides society into various functional groups—agricultural producers, industrial producers, entrepreneurs, white-collar workers, the armed forces—and fosters organic links between each and the state.[29] The precise composition of corporatist groups and the nature of the arrangements between them vary across Middle Eastern countries and depend on prevailing class alliances and preferences within each country. Nevertheless, all Middle Eastern states have identified at least three functional groups whose corporatization into the state's orbit they deem essential: civil servants, entrepreneurs, and the armed forces. The oil monarchies of the Arabian peninsula, which do not have an indigenous labor force of their own and import practically all of their necessary labor, have no need to include immigrant laborers in the state's corporatist arrangement. The opposite is true of countries with an expansive class of laborers—that is, virtually all the other countries of the Middle East—where states have devised elaborate institutional and organizational arrangements to ensure labor's corporatization.[30] Within the oil monarchies themselves, Saudi Arabia appears to have gone the furthest in inculcating corporatist ties between the state and the kingdom's selected tribes, although lesser forms of the phenomenon can also be found elsewhere in the peninsula.[31] In Saudi Arabia, this was traditionally done through the institution of the *majlis,* or council, in which the monarch or his representatives, usually one of the royal princes, met with tribal leaders and ensured their co-option into the system.[32]

The three features of the ruling bargain discussed so far—nationalism, patrimonialism, and corporatism—may be necessary for keeping the state-society modus vivendi operational, but insofar as the state is concerned, they are seldom sufficient to ensure the state's supremacy over society. In fact, each of the three features of the ruling bargain either already has encountered or is in the process of encountering significant problems of its own. Official nationalism, as already mentioned, hardly holds the sway today that it once did, and Middle Eastern states are finding it increasingly hard to manipulate popular nationalist sentiments for political purposes. Patrimonialism has also become difficult to maintain in recent decades as declining state largesse has tended to weaken some of the systemic bonds of loyalty between successive layers of patrons and clients. Similar problems have also plagued corporatist arrangements, which, by bestowing on various groups organizational skills and mobilization, have the potential to get out of the state's control and turn on it. In fact, the state's deliberate effort to corporatize industrial laborers in Turkey has had the paradoxical effect of enhancing their autonomy and potential as an irritant to the state.[33]

The upshot has been a keen awareness on the part of Middle Eastern states that they must underwrite their ruling bargains with high levels of coercion, or at least the threat of coercion. The message given by the state to social actors is clear and simple: comply with the dictates of the state—buy into the ruling bargain—or face the consequences. Repression, or its implied threat, is ever-present in the world of politics. Some four decades ago, Samuel Huntington described such "praetorian" polities as those in which "social forces confront each other nakedly; no political institutions, no crop of professional political leaders are recognized or accepted as the legitimate intermediaries to moderate group conflict. Equally important, no agreement exists among the groups as to the legitimate and authoritative methods of resolving conflict."[34] In the praetorian polities of the Middle East, repression is viewed as a necessary survival tool by state actors who often consider themselves besieged by potential adversaries from within the different societal strata. A sense of paranoia pervades state-society relations, whereby each side suspects the intentions and motives of the other. The steady decline in states' legitimacy in recent decades, manifested in recurrent and multifaceted challenges to the ruling bargain, has made states' resort to coercion all the more frequent.

The state's attempts to give popular currency to a "ruling bargain" among the urban middle classes and its resort to coercion when necessary have had two larger consequences for overall state-society relations in the Middle East. First, although in some respects the state's attempts to forge subjective, extrainstitutional links with society have been futile or have elicited sharp adverse reactions, its efforts to corporatize functional groups, its use of patrimonial linkages, and its championing of (official) nationalism have, in some ways, helped it retain a certain relevance to the life and identity of society. In other words, although the institutional links between the state and society may be designed to help maintain the state's primacy and dominance over society, some extrainstitutional links, however weak, continue to bind the two together subjectively.

This is quite unlike the cases of South America and eastern Europe in the 1980s. There the state unintentionally severed crucial subjective links with society, uncaring or unaware of many sociocultural dynamics about which people cared deeply. This in turn led to the development of a "parallel" or "alternative" society in contrast to the "official" society that the state sought to define and control.[35] But virtually all the states in the Middle East, to one extent or another, have sought to carve out a cultural niche for themselves, and some have been far more successful at it than others. A few states have pointed to a favorite cultural disposition, monopolized its interpretation, and made it their primary source of cultural legitimacy. For Sudan, Saudi Arabia, and Iran this has been religion; at the opposite extreme, for Turkey it has been secular Kemalism. For most others, attempts at cultural legitimation have been more nuanced and mixed. The states of Morocco, Algeria, Tunisia, Egypt, Syria, and Jordan, to name a few, have tried to strike a careful balance in their attention to the prevailing cultural norms of society. Invariably, however, they have alienated one of the strata in society, the Islamists, for whom the state's attention to religion has been both insufficient and disingenuous. Each state has faced its own Islamist challenge as a result, which itself has been multilayered and highly differentiated.[36]

A second consequence of the prevailing patterns of state-society relations in the Middle East is the overall "exit" of society from the political process. The perceived costs of political activity are too high and the risks involved too perilous for the average urban middle-class person to willingly and voluntarily engage in it. Fear, paranoia, and a perception of the omnipresence of the dreaded secret police, the *mukhaberat,* in addition to a series of lofty broken promises, have helped deepen a pervasive political skepticism among the urban middle classes. With diminished belief in one's overall political efficacy, routine political involvement becomes pro forma and an act of prudent obligation. The most common instance of this type of political participation is voting in elections whose outcome everyone knows to be predetermined. If springing from genuine conviction, political activism is likely to take the form of participation in extralegal organizations and means to overthrow the state. Prime examples include organizations such as the Gama'a Islamiyya in Egypt, the Muslim Brotherhood in Syria, and the Islamic Salvation Front (FIS) in Algeria. Other politically active social organizations—for example, Adl wal-Ihsan in Morocco—may not be as radical as the Gama'a or the FIS, but by and large, they are just as committed to basically reconstituting the state.[37] Especially in *mukhaberat* states like Iraq before Saddam's overthrow, Egypt, and Algeria, therefore, most people participate in presidential elections knowing full well that the outcome is predetermined. But they do so anyway to get the appropriate stamp on their identity cards or birth certificates that may come in handy at some later date. The basic attitudes of urban society toward the state are those of avoidance wherever possible, passive compliance whenever appropriate, and begrudging acceptance in the absence of viable alternatives.

These are some of the more pronounced, *general* features of state-society relations in Middle Eastern countries, and the foregoing analysis does not take into account some of the more subtle sociopolitical dynamics percolating beneath the surface in many parts of the region. This section has demonstrated that social and political conditions in most countries of the Middle East reduce the possibility that CSOs will emerge and bring about civil society–driven democratic transitions. By itself, however, this does not lessen the possibility of democratization in the Middle East. In fact, as the following section argues, the gradual but steady weakening of the ruling bargain over the last couple of decades has set in motion a subtle, at times painfully slow process whereby state elites have been forced to negotiate over some of the premises of the bargain with selected social actors. In two countries—Iran and Morocco—this slow process of negotiation, which is at this point far from over, at some point appeared to be heading in a generally democratic direction. To ensure that the liberalization process did not get out of hand and erode too many of its privileges, however, in both countries the state stepped in before too long and stalled or reversed many of the democratic gains society had or was about to win. In Lebanon, in the meanwhile, a top-down democratic polity is once again being reconstituted for somewhat different reasons. The forces at work here are not so much bargaining state and social elites as intraelite strategic decisions based on the perceived benefits of reconstituting a collapsed democratic state. As these three examples indicate, political liberalization—of a prolonged, painfully slow, variety—may still have some breathing room in the Middle East. The next section considers these prospects.

PROSPECTS FOR DEMOCRATIZATION IN THE MIDDLE EAST

As already argued, democratic transitions based primarily on the efforts of civil society or originating from above are unlikely to take place in the Middle East in the near future. Instead, the most likely pattern of democratization is one involving a gradual redefinition of the state's role in relation to society as a result of the efforts of newly emerging actors within the state or the rise of actors loosely affiliated with the state. Before going into further detail about the dynamics involved in these types of transitions, let us examine the reasons for the absence so far of transitions from above and those propelled by civil society.

The most important reason that neither of these two types of transitions has occurred yet in the Middle East is the relative strength and viability of the nondemocratic state in relation to society. Insofar as democratization from above is concerned, throughout the Middle East, state elites have been able to respond to crises of legitimacy and control in ways that have not necessitated a wholesale abdication of power to potential democratic successors. When confronted with these types of crises in the late 1970s, the shah of Iran first tried suppression and then, once that failed, opted for concessions. But his concessions were too little, too late, and before long an increasingly radicalized revolutionary movement overthrew the entire monarchical system and all of its institutional vestiges. To preempt the possibility of a similar fate befalling them, in the 1980s state leaders throughout the Middle East embarked on a strategy combining increased authoritarianism and a more vocal championing of the rhetoric of democracy.

This careful balancing act became all the more prevalent toward the end of the 1980s as Middle Eastern leaders scrambled to find ways of staying out of the "third wave." In a move that at the time appeared to be the beginning of meaningful democratic transitions, most took to drafting "national charters" (al-Mithaq). Although slightly different in each case, the national charters invariably reaffirmed the commitment of social actors to the basic tenets of the state and committed the state to a process of liberalization. This was the case in Morocco, Algeria, Tunisia, and Jordan, where in the final years of the 1980s national charters were drawn up with great fanfare. Major constitutional changes were also undertaken in Iran, and a less doctrinaire, comparatively more open "Second Republic" began to take shape. In a less formal way, in 1993 the Egyptian state called for the initiation of a "national dialogue" *(al-hiwar al-qawmi)*. Buffered by their oil wealth, the oil monarchies of the Arabian peninsula did not go so far as to draw up national charters, but most did clean up their public image and strengthened their traditional bonds of patronage. Beginning in 1992, for example, the king of Saudi Arabia adopted a new title, Custodian of Islam's Two Holy Sites. The Iraqi state, desperate after an inconclusive, bloody war with Iran, resorted to a radically different tactic, but one with which President Saddam Hussein was familiar: invasion, in this case the invasion of Kuwait.

Despite the considerable initial excitement generated by the drafting of national charters and by other promises of liberalization implicitly or explicitly given by the state, it soon became obvious that the concessions of the late 1980s and early 1990s were, for the most part, tactical retreats by state elites who in the long run were unwilling to institute power-sharing arrangements. The most stunning and dramatic reversal occurred in Algeria, where electoral successes by the FIS in the first round of parliamentary elections in December 1991 triggered a military coup and plunged the country into civil war for much of the 1990s. Hopes for a democratic opening were once again raised in the run-up to presidential elections in 1999, for which some fifty candidates initially signed up. But the number of the candidates was reduced first to twelve, then seven, and eventually only one, Abdelaziz Bouteflika, the military's so-called "national consensus candidate."[38] Elected to a second term in 2009, Bouteflika's presidency has brought an end to the civil war but has not resulted in any tangible changes in the state's overall nature. Next door in Tunisia, alarmed that a similar Islamist victory might take place at the polls, President Zein el-Abidine Ben Ali also constricted the narrow political space he had initially allowed and banned the religiously oriented al-Nahda Party. There was also a reinvigoration of authoritarianism in Egypt beginning in the early 1990s: the state asserted its control over many professional syndicates, terminated the elected position of village mayors and deputy mayors, manipulated election laws ahead of the 1995 parliamentary elections, and arrested scores of journalists, parliamentary candidates, and members of the Muslim Brotherhood.[39] Elections did proceed as scheduled in Morocco and Jordan, but in both cases the states' vocal opponents were harassed and some were even arrested.

Compared to the rest of the Arab world, the advent of multipartyism *(ta'addudiyya)* brought significant political liberalization to Jordan and Morocco. But in each of these cases, it also soon became apparent that the political opening did not extend beyond mostly cosmetic changes. By showing greater tolerance toward the emerging "loyal opposition" and allowing parliamentary elections to go ahead, the Jordanian and Moroccan monarchies helped promote the appearance of a more open political space, hoping to thereby marginalize the more radical elements of the opposition. But neither state was willing to loosen its tight control of the liberalization process, and some of the state's core policies (e.g., the monarchy's powers and privileges, the conduct of foreign policy, the state's treatment of the opposition) remained closed to discussion and debate by the parliament. Before long, it became obvious that the ongoing processes of liberalization were mostly cosmetic and that multipartyism was having little structural impact.[40] The two states have remained sultanistic monarchies that continue to rule through royal patronage and the dispensing of favors through the *makhzen*.[41]

In each Middle Eastern country, the unfolding of events was influenced by what was occurring elsewhere. Each state was, of course, trying to prevent the emergence of conditions similar to those that had engulfed East European dictatorships. But, more importantly, the controlled liberalization processes set into motion in Jordan and Morocco, and more briefly in Algeria and Tunisia, were motivated by a series of perceived international economic and diplomatic benefits that each state hoped to accrue. Both the Jordanian and Moroccan states faced crushing debt burdens, and loans and grants from the International Monetary Fund served as important catalysts for the initial impulse to liberalize and, as time went by, to appear less authoritarian. Image appears to have been the primary motivator in Algeria and Tunisia, where state elites sought to look less like "Oriental despots," especially before the French and others in the international community. Earlier in the 1980s this concern with image had prompted Turkish generals to give up power almost completely, move to behind the scenes, and let elected, approved, civilian politicians enhance Turkey's image as a European country worthy of membership in the European Union. The greater immediacy of an "image problem," or at least the perceived immediacy of its consequences, appears to have been a factor resulting in a unique process of democratization from above in Turkey, whereas other Middle Eastern states only partially liberalized.

Even in Turkey, as discussed in Chapter 9, the military establishment continues to exert considerable political influence through the powerful National Security Council, to the extent that in 1997 it launched a "silent coup" against an elected prime minister and banned his political party.[42]

The continued dominance of nondemocratic state institutions in the Middle East is matched by a number of inherent weaknesses within CSOs. Earlier in the chapter, CSOs were defined as self-organized, politically autonomous organizations that serve as unofficial gathering places for interest articulation, cultural and/or political expression, and participation in the public arena. To be sure, there is a rich and varied history of associational activism throughout the Middle East, and self-organized, interest-driven groups have long existed and operated in every country of the region from Iran in the east to Morocco in the west. These have ranged from merchants' guilds and associations to syndicates belonging to writers, artisans, various professional groups (pharmacists, physicians, journalists, lawyers, dentists, etc.), and even Freemasons. The Middle East also has a rich tradition of activism, at times going all the way back to Ottoman times, by other self-organized, associative groups such as Sufi orders (in Egypt), clerics (in Iran's 1906–11 Constitutional Revolution), women's rights advocates (in the 1920s in Iran), minority rights groups, and secular members of the intelligentsia (the Young Turks, and nationalists in Palestine and elsewhere before and after World War I).[43] Beginning in the 1980s, as economic difficulties and *infitah* (open-door) policies reduced the role of the state in the economy somewhat, associations proliferated. In Egypt, for example, the number of business groups grew from 26 in 1970 to 40 in 1980, professional groups from 36 to 68, and cultural organizations from 86 to 215.[44] In Morocco, by the 1980s an estimated 3,000 associations were said to be active.[45] Algeria saw an even more dramatic explosion of associational activism in the late 1980s, especially after the enactment of liberal laws in 1987–88 removing the need for government approval in establishing associations. By 1991, some 7,350 associations were in existence there.[46]

But the depth and prevalence of associational life have not necessarily meant its political independence and autonomy. Again and again, both historically and in contemporary times, the state has stepped in to curtail the degree to which these groups can act independently and serve as potential forums for political activism or the articulation of nonstate ideologies. Surprised by their quick proliferation and unexpected vibrancy, each of the states hurriedly drafted laws designed to curtail the associations' autonomy and thus their efficacy as alternative sources of interest articulation and mobilization. In Egypt, where today there may be as many as fourteen thousand voluntary associations, the government has insisted that they had to engage only in social activities and remain apolitical or risk being banned. In a law enacted in 1993, the government also tried to regulate elections within voluntary associations—in which oppositional Islamists were scoring impressive victories—and to tighten its control over them.[47] In Jordan, where most associations have remained relatively passive and have interested themselves in parochial, largely nonpolitical issues, the government nevertheless decreed laws tightening control over the press and placed burdensome financial requirements on independent publications, resulting in the closure of twelve weeklies.[48] In Morocco, the government's efforts aimed at curtailing the independence of associations took a slightly different form—co-optation and penetration. The state placed its "faithful representatives and cronies" in leadership positions of the associations and "supplied them with financial and infrastructure support."[49] Clientalization caused these voluntary associations to lose any semblance of political autonomy they had once had. Even in Palestinian territories, the fledgling Palestinian Authority, alarmed at the popularity of Islamists within the various Palestinian nongovernmental organizations, made certain early on, through legislation, that the powers and independence of the NGOs would remain checked.[50] Thus, throughout the Middle East, the state has gone to great lengths to ensure its continued and unimpeded dominance over society, seeing to it that civil society would suffer an embryonic death.

Given the effective subjugation of voluntary associations and NGOs to state organs, the only effective vehicle for change in state-society relations is the state itself. More specifically, state institutions such as parliamentary bodies and officially approved political parties—if not the state party itself—can often act as catalysts for subtle changes in the way the state relates to society. For quite different reasons, this is what has been taking place in Iran and Lebanon and, to a somewhat lesser extent, in Morocco. Baaklini, Denoeux, and Springborg have labeled the ensuing process a "negotiated transition" to democracy:

> [R]egime and opposition alike realize that the system is becoming more open. They are aware that the rules of the game are being more liberalized, yet neither knows exactly what the rules will end up being. The regime appears confident that it can control the pace at which, and the extent to which, the rules are being altered. It is orchestrating reforms on the assumption that these reforms will ultimately strengthen its position. The opposition, for its part, believes that its bargaining power

is increasing with every concession made by the regime. It hopes that, in the long run, the small and incremental changes that are being implemented will amount to a significant shift in the balance of power between state and society.[51]

In each of these three cases, the elected members of the legislature have set into motion a subtle process whereby some of the state's traditional policies and practices are being openly debated. Significantly, the primary impetus for such a debate is the internal makeup of the state itself, the unintended outgrowth of a highly controlled process of liberalization that has given rise to a larger debate over the general state of politics. In both Iran and Morocco, the state has done whatever it can to muffle the debate and direct it in ways suited to its own purposes. The response by elements within the Iranian state has been particularly brutal, leading to the serial murder of a number of noted journalists and writers in the late 1990s and blanket repression, mass arrests, and show trials of hundreds of political activists and state opponents in 2009. Countless newspapers and journals have also been closed down in recent years. In 2004 thousands of reformist candidates were barred from running in parliamentary elections, and the "stolen" 2009 presidential elections left hundreds dead and imprisoned in its painful wake. Nevertheless, talk of a loosely defined "reformation" abounds in Iran. The Iranian parliament, interestingly, had earlier emerged as one of the primary articulators and defenders of what is turning out to be a uniquely Iranian brand of democracy.[52] Whether this trend will continue remains to be seen.

A similar but somewhat less noisy and contentious process has been unfolding in Morocco, where, beginning in the mid-1990s, the late King Hassan II strengthened the role of the parliament and allowed the unprecedented public airing of often-heated parliamentary debates and proceedings. Political prisoners were granted a royal amnesty in 1993, and a constitutional amendment in 1996 allowed for the direct election of deputies to the lower house of the parliament, one of the main demands of the opposition.[53] Most importantly, in April 2004, the country's new monarch, Mohammed VI, established an Equity and Reconciliation Commission (Instance Équité et Réconciliation [IER]) charged with investigating and, through monetary and other forms of compensation, healing the wounds left by the country's bitter legacy of arbitrary arrests and the ill treatment of prisoners. As a report by the International Center for Transitional Justice maintained at the time, "The Commission represents a groundbreaking approach for the entire region and is exceptional in many respects. It has the blessing of a King examining the crimes of his own father; its membership comprises many victims of arbitrary detention and torture; it is the only truth commission to ever have possessed the power to grant compensation directly to victims; and it is the first truth commission in the Arab world. For these and other reasons, the IER has the potential for significant regional and international influence, both in the short and long term."[54] The IER's final report, issued in December 2005 and released to the public a few weeks later, revealed that previous governments were responsible for disappearances or forced exile of political opponents, arbitrary detentions that were often followed by execution, numerous violations of civil liberties, and sexual violence committed against prisoners and detainees. In addition to awarding monetary compensation to the victims, the report made a number of important recommendations, the most important of which were "consolidating constitutional guarantees to human rights"; "adopting and implementing an integrated national strategy to struggle against impunity"; and "reforms in the sectors of security, justice, law, and penal policy."[55]

Despite the hopes raised by the commission's appointment and its report, Morocco's much-anticipated process of democratic opening has so far failed to materialize. The monarch remains the undisputed fount of all power. It appears that the efforts of King Hassan were designed to "reinvent" the monarchy and make it easier for his heir to rule.[56] His son, King Mohammed VI, has sought to change the public appearance of the political system but has left intact its unaccountable and largely unresponsive relationship with society. Within only months of the IER's report, an examination of the state of the country's political opening reached the following conclusion: "There is no indication that Morocco is becoming a democratic country in which power resides in institutions accountable to the electorate. Instead, the king remains the dominant religious and political authority in the country and the main driver of the reform process. All new measures have been introduced from the top, as the result of decisions taken by the king and on the basis of studies carried out by commissions he appointed. Moreover, none of the measures impose limits on his power."[57]

In Morocco, as in Iran, there is also a problem of routinized popular participation in NGOs, as lack of skills, limited opportunities, and fear of possible risks keep most urban middle classes away from voluntary associations.[58] This is likely to hamper the emergence of a "culture of debate" in the country, though democratic aspirations continue to manifest themselves across the social spectrum.[59]

The other Middle Eastern country in which parliamentary democracy has been taking shape in recent years is Lebanon. The collapse of the

1943 National Pact (al-Mithaq al-Watani) set off a bloody civil war that raged from 1975 to 1990.[60] The civil war was precipitated by, among other things, the inherent fragility of Lebanon's consociational democracy and the institutions on which it relied. Also important were bitter inter- and intraelite factionalism and the stresses associated with the 1967 and 1973 Arab-Israeli wars, chief among which was an influx of armed Palestinian guerrillas into the country following their expulsion from Jordan in 1970. For nearly fifteen years, the civil war was sustained by the convergence of international and domestic factors. One of the domestic factors was the interests of local bosses (zu'ama), who found the crippled but still service-able institutions and processes of the state beneficial.[61] By the late 1980s, however, Lebanon's self-destruction had become too costly, and members of the last elected parliament, from 1972, gathered in Ta'if, Saudi Arabia, to negotiate an end to the war and foster a new national consensus. Although the civil war continued for another year, the Ta'if Accord was meant to serve as the basis of a reconstituted democratic system. Finally, in October 1990, the Lebanese civil war came to an end.

The spirit of Ta'if did not outlast the civil war by much. Initially, opposition candidates, mostly Christian, boycotted the 1992 parliamentary elections, primarily because of Syria's heavy-handed presence in the country. By the time the 1996 elections came around, talk of a boycott was abandoned by those opposed to the Ta'if formula, and a reinvigorated democracy appeared to be in the offing. But it did not take long for the state elites to ensure that election laws favored their reelection and continued dominance of the system.[62] As an indication of other limits of Lebanon's democracy, various acts of intimidation of opposition figures and state-imposed restrictions continued to occur throughout the 1990s. In 1998, for example, the government banned public gatherings and demonstrations and prevented the broadcast of a television interview with the exiled Aoun.[63] Parliament's election in 1999 of a new president—Emile Lahoud, formerly commander of the army—and the subsequent resignation of a prime minister widely perceived to be corrupt—Rafiq Hariri—held promises of a greater democratization of the Lebanese polity.

Because the Lebanese have historically found themselves in the firing line of much more powerful rivals—the Israelis, the Palestinians, the Syrians, and more recently the Iranians—their domestic politics has been shaped, perhaps more so than in any other regional state, by international cross-currents over which they have had little or no control. Repeatedly, Lebanon's various factions have failed to demonstrate their own resolve to sustain the country's constitutionally democratic political system. But the constant machinations of overbearing external players have done even more harm to the consolidation of a consolidated democracy. Although the Ta'if Accord mandated the departure of Syrian troops from Lebanon, who had been present since 1976, it was not until April 2005 that the Syrian army finally withdrew from the country. Up until that point, "Damascus essentially controlled Lebanon—dominating government, interfering in elections, naming presidents and prime ministers, making major policy decisions."[64] Syria's withdrawal was prompted by Hariri's assassination the previous February, once again plunging Lebanon into chaos and leading to bitter acrimony among the country's multiple factions. The animosities were temporarily set aside in the aftermath of Israel's devastating war on the country in 2006 but resurfaced again shortly thereafter. Iran, meanwhile, found in its ally the Hezbollah a highly effective deterrent against possible Israeli attacks on its soil.

On the one hand, Lebanon's various factions are too divided and acrimonious to enter into lasting, viable alliances. On the other hand, none is strong or numerous enough to effectively overwhelm the others and impose its will on them. Not surprisingly, early on in the life of the republic a consociational democracy was determined to be the most appropriate form of political system for the country.[65] But neither the Lebanese elites themselves nor the external actors interested in the country have done much to make the system meaningfully effective. If anything, they have often deliberately eroded its efficacy. Nevertheless, despite its chronic precarious balance, at times its teetering on the edge of collapse, the political system has somehow withstood the test of time since the civil war ended. How much more meaningfully democratic it will become over time is yet to be determined.

As the examples of Iran, Morocco, and Lebanon show, so far in the Middle East the pace, depth, and meaningfulness of liberalization processes all have been a product of the agendas, priorities, and overall nature of dynamics within the state. Iran offers a paradigmatic example of a state-led transition arising from tensions between "hard-liners" and "soft-liners." These internal tensions are far less apparent in Morocco, where the state remains far more cohesive in its goals and priorities, so the transition process there has been considerably slower and far more controlled. In Lebanon, the ruling elite's commitment to the spirit of the Ta'if Accord has proven paramount in maintaining the overall vibrancy of the country's democracy. Up until the late 1990s the locus of the elite's commitment lay elsewhere. The election of a new president in 1999 and the slow emergence of a new cadre of politicians appear to have brightened the prospects for

Lebanon's democracy.[66] The degree to which society eventually becomes involved in the transition process and the timing of such involvement depend on specific conditions within each country. The frequency of political mobilization in Iran over the last two decades appears to have been instrumental in giving Iran's transition greater societal resonance so far, whereas a history of statist absolutism has made most Moroccans take a wait-and-see attitude toward the state's proclaimed championing of democracy. In Lebanon, where sectarian and community leaders have long held sway among their respective clients, the popular scope of the country's democracy has been defined more sharply by elite agendas and priorities.

The most obvious comparative conclusion for the rest of the Middle East based on these three diverse cases is the resilience of the nondemocratic state as a viable entity and of statism as a phenomenon. Specific national circumstances notwithstanding, barring dramatic developments such as palace coups and military takeovers, it appears that for the foreseeable future, the direction, depth, and pace of democratic transitions in the Middle East will be determined primarily by the priorities of state actors and the extent to which they are willing to share state resources and institutions—especially the legislature—with more democratically committed actors. These internal state developments have varied from slow and then halted moves toward democratization in Iran and Morocco, to frozen liberalization in Jordan, authoritarian retrenchment in Algeria and Egypt, civil war in the Sudan, and a timid but functioning democracy in Lebanon. As history has demonstrated, more often than not the spread of democracy is a regionwide phenomenon, frequently engulfing nondemocratic neighbors in relatively rapid succession. Whether a regional role model will emerge remains to be seen, as does its potential for triggering similar processes elsewhere. If one of the Middle East's authoritarian states were to become meaningfully democratic, however, the remaining holdouts could find it much harder to keep democracy at bay.

Despite the global resurgence of democracy in recent decades and the spread of the "third wave" of democratization across South America and eastern Europe, authoritarianism has shown remarkable resilience and staying power in the Middle East. Several factors underlie this resilience, chiefly the weakness of civil society, the continued strength of state institutions, and the societal relevance of state institutions as guaranteed through ruling bargains that rest on nationalism, patrimonialism, and corporatism. Equally important has been the absence of international pressures for democratization, which were of paramount significance in influencing the demise of authoritarian polities in eastern Europe and South America. In the Middle East, only Turkey has let international forces directly shape its domestic priorities. As a result, the desire to be considered European and be admitted into the European Union has prompted state elites to consistently maintain an imperfect but functioning democratic system since 1983. No state, of course, is completely immune from the unfolding of international events and their potential consequences for domestic politics. Nevertheless, so far a vast majority of Middle Eastern states have not confronted international developments that have had domestic consequences for democratization. Ironically, the United States' invasion of Iraq and its subsequent overthrow of the Iraqi state in 2003 appear to have strengthened authoritarian hard-liners throughout the Middle East.

Given that in the Middle East the state is by far the more dominant and powerful partner in state-society relations, any meaningful moves toward a greater opening of the political process are likely to be initiated from within the state itself. The most likely course of a democratic transition in the Middle East is that certain actors within the state will begin using the state resources and institutions at their disposal to reform the system from within and make it more democratic. The internal tensions within the state—the competition between "soft-liners" and "hard-liners"—will set off a slow, nonlinear process whereby the state becomes increasingly less authoritarian and more democratic. In turn, the more open political atmosphere that ensues will allow members of the intelligentsia and other state-affiliated or state-approved figures to engage in dialogues over the essence and propriety of state-society relations. The defining characteristics of the dialogue—its main premises, its intellectual content, the venues of its expression, and its censorship or tolerance—will all vary from case to case and country to country. Such dialogues started but met with embryonic deaths in Iran and Morocco. Whether the states concerned can indefinitely keep defining the national political agenda, and thereby the very essence of politics, depends on specific circumstances within each country. We have seen so far that authoritarian retrenchment is as much of a possibility as is meaningful political liberalization. Only time, and state capabilities and agendas, will tell which option will prevail.

11 Challenges Facing the Middle East

The political history of the Middle East has been fraught with turmoil and political instability. By the middle of the twentieth century, most of the region had experienced two separate, qualitatively different periods of colonial subjugation. First came Ottoman rule, from the early to mid-1500s up until the late 1910s, and then British and French rule, beginning with the end of the First World War and lasting until the late 1940s. Not surprisingly, the state-building processes of the 1940s and 1950s—like those in Turkey in the 1920s and in Iran in the 1930s—took on an urgent and feverish character. A similar sense of urgency characterized the modernization drive of the 1960s and 1970s. Dictatorships were established, overthrown, and reestablished; wars were fought, lost, and refought; a new state was born and another died; and the wretched history of one diaspora came to an end but the misery of another got under way. The last three decades have brought more of the same, though with slightly different features and added layers of complexity.

Not every aspect of Middle Eastern history has been cyclical. In the 1960s and 1970s, the physical character of the Middle East changed tremendously. Cities were expanded, massive monuments, roads, and factories were built, and the march toward "development" yielded some tangible results. The region's countless monarchs—both official ones and the others who chose to label themselves "president"—could point to their countries' economic and industrial progress with a measure of justified pride. But many in the Middle East remained poor, and the fruits of industrial development were not shared evenly anywhere. More fundamentally, as the United Nations has pointed out, much of the Middle East, especially the Arab world and Iran, continues to suffer from three glaring deficits—in freedom, in women's empowerment, and in human capabilities and knowledge relative to income.[1] Nevertheless, industrial development became less of a dream and more of a reality throughout the Middle East in the twentieth century. What differed greatly was its depth compared to other parts of the world and the different levels to which it spread in the various parts of the region.

Industrial development, uneven as it has been, has had several adverse side effects with which the countries of the Middle East must now contend. For the past century or so, the challenges facing the Middle East have been those of state building, military security, political consolidation, and economic development. Far from being resolved or somehow withering away, these challenges are now being compounded by the negative consequences of industrial modernization. Of these, three seem particularly pressing: astoundingly high rates of population growth; the increasing scarcity of water resources; and the pollution of various environmental resources, especially air. This chapter examines the magnitude of each of these problems and highlights the negative consequences each has had so far for the countries of the Middle East. These are the defining challenges that the Middle East must confront in the twenty-first century. Failure to resolve them could well end up being more consequential than the wars and revolutions that became such hallmarks of the last hundred years.

POPULATION GROWTH

With a few exceptions in sub-Saharan Africa, the countries of the Middle East tend to have the highest rates of population growth in the world (table 12). Overall, according to the World Bank, between 1990 and 2007 the population of the Middle East grew at an average rate of 2.0 percent annually, compared to 2.6 percent for sub-Saharan Africa, 1.8 percent for East Asia and the Pacific, and 1.5 percent for Latin America and the Caribbean.[2] Tragically, in sub-Saharan Africa, infant mortality rates are much higher than in the Middle East (89 per 1,000 live births compared to 32 in the Middle East in 2007) and life expectancy is much lower (fifty-one years in Africa compared to seventy in the Middle East in 2007). As a result, the slightly higher annual rates of population growth in Africa are offset by higher levels of infant mortality and shorter life spans. At current rates, the population of the Middle East is estimated to double in approximately twenty-seven years.[3]

As with the rest of the developing world, population growth rates in the Middle East accelerated beginning especially in the 1950s and 1960s, when advances in medical technology and hygiene resulted in declining

Table 12. Population Characteristics of the Middle East

	Population (millions)			Average Annual Population Increase (%)		Average Annual Labor Force Increase (%)	% Urban Population		Life Expectancy at Birth (years)		Infant Mortality (per 1,000)		Adult Literacy Rate (% of population over age 15)	
	1990	2007	2015 (est.)	1990–2007	2007–2015 (est.)	1990–2007	1990	2007	1990	2007	1990	2007	Male (2005–7)	Female (2005–7)
Algeria	25.3	33.9	38.0	1.7	1.5	4.0	52	65	67	72	54	33	84	66
Bahrain		0.75			1.9ᵃ					76				
Egypt	55.1	75.5	86.2	1.8	1.7	2.4	44	43	62	71	68	30	75	58
Iran	54.4	71.0	78.9	1.6	1.3	3.4	56	68	65	71	54	29	87	77
Iraq	18.5	—	—	—	—	—	70	67	62	—	42	—	—	—
Israel	4.7	7.2	8.1	2.5	1.6	3.2	90	92	77	81	10	4	—	—
Jordan	3.2	5.7	6.8	3.5	2.1	5.0	72	78	67	73	33	21	95	87
Kuwait	2.1	2.7	3.2	1.3	2.1	2.9	98	98	75	78	13	9	95	93
Lebanon	3.0	4.1	4.4	1.9	1.0	2.4	83	87	69	72	32	26	95	86

Libya	4.4	6.2	7.1	2.0	1.8	3.6	76	77	68	74	35	17	94	78
Morocco	24.2	30.9	33.9	1.4	1.2	2.3	48	56	64	71	69	32	69	43
Oman	1.8	2.6	3.0	2.0	2.0	3.0	66	72	70	76	25	11	89	77
Qatar		0.84			1.8[a]					76				
Saudi Arabia	16.4	24.2	28.3	2.3	2.0	3.2	77	81	68	73	35	20	89	79
Sudan	25.9	38.6	45.6	2.3	3.1	2.9	27	43	53	59	79	69	—	—
Syria	12.7	19.9	23.5	2.6	2.1	4.0	49	54	68	74	30	15	90	76
Tunisia	8.2	10.2	11.2	1.3	1.1	2.5	58	66	70	74	41	18	86	69
Turkey	56.2	73.9	81.0	1.6	1.2	0.8	59	68	66	72	67	21	96	81
UAE	1.9	4.4	5.3	5.0	2.4	6.2	79	78	73	79	13	7	89	91
Yemen	12.3	22.4	28.2	3.5	2.9	4.6	21	30	54	63	90	55	77	40

SOURCES: World Bank, *World Development Indicators, 2009* (Washington, DC: World Bank, 2009), pp. 40–42, 44–46, 92–94, 122–24, 174–76; World Bank Online Country Profiles.
[a] 2007.

levels of infant mortality and longer life expectancy. In specific relation to the Middle East, two additional factors account for the region's high rate of population growth. The first has to do with the relatively high rates of fertility among Middle Eastern women as compared to women elsewhere. In 1991, women in the Middle East on average had 4.8 children, a figure that dropped to 3.6 a decade later and to 2.8 in 2007 (table 13). By contrast, fertility rates were lower in all other regions of the developing world except sub-Saharan Africa.

Fertility rates tend to be higher in sub-Saharan Africa because of pervasive insecurity and fears about the future, in turn prompting parents to procreate for posterity's sake. In the Middle East, high fertility rates tend to be a product of factors that are mostly cultural rather than economic. Women in the Middle East and in other Islamic countries tend to get married at a much younger age. Overall, the prevalence of teenage brides tends to be higher in Muslim countries than in other parts of the developing world. Although cultural norms regarding marriage appear to be changing, women in the Middle East are likely to get pregnant earlier and more frequently. Early marriages are encouraged by social and cultural values that attach high esteem to the institution of the family and uphold the virtues of motherhood.[4] For many parents, especially those from more traditional backgrounds, there is also the fear that their daughter, if not quickly married off, may engage in premarital sex and bring dishonor to herself and her family.[5] Although not unique to the region, greater prestige attached to having male children also accounts for high fertility rates in the Middle East. Male offspring are often seen as carriers of the family name and tradition, as well as protectors of parents in old age and in times of need. They are, in essence, guarantors of the continuance of the family in the uncertain world of the future. Most parents, therefore, continue having children until they have produced the number of boys that they consider sufficient.

The low availability and use of contraceptives also account for the high rate of fertility among women in the Middle East. According to most interpretations of the *sharia* (Islamic law), Islam does not prohibit the use of contraceptives as such, and couples are able to exercise some control over reproduction.[6] This does not extend to abortion, however, which as a method of birth control is legally banned in almost all countries of the Middle East.[7] Nevertheless, despite a general lack of religious prohibitions on the use of contraceptives, married women in the Middle East are half as likely as women elsewhere in the developing world to be using some form of birth control: 22 percent in the Middle East as compared to 54 percent

Table 13. Fertility Rates in the Middle East as Compared to Other World Regions (births per woman)

	1991	2001	2007
Algeria	4.3	2.9	2.4
Bahrain	3.6	2.4	2.3
Egypt	4.0	3.0	2.9
Iran	4.8	2.9	2.0
Iraq	5.8	4.9	...
Israel	3.0	2.8	2.9
Jordan	5.7	4.4	3.6
Kuwait	3.4	2.7	2.2
Lebanon	3.1	2.2	2.2
Libya	4.6	3.5	2.7
Morocco	4.1	3.1	2.4
Oman	6.9	5.6	3.0
Qatar	4.3	3.4	2.7
Saudi Arabia	6.8	5.7	3.2
Sudan	5.4	4.6	4.2
Syria	5.3	3.8	3.1
Tunisia	3.4	2.2	2.0
Turkey	3.3	2.4	2.2
UAE	4.0	3.0	2.3
Yemen	7.6	7.6	5.5
East Asia and Pacific	3.0	2.5	1.9
Latin America and Carib.	3.2	2.8	2.4
Middle East and N. Africa	4.8	3.6	2.8
South Asia	4.1	3.3	2.9
Sub-Saharan Africa	6.2	5.4	5.1

SOURCES: World Bank, *World Development Indicators, 2009* (Washington, DC: World Bank, 2009), pp. 106–8; World Bank Online Country Profiles.

in other developing countries.[8] Statistics published by the World Bank in 2007 place the average prevalence of contraceptives among women in the Middle East and North Africa, married and unmarried alike, at 39.0 percent, compared to 41.4 percent in Asia and the Pacific and 49.4 percent in Latin America and the Caribbean.[9] Again, most of the reasons for avoiding contraception appear to be cultural: men do not like using them, and, given that sex as a subject remains taboo and sex education tends to be nonexistent, most couples depend on natural, unreliable methods of contraception (such as withdrawal).[10]

A second reason for the high rate of population growth in the Middle East is the migration of many "guest workers" to the oil-rich countries of the Arabian peninsula in search of employment. The oil boom created vast employment opportunities in the oil monarchies, which had insufficient labor resources. As a result, beginning in the 1960s and 1970s, expatriate workers began streaming into the oil monarchies in search of jobs and better opportunities. By 2000, foreigners composed some 72 percent of the total labor force in the oil-rich countries of the Arabian peninsula (table 14). Most of the earlier immigrants came from the less wealthy parts of the Arab world, such as Egypt, Syria, Lebanon, Jordan, the Palestinian territories, and Yemen. Significant numbers also came from South Asia, especially India, Bangladesh, Sri Lanka, Nepal, and Pakistan. Although they could not enjoy many of the economic privileges that citizens enjoyed, many expatriates decided to stay and have now become part of the population. In fact, as much as 85 percent of the populations of Qatar and the UAE are made up of noncitizens. After the Gulf War, Kuwait and some of the other Gulf states compelled many Palestinians and other Arab expatriates to leave—in retaliation for the PLO's siding with Iraq during the conflict— and in recent years there has been an attempt to encourage the immigration of workers from the Indian subcontinent and the Philippines instead of other Arab countries. Nevertheless, the overall structure of the population remains largely intact, as does overdependence on foreign laborers.

The consequences of rapid population growth rates, whether due to natural increases or immigration, are manifold. To begin with, the population of the Middle East tends to be skewed in favor of the young, especially those under the age of fourteen, who compose some 32 percent of the total population (table 15). Such a young population poses particular challenges, especially in such areas as adequate schooling (at both high school and university levels), the provision of health care and other necessary facilities, and future employment opportunities. There are other, more immediate ramifications as well. Adequate and affordable housing is a major concern;

Table 14. Foreign Labor Force in the Oil Monarchies, 1975–2000

Country	Foreign Labor Force (1,000s)			Foreigners as % of Total Labor Force Participation		
	1975	1990	2000	1975	1990	2000
Bahrain	39	132	168	46	51	61.9
Kuwait	218	731	1,261[a]	70	86	81.3[a]
Oman	103	442	552	54	70	64.3
Qatar	57	230	98	83	92	81.6
Saudi Arabia	475	2,878	4,004	32	60	55.8
UAE	234	805	1,207	84	89	89
All GCC Countries	1,126	5,218	7,772	47	74	72.3

SOURCES: Nasra M. Shah, "Restrictive Labour Immigration Policies in the Oil-Rich Gulf: Effectiveness and Implications for Sending Asian Countries," in *United Nations Expert Group Meeting on International Migration and Development in the Arab Region* (Beirut: United Nations Secretariat, 2006), p. 17; Michael Bonine, "Population, Poverty, and Politics: Contemporary Middle East Cities in Crisis," in *Population, Poverty, and Politics in Middle East Cities*, ed. Michael Bonine (Gainesville: University Press of Florida, 1997), p. 7.
[a]2005.

its insufficient availability has resulted in the growth of vast shantytowns on the margins of all Middle Eastern cities.[11] Overpopulation and housing shortages are endemic throughout the Middle East. Those who can afford to live outside squatter settlements often either build unsafe dwellings without official permits or stay with family and friends. In Fez, Morocco, for example, one-family houses sometimes have thirty families living within them, with as many as three families occupying a single room.[12]

Also, as Chapter 8 argued, most Middle Eastern countries have been paying far more attention to industrial development than to the development of the agricultural sector. Added stress on available food supplies increases the need for additional food imports, thus deepening international dependence on foreign suppliers and vulnerabilities to market fluctuations. Currently, the Middle East as a whole imports more than 50 percent of its food supplies. This reliance on food imports is expected to grow significantly over the next few decades.[13]

Moreover, high fertility rates appear to have negative effects at the household and individual levels. In particular, mothers with multiple pregnancies run higher risks of disease or even death. And children, especially girls, who have multiple siblings are more likely to be deprived in various ways.[14]

Table 15. Age Structure in the Middle East, 2007
(% of population)

	0–14 Years Old	15–64 Years Old	65 and Over
Algeria	28	67	5
Bahrain	26[a]	70[a]	4[a]
Egypt	33	62	5
Iran	27	69	4
Iraq	—	—	—
Israel	28	62	10
Jordan	36	61	3
Kuwait	23	75	2
Lebanon	28	65	7
Libya	30	66	4
Morocco	29	65	5
Oman	32	65	3
Qatar	29[a]	77[a]	1[a]
Saudi Arabia	33	65	3
Sudan	40	56	4
Syria	36	61	3
Tunisia	25	69	6
Turkey	27	67	6
UAE	20	79	1
Yemen	45	53	2
Middle East/N. Afr. Average	32	63	4

SOURCE: World Bank, *World Development Indicators, 2009* (Washington, DC: World Bank, 2009), pp. 40–42; Central Intelligence Agency, *CIA World Fact Book, 2009.*
[a]2009.

Equally consequential are the effects of high population growth rates on the uncontrollable growth of cities. An examination of the dilemmas associated with rampant and unplanned urbanization in the Middle East is beyond the scope of this book. But urban populations expanding not only from high birthrates but also from migration from rural areas into the cities have created multiple problems in Middle Eastern (and other developing world) cities. From the megacities of Tehran, Istanbul, Cairo, and Algiers to the smaller, "secondary" cities of Shiraz, Izmir, Ismailiyya, and Oran, and everywhere in between, urban infrastructures and services have been pushed to the breaking point and, in many instances, have collapsed under pressure. Numbers and statistics cannot adequately capture the magnitude of the difficulties that cities and their inhabitants face. In the words of one observer, "The rapid urbanization and burgeoning city populations, similar to most of the Third World, have led to problems and to declines of quality of urban life. There are too many people, insufficient jobs, inadequate infrastructures, shortages of basic services, deficient nutrition, poor health, and a deterioration of the physical environment. Middle Eastern cities are in crisis."[15]

It is little wonder that the Middle East as a whole and its cities in particular are facing such acute crises of environmental degradation. In many of the Middle East's larger cities, the air is often unbreathable and there are looming shortages of water for drinking and irrigation. If left unattended, environmental pollution is likely to have disastrous consequences for the Middle East.

ENVIRONMENTAL POLLUTION

Throughout the developing world, preoccupation with industrial development and the many struggles of daily life relegates popular concerns about the environment to the back burner. Especially in the inner cities and in other urban areas, where employment, housing, and other economic considerations are primary, protecting the environment is not a concern for the average person. Especially outside the oil monarchies, life for the popular classes can be harsh and constricting or at least beset with bureaucratic obstacles and other economic difficulties. Thus the average person is either unaware of the need to safeguard environmental resources or unwilling to take on the added economic costs of such an undertaking.

Environmental pollution takes a variety of forms, most commonly air, water, and soil pollution. Of these, air pollution has reached critical levels in many of the Middle East's larger cities—such as Tehran, Istanbul, and Cairo—and has already had adverse consequences for public health, especially in the form of various respiratory ailments. Air pollution has two main sources, both of which are plentiful in the Middle East (and elsewhere in the developing world): motor vehicles and industrial complexes and factories. As far as industrial complexes are concerned, most of the larger enterprises tend to employ older imported technology that is not always fully efficient and is often a major source of environmental pollution.[16] Air and especially soil pollution also results from the operations of small work-shops and business establishments—coppersmiths, mechanics, furniture makers, and so on—of which every Middle Eastern city has thousands. Many of these semiformal businesses, often family owned and operated, are too small to enable their proprietors to invest in environmentally friendly technology and practices. Again, the question confronting these small business owners is one of priorities. Given the importance of ensuring the viability of the family business by maximizing profits and keeping overhead to a minimum, protecting the air or the ground from pollutants often becomes a nonissue.

Motor vehicles are an even bigger source of air pollution. For example, in Tehran, whose air is among the most polluted in the world, 71 percent of the air pollution comes from the city's estimated two million cars.[17] In the relationship between vehicles and air pollution, three factors are important: the sheer numbers of commercial and private vehicles in circulation, the toxicity and levels of their exhaust emissions, and the type of gasoline used. Recent decades have seen an astounding rise in the numbers of vehicles in the Middle East, so much so that traffic jams have become daily features of even smaller cities and towns throughout the region. For example, in 1974 there were 674,947 motor vehicles in operation in Turkey, but by November 2000 the number had jumped to 7,109,844, an increase of over 1,053 percent. During the same period, the number of buses increased by 551 percent and trucks by more than 412 percent. There were similar rises in the number of minibuses and small trucks, though by far the biggest rise, by some 1,400 percent, was in the number of passenger cars.[18] Added to these staggering numbers in Turkey and elsewhere is the continued and widespread use of leaded gasoline and diesel fuel by both passenger cars and trucks and buses throughout the Middle East, thus increasing the emission of harmful pollutants to the environment.

Little information is available on environmental degradation in the Middle East. However, some statistics from Iran can help put things in perspective. Although the average life span of a car is estimated at 15.9 years, the government's ban on car imports has pushed the age of most cars in Iran to between 10 and 22 years old. Every twenty-four hours, cars operating in Tehran alone produce sixteen tons of tire particles, seven tons of asbestos (used in their brake shoes), and five tons of lead. Every year, 495,000 tons of pollutants are produced in Tehran alone, accounting for 25 percent of all the pollutants produced in the country. The city's population, meanwhile, is estimated at around twelve million inhabitants. Tehran officials estimate that air pollution kills on average 4,600 residents every year. Countless others suffer from poor vision, burning eyes, and respiratory problems because of the city's heavy, soupy air.[19] Meanwhile, demands for even more cars far surpasses the available supply.

These and other similar statistics have made it difficult for officials in Iran and elsewhere to continue ignoring the adverse effects of environmental pollution. As pollution rates approach crisis levels, government agencies and to a lesser extent nongovernmental organizations have become active in trying to reverse some of these alarming trends. Every government in the region has set up a cabinet-level agency or a separate ministry devoted to the environment.[20] In several countries popular awareness of the importance of environmental protection has increased. In Iran, for example, a Green Party has started low-key operations and is trying to attract members. A study conducted in Sharjah in the UAE found that there has been a steady rise in environmental awareness among women in the emirate.[21]

Official measures and popular attitudes regarding protecting the environment still have a long way to go, however. The demands for industrial and economic development are far too great to allow policy makers to devote financial and technological resources toward environmental protection. Official rhetoric notwithstanding, the rates at which the air gets polluted, landfills are capped with refuse, and industrial and domestic waste is generated dwarf the limited resources that governments allocate to environmental initiatives or the small steps that people take on their own. In many of the more populous and less wealthy countries—Iran, Iraq, Egypt, and Morocco chief among them—environmental pollution has already reached crisis levels, yet many of the developments that lead to environmental degradation continue full speed ahead. Environmental pollution in the Middle East is not simply a challenge of the future; it is a crisis of the present. Neglect or insufficient attention will only deepen the crisis.

WATER SCARCITY

Equally troublesome is the increasing scarcity of water in the region. Most parts of the Middle East are among the most arid in the world, and in many Middle Eastern countries rainfall levels tend to be irregular, localized, and unpredictable. Of all the countries of the region, only Iran, Turkey, and Lebanon have adequate rainfall and other water resources to meet their present and future needs, including those of agriculture. More than half the countries of the Middle East, however, are currently facing serious water shortages.[22] Per capita water supplies are projected to decline throughout the region over the next two decades or so, and, as table 16

Table 16. Per Capita Water Availability and the Ratio of Supply and Demand in the Middle East

Country	Per Capita Water Availability 1990 (m^3 per person per year)	Projected per Capita Water Availability, 2025 (m^3 per person per year)	Water Withdrawal as % of Renewable Supplies
Qatar	60	20	174
UAE	190	110	140
Yemen	240	80	135
Jordan	260	80	110
Israel	470	310	110
Saudi Arabia	160	50	106
Kuwait	< 10	< 10	> 100
Bahrain	< 10	< 10	> 100
Egypt	1,070	620	97
Iraq	5,500	n.a.	43
Iran	2,080	960	39
Oman	1,330	470	22
Lebanon	1,600	960	16
Syria	610	n.a.	9
Turkey	3,520	n.a.	8

SOURCE: Mostafa Dolatyar and Tim Gray, *Water Politics in the Middle East: A Context for Conflict or Cooperation?* (New York: Macmillan, 2000), p. 81.

demonstrates, many Middle Eastern countries are already withdrawing a greater percentage of water from renewable supplies than is being replenished. The costs of water supply and sanitation are estimated to be higher in the Middle East than in any other part of the world, being twice over those in North America and five times those in Southeast Asia. It is estimated that by 2025 Middle Eastern countries will need four times as much water as they now have available in their indigenous natural resources.[23]

Regarding the role and importance of water in the future of the Middle East, two factors must be kept in mind. First, extremely high rates of population growth and inefficient water usage practices have aggravated and will continue to aggravate the scarcity of water supplies caused by the Middle East's climate. Some of the main causes and consequences of rapid population growth in the Middle East were discussed in the last section.

Further exacerbating the problems of water scarcity (as well as poor water quality) is the inadequate management of what little is available. Inefficient use of water for irrigation and industrial purposes is widespread throughout the Middle East. As one observer has noted, "Great quantities of water are lost through inefficient irrigation systems such as flood irrigation of fields, unlined or uncovered canals, and evaporation from reservoirs behind dams. Pollution from agriculture, including fertilizer and pesticide runoffs as well as increased salts, added to increasing amounts of industrial and toxic waste and urban pollutants, combine to lower the quality of water for countries downstream . . . increasing their costs, and provoke dissatisfaction and frustration, . . . creating irritations that can lead to conflicts."[24]

A second factor to consider is that except for the three countries of Lebanon, Turkey, and Iran, countries of the Middle East are dependent on exogenous sources of water. Apart from rainfall, whose levels are almost uniformly low throughout the region, there are two major sources of freshwater in the Middle East, namely rivers and aquifers (underground water formations). Both of these sources, especially rivers, traverse international boundaries, with one country having the ability to significantly influence the flow of water into neighboring countries.

The significance of water is particularly magnified in Israel and the Occupied Territories, where close geographic locations and contending claims to the same pieces of land have given a special urgency to scarcity of water resources. This importance is far greater than there is room here to discuss. Briefly, however, a couple of points merit mentioning. Within the Occupied Territories, the average aggregate per capita water consumption for Jewish settlements ranges between 90 and 120 cubic meters, whereas for Palestinians it is 25 to 35 cubic meters. Israeli authorities do not allow Palestinians to dig new wells. Israeli settlers and military authorities, however, are allowed to dig new wells, which Palestinians claim are often deeper than existing ones and thus dry up Palestinian wells. Also, Israelis in general and Israeli settlers in particular pay a much lower price for water than do Palestinians in the Occupied Territories.[25] Altogether, some 40 to 50 percent of Israel's water is estimated to come from aquifers in the West Bank and Gaza, thus adding to the practical needs of the Jewish state to hold on to biblical "Judea and Samaria."[26] Another 20 percent of Israel's water supply is estimated to come from the Golan Heights. Combined, Israel receives some two-thirds of its water from the areas it occupied in 1967.[27]

The potential for international hostilities and cross-border conflicts over water is greatest, however, along the region's three major river basins, the Tigris-Euphrates, the Nile, and the Jordan. The Tigris and Euphrates rivers originate in Turkey and flow down to Syria (only a small portion of the Tigris goes through Syria) and then Iraq, forming the Shatt al-Arab in the south and then pouring into the Persian Gulf. Up until the 1960s, all three countries shared the water resources without tension. However, in the 1960s and especially the 1970s, Syria and Turkey began exploiting water from the Euphrates in significant amounts, resulting in the initiation of a series of trilateral agreements among the countries. The easing of tensions did not last long, however, as in the mid-1980s Turkey announced the initiation of an ambitious plan to build twenty-two dams on the Euphrates under a scheme called the Southeast Anatolian Development Project (Turkish acronym GAP). If and when the GAP is completed, it is estimated to reduce the river's flow to Syria by some 30 to 50 percent over the next fifty years.[28]

As for the Nile basin, the stakes are especially high for Egypt, which is completely dependent on the Nile and whose population continues to grow at alarming rates. Over 95 percent of Egypt's agricultural production is from irrigated land, but about 85 percent of the flow of the Nile into Egypt originates in the Ethiopian plateau.[29] Ten states share the Nile or one of its two main tributaries—the Blue Nile and the White Nile—and chronic political instability in these states, especially in Ethiopia and the Sudan, is of particular concern to Egypt. Despite long-standing plans, Ethiopia has not been able to attract sufficient international investments and technical knowledge to fully exploit the Blue Nile's potential, a failure about which Egypt has been quite happy so far. However, if Ethiopia's domestic turmoil gives way to political stability and then economic development, the water situation for Egypt and the other countries concerned could greatly change for the worse.[30]

Because of its strategic location and the long history of open hostilities among the countries that share its water, the Jordan River has received the most attention as a source of future conflict over water in the Middle East, even though it is actually more of a rivulet than a river in the proper sense of the word. In fact, the average intact flow of the Jordan River is less than 2 percent of the Nile, 5 percent of the Euphrates, and slightly more than 3 percent of the Tigris.[31] The river is also subject to great seasonal fluctuations, carrying as much as 40 percent of its total annual flow in winter months and as little as 3 to 4 percent in the summer.[32] From 1987 to 1991, the area surrounding the river experienced a severe drought that further reduced its annual discharge. Added to this were the adverse consequences of a series of development projects Syria started in the late 1980s in the upper Yarmuk River, a major tributary of the Jordan River, which in turn increased salinity in the Jordan and lowered water levels in the Dead Sea.[33]

The potential for conflict over the waters of the Jordan River has been reduced in recent years since the signing of the Jordanian-Israeli peace treaty in October 1994, a major aspect of which revolved around terms for sharing the river.[34] Israel's withdrawal from southern Lebanon in 2000 reduced previous water tensions between Israel and Lebanon as well, this time over the Litani River. Nevertheless, tensions over the water-rich Golan Heights and the Yarmuk River continue between Israel and Syria.

The ongoing conflict between Syria and Israel over the Golan Heights tells us much about the larger issue of water in the Middle East. Throughout the region, water resources have been an afterthought in justifying larger military objectives and territorial ambitions once the conquests had already taken place. They have constituted additional benefits accrued to victorious parties, especially Israel, rather than serving as the original catalyst for a conflict. Rich underground water deposits, such as the aquifers in the West Bank, Gaza, and the Golan Heights, or fertile river basins, such as the land along the Nile, the Jordan, and the Tigris and Euphrates Rivers, have made the stakes higher in conflicts whose genesis had little to do with water. The harsh rhetoric of many of the warring parties, who often happen to share a river, has muddled the distinction between *water scarcity* and *water conflict*. The crisis facing the Middle East today is one of water scarcity, not necessarily one of impending water conflict.

In fact, given the Middle East's long history of aridity and scarce water resources, the region has a rich tradition of cooperation rather than conflict over water. Such a cooperative tradition, along with the calculated benefits of cooperation compared to the costs of conflict, is likely to foster future agreements and further cooperation among the contending parties. In the words of two observers of the issue: "Middle Eastern water problems are not inherently different from those in other parts of the globe, and the doom-laden hypotheses which represent the dominant view in the literature of hydropolitics are greatly exaggerated. . . . Far from leading to military conflict, increasing water scarcity will concentrate the minds of those involved to find sustainable solutions and, to achieve this goal, the concerned parties will increasingly resort to coordinated, cooperative, and conciliatory arrangements."[35]

Nevertheless, although the potential for international wars over water is not that great, the crisis of water scarcity continues, and it is projected to get more acute in the future as population levels rise and available freshwater sources decline. Numerous academic and practical solutions have been proposed, some more realistic and feasible than others.[36] Each country has already embarked on ambitious water conservation schemes of its own, but it is unclear whether such measures are enough to address existing or impending scarcities. Averting a real crisis requires progress on a number of fronts, from lowering population growth rates to making water usage more efficient and ensuring more equitable access to all concerned. These are weighty tasks. The challenge lies in performing them.

On a trip to Iran in 2003, I was struck by the pervasive gloom I witnessed among people of all colors, rich and poor, urban and rural. Although my trip took place some fifteen years after the end of the Iran-Iraq War, the awful memory of that bloody and devastating conflict still cast a dark shadow over many people. The wars in Iraq and Afghanistan and continued tensions between Iran, Israel, and the United States also weighed heavily on people's minds. But most of the complaints I heard had to do with people's more immediate circumstances: high prices, traffic, overcrowded cities and unaffordable housing, unemployment, air pollution, petty restrictions, arbitrary officials and unpredictable government policies, unavailability of certain goods and services, lack of real democracy, and so on. Although this was in Tehran, I could have been talking to an average person almost anywhere in the Middle East, whether in Cairo or Tripoli, Damascus or Amman. After a while, I found the experience so dispiriting that I stopped asking people what issues concerned them the most.

At least among a significant segment of the population, hopelessness and despair abound. Add to this the crushing poverty that pervades most urban centers of the Middle East, along with unresponsive and autocratic rulers, and a fertile breeding ground emerges for extremist ideologies and movements. Political groups that preach and practice the most brutal forms of violence—Hamas and the Islamic Jihad in Palestine, the Gama'a in Egypt, the former Islamic Salvation Front in Algeria, and the few but lethal sympathizers of Osama bin Laden across the region—are a product of, and are in turn fueled by, the dire socioeconomic and political predicaments of their larger environments. For these and other similar groups, the potential pool of recruits is endless. The less a person has to look forward to in this life, the more likely it is that he or she will fall for promises of eternal glory in the afterlife. That such promises are based on blatant corruptions of Islamic precepts matters little to those who are desperate for quick remedies. The yearning for immediate action leaves little room for reasoned discourse over Islam or any other ideology. The realities are harsh, and state terror is ever-present. The best solution, the *only* solution, is to strike hard at the state or, better yet, at its powerful patron, the United States.

Suicide bombers, plane hijackers, and self-described holy warriors do not come out of thin air. Nor are they, despite what some in the West believe, manifestations of an ongoing or impending "clash of civilizations."[37] And again, despite what some in the West think, they do not represent supposedly innate violent tendencies within Islam.[38] For a fringe but vocal minority in the Middle East, terror has become the only viable outlet. It has become an instrument of both political expression and self-actualization. The reason it often assumes an Islamic tinge is that the enemy—that is, the state—is secular and non-Islamic. The politicization of Islam dates back to the 1960s and 1970s, when one secular leader after another turned out to be corrupt, repressive, and incompetent. The state's continued repression of Islam, as in Egypt and Algeria, or its shameless manipulation of the religion, as in Saudi Arabia, has only further inflamed those whose religious sensibilities are offended. These individuals have in turn manipulated Islam for their own purposes, this time toward violent, antistate ends.

The manifestations of political violence in the Middle East are often both dramatic and tragic. And as demonstrated by the attacks on the World Trade Center in New York City and the Pentagon in Washington, D.C., on September 11, 2001, they now have the potential to spill over into other parts of the world. But the problems that gave rise to the violence in the first place are rooted deep in the politics and economies of the region. Waging "war on terrorism" must entail addressing the economic and political problems that give rise to the likes of Osama bin Laden. Unleashing the full force of the state to combat terrorism, and even worse the full might of the American army, is only likely to perpetuate the cycle of violence.

But the prognosis is not all gloomy. Amid the despair, there are numerous signs of hope and a better future. One of the last conversations I had in Iran was with a group of young university students whose thoughts made the biggest impression on me. "Our parents' and our generations have sacrificed a lot and have suffered a great deal," they all agreed, "but the outlook for future generations is much brighter." They pointed to their own skills and priorities, to their sense of empowerment and their accomplishments, and to larger trends internationally and domestically that made them optimistic. They impressed upon me that the wars and conflicts of the past and the limitations of today are not as important as the potentialities of tomorrow. Again, I felt as if I could be having this conversation anywhere in the Middle East.

The political history of the Middle East has indeed been tormented and painful. And the challenges of the future are both formidable and numerous. But it does appear that the horrors of the past—though still possible to resurrect—are less and less likely to reemerge in the future. A quick glance at some of the challenges facing the region today and in the past is quite revealing. In the 1920s and 1930s, the primary task facing the elites and masses of the Middle East was to build viable territorial and political entities out of the ashes of the Ottoman Empire or the carvings of European colonial powers. In the 1940s, 1950s, and 1960s, the region was torn by the forces of nationalism, military ascension and conquest, exile, defeat, and subjugation. The 1970s and 1980s brought more wars and chaos, capped by the devastation of the Second Gulf War in 1990–91. The forces and dynamics that gave rise to these bloody conflicts have not fully died down. Also, as long as the occupation of Palestinian territories by Israel continues and central authority has not been established in postinvasion Iraq and Afghanistan, there is bound to be more violence and bloodshed. But the challenges facing the Middle East today are qualitatively different from those of the past. The great problems today concern the environment, sustainable economic development, scientific progress, global economic competition, and overall quality of life. These are, of course, major challenges, and the ability or willingness of the current slate of Middle Eastern policy makers to adequately address them is far from certain. But they are unlikely to directly or even indirectly cause international wars and bloodshed. If anything, they may foster greater regionwide cooperation and consensus. The future is not nearly as bleak as the past. In fact, it looks much brighter.

Notes

INTRODUCTION

1. Fouad Ajami, *The Dream Palace of the Arabs: A Generation's Odyssey* (New York: Pantheon Books, 1998), p. 80.

1. FROM ISLAM TO THE GREAT WAR

1. Ira Lapidus, *A History of Islamic Societies* (New York: Cambridge University Press, 1988), p. 7.

2. In the southern city of Mecca, where Islam first appeared, the three pagan goddesses of Lat, Manat, and Uzza would later become sources of great controversy in Islamic history, inspiring, in the late twentieth century, a controversial novel entitled *The Satanic Verses* by Salman Rushdie (New York: Viking Books, 1989).

3. While viewing themselves as the defenders of Christianity in the East, the Byzantines are said to have held a more tolerant attitude toward Muslims and other "infidels" than their European co-religionists further west. Sir Steven Runciman, *The Fall of Constantinople, 1453* (New York: Cambridge University Press, 1965), p. 2.

4. Albert Hourani, *A History of the Arab Peoples* (Cambridge, MA: Belknap Press, 1991), p. 128. For more on markets and trade in the ancient Middle East, see Morris Silver, *Economic Structures of the Ancient Near East* (London: Croom Helm, 1985), especially chs. 5 and 6.

5. Fred M. Donner, "Muhammad and the Caliphate: Political History of the Islamic Empire up to the Mongol Conquest," in *The Oxford History of Islam*, ed. John Esposito (New York: Oxford University Press, 1999), p. 13.

6. The dog had been domesticated as early as 9000 B.C. The specific animals domesticated during the Neolithic revolution included the sheep, pig, and cow.

7. Archeological evidence from ancient Mesopotamia (modern-day Iraq) suggests that cities were first established and grew sometime between 3100 and 2800 B.C. Daniel Snell, *Life in the Ancient Near East, 3100–332 B.C.E.*

393

(New Haven, CT: Yale University Press, 1997), p. 19. Jericho, first a village and now a city in present-day Palestine, was the earliest continually occupied settlement, dating from 8000 B.C. to the present.

8. Hourani, *History of the Arab Peoples*, p. 104.

9. For the role of irrigation in the rise of states, see Karl Wittfogel, "Hydraulic Civilizations," in *Man's Role in Changing the Face of the Earth*, ed. William Thomas (Chicago: University of Chicago Press, 1956), pp. 152–64; Theodore Downing and McGuire Gibson, eds., *Irrigation's Impact on Society* (Tucson: University of Arizona Press, 1974); and Walter Coward, ed., *Irrigation and Agricultural Development in Asia: Perspectives from the Social Sciences* (Ithaca, NY: Cornell University Press, 1980).

10. Works on the geography of the Middle East are few and far between. For three of the better examples, see Colbert C. Held, *Middle East Patterns: Places, Peoples, and Politics*, 2nd ed. (Boulder, CO: Westview Press, 1994); Alasdair Drysdale and Gerald Blake, *The Middle East and North Africa: A Political Geography* (New York: Oxford University Press, 1985); and Graham Chapman and Kathleen Baker, eds., *The Changing Geography of Africa and the Middle East* (London: Routledge, 1992).

11. Held, *Middle East Patterns*, pp. 160–61.

12. Ibid., pp. 384, 404.

13. World Bank, *World Development Indicators 1997* (Washington, DC: World Bank, 1997), pp. 114–16.

14. United Nations Development Program, *Arab Human Development Report 2002; Creating Opportunities for Future Generations* (New York: United Nations Development Program, 2002), p. 46. Given increased rates of rural-urban migration in recent decades across the Middle East, as in much of the rest of the developing world, it is increasingly difficult to draw cultural, and in some respects spatial, distinctions between the city and the countryside. Therefore, even in Middle Eastern countries with large urban-based populations—Iran at 67 percent, Iraq at 68 percent, Jordan at 79 percent, and Turkey at 66 percent—growth in the number of urban residents does not necessarily imply assimilation into the urban mainstream, or what social scientists generally refer to as "urbanization." Data collected from Barry Truner, ed., *The Statesman's Yearbook, 2009* (New York: Palgrave Macmillan, 2008).

15. Snell, *Life in the Ancient Near East*, p. 148.

16. Such works are too numerous to mention individually here, but some of the more notable ones are Hourani, *History of the Arab Peoples*; Lapidus, *History of Islamic Societies*; Esposito, *Oxford History of Islam*; and Arthur Goldschmidt, Jr., *A Concise History of the Middle East*, 6th ed. (Boulder, CO: Westview Press, 1999).

17. What follows is a brief account of Prophet Muhammad's life based on traditional narratives. Problems facing historians writing on the life of the Prophet are the lack of original, contemporary documentation and the interpretative nature of many later accounts of his life. See Donner, "Muhammad and the Caliphate," pp. 5–6. For a detailed account of the Prophet's life based

on early Islamic sources, see Martin Lings, *Muhammad: His Life Based on the Earliest Sources* (Cambridge: Islamic Text Society, 1995).

18. See Richard Bulliet, *The Camel and the Wheel* (Cambridge, MA: Harvard University Press, 1975), pp. 105–6.

19. Maxime Rodinson, *Muhammad* (New York: Pantheon Books, 1980), pp. 103–5.

20. See ibid., pp. 106–7.

21. Goldschmidt's insight into the *hijrah* is worth repeating here: "Rather than a 'flight,' as some have referred to it, the *hijrah* was a carefully planned maneuver by Muhammad in response to an invitation by the citizens of Yathrib. It enabled him to unite his followers as a community, as a nation. . . . From then on, Muhammad was both a prophet and a lawgiver, both a religious and a political leader." Goldschmidt, *Concise History*, pp. 29–30.

22. Hourani, *History of the Arab Peoples*, p. 17.

23. Marshall G. S. Hodgson, *The Venture of Islam*, vol. 1, *The Classical Age of Islam* (Chicago: University of Chicago Press, 1974), p. 183.

24. Quoted in Rafiq Zakaria, *Muhammad and the Quran* (New York: Penguin Books, 1991), p. 30.

25. Fazlur Rahman, *Islam*, 2nd ed. (Chicago: University of Chicago Press, 1979), p. 69.

26. Ibid., p. 68.

27. Ibid., p. 101. Emphasis in original.

28. See Zakaria, *Muhammad and the Quran*, pp. 395–400.

29. For a chronological arrangement of the Quran, see Fathi Osman, *Concepts from the Quran: A Topical Reading* (Los Angeles: MVI Publications, 1997).

30. Michael Rogers, *The Spread of Islam* (New York: Elsevier, 1976), pp. 24–25.

31. See Wilferd Madelung, *The Succession to Muhammad: A Study of the Early Caliphate* (New York: Cambridge University Press, 1997), especially pp. 1–27.

32. Lapidus, *History of Islamic Societies*, pp. 56–57.

33. S. Husain Jafri, *Origins and Early Development of Shi'a Islam* (London: Longman, 1979), p. 92.

34. G. E. Von Grunebaum, *Classical Islam: A History, 600–1258*, trans. Katherine Watson (London: George Allen and Unwin, 1970), p. 74.

35. The *mawali* (literally, clients) were foreigners who had converted to Islam. Since their foreign birth did not allow them to be incorporated into the kinship-based society of Arabs, they had to be voluntarily placed into the protection of a clan, thereby becoming their "client." For the most part, the *mawali* were treated as second-class citizens. See Jamil Ahmad Chaudry, "Muslims and Mawali," *Hamdard Islamicus* 27 (Winter 1994): 85–98.

36. Adam Mez, *The Renaissance of Islam*, trans. Salahuddin Khuda Bukhsh and D. S. Margoliouth (London: Luzac, 1937), p. 51.

37. Von Grunebaum, *Classical Islam*, p. 81.

38. Goldschmidt, *Concise History*, p. 67.

39. For a fascinating account of life in the city and in the royal court at the time, see G. Le Strange, *Baghdad during the Abbasid Caliphate, from Contemporary Arabic and Persian Sources* (Oxford: Clarendon Press, 1924).

40. Von Grunebaum, *Classical Islam*, p. 85. An insightful account of Napoleon's Egyptian campaign is presented by Juan Cole in *Napoleon's Egypt: Invading the Middle East* (New York: Palgrave Macmillan, 2007).

41. See, for example, Paula Sanders, *Ritual, Politics, and the City in Fatimid Cairo* (Albany: SUNY Press, 1994); Janet Abu-Lughod, *Cairo: 1001 Years of the City Victorious* (Princeton, NJ: Princeton University Press, 1971), pp. 13–36; and Desmond Steward, *Great Cairo: Mother of the World* (London: Rupert Hart-Davis, 1969), pp. 63–84.

42. Goldschmidt, *Concise History*, p. 86.

43. Lapidus, *History of Islamic Societies*, p. 279.

44. Ibid., p. 145.

45. Lord Kinross, *The Ottoman Centuries: The Rise and Fall of the Turkish Empire* (New York: William Morrow, 1977), p. 42.

46. Ira Lapidus, "Sultanates and Gunpowder Empires: The Middle East," in Esposito, *Oxford History of Islam*, p. 377.

47. Ibid.

48. Goldschmidt, *Concise History*, pp. 133–34.

49. Andrew Wheatcroft, *The Ottomans: Dissolving Images* (London: Penguin Books, 1995), p. 65.

50. Ibid.

51. Kinross, *Ottoman Centuries*, p. 457.

52. See Bernard Lewis, *The Emergence of Modern Turkey*, 2nd ed. (New York: Oxford University Press, 1968), ch. 4.

53. Hourani, *History of the Arab Peoples*, pp. 258–59.

54. Wheatcroft, *Ottomans*, p. 69.

55. Kinross, *Ottoman Centuries*, p. 418.

56. Lapidus, *History of Islamic Societies*, p. 598.

57. Quoted in Rudolph Peters, "Religious Attitudes towards Modernization in the Ottoman Empire: A Nineteenth Century Pious Text on Steamships, Factories and the Telegraph," *Die Welt des Islams* 26 (1986): 95.

58. See Robin Okey, *The Habsburg Monarchy: From Enlightenment to Eclipse* (New York: St. Martin's Press, 2001).

59. Lewis, *Emergence of Modern Turkey*, pp. 218–19.

60. Kinross tends to downplay the extent of the "Armenian genocide" by putting the number of dead at half a million. Most other historians, however, including Lewis, put the number of those who perished at one and a half million. See Kinross, *Ottoman Centuries*, p. 607, and Lewis, *Emergence of Modern Turkey*, p. 356.

61. As Lewis puts it, the Young Turks may have given Istanbul drains, but they did not give Turkey a constitutional government. Lewis, *Emergence of Modern Turkey*, p. 228.

62. Kinross, *Ottoman Centuries,* p. 608.

63. Sufism dates back to the ninth century and arose as a result of mystical influences predating Islam as well as the mystical reading of the Quran (what is called *istinbad*). Raymond Nicholson, *The Mystics of Islam* (1914; repr., London: Arkana, 1989), pp. 23–24.

64. Said Amir Arjomand, *The Shadow of God and the Hidden Imam: Religion, Political Order, and Societal Change in Shi'ite Iran from the Beginning to 1890* (Chicago: University of Chicago Press, 1984), p. 106.

65. Haneda has compiled a list of some seventy principal religious buildings that the Safavid constructed in Esfahan. See Masashi Haneda, "The Character of the Urbanization of Isfahan in the Later Safavid Period," in *Safavid Persia,* ed. Charles Melville (London: I. B. Tauris, 1996), pp. 378–82.

66. Lapidus, "Sultanates and Gunpowder Empires," p. 366.

67. Willem Floor, *Safavid Government Institutions* (Costa Mesa, CA: Mazda, 2001), p. 1.

68. Shah Abbas II's (r. 1642–66) reported fondness for wine and dancing girls, for example, did not help win him favors with the *ulama.* See Arjomand, *Shadow of God,* p. 200.

69. Lapidus, "Sultanates and Gunpowder Empires," p. 370.

70. Ann K. S. Lambton, *Qajar Persia: Eleven Studies* (London: I. B. Tauris, 1987), p. 96.

71. Rouhollah K. Ramazani, *The Foreign Policy of Iran, 1500 to 1941* (Charlottesville: University of Virginia Press, 1966), pp. 66–67.

72. Ishtiaq Ahmad, *Anglo-Iranian Relations, 1905–1919* (Bombay: Asia Publishing House, 1975), p. 48.

73. Hamid Algar, *Religion and State in Iran, 1785–1906: The Role of the Ulama in the Qajar Period* (Berkeley: University of California Press, 1969), p. 242.

74. Lambton, *Qajar Persia,* pp. 321–22.

2. FROM TERRITORIES TO INDEPENDENT STATES

1. Ann Williams, *Britain and France in the Middle East and North Africa, 1914–1967* (New York: Macmillan, 1968), p. 4.

2. Roger Adelson, *London and the Invention of the Middle East: Money, Power, and War, 1902–1922* (New Haven, CT: Yale University Press, 1995), p. 7.

3. Elie Kedourie, *England and the Middle East: The Destruction of the Ottoman Empire, 1914–1921* (London: Mansell, 1987), p. 15.

4. Williams, *Britain and France,* p. 6.

5. J. C. Hurewitz, *Diplomacy in the Near and Middle East: A Documentary Record,* vol. 1, *1535–1914* (Princeton, NJ: D. Van Nostrand, 1956), p. 264.

6. Jukka Nevakivi, *Britain, France, and the Middle East, 1914–1920* (London: Athlone, 1969), p. 5.

7. The Ottomans had already lost Egypt, first to the ambitious Muhammad Ali and then to the British in 1882.

8. M. E. Yapp, *The Making of the Modern Middle East, 1792–1923* (London: Longman, 1987), p. 301.

9. More specifically, Hussein claimed to be from the same Hashemite clan of the Quraysh as the Prophet had been. Despite their eventual eclipse in the Hijaz, the Hashemites later became powerful in Jordan, where they still remain the ruling family.

10. The territorial promises contained in the Hussein-McMahon Correspondence, which later came to be called the "Damascus Protocol," can be found in Randall Baker, *King Husain and the Kingdom of Hejaz* (New York: Oleander, 1979), p. 65.

11. On popular portrayals of T. E. Lawrence, the historian Arthur Goldschmidt has said it best: "I will not deny that Lawrence's *Seven Pillars of Wisdom* is a book worth reading or that *Lawrence of Arabia* is a great film. But neither one is history." Arthur Goldschmidt, Jr., *A Concise History of the Middle East*, 6th ed. (Boulder, CO: Westview Press, 1999), p. 183.

12. Hurewitz, *Diplomacy*, p. 19.

13. Quoted in Philip Graves, *Memoirs of King Abdullah of Transjordan* (London: Jonathan Cape, 1951), p. 203.

14. The decision to change the country's name from Transjordan to Jordan was adopted, following the country's independence, in the same parliamentary session (on May 22, 1946) that changed Abdullah's official title from emir (i.e., commander) to king. Kamal Salibi, *The Modern History of Jordan* (London: I. B. Tauris, 1993), p. 153.

15. Adelson, *London*, pp. 149–50.

16. Quoted in Doreen Ingrams, *Palestine Papers, 1917–1922: Seeds of Conflict* (London: John Murray, 1972), p. 18. For a full treatment of the declaration, see Leonard Stein, *The Balfour Declaration* (New York: Simon and Schuster, 1961), especially pp. 543–56.

17. Yapp, *Making of the Modern Middle East*, pp. 290–91.

18. Quoted in Adelson, *London*, p. 151.

19. Sykes's commitment to the Zionist cause actually sprang from his fervent desire to keep the French out of Palestine. See Stein, *Balfour Declaration*, pp. 233–39.

20. Quoted in Peter Mansfield, *The Ottoman Empire and Its Successors* (New York: Macmillan, 1973), p. 50.

21. Quoted in Joshua Baylson, *Territorial Allocation by Imperial Rivalry: The Human Legacy in the Near East* (Chicago: University of Chicago, Department of Geography, 1987), p. 104.

22. Yapp, *Making of the Modern Middle East*, pp. 335–36.

23. Ibid., pp. 329–30.

24. Not surprisingly, Churchill's views on the matter are somewhat different. In his memoirs he writes: "I never felt that the Arab countries had had anything from us but fair play. To Britain, and Britain alone, they owed their very existence as nations. We created them; British money and British advisers set the pace of their advance; British arms protected them." Winston

Churchill, *Memoirs of the Second World War* (Boston: Houghton Mifflin, 1959), p. 1014.

25. Baylson, *Territorial Allocation*, p. 106.

26. Eliezer Tauber, *The Formation of Modern Syria and Iraq* (London: Frank Cass, 1995), p. 67.

27. According to Baylson, Transjordan served two purposes for the British: it provided a buffer against Syria, and it facilitated the construction of a railway line from the Mediterranean to India through Iraq. Baylson, *Territorial Allocation*, p. 108.

28. In the words of a British cabinet minister at the time, "[I]t is now *the Canal and India;* there is no such thing now to us as India alone. India is any number of cyphers; but the Canal is the unit that makes these cyphers valuable" (emphasis in original). Quoted in Yapp, *Making of the Modern Middle East*, p. 226.

29. Yapp, *Making of the Modern Middle East*, p. 229.

30. Albert Hourani, *A History of the Arab Peoples* (Cambridge, MA: Belknap Press, 1991), p. 228.

31. Charles-André Julien, *History of North Africa: Tunisia, Algeria, Morocco,* trans. John Petrie (New York: Frederick A. Praeger, 1970), p. 270.

32. For an example of the first view, see Robin Bidwell, *Morocco under Colonial Rule: French Administration of Tribal Areas, 1912–1956* (London: Frank Cass, 1973), p. 33; for an example of the second, see C. R. Pennell, *Morocco since 1830: A History* (New York: NYU Press, 2000), p. 28.

33. Quoted in John Ruedy, *Modern Algeria: The Origins and Development of a Nation* (Bloomington: Indiana University Press, 1992), p. 50.

34. Ibid.

35. Lisa Anderson, *The State and Social Transformation in Tunisia and Libya, 1830–1980* (Princeton, NJ: Princeton University Press, 1986), p. 186.

36. Ali Abdullatif Ahmida, *The Making of Modern Libya: State Formation, Colonization, and Resistance, 1830–1932* (Albany: SUNY Press, 1994), p. 104.

37. S. N. Eisenstadt, "The Kemalist Regime and Modernization: Some Comparative and Analytical Remarks," in *Atatürk and the Modernization of Turkey,* ed. Jacob Landau (Boulder, CO: Westview Press, 1984), pp. 7–9. As will be seen shortly, "revolutionism," the translation for Atatürk's *inkilabçilik,* was also one of the six "arrows" or principles on which the Kemalist ideology was based.

38. Paul Dumont, "The Origins of the Kemalist Ideology," in Landau, *Atatürk,* p. 35.

39. See Niyazi Berkes, *The Development of Secularism in Turkey* (Montreal: McGill University Press, 1964), pp. 192–93.

40. Quoted in Bernard Lewis, *The Emergence of Modern Turkey,* 2nd ed. (New York: Oxford University Press, 1968), p. 257.

41. Ibid., p. 353.

42. Ibid., p. 354.

43. Feroz Ahmad, *The Making of Modern Turkey* (London: Routledge, 1993), pp. 61–63.

44. Ibid., p. 58.

45. Lewis, *Emergence of Modern Turkey*, pp. 370–71.

46. Quoted in Andrew Mango, *Atatürk* (Woodstock, NY: Overlook Press, 2000), p. 463.

47. This was in contrast to similar prohibitions imposed on the veil at about the same time in Iran and Afghanistan. On hearing about the prohibition of veiling in Afghanistan, Kemal is said to have predicted the overthrow of the country's King Amanullah as a result. Ahmad, *Making of Modern Turkey*, p. 87.

48. Quoted in Lewis, *Emergence of Modern Turkey*, p. 278.

49. Ibid., p. 289.

50. Ahmad, *Making of Modern Turkey*, p. 97.

51. Ibid., p. 98.

52. Lord Kinross, *Ataturk: A Biography of Mustafa Kemal, Father of Modern Turkey* (New York: William Morrow, 1965), pp. 539–40.

53. *Khan* is a term of respect, the closest translation for which is "Lord," although it does not necessarily have the latter's feudal connotation.

54. One of the most lucid and accessible accounts of this time period can be found in Ervand Abrahamian's *Iran between Two Revolutions* (Princeton, NJ: Princeton University Press, 1982), especially pp. 92–120.

55. Donald Wilber, *Riza Shah Pahlavi: The Resurrection and Reconstruction of Iran, 1878–1944* (Hicksville, NY: Exposition Press, 1975), p. 75.

56. The poetry of Mirza Abolqassem Aref Qazvini, who had earlier supported the constitutionalist cause, is most representative. An interesting example reads, in part:

> Now that the banner of republic comes from afar,
> Under its shadow, life will be blessed.
>
> After the calamity of Qajar comes the festival of the republic.
> Be certain that today is the best of times.
>
> I'm happy that destiny's hand placed in the royal court
> The light of dynasty that the shah extinguished.
>
> With one look toward Europe the shah lost his will,
> In this costly gamble losing his throne.
>
> Say a dying prayer for dynasty, Aref.
> God forgive it for its evil harms.
>
> It ruined our country all throughout.
> From now on the country will prosper.
>
> Whoever holds the republic's reins,
> There will always be noble men among the people.
>
> > Mirza Abolqassem Aref Qazvini, *Koliyyat-e Divan*
> > [Complete works] (Tehran: Chapp-e Jadid,
> > 1357/1978), p. 283.

57. Shahrough Akhavi, *Religion and Politics in Contemporary Iran: Clergy-State Relations in the Pahlavi Period* (Albany: SUNY Press, 1980), pp. 28–29.

58. Abrahamian, *Iran between Two Revolutions*, p. 135.

59. Reza Khan is said not to have been certain of the precise meaning of Pahlavi for a number of years after adopting it as his last name, and anecdotal evidence suggests he had thought about choosing Pahlavan (literally, champion) instead. Wilber, *Riza Shah Pahlavi*, p. 229.

60. Ibid., pp. 157–58.

61. Abrahamian, *Iran between Two Revolutions*, p. 141.

62. Homa Katouzian, *The Political Economy of Modern Iran, 1926–1979* (New York: NYU Press, 1981), p. 116.

63. Wilber, *Riza Shah Pahlavi*, p. 148.

64. Katouzian, *Political Economy of Modern Iran*, p. 113.

65. Abrahamian, *Iran between Two Revolutions*, pp. 136–37.

66. The new civil code exemplified the less sweeping nature of state-sponsored social change in Iran as compared to Turkey; it continued to retain a number of *sharia* features, especially with regard to inheritance and family relations.

67. Akhavi, *Religion and Politics*, p. 38.

68. This restriction, which had the ironic effect of making many women prisoners in their own homes, was lifted in 1941.

69. Wilber, *Riza Shah Pahlavi*, p. 185.

70. Katouzian, *Political Economy of Modern Iran*, pp. 116–17.

71. Abrahamian, *Iran between Two Revolutions*, pp. 162–63.

72. Wilber, *Riza Shah Pahlavi*, p. 244.

73. Two of these financial experts were William Morgan Shuster and Arthur C. Millspaugh, who later published their memoirs. See William M. Shuster, *The Strangling of Persia* (New York: Greenwood, 1939), and Arthur C. Millspaugh, *The American Task in Persia* (New York: Century, 1925).

74. Wilber estimates the total number of Germans in Iran at this time, including their dependents, at around 1,200 to 2,000. Wilber, *Riza Shah Pahlavi*, p. 201.

75. Frederick Anscombe, *The Ottoman Gulf: The Creation of Kuwait, Saudi Arabia, and Qatar* (New York: Columbia University Press, 1997), pp. 143–44.

76. For such accounts, see Leslie McLoughlin, *Ibn Saud: Founder of a Kingdom* (New York: St. Martin's Press, 1993); Mohammed Almana, *Arabia Unified: A Portrait of Ibn Saud* (London: Hutchinson Benham, 1980); and Gary Troeller, *The Birth of Saudi Arabia: Britain and the Rise of the House of Sa'ud* (London: Frank Cass, 1976).

77. Almana, a sympathetic chronicler, records at least twenty-two battles fought by Abdel Aziz (b. 1880) between 1900 and his death in 1953. For details, see Almana, *Arabia Unified*, pp. 271–73.

78. Troeller, *Birth of Saudi Arabia*, pp. 83–91.

79. Almana, *Arabia Unified*, p. 218.

80. Ibid., p. 226.

81. Troeller, *Birth of Saudi Arabia*, p. 241.

82. Anthony Cave Brown, *Oil, God, and Gold: The Story of Aramco and the Saudi Kings* (Boston: Houghton Mifflin, 1999), p. 139.

83. "ARAMCO's operations in the oil town," writes the political scientist Robert Vitalis, "rested on a set of exclusionary practices and norms that were themselves legacies of earlier mining booms and market formation in the American West and Southwest. This was a system of privilege and inequality, which we know as Jim Crow in the United States, as Apartheid in South Africa, and as racism more generally." The company, Vitalis goes on to argue, forbade Saudis employees to live with their families and deported those American employees that sought to have contacts with nearby Arab families. Robert Vitalis, *America's Kingdom: Mythmaking on the Saudi Oil Frontier* (Stanford, CA: Stanford University Press, 2007), p. xiii.

84. Brown, *Oil, God, and Gold*, p. 150.

85. Ralph Braibanti, "Saudi Arabia in the Context of Political Development Theory," in *King Faisal and the Modernization of Saudi Arabia*, ed. Willard Beling (London: Croom Helm, 1980), p. 35.

3. THE AGE OF NATIONALISM

1. There are numerous anthologies on nationalism. Two of the more significant ones are John Hutchinson and Anthony Smith, eds., *Nationalism* (New York: Oxford University Press, 1994), and Geoff Eley and Ronald Grigor Suny, eds., *Becoming National: A Reader* (New York: Oxford University Press, 1996). A representative definition of nationalism in the current literature is offered by Guibernau: "By 'nationalism' I mean the sentiment of belonging to a community whose members identify with a set of symbols, beliefs and ways of life, and have the will to decide upon their common political destiny." Montserrat Guibernau, *Nationalisms: The Nation-State and Nationalism in the Twentieth Century* (Cambridge: Polity Press, 1996), p. 47.

2. Eley and Suny, *Becoming National*.

3. Benedict Anderson, *Imagined Communities* (London: Verso, 1991), p. 46.

4. Ernest Gellner, *Nations and Nationalism* (Ithaca, NY: Cornell University Press, 1983), p. 40.

5. Bernard Lewis, *The Emergence of Modern Turkey*, 2nd ed. (New York: Oxford University Press, 1968), p. 354. For more on issues related to the construction of national identities after World War I, see Aviel Roshwald, *Ethnic Nationalism and the Fall of Empires: Central Europe, Russia and the Middle East, 1914–1923* (London: Routledge, 2001).

6. Theodor Herzl, the founder of modern Zionism, was so determined to secure a national home for Jews that he considered locating it in Uganda. See Howard Sachar, *A History of Israel: From the Rise of Zionism to Our Time*, 2nd ed. (New York: Alfred A. Knopf, 1996), pp. 59–63.

7. Ella Shohat, "The Invention of the Mizrahim," *Journal of Palestine Studies* 29 (Autumn 1999): 8.

8. Rashid Khalidi, "The Origins of Arab Nationalism: Introduction," in *The Origins of Arab Nationalism*, ed. Rashid Khalidi et al. (New York: Columbia University Press, 1991), pp. ix–xii.

9. The case of the Hijaz illustrates the diverse nature of the beginnings of Arab nationalism. Whereas elsewhere Arabism rose in opposition to the centralizing policies of the Committee of Union and Progress, Hijazi nationalism was initially less a product of the confluence of an emerging nation and a state than a pragmatic tool employed by Hussein in achieving power. Mary C. Wilson, "The Hashemites, the Arab Revolt, and Arab Nationalism," in Khalidi et al., *Origins of Arab Nationalism*, p. 214.

10. Following Stephen Krasner, Fred Lawson attributes this shift to the emergence of "Westphalian sovereignty": nationalist leaders "came to recognize the territorial boundaries of one another's domains, and to reject as inherently illegitimate any attempt by surrounding leaderships to interfere in the internal affairs of their respective polities. . . . Nationalist leaders consciously and deliberately restricted their political ambitions to specific geographical zones, and stopped trying, or even claiming, to exercise authority over the Arab world as a whole." Fred H. Lawson, *Constructing International Relations in the Arab World* (Stanford, CA: Stanford University Press, 2006), p. 12.

11. An accessible collection in English of some nationalist writings of the period can be found in Sylvia Haim, ed., *Arab Nationalism: An Anthology* (Berkeley: University of California Press, 1962).

12. Mark Tessler, *A History of the Israeli-Palestinian Conflict* (Bloomington: Indiana University Press, 1994), p. 20.

13. Ibid.

14. The precise significance of the *haskala* for the development of the modern Zionist movement is a matter of scholarly debate. See, for example, Tessler, *History*, pp. 26–36; Sachar, *History of Israel*, pp. 8–10. More conservative Jews speak of it disparagingly, as did David Ben-Gurion, one of Zionism's most ardent advocates and the first prime minister of Israel, who wrote that because of the *haskala* "adherence to traditional forms of faith and law was shaken . . . [as] the upper strata of Jews started to use the languages of the secular rulers and began to imitate the dress, customs, and education of the Gentiles." David Ben-Gurion, *Israel: A Personal History* (New York: Funk and Wagnalls, 1971), p. 8.

15. In 1894, French authorities accused Captain Alfred Dreyfus of spying for Germany and court-martialed him; the charges were motivated largely by the accused's Jewish background. After some twelve years of heightened anti-Semitism, Dreyfus was eventually found innocent of the charges. See Michael Burns, *France and the Dreyfus Affair: A Documentary History* (New York: St. Martin's Press, 1999).

16. Extract from Theodor Herzl, *The Jewish State*, in Walter Laqueur and Barry Rubin, eds., *The Israeli-Arab Reader: A Documentary History of the Middle East Conflict*, 5th ed. (New York: Penguin Books, 1995), pp. 5–10.

17. Ibid., p. 10.

18. Quoted in ibid., pp. 10–11.

19. Tessler, *History*, p. 53.

20. Sachar, *History of Israel*, pp. 56–57.

21. Other incipient state institutions included the Palestine Foundation Fund, the Palestine Jewish Colonization Association, the Palestine Land Development Company, and the Jewish Colonization Association, to name a few.

22. Tessler, *History*, p. 59.

23. Samih K. Farsoun and Christina E. Zacharia, *Palestine and the Palestinians* (Boulder, CO: Westview Press, 1997), p. 78.

24. Tessler, *History*, p. 61.

25. Sachar, *History of Israel*, pp. 154–55.

26. Tessler, *History*, p. 208.

27. For more on the ideological formation of early Zionism, see David Vital, *Zionism: The Crucial Phase* (Oxford: Clarendon Press, 1987); Shmuel Almog, *Zionism and History: The Rise of a New Jewish Consciousness* (New York: St. Martin's Press, 1987); Michael Berkowitz, *Zionist Culture and West European Jewry before the First World War* (New York: Cambridge University Press, 1993). For a useful collection of the writings of some of the early articulators of Zionist ideology, see Arthur Hertzberg, ed., *The Zionist Idea: A Historical Analysis and Reader* (New York: Atheneum, 1959).

28. Quoted in Edward Said, *The Question of Palestine* (New York: Times Books, 1981), pp. 16–17.

29. In an interview published in the London *Times* (June 15, 1969, p. 12), quoted in Rashid Khalidi, *Palestinian Identity: The Construction of Modern National Consciousness* (New York: Columbia University Press, 1997), p. 181.

30. Ben-Gurion, *Israel*, especially pp. 9–78. The closest Ben-Gurion comes to mentioning the Palestinians is through occasional generic references to "Arabs."

31. David Ben-Gurion, *Memoirs* (New York: World, 1970), p. 26.

32. W. T. Mallison, Jr., "The Balfour Declaration: An Appraisal in International Law," in *The Transformation of Palestine: Essays on the Origin and Development of the Arab-Israeli Conflict*, ed. Ibrahim Abu-Lughod (Evanston, IL: Northwestern University Press, 1971), p. 98.

33. Quoted in Said, *Question of Palestine*, p. 13.

34. For a detailed analysis of land sales in Palestine, see Khalidi, *Palestinian Identity*, pp. 111–17.

35. Professor Israel Shahak's research is quoted in Said, *Question of Palestine*, p. 14. Said quotes another set of statistics, this time from the London *Times*, claiming that in the West Bank and Gaza some 7,554 Arab houses were razed from 1967 to 1969, and another 9,000 by 1971.

36. Sachar, *History of Israel*, p. 215.

37. By some accounts, the UN Partition Plan was based on the Zionists' own plan endorsed by the United States in August 1946. Farsoun and Zacharia, *Palestine and the Palestinians*, p. 111.

NOTES TO PAGES 83-88 / **405**

38. See, for example, Shimon Peres, *The New Middle East* (New York: Henry Holt, 1993), p. 166.

39. Israeli thinkers Simha Flapan and Zeev Sternhell are two cases in point. See Zeev Sternhell, *The Founding Myths of Israel*, trans. David Maisel (Princeton, NJ: Princeton University Press, 1998), and Simha Flapan, *The Birth of Israel: Myths and Realities* (New York: Pantheon Books, 1987), p. 33. Not surprisingly, these "new historians" are not without their detractors, one of whom is Professor Joseph Heller of the Hebrew University of Jerusalem. For Heller's critique of the "new historians," see his *The Birth of Israel: Ben-Gurion and His Critics* (Gainesville: University of Florida Press, 2000), pp. 295–307.

40. Flapan, *Birth of Israel*, p. 33.

41. For more on this, see the collection of essays in Edward Said and Christopher Hitchens, eds., *Blaming the Victims: Spurious Scholarship and the Palestinian Question* (New York: Verso, 1988).

42. Farsoun and Zacharia, *Palestine and the Palestinians*, p. 113.

43. Sachar, *History of Israel*, p. 333. Farsoun and Zacharia, in *Palestine and the Palestinians*, p. 114, put the number of those massacred at 245. As Sachar points out, the Zionists were not alone in committing atrocities, the Palestinians having been guilty as well on previous occasions. But the Deir Yassin massacre stands out both for its brutality and for the fear it instilled in the remaining Palestinian population.

44. Farsoun and Zacharia, *Palestine and the Palestinians*, p. 114.

45. Baruch Kimmerling and Joel Migdal, *Palestinians: The Making of a People* (Cambridge, MA: Harvard University Press, 1993), p. 147. Britain estimated the number of refugees at between 600,000 and 760,000.

46. For the interpretations of one of Israel's leading "new historians," see Benny Morris, *The Birth of the Palestinian Refugee Problem, 1947–1949* (New York: Cambridge University Press, 1987).

47. Sachar, *History of Israel*, p. 332; Flapan, *Birth of Israel*, p. 85.

48. Flapan, *Birth of Israel*, p. 93.

49. Farsoun and Zacharia, *Palestine and the Palestinians*, pp. 132–35.

50. Quoted in Flapan, *Birth of Israel*, p. 42.

51. Ilan Pappe, *The Ethnic Cleansing of Palestine* (Oxford: Oneworld, 2006), p. 49.

52. Kimmerling and Migdal, *Palestinians*, p. 152.

53. Joseph Nevo, *King Abdallah and Palestine: A Territorial Ambition* (New York: St. Martin's Press, 1996), pp. 108–21.

54. Rashid Khalidi makes a similar, though slightly different, argument. See Khalidi, *Palestinian Identity*, pp. 145–50.

55. For the sake of chronological consistency, this chapter examines only the first two of these phases of Palestinian nationalism, leaving the subsequent three to be discussed in Chapter 7.

56. Bassam Tibi, *Arab Nationalism: A Critical Inquiry*, 2nd ed., trans. Marion Farouk-Sluglett and Peter Sluglett (New York: St. Martin's Press, 1990), pp. 106–16.

57. For a rare and perceptive examination of these and other early Palestinian periodicals, see Khalidi, *Palestinian Identity*, pp. 119–44.

58. Adnan Mohammed Abu-Ghazaleh, *Arab Cultural Nationalism in Palestine during the British Mandate* (Beirut: Institute for Palestine Studies, 1973), p. 102. These individuals included men like Said al-Huseini, Ruhi al-Khalidi, Muhammad Hasan al-Budayri, and Khalil al-Sakakini.

59. William Quandt, Fuad Jabber, and Ann Mosley Lesch, *The Politics of Palestinian Nationalism* (Berkeley: University of California Press, 1973), p. 25.

60. Benny Morris, *Righteous Victims: A History of the Zionist-Arab Conflict, 1881–2001* (New York: Vintage Books, 2001), p. 145.

61. Ibid.

62. Khalidi, *Palestinian Identity*, p. 190.

63. Yehoyada Haim, *Abandonment of Illusions: Zionist Political Attitudes toward Palestinian Arab Nationalism, 1936–1939* (Boulder, CO: Westview Press, 1983), p. 50.

64. For repeated efforts by Palestinian leadership to see glory in defeat, see Khalidi, *Palestinian Identity*, pp. 197–98.

65. See Bassam Tibi, *Arab Nationalism: Between Islam and the Nation-State*, 3rd ed. (New York: St. Martin's Press, 1997), pp. 116–22.

66. P. J. Vatikiotis, *Nasser and His Generation* (New York: St. Martin's Press, 1978), p. 49.

67. Partly out of self-delusion and partly to placate their military officers, the Arab armies that took part in the 1948 war handed out lavish promotions to their officers, often promoting individuals without regard to their qualifications or experience.

68. Gamal Abdel Nasser, *The Philosophy of the Revolution* (Buffalo, NY: Economica Books, 1959), p. 28.

69. Ibid., pp. 36–37.

70. Ibid., pp. 32–33.

71. Joel Gordon, *Nasser's Blessed Movement: Egypt's Free Officers and the July Revolution* (New York: Oxford University Press, 1992), p. 13.

72. Quoted in ibid., p. 179. Upon his return to Cairo, Nasser's train was met by throngs of cheering masses.

73. For details of the Agrarian Reform Law, see Vatikiotis, *Nasser and His Generation*, pp. 205–9.

74. R. Hrair Dekmejian, *Egypt under Nasir: A Study in Political Dynamics* (Albany: SUNY Press, 1971), p. 43.

75. Fred J. Khouri, *The Arab-Israeli Dilemma*, 3rd ed. (Syracuse, NY: Syracuse University Press, 1985), pp. 215–16.

76. Quoted in Vatikiotis, *Nasser and His Generation*, p. 275.

77. Clement Henry Moore, *Politics in North Africa: Algeria, Morocco, and Tunisia* (Boston: Little, Brown, 1970), p. 38.

78. Ibid., p. 35.

79. Ibid., p. 36.

80. Ibid.

81. C. R. Pennell, *Morocco since 1830: A History* (New York: NYU Press, 2000), p. 280.

82. Lorna Hahn, *North Africa, Nationalism to Nationhood* (Washington, DC: Public Affairs Press, 1960), p. 280.

83. Elbaki Hermassi, *Leadership and National Development in North Africa: A Comparative Study* (Berkeley: University of California Press, 1972), pp. 103–4.

84. Although many Moroccans aspired to acquire *baraka,* few were actually perceived by others to be so blessed. "*Baraka* can be defined as a beneficial force derived from a divine origin yielding abundance and prosperity in the physical order. The ultimate sources of *baraka* are the sayings of God in the Koran and those of his Messenger, the Prophet Muhammad. By a sort of transmission, God has empowered all the descendants of the Prophet and all those who are close to God (that is, saints) with *baraka.*" Rahma Bourqia, "The Cultural Legacy of Power in Morocco," in *In the Shadow of the Sultan: Culture, Power, and Politics in Morocco,* ed. Rahma Bourqia and Susan Gilson Miller (Cambridge, MA: Harvard University Press, 1999), p. 246.

85. Pennell, *Morocco since 1830,* p. 291.

86. Moore, *Politics in North Africa,* p. 40.

87. Ibid., p. 40.

88. Hermassi, *Leadership and National Development,* pp. 133–34.

89. John Ruedy, *Modern Algeria: The Origins and Development of a Nation* (Bloomington: Indiana University Press, 1992), p. 173.

90. Moore, *Politics in North Africa,* p. 69.

91. Hermassi, *Leadership and National Development,* p. 121.

92. Lisa Anderson, *The State and Social Formation in Tunisia and Libya, 1830–1980* (Princeton, NJ: Princeton University Press, 1986), p. 175.

93. Clement Henry Moore, *Tunisia since Independence: The Dynamics of One-Party Government* (Berkeley: University of California Press, 1965), pp. 51–56.

94. Farsoun and Zacharia, *Palestine and the Palestinians,* p. 144.

4. THE ARAB-ISRAELI WARS

1. For a detailed account of Syrian politics in the 1940s and 1950s, see Patrick Seale, *The Struggle for Syria: A Study of Post-War Arab Politics, 1945–1958* (New Haven, CT: Yale University Press, 1986).

2. Alan R. Taylor, *The Superpowers and the Middle East* (Syracuse, NY: Syracuse University Press, 1991), p. 40.

3. Anthony Nutting, *Nasser* (New York: E. P. Dutton, 1972), pp. 316–17.

4. Taylor, *Superpowers and the Middle East,* p. 31.

5. Quoted in Dan Hofstadter, ed., *Egypt and Nasser,* vol. 2, *1957–66* (New York: Facts on File, 1973), p. 5.

6. Taylor, *Superpowers and the Middle East,* p. 60.

7. Seale, *Struggle for Syria,* p. 293.

8. Hofstadter, *Egypt and Nasser*, p. 37.

9. Quwatli, for example, was retired and given the honorific title of "First Citizen of the UAR." Malcolm Kerr, *The Arab Cold War, 1958–1964: A Study in Ideological Politics* (New York: Oxford University Press, 1965), p. 15.

10. Ibid., pp. 16–17.

11. Nutting, *Nasser*, p. 263.

12. Quoted in Hofstadter, *Egypt and Nasser*, p. 109.

13. Quoted in ibid., p. 106.

14. Kerr, *Arab Cold War*, p. 35.

15. Robert W. Stookey, *Yemen: The Politics of the Yemen Arab Republic* (Boulder, CO: Westview Press, 1978), p. 186.

16. Nutting, *Nasser*, p. 338.

17. All Abdel Rahman Rahmy, *The Egyptian Policy in the Arab World: Intervention in Yemen, 1962–1967. Case Study* (Washington, DC: University Press of America, 1983), p. 96.

18. Tawfiq Y. Hasou, *The Struggle for the Arab World: Egypt's Nasser and the Arab League* (London: KPI, 1985), pp. 138–39.

19. Rahmy, *Egyptian Policy*, p. 147.

20. Stookey, *Yemen*, p. 244.

21. Hasou, *Struggle for the Arab World*, p. 157.

22. Soon after the Egyptian withdrawal, Yemen's President Abdullah Salal, who had led the republicans in their fight against the royalists, was overthrown in a military coup and replaced by Said Abdel Rahman Iriani.

23. Nutting, *Nasser*, p. 285.

24. The most serious attacks occurred on May 27, 1965, September 5, 1965, April 30, 1966, July 14, 1966, and April 7, 1967.

25. Edgar O'Ballance, *The Third Arab-Israeli War* (Hamden, CT: Archon Books, 1972), p. 20.

26. Fred J. Khouri, *The Arab-Israeli Dilemma*, 3rd ed. (Syracuse, NY: Syracuse University Press, 1985), p. 247.

27. Quoted in Hisham Sharabi, "Prelude to War: The Crisis of May–June 1967," in *The Arab-Israeli Confrontation of June 1967: An Arab Perspective*, ed. Ibrahim Abu-Lughod (Evanston, IL: Northwestern University Press, 1970), p. 53.

28. Khouri, *Arab-Israeli Dilemma*, p. 243.

29. For details of parliamentary challenges to Eshkol's premiership, see O'Ballance, *Third Arab-Israeli War*, pp. 32–33.

30. Ibid., p. 21.

31. Khouri, *Arab-Israeli Dilemma*, p. 258.

32. O'Ballance, *Third Arab-Israeli War*, p. 67.

33. Ibid., pp. 78–79.

34. Ibid., p. 232.

35. Ibid., p. 272. The IDF later claimed that 778 Israeli soldiers and 26 civilians had been killed and that another 2,586 soldiers had been wounded along with 195 civilians.

36. Sharabi, "Prelude to War," p. 57.

37. Fouad Ajami, *The Arab Predicament: Arab Political Thought and Practice since 1967* (New York: Cambridge University Press, 1992), pp. 32–33.

38. Ibid., p. 30.

39. Bassam Tibi, *Conflict and War in the Middle East: From Interstate War to New Security*, 2nd ed. (New York: St. Martin's Press, 1998), p. 83.

40. Ajami, *Arab Predicament*, p. 41.

41. O'Ballance, *Third Arab-Israeli War*, p. 142. This proved especially damaging to Egypt's own progress in the war, as many Egyptian officers, having lost their lines of communication with their commanders, were initially relying on reports by Cairo Radio to make decisions.

42. Kirk Beattie, *Egypt during the Nasser Years: Ideology, Politics, and Civil Society* (Boulder, CO: Westview Press, 1994), p. 209.

43. For a text of Nasser's resignation speech, see "Nasser's Resignation Broadcast, June 9, 1967," in *The Israeli-Arab Reader: A Documentary History of the Middle East Conflict*, ed. Walter Laqueur and Barry Rubin, 5th ed. (New York: Penguin Books, 1995), pp. 160–65.

44. Tibi, *Conflict and War*, pp. 90–91.

45. Beattie, *Egypt during the Nasser Years*, pp. 213–15.

46. Samih K. Farsoun and Christina E. Zacharia, *Palestine and the Palestinians* (Boulder, CO: Westview Press, 1997), p. 134.

47. Quoted in Adnan Abu-Odeh, *Jordanians, Palestinians and the Hashemite Kingdom in the Middle East Peace Process* (Washington, DC: U.S. Institute for Peace Press, 1999), pp. 184.

48. "Security Council Resolution on the Middle East, November 22, 1967," in Laqueur and Rubin, *Israeli-Arab Reader*, pp. 217–18.

49. For an analysis of the writings and arguments of some of these intellectuals (e.g., Hisham Sharabi, Anwar Abdel Malik, Jalal Amin, and Samir Amin), see Issa Boullata, *Trends and Issues in Contemporary Arab Thought* (Albany: SUNY Press, 1990), pp. 87–118.

50. Rasheed el-Enany, *Naguib Mahfouz: The Pursuit of Meaning* (London: Routledge, 1993), p. 26.

51. Felipe Fernández-Armesto, *Sadat and His Statecraft* (London: Kensal, 1982), p. 48.

52. Raymond Hinnebusch, *Egyptian Politics under Sadat: The Post-Populist Development of an Authoritarian-Modernizing State* (New York: Cambridge University Press, 1985), p. 46.

53. Avi Shlaim, *The Iron Wall: Israel and the Arab World* (New York: W. W. Norton, 2001), p. 289.

54. Anwar el-Sadat, *The Public Diary of Anwar Sadat: Part One, The Road to War*, ed. Raphael Israeli (Leiden: E. J. Brill, 1978), p. 109.

55. Because the October 1973 War occurred during Ramadan and Yom Kippur, the Arabs refer to it as the Ramadan War and the Israelis as the Yom Kippur War. More objective observers, however, simply refer to it as the 1973 War.

56. For the increasing professionalization of Middle Eastern militaries after the 1967 War, see Mehran Kamrava, "Military Professionalization and Civil-Military Relations in the Middle East," *Political Science Quarterly* 115 (Spring 2000): 67–92.

57. On crossing the Suez, which the Egyptians did in a matter of hours, Dayan later said: "I had a theory that it would take them all night to set up the bridges . . . and that we would be able to prevent this with our armor." Quoted in Frank Aker, *October 1973: The Arab-Israeli War* (Hamden, CT: Archon Books, 1985), p. 23.

58. Ibid., p. 21.

59. Tibi, *Conflict and War*, pp. 109–10. The airlift is said to have included some seven hundred to eight hundred tons of military equipment daily. Peter Allen, *The Yom Kippur War* (New York: Charles Scribner's Sons, 1982), pp. 208–9.

60. Aker, *October 1973*, p. 57.

61. Kamal Salibi, *The Modern History of Jordan* (London: I. B. Tauris, 1993), pp. 254–55.

62. Quoted in Joseph Lorenz, *Egypt and the Arabs: Foreign Policy and the Search for National Identity* (Boulder, CO: Westview Press, 1990), p. 47.

63. Tibi, *Conflict and War*, p. 116.

64. Quoted in Hassan el Badri, Taha el Magdoub, and Mohammed Dia el Din Zohdy, *The Ramadan War, 1973* (Dunn Loring, VA: T. N. Dupuy Associates, 1978), p. 201.

65. Ibid., p. 202. This book was originally published in Arabic in Cairo under the title *Harb Ramadan*.

66. Aker, *October 1973*, p. 58.

67. Ajami, *Arab Predicament*, p. 116.

68. Hinnebusch, *Egyptian Politics under Sadat*, pp. 56–57.

69. "My main concern in this connection," he wrote, "is whether Israel really and truly wants peace. For my part I really want peace and have proved it beyond a shadow of doubt." Anwar el-Sadat, *In Search of Identity: An Autobiography* (New York: Harper and Row, 1978), p. 306.

70. Khouri, *Arab-Israeli Dilemma*, p. 414.

71. John Waterbury, *The Egypt of Nasser and Sadat: The Political Economy of Two Regimes* (Princeton, NJ: Princeton University Press, 1983), p. 240.

72. Ibid., p. 370.

73. Howard Sachar, *A History of Israel: From the Rise of Zionism to Our Time*, 2nd ed. (New York: Alfred A. Knopf, 1996), p. 801.

74. Ibid., p. 805.

75. Shlaim, *Iron Wall*, p. 325.

76. Ibid., p. 801.

77. Charles D. Smith, *Palestine and the Arab-Israeli Conflict*, 4th ed. (New York: St. Martin's Press, 2001), p. 329.

78. Shlaim, *Iron Wall*, p. 328.

79. Khalil Nakhleh, "The Political Effects of the October War on Israeli

Society," in *Middle East Crucible: Studies on the Arab-Israeli War of October 1973*, ed. Nasser Aruri (Wilmette, IL: Medina University Press International, 1975), p. 167.

80. Ibid.

81. King Hussein of Jordan, "Disengagement from the West Bank (July 31, 1988)," in Laqueur and Rubin, *Israeli-Arab Reader*, p. 340.

82. Tareq Ismael, *International Relations of the Contemporary Middle East: A Study in World Politics* (Syracuse, NY: Syracuse University Press, 1986), pp. 104–5.

83. Joe Stork, "The Oil Weapon," in Aruri, *Middle East Crucible*, p. 352.

84. Giacomo Luciani, "Oil and Political Economy in the International Relations of the Middle East," in *International Relations of the Middle East*, ed. Louise Fawcett (Oxford: Oxford University Press, 2005), p. 89.

85. Ibid; emphasis added.

86. Ibid.

5. THE IRANIAN REVOLUTION

1. There is a rich theoretical literature on revolutions; some of the more notable works are Peter Calvert, *Revolution and Counter-Revolution* (Minneapolis: University of Minnesota Press, 1990); Jack Goldstone, ed., *Revolutions: Theoretical, Comparative, and Historical Studies*, 2nd ed. (New York: Harcourt Brace, 1994); and Theda Skocpol, *States and Social Revolutions* (New York: Cambridge University Press, 1979), and *Social Revolutions in the Modern World* (New York: Cambridge University Press, 1994). For my own writings on the subject, see Mehran Kamrava, *Revolutionary Politics* (Westport, CT: Praeger, 1992), and "Revolution Revisited: Revolutionary Types and the Structuralist vs. Voluntarist Debate," *Canadian Journal of Political Science* 32 (June 1999): 1–29.

2. As the Iran-Iraq War is covered in detail in the next chapter, the only references to that event here are in passing.

3. Approximately 60 percent of Iran's population of about sixty-six million is thought to have been born after the revolution. Because of concerted efforts by the government, however, the fertility rate declined from seven children per woman in 1986 to 3.5 in 1993. Fariba Adelkhah, *Being Modern in Iran*, trans. Jonathan Derrick (New York: Columbia University Press, 2000), p. 156.

4. Richard Cottam, *Nationalism in Iran* (Pittsburgh, PA: University of Pittsburgh Press, 1979), pp. 60–61.

5. Shahrough Akhavi, *Religion and Politics in Contemporary Iran: Clergy-State Relations in the Pahlavi Period* (Albany: SUNY Press, 1980), p. 59.

6. For an insightful, succinct analysis of the causes of the collapse of the Azerbaijan rebellion, see Homa Katouzian, *The Political Economy of Modern Iran, 1926–1979* (New York: NYU Press, 1981), pp. 150–53.

7. Fakhreddin Azimi, *Iran: The Crisis of Democracy* (New York: St. Martin's Press, 1989), p. 340.

8. James Goode, *The United States and Iran, 1946–51: The Diplomacy of Neglect* (New York: St. Martin's Press, 1989), p. 10.

9. Peter Avery, *Modern Iran* (New York: Frederick A. Praeger, 1965), p. 405.

10. Sepehr Zabih, *The Mossadegh Era: Roots of the Iranian Revolution* (Chicago: Lake View Press, 1982), p. 111.

11. For obvious reasons, the precise role of the Central Intelligence Agency in the coup that overthrew Musaddiq is shrouded in mystery. Nevertheless, on the eve of the 1978–79 revolution, the CIA's principal organizer of the coup, Kermit Roosevelt, wrote what remains a unique, if not thorough, account of the CIA's efforts. See his *Countercoup: The Struggle for the Control of Iran* (New York: McGraw-Hill, 1979). Equally interesting, and more thorough and objective, are a series of CIA reports and other documents related to the coup compiled by the *New York Times* and posted on the paper's Web site: James Risen, "Secrets of History: The CIA in Iran," 2000, www.nytimes.com/library/world/mideast/041600iran-cia-index.html.

12. Cottam, *Nationalism in Iran*, pp. 226–27. This is not to imply that everyone who took part in anti-Musaddiq demonstrations had been paid to do so. As Cottam correctly notes (on p. 229), "[R]egardless of foreign participation, Mossadeq could not have been overthrown if significant elements of the population had not lost faith in his leadership."

13. Shahrough Akhavi, "The Role of the Clergy in Iranian Politics, 1949–1954," in *Musaddiq, Iranian Nationalism, and Oil*, ed. James A. Bill and William Roger Louis (Austin: University of Texas Press, 1988), p. 92.

14. For a detailed account of Musaddiq's trial, see Homa Katouzian, *Musaddiq and the Struggle for Power in Iran* (London: I. B. Tauris, 1990), pp. 294–307.

15. Ervand Abrahamian, *Iran between Two Revolutions* (Princeton, NJ: Princeton University Press, 1982), p. 420.

16. This actually happened to a close former associate of Dr. Musaddiq, Alahyar Saleh, a popular nationalist in his own right. Cottam, *Nationalism in Iran*, p. 301.

17. Asadollah Alam, *The Shah and I: The Confidential Diaries of Iran's Royal Court, 1969–1977*, trans. Alinaghi Alikhani and Nicholas Vincent (New York: St. Martin's Press, 1991), p. 390.

18. Mohammad Reza Pahlavi, *Mission for My Country* (London: Hutchinson, 1961), p. 125.

19. Mohammad Reza Pahlavi, *Answer to History* (New York: Stein and Day, 1980), p. 176.

20. Mohammad Reza Pahlavi, *Inqilab-e Sefeed* [The White Revolution] (Tehran: Imperial Pahlavi Library, 1967), p. 25.

21. Akhavi, *Religion and Politics*, p. 102.

22. Unlike their Sunni counterparts, who have no formal hierarchy, the Shi'ite clergy are hierarchically divided into four strata: from lowest to highest, the *muezzin* or *akhunds*, the *hojjatoleslams*, the ayatollahs, and the grand ayatollahs *(Ayatollah Uzma)*. The 1978–79 revolution gave rise to the innova-

tive position of *velayat faqih*, or supreme jurisconsult, to be occupied first by the revolution's leader, Ayatollah Khomeini.

23. For the White Revolution's various principles and the dates of their enactment, see Pahlavi, *Answer to History*, pp. 193–94.

24. For the first view, see Katouzian, *Political Economy of Modern Iran*, p. 241; for the second, see Gholam R. Afkhami, *The Iranian Revolution: Thanatos on a National Scale* (Washington, DC: Middle East Institute, 1985), p. 56.

25. Ibid. For a rare and recent study of Hoveida and his tenure in office, see Abbas Milani, *The Persian Sphinx: Amir Abbas Hoveyda and the Riddle of the Iranian Revolution* (Washington, DC: Mage, 2000).

26. Even regime insiders knew this. Of the party's first congress, the shah's court minister wrote in his diaries: "The whole thing was excellently state-managed, but hollow; utterly hollow and false." Alam, *Shah and I*, p. 422.

27. Ibid., p. 494.

28. Pahlavi, *Answer to History*, p. 145.

29. Hushang Moghtader, "The Impact of Increased Oil Revenue on Iran's Economic Development, 1973–76," in *Towards a Modern Iran: Studies in Thought, Politics and Society*, ed. Elie Kedouri and Sylvia Haim (London: Frank Cass, 1980), p. 241.

30. Ibid., pp. 254–55.

31. Ibid., pp. 259–60.

32. Alam, *Shah and I*, p. 535.

33. Ibid., p. 548.

34. There is a vast and rich literature dealing with the role and influence of U.S. foreign policy toward Iran in the final months of the Pahlavi regime. Perhaps the most authoritative work is James Bill, *The Eagle and the Lion: The Tragedy of American-Iranian Relations* (New Haven, CT: Yale University Press, 1988).

35. Pahlavi, *Answer to History*, p. 165.

36. For an analysis of the main parties forming the National Front, see Cottam, *Nationalism in Iran*, pp. 264–68.

37. Abrahamian, *Iran between Two Revolutions*, p. 451.

38. Mujahedeen Khalq, *Sharh-e Ta'sis va Tarikhche-ye Vaqaye' Sazman-e Mujahedeen-e Khalq-e Iran az Sal-e 1344 ta Sal-e 1350* [Explanation of the foundation and a history of the People's Mujahedeen Organization of Iran from the year 1965 to the year 1971] (Tehran: Sazman-e Mujahedeen, 1358/1979), p. 45.

39. For more on this, see ibid., pp. 58–72.

40. For an account of the activities of the Mujahedeen and the Fedayeen before the revolution, see Mehran Kamrava, *Revolution in Iran: The Roots of Turmoil* (London: Routledge, 1990), pp. 60–65.

41. For an English translation of Al-e Ahmad's major work, see *West-struckness*, trans. John Green and Ahmad Alizadeh (Lexington, KY: Mazda, 1982). See also Michael C. Hillmann, ed., *Iranian Society: An Anthology of Writings by Jalal Al-e Ahmad* (Lexington, KY: Mazda, 1982).

42. See Ali Rahnema, *An Islamic Utopian: A Political Biography of Ali Sharia'ti* (London: I. B. Tauris, 1998).

43. Hamid Dabashi, *Theology of Discontent: The Ideological Foundations of the Islamic Revolution in Iran* (New York: NYU Press, 1993).

44. Kamrava, *Revolution in Iran*, p. 47.

45. Dilip Hiro, *Iran under the Ayatollahs* (London: Routledge and Kegan Paul, 1985), p. 93.

46. Ibid., pp. 106–7.

47. See, for example, the U.S. secretary of state's views in Cyrus Vance, *Hard Choices: Critical Years in America's Foreign Policy* (New York: Simon and Schuster, 1983), pp. 370–75.

48. Pahlavi, *Answer to History*, p. 15.

49. Hamid Algar, trans., *Constitution of the Islamic Republic of Iran* (Berkeley, CA: Mizan Press, 1980), p. 29.

50. This included especially the hostages themselves, who believed the takeover would last only a few hours, as had been the case the previous February, or a couple of days at most. See, for example, the thoughts of a former hostage, Richard Queen, *Inside and Out: Hostage to Iran, Hostage to Myself* (New York: G. P. Putnam's Sons, 1981), p. 57.

51. Gary Sick, who worked at the White House at the time and was involved in many of the initiatives to free the hostages, writes in detail of efforts by two private attorneys hired by Iran's foreign minister, Sadeq Qotbzadeh, to broker a deal for the hostages' release. See Gary Sick, *All Fall Down: America's Tragic Encounter with Iran* (New York: Penguin Books, 1985), pp. 294–328.

52. For more on the planning and execution of the rescue mission, see Paul Ryan, *The Iranian Rescue Mission: Why It Failed* (Annapolis, MD: Naval Institute Press, 1985).

53. This position was taken chiefly by President Carter's national security advisor, Zbigniew Brzezinski. See his *Power and Principle: Memoirs of the National Security Advisor, 1977–1981* (New York: Farrar, Straus, Giroux, 1985), p. 499.

54. Sick, *All Fall Down*, p. 364.

55. The scenario that follows is based on Gary Sick's *October Surprise: America's Hostages in Iran and the Election of Ronald Reagan* (New York: Times Books, 1991). Sick's claims are corroborated by Iran's president at the time, Abol Hassan Bani-Sadr. See Abol Hassan Bani-Sadr, *My Turn to Speak: Iran, the Revolution, and Secret Deals with the U.S.* (Washington, DC: Brassey's, 1991).

56. Trita Parsi, *Treacherous Alliance: The Secret Dealings of Israel, Iran, and the United States* (New Haven, CT: Yale University Press, 2007), pp. 105–9.

57. The Iran-Contra Affair came to light when it was revealed that the United States had secretly sold arms to Iran and had used the proceeds to fund the Contra guerrillas fighting the revolutionary Sandinista regime in Nicaragua.

58. Hiro, *Iran under the Ayatollahs*, p. 196.

59. Guity Nashat, "Women in the Ideology of the Islamic Republic," in *Women and Revolution in Iran*, ed. Guity Nashat (Boulder, CO: Westview Press, 1983), p. 195.

60. Sohrab Behdad, "The Post-Revolutionary Economic Crisis," in *Iran after the Revolution: Crisis of an Islamic State*, ed. Saeed Rahnema and Sohrab Behdad (London: I. B. Tauris, 1996), pp. 108–9.

61. Anoushiravan Ehteshami, *After Khomeini: The Iranian Second Republic* (London: Routledge, 1995), p. 55.

62. Quoted in ibid., p. 100.

63. Bahman Baktiar, *Parliamentary Politics in Revolutionary Iran: The Institutionalization of Factional Politics* (Gainesville: University Press of Florida, 1996), pp. 218–19.

64. For a detailed and unique examination of the Islamic Republic's constitution, see Asghar Schirazi, *The Constitution of Iran: Politics and the State in the Islamic Republic*, trans. John O'Kane (London: I. B. Tauris, 1998).

65. Hooshang Amirahmadi, *Revolution and Economic Transition: The Iranian Experience* (Albany: SUNY Press, 1990), pp. 86–87.

66. Behdad, "Post-Revolutionary Economic Crisis," p. 123.

67. Anoushiravan Ehteshami, "Iran and its Immediate Neighbourhood," in *Iran's Foreign Policy from Khatami to Ahmadinejad*, ed. Anoushiravan Ehteshami and Mahjoob Zweiri (London: Ithaca Press, 2008), p. 136.

68. Mehran Kamrava, *Iran's Intellectual Revolution* (Cambridge: Cambridge University Press, 2008).

6. THE GULF WARS AND BEYOND

1. Alan R. Taylor, *The Superpowers and the Middle East* (Syracuse, NY: Syracuse University Press, 1991), p. 133.

2. Tareq Y. Ismael, *International Relations of the Contemporary Middle East: A Study in World Politics* (Syracuse, NY: Syracuse University Press, 1986), pp. 155–56.

3. Perhaps the most detailed chronological account of the Iran-Iraq War can be found in Dilip Hiro, *The Longest War: The Iran-Iraq Military Conflict* (New York: Routledge, Chapman, and Hall, 1991), pp. 288–96.

4. Efraim Karsh and Inari Rautsi, *Saddam Hussein: A Political Biography* (New York: Free Press, 1991), p. 18.

5. Ibid., p. 19.

6. Ibid., p. 86.

7. Ibid., p. 88. Later, in 1982, the president had himself promoted to the rank of field marshal.

8. Samir al-Khalil, *Republic of Fear: The Inside Story of Saddam's Iraq* (New York: Pantheon Books, 1989), p. xxxi.

9. Ofra Bengio, *Saddam's Word: Political Discourse in Iraq* (New York: Oxford University Press, 1998), p. 83. As Bengio demonstrates, the same type

of hyperbole and exaggerated sense of importance marked the regime's propaganda later on, especially during "the mother of all battles."

10. al-Khalil, *Republic of Fear,* p. 270.

11. Shaul Bakhash, *The Reign of the Ayatollahs: Iran and the Islamic Revolution* (London: I. B. Tauris, 1985), pp. 112–13.

12. Quoted in Rouhollah K. Ramazani, *Revolutionary Iran: Challenge and Response in the Middle East* (Baltimore, MD: Johns Hopkins University Press, 1986), p. 24.

13. Quoted in Karsh and Rautsi, *Saddam Hussein,* p. 124.

14. Edgar O'Ballance, *The Gulf War* (London: Brassey's Defence, 1988), p. 38.

15. Stephen C. Pelletiere, *The Iran-Iraq War: Chaos in a Vacuum* (Westport, CT: Praeger, 1992), pp. 35–36.

16. Hiro, *Longest War,* p. 45.

17. Ibid., pp. 297–98. These numbers, of course, cannot be verified, and different observers have presented different figures. Nevertheless, the varying figures all confirm the overall trend in the growth of both countries' forces. See, for example, Anthony H. Cordesman, *The Iran-Iraq War and Western Security, 1984–87: Strategic Implications and Policy Options* (London: Royal United Services Institute, 1987), p. 42.

18. Quoted in W. Thom Workman, *The Social Origins of the Iran-Iraq War* (Boulder, CO: Lynne Rienner, 1994), p. 124.

19. For Bani-Sadr's own account of his removal, see Abol Hassan Bani-Sadr, *My Turn to Speak: Iran, the Revolution, and Secret Deals with the U.S.* (Washington, DC: Brassey's, 1991), pp. 161–72.

20. For an account of Israel's daring raid on the Iraqi nuclear reactor, see Adel Darwish and Gregory Alexander, *Unholy Babylon: The Secret History of Saddam's War* (New York: St. Martin's Press, 1991), pp. 123–27.

21. Pelletiere, *Iran-Iraq War,* pp. 40–41.

22. Stephen C. Pelletiere and Douglas V. Johnson II, *Lessons Learned: The Iran-Iraq War* (Carlisle Barracks, PA: Strategic Studies Institute, U.S. Army War College, 1991), p. 10.

23. O'Ballance, *Gulf War,* pp. 116–17.

24. Pelletiere and Johnson, *Lessons Learned,* p. 32.

25. Agence France-Presse, March 13, 2000.

26. Islamic Republic News Agency, November 13, 2000.

27. More than a decade after the downing of the Iran Air flight and a U.S. congressional investigation into the incident, many details of the tragedy remain buried. For an examination of some of the continuing controversies, see John Barry and Roger Charles, "Sea of Lies," *Newsweek,* July 13, 1992, pp. 29–39.

28. Hiro, *Longest War,* p. 250; Islamic Republic News Agency, September 23, 2000.

29. Ibid.

30. Karsh and Rautsi, *Saddam Hussein,* p. 201.

31. Simon Henderson, *Instant Empire: Saddam Hussein's Ambition for Iraq* (San Francisco: Mercury House, 1991), p. 219.

32. Quoted in Laurie Mylroie, "Saddam Hussein's Invasion of Kuwait: A Premeditated Act," in *The Iraqi Aggression against Kuwait: Strategic Lessons and Implications for Europe,* ed. Wolfgang F. Danspeckgruber and Charles Tripp (Boulder, CO: Westview Press, 1996), p. 44.

33. Hiro, *Longest War,* pp. 60–61.

34. Bruce W. Jentleson, *With Friends Like These: Reagan, Bush, and Saddam, 1982–1990* (New York: W. W. Norton, 1994), p. 46. For other examples of U.S.-Iraqi cooperation during the Iran-Iraq War, see Adam Tarock, *The Superpowers' Involvement in the Iran-Iraq War* (Commack, NY: Nova Science, 1998), pp. 80–90.

35. Jean Edward Smith, *George Bush's War* (New York: Henry Holt, 1992), p. 9.

36. Members of the coalition included Afghanistan, Argentina, Australia, Bahrain, Bangladesh, Belgium, Canada, Czechoslovakia, Denmark, Egypt, France, Germany, Greece, Hungary, Honduras, Italy, Kuwait, Morocco, the Netherlands, New Zealand, Niger, Norway, Oman, Pakistan, Poland, Portugal, Qatar, Saudi Arabia, Senegal, South Korea, Spain, Syria, Turkey, the United Arab Emirates, the United Kingdom, and the United States. The contribution of some of the countries was almost purely symbolic: 300 troops by Afghanistan, 150 by Honduras, 500 by Niger, and so on.

37. The resolution was supported by Bahrain, Djibouti, Egypt, Kuwait, Lebanon, Morocco, Oman, Qatar, Saudi Arabia, Somalia, Syria, and the UAE. Iraq, the PLO, and Libya opposed it. Algeria and Yemen abstained, and Jordan, Mauritania, and Sudan expressed reservations about the resolution. Dilip Hiro, *Desert Shield to Desert Storm: The Second Gulf War* (New York: Routledge, 1992), p. 128.

38. Lawrence Freedman and Efraim Karsh, *The Gulf Conflict, 1990–1991: Diplomacy and War in the New World Order* (Princeton, NJ: Princeton University Press, 1993), p. 325. Nevertheless, Freedman and Karsh cite an analyst (p. 312) who claimed that some fifty out of the eight hundred strategic targets had been misidentified.

39. Ibid., pp. 333–37.

40. Quoted in Hiro, *Desert Shield to Desert Storm,* p. 387.

41. The Iraqi government's maltreatment of Shi'ites and Kurds has been well documented. See, for example, Saïd K. Aburish, *Saddam Hussein: The Politics of Revenge* (New York: Bloomsbury, 2000), pp. 122–23, and Kanan Makiya, *Cruelty and Silence: War, Tyranny, Uprising and the Arab World* (New York: W. W. Norton, 1993), pp. 152–53.

42. Makiya, *Cruelty and Silence,* p. 152. According to Makiya, Kurdish leaders put the number of killed at 180,000.

43. Ibid., p. 219.

44. Ismael, *International Relations,* pp. 52–56.

45. See Hussein J. Agha and Ahmad S. Khalidi, *Syria and Iran: Rivalry and Cooperation* (New York: Council on Foreign Relations Press, 1995).

46. R. Stephen Humphreys, *Between Memory and Desire: The Middle East in a Troubled Age* (Berkeley: University of California Press, 1999), p. 82.

47. Raymond Hinnebusch, "The Middle East Regional System," in *The Foreign Policies of Middle East States*, ed. Raymond Hinnebusch and Anoushiravan Ehteshami (Boulder, CO: Lynne Rienner, 2002), p. 49.

48. Richard K. Herrmann and R. William Ayres, "The New Geo-Politics of the Gulf: Forces for Change and Stability," in *The Persian Gulf at the Millennium: Essays in Politics, Economy, Security, and Religion*, ed. Gary G. Sick and Lawrence G. Potter (New York: St. Martin's Press, 1997), p. 38.

49. Bahgat Korany, "The Arab World and the New Balance of Power in the New Middle East," in *Middle East Dilemma: The Politics and Economics of Arab Integration*, ed. Michael C. Hudson (New York: Columbia University Press, 1999), pp. 47–48.

50. Michael N. Barnett, *Dialogues in Arab Politics: Negotiations in Regional Order* (New York: Columbia University Press, 1998), p. ix.

51. Shibley Telhami and Michael Barnett, "Introduction: Identity and Foreign Policy in the Middle East," in *Identity and Foreign Policy in the Middle East*, ed. Shibley Telhami and Michael Barnett (Ithaca, NY: Cornell University Press, 2002), pp. 13–14.

52. Hinnebusch, "Middle East Regional System," p. 49.

53. Shimon Peres, *The New Middle East* (New York: Henry Holt, 1993), p. 60.

54. Hinnebusch, "Middle East Regional System," p. 48.

55. Korany, "Arab World," pp. 51–52.

56. Ibid., p. 51.

57. To keep the historical narrative unbroken, the following section examines the role of Islamic fundamentalism insofar as the specific events surrounding the September 11 attacks are concerned. Chapter 7 offers a more detailed analysis of the multiple causes and consequences, and the various manifestations, of political Islam, including Islamic fundamentalism.

58. David A. Kaplan, *The Accidental President* (New York: HarperCollins, 2001).

59. Fouad Ajami, "The Uneasy Imperium: Pax Americana in the Middle East," in *How Did This Happen? Terrorism and the New War*, ed. James F. Hoge and Gideon Rose (New York: Council on Foreign Relations, 2001), p. 15.

60. On American support for Israel, in their best-selling and controversial book *The Israel Lobby and U.S. Foreign Policy*, John Mearsheimer and Stephen Walt write: "For the past four decades, the United States has provided Israel with a level of material and diplomatic support that dwarfs what it provides to other countries. That aid is largely unconditional: no matter what Israel does, the level of support remains largely unchanged." They go on to argue that "the United States has also undertaken policies in the broader Middle East that reflect Israel's preferences," a situation that "has no equal in American history" and "is due primarily to the activities of the Israel lobby." John J. Mearsheimer and Stephen M. Walt, *The Israel*

Lobby and U.S. Foreign Policy (New York: Farrar, Straus and Giroux, 2008), pp. 7–8.

61. Alvin Rabushka, "Why Aid to Israel Hurts . . . Israelis," *Hoover Digest,* no. 3 (1998): 109–12. According to Rabushka, from the early 1970s to the mid-1980s, American aid to Israel totaled around $1 billion a year. It has steadily increased ever since, reaching some $4 billion by the late 1990s. A 2008 report by the Congressional Research Service, prepared for members of the U.S. Congress, puts the total annual U.S. aid to Israel at around $3.1 billion. According to the report, in 2007 the Bush administration asked the U.S. Congress to increase U.S. assistance to Israel by $6 billion over the next decade. Jeremy Sharp, "U.S. Foreign Aid to Israel," Congressional Research Service [CRS] Report RL33222, January 2008, www.au.af.mil/au/awc/awcgate/crs/rl33222.pdf, p. 2.

62. Taylor, *Superpowers and the Middle East,* p. 62.

63. Paul Findley, *They Dare to Speak Out: People and Institutions Confront Israel's Lobby* (Chicago: Lawrence Hill, 1989), p. 25. For more on how in the United States the Israel lobby guides the policy process, dominates public discourse on issues related to Israel and its foes, and influences foreign policy toward Syria, Lebanon, and Iran, see Mearsheimer and Walt, *Israel Lobby.*

64. Shibley Telhami, *2006 Annual Arab Public Opinion Survey,* 2006, www.brookings.edu/views/speeches/telhami20070208.pdf; *2008 Annual Arab Public Opinion Survey,* 2008, www.brookings.edu/topics/~/media/Files/events/2008/0414_middle_east/0414_middle_east_telhami.pdf; and *2009 Annual Arab Public Opinion Survey,* 2009, www.brookings.edu/~/media/Files/events/2009/0519_arab_opinion/2009_arab_public_opinion_poll.pdf, all three prepared by the University of Maryland with Zogby International.

65. Telhami, *2006 Annual Arab Public Opinion Survey.*

66. Telhami, *2009 Annual Arab Public Opinion Survey.*

67. Nadia El-Shazly and Raymond Hinnebusch, "The Challenge of Security in the Post–Gulf War Middle East System," in Hinnebusch and Ehteshami, *Foreign Policies,* p. 73.

68. Neamatollah Najoumi, *The Rise of the Taliban in Afghanistan: Mass Mobilization, Civil War, and the Future of the Region* (New York: Palgrave Press, 2002), p. 222.

69. Ahmad Rashid, *Taliban* (New Haven, CT: Yale University Press, 2001), p. 130.

70. Ibid., p. 133.

71. Jeffrey Legro and Andrew Moravcsik, "Faux Realism: Spin versus Substance in the Bush Foreign Policy Doctrine," *Foreign Policy,* no. 125 (July-August 2001): 81–82.

72. The 2002 *U.S. National Security Strategy* report, issued by the White House, states, "We will not hesitate to act alone, if necessary, to exercise our right of self defense by acting preemptively against such terrorists, to prevent them from doing harm against our people and our country." White House, *The National Security Strategy of the United States, September 2002* (Washington, DC: White House, 2002), p. 6. For more on the Bush Doctrine, see also

François Heisbourg, "A Work in Progress: The Bush Doctrine and Its Consequences," *Washington Quarterly* 26 (Spring 2003): 75–88.

73. The full text of President Bush's 2002 State of the Union speech is available through the electronic archives of the White House, at "President Delivers State of the Union Address," January 29, 2002, http://georgewbush -whitehouse.archives.gov/news/releases/2002/01/20020129–11.html.

74. Department of Defense, *Base Structure Report, Fiscal Year 2008 Baseline* (Washington, DC: Department of Defense, 2008), p. 2.

75. Richard L. Berke and Janet Elder, "After the Attacks: The Poll; Public Voices Overwhelming Support for the Use of Force against Terrorism," *New York Times*, September 17, 2001, p. 5. Only a month before the attacks, the president's popularity was as low as 50 percent.

76. By far the most thorough account of such plans is presented by the investigative journalist Bob Woodward in his *Plan of Attack* (New York: Simon and Schuster, 2004).

77. The full text of President Bush's 2003 State of the Union speech is available through the electronic archives of the White House, at "President Delivers 'State of the Union,'" January 28, 2003, http://georgewbush-whitehouse .archives.gov/news/releases/2003/01/20030128–19.html.

78. Data collected from the U.S. Energy Information Administration, "Iraq Energy Profile," http://tonto.eia.doe.gov/country/country_energy_data.cfm?fips =IZ.

79. On Feith, see, for example, Douglas Feith and Frank Gaffney, "A Continuing Botch-up of U.S. Policy," *Jerusalem Post*, March 9, 1992, and Douglas Feith, "An Alliance That Threatens World Order," *Jerusalem Post*, May 30, 1991. On Perle, see Chris Toensing and Ian Urbina, "Bush's Middle East Policy: Look to His Advisors," *Foreign Policy in Focus*, December 19, 2001, www .merip.org/newspaper_opeds/CT-IA-Bush-middle-east.html, pp. 9–12.

80. In January 1998, a group of well-known conservative intellectuals and political figures affiliated with the Project for the New American Century, a nonprofit organization set up "to promote American global leadership," wrote an open letter to President Clinton calling on his administration to remove Saddam Hussein from power and to "undertake military action [against Iraq] as diplomacy is clearly failing." The authors of the letter included, among others, future Secretary of Defense Donald Rumsfeld, his deputy Paul Wolfowitz, and a number of other highly influential figures in the Bush administration, such as Elliott Abrams, Richard L. Armitage, John Bolton, Zalmay Khalilzad, and Richard Perle. The text of the letter is available on the group's Web site: "Letter to President Clinton on Iraq," January 26, 1998, www.newamerican century.org/iraqclintonletter.htm.

81. United Nations Security Council, Resolution 1441, November 8, 2002, pp. 3, 5.

82. Hans Blix, "Briefing of the Security Council," *UN News Service*, February 14, 2003.

83. Judith S. Yaphe, "War and Occupation in Iraq: What Went Right? What Could Go Wrong?" *Middle East Journal* 57 (Summer 2003): 393.

84. Gilbert Burnham et al., "Mortality after the 2003 Invasion of Iraq: A Cross-Sectional Cluster Sample Survey," *Lancet* 369 (October 21–27, 2006): 1421. The cited study did face criticism on grounds of its methodology and the accuracy of its data, although the authors have stood by their assertions. For some of the criticism against the study and its authors' rebuttal, see Johan von Schreeb et al., "Mortality in Iraq/Authors' Reply," *Lancet* 369 (January 13–19, 2007): 101–5.

85. Patricia Weiss Fagen, "Iraqi Refugees: Seeking Stability in Syria and Jordan," occasional paper, Georgetown University, School of Foreign Service in Qatar, Center for International and Regional Studies, 2009, http://isim.george town.edu/Publications/PatPubs/Iraqi%20Refugees.pdf, p. 4.

86. Susan G. Chesser, "Iraq: U.S. Casualties," Congressional Research Service [CRS] Report RS21578, May 28, 2009, http://fpc.state.gov/documents/organization/125559.pdf, p. 1.

87. Bassam Tibi first predicted this possibility years before the September 11, 2001, attacks. See his *Conflict and War in the Middle East: From Interstate War to New Security*, 2nd ed. (New York: St. Martin's Press, 1998), pp. 189–93.

7. THE PALESTINIAN-ISRAELI CONFLICT

1. Deborah Gerner, *One Land, Two Peoples: The Conflict over Palestine*, 2nd ed. (Boulder, CO: Westview Press, 1994).

2. Dilip Hiro, *Sharing the Promised Land: A Tale of Israelis and Palestinians* (New York: Olive Branch Press, 1999).

3. Paloma Díaz-Mas, *Sephardim: The Jews from Spain*, trans. George K. Zucker (Chicago: University of Chicago Press, 1992), p. 7.

4. Central Bureau of Statistics, *Statistical Abstract of Israel, 2008*, no. 59 (Tel Aviv: Government Publishing House, 2003), p. 152.

5. Ibid., p. 158.

6. Eliezer Ben-Rafael, *Language, Identity, and Social Division: The Case of Israel* (New York: Oxford University Press, 1994), p. 89.

7. The Reform movement started in Germany around 1800 in reaction to the strict dictates of Orthodox Judaism. Other, smaller non-Orthodox movements within Judaism include the Reconstructionist, Conservadox, Renewal, and Humanistic Judaism. For more on these and other tendencies within Judaism, see Michael A. Meyer, *Judaism within Modernity: Essays on Jewish History and Religion* (Detroit, MI: Wayne State University Press, 2001).

8. Ran Greenstein, *Genealogies of Conflict: Class, Identity, and the State in Palestine/Israel and South Africa* (Hanover, NH: Wesleyan University Press, 1995), pp. 85–86.

9. Ella Shohat, "The Invention of the Mizrahim," *Journal of Palestine Studies* 29 (Autumn 1999): 8.

10. Yoav Peled, "Towards a Redefinition of Jewish Nationalism in Israel? The Enigma of Shas," *Ethnic and Racial Studies* 21 (July 1998): 706.

11. These and other statistics in this paragraph are drawn from Hiro, *Sharing the Promised Land*, p. 53.

12. Peled, "Towards a Redefinition," p. 708.

13. Ibid., p. 709.

14. Hiro, *Sharing the Promised Land*, pp. 54–55.

15. See, for example, Amos Elon, *The Israelis: Founders and Sons* (New York: Holt, Rinehart, and Winston, 1971); Dan V. Segre, *A Crisis of Identity: Israel and Zionism* (New York: Oxford University Press, 1980); and Yosef Gorny, *The State of Israel in Jewish Public Thought: The Quest for Collective Identity* (New York: NYU Press, 1994). A notable exception is Akiva Orr, who left the Israeli Communist Party in 1962. He writes:

> Instead of alleviating identity complexes this state has created new ones, not the least of which is a principled insistence on maintaining internal ethnic discrimination. Not only is every Israeli citizen required to register by ethnic origin and to carry an identity card stating ethnic origin, but the declaration of independence which pledges itself to "uphold full social and political rights to all citizens without discrimination of religion, race or sex" deliberately omits the phrase "or ethnic origin." Social and demographic statistical surveys in Israel categorise the population into two ethnic groups, namely Jews and non-Jews . . . , which indicates that ethnic discrimination is not some minor flaw in the structure of Israel but its fundamental feature.
>
> > Akiva Orr, *Israel: Politics, Myths and Identity Crisis*
> > (London: Pluto, 1994), p. 35

16. Hiro, *Sharing the Promised Land*, p. 49.

17. Ben-Raphael, *Language, Identity*, p. 96.

18. Hiro, *Sharing the Promised Land*, p. 45.

19. Peled, "Towards a Redefinition," p. 703; Etta Bick, "The Shas Phenomenon and Religious Parties in the 1999 Elections," *Israel Affairs* 7, no. 2/3 (2001): 55.

20. Nina Sovich, "Shas Courts Israel's Bedouin," *Middle East International*, no. 593 (February 12, 1999): 24.

21. Bick, "Shas Phenomenon," pp. 59–60.

22. Ben-Rafael, *Language, Identity*, p. 99.

23. Peled, "Towards a Redefinition," pp. 706–7.

24. Eliezer Ben-Rafael, "Mizrahi and Russian Challenges to Israel's Dominant Culture: Divergences and Convergences," *Israel Studies* 12 (Fall 2007): 76.

25. For an insightful examination of the writings of Israeli scholars over issues of identity, see Gorny, *State of Israel*, pp. 197–231.

26. See, for example, the chapter on "Israeliness" in Orr, *Israel*, pp. 44–52.

27. Segre, *Crisis of Identity*, pp. 32–33.

28. In his famous speech before the UN General Assembly on November 13, 1974, Yasser Arafat said: "The Palestine Liberation Organization has . . . gained its legitimacy by representing every faction, union or group as well as every Palestinian talent, either in the National Council or in people's institutions. . . . The Palestine Liberation Organization represents the Palestinian people legitimately and uniquely." "Address to the UN General Assembly (November 13, 1974)," in *The Israeli-Arab Reader: A Documentary History of the Middle East Conflict,* ed. Walter Laqueur and Barry Rubin, 5th ed. (New York: Penguin Books, 1995), p. 338.

29. James Kellas, *The Politics of Nationalism and Ethnicity,* 2nd ed. (New York: St. Martin's Press, 1998), p. 215.

30. Article 4 of the Palestinian National Charter, drafted by the PLO's Palestine National Council in 1968, is revealing in its attempt to defend Palestinian identity: "The Palestinian identity is a genuine, essential, and inherent characteristic; it is transmitted from parents to children. The Zionist occupation and the dispersal of the Palestinian Arab people, through the disasters which befell them, do not make them lose their Palestinian identity and their membership in the Palestinian community, nor do they negate them." "Palestinian National Charter: Resolutions of the Palestinian National Council," in Laqueur and Rubin, *Israeli-Arab Reader,* p. 218.

31. For more on Palestinian civil society organizations, see Denis Sullivan, "NGOs in Palestine: Agents of Development and Foundation of Civil Society," *Journal of Palestine Studies* 25 (Spring 1996): 93–100, and Mehran Kamrava, "What Stands between the Palestinians and Democracy?" *Middle East Quarterly* 6 (June 1999): 3–12.

32. Data collected from the Palestinian Central Bureau of Statistics, at www.pcbs.gov.ps. The most recent Palestinian census was conducted in 2007, the results of which are available in Palestinian Central Bureau of Statistics, *Population, Housing and Establishment Census, 2007* (Ramallah: Palestinian Central Bureau of Statistics, 2009).

33. Data collected from the United Nations Relief and Works Agency for Palestine Refugees, "UNRWA in Figures," December 2008, www.unrwa.org/userfiles/uif-dec08_2.pdf.

34. The 2008 estimate is from the Israel Central Bureau of Statistics, under "Tools," then "Time Series (Data Bank)," then "Population," then"Population, by Population Group," www.cbs.gov.il/reader/?MIval=cw_usr_view_Folder&ID =141.

35. Laurie Brand, *Palestinians in the Arab World: Institution Building and the Search for State* (New York: Columbia University Press, 1988), p. 222.

36. In fact, Israelis often discuss with relative ease the exact opposite of Palestinian repatriation: "transfer," by which they mean the removal of additional Palestinians from the Occupied Territories and Israel.

37. Mark Tessler, *A History of the Israeli-Palestinian Conflict* (Bloomington: University of Indiana Press, 1994), p. 436. Secularism, of course, fit the general ideological tenor of the 1960s and much of the 1970s. Tessler quotes the Syr-

ian poet and intellectual Adonis, who in 1968 wrote: "We must realize that the societies that modernized did so only after they rebelled against their history, tradition, and values. . . . We must ask our religious heritage what it can do for us in our present and future. . . . If it cannot do much for us we must abandon it."

38. Beverley Milton-Edwards, *Islamic Politics in Palestine* (London: I. B. Tauris, 1999), p. 103.

39. Over the years, a few young Palestinians from Gaza and West Bank refugee camps were given grants and scholarships to study in universities abroad, especially in Egypt, and returned home as members of the middle or even upper middle classes (many as high school and university instructors, engineers, or physicians).

40. Glenn E. Robinson, *Building a Palestinian State: The Incomplete Revolution* (Bloomington: Indiana University Press, 1997), p. 19.

41. Ibid., p. 20.

42. James A. Graff and Mohamed Abdollel, *Palestinian Children and Israeli State Violence* (Toronto: Near East Cultural and Educational Foundation of Canada, 1991), p. 169. This source contains valuable statistical data on injuries sustained by Palestinian children in the first two years of the *intifada*.

43. Ziad Abu-Amr, *Islamic Fundamentalism in the West Bank and Gaza* (Bloomington: Indiana University Press, 1994), p. 15.

44. For the founding of the Muslim Brotherhood and its spread elsewhere in the Middle East, see Nazih Ayubi, *Political Islam: Religion and Politics in the Arab World* (London: Routledge, 1991), pp. 70–98. For the activities of the Muslim Brotherhood first in Palestine and later in the Occupied Territories, see Abu Amr, *Islamic Fundamentalism*, especially pp. 1–52, and Milton-Edwards, *Islamic Politics in Palestine*.

45. Abu-Amr, *Islamic Fundamentalism*, p. 95.

46. Ibid., p. 115.

47. Shaul Mishal and Avraham Sela, *The Palestinian Hamas: Vision, Violence, and Coexistence* (New York: Columbia University Press, 2000), p. 9.

48. Both during the *intifada* and afterward, conflicts emerged between Hamas and first the ULU and later the PNA, especially following a number of suicide bombings attributed to the military wing of Hamas called the al-Qassam Brigade after the famous Muslim activist Sheikh Izz al-Din al-Qassam (1882–1935).

49. Mishal and Sela, *Palestinian Hamas*, p. 57.

50. Few observers of the Palestinian-Israeli conflict have paid sufficient attention to living conditions in the Occupied Territories and the consequences of these living conditions in sparking the *intifada* and the eventual signing of various peace agreements between the Israeli government and Palestinian representatives. For a moving portrait of life in Gaza written by an Israeli activist, see Amira Hass, *Drinking the Sea at Gaza: Days and Nights in a Land under Siege* (New York: Henry Holt, 1999). For a glimpse of life in the West Bank, see Saïd K. Aburish, *Cry Palestine: Inside the West Bank* (Boulder, CO: Westview Press, 1993).

51. For a typical Israeli explanation for the departure of the Palestinians in 1947–48, see excerpts from the speech before the United Nations (November 17, 1958) by Israel's ambassador to the body and later its foreign minister, Abba Eban, in "Abba Eban: The Refugee Problem," in Laqueur and Rubin, *Israeli-Arab Reader*, pp. 129–40. For one of the earliest critical analyses of this line of explanation, see the reprint of a 1961 article, "The Other Exodus," by Irish journalist Erskine Childers, also in Laqueur and Rubin, *Israeli-Arab Reader*, pp. 122–28.

52. Ilan Pappe, *The Ethnic Cleansing of Palestine* (Oxford: Oneworld, 2006); Benny Morris, *The Birth of the Palestinian Refugee Problem, 1947–1949* (New York: Cambridge University Press, 1987). See also Samih K. Farsoun and Christina E. Zacharia, *Palestine and the Palestinians* (Boulder, CO: Westview Press, 1997), pp. 130–40, and Orr, *Israel*, pp. 68–74.

53. Don Peretz, *Palestinians, Refugees, and the Middle East Peace Process* (Washington, DC: U.S. Institute for Peace Press, 1993), p. 13.

54. It is worth quoting at length passages from the U.S. Department of State's *Country Report on Human Rights Practices—2000:*

> Members of the Israeli security forces committed numerous serious human rights abuses, particularly following the outbreak of violence in late September. . . .
>
> Israel's overall human rights record in the occupied territories was poor. . . . Prolonged detention, limits on due process, and infringements on privacy rights remained problems. Israeli security forces sometimes impeded the provision of medical assistance to Palestinian civilians. Israeli security forces destroyed Palestinian-owned agricultural land. Israeli authorities censored Palestinian publications, placed limits on freedom of assembly, and restricted freedom of movement for Palestinians. . . .
>
> Israeli settlers harass, attack, and occasionally kill Palestinians in the West bank and Gaza Strip. There were credible reports that settlers injured a number of Palestinians during the "al-Aqsa intifada," usually by stoning their vehicles, which at times caused fatal accidents, shooting them, or hitting them with moving vehicles. Human rights groups received several dozen reports during the year that Israeli settlers in the West Bank beat Palestinians and destroyed the property of Palestinians living or farming near Israeli settlements.
>
> U.S. Department of State, "Israel and the Occupied Territories," in *Country Report on Human Rights Practices—2000* (Washington, DC: U.S. Department of State, 2001)

The same report, it must be mentioned, goes on to list a variety of acts of harassment and other human rights violations committed against Israeli settlers by Palestinians, including shootings, beatings, and stabbings.

55. Ibid.

56. David McDowall, *The Palestinians: The Road to Nationhood* (London: Minority Rights Group, 1995), pp. 82–84.

57. Anthony Coon, *Israel and the Occupied Territories, Demolition and Dispossession: The Destruction of Palestinian Homes* (London: Amnesty International, 1999), p. 11.

58. Ibid., p. 1.

59. Amnesty International, "Palestinian Homes Demolished without Warning," March 11, 2008, www.amnesty.org/en/news-and-updates/news/palestinian-homes-demolished-without-warning-20080311.

60. Coon, *Israel and the Occupied Territories,* p. 9.

61. Ibid., p. 12.

62. Central Bureau of Statistics, *Statistical Abstract of Israel, 2000,* no. 51 (Tel Aviv: Government Publishing House, 2000), pp. 16–17.

63. United Nations Commission on Human Rights, "Mission Report on Israel's Violations of Human Rights in the Palestinian Territories Occupied since 1967," E/CN.4/S-5/3, October 27, 2000.

64. B'Tselem, "Planning and Building," n.d., www.btselem.org/english/Planning_and_Building/Index.asp, accessed August 9, 2009.

65. Palestinian homes are often destroyed under the pretext of not having the proper building permits. The same requirement does not apply to the homes of Israeli settlers, however. According to a statement by the Israel Committee Against Home Demolitions,

> With three unusual exceptions, in the past 30 years NO Jewish house on the West Bank has ever been threatened with demolition. The entire notion is absolutely unthinkable to an Israeli. Moreover, any comparison of the legal status of the Palestinian and Jewish residents of the West Bank reveals completely different sets of rights, protections, and penalties.
>
> Israeli settlers are citizens of Israel and are subject only to Israeli law. None of the planning guidelines, procedures for obtaining building permits from the civilian administration or house demolition penalties applies to them. The first 21 Jewish settlements on the West Bank were done so without plans or permits and, indeed, against the stated policies and wishes of the Israeli government. Erecting structures in order to "create facts" on the ground is still a favorite tactic of the settlers, and thousands of Jewish housing units have been built without permits.
>
> Jeff Halper, *On the Policy of House Demolition by the Israeli Army in the West Bank* (Hebron: Israel Committee against House Demolitions, 1998)

66. Charles D. Smith, *Palestine and the Arab-Israeli Conflict,* 4th ed. (New York: St. Martin's Press, 2001), pp. 303–4.

67. Central Bureau of Statistics of Israel, "Survey of New Dwellings for Sale in the Private Sector," January–March 2009, table 1.1, p. 15.

68. Craig Horowitz, "A Tale of Two Cities," *New York*, April 7, 1997, p. 34.

69. Ian S. Lustick, *For the Land and the Lord: Jewish Fundamentalism in Israel* (New York: Council on Foreign Relations Press, 1988), pp. 45–46.

70. McDowall, *Palestinians*, p. 87.

71. United Nations, "The Impact of Prolonged Closure on Palestinian Poverty," *United Nations Report*, November 1, 2000, p. 1.

72. Colin MacKinnon, "Costs of the Closure: Gaza Hard Hit," *Washington Report on Middle East Affairs*, July 1996, p. 85.

73. All data in this paragraph come from the World Bank, *Investing in Palestinian Economic Reform and Development* (Washington, DC: World Bank, 2007).

74. In February–March 1996, for example, Hamas claimed responsibility for three suicide car bombings in Tel Aviv and Jerusalem that killed fifty-seven civilian Israelis. For an account of some of the terrorist activities committed by Palestinian guerrillas and suicide bombers against Israeli targets, see U.S. Department of State, "Israel and the Occupied Territories," in *Country Report on Human Rights Practices—2000* (Washington, DC: U.S. Department of State, 2001).

75. U.S. Department of State, "Israel and the Occupied Territories," in *Country Reports on Human Rights Practices—2002* (Washington, DC: U.S. Department of State, 2003).

76. Mishal and Sela, *Palestinian Hamas*, p. 62.

77. See, for example, Shimon Peres, *The New Middle East* (New York: Henry Holt, 1993); and Shimon Peres and Robert Littell, *For the Future of Israel* (Baltimore, MD: Johns Hopkins University Press, 1998).

78. Uri Savir, *The Process: 1,100 Days That Changed the Middle East* (New York: Vintage Books, 1998), p. 77.

79. Nicholas Guyatt, *The Absence of Peace: Understanding the Israeli-Palestinian Conflict* (London: Zed, 1998), p. 35.

80. For a detailed account of Sadat's trip to Israel and other events leading up to the Camp David Accords, see Kenneth Stein, *Heroic Diplomacy: Sadat, Kissinger, Carter, Begin, and the Quest for Arab-Israeli Peace* (London: Routledge, 1999), pp. 187–228.

81. Quoted in Laqueur and Rubin, *Israeli-Arab Reader*, p. 396.

82. Quoted in Fred Khouri, *The Arab-Israeli Dilemma*, 3rd ed. (Syracuse, NY: Syracuse University Press, 1985), p. 403.

83. Publicly, the PLO and Syria condemned Sadat's initiative but tried to keep their options open, while Saudi Arabia and Jordan took a wait-and-see attitude. Iraq, Libya, and South Yemen, however, were most vocal in condemning Sadat and succeeded in getting Egypt ejected, temporarily as it turned out, from the Arab League. Khouri, *Arab-Israeli Dilemma*, p. 404.

84. Ibid., p. 407.

85. Quoted in ibid., pp. 407–8.

86. Stein, *Heroic Diplomacy*, p. 254.

87. In announcing Jordan's "administrative and legal disengagement from

the West Bank," the king argued that continued Jordanian administration of the territory "would be an obstacle to the Palestinian struggle, which seeks to win international support for the Palestinian question, considering that it is a just national issue of a people struggling against foreign occupation." Quoted in Adnan Abu-Odeh, *Jordanians, Palestinians and the Hashemite Kingdom in the Middle East Peace Process* (Washington, DC: U.S. Institute of Peace Press, 1999), p. 226.

88. Savir, *Process*, p. 5.

89. Uri Savir was the chief Israeli diplomat who negotiated with the PLO in Oslo. For a most fascinating account of his efforts and his perspective, see Savir, *Process*.

90. On several occasions, for example, Israeli negotiators presented the PLO teams with a "take it or leave it" option, and the Palestinians almost always caved in. See, for example, ibid., p. 43.

91. Ibid., p. 59.

92. For a full text of the DOP, see Laqueur and Rubin, *Israeli-Arab Reader*, pp. 599–611. For this and other related documents, see also Institute for Palestine Studies, *The Palestinian-Israeli Peace Agreement: A Documentary Record* (Washington, DC: Institute for Palestine Studies, 1994).

93. Avi Shlaim, "The Oslo Accord," *Journal of Palestine Studies* 23 (Spring 1994): 34.

94. Guyatt, *Absence of Peace*, p. 35.

95. Edward Said, *Peace and Its Discontents: Essays on Palestine in the Middle East Peace Process* (New York: Vintage Books, 1995), p. 7.

96. Ibid., pp. 3–4.

97. Hillel Frisch, *Countdown to Statehood: Palestinian State Formation in the West Bank and Gaza* (Albany: SUNY Press, 1998), pp. 132–35.

98. Quoted in Jimmy Carter, *Palestine, Peace not Apartheid* (New York: Simon and Schuster, 2006), p. 147.

99. Naseer H. Aruri, "The Wye Memorandum: Netanyahu's Oslo and Unreciprocal Reciprocity," *Journal of Palestine Studies* 28 (Winter 1999): 17–28; Norman Finkelstein, "Securing Occupation: The Real Meaning of the Wye River Memorandum," *New Left Review*, no. 232 (1998): 128–39.

100. Finkelstein, "Securing Occupation," p. 137.

101. Avi Shlaim, *The Iron Wall: Israel and the Arab World* (New York: W. W. Norton, 2001), p. 600.

102. Don Peretz, "Barak's Israel," *Current History* 100 (January 2001): 22.

103. Sara Roy, "Why Peace Failed: An Oslo Autopsy," *Current History* 101 (January 2002): 9.

104. Akram Hanieh, "The Camp David Papers," *Journal of Palestine Studies* 30 (Winter 2001): 76.

105. Robert Malley and Hussein Agha, "Camp David: Tragedy of Errors," *New York Review of Books*, August 9, 2001.

106. Shibley Telhami, "Camp David II: Assumptions and Consequences," *Current History* 100 (January 2001): 11.

107. Tim Youngs, "The Middle East Crisis: Camp David, the 'Al-Aqsa Intifada' and the Prospects for the Peace Process," United Kingdom House of Commons Library, Research Paper 01/09, January 24, 2001, p. 15.

108. Roy, "Why Peace Failed," p. 15.

109. Ibid., p. 19.

110. Malley and Agha, "Camp David," p. 71.

111. For a discussion of the Sabra and Shatila massacres and Sharon's role, see Tessler, *History*, pp. 590–99.

112. For excerpts of the Mitchell Report, see Mitchell Report, "The Sharm al-Shaykh Fact-Finding Committee, 'The Mitchell Report,' 20 May 2001," *Journal of Palestine Studies* 30 (Spring 2001): 146–50.

113. U.S. Department of State, "Israel and the Occupied Territories," in *Country Report on Human Rights Practices—2001* (Washington, DC: U.S. Department of State, 2002).

114. Ibid.

115. Quoted in Edward R. F. Sheehan, "The Map and the Fence," *New York Review of Books*, July 3, 2003, 8.

116. See, for example, Milton Viorst, "The Road Map to Nowhere," *Washington Quarterly* 26 (Summer 2003): 177–90.

117. Sheehan, "Map and the Fence," pp. 8–9.

118. Ariel Sharon's address to the Fourth Herzliya Conference, December 18, 2003, www.mfa.gov.il.

119. David Rose, "The Gaza Bombshell," *Vanity Fair*, April 2008, pp. 192–98, 247–51.

120. United Nations Office for the Coordination of Humanitarian Affairs, "Field Update on Gaza from the Humanitarian Coordinator, 24–26 January 2009," East Jerusalem, 2009, www.ochaopt.org/documents/ocha_opt_gaza_humanitarian_situation_report_2009_01_14_english.pdf.

121. Clancy Chassay and Julian Borger, "New Evidence of Israel's Gaza War Crimes Revealed: Investigation Finds Medical Staff Hit and Civilians 'Used as Shields,'" *Guardian*, March 24, 2009, p. 1.

122. Shlaim, *Iron Wall*, p. xx.

123. See, for example, Said, *Peace and Its Discontents*, p. 121.

124. Aharon Klieman, *Compromising Palestine: A Guide to Final Status Negotiations* (New York: Columbia University Press, 2000), pp. 239–42.

8. THE CHALLENGE OF ECONOMIC DEVELOPMENT

1. Roger Owen and Sevket Pamuk, *A History of Middle East Economies in the Twentieth Century* (Cambridge, MA: Harvard University Press, 1999), p. 7.

2. Charles Issawi, *The Middle East Economy: Decline and Recovery* (Princeton, NJ: Markus Wiener, 1995), p. 101.

3. Owen and Pamuk, *History of Middle East Economies*, p. 7.

4. Michael P. Todaro, *Economic Development*, 6th ed. (Reading, MA: Addison-Wesley, 1997), p. 721.

5. Alan Richards and John Waterbury, *A Political Economy of the Middle East*, 2nd ed. (Boulder, CO: Westview Press, 1996), p. 175.

6. Ibid., p. 201.

7. Interventionism and heavy regulation of the economy can make a state appear socialist. Nazih Ayubi discusses at great length the question of whether the Middle Eastern state is socialist or what he calls "populist-corporatist," arguing that despite the adoption of socialist slogans and even certain organizational structures, what predominates in the Middle East is not socialism but *etatism*. See Nazih N. Ayubi, *Over-Stating the Arab State: Politics and Society in the Middle East* (London: I. B. Tauris, 1999), pp. 196–203.

8. Monte Palmer, *Political Development: Dilemmas and Challenges* (Itasca, IL: F. E. Peacock, 1997), p. 30.

9. Cited in Richards and Waterbury, *Political Economy*, p. 180.

10. John Waterbury, *The Egypt of Nasser and Sadat: The Political Economy of Two Regimes* (Princeton, NJ: Princeton University Press, 1983), p. 160.

11. Richards and Waterbury, *Political Economy*, p. 184.

12. Volker Perthes, *The Political Economy of Syria under Asad* (London: I. B. Tauris, 1997), p. 141.

13. Data collected from the Syrian Central Bureau of Statistics, www.cbssyr.org.

14. John Ruedy, *Modern Algeria: The Origins and Development of a Nation* (Bloomington: Indiana University Press, 1992), p. 216.

15. Richards and Waterbury, *Political Economy*, p. 187.

16. Ibid., p. 188.

17. Ibid., p. 195.

18. Hooshang Amirahmadi, *Revolution and Economic Transition: The Iranian Experience* (Albany: SUNY Press, 1990), p. 189.

19. Anne Marie Baylouny, "Militarizing Welfare: Neo-Liberalism and Jordanian Policy," *Middle East Journal* 62 (Spring 2008): 287.

20. Central Intelligence Agency, *CIA World Factbook, 2009*, https://www.cia.gov/library/publications/the-world-factbook/.

21. Ibid.

22. "Cleanup" efforts have been largely unsuccessful. See Kate Gillespie and Gwenn Okruhlik, "Cleaning Up Corruption in the Middle East," *Middle East Journal* 42 (Winter 1988): 59–82.

23. Owen and Pamuk, *History of Middle East Economies*, pp. 141–44. Andre Croppenstadt, "Measuring Technical Efficiency of Wheat Farmers in Egypt," ESA Working Paper No. 05–06, Food and Agriculture Organization of the United Nations, July 2005, p. 1.

24. Richards and Waterbury, *Political Economy*, p. 153.

25. Ibid., p. 206.

26. Ruedy, *Modern Algeria*, p. 220.

27. Richards and Waterbury, *Political Economy*, p. 216.

28. Perthes, *Political Economy of Syria*, p. 204.

29. Richards and Waterbury, *Political Economy*, pp. 233–37.

30. World Bank, *World Development Indicators, 2003* (Washington, DC: World Bank, 2003), pp. 258–60.

31. Iliya Harik, "Privatization: The Issues, the Prospects, and the Fears," in *Privatization and Liberalization in the Middle East,* ed. Iliya Harik and Denis Sullivan (Bloomington: Indiana University Press, 1992), pp. 18–19.

32. John Page and Linda Van Gelder, "Missing Links: Institutional Capability, Policy Reform, and Growth in the Middle East and North Africa," in *The State and Global Change: The Political Economy of Transition in the Middle East and North Africa,* ed. Hassan Hakimian and Ziba Moshaver (London: Curzon, 2001), p. 46.

33. Ibid., p. 28.

34. Put differently, rentierism is the product of "unearned income not generated by the productive operation of the national economy." Khaldoun Hasan Al-Naqeeb, *Society and State in the Gulf and Arab Peninsula: A Different Perspective,* trans. L. M. Kenny (London: Routledge, 1990), pp. 78–79. Todaro offers a more precise definition of economic rent: "the payment to a factor of production (i.e. resources or inputs such as land, labor, or capital) required to produce a good or a service over and above its highest opportunity cost." Todaro, *Economic Development,* p. 716.

35. Laurie Brand, "Economic and Political Liberalization in a Rentier Economy: The Case of the Hashemite Kingdom of Jordan," in Harik and Sullivan, *Privatization and Liberalization,* p. 168.

36. Peter Evans, *Embedded Autonomy: States and Industrial Transformation* (Princeton, NJ: Princeton University Press, 1995), p. 23. Nevertheless, especially in relation to the Middle East, a rentier state is generally seen as one that "depends on external sources for a large portion of its revenues. These revenues from abroad are called rent. Rent is not the only income, but it certainly predominates. In the past, rentier states have been based on international trade in gold or bat guano. Today, the term refers most often to the oil states whose income is derived from the international sale of petroleum." Gwenn Okruhlik, "Rentier Wealth, Unruly Law, and the Rise of Opposition: The Political Economy of Oil States," *Comparative Politics* 31 (April 1999): 295.

37. Timothy J. Piro, *The Political Economy of Market Reform in Jordan* (Lanham, MD: Rowman and Littlefield, 1998), p. 11.

38. Brand, "Economic and Political Liberalization," p. 168.

39. Gregory S. Mahler, *Politics and Government in Israel* (Lanham, MD: Rowman and Littlefield, 2004), p. 105. For more on Israel's "imported money," see Asher Arian, *Politics in Israel: The Second Republic,* 2nd ed. (Washington, DC: CQ Press, 2005), pp. 71–72.

40. Brand, "Economic and Political Liberalization," p. 168.

41. Ibid., p. 169.

42. Kiren Chaudhry rejects the argument that the state deliberately seeks to foster clientalism and patronage, instead maintaining that social outcomes can be best explained by examining "the interaction of laissez-faire distributive imperatives *undertaken for growth alone,* the lack of economic informa-

tion, and the preexisting composition of the bureaucracy" (emphasis added). Kiren Aziz Chaudhry, *The Price of Wealth: Economies and Institutions in the Middle East* (Ithaca, NY: Cornell University Press, 1997), p. 191. Nevertheless, the outcome, namely the acquiescence of important economically active sectors of the population to state authoritarianism, remains the same.

43. There is a rich body of literature on rentierism in the Middle East. A sample of this literature includes Rex Brynen, "Economic Crisis and Post-Rentier Democratization in the Arab World: The Case of Jordan," *Canadian Journal of Political Science* 25 (March 1992): 69–97; Barnett Rubin, "Political Elites in Afghanistan: Rentier State Building, Rentier State Wrecking," *International Journal of Middle East Studies* 24 (February 1992): 77–99; Hootan Shambayati, "The Rentier State, Interest Groups, and the Paradox of Autonomy: State and Business in Turkey and Iran," *Comparative Politics* 26 (April 1994): 307–31; and Eva Bellin, "The Politics of Profit in Tunisia: Utility of the Rentier Paradigm?" *World Development* 22, no. 3 (1994): 427–36.

44. This take on rentierism is shared by most but not all students of the phenomenon. Okruhlik, for example, maintains that in Saudi Arabia "rent did not buy the support or loyalty of different social groups even during the boom," as the uneven distribution of its proceeds led to resentment and opposition. Okruhlik, "Rentier Wealth," p. 297.

45. Daniel Brumberg, "Authoritarian Legacies and Reform Strategies in the Arab World," in *Political Liberalization and Democratization in the Arab World*, vol. 1, *Theoretical Perspectives*, ed. Rex Brynen, Bahgat Korany, and Paul Noble (Boulder, CO: Lynne Rienner, 1995), p. 233. For more on the "ruling bargain," see Chapter 9.

46. Although almost the rule, rent seeking in the Middle East has been a highly risky endeavor, especially lately, as the amount of revenues accrued from it—namely from oil, labor, and tourism—has been volatile and unpredictable.

47. Brumberg, "Authoritarian Legacies," p. 239.

48. For essays on the different liberalization experiences in the Middle East in the 1980s, see Harik and Sullivan, *Privatization and Liberalization*. See also Henri Barkey, ed., *The Politics of Economic Reform in the Middle East* (New York: St. Martin's Press, 1992).

49. As Okruhlik puts it, Middle Eastern states have opted for "system maintenance in the guise of liberalization from above . . . [hoping to] coopt wider circles of the political public and direct political and religious organizations into acceptable and controllable channels." Okruhlik, "Rentier Wealth," p. 305.

50. David Waldner, *State Building and Late Development* (Ithaca, NY: Cornell University Press, 1999), pp. 198–99.

51. Ibid., pp. 49–51.

52. Robert Looney, "Reforming the Rentier State: The Imperative for Change in the Gulf," in *Critical Issues Facing the Middle East: Security, Politics, and Economics*, ed. James A. Russell (New York: Macmillan, 2006), p. 43.

53. The linkages between declines in economic rents and political instability are not as direct as they may appear on the surface. Even in times of

economic difficulty, in many instances the state is still seen as an important source of patronage and protection under adverse circumstances, and as the only ally that can turn the economy around and once again funnel capital into private hands.

54. Richard Auty, "The Political State and the Management of Mineral Rents in Capital-Surplus Economies," *Resources Policy* 27 (2001): 79.

55. See, for example, Amirahmadi, *Revolution and Economic Transition;* Chaudhry, *Price of Wealth;* Manochehr Dorraj, "State, Petroleum, and Democratization in the Middle East and North Africa," in *The Changing Political Economy of the Third World,* ed. Manochehr Dorraj (Boulder, CO: Lynne Rienner, 1995), pp. 119–43; Ellis Jay Goldberg, ed., *The Social History of Labor in the Middle East* (Boulder, CO: Westview Press, 1996); Harik and Sullivan, *Privatization and Liberalization;* Homa Katouzian, *The Political Economy of Modern Iran, 1926–1979* (New York: NYU Press, 1981); Piro, *Political Economy;* and Richards and Waterbury, *Political Economy.*

56. Edmund Burke, ed., *Struggle and Survival in the Modern Middle East* (Berkeley: University of California Press, 1993).

57. For a study on informal networks, see Guilain Denoeux, *Urban Unrest in the Middle East: A Comparative Study of Informal Networks in Egypt, Iran, and Lebanon* (Albany: SUNY Press, 1993). Sanchez, Palmiero, and Ferrero do discuss a "quasi-formal" sector, although they apply the concept to "those earning a high income either because of advanced skills, or because of high capital intensity or because of oligarchical market environment," embodying "self-employed professionals like doctors, lawyers, etc.; small engineering units and manufacturing activities with significant amounts of skills and investment; self-employed construction workers including plumbers and electricians and the like; and commercial activities with a substantial capital input." Carlos Sanchez, Horacio Palmiero, and Fernando Ferrero, "The Informal and Quasi-Formal Sectors in Cordoba," in *The Urban Informal Sector in Developing Countries: Employment, Poverty and Environment,* ed. S. V. Sethuraman (Geneva: International Labour Office, 1981), pp. 144–45.

58. John Waterbury, *Exposed to Innumerable Delusions: Public Enterprise and State Power in Egypt, India, Mexico, and Turkey* (New York: Cambridge University Press, 1993), p. 1.

59. Monte Palmer, Ali Leila, and El Sayed Yassin, *The Egyptian Bureaucracy* (Cairo: American University of Cairo Press, 1988).

60. Piro, *Political Economy,* pp. 96–97.

61. Richards and Waterbury quote an Egyptian study that found four different subsectors within Egypt's informal sector: (1) small-scale manufacturing and handicraft work; (2) itinerant and jobbing artisanry (masons, carpenters, tailors); (3) personal services (servants, porters, watchmen); and (4) petty services and retailing activities (car washers, street hawkers and vendors, garbage collectors). According to the broader classification used here, subsectors 1 and 2 are stationary, while 3 and 4 are mobile members of the informal sector. Richards and Waterbury, *Political Economy,* p. 139.

62. Richard Adams, "Bureaucrats, Peasants and the Dominant Coalition: An Egyptian Case Study," *Journal of Development Studies* 2, no. 2 (1986): 236–54.

63. Alan Richards, "Economic Imperatives and Political Systems," *Middle East Journal* 47, no. 2 (1993): 219–20.

64. Giacomo Luciani, "The Oil Rent, Fiscal Crisis of the State and Democratization," in *Democracy without Democrats? The Renewal of Politics in the Muslim World*, ed. Ghassan Salame (London: I. B. Tauris, 1994), pp. 130–55.

65. S. V. Sethuraman, "The Role of the Urban Informal Sector," in Sethuraman, *Urban Informal Sector*, p. 28.

66. In 1977, the Iranian state hired university students to conduct price checks on *bazaari* merchants (but not on smaller-scale, less economically visible businesses); more on this below.

67. Mehran Kamrava, *Democracy in the Balance: Culture and Society in the Middle East* (Chatham, NJ: Chatham House, 1998), p. 65.

68. There have been no systematic studies of the punishment of criminals by economic and/or social status in the Middle East. Studies focusing on Latin America and Africa show, however, that marginal elements within society, especially the homeless and street children, often receive harsh and indiscriminate punishment from the police and other security forces. See, for example, European Conference on Street Children Worldwide, *Street Children in North and South: A Comparative Summary* (Amsterdam: Royal Tropical Institute, 1996).

69. Achille Mbembe, "Power and Obscenity in the Post-Colonial Period: The Case of Cameroon," in *Rethinking Third World Politics*, ed. James Manor (London: Longman, 1991), pp. 166–82.

70. Amnesty International, *Challenging Repression: Human Rights Defenders in the Middle East and North Africa* (London: Amnesty International, 2008).

71. Amnesty International, *Affront to Justice: The Death Penalty in Saudi Arabia* (London: Amnesty International, 2008). See also Amnesty International, *Kuwait: Five Years of Impunity since the Withdrawal of Iraqi Forces* (London: Amnesty International, 1996).

72. Safia K. Mohsen, "New Images, Old Reflections: Working Middle-Class Women in Egypt," in *Women and the Family in the Middle East: New Voices for Change*, ed. Elizabeth Wamock Fernea (Austin: University of Texas Press, 1985), p. 57.

73. Waterbury, *Exposed to Innumerable Delusions*, p. 5.

74. Joel Migdal, "Studying the State," in *Comparative Politics: Rationality, Culture, and Structure*, ed. Mark Irving Lichbach and Alan Zuckerman (New York: Cambridge University Press, 1997), p. 214.

75. Ibid., p. 222.

76. Palmer, Leila, and Yassin, *Egyptian Bureaucracy*, p. 119.

77. Denis Sullivan, "Extra-State Actors and Privatization in Egypt," in Harik and Sullivan, *Privatization and Liberalization*, pp. 24–45.

78. Michael Field, *The Merchants: The Big Business Families of Saudi Arabia and the Gulf States* (Woodstock, NY: Overlook Press, 1985).

79. Shaul Bakhash, *The Reign of the Ayatollahs: Iran and the Islamic Revolution* (London: I. B. Tauris, 1985), p. 192.

80. Louis Cantori, "Civil Society, Liberalism and the Corporatist Alternative in the Middle East," *Middle East Studies Association Bulletin* 31 (July 1997): 37–38.

81. One of the most perceptive treatments of globalization, and especially its engagement with the Middle East, can be found in Anoushiravan Ehteshami, *Globalization and Geopolitics in the Middle East: Old Games, New Rules* (London: Routledge, 2007).

82. See, for example, Indra de Soysa, *Foreign Direct Investment, Democracy, and Development: Assessing Contours, Correlates, and Concomitants of Globalization* (London: Routledge, 2003).

83. Given the scales of the economies involved and the number of countries in each of the two regions, the average net FDI inflow into (and the percentage of high-technology export from) South Asia is actually higher than that of the Middle East/North Africa region.

84. The percentage of high-technology goods as compared to the total of manufactured exports indicates levels of industrial development and global competitiveness, and is therefore a key index of globalization.

85. Ehteshami, *Globalization and Geopolitics*, p. 51.

86. Roger Owen, "Inter-Arab Economic Relations during the Twentieth Century: World Market vs. Regional Market?" in *Middle East Dilemma: The Politics and Economics of Arab Integration*, ed. Michael C. Hudson (New York: Columbia University Press, 1999), p. 220.

87. Yusif A. Sayigh, "Arab Economic Integration: The Poor Harvest of the 1980s," in *Middle East Dilemma: The Politics and Economics of Arab Integration*, ed. Michael C. Hudson (New York: Columbia University Press, 1999), pp. 233–58.

88. On the Euro-Mediterranean agreement, see Owen, "Inter-Arab Economic Relations," p. 227.

89. Enrico Gisolo, "The Degree of Central Bank Independence in MENA Countries," in *Monetary Policy and Central Banking in the Middle East and North Africa*, ed. David Cobhan and Ghassan Dibeh (London: Routledge, 2009), p. 48.

90. Ibid., p. 50.

91. For more on this, see Mehran Kamrava, "Structural Impediments to Economic Globalization in the Middle East," *Middle East Policy* 11 (Winter 2004): 96–112.

92. Jacob Skovgaard-Petersen, "The Global Mufti," in *Globalization and the Muslim World: Culture, Religion, and Modernity*, ed. Bright Schaebler and Leif Stenberg (Syracuse, NY: Syracuse University Press, 2004), pp. 153–65.

9. STATES AND THEIR OPPONENTS

1. James Lee Ray, "The Democratic Path to Peace," *Journal of Democracy* 8 (April 1997): 49–64. For critical discussions of the "democratic peace theory," see Tarak Barkawi and Mark Laffey, eds., *Democracy, Liberalism, and War: Rethinking the Democratic Peace Debate* (Boulder, CO: Lynne Rienner, 2001).

2. Although these labels or their variations appear elsewhere, my usage of them here is inspired by Jeff Goodwin and Theda Skocpol's "Explaining Revolutions in the Contemporary Third World," *Politics and Society* 17 (1989): 489–509. For other state typologies, see Anton Bebler and Jim Seroka, eds., *Contemporary Political Systems: Classifications and Typologies* (Boulder, CO: Lynne Rienner, 1990), especially Bahgat Korany's chapter, "Arab Political Systems," pp. 303–29. See also Iliya Harik, "The Origins of the Arab State System," in *The Foundations of the Arab State*, ed. Ghassan Salame (London: Croom Helm, 1987), pp. 19–46.

3. Praetorian systems are dictatorships in which "social forces confront each other nakedly; no political institutions, no corps of professional political leaders are recognized or accepted as legitimate intermediaries to moderate group conflict. Equally important, no agreement exists among groups as to the legitimate and authoritative methods for resolving conflicts." Samuel P. Huntington, *Political Order in Changing Societies* (New Haven, CT: Yale University Press, 1968), p. 196.

4. Khaldoun Hasan Al-Naqeeb, *Society and State in the Gulf and Arab Peninsula: A Different Perspective*, trans. L. M. Kenney (London: Routledge, 1990), p. 6.

5. Dirk Vandewalle, "From the New State to the New Era: Toward a Second Republic in Tunisia," *Middle East Journal* 42, no. 4 (1988): 618.

6. Rosemarie Said Zahlan, *The Making of the Modern Gulf States: Kuwait, Bahrain, Qatar, the United Arab Emirates, and Oman* (London: Unwin Hyman, 1989), p. 63.

7. Most of the top leaders in the Syrian state are members of the Al-Assad family. Hanna Battatu, "Political Power and Social Structure in Syria and Iraq," in *Arab Society: Continuity and Change*, ed. Samih K. Farsoun (London: Croom Helm, 1985), p. 37.

8. For an interesting study of the media in the Arab world, see William Rugh, *The Arab Press* (Syracuse, NY: Syracuse University Press, 1987). Rugh does not discuss the Arab press's coverage of local issues.

9. James Rosberg, "Causes and Consequences of Judicial Independence in Contemporary Egypt," paper presented at the Middle East Studies Association Conference, Phoenix, AZ, November 1994.

10. Ismail Boulahia, vice president of the Democratic Socialist Movement (MDS) Party, interview by author, Tunis, May 27, 1996.

11. Lisa Anderson, "Absolutism and the Resilience of Monarchy in the Middle East," *Political Science Quarterly* 106, no. 1 (1991): 5–6.

12. Daniel Brumberg, "Authoritarian Legacies and Reform Strategies in

the Arab World," in *Political Liberalization and Democratization in the Arab World,* vol. 1, *Theoretical Perspectives,* ed. Rex Brynen, Bahgat Korany, and Paul Noble (Boulder, CO: Lynne Rienner, 1995), p. 233. For more on the "ruling bargain," see Chapter 10.

13. Monte Palmer, Ali Leila, and El Sayed Yassin, *The Egyptian Bureaucracy* (Cairo: American University of Cairo Press, 1988), p. 4.

14. Ibid.

15. Alan Richards and John Waterbury, *A Political Economy of the Middle East,* 2nd ed. (Boulder, CO: Westview Press, 1996), p. 192.

16. Dirk Vandewalle, "Breaking with Socialism: Economic Liberalization and Privatization in Algeria," in *Privatization and Liberalization in the Middle East,* ed. Iliya Harik and Denis Sullivan (Bloomington: Indiana University Press, 1992), p. 189.

17. Brumberg, "Authoritarian Legacies," p. 235.

18. Richards and Waterbury, *Political Economy,* pp. 257–58.

19. Fouad Ajami, *The Arab Predicament: Arab Political Thought and Practice since 1967* (New York: Cambridge University Press, 1992), p. 104.

20. Anthony McDermott, *Egypt from Nasser to Mubarak: A Flawed Revolution* (London: Croom Helm, 1988), p. 198.

21. Raymond Hinnebusch, "State and Civil Society in Syria," *Middle East Journal* 47, no. 2 (1993): 247.

22. Max Weber, *On Charisma and Institution Building* (Chicago: University of Chicago Press, 1968), p. 46.

23. After the Iran-Iraq War and its invasion of Kuwait, Iraq fit more appropriately into the inclusionary than the exclusionary category of states. Nevertheless, even Saddam Hussein, who never served in the Iraqi army, was given the rank of general by his then superior, President Bakr. Before the two wars, Saddam often wore civilian suits, although in the months leading up to the U.S. invasion of Iraq and his overthrow, he was hardly seen not wearing his military uniform.

24. James Bill and Robert Springborg, *Politics in the Middle East,* 4th ed. (New York: HarperCollins, 1994), p. 247.

25. Ibid., p. 267.

26. Patrick Seale, "Asad: Between Institutions and Autocracy," in *Syria: Society, Culture, and Polity,* ed. Richard Antoun and Donald Quataert (Albany: SUNY Press, 1991), p. 107.

27. Foreign Broadcast Information Service: Near East and South Asia (FBIS-NES), November 8, 1995, p. 21.

28. For an insightful look at Egypt's al-Gama'a, see Hamied Ansari, *Egypt: The Stalled Society* (Albany: SUNY Press, 1986), pp. 212–30.

29. See Michael Collins Dunn, "The Al-Nahda Movement in Tunisia: From Renaissance to Revolution," in *Islamism and Secularism in North Africa,* ed. John Ruedy (New York: St. Martin's Press, 1994), pp. 149–65. At best, leaders of al-Nahda, most of whom are in exile in Europe, denounce President Ben Ali through fax transmissions into the country. Western diplomat (who chose to remain unnamed), interview by author, Tunis, May 1996.

30. Lisa Anderson, "Political Pacts, Liberalism, and Democracy: The Tunisian National Pact of 1988," *Government and Opposition* 26 (Spring 1991): 244–60; U.S. Department of State, "Tunisia," in *Country Report on Human Rights Practices—1995* (Washington, DC: U.S. Department of State, 1996), pp. 2–3.

31. For a vivid account of the events at Hama, see Thomas Friedman, *From Beirut to Jerusalem* (New York: Farrar Straus Giroux, 1989), pp. 76–87.

32. John Ruedy, *Modern Algeria: The Origins and Development of a Nation* (Bloomington: Indiana University Press, 1992), p. 209.

33. Pictorial or symbolic representations of the president (in terms of public places named after him) vary from one exclusionary state to another. President Hafiz Al-Assad's larger-than-life photographs and statues can be found throughout Damascus and other Syrian cities, even now that he is deceased and has been succeeded by his son. President Ben Ali's portraits are somewhat less omnipresent in Tunisia, although there is no shortage of his photographs in various poses throughout Tunisia. Although there were many giant portraits of Sadat in Egyptian cities when he was in power, today there are few of President Mubarak, though some can still be found in Cairo and elsewhere.

34. Ervand Abrahamian, *Khomeinism: Essays on the Islamic Republic* (Berkeley: University of California Press, 1993), p. 38.

35. Mohsen Milani, "Shi'ism and the State in the Constitution of the Islamic Republic of Iran," in *Iran: Political Culture in the Islamic Republic*, ed. Samih Farsoun and Mehrdad Mashayekhi (London: Routledge, 1992), p. 152.

36. Dirk Vandewalle, "Qadhafi's 'Perestroika': Economic and Political Liberalization in Libya," *Middle East Journal* 45, no. 2 (1991): 217.

37. Bill and Springborg, *Politics in the Middle East*, pp. 291–92.

38. Nikola Schahgaldian, *The Iranian Military under the Islamic Republic* (Santa Monica, CA: Rand Corporation, 1987), p. 34.

39. Anoushiravan Ehteshami, *After Khomeini: The Iranian Second Republic* (London: Routledge, 1995), pp. 27–29, 71.

40. Fredric Wehrey et al., *The Rise of the Pasdaran: Assessing the Domestic Role of Iran's Islamic Revolutionary Guards Corps* (Santa Monica, CA: Rand, 2009).

41. Hooshang Amirahmadi, *Revolution and Economic Transition: The Iranian Experience* (Albany: SUNY Press, 1990), p. 89.

42. Samir al-Khalil, *Republic of Fear: The Inside Story of Saddam's Iraq* (New York: Pantheon Books, 1989). Referring to alleged plotters within the Ba'th Party, Saddam himself is quoted as having once said: "We are now in our Stalinist era. We shall strike with an iron fist against the slightest deviation or backsliding beginning with the Ba'thists themselves." Quoted in Efraim Karsh and Inari Rautsi, *Saddam Hussein: A Political Biography* (New York: Free Press, 1991), p. 117.

43. F. Gregory Gause, "Regional Influences on Experiments in Political Liberalization in the Arab World," in Brynen, Korany, and Noble, *Political Liber-*

alization, vol. 1, p. 286. Comparable data for the same years include 20.5 percent for Saudi Arabia and 18.8 percent for PDR Yemen.

44. Following the Gulf War, this number was reported to have been reduced to 350,000. John Paxton, ed., *The Statesman's Yearbook, 1988–89* (New York: St. Martin's Press, 1988); Brian Hunter, ed., *The Statesman's Yearbook, 1993–94* (New York: St. Martin's Press, 1993).

45. al-Khalil, *Republic of Fear,* pp. 30–31.

46. Karsh and Rautsi, *Saddam Hussein,* p. 176. See also Marion Farouk-Sluglett and Peter Sluglett, "The Iraqi Bath Party," in *Political Parties in the Third World,* ed. Vicky Randall (Newbury Park, CA: Sage Publications, 1988), pp. 57–74.

47. Karsh and Rautsi, *Saddam Hussein,* pp. 176–77.

48. Vandewalle, "Qadhafi's 'Perestroika,'" pp. 218–19.

49. Samir al-Khalil, *The Monument: Art and Vulgarity in Iraq* (Berkeley: University of California Press, 1991); Donald Malcom Reid, "The Postage Stamp: A Window on Saddam Hussein's Iraq," *Middle East Journal* 47, no. 1 (1993): 77–89.

50. Karsh and Rautsi, *Saddam Hussein,* p. 224.

51. Bill and Springborg, *Politics in the Middle East,* pp. 151–71.

52. Ruedy, *Modern Algeria,* p. 240.

53. Manoucher Parvin and Mostafa Vaziri, "Islamic Man and Society in the Islamic Republic of Iran," in Farsoun and Mashayekhi, *Iran,* pp. 123–24.

54. Abrahamian, *Khomeinism,* p. 38.

55. Zahlan, *Making of the Modern Gulf States,* pp. 27–30.

56. Rex Brynen, "Economic Crisis and Post-Rentier Democratization in the Arab World: The Case of Jordan," *Canadian Journal of Political Science* 25 (March 1992): 70.

57. Albert Hourani, *A History of the Arab Peoples* (Cambridge, MA: Belknap Press, 1991), p. 115.

58. Today, the Moroccan state relies for its legitimacy not so much on the country's history of monarchic rule as on the "struggles" of the founder of the modern state, Muhammad V, against the French.

59. Al-Naqeeb, *Society and State,* p. 102.

60. Weber, *On Charisma,* p. 46.

61. Ibid., emphasis in original.

62. Al-Naqeeb, *Society and State,* p. 107.

63. F. Gregory Gause, *Oil Monarchies: Domestic and Security Challenges in the Arab Gulf States* (New York: Council on Foreign Relations Press, 1994), p. 23.

64. Ibid., p. 25.

65. Zahlan, *Making of the Modern Gulf States,* p. 79.

66. Ibid., p. 88.

67. Peter Wilson and Douglas Graham, *Saudi Arabia: The Coming Storm* (Armonk, NY: M. E. Sharpe, 1994), pp. 20–21.

68. Nevertheless, princely privileges appear more extensive in Saudi Ara-

bia than in the other Gulf monarchies. The Saudi royal family has a separate satellite telephone network of its own, and all princes receive annual salaries ranging from $200,000 to $500,000. See ibid., pp. 19–22.

69. Gause, *Oil Monarchies*, pp. 56–57.

70. Ibid., p. 54.

71. In 1986, in an attempt to shore up his Islamic credentials, King Fahd dropped the title of "His Majesty" and instead adopted the more humble "Custodian of the Two Holy Mosques."

72. In this respect, in fact, family control over state institutions is far more extensive in Syria than in Jordan.

73. Omar Bendourou, "Power and Opposition in Morocco," *Journal of Democracy* 7, no. 3 (1996): 110–11.

74. Ibid., p. 110.

75. Quoted in ibid., p. 114.

76. Saad Eddin Ibrahim, "Liberalization and Democratization in the Arab World: An Overview," in Brynen, Korany, and Noble, *Political Liberalization*, vol. 1, pp. 46–47.

77. For a detailed discussion of the distinctions between "viable" and quasi-democracies, see Mehran Kamrava, *Politics and Society in the Developing World*, 2nd ed. (London: Routledge, 2000), pp. 198–205.

78. Jeremy Salt, "Turkey's Military 'Democracy,'" *Current History* 98 (February 1999): 72–78, and Mehran Kamrava, "Military-Professionalization and Civil-Military Relations in the Middle East," *Political Science Quarterly* 115 (Spring 2000): 70–76.

79. Henri Barkey and Graham Fuller, *Turkey's Kurdish Question* (Lanham, MD: Rowman and Littlefield, 1998), p. 12.

80. Feroz Ahmad, *The Making of Modern Turkey* (London: Routledge, 1993), p. 12.

81. Quoted in ibid., p. 181.

82. Ahmet Evin, "Demilitarization and Civilianization of the Regime," in *Politics in the Third Turkish Republic*, ed. Metin Heper and Ahmet Evin (Boulder, CO: Westview Press, 1994), pp. 30–32.

83. Mehran Kamrava, "Pseudo-Democratic Politics and Populist Possibilities: The Rise and Demise of Turkey's Refah Party," *British Journal of Middle Eastern Studies* 25 (November 1998): 288.

84. Barkey and Fuller, *Turkey's Kurdish Question*, p. 140.

85. The 1996 and 1999 elections have shown that the electoral reforms of 1992 have not had their intended consequences of strengthening the prime minister's hand in dealing with the Knesset. See Gideon Doron and Michael Harris, *Public Policy and Electoral Reform: The Case of Israel* (Lanham, MD: Lexington Books, 2000), pp. 71–73.

86. Asher Arian, *The Second Republic: Politics in Israel* (Chatham, NJ: Chatham House, 1998), p. 266.

87. Central Bureau of Statistics of Israel, *Statistical Abstract of Israel, 2008*, no. 59 (Tel Aviv: Government Publishing House, 2008), pp. 85–86. Of

Arab Israelis, approximately 78 percent are Muslim, 14 percent Christian, and 9 percent Druze. Although Israeli authorities consider the two as members of separate communities, the Druze are actually Muslims with their own ethno-sectarian identity.

88. Don Peretz and Gideon Doron, *The Government and Politics of Israel*, 3rd ed. (Boulder, CO: Westview Press, 1997), p. 56.

89. Arian, *Second Republic*, p. 38.

90. Peretz and Doron, *Government and Politics*, p. 7.

91. Arian, *Second Republic*, p. 294.

92. Ibid., p. 297.

93. Eva Etzioni-Halvey, "Civil-Military Relations and Democracy: The Case of the Military-Political Elites' Connection in Israel," *Armed Forces and Society* 22 (Spring 1996): 413.

94. Tom Najem, *The Collapse and Reconstruction of Lebanon*, Durham Middle East Papers 59 (Durham, NC: University of Durham Center for Middle Eastern Studies, 1998), p. 7.

95. Charles Winslow, *Lebanon: War and Politics in a Fragmented Society* (London: Routledge, 1996), p. 80.

96. Arend Lijphart, "Consociational Democracy," *World Politics* 21, no. 2 (1969): 216. See also Arend Lijphart, *Patterns of Democracy: Government Forms and Performance in Thirty-Six Countries* (New Haven, CT: Yale University Press, 1999), pp. 31–47.

97. Winslow, *Lebanon*, p. 274.

98. See Human Rights Watch, *Fatal Strikes: Israel's Indiscriminate Attacks against Civilians in Lebanon* (New York: Human Rights Watch, 2006).

99. The phrase "Ministry of Mobilization" was originally used by I. William Zartman, quoted in Ibrahim Karawan, "Political Parties between State Power and Islamist Opposition," in *Between the State and Islam*, ed. Charles E. Butterworth and I. William Zartman (New York: Cambridge University Press, 2001), p. 179.

100. Karawan, "Political Parties," p. 182.

101. Timothy Piro, "Liberal Professionals in the Contemporary Arab World," in Butterworth and Zartman, *Between the State and Islam*, p. 186.

102. Fouad Ajami, *The Dream Palace of the Arabs: A Generation's Odyssey* (New York: Pantheon Books, 1998), p. 7.

103. For an account of these and other Arab intellectuals of their generation, see ibid.

104. John E. Esposito and John O. Voll, *The Makers of Contemporary Islam* (New York: Oxford University Press, 2001), pp. 16–17.

105. Much of the information contained in this and the following paragraph comes from ibid.

106. Suha Taji-Farouki, "Islamic State Theories and Contemporary Realities," in *Islamic Fundamentalism*, ed. Abdel Salam Sidahmed and Anoushiravan Ehteshami (Boulder, CO: Westview Press, 1996), p. 38.

107. Maha Azzam, "Egypt: The Islamists and the State under Mubarak," in Salam Sidahmed and Ehteshami, *Islamic Fundamentalism*, p. 111.

108. *Jihad*, which literally means "struggle," has been given different meanings by observers and practitioners of Islam since the earliest days, with some believing it to connote an inner-self struggle for personal betterment while others see it as a call to fight Islam's enemies, and still others take it to mean a combination of both alternatives. As the scholar John Esposito has observed:

> [T]here is no single doctrine of jihad that has always and everywhere existed or been universally accepted. Muslim understanding of what is required by the Quran and the practice of the Prophet regarding jihad has changed over time. The doctrine of jihad is not a product of a single authoritative individual or organization's interpretation. It is rather a product of diverse individuals and authorities interpreting and applying the principles of sacred texts in specific historical and political contexts.
>
> John Esposito, *Unholy War: Terror in the Name of Islam* (New York: Oxford University Press, 2002), p. 64

10. THE QUESTION OF DEMOCRACY

1. Samuel P. Huntington, *The Third Wave: Democratization in the Late Twentieth Century* (Norman: University of Oklahoma Press, 1991).

2. See, for example, Augustus Richard Norton, ed., *Civil Society in the Middle East* (Leiden: E. J. Brill, 1995).

3. Abdo Baaklini, Guilain Denoeux, and Robert Springborg, *Legislative Politics in the Arab World: The Resurgence of Democratic Institutions* (Boulder, CO: Lynne Rienner, 1999), p. 44.

4. James Bill, "The Study of Middle East Politics, 1946–1996: A Stockpiling," *Middle East Journal* 50 (Autumn 1996): 502.

5. As Chapter 5 demonstrated, in Iran's Third Republic political pragmatism has in many ways started to eclipse, or at least in some ways challenge, the once-dominant political Islam.

6. The absence of democracy from below is not, of course, unique to the Middle East. The same holds true for a number of countries in East Asia (most notably South Korea and Taiwan) and sub-Saharan Africa (with the notable exception of South Africa). See, for example, Howard Wiarda, ed., *Comparative Democracy and Democratization* (Fort Worth, TX: Harcourt, 2002), and Robert Pinkney, *Democracy in the Third World* (Boulder, CO: Lynne Rienner, 1994).

7. Terry Lynn Karl, "Dilemmas of Democratization in Latin America," in *Democracy in Latin America: Patterns and Cycles*, ed. Roderic Ai Camp (Wilmington, DE: Scholarly Resources Books, 1996), pp. 31–32. Earlier, in the mid-1970s, this pattern of transition had taken place in southern Europe in Greece (1974), Portugal (1975), and Spain (1975). See Philippe C. Schmitter,

"An Introduction to Southern European Transitions from Authoritarian Rule: Italy, Portugal, Spain, and Turkey," in *Transitions from Authoritarian Rule: Southern Europe*, ed. Guillermo O'Donnell, Philippe C. Schmitter, and Laurence Whitehead (Baltimore, MD: Johns Hopkins University Press, 1986), pp. 3–10.

8. John Peeler, *Building Democracy in Latin America* (Boulder, CO: Lynne Rienner, 1998), p. 157.

9. Andrew Arato, "Civil Society against the State: Poland 1980–81," *Telos* 47 (1981): 29.

10. Sabrina Petra Ramet, *Social Currents in Eastern Europe: The Sources and Consequences of the Great Transformation*, 2nd ed. (Durham, NC: Duke University Press, 1995), pp. 120–23; Brian H. Smith, *The Church and Politics in Chile: Challenges to Modern Catholicism* (Princeton, NJ: Princeton University Press, 1982), p. 340.

11. Juan Linz and Alfred Stepan, *Problems of Democratic Transition and Consolidation: Southern Europe, South America, and Post-Communist Europe* (Baltimore, MD: Johns Hopkins University Press, 1996), p. 8.

12. Michael Ignatieff, "On Civil Society: Why Eastern Europe's Revolutions Could Succeed," *Foreign Affairs* 74 (March/April 1995): 130.

13. See Giuseppe Di Palma, *To Craft Democracies: An Essay on Democratic Transitions* (Berkeley: University of California Press, 1990), p. 86.

14. Karen L. Remmer, "Democratization in Latin America," in *Global Transformation and the Third World*, ed. Robert O. Slater, Barry M. Schutz, and Steven Dorr (Boulder, CO: Lynne Rienner, 1993), p. 99.

15. Peeler, *Building Democracy*, pp. 75–76.

16. Schmitter, "Introduction to Southern European Transitions," p. 5.

17. The notion of the division of ruling elites into "hard-liners" and "softliners" (or "liberalizers") was first introduced by Adam Przeworski, *Democracy and the Market: Political and Economic Reforms in Eastern Europe and Latin America* (New York: Cambridge University Press, 1991), pp. 54–66. It has since been adopted by various students of democratization, the most notable of whom are Stephen Haggard and Robert R. Kaufman, *The Political Economy of Democratic Transitions* (Princeton, NJ: Princeton University Press, 1995), p. 32. For an application of the notion to the Middle East, see Farhad Kazemi and Augustus Richard Norton, "Hardliners and Softliners in the Middle East: Problems of Governance and Prospects for Liberalization in Authoritarian Political Systems," in *Democracy and Its Limits: Lessons from Asia, Latin America, and the Middle East*, ed. Howard Handelman and Mark Tessler (Notre Dame, IN: University of Notre Dame Press, 1999), pp. 69–89.

18. Haggard and Kaufman do not see the division between the two groups as a result of differing visions over the proper nature of state-society relations. Instead, they argue, "'Softliners' begin to calculate that the corporate interests of the ruling elite are best guarded by conciliation, rather than further repression. Even when the objective is a 'broadened dictatorship' rather than a transition to democratic rule, the division within the government between

softliners and hardline defenders of the status quo provides the opportunity for the opposition to press for broader political reforms." Haggard and Kaufman, *Political Economy,* p. 32.

19. Mehran Kamrava, "Military Professionalization and Civil-Military Relations in the Middle East," *Political Science Quarterly* 115 (Spring 2000): 67–69.

20. Saad Eddin Ibrahim, "Liberalization and Democratization in the Arab World: An Overview," in *Political Liberalization and Democratization in the Arab World,* vol. 1, *Theoretical Perspectives,* ed. Rex Brynen, Bahgat Korany, and Paul Noble (Boulder, CO: Lynne Rienner, 1995), p. 36.

21. Emad Eldin Shahin, *Political Ascent: Contemporary Islamic Movements in North Africa* (Boulder, CO: Westview Press, 1998), pp. 167–68.

22. F. Gregory Gause, *Oil Monarchies: Domestic and Security Challenges in the Arab Gulf States* (New York: Council on Foreign Relations Press, 1994), p. 12.

23. Khaldoun Hasan Al-Naqeeb, *Society and the State in the Gulf and Arab Peninsula: A Different Perspective,* trans. L. M. Kenny (London: Routledge, 1900), pp. 105–6.

24. Gause, *Oil Monarchies,* p. 155.

25. Daniel Brumberg, "Authoritarian Legacies and Reform Strategies in the Arab World," in Brynen, Korany, and Noble, *Political Liberalization,* vol. 1, pp. 229–30.

26. Ibid., p. 229.

27. James A. Bill and Robert Springborg, *Politics in the Middle East,* 5th ed. (New York: Addison Wesley Longman, 2000), pp. 113–14.

28. Alan Richards and John Waterbury, *A Political Economy of the Middle East,* 2nd ed. (Boulder, CO: Westview Press, 1996), p. 314.

29. Ibid.

30. See, for example, Robert Bianchi, "The Corporatization of the Egyptian Labor Movement," *Middle East Journal* 40 (Summer 1986): 429–40.

31. Al-Naqeeb, *Society and State,* p. 127.

32. Peter Wilson and Douglas Graham, *Saudi Arabia: The Coming Storm* (Armonk, NY: M. E. Sharpe, 1994), p. 82.

33. Richards and Waterbury, *Political Economy,* p. 318.

34. Samuel P. Huntington, *Political Order in Changing Societies* (New Haven, CT: Yale University Press, 1968), p. 196.

35. Ramet, *Social Currents,* p. 84.

36. See especially Shahin, *Political Ascent,* and John Ruedy, ed., *Islamism and Secularism in North Africa* (New York: St. Martin's Press, 1994).

37. On Adl wal-Ihsan, see Shahin, *Political Ascent,* p. 193.

38. Faisal Kutty, "Hopes for Multi-Party Election to End Algeria's Nightmare Die with April 15 One-Candidate Choice," *Washington Report on the Middle East,* June 1999, p. 34.

39. Baaklini, Denoeux, and Springborg, *Legislative Politics,* p. 233.

40. Bahgat Korany, "Monarchical Islam with a Democratic Veneer: Morocco,"

in *Political Liberalization and Democratization in the Arab World,* vol. 2, *Comparative Experiences,* ed. Rex Brynen, Bahgat Korany, and Paul Noble (Boulder, CO: Lynne Rienner, 1998), p. 170.

41. In Arabic, *makhzen* literally means the warehouse where goods and provisions are stored. "In Morocco's political context, specialists use it to denote government as a network of power and grants from the top rather than balance and mutual concessions among the different organs. The top or the center is then in control, and it exercises its control through arbitration and distribution of rewards." Ibid., p. 157.

42. Mehran Kamrava, "Pseudo-Democratic Politics and Populist Possibilities: The Rise and Demise of Turkey's Refah Party," *British Journal of Middle Eastern Studies* 25 (November 1998): 275–301.

43. On Sufis in Egypt, see Bahgat Korany, "Restricted Democratization from Above: Egypt," in Brynen, Korany, and Noble, *Political Liberalization,* vol. 2, p. 50; on clerics in Iran, see Janet Afary, *The Iranian Constitutional Revolution, 1906–1911: Grassroots Democracy, Social Democracy, and the Origins of Feminism* (New York: Columbia University Press, 1996), p. 23; on women's rights advocates in Iran, see Eliz Sanasarian, *The Women's Rights Movement in Iran: Mutiny, Appeasement, and Repression from 1900 to Khomeini* (New York: Frederick A. Praeger, 1982); on minority rights groups and secular members of the intelligentsia, see the various chapters in Rashid Khalidi et al., eds., *The Origins of Arab Nationalism* (New York: Columbia University Press, 1991).

44. Korany, "Restricted Democratization," p. 60.

45. Korany, "Monarchical Islam," p. 174.

46. Bahgat Korany and Saad Amrani, "Explosive Civil Society and Democratization from Below: Algeria," in Brynen, Korany, and Noble, *Political Liberalization,* vol. 2, p. 27.

47. Korany, "Restricted Democratization," pp. 61–62.

48. Rex Brynen, "The Politics of Monarchical Liberalism: Jordan," in Brynen, Korany, and Noble, *Political Liberalization,* vol. 2, p. 84.

49. Korany, "Monarchical Islam," p. 175.

50. Rex Brynen, "From Occupation to Uncertainty: Palestine," in Brynen, Korany, and Noble, *Political Liberalization,* vol. 2, p. 194.

51. Baaklini, Denoeux, and Springborg, *Legislative Politics,* p. 119.

52. Kazem Alamdari, "Iran Parliamentary Election: The Third Consecutive Victory for the Reformists," *ISIM Newsletter* 6 (October 2000); 22. See also Stephen Fairbanks, "Theocracy versus Democracy: Iran Considers Political Parties," *Middle East Journal* 52 (Winter 1998): 17–31.

53. Baaklini, Denoeux, and Springborg, *Legislative Politics,* p. 124.

54. Veerle Opgenhaffen and Mark Freeman, *Transitional Justice in Morocco: A Progress Report* (New York: International Center for Transitional Justice, 2005), p. 2.

55. See "Kingdom of Morocco, the Moroccan Equity and Reconciliation Commission: Three-Part Summary of the Final Report," 2005, www.ictj.org/static/MENA/Morocco/IERreport.findingssummary.eng.pdf.

56. Baaklini, Denoeux, and Springborg, *Legislative Politics*, pp. 130–31.

57. Marina Ottaway and Meredith Riley, *Morocco: From Top-Down Reform to Democratic Transition?*, Carnegie Papers, no. 71 (Washington, DC: Carnegie Endowment for International Peace, 2006), www.carnegieendowment.org/files/cp71_ottaway_final.pdf, 3.

58. Halima El-Glaoui, "Contributing to a Culture of Debate in Morocco," *Journal of Democracy* 10 (January 1999): 160.

59. Ibid., p. 157.

60. See Chapter 9.

61. Judith Palmer Harik, "Democracy (Again) Derailed: Lebanon's Ta'if Paradox," in Korany, Brynen, and Noble, *Political Liberalization*, vol. 2, p. 137.

62. Ibid., p. 147.

63. Carole Dagher, "A Crucial Year for Democracy in Lebanon Opens with a Warming of U.S.-Lebanese Relations," *Washington Report on Middle East Affairs*, March 1998, p. 85.

64. Paul Salem, "The Future of Lebanon," *Foreign Affairs* 58 (November/December 2006): 14.

65. The classic discussion of consociational democracies is offered by Arend Lijphart, "Consociational Democracy," *World Politics* 21, no. 2 (1969): 207–25.

66. Carole Dagher, "New Lebanese President Lahoud Announces New, Trimmed-Down Cabinet and Wide-Ranging Reforms," *Washington Report on Middle East Affairs*, January–February 1999, pp. 52, 95.

11. CHALLENGES FACING THE MIDDLE EAST

1. United Nations Development Program, *The Arab Human Development Report, 2002: Creating Opportunities for Future Generations* (New York: United Nations Development Program, 2002), p. 27.

2. Data compiled from World Bank, *Country at a Glance, February 2000* (Washington, DC: World Bank, 2000).

3. This estimate is based on figures provided in Michael Bonine, "Population, Poverty, and Politics: Contemporary Middle East Cities in Crisis," in *Population, Poverty, and Politics in Middle East Cities*, ed. Michael Bonine (Gainesville: University Press of Florida, 1997), p. 4.

4. For more on the significance of the family in the Middle East, see Halim Barakat, *The Arab World: Society, Culture, and State* (Berkeley: University of California Press, 1993), pp. 97–107.

5. John Weeks, "The Demography of Islamic Nations," *Population Bulletin* 43 (December 1988): 21.

6. Ibid., p. 19.

7. See, for example, Sandra Hale, "Gender and Health: Abortion in Urban Egypt," in Bonine, *Population, Poverty, and Politics*, pp. 208–34.

8. Weeks, "Demography of Islamic Nations," p. 21.

9. Elizabeth Lule, Rifat Hasan, and Kanako Yamashita-Allen, "Global Trends in Fertility, Contraceptive Use and Unintended Pregnancies," in *Fertility Regu-*

lation Behaviors and Their Costs: Contraception and Unintended Pregnancies in Africa and Eastern Europe and Central Asia, ed. Elizabeth Lule, Susheela Singh and Sadia Afroze Chowdhury (Washington, DC: World Bank, 2007), p. 20.

10. The Iranian government has made significant strides in changing popular attitudes toward contraception, requiring, among other things, that couples enroll in family planning classes before obtaining marriage licenses. See Robin Wright, *The Last Great Revolution: Turmoil and Transformation in Iran* (New York: Vintage Books, 2001), pp. 160–87.

11. Bonine, "Population, Poverty, and Politics," p. 12.

12. Kirk S. Bowman and Jerrold D. Green, "Urbanization and Political Instability in the Middle East," in Bonine, *Population, Poverty, and Politics,* p. 242.

13. Abdul-Karim Sadik and Shawki Barghouti, "The Water Problems of the Arab World: Management of Scarce Resources," in *Water in the Arab World: Perspectives and Prognoses,* ed. Peter Rogers and Peter Lydon (Cambridge, MA: Harvard University Press, 1994), p. 8.

14. Robert Cassen, "Population and Development: Old Debates, New Conclusions," in *Population and Development: Old Debates, New Conclusions,* ed. Robert Cassen (New Brunswick, NJ: Transaction Books, 1994), p. 4.

15. Bonine, "Population, Poverty, and Politics," p. 1.

16. Having adopted import-substitution industrialization policies, most Middle Eastern countries import goods and technology from Japan, western Europe, and the United States, although in recent years new suppliers from eastern Europe, South Korea, and China have also become important.

17. "Tehran Air Reportedly Causing Health Risks," IRNA News Agency, Tehran, February 3, 2001.

18. Data compiled from *The Number of Motor Vehicles, November 2000* (Ankara: State Institute of Statistics, 2001).

19. "Tehran Air."

20. Besides the necessary political hyperbole, the following statement by Oman's minister of the environment exemplifies the increased attention of Middle Eastern policy makers to the importance of environmental protection: "From the time of its inception in 1970, the government of Sultan Qaboos has been keenly aware of the need to protect the environment in all its aspects. The government has had one particular advantage in this respect in that it has not been faced with the problem of rectifying the ravages of earlier industrialisation. It has been possible to monitor closely the progressive development of industrial plants throughout the Sultanate and control any possible pollution of the environment." Quoted in Hussein Shehadeh, "Progress and Preservation in Oman," *Middle East,* no. 220 (February 1993): 46.

21. "Women Carry the Torch of Environmental Awareness," Global News Wire, March 3, 2001.

22. Mostafa Dolatyar and Tim Gray, *Water Politics in the Middle East: A Context for Conflict or Cooperation?* (New York: Macmillan, 2000), pp. 79–80.

23. Ibid., p. 80.

24. Christine Drake, "Water Resource Conflicts in the Middle East," *Journal of Geography* 96 (January 1997): 6.

25. For more on this, see Amikam Nachmani, "Water Jitters in the Middle East," *Studies in Conflict and Terrorism* 20 (January 1997): 67–93; Alwyn Rouyer, *Turning Water into Politics: The Water Issue in the Palestinian Israeli Conflict* (New York: Macmillan, 2000); and, for an Israeli perspective, Martin Sherman, *The Politics of Water in the Middle East: An Israeli Perspective on the Hydro-Political Aspects of the Conflict* (New York: St. Martin's Press, 1999).

26. Drake, "Water Resource Conflicts," p. 6.

27. Mary E. Morris, "Water and Conflict in the Middle East: Threats and Opportunities," *Studies in Conflict and Terrorism* 20 (January 1997): 8.

28. Drake, "Water Resource Conflicts," p. 7. For more on GAP and Syria and Iraq's reactions, see Dolatyar and Gray, *Water Politics*, pp. 143–47.

29. Drake, "Water Resource Conflicts," p. 8.

30. Greg Shapland, *Rivers of Discord: International Water Disputes in the Middle East* (New York: St. Martin's Press, 1997), p. 99.

31. Dolatyar and Gray, *Water Politics*, p. 85.

32. Ibid.

33. Morris, "Water and Conflict," p. 1.

34. For details of the agreement in relation to the Jordan River, see Shapland, *Rivers of Discord*, pp. 29–31.

35. Dolatyar and Gray, *Water Politics*, p. 9.

36. One of the more far-fetched ideas mentioned is dragging a chunk of polar iceberg to the Persian Gulf.

37. The thesis of clash of civilizations was introduced by Samuel Huntington in the 1990s, first in a 1993 article and then in a 1996 book, in which he envisioned the world as moving into the two opposing camps of "the West versus the rest," the "rest" being an alliance of Sino-Islamic civilizations. See Samuel P. Huntington, *The Clash of Civilizations and the Remaking of World Order* (New York: Simon and Schuster, 1996). For an insightful critique of Huntington's thesis, see Fouad Ajami, "The Summoning," *Foreign Affairs* 72, no. 4 (1993): 2–9.

38. Western (mis)perceptions of Islam are explored in a number of useful works. See, for example, John L. Esposito, *The Islamic Threat: Myth or Reality* (New York: Oxford University Press, 1995), and Fred Halliday, *Islam and the Myth of Confrontation: Religion and Politics in the Middle East* (London: I. B. Tauris, 1996).

Bibliography

Abrahamian, Ervand. *Iran between Two Revolutions.* Princeton, NJ: Princeton University Press, 1982.

———. *Khomeinism: Essays on the Islamic Republic.* Berkeley: University of California Press, 1993.

Abu-Amr, Ziad. *Islamic Fundamentalism in the West Bank and Gaza.* Bloomington: Indiana University Press, 1994.

Abu-Ghazaleh, Adnan Mohammed. *Arab Cultural Nationalism in Palestine during the British Mandate.* Beirut: Institute for Palestine Studies, 1973.

Abu-Lughod, Janet. *Cairo: 1001 Years of the City Victorious.* Princeton, NJ: Princeton University Press, 1971.

Abu-Odeh, Adnan. *Jordanians, Palestinians and the Hashemite Kingdom in the Middle East Peace Process.* Washington, DC: U.S. Institute for Peace Press, 1999.

Aburish, Saïd K. *Cry Palestine: Inside the West Bank.* Boulder, CO: Westview Press, 1993.

———. *Saddam Hussein: The Politics of Revenge.* New York: Bloomsbury, 2000.

Ackerman, Seth. "Al-Aqsa Intifada and the U.S. Media." *Journal of Palestine Studies* 30 (Winter 2001): 61–74.

Adams, Richard. "Bureaucrats, Peasants and the Dominant Coalition: An Egyptian Case Study." *Journal of Development Studies* 2, no. 2 (1986): 236–54.

Adelkhah, Fariba. *Being Modern in Iran.* Translated by Jonathan Derrick. New York: Columbia University Press, 2000.

Adelson, Roger. *London and the Invention of the Middle East: Money, Power, and War, 1902–1922.* New Haven, CT: Yale University Press, 1995.

Afary, Janet. *The Iranian Constitutional Revolution, 1906–1911: Grassroots Democracy, Social Democracy, and the Origins of Feminism.* New York: Columbia University Press, 1996.

Afkhami, Gholam R. *The Iranian Revolution: Thanatos on a National Scale.* Washington, DC: Middle East Institute, 1985.

Aftandilian, Gregory. *Egypt's Bid for Arab Leadership: Implications for U.S. Policy.* New York: Council on Foreign Relations, 1993.

Agha, Hussein J., and Ahmad S. Khalidi. *Syria and Iran: Rivalry and Cooperation.* New York: Council on Foreign Relations Press, 1995.

Ahmad, Feroz. *The Making of Modern Turkey.* London: Routledge, 1993.

Ahmad, Ishtiaq. *Anglo-Iranian Relations, 1905–1919.* Bombay: Asia Publishing House, 1975.

Al-e Ahmad, Jalal. *Weststruckness.* Translated by John Green and Ahmad Alizadeh. Lexington, KY: Mazda, 1982.

Ahmida, Ali Abdullatif. *The Making of Modern Libya: State Formation, Colonization, and Resistance, 1830–1932.* Albany: SUNY Press, 1994.

Ajami, Fouad. *The Arab Predicament: Arab Political Thought and Practice since 1967.* New York: Cambridge University Press, 1992.

———. *The Dream Palace of the Arabs: A Generation's Odyssey.* New York: Pantheon Books, 1998.

———. "The Summoning." *Foreign Affairs* 72, no. 4 (1993): 2–9.

———. "The Uneasy Imperium: Pax Americana in the Middle East." In *How Did This Happen? Terrorism and the New War,* edited by James F. Hoge and Gideon Rose, pp. 15–30. New York: Council on Foreign Relations, 2001.

Aker, Frank. *October 1973: The Arab-Israeli War.* Hamden, CT: Archon Books, 1985.

Akhavi, Shahrough. *Religion and Politics in Contemporary Iran: Clergy-State Relations in the Pahlavi Period.* Albany: SUNY Press, 1980.

———. "The Role of the Clergy in Iranian Politics, 1949–1954." In *Musaddiq, Iranian Nationalism, and Oil,* edited by James A. Bill and William Roger Louis, pp. 91–117. Austin: University of Texas Press, 1988.

Alam, Asadollah. *The Shah and I: The Confidential Diaries of Iran's Royal Court, 1969–1977.* Translated by Alinaghi Alikhani and Nicholas Vincent. New York: St. Martin's Press, 1991.

Alamdari, Kazem. "Iran Parliamentary Election: The Third Consecutive Victory for Reformists." *ISIM Newsletter* 6 (October 2000): 22.

Algar, Hamid, trans. *Constitution of the Islamic Republic of Iran.* Berkeley, CA: Mizan Press, 1980.

———. *Religion and State in Iran, 1785–1906: The Role of the Ulama in the Qajar Period.* Berkeley: University of California Press, 1969.

Allen, Peter. *The Yom Kippur War.* New York: Charles Scribner's Sons, 1982.

Almana, Mohammed. *Arabia United: A Portrait of Ibn Saud.* London: Hutchinson Benham, 1980.

Almog, Shmuel. *Zionism and History: The Rise of a New Jewish Consciousness.* New York: St. Martin's Press, 1987.

Amirahmadi, Hooshang. *Revolution and Economic Transition: The Iranian Experience.* Albany: SUNY Press, 1990.

Amnesty International. *Affront to Justice: The Death Penalty in Saudi Arabia.* London: Amnesty International, 2008.

———. *Annual Report, 1998.* London: Amnesty International, 1998.

————. *Challenging Repression: Human Rights Defenders in the Middle East and North Africa.* London: Amnesty International, 2008.

————. *Kuwait: Five Years of Impunity since the Withdrawal of Iraqi Forces.* London: Amnesty International, 1996.

Anderson, Benedict. *Imagined Communities.* London: Verso, 1991.

Anderson, Lisa. "Absolutism and the Resilience of Monarchy in the Middle East." *Political Science Quarterly* 106, no. 1 (1991): 1–15.

————. "Political Pacts, Liberalism, and Democracy: The Tunisian National Pact of 1988." *Government and Opposition* 26 (Spring 1991): 244–60.

————. *The State and Social Transformation in Tunisia and Libya, 1830–1980.* Princeton, NJ: Princeton University Press, 1986.

Ansari, Hamied. *Egypt: The Stalled Society.* Albany: SUNY Press, 1986.

Anscombe, Frederick. *The Ottoman Gulf: The Creation of Kuwait, Saudi Arabia, and Qatar.* New York: Columbia University Press, 1997.

Arab Monetary Fund. *The Joint Arab Economic Report, September 2008.* Abu Dhabi: The Arab Monetary Fund, 2008.

Arato, Andrew. "Civil Society against the State: Poland." *Telos* 47 (1981): 23–47.

Aref Qazvini, Mirza Abolqassem. *Koliyyat-e Divan* [Complete works]. Tehran: Chapp-e Jadid, 1357/1978.

Arian, Asher. *Politics in Israel: The Second Republic.* 2nd ed. Washington, DC: CQ Press, 2005.

————. *The Second Republic: Politics in Israel.* Chatham, NJ: Chatham House, 1998.

Arjomand, Said Amir. *The Shadow of·God and the Hidden Imam: Religion, Political Order, and Societal Change in Shi'ite Iran from the Beginning to 1890.* Chicago: University of Chicago Press, 1984.

Aruri, Naseer H. "The Wye Memorandum: Netanyahu's Oslo and Unreciprocal Reciprocity." *Journal of Palestine Studies* 28 (Winter 1999): 17–28.

Auty, Richard. "The Political State and the Management of Mineral Rents in Capital-Surplus Economies." *Resources Policy* 27 (2001): 77–86.

Avery, Peter. *Modern Iran.* New York: Frederick A. Praeger, 1965.

Ayubi, Nazih N. *Over-Stating the Arab State: Politics and Society in the Middle East.* London: I. B. Tauris, 1999.

————. *Political Islam: Religion and Politics in the Arab World.* London: Routledge, 1991.

Azimi, Fakhreddin. *Iran: The Crisis of Democracy.* New York: St. Martin's Press, 1989.

Azzam, Maha. "Egypt: The Islamists and the State under Mubarak." In *Islamic Fundamentalism*, edited by Abdel Salam Sidahmed and Anoushiravan Ehteshami, pp. 109–22. Boulder, CO: Westview Press, 1996.

Baaklini, Abdo, Guilain Denoeux, and Robert Springborg. *Legislative Politics in the Arab World: The Resurgence of Democratic Institutions.* Boulder, CO: Lynne Rienner, 1999.

el Badri, Hassan, Taha el Magdoub, and Mohammad Dia el Din Zohdy. *The Ramadan War, 1973.* Dunn Loring, VA: T. N. Dupuy Associates, 1978.

Baker, Randall. *King Husain and the Kingdom of Hejaz.* New York: Oleander, 1979.

Bakhash, Shaul. *The Reign of the Ayatollahs: Iran and the Islamic Revolution.* London: I. B. Tauris, 1985.

Baktiar, Bahman. *Parliamentary Politics in Revolutionary Iran: The Institutionalization of Factional Politics.* Gainesville: University Press of Florida, 1996.

Bani-Sadr, Abol Hassan. *My Turn to Speak: Iran, the Revolution, and Secret Deals with the U.S.* Washington, DC: Brassey's, 1991.

Barakat, Halim. *The Arab World: Society, Culture, and State.* Berkeley: University of California Press, 1993.

Barber, Brian. "Political Violence, Social Integration, and Youth Functioning: Palestinian Youth from the Intifada." *Journal of Community Psychology* 29, no. 3 (2001): 259–80.

Barkawi, Tarak, and Mark Laffey, eds. *Democracy, Liberalism, and War: Rethinking the Democratic Peace Debate.* Boulder, CO: Lynne Rienner, 2001.

Barkey, Henri, ed. *The Politics of Economic Reform in the Middle East.* New York: St. Martin's Press, 1992.

Barkey, Henri, and Graham Fuller. *Turkey's Kurdish Question.* Lanham, MD: Rowman and Littlefield, 1998.

Barnett, Michael N. *Dialogues in Arab Politics: Negotiations in Regional Order.* New York: Columbia University Press, 1998.

Barry, John, and Roger Charles. "Sea of Lies." *Newsweek,* July 13, 1992, pp. 29–39.

Battatu, Hanna. "Political Power and Social Structure in Syria and Iraq." In *Arab Society: Continuity and Change,* edited by Samih K. Farsoun, pp. 34–47. London: Croom Helm, 1985.

Bayat, Mangol. *Mysticism and Dissent: Socioreligious Thought in Qajar Iran.* Syracuse, NY: Syracuse University Press, 1982.

Baylouny, Anne Marie. "Militarizing Welfare: Neo-Liberalism and Jordanian Policy." *Middle East Journal* 62 (Spring 2008): 277–303.

Baylson, Joshua. *Territorial Allocation by Imperial Rivalry: The Human Legacy in the Near East.* Chicago: University of Chicago, Department of Geography, 1987.

Beattie, Kirk. *Egypt during the Nasser Years: Ideology, Politics, and Civil Society.* Boulder, CO: Westview Press, 1994.

Bebler, Anton, and Jim Seroka, eds. *Contemporary Political Systems: Classifications and Typologies.* Boulder, CO: Lynne Rienner, 1990.

Behdad, Sohrab. "The Post-Revolutionary Economic Crisis." In *Iran after the Revolution,* edited by Saeed Rahnema and Sohrab Behdad, pp. 97–128. London: I. B. Tauris, 1996.

Bellin, Eva. "The Politics of Profit in Tunisia: Utility of the Rentier Paradigm?" *World Development* 22, no. 3 (1994): 427–36.

Bendourou, Omar. "Power and Opposition in Morocco." *Journal of Democracy* 7, no. 3 (1996): 108–22.

Bengio, Ofra. *Saddam's Word: Political Discourse in Iraq.* New York: Oxford University Press, 1998.

Bengio, Ofra, and Gabriel Ben-Dor, eds. *Minorities and the State in the Arab World.* Boulder, CO: Lynne Rienner, 1999.

Ben-Gurion, David. *Israel: A Personal History.* New York: Funk and Wagnalls, 1971.

———. *Memoirs.* New York: World, 1970.

Ben-Meir, Alon. "Behind the Palestinian-Israeli Violence and Beyond." *Middle East Policy* 3 (March 2001): 81–88.

Ben-Rafael, Eliezer. *Language, Identity, and Social Division: The Case of Israel.* New York: Oxford University Press, 1994.

———. "Mizrahi and Russian Challenges to Israel's Dominant Culture: Divergences and Convergences." *Israel Studies* 12 (Fall 2007): 68–91.

Berkes, Niyazi. *The Development of Secularism in Turkey.* Montreal: McGill University Press, 1964.

Berkowitz, Michael. *Zionist Culture and West European Jewry before the First World War.* New York: Cambridge University Press, 1993.

Bertelsen, Judy. *The Palestinian Arabs: A Non-State Nation Systems Analysis.* Beverly Hills, CA: Sage Publications, 1976.

Bianchi, Robert. "The Corporatization of the Egyptian Labor Movement." *Middle East Journal* 40, no. 3 (1986): 429–40.

Bick, Etta. "The Shas Phenomenon and Religious Parties in the 1999 Elections." *Israel Affairs* 7, no. 2/3 (2001): 55–100.

Bidwell, Charles. *Morocco under Colonial Rule: French Administration of Tribal Areas, 1912–1956.* London: Frank Cass, 1973.

Bill, James. *The Eagle and the Lion: The Tragedy of American-Iranian Relations.* New Haven, CT: Yale University Press, 1988.

———. "The Study of Middle East Politics, 1946–1996: A Stockpiling." *Middle East Journal* 50 (Autumn 1996): 501–21.

Bill, James, and Robert Springborg. *Politics in the Middle East.* 4th ed. New York: HarperCollins, 1994.

———. *Politics in the Middle East.* 5th ed. New York: Addison Wesley Longman, 2000.

Bonine, Michael. "Population, Poverty, and Politics: Contemporary Middle East Cities in Crisis." In *Population, Poverty, and Politics in Middle East Cities,* edited by Michael Bonine, pp. 1–21. Gainesville: University Press of Florida, 1997.

———, ed. *Population, Poverty, and Politics in Middle East Cities.* Gainesville: University Press of Florida, 1997.

Boullata, Issa. *Trends and Issues in Contemporary Arab Thought.* Albany: SUNY Press, 1990.

Bourqia, Rahma. "The Cultural Legacy of Power in Morocco." In *In the Shadow of the Sultan: Culture, Power, and Politics in Morocco,* edited by Rahma

Bourqia and Susan Gilson Miller, pp. 243–58. Cambridge, MA: Harvard University Press, 1999.

Bowman, Kirk S., and Jerrold D. Green. "Urbanization and Political Instability in the Middle East." In *Population, Poverty, and Politics in Middle East Cities,* edited by Michael Bonine, pp. 237–55. Gainesville: University Press of Florida, 1997.

Braibanti, Ralph. "Saudi Arabia in the Context of Political Development Theory." In *King Faisal and the Modernization of Saudi Arabia,* edited by Willard Beling, pp. 35–57. London: Croom Helm, 1980.

Brand, Laurie. "Economic and Political Liberalization in a Rentier Economy: The Case of the Hashemite Kingdom of Jordan." In *Privatization and Liberalization in the Middle East,* edited by Iliya Harik and Denis Sullivan, pp. 167–88. Bloomington: Indiana University Press, 1992.

———. *Palestinians in the Arab World: Institution Building and the Search for State.* New York: Columbia University Press, 1988.

Bromley, Simon. *Rethinking Middle East Politics.* Austin: University of Texas Press, 1994.

Brown, Anthony Cave. *Oil, God, and Gold: The Story of Aramco and the Saudi Kings.* Boston: Houghton Mifflin, 1999.

Brown, L. Carl. *International Politics and the Middle East: Old Rules, Dangerous Game.* Princeton, NJ: Princeton University Press, 1984.

Brumberg, Daniel. "Authoritarian Legacies and Reform Strategies in the Arab World." In *Political Liberalization and Democratization in the Arab World,* vol. 1, *Theoretical Perspectives,* edited by Rex Brynen, Bahgat Korany, and Paul Noble, pp. 229–59. Boulder, CO: Lynne Rienner, 1995.

Brynen, Rex. "Economic Crisis and Post-Rentier Democratization in the Arab World: The Case of Jordan." *Canadian Journal of Political Science* 25 (March 1992): 69–97.

———. "From Occupation to Uncertainty: Palestine." In *Political Liberalization and Democratization in the Arab World,* vol. 2, *Comparative Experiences,* edited by Rex Brynen, Bahgat Korany, and Paul Noble, pp. 185–202. Boulder, CO: Lynne Rienner, 1998.

———. "The Politics of Monarchical Liberalism: Jordan." In *Political Liberalization and Democratization in the Arab World,* vol. 2, *Comparative Experiences,* edited by Rex Brynen, Bahgat Korany, and Paul Noble, pp. 71–100. Boulder, CO: Lynne Rienner, 1998.

Brzezinski, Zbigniew. *Power and Principle: Memoirs of the National Security Advisor, 1977–1981.* New York: Farrar, Straus, Giroux, 1985.

B'Tselem. *Fatalities in the Al-Aqsa Intifada.* Jerusalem: B'Tselem, 2002.

Bulliet, Richard. *The Camel and the Wheel.* Cambridge, MA: Harvard University Press, 1975.

Bulloch, John, and Harvey Morris. *Saddam's War: The Origins of the Kuwait Conflict and the International Response.* London: Faber and Faber, 1991.

Burke, Edmund, ed. *Struggle and Survival in the Modern Middle East.* Berkeley: University of California Press, 1993.

Burnham, Gilbert, Riyadh Lafta, Shannon Doocy, and Les Roberts. "Mortality after the 2003 Invasion of Iraq: A Cross-Sectional Cluster Sample Survey." *Lancet* 369 (October 21–27, 2006): 1421–28.

Burns, Michael. *France and the Dreyfus Affair: A Documentary History.* New York: St. Martin's Press, 1999.

Calvert, Peter. *Revolution and Counter-Revolution.* Minneapolis: University of Minnesota Press, 1990.

Camp, Roderick Ai. *Democracy in Latin America: Patterns and Cycles.* Wilmington, DE: Scholarly Resources Books, 1996.

Cantori, Louis. "Civil Society, Liberalism and the Corporatist Alternative in the Middle East." *Middle East Studies Association Bulletin* 31 (July 1997): 34–41.

Carter, Jimmy. *Palestine, Peace not Apartheid.* New York: Simon and Schuster, 2006.

Cassen, Robert. "Population and Development: Old Debates, New Conclusions." In *Population and Development: Old Debates, New Conclusions,* edited by Robert Cassen, pp. 1–26. New Brunswick, NJ: Transaction Books, 1994.

Central Bureau of Statistics of Israel. *Statistical Abstract of Israel, 2000.* No. 51. Tel Aviv: Government Publishing House, 2001.

———. *Statistical Abstract of Israel, 2003.* No. 54. Tel Aviv: Government Publishing House, 2003.

———. *Statistical Abstract of Israel, 2008.* No. 59. Tel Aviv: Government Publishing House, 2008.

Central Intelligence Agency. *CIA World Factbook, 2009.* https://www.cia.gov/library/publications/the-world-factbook/.

Chapman, Graham, and Kathleen Baker, eds. *The Changing Geography of Africa and the Middle East.* London: Routledge, 1992.

Chaudhry, Kiren Aziz. *The Price of Wealth: Economies and Institutions in the Middle East.* Ithaca, NY: Cornell University Press, 1997.

Chaudry, Jamil Ahmad. "Muslims and Mawali." *Hamdard Islamicus* 27 (Winter 1994): 85–98.

Chesser, Susan G. "Iraq: U.S. Casualties." Congressional Research Service [CRS] Report RS21578, May 28, 2009, http://fpc.state.gov/documents/organization/125559.pdf.

Choueiri, Youssef. "The Political Discourse of Contemporary Islamist Movements." In *Islamic Fundamentalism,* edited by Abdel Salam Sidahmed and Anoushiravan Ehteshami, pp. 19–33. Boulder, CO: Westview Press, 1996.

Chubin, Shahram. "Iran and the War: From Stalemate to Ceasefire." In *The Iran-Iraq War: Impact and Implications,* edited by Efraim Karsh, pp. 13–25. New York: St. Martin's Press, 1989.

Churchill, Winston. *Memoirs of the Second World War.* Boston: Houghton Mifflin, 1959.

Cole, Juan. *Napoleon's Egypt: Invading the Middle East.* New York: Palgrave Macmillan, 2007.

Coon, Anthony. *Israel and the Occupied Territories, Demolition and Dispos-*

session: The Destruction of Palestinian Homes. London: Amnesty International, 1999.

Cordesman, Anthony H. *The Iran-Iraq War and Western Security, 1984–87: Strategic Implications and Policy Options.* London: Royal United Services Institute, 1987.

Cottam, Richard. *Nationalism in Iran.* Pittsburgh, PA: University of Pittsburgh Press, 1979.

Coward, Walter, ed. *Irrigation and Agricultural Development in Asia: Perspectives from the Social Sciences.* Ithaca, NY: Cornell University Press, 1980.

Croppenstadt, Andre. "Measuring Technical Efficiency of Wheat Farmers in Egypt." ESA Working Paper No. 05–06, Food and Agriculture Organization of the United Nations, July 2005.

Dabashi, Hamid. *Theology of Discontent: The Ideological Foundations of the Islamic Revolution in Iran.* New York: NYU Press, 1993.

Dagher, Carole. "A Crucial Year for Democracy in Lebanon Opens with a Warming of U.S.-Lebanese Relations." *Washington Report on Middle East Affairs,* March 1998, pp. 42, 85.

———. "New Lebanese President Lahoud Announces New, Trimmed-Down Cabinet and Wide-Ranging Reforms." *Washington Report on Middle East Affairs,* January–February 1999, pp. 52, 95.

Darwish, Adel, and Gregory Alexander. *Unholy Babylon: The Secret History of Saddam's War.* New York: St. Martin's Press, 1991.

de Soysa, Indra. *Foreign Direct Investment, Democracy, and Development: Assessing Contours, Correlates, and Concomitants of Globalization.* London: Routledge, 2003.

Dekmejian, R. Hrair. *Egypt under Nasir: A Study in Political Dynamics.* Albany: SUNY Press, 1971.

———. "The Rise of Political Islamism in Saudi Arabia." *Middle East Journal* 48, no. 4 (1994): 627–43.

Denoeux, Guilain. *Urban Unrest in the Middle East: A Comparative Study of Informal Networks in Egypt, Iran, and Lebanon.* Albany: SUNY Press, 1993.

Di Palma, Giuseppe. *To Craft Democracies: An Essay on Democratic Transitions.* Berkeley: University of California Press, 1990.

Díaz-Mas, Paloma. *Sephardim: The Jews from Spain.* Translated by George K. Zucker. Chicago: University of Chicago Press, 1992.

Dillman, Bradford. "Global Markets and Democratization in North Africa." Paper presented at the Twenty-Eighth World Congress of the International Political Science Association, August 1–5, 2000, Québec, Canada.

Dolatyar, Mostafa, and Tim Gray. *Water Politics in the Middle East: A Context for Conflict or Cooperation?* New York: Macmillan, 2000.

Donner, Fred M. "Muhammad and the Caliphate: Political History of the Islamic Empire up to the Mongol Conquest." In *The Oxford History of Islam,* edited by John Esposito, pp. 1–61. New York: Oxford University Press, 1999.

Doron, Gideon, and Michael Harris. *Public Policy and Electoral Reform: The Case of Israel.* Lanham, MD: Lexington Books, 2000.

Dorr, Steven R. "Democratization in the Middle East." In *Global Transformation and the Third World,* edited by Robert Slater, Barry Shutz, and Steven Dorr, pp. 131–57. Boulder, CO: Lynne Rienner, 1993.

Dorraj, Manochehr. "State, Petroleum, and Democratization in the Middle East and North Africa." In *The Changing Political Economy of the Third World,* edited by Manochehr Dorraj, pp. 119–43. Boulder, CO: Lynne Rienner, 1995.

Downing, Theodore, and McGuire Gibson, eds. *Irrigation's Impact on Society.* Tucson: University of Arizona Press, 1974.

Drake, Christine. "Water Resource Conflicts in the Middle East." *Journal of Geography* 96 (January 1997): 4–12.

Drysdale, Alasdair, and Gerald Blake. *The Middle East and North Africa: A Political Geography.* New York: Oxford University Press, 1985.

Dumont, Paul. "The Origins of the Kemalist Ideology." In *Atatürk and the Modernization of Turkey,* edited by Jacob Landau, pp. 25–44. Boulder, CO: Westview Press, 1984.

Dunn, Michael Collins. "The Al-Nahda Movement in Tunisia: From Renaissance to Revolution." In *Islamism and Secularism in North Africa,* edited by John Ruedy, pp. 149–65. New York: St. Martin's Press, 1994.

Ehteshami, Anoushiravan. *After Khomeini: The Iranian Second Republic.* London: Routledge, 1995.

———. *Globalization and Geopolitics in the Middle East: Old Games, New Rules.* London: Routledge, 2007.

———. "Iran and Its Immediate Neighbourhood." In *Iran's Foreign Policy from Khatami to Ahmadinejad,* edited by Anoushiravan Ehteshami and Mahjoob Zweiri, pp. 129–39. London: Ithaca Press, 2008.

Eickelman, Eric. "Bin Laden, the Arab 'Street,' and the Middle East's Democracy Deficit." *Current History* 101 (January 2002): 36–39.

Eisenstadt, S. N. "The Kemalist Regime and Modernization: Some Comparative and Analytical Remarks." In *Atatürk and the Modernization of Turkey,* edited by Jacob Landau, pp. 3–15. Boulder, CO: Westview Press, 1984.

Eley, Geoff, and Ronald Grigor Suny, eds. *Becoming National: A Reader.* New York: Oxford University Press, 1996.

Elon, Amos. *The Israelis: Founders and Sons.* New York: Holt, Rinehart, and Winston, 1971.

el-Enany, Rasheed. *Naguib Mahfouz: The Pursuit of Meaning.* London: Routledge, 1993.

Esposito, John. *The Islamic Threat: Myth or Reality.* New York: Oxford University Press, 1995.

———, ed. *The Oxford History of Islam.* New York: Oxford University Press, 1999.

———. *Unholy War: Terror in the Name of Islam.* New York: Oxford University Press, 2002.

Esposito, John E., and John O. Voll. *Islam and Democracy.* New York: Oxford University Press, 1996.

———. *Makers of Contemporary Islam.* New York: Oxford University Press, 2001.

Etzioni-Halvey, Eva. "Civil-Military Relations and Democracy: The Case of the Military-Political Elites' Connection in Israel." *Armed Forces and Society* 22 (Spring 1996): 401–17.

Euromonitor. *Middle East Economic Handbook.* London: Euromonitor, 1986.

European Conference on Street Children Worldwide. *Street Children in North and South: A Comparative Summary.* Amsterdam: Royal Tropical Institute, 1996.

Evans, Peter. *Embedded Autonomy: States and Industrial Transformation.* Princeton, NJ: Princeton University Press, 1995.

Evin, Ahmet. "Demilitarization and Civilianization of the Regime." In *Politics in the Third Turkish Republic,* edited by Metin Heper and Ahmet Evin, pp. 23–48. Boulder, CO: Westview Press, 1994.

Fagen, Patricia Weiss. "Iraqi Refugees: Seeking Stability in Syria and Jordan." Occasional paper, Georgetown University, School of Foreign Service in Qatar, Center for International and Regional Studies, 2009, http://isim.georgetown .edu/Publications/PatPubs/Iraqi%20Refugees.pdf.

Fairbanks, Stephen. "Theocracy versus Democracy: Iran Considers Political Parties." *Middle East Journal* 52 (Winter 1998): 17–31.

Falk, Richard. "International Law and the Al-Aqsa Intifada." *Middle East Report* 30 (Winter 2000): 16–18.

Farouk-Sluglett, Marion, and Peter Sluglett. "The Iraqi Bath Party." In *Political Parties in the Third World,* edited by Vicky Randall, pp. 57–74. Newbury Park, CA: Sage Publications, 1988.

Farsoun, Samih K., and Christina E. Zacharia. *Palestine and the Palestinians.* Boulder, CO: Westview Press, 1997.

Fecci, JoMarie. "The Al-Aqsa Intifada: The Unseen Consequences of Violence on Palestinian Women and Children." *Washington Report on Middle East Affairs,* January/February 2000, pp. 9–11.

Fernández-Armesto, Felipe. *Sadat and His Statecraft.* London: Kensal, 1982.

Field, Michael. *The Merchants: The Big Business Families of Saudi Arabia and the Gulf States.* Woodstock, NY: Overlook Press, 1985.

Findley, Paul. *They Dare to Speak Out: People and Institutions Confront Israel's Lobby.* Chicago: Lawrence Hill, 1989.

Finkelstein, Norman. "Securing Occupation: The Real Meaning of the Wye River Memorandum." *New Left Review,* no. 232 (1998): 128–39.

Flapan, Simha. *The Birth of Israel: Myths and Realities.* New York: Pantheon Books, 1987.

Floor, Willem. *Safavid Government Institutions.* Costa Mesa, CA: Mazda, 2001.

Fraser, T. G. *The Arab-Israeli Conflict.* New York: St. Martin's Press, 1995.

Freedman, Lawrence, and Efraim Karsh. *The Gulf Conflict, 1990–1991: Diplo-

macy and War in the New World Order. Princeton, NJ: Princeton University Press, 1993.

Freiberger, Steven. *Dawn over Suez: The Rise of American Power in the Middle East, 1953–1957.* Chicago: Ivan R. Dee, 1992.

Friedman, Norman. *Desert Victory: The War for Kuwait.* Annapolis, MD: Naval Institute Press, 1991.

Friedman, Thomas. *From Beirut to Jerusalem.* New York: Farrar Straus Giroux, 1989.

Frisch, Hillel. *Countdown to Statehood: Palestinian State Formation in the West Bank and Gaza.* Albany: SUNY Press, 1998.

Fukuyama, Francis. *The End of History and the Last Man.* New York: Avon Books, 1992.

Gause, F. Gregory. *Oil Monarchies: Domestic and Security Challenges in the Arab Gulf States.* New York: Council on Foreign Relations Press, 1994.

———. "Regional Influences on Experiments in Political Liberalization in the Arab World." In *Political Liberalization and Democratization in the Arab World,* vol. 1, *Theoretical Perspectives,* edited by Rex Brynen, Bahgat Korany, and Paul Noble, pp. 283–306. Boulder, CO: Lynne Rienner, 1995.

Gellner, Ernest. *Nations and Nationalism.* Ithaca, NY: Cornell University Press, 1983.

Gerner, Deborah. *One Land, Two Peoples: The Conflict over Palestine.* 2nd ed. Boulder, CO: Westview Press, 1994.

Ghadbian, Najib. *Democratization and the Islamist Challenge in the Arab World.* Boulder, CO: Westview Press, 1997.

Ghods, M. Reza. *Iran in the Twentieth Century: A Political History.* Boulder, CO: Lynne Rienner, 1989.

Gillespie, Kate, and Gwenn Okruhlik. "Cleaning Up Corruption in the Middle East." *Middle East Journal* 42 (Winter 1988): 59–82.

Gisolo, Enrico. "The Degree of Central Bank Independence in MENA Countries." In *Monetary Policy and Central Banking in the Middle East and North Africa,* edited by David Cobham and Ghassan Dibeh, pp. 27–65. London: Routledge, 2009.

El-Glaoui, Halima. "Contributing to a Culture of Debate in Morocco." *Journal of Democracy* 10 (January 1999): 157–65.

Goldberg, Ellis Jay, ed. *The Social History of Labor in the Middle East.* Boulder, CO: Westview Press, 1996.

Goldschmidt, Arthur, Jr. *A Concise History of the Middle East.* 6th ed. Boulder, CO: Westview Press, 1999.

Goldstone, Jack, ed. *Revolutions: Theoretical, Comparative, and Historical Studies.* 2nd ed. New York: Harcourt Brace, 1994.

Goode, James. *The United States and Iran, 1946–51: The Diplomacy of Neglect.* New York: St. Martin's Press, 1989.

Goodwin, Jeff, and Theda Skocpol. "Explaining Revolutions in the Contemporary Third World." *Politics and Society* 17 (1989): 489–509.

Gordon, Joel. *Nasser's Blessed Movement: Egypt's Free Officers and the July Revolution.* New York: Oxford University Press, 1992.

Gorny, Yosef. *The State of Israel in Jewish Public Thought: The Quest for Collective Identity.* New York: NYU Press, 1994.

Graff, James A., and Mohamed Abdollel. *Palestinian Children and Israeli State Violence.* Toronto: Near East Cultural and Educational Foundation of Canada, 1991.

Graves, Philip. *Memoirs of King Abdullah of Transjordan.* London: Jonathan Cape, 1951.

Greenstein, Ran. *Genealogies of Conflict: Class, Identity, and the State in Palestine/Israel and South Africa.* Hanover, NH: Wesleyan University Press, 1995.

Guibernau, Montserrat. *Nationalisms: The Nation-State and Nationalism in the Twentieth Century.* Cambridge: Polity Press, 1996.

Guyatt, Nicholas. *The Absence of Peace: Understanding the Israeli-Palestinian Conflict.* London: Zed, 1998.

Haggard, Stephen, and Robert R. Kaufman. *The Political Economy of Democratic Transitions.* Princeton, NJ: Princeton University Press, 1995.

Hahn, Lorna. *North Africa, Nationalism to Nationhood.* Washington, DC: Public Affairs Press, 1960.

Haim, Sylvia, ed. *Arab Nationalism: An Anthology.* Berkeley: University of California Press, 1962.

Haim, Yehoyada. *Abandonment of Illusions: Zionist Political Attitudes toward Palestinian Arab Nationalism, 1936–1939.* Boulder, CO: Westview Press, 1983.

Hale, Sandra. "Gender and Health: Abortion in Urban Egypt." In *Population, Poverty, and Politics in Middle East Cities,* edited by Michael Bonine, pp. 208–34. Gainesville: University Press of Florida, 1997.

Halliday, Fred. *Islam and the Myth of Confrontation: Religion and Politics in the Middle East.* London: I. B. Tauris, 1996.

Halliday, Fred, and Hamza Alavi, eds. *State and Ideology in the Middle East and Pakistan.* New York: Monthly Review Press, 1988.

Halper, Jeff. *On the Policy of House Demolition by the Israeli Army in the West Bank.* Hebron: Israel Committee against House Demolitions, 1998.

Hamid, Mohamed. *The Politicization of Islam: A Case Study of Tunisia.* Boulder, CO: Westview Press, 1998.

Hammami, Rema, and Salim Tamari. "The Second Uprising: End or New Beginning?" *Journal of Palestine Studies* 30 (Winter 2001): 5–25.

Haneda, Masashi. "The Character of the Urbanization of Isfahan in the Later Safavid Period." In *Safavid Persia,* edited by Charles Melville, pp. 369–87. London: I. B. Tauris, 1996.

Hanieh, Akram. "The Camp David Papers." *Journal of Palestine Studies* 30 (Winter 2001): 75–97.

Harik, Iliya. "The Origins of the Arab State System." In *The Foundations of the Arab State,* edited by Ghassan Salame, pp. 19–46. London: Croom Helm, 1987.

————. "Privatization: The Issues, the Prospects, and the Fears." In *Privatization and Liberalization in the Middle East*, edited by Iliya Harik and Denis Sullivan, pp. 1–23. Bloomington: Indiana University Press, 1992.

Harik, Iliya, and Denis Sullivan, eds. *Privatization and Liberalization in the Middle East*. Bloomington: Indiana University Press, 1992.

Harik, Judith Palmer. "Democracy (Again) Derailed: Lebanon's Ta'if Paradox." In *Political Liberalization and Democratization in the Arab World*, vol. 2, *Comparative Experiences*, edited by Rex Brynen, Bahgat Korany, and Paul Noble, pp. 127–55. Boulder, CO: Lynne Rienner, 1998.

Hasou, Tawfiq Y. *The Struggle for the Arab World: Egypt's Nasser and the Arab League*. London: KPI, 1985.

Hass, Amira. *Drinking the Sea at Gaza: Days and Nights in a Land under Siege*. New York: Henry Holt, 1999.

Hatem, Mervat. "Egypt's Middle Class in Crisis: The Sexual Division of Labor." *Middle East Journal* 42, no. 3 (1988): 407–22.

Heisbourg, François. "A Work in Progress: The Bush Doctrine and Its Consequences." *Washington Quarterly* 26 (Spring 2003): 75–88.

Held, Colbert C. *Middle East Patterns: Places, Peoples, and Politics*. 2nd ed. Boulder, CO: Westview Press, 1994.

Heller, Joseph. *The Birth of Israel: Ben-Gurion and His Critics*. Gainesville: University of Florida Press, 2000.

Henderson, Simon. *Instant Empire: Saddam Hussein's Ambition for Iraq*. San Francisco: Mercury House, 1991.

Herf, Jeffrey. "What Is Old and What Is New in the Terrorism of Islamic Fundamentalism?" *Partisan Review* 69, no. 1 (2002): 25–31.

Hermassi, Elbaki. *Leadership and National Development in North Africa: A Comparative Study*. Berkeley: University of California Press, 1972.

Herrmann, Richard K., and R. William Ayres. "The New Geo-Politics of the Gulf: Forces for Change and Stability." In *The Persian Gulf at the Millennium: Essays in Politics, Economy, Security, and Religion*, edited by Gary G. Sick and Lawrence G. Potter, pp. 31–60. New York: St. Martin's Press, 1997.

Hertzberg, Arthur, ed. *The Zionist Idea: A Historical Analysis and Reader*. New York: Atheneum, 1959.

Higgins, Patricia. "Minority-State Relations in Contemporary Iran." In *The State, Religion, and Ethnic Politics: Afghanistan, Iran, and Pakistan*, edited by Ali Banuazizi and Myron Weiner, pp. 167–97. Syracuse, NY: Syracuse University Press, 1986.

Hillmann, Michael C., ed. *Iranian Society: An Anthology of Writings by Jalal Al-e Ahmad*. Lexington, KY: Mazda, 1982.

Hinnebusch, Raymond. *Egyptian Politics under Sadat: The Post-Populist Development of an Authoritarian-Modernizing State*. New York: Cambridge University Press, 1985.

————. "The Middle East Regional System." In *The Foreign Policies of Middle East States*, edited by Raymond Hinnebusch and Anoushiravan Ehteshami, pp. 29–53. Boulder, CO: Lynne Rienner, 2002.

———. "State and Civil Society in Syria." *Middle East Journal* 47, no. 2 (1993): 243–59.

Hiro, Dilip. *Desert Shield to Desert Storm: The Second Gulf War*. New York: Routledge, 1992.

———. *Iran under the Ayatollahs*. London: Routledge and Kegan Paul, 1985.

———. *The Longest War: The Iran-Iraq Military Conflict*. New York: Routledge, Chapman, and Hall, 1991.

———. "The Rise of Hamas: (1) Israel's Nemesis." *Middle East International*, no. 562 (November 7, 1997): 17–18.

———. "The Rise of Hamas: (2) In the Driving Seat." *Middle East International*, no. 563 (November 21, 1997): 19–20.

———. *Sharing the Promised Land: A Tale of Israelis and Palestinians*. New York: Olive Branch Press, 1999.

Hirst, David, and Irene Beeson. *Sadat*. London: Faber and Faber, 1981.

Hodgson, Marshall G. S. *The Venture of Islam*. Vol. 1. *The Classical Age of Islam*. Chicago: University of Chicago Press, 1974.

Hofstadter, Dan, ed. *Egypt and Nasser*. Vol. 2. *1957–66*. New York: Facts on File, 1973.

Horowitz, Craig. "A Tale of Two Cities." *New York*, April 7, 1997, pp. 34–39, 72.

Hourani, Albert. *A History of the Arab Peoples*. Cambridge, MA: Belknap Press, 1991.

Human Rights Watch. *Fatal Strikes: Israel's Indiscriminate Attacks against Civilians in Lebanon*. New York: Human Rights Watch, 2006.

Humphreys, R. Stephen. *Between Memory and Desire: The Middle East in a Troubled Age*. Berkeley: University of California Press, 1999.

Hunter, Brian, ed. *The Statesman's Yearbook, 1993–94*. New York: St. Martins, 1993.

Huntington, Samuel P. *The Clash of Civilizations and the Remaking of World Order*. New York: Simon and Schuster, 1996.

———. *Political Order in Changing Societies*. New Haven, CT: Yale University Press, 1968.

———. *The Third Wave: Democratization in the Late Twentieth Century*. Norman: University of Oklahoma Press, 1991.

Hurewitz, J. C. *Diplomacy in the Near and Middle East: A Documentary Record*. Vol. 1. *1535–1914*. Princeton, NJ: D. Van Nostrand, 1956.

———. *Diplomacy in the Near and Middle East: A Documentary Record*. Vol. 2. *1914–1956*. Princeton, NJ: D. Van Nostrand, 1956.

Hutchinson, John, and Anthony Smith, eds. *Nationalism*. New York: Oxford University Press, 1994.

Hutchison, Kevin Don. *Operation Desert Shield/Desert Storm: Chronology and Factbook*. Westport, CT: Greenwood, 1995.

Ibrahim, Saad Eddin. "Crises, Elites, and Democratization in the Arab World." *Middle East Journal* 47, no. 2 (1993): 292–305.

———. "Liberalization and Democratization in the Arab World: An Overview." In *Political Liberalization and Democratization in the Arab World*, vol. 1, *Theoretical Perspectives,* edited by Rex Brynen, Bahgat Korany, and Paul Noble, pp. 29–57. Boulder, CO: Lynne Rienner, 1995.

Ignatieff, Michael. "On Civil Society: Why Eastern Europe's Revolutions Could Succeed." *Foreign Affairs* 47 (March/April 1995): 128–36.

Ingrams, Doreen. *Palestine Papers, 1917–1922: Seeds of Conflict.* London: John Murray, 1972.

Institute for Palestine Studies. *The Palestinian-Israeli Peace Agreement: A Documentary Record.* Washington, DC: Institute for Palestine Studies, 1994.

Ismael, Tareq Y. *International Relations of the Contemporary Middle East: A Study in World Politics.* Syracuse, NY: Syracuse University Press, 1986.

Israeli, Raphael. *Man of Defiance: A Political Biography of Anwar Sadat.* London: Weidenfeld and Nicolson, 1985.

Issawi, Charles. *The Middle East Economy: Decline and Recovery.* Princeton, NJ: Markus Wiener, 1995.

Jafri, S. Husain. *Origins and Early Development of Shi'a Islam.* London: Longman, 1979.

Jentleson, Bruce W. *With Friends Like These: Reagan, Bush, and Saddam, 1982–1990.* New York: W. W. Norton, 1994.

Jreisat, Jamil. *Politics without Process: Administering Development in the Arab World.* Boulder, CO: Lynne Rienner, 1997.

Julien, Charles-André. *History of North Africa: Tunisia, Algeria, Morocco.* Translated by John Petrie. New York: Frederick A. Praeger, 1970.

Kamil, Omar. "The Synagogue as Civil Society, or How We Can Understand the Shas Party." *Mediterranean Quarterly* 12, no. 3 (2001): 128–43.

Kamrava, Mehran. *Cultural Politics in the Third World.* London: University College of London Press, 1999.

———. *Democracy in the Balance: Culture and Society in the Middle East.* Chatham, NJ: Chatham House, 1998.

———. "Domestic Political Obstacles to Democracy in Palestine." *Middle East Affairs Journal* 4 (Winter/Spring 1998): 109–27.

———. *Iran's Intellectual Revolution.* Cambridge: Cambridge University Press, 2008.

———. "Military Professionalization and Civil-Military Relations in the Middle East." *Political Science Quarterly* 115 (Spring 2000): 67–92.

———. "Non-Democratic States and Political Liberalisation in the Middle East: A Structural Analysis." *Third World Quarterly* 19, no. 1 (1998): 63–85.

———. *Politics and Society in the Developing World.* 2nd ed. London: Routledge, 2000.

———. "Pseudo-Democratic Politics and Populist Possibilities: The Rise and Demise of Turkey's Refah Party." *British Journal of Middle Eastern Studies* 25 (November 1998): 275–301.

———. *Revolution in Iran: The Roots of Turmoil.* London: Routledge, 1990.

———. "Revolution Revisited: Revolutionary Types and the Structuralist vs. Voluntarist Debate." *Canadian Journal of Political Science* 32 (June 1999): 1–29.

———. *Revolutionary Politics*. Westport, CT: Praeger, 1992.

———. "Structural Impediments to Economic Globalization in the Middle East." *Middle East Policy* 11 (Winter 2004): 96–112.

———. "What Stands between the Palestinians and Democracy?" *Middle East Quarterly* 6 (June 1999): 3–12.

Kaplan, David A. *The Accidental President*. New York: HarperCollins, 2001.

Karawan, Ibrahim. "Political Parties between State Power and Islamist Opposition." In *Between the State and Islam*, edited by Charles E. Butterworth and I. William Zartman, pp. 158–83. New York: Cambridge University Press, 2001.

Karl, Terry Lynn. "Dilemmas of Democratization in Latin America." In *Democracy in Latin America: Patterns and Cycles*, edited by Roderic Ai Camp, pp. 21–46. Wilmington, DE: Scholarly Resources Books, 1996.

Karsh, Efraim, and Inari Rautsi. *Saddam Hussein: A Political Biography*. New York: Free Press, 1991.

Katouzian, Homa. *Musaddiq and the Struggle for Power in Iran*. London: I. B. Tauris, 1990.

———. *The Political Economy of Modern Iran, 1926–1979*. New York: NYU Press, 1981.

Kazemi, Farhad, and Augustus Richard Norton. "Hardliners and Softliners in the Middle East: Problems of Governance and Prospects for Liberalization in Authoritarian Political Systems." In *Democracy and Its Limits: Lessons from Asia, Latin America, and the Middle East*, edited by Howard Handelman and Mark Tessler, pp. 69–89. Notre Dame, IN: University of Notre Dame Press, 1999.

Keddie, Nikki R., ed. *Religion and Politics in Iran: Shi'ism from Quietism to Revolution*. New Haven, CT: Yale University Press, 1983.

Kedourie, Elie. *England and the Middle East: The Destruction of the Ottoman Empire, 1914–1921*. London: Mansell, 1987.

Kellas, James. *The Politics of Nationalism and Ethnicity*. 2nd ed. New York: St. Martin's Press, 1998.

Kerr, Malcolm. *The Arab Cold War, 1958–1964: A Study in Ideological Politics*. New York: Oxford University Press, 1965.

Khalidi, Rashid. "The Origins of Arab Nationalism: Introduction." In *The Origins of Arab Nationalism*, edited by Rashid Khalidi, Lisa Anderson, Muhammad Muslih, and Reeva Simon, pp. vii–xix. New York: Columbia University Press, 1991.

———. *Palestinian Identity: The Construction of Modern National Consciousness*. New York: Columbia University Press, 1997.

Khalidi, Rashid, Lisa Anderson, Muhammad Muslih, and Reeva Simon, eds. *The Origins of Arab Nationalism*. New York: Columbia University Press, 1991.

al-Khalil, Samir. *The Monument: Art and Vulgarity in Iraq*. Berkeley: University of California Press, 1991.

———. *Republic of Fear: The Inside Story of Saddam's Iraq*. New York: Pantheon Books, 1989.

Khan, M. A. Muqtadar. "The Compact of Medina as the First Islamic Constitution." *Mirror International,* May 30, 2001, p. 23.

Khouri, Fred J. *The Arab-Israeli Dilemma.* 3rd ed. Syracuse, NY: Syracuse University Press, 1985.

Kimche, David, and Dan Bawly. *The Sandstorm: The Arab-Israeli War of June 1967.* New York: Stein and Day, 1968.

Kimmerling, Baruch, and Joel Migdal. *Palestinians: The Making of a People.* Cambridge, MA: Harvard University Press, 1993.

Kingston, Paul. "Contextualizing Islamic Fundamentalism." *International Journal* 54 (Autumn 1999): 695–704.

Kinross, Lord. *Ataturk: A Biography of Mustafa Kemal, Father of Modern Turkey.* New York: William Morrow, 1965.

———. *The Ottoman Centuries: The Rise and Fall of the Turkish Empire.* New York: William Morrow, 1977.

Klieman, Aharon. *Compromising Palestine: A Guide to Final Status Negotiations.* New York: Columbia University Press, 2000.

Korany, Bahgat. "The Arab World and the New Balance of Power in the New Middle East." In *Middle East Dilemma: The Politics and Economics of Arab Integration,* edited by Michael C. Hudson, pp. 35–59. New York: Columbia University Press, 1999.

———. "Monarchical Islam with a Democratic Veneer: Morocco." In *Political Liberalization and Democratization in the Arab World,* vol. 2, *Comparative Experiences,* edited by Rex Brynen, Bahgat Korany, and Paul Noble, pp. 157–84. Boulder, CO: Lynne Rienner, 1998.

———. "Restricted Democratization from Above: Egypt." In *Political Liberalization and Democratization in the Arab World,* vol. 2, *Comparative Experiences,* edited by Rex Brynen, Bahgat Korany, and Paul Noble, pp. 39–69. Boulder, CO: Lynne Rienner, 1998.

Korany, Bahgat, and Saad Amrani. "Explosive Civil Society and Democratization from Below: Algeria." In *Political Liberalization and Democratization in the Arab World,* vol. 2, *Comparative Experiences,* edited by Rex Brynen, Bahgat Korany, and Paul Noble, pp. 11–38. Boulder, CO: Lynne Rienner, 1998.

Kosut, Hal. *Israel and the Arabs: The June 1967 War.* New York: Facts on File, 1968.

Kramer, Gudrun. "The Integration of the Integrists: A Comparative Study of Egypt, Jordan and Tunisia." In *Democracy without Democrats? The Renewal of Politics in the Muslim World,* edited by Ghassan Salame, pp. 200–226. London: I. B. Tauris, 1994.

Kutty, Faisal. "Hopes for Multi-Party Election to End Algeria's Nightmare Die with April 15 One Candidate Choice." *Washington Report on the Middle East,* June 1999, pp. 34, 36.

Lambton, Ann K. S. *Qajar Persia: Eleven Studies.* London: I. B. Tauris, 1987.

Lapidus, Ira. *A History of Islamic Societies.* New York: Cambridge University Press, 1988.

————. "Sultanates and Gunpowder Empires: The Middle East." In *The Oxford History of Islam*, edited by John Esposito, pp. 347–93. New York: Oxford University Press, 1999.

Laqueur, Walter. *The Road to Jerusalem: The Origins of the Arab-Israeli Conflict*. New York: Macmillan, 1968.

Laqueur, Walter, and Barry Rubin, eds. *The Israeli-Arab Reader: A Documentary History of the Middle East Conflict*. 5th ed. New York: Penguin Books, 1995.

Lawson, Fred H. *Constructing International Relations in the Arab World*. Stanford, CA: Stanford University Press, 2006.

Le Strange, G. *Baghdad during the Abbasid Caliphate, from Contemporary Persian and Arabic Sources*. Oxford: Clarendon Press, 1924.

Legro, Jeffrey, and Andrew Moravcsik. "Faux Realism: Spin versus Substance in the Bush Foreign Policy Doctrine." *Foreign Policy*, no. 125 (July–August 2001): 80–83.

Lenczowski, George. *The Middle East in World Affairs*. 3rd ed. Ithaca, NY: Cornell University Press, 1971.

Lewis, Bernard. *The Emergence of Modern Turkey*. 2nd ed. New York: Oxford University Press, 1968.

Lijphart, Arend. "Consociational Democracy." *World Politics* 21, no. 2 (1969): 207–25.

————. *Patterns of Democracy: Government Forms and Performance in Thirty-Six Countries*. New Haven, CT: Yale University Press, 1999.

Lings, Martin. *Muhammad: His Life Based on the Earliest Sources*. Cambridge: Islamic Text Society, 1995.

Linz, Juan, and Alfred Stepan. *Problems of Democratic Transition and Consolidation: Southern Europe, South America, and Post-Communist Europe*. Baltimore, MD: Johns Hopkins University Press, 1996.

Looney, Robert. "Reforming the Rentier State: The Imperative for Change in the Gulf." In *Critical Issues Facing the Middle East: Security, Politics, and Economics*, edited by James A. Russell, 37–73. New York: Macmillan, 2006.

Lorenz, Joseph. *Egypt and the Arabs: Foreign Policy and the Search for National Identity*. Boulder, CO: Westview Press, 1990.

Luciani, Giacomo. "Oil and Political Economy in the International Relations of the Middle East." In *International Relations of the Middle East*, edited by Louise Fawcett, pp. 79–104. Oxford: Oxford University Press, 2005.

————. "The Oil Rent, Fiscal Crisis of the State and Democratization." In *Democracy without Democrats? The Renewal of Politics in the Muslim World*, edited by Ghassan Salame, pp. 130–55. London: I. B. Tauris, 1994.

Lule, Elizabeth, Rifat Hasan, and Kanako Yamashita-Allen. "Global Trends in Fertility, Contraceptive Use and Unintended Pregnancies." In *Fertility Regulation Behaviors and Their Costs: Contraception and Unintended Pregnancies in Africa and Eastern Europe and Central Asia*, edited by Elizabeth Lule, Susheela Singh, and Sadia Afroze Chowdhury, pp. 8–36. Washington, DC: World Bank, 2007.

Lustick, Ian S. *For the Land and the Lord: Jewish Fundamentalism in Israel.* New York: Council on Foreign Relations Press, 1988.

MacKinnon, Colin. "Costs of the Closure: Gaza Hard Hit." *Washington Report on Middle East Affairs,* July 1996, pp. 85, 107.

Madelung, Wilferd. *The Succession to Muhammad: A Study of the Early Caliphate.* New York: Cambridge University Press, 1997.

Mahler, Gregory S. *Politics and Government in Israel.* Lanham, MD: Rowman and Littlefield, 2004.

Makiya, Kanan. *Cruelty and Silence: War, Tyranny, Uprising and the Arab World.* New York: W. W. Norton, 1993.

———. "Toleration and the New Arab Politics." *Journal of Democracy* 6, no. 1 (1995): 90–103.

Malley, Robert, and Hussein Agha. "Camp David: Tragedy of Errors." *New York Review of Books,* August 9, 2001.

Mallison, W. T., Jr. "The Balfour Declaration: An Appraisal in International Law." In *The Transformation of Palestine: Essays on the Origin and Development of the Arab-Israeli Conflict,* edited by Ibrahim Abu-Lughod, pp. 66–111. Evanston, IL: Northwestern University Press, 1971.

Mango, Andrew. *Atatürk.* Woodstock, NY: Overlook Press, 2000.

Mansfield, Peter. *A History of the Middle East.* New York: Penguin Books, 1991.

———. *The Ottoman Empire and Its Successors.* New York: Macmillan, 1973.

Mansoor, Camile. "Israel's Colonial Impasse." *Journal of Palestine Studies* 30 (Summer 2001): 83–88.

Masci, David. "Islamic Fundamentalism." *Congressional Quarterly* 10 (March 24, 2000): 241–56.

Mbembe, Achille. "Power and Obscenity in the Post-Colonial Period: The Case of Cameroon." In *Rethinking Third World Politics,* edited by James Manor, pp. 166–82. London: Longman, 1991.

McArthur, Shirl. "'Suspended' Wye River Agreement May Have Positive Congressional Side Effects." *Washington Report on Middle East Affairs,* March 1999, pp. 45, 102.

McDermott, Anthony. *Egypt from Nasser to Mubarak: A Flawed Revolution.* London: Croom Helm, 1988.

McDowall, David. *The Palestinians: The Road to Nationhood.* London: Minority Rights Group, 1995.

McLoughlin, Frederick. *Ibn Saud: Founder of a Kingdom.* New York: St. Martin's Press, 1993.

Mearsheimer, John J., and Stephen M. Walt. *The Israel Lobby and U.S. Foreign Policy.* New York: Farrar, Straus and Giroux, 2008.

Meyer, Michael A. *Judaism within Modernity: Essays on Jewish History and Religion.* Detroit, MI: Wayne State University Press, 2001.

Mez, Adam. *The Renaissance of Islam.* Translated by Salahuddin Khuda Bukhsh and D. S. Margoliouth. London: Luzac, 1937.

Migdal, Joel. "The State in Society: An Approach to Struggles for Domination." In *State Power and Social Forces: Domination and Transformation in the Third World,* edited by Joel Migdal, Atul Kohli, and Vivienne Shue, pp. 7–34. New York: Cambridge University Press, 1994.

————. "Studying the State." In *Comparative Politics: Rationality, Culture, and Structure,* edited by Mark Irving Lichbach and Alan Zuckerman, pp. 208–35. New York: Cambridge University Press, 1997.

Migdal, Joel, Atul Kohli, and Vivienne Shue, eds. *State Power and Social Forces: Domination and Transformation in the Third World.* New York: Cambridge University Press, 1994.

Milani, Abbas. *The Persian Sphinx: Amir Abbas Hoveyda and the Riddle of the Iranian Revolution.* Washington, DC: Mage, 2000.

Milani, Mohsen. "Shi'ism and the State in the Constitution of the Islamic Republic of Iran." In *Iran: Political Culture in the Islamic Republic,* edited by Samih Farsoun and Mehrdad Mashayekhi, pp. 133–59. London: Routledge, 1992.

Millspaugh, Arthur C. *The American Task in Persia.* New York: Century, 1925.

Milton-Edwards, Beverley. *Islamic Politics in Palestine.* London: I. B. Tauris, 1999.

Mishal, Shaul, and Avraham Sela. *The Palestinian Hamas: Vision, Violence, and Coexistence.* New York: Columbia University Press, 2000.

Mitchell Report. "The Sharm al-Shaykh Fact-Finding Committee, 'The Mitchell Report,' 20 May 2001." *Journal of Palestine Studies* 30 (Spring 2001): 146–50.

Moaddel, Mansoor. "Religion and Women: Islamic Modernism versus Fundamentalism." *Journal for the Scientific Study of Religion* 37, no. 1 (1998): 108–30.

Moghtader, Hushang. "The Impact of Increased Oil Revenue on Iran's Economic Development, 1973–76." In *Towards a Modern Iran: Studies in Thought, Politics and Society,* edited by Elie Kedouri and Sylvia Haim, pp. 241–62. London: Frank Cass, 1980.

Mohsen, Safia K. "New Images, Old Reflections: Working Middle-Class Women in Egypt." In *Women and the Family in the Middle East: New Voices for Change,* edited by Elizabeth Warnock Fernea, pp. 56–72. Austin: University of Texas Press, 1985.

Moore, Clement Henry. *Politics in North Africa: Algeria, Morocco, and Tunisia.* Boston: Little, Brown, 1970.

————. *Tunisia since Independence: The Dynamics of One-Party Government.* Berkeley: University of California Press, 1965.

Morris, Benny. *The Birth of the Palestinian Refugee Problem, 1947–1949.* New York: Cambridge University Press, 1987.

————. *Righteous Victims: A History of the Zionist-Arab Conflict, 1881–2001.* New York: Vintage Books, 2001.

Morris, Mary E. "Water and Conflict in the Middle East: Threats and Opportunities." *Studies in Conflict and Terrorism* 20 (January 1997): 1–13.

Mujahedeen Khalq. *Sharh-e Ta'sis va Tarikhche-ye Vaqaye' Sazman-e Mujahedeen-e Khalq-e Iran az Sal-e 1344 ta Sal-e 1350* [Explanation of the foundation and a history of the People's Organization of Iran from the year 1965 to the year 1971]. Tehran: Sazman-e Mujahedeen, 1358/1979.

Mylroie, Laurie. "Saddam Hussein's Invasion of Kuwait: A Premeditated Act." In *The Iraqi Aggression against Kuwait: Strategic Lessons and Implications for Europe,* edited by Wolfgang F. Danspeckgruber and Charles Tripp, pp. 39–50. Boulder, CO: Westview Press, 1996.

Nachmani, Amikam. "Water Jitters in the Middle East." *Studies in Conflict and Terrorism* 20 (January 1997): 67–93.

Najem, Tom. *The Collapse and Reconstruction of Lebanon.* Durham Middle East Papers 59. Durham, NC: University of Durham Center for Middle Eastern Studies, 1998.

Najoumi, Neamatollah. *The Rise of the Taliban in Afghanistan: Mass Mobilization, Civil War, and the Future of the Region.* New York: Palgrave Press, 2002.

Nakhleh, Khalil. "The Political Effects of the October War on Israeli Society." In *Middle East Crucible: Studies on the Arab-Israeli War of October 1973,* edited by Nasser Aruri, pp. 156–72. Wilmette, IL: Medina University Press International, 1975.

Al-Naqeeb, Khaldoun Hasan. *Society and the State in the Gulf and Arab Peninsula: A Different Perspective.* Translated by L. M. Kenney. London: Routledge, 1990.

Nashat, Guity. "Women in the Ideology of the Islamic Republic." In *Women and Revolution in Iran,* edited by Guity Nashat. Boulder, CO: Westview Press, 1983.

Nasser, Gamal Abdel. *The Philosophy of the Revolution.* Buffalo, NY: Economica Books, 1959.

Nevakivi, Jukka. *Britain, France, and the Middle East, 1914–1920.* London: Athlone, 1969.

Nevo, Joseph. *King Abdullah and Palestine: A Territorial Ambition.* New York: St. Martin's Press, 1996.

Nicholson, Raymond. *The Mystics of Islam.* 1914. Repr., London: Arkana, 1989.

Norton, Augustus Richard. "America's Middle East Peace Crisis." *Current History* 100 (January 2001): 3–9.

——, ed. *Civil Society in the Middle East.* Leiden: E. J. Brill, 1995.

Nutting, Anthony. *Nasser.* New York: E. P. Dutton, 1972.

O'Ballance, Edgar. *The Gulf War.* London: Brassey's Defence, 1988.

——. *The Third Arab-Israeli War.* Hamden, CT: Archon Books, 1972.

O'Donnell, Guillermo, Philippe C. Schmitter, and Laurence Whitehead, eds. *Transitions from Authoritarian Rule: Southern Europe.* Baltimore, MD: Johns Hopkins University Press, 1986.

Okey, Robin. *The Habsburg Monarchy: From Enlightenment to Eclipse.* New York: St. Martin's Press, 2001.

Okruhlik, Gwenn. "Rentier Wealth, Unruly Law, and the Rise of Opposition:

The Political Economy of Oil States." *Comparative Politics* 31 (April 1999): 295–315.

Opgenhaffen, Veerle, and Mark Freeman. *Transitional Justice in Morocco: A Progress Report.* NY: International Center for Transitional Justice, 2005.

Orr, Akiva. *Israel: Politics, Myths and Identity Crisis.* London: Pluto, 1994.

Osman, Fathi. *Concepts from the Quran: A Topical Reading.* Los Angeles: MVI Publications, 1997.

Ottaway, Marina, and Meredith Riley. *Morocco: From Top-Down Reform to Democratic Transition?* Carnegie Papers, no. 71. Washington, DC: Carnegie Endowment for International Peace, 2006. www.carnegieendowment .org/files/cp71_ottaway_final.pdf.

Owen, Roger. "Inter-Arab Economic Relations during the Twentieth Century: World Market vs. Regional Market?" in *Middle East Dilemma: The Politics and Economics of Arab Integration,* edited by Michael C. Hudson, pp. 215–32. New York: Columbia University Press, 1999.

———. "Reflections on the Meaning and Consequences of the Gulf Crisis." In *The Arab World Today,* edited by Dan Tschirgi, pp. 13–20. Boulder, CO: Lynne Rienner, 1994.

———. *State, Power and Politics in the Making of the Modern Middle East.* London: Routledge, 1992.

Owen, Roger, and Sevket Pamuk. *A History of Middle East Economies in the Twentieth Century.* Cambridge, MA: Harvard University Press, 1999.

Page, John, and Linda Van Gelder. "Missing Links: Institutional Capability, Policy Reform, and Growth in the Middle East and North Africa." In *The State and Global Change: The Political Economy of Transition in the Middle East and North Africa,* edited by Hassan Hakimian and Ziba Moshaver, pp. 15–58. London: Curzon, 2001.

Pahlavi, Mohammad Reza. *Answer to History.* New York: Stein and Day, 1980.

———. *Inqilab-e Sefeed* [The White Revolution]. Tehran: Imperial Pahlavi Library, 1967.

———. *Mission for My Country.* London: Hutchinson, 1961.

Palestinian Central Bureau of Statistics. *Population, Housing and Establishment Census, 2007.* Ramallah: Palestinian Central Bureau of Statistics, 2009.

Palmer, Michael. *Guardians of the Gulf: A History of America's Expanding Role in the Persian Gulf, 1833–1992.* New York: Free Press, 1992.

Palmer, Monte. *Political Development: Dilemmas and Challenges.* Itasca, IL: F. E. Peacock, 1997.

Palmer, Monte, Ali Leila, and El Sayed Yassin. *The Egyptian Bureaucracy.* Cairo: American University of Cairo Press, 1988.

Pappe, Ilan. *The Ethnic Cleansing of Palestine.* Oxford: Oneworld, 2006.

Parsa, Misagh. *Social Origins of the Iranian Revolution.* New Brunswick, NJ: Rutgers University Press, 1989.

Parsi, Trita. *Treacherous Alliance: The Secret Dealings of Israel, Iran, and the United States.* New Haven, CT: Yale University Press, 2007.

Parvin, Manoucher, and Mostafa Vaziri. "Islamic Man and Society in the Islamic

Republic of Iran." In *Iran: Political Culture in the Islamic Republic*, edited by Samih Farsoun and Mehrdad Mashayekhi, pp. 116–32. London: Routledge, 1992.

Paxton, John, ed. *The Statesman's Yearbook, 1988–89*. New York: St. Martins, 1988.

Peeler, John. *Building Democracy in Latin America*. Boulder, CO: Lynne Rienner, 1998.

Peled, Yoav. "Toward a Redefinition of Jewish Nationalism in Israel? The Enigma of Shas." *Ethnic and Racial Studies* 21 (July 1998): 703–27.

Pelletiere, Stephen C. *The Iran-Iraq War: Chaos in a Vacuum*. Westport, CT: Praeger, 1992.

Pelletiere, Stephen C., and Douglas V. Johnson II. *Lessons Learned: The Iran-Iraq War*. Carlisle Barracks, PA: Strategic Studies Institute, U.S. Army War College, 1991.

Pennell, C. R. *Morocco since 1830: A History*. New York: NYU Press, 2000.

Peres, Shimon. *The New Middle East*. New York: Henry Holt, 1993.

Peres, Shimon, and Robert Littell. *For the Future of Israel*. Baltimore, MD: Johns Hopkins University Press, 1998.

Peretz, Don. "Barak's Israel." *Current History* 100 (January 2001): 21–26.

———. *Palestinians, Refugees, and the Middle East Peace Process*. Washington, DC: U.S. Institute for Peace Press, 1993.

Peretz, Don, and Gideon Doron. *The Government and Politics of Israel*. 3rd ed. Boulder, CO: Westview Press, 1997.

Perlmutter, Amos. *Politics and the Military in Israel, 1967–1977*. London: Frank Cass, 1978.

Perthes, Volker. *The Political Economy of Syria under Asad*. London: I. B. Tauris, 1997.

Peters, Rudolph. "Religious Attitudes towards Modernization in the Ottoman Empire: A Nineteenth Century Pious Text on Steamships, Factories and the Telegraph." *Die Welt des Islams* 26 (1986): 76–105.

Peterson, J. E. *Yemen: The Search for a Modern State*. Baltimore, MD: Johns Hopkins University Press, 1982.

Pinkney, Robert. *Democracy in the Third World*. Boulder, CO: Lynne Rienner, 1994.

Pipes, Daniel. *The Hidden Hand: Middle Eastern Fears of Conspiracy*. New York: St. Martin's Griffin, 1996.

Piro, Timothy. "Liberal Professionals in the Contemporary Arab World." In *Between the State and Islam*, edited by Charles E. Butterworth and I. William Zartman, pp. 184–206. New York: Cambridge University Press, 2001.

———. *The Political Economy of Market Reform in Jordan*. New York: Rowman and Littlefield, 1998.

Posusney, Marsha Pripstein. *Labor and the State in Egypt: Workers, Unions, and Economic Restructuring*. New York: Columbia University Press, 1997.

Przeworski, Adam. *Democracy and the Market: Political and Economic Re-*

forms in Eastern Europe and Latin America. New York: Cambridge University Press, 1991.

Quandt, William, Fuad Jabber, and Ann Mosley Lesch. *The Politics of Palestinian Nationalism.* Berkeley: University of California Press, 1973.

Queen, Richard. *Inside and Out: Hostage to Iran, Hostage to Myself.* New York: G. P. Putnam's Sons, 1981.

Rabushka, Alvin. "Why Aid to Israel Hurts . . . Israelis." *Hoover Digest,* no. 3 (1998): 109–12.

Rahman, Fazlur. *Islam.* 2nd ed. Chicago: University of Chicago Press, 1979.

Rahmy, Ali Abdel Rahman. *The Egyptian Policy in the Arab World: Intervention in Yemen, 1962–1967. Case Study.* Washington, DC: University Press of America, 1983.

Rahnema, Ali. *An Islamic Utopian: A Political Biography of Ali Sharia'ti.* London: I. B. Tauris, 1998.

Ramazani, Rouhollah K. *The Foreign Policy of Iran, 1500 to 1941.* Charlottesville: University of Virginia Press, 1966.

———. *Revolutionary Iran: Challenge and Response in the Middle East.* Baltimore, MD: Johns Hopkins University Press, 1986.

Ramet, Sabrina Petra. *Social Currents in Eastern Europe: The Sources and Consequences of the Great Transformation.* 2nd ed. Durham, NC: Duke University Press, 1995.

al-Rasheed, Madawi. "God, King and the Nation: Political Rhetoric in Saudi Arabia." *Middle East Journal* 50, no. 3 (1996): 359–71.

Rashid, Ahmad. *Taliban.* New Haven, CT: Yale University Press, 2001.

Ray, James Lee. "The Democratic Path to Peace." *Journal of Democracy* 8 (April 1997): 49–64.

Reid, Donald Malcom. "The Postage Stamp: A Window on Saddam Hussein's Iraq." *Middle East Journal* 47, no. 1 (1993): 77–89.

Remmer, Karen. "Democratization in Latin America." In *Global Transformations and the Third World,* edited by Robert O. Slater, Barry M. Schutz, and Steven Dorr, pp. 91–111. Boulder, CO: Lynne Rienner, 1993.

Richards, Alan. "Economic Imperatives and Political Systems." *Middle East Journal* 47, no. 2 (1993): 217–27.

Richards, Alan, and John Waterbury. *A Political Economy of the Middle East.* 2nd ed. Boulder, CO: Westview Press, 1996.

Risen, James. "Secrets of History: The CIA in Iran." 2000. www.nytimes.com/library/world/mideast/041600iran-cia-index.html.

Robinson, Glenn E. *Building a Palestinian State: The Incomplete Revolution.* Bloomington: Indiana University Press, 1997.

———. "Israel and the Palestinians: The Bitter Fruits of Hegemonic Peace." *Current History* 100 (January 2001): 15–20.

Rodinson, Maxime. *Muhammad.* New York: Pantheon Books, 1980.

Rogers, Michael. *The Spread of Islam.* New York: Elsevier, 1976.

Roosevelt, Kermit. *Countercoup: The Struggle for the Control of Iran.* New York: McGraw-Hill, 1979.

Rosberg, James. "Causes and Consequences of Judicial Independence in Contemporary Egypt." Paper presented at the Middle East Studies Association Conference, Phoenix, AZ, 1994.

Rose, David. "The Gaza Bombshell," *Vanity Fair,* April 2008, 192–98, 247–51.

Roshwald, Aviel. *Ethnic Nationalism and the Fall of Empires: Central Europe, Russia and the Middle East, 1914–1923.* London: Routledge, 2001.

Rouyer, Alwyn. *Turning Water into Politics: The Water Issue in the Palestinian Israeli Conflict.* New York: Macmillan, 2000.

Roy, Sara. "Palestinian Society and Economy: The Continued Denial of Possibility." *Journal of Palestine Studies* 30 (Summer 2001): 5–20.

———. "Why Peace Failed: An Oslo Autopsy." *Current History* 101 (January 2002): 8–16.

Rubin, Barnett. "Political Elites in Afghanistan: Rentier State Building, Rentier State Wrecking." *International Journal of Middle East Studies* 24 (February 1992): 77–99.

Ruedy, John, ed. *Islamism and Secularism in North Africa.* New York: St. Martin's Press, 1994.

———. *Modern Algeria: The Origins and Development of a Nation.* Bloomington: Indiana University Press, 1992.

Rugh, William. *The Arab Press.* Syracuse, NY: Syracuse University Press, 1987.

Runciman, Sir Steven. *The Fall of Constantinople, 1453.* New York: Cambridge University Press, 1965.

Rushdie, Salman. *The Satanic Verses.* New York: Viking Books, 1989.

Ryan, Paul. *The Iranian Rescue Mission: Why It Failed.* Annapolis, MD: Naval Institute Press, 1985.

Sachar, Howard. *A History of Israel: From the Rise of Zionism to Our Time.* 2nd ed. New York: Alfred A. Knopf, 1996.

el-Sadat, Anwar. *In Search of Identity: An Autobiography.* New York: Harper and Row, 1978.

———. *The Public Diary of Anwar Sadat: Part One, The Road to War.* Edited by Raphael Israeli. Leiden: E. J. Brill, 1978.

Sadik, Abdul-Karim, and Shawki Barghouti. "The Water Problems of the Arab World: Management of Scarce Resources." In *Water in the Arab World: Perspectives and Prognoses,* edited by Peter Rogers and Peter Lydon, pp. 1–37. Cambridge, MA: Harvard University Press, 1994.

Safran, Nadav. *From War to War: The Arab-Israeli Confrontation, 1948–1967.* New York: Pegasus, 1969.

Said, Edward. *Peace and Its Discontents: Essays on Palestine in the Middle East Peace Process.* New York: Vintage Books, 1995.

———. *The Question of Palestine.* New York: Times Books, 1981.

Said, Edward, and Christopher Hitchens, eds. *Blaming the Victims: Spurious Scholarship and the Palestinian Question.* New York: Verso, 1988.

Salame, Ghassan, ed. *The Foundations of the Arab State.* London: Croom Helm, 1987.

Salem, Paul. "The Future of Lebanon." *Foreign Affairs* 58 (November/December 2006): 13–22.

Salibi, Kamal. *The Modern History of Jordan.* London: I. B. Tauris, 1993.

Salinger, Pierre. *America Held Hostage: The Secret Negotiations.* Garden City, NY: Doubleday, 1981.

Salt, Jeremy. "Turkey's Military 'Democracy.'" *Current History* 98 (February 1999): 72–78.

Sanasarian, Eliz. *The Women's Rights Movement in Iran: Mutiny, Appeasement, and Repression from 1900 to Khomeini.* New York: Frederick A. Praeger, 1982.

Sanchez, Carlos, Horacio Palmiero, and Fernando Ferrero. "The Informal and Quasi-Formal Sectors in Cordoba." In *The Urban Informal Sector in Developing Countries: Employment, Poverty and Environment,* edited by S. V. Sethuraman, pp. 144–58. Geneva: International Labour Office, 1981.

Sanders, Paula. *Ritual, Politics, and the City in Fatimid Cairo.* Albany: SUNY Press, 1994.

Savir, Uri. *The Process: 1,100 Days That Changed the Middle East.* New York: Vintage Books, 1998.

Sayigh, Yusif A. "Arab Economic Integration: The Poor Harvest of the 1980s," in *Middle East Dilemma: The Politics and Economics of Arab Integration,* edited by Michael C. Hudson, pp. 233–58. New York: Columbia University Press, 1999.

Schahgaldian, Nikola. *The Iranian Military under the Islamic Republic.* Santa Monica, CA: Rand Corporation, 1987.

Schirazi, Asghar. *The Constitution of Iran: Politics and the State in the Islamic Republic.* Translated by John O'Kane. London: I. B. Tauris, 1998.

Schmitter, Philippe. "An Introduction to Southern European Transitions from Authoritarian Rule: Italy, Portugal, Spain, and Turkey." In *Transitions from Authoritarian Rule: Southern Europe,* edited by Guillermo O'Donnell, Philippe C. Schmitter, and Laurence Whitehead, pp. 3–10. Baltimore, MD: Johns Hopkins University Press, 1986.

Seale, Patrick. "Asad: Between Institutions and Autocracy." In *Syria: Society, Culture, and Polity,* edited by Richard Antoun and Donald Quataert, pp. 97–110. Albany: SUNY Press, 1991.

———. *The Struggle for Syria: A Study of Post-War Arab Politics, 1945–1958.* New Haven, CT: Yale University Press, 1986.

———. "The Syria-Israel Negotiations: Who Is Telling the Truth?" *Journal of Palestine Studies* 29 (Winter 2000): 65–77.

Segre, Dan V. *A Crisis of Identity: Israel and Zionism.* New York: Oxford University Press, 1980.

Seitz, Charmaine. "Hamas Stands Down?" *Middle East Report* 31, no. 4 (2001): 4–7.

Sela, Avraham. *The Decline of the Arab-Israeli Conflict: Middle East and the Quest for Regional Order.* Albany: SUNY Press, 1998.

Sethuraman, S. V. "The Role of the Urban Informal Sector." In *The Urban*

Informal Sector in Developing Countries: Employment, Poverty and Environment, edited by S. V. Sethuraman, pp. 3–47. Geneva: International Labour Office, 1981.

Shah, Nasra M. "Restrictive Labour Immigration Policies in the Oil-Rich Gulf: Effectiveness and Implications for Sending Asian Countries." In *United Nations Expert Group Meeting on International Migration and Development in the Arab Region.* Beirut: United Nations Secretariat, 2006.

Shahin, Emad Eldin. *Political Ascent: Contemporary Islamic Movements in North Africa.* Boulder, CO: Westview Press, 1998.

Shambayati, Hootan. "The Rentier State, Interest Groups, and the Paradox of Autonomy: State and Business in Turkey and Iran." *Comparative Politics* 26 (April 1994): 307–31.

Shapland, Greg. *Rivers of Discord: International Water Disputes in the Middle East.* New York: St. Martin's Press, 1997.

Sharabi, Hisham. "Prelude to War: The Crisis of May–June 1967." In *The Arab-Israeli Confrontation of June 1967: An Arab Perspective*, edited by Ibrahim Abu-Lughod, pp. 49–65. Evanston, IL: Northwestern University Press, 1970.

Sharp, Jeremy. "U.S. Foreign Aid to Israel." Congressional Research Service [CRS] ReportRL33222, January 2008, www.au.af.mil/au/awc/awcgate/crs/rl33222.pdf.

Shay, Shaul, and Yoram Scheitzer. "Al-Aqsa Intifada: Strategies of Asymmetric Confrontation." *Faultlines* 8 (2001): 81–104.

El-Shazly, Nadia, and Raymond Hinnebusch. "The Challenge of Security in the Post–Gulf War Middle East System." In *The Foreign Policies of Middle East States*, edited by Raymond Hinnebusch and Anoushiravan Ehteshami, pp. 71–90. Boulder, CO: Lynne Rienner, 2002.

Sheehan, Edward R. F. "The Map and the Fence." *New York Review of Books*, July 3, 2003, 8–13.

Shehadeh, Hussein. "Progress and Preservation in Oman." *Middle East*, no. 220 (February 1993): 46.

Sherman, Martin. *The Politics of Water in the Middle East: An Israeli Perspective on the Hydro-Political Aspects of the Conflict.* New York: St. Martin's Press, 1999.

Shlaim, Avi. *The Iron Wall: Israel and the Arab World.* New York: W. W. Norton, 2001.

———. "The Oslo Accord." *Journal of Palestine Studies* 23 (Spring 1994): 24–40.

Shohat, Ella. "The Invention of the Mizrahim." *Journal of Palestine Studies* 29 (Autumn 1999): 5–20.

Shuster, William M. *The Strangling of Persia.* New York: Greenwood, 1939.

Sick, Gary. *All Fall Down: America's Tragic Encounter with Iran.* New York: Penguin Books, 1985.

———. *October Surprise: America's Hostages in Iran and the Election of Ronald Reagan.* New York: Times Books, 1991.

Sickman, Rocky. *Iranian Hostage: A Personal Diary*. Topeka, KS: Crawford Press, 1982.

Silver, Morris. *Economic Structures of the Ancient Near East*. London: Croom Helm, 1985.

Skocpol, Theda. *Social Revolutions in the Modern World*. New York: Cambridge University Press, 1994.

———. *States and Social Revolutions*. New York: Cambridge University Press, 1979.

Skovgaard-Petersen, Jacob. "The Global Mufti," in *Globalization and the Muslim World: Culture, Religion, and Modernity*, edited by Bright Schaebler and Leif Stenberg, pp. 153–65. Syracuse, NY: Syracuse University Press, 2004.

Smith, Anthony, ed. *Nationalism*. New York: Oxford University Press, 1994.

Smith, Brian H. *The Church and Politics in Chile: Challenges to Modern Catholicism*. Princeton, NJ: Princeton University Press, 1982.

Smith, Charles D. *Palestine and the Arab-Israeli Conflict*. 4th ed. New York: St. Martin's Press, 2001.

Smith, Jean Edward. *George Bush's War*. New York: Henry Holt, 1992.

Snell, Daniel. *Life in the Ancient Near East, 3100–332 B.C.E.* New Haven, CT: Yale University Press, 1997.

Sobel, Lester, ed. *Israel and the Arabs: The October 1973 War*. New York: Facts on File, 1974.

Sovich, Nina. "Shas Courts Israel's Bedouin." *Middle East International*, no. 593 (February 12, 1999): 24–26.

Springborg, Robert. *Mubarak's Egypt: Fragmentation of the Political Order*. Boulder, CO: Westview Press, 1989.

Stein, Kenneth. *Heroic Diplomacy: Sadat, Kissinger, Carter, Begin, and the Quest for Arab-Israeli Peace*. London: Routledge, 1999.

Stein, Leonard. *The Balfour Declaration*. New York: Simon and Schuster, 1961.

Stepan, Alfred. *State and Society: Peru in Comparative Perspective*. Princeton, NJ: Princeton University Press, 1978.

Sternhell, Zeev. *The Founding Myths of Israel*. Translated by David Maisel. Princeton, NJ: Princeton University Press, 1998.

Steward, Desmond. *Great Cairo: Mother of the World*. London: Rupert Hart-Davis, 1969.

Stookey, Robert W. *Yemen: The Politics of the Yemen Arab Republic*. Boulder, CO: Westview Press, 1978.

Stork, Joe. "The Oil Weapon." In *Middle East Crucible: Studies on the Arab-Israeli War of October 1973*, edited by Nasser Aruri, pp. 340–85. Wilmette, IL: Medina University Press International, 1975.

Sullivan, Denis. "Extra-State Actors and Privatization in Egypt." In *Privatization and Liberalization in the Middle East*, edited by Iliya Harik and Denis Sullivan, pp. 24–45. Bloomington: Indiana University Press, 1992.

———. "NGOs in Palestine: Agents of Development and Foundation of Civil Society." *Journal of Palestine Studies* 25 (Spring 1996): 93–100.

Taji-Farouki, Suha. "Islamic State Theories and Contemporary Realities." In *Islamic Fundamentalism,* edited by Abdel Salam Sidahmed and Anoushiravan Ehteshami, pp. 35–50. Boulder, CO: Westview Press, 1996.

Tarock, Adam. *The Superpowers' Involvement in the Iran-Iraq War.* Commack, NY: Nova Science, 1998.

Tauber, Eliezer. *The Formation of Modern Syria and Iraq.* London: Frank Cass, 1995.

Taylor, Alan R. *The Superpowers and the Middle East.* Syracuse, NY: Syracuse University Press, 1991.

Telhami, Shibley. "Camp David II: Assumptions and Consequences." *Current History* 100 (January 2001): 10–14.

———. *2006 Annual Arab Public Opinion Survey,* prepared by the University of Maryland with Zogby International, 2006, www.brookings.edu/views/speeches/telhami20070208.pdf.

———. *2008 Annual Arab Public Opinion Survey,* prepared by the University of Maryland with Zogby International, 2008, www.brookings.edu/topics/~/media/Files/events/2008/0414_middle_east/0414_middle_east_telhami.pdf.

———. *2009 Annual Arab Public Opinion Survey,* prepared by the University of Maryland with Zogby International, 2009, www.brookings.edu/~/media/Files/events/2009/0519_arab_opinion/2009_arab_public_opinion_poll.pdf.

Telhami, Shibley, and Michael Barnett. "Introduction: Identity and Foreign Policy in the Middle East." In *Identity and Foreign Policy in the Middle East,* edited by Shibley Telhami and Michael Barnett, pp. 1–25. Ithaca, NY: Cornell University Press, 2002.

Tessler, Mark. *A History of the Israeli-Palestinian Conflict.* Bloomington: Indiana University Press, 1994.

———. "The Origins of Popular Support for Islamic Movements: A Political Economy Analysis." In *Islam, Democracy, and the State in North Africa,* edited by John Entelis, pp. 93–126. Bloomington: Indiana University Press, 1997.

Tibi, Bassam. *Arab Nationalism: A Critical Inquiry.* 2nd ed. Translated by Marion Farouk-Sluglett and Peter Sluglett. New York: St. Martin's Press, 1990.

———. *Arab Nationalism: Between Islam and the Nation-State.* 3rd ed. New York: St. Martin's Press, 1997.

———. *Conflict and War in the Middle East: From Interstate War to New Security.* 2nd ed. New York: St. Martin's Press, 1998.

Todaro, Michael P. *Economic Development.* 6th ed. New York: Addison-Wesley, 1997.

Troeller, Gary. *The Birth of Saudi Arabia: Britain and the Rise of the House of Sa'ud.* London: Frank Cass, 1976.

Turner, Barry, ed. *The Statesman's Yearbook, 2009.* New York: Palgrave Macmillan, 2008.

United Nations. "The Impact of Prolonged Closure on Palestinian Poverty." *United Nations Report,* November 1, 2000.

United Nations Commission on Human Rights. "Mission Report on Israel's Violations of Human Rights in the Palestinian Territories Occupied since 1967." E/CN.4/S-5/3. October 17, 2000.

United Nations Development Program. *Arab Human Development Report, 2002: Creating Opportunities for Future Generations.* New York: United Nations Development Program, 2002.

United Nations Office for the Coordination of Humanitarian Affairs. "Field Update on Gaza from the Humanitarian Coordinator, 24–26 January 2009." East Jerusalem, 2009. www.ochaopt.org/documents/ocha_opt_gaza_human itarian_situation_report_2009_01_14_english.pdf.

U.S. Department of Defense. *Base Structure Report, Fiscal Year 2008 Baseline.* Washington, DC: Department of Defense, 2008.

U.S. Department of State. "Israel and the Occupied Territories." In *Country Report on Human Rights Practices—2000.* Washington, DC: U.S. Department of State, 2001.

———. "Israel and the Occupied Territories." In *Country Report on Human Rights Practices—2001.* Washington, DC: U.S. Department of State, 2002.

———. "Tunisia." In *Country Report on Human Rights Practices—1995.* Washington, DC: U.S. Department of State, 1996.

Vance, Cyrus. *Hard Choices: Critical Years in America's Foreign Policy.* New York: Simon and Schuster, 1983.

Vandewalle, Dirk. "Breaking with Socialism: Economic Liberalization and Privatization in Algeria." In *Privatization and Liberalization in the Middle East,* edited by Iliya Harik and Denis Sullivan, pp. 189–209. Bloomington: Indiana University Press, 1992.

———. "From the New State to the New Era: Toward a Second Republic in Tunisia." *Middle East Journal* 42, no. 4 (1988): 602–20.

———. "Qadhafi's 'Perestroika': Economic and Political Liberalization in Libya." *Middle East Journal* 45, no. 2 (1991): 216–31.

Vatikiotis, P. J. *Nasser and His Generation.* New York: St. Martin's Press, 1978.

Viorst, Milton. "The Road Map to Nowhere." *Washington Quarterly* 26 (Summer 2003): 177–90.

Vital, David. *Zionism: The Crucial Phase.* Oxford: Clarendon Press, 1987.

Vitalis, Robert. *America's Kingdom: Mythmaking on the Saudi Oil Frontier.* Stanford, CA: Stanford University Press, 2007.

von Grunebaum, G. E. *Classical Islam: A History, 600–1258.* Translated by Kathleen Watson. London: George Allen and Unwin, 1970.

von Schreeb, Johan, Hans Rosling, Richard Garfield, Prabhat Jha, et al. "Mortality in Iraq/Authors' Reply." *Lancet* 369 (January 13–19, 2007): 101–5.

Waldner, David. *State Building and Late Development.* Ithaca, NY: Cornell University Press, 1999.

Waterbury, John. "Democracy without Democrats? The Potential for Political Liberalization in the Middle East." In *Democracy without Democrats? The Renewal of Politics in the Muslim World,* edited by Ghassan Salame, pp. 23–47. London: I. B. Tauris, 1994.

———. *The Egypt of Nasser and Sadat: The Political Economy of Two Regimes.* Princeton, NJ: Princeton University Press, 1983.

———. *Exposed to Innumerable Delusions: Public Enterprise and State Power in Egypt, India, Mexico, and Turkey.* New York: Cambridge University Press, 1993.

Weber, Max. *On Charisma and Institution Building.* Chicago: University of Chicago Press, 1968.

Weeks, John. "The Demography of Islamic Nations." *Population Bulletin* 43 (December 1988): 1–53.

Wehrey, Fredric, et al. *The Rise of the Pasdaran: Assessing the Domestic Role of Iran's Islamic Revolutionary Guards Corps.* Santa Monica, CA: Rand, 2009.

Weighill, Marie-Louise. "Palestinians in Lebanon: The Politics of Assistance." *Journal of Refugee Studies* 10, no. 3 (1997): 294–313.

Wells, Tim. *444 Days: The Hostages Remember.* New York: Harcourt Brace Jovanovich, 1985.

Wheatcroft, Andrew. *The Ottomans: Dissolving Images.* London: Penguin Books, 1995.

White House. *The National Security Strategy of the United States, September 2002.* Washington, DC: White House, 2002.

Wiarda, Howard, ed. *Comparative Democracy and Democratization.* Fort Worth, TX: Harcourt, 2002.

Wilber, Donald. *Riza Shah Pahlavi: The Resurrection and Reconstruction of Iran, 1878–1944.* Hicksville, NY: Exposition Press, 1975.

Williams, Ann. *Britain and France in the Middle East and North Africa, 1914–1967.* New York: Macmillan, 1968.

Wilson, Mary C. "The Hashemites, the Arab Revolt, and Arab Nationalism." In *The Origins of Arab Nationalism,* edited by Rashid Khalidi, Lisa Anderson, Muhammad Muslih, and Reeva Simon, pp. 204–21. New York: Columbia University Press, 1991.

Wilson, Peter, and Douglas Graham. *Saudi Arabia: The Coming Storm.* Armonk, NY: M. E. Sharpe, 1994.

Winslow, Charles. *Lebanon: War and Politics in a Fragmented Society.* London: Routledge, 1996.

Wittfogel, Karl. "Hydraulic Civilizations." In *Man's Role in Changing the Face of the Earth,* edited by William Thomas, pp. 152–64. Chicago: Chicago University Press, 1956.

Woodward, Bob. *Plan of Attack.* New York: Simon and Schuster, 2004.

Workman, W. Thom. *The Social Origins of the Iran-Iraq War.* Boulder, CO: Lynne Rienner, 1994.

World Bank. *Country at a Glance, February 2000.* Washington, DC: World Bank, 2000.

———. *Investing in Palestinian Economic Reform and Development.* Washington, DC: World Bank, 2007.

———. *World Development Indicators, 1997.* Washington, DC: World Bank, 1997.

————. *World Development Indicators, 2003.* Washington, DC: World Bank, 2003.

————. *World Development Indicators, 2009.* Washington, DC: World Bank, 2009.

————. *World Development Report, 1999/2000.* Washington, DC: World Bank, 2000.

World Trade Organization. *International Trade Statistics, 2008.* Washington, DC: World Trade Organization, 2008.

Wright, Robin. *The Last Great Revolution: Turmoil and Transformation in Iran.* New York: Vintage Books, 2001.

Yaphe, Judith S. "War and Occupation in Iraq: What Went Right? What Could Go Wrong?" *Middle East Journal* 57 (Summer 2003): 381–99.

Yapp, M.E. *The Making of the Modern Middle East, 1792–1923.* London: Longman, 1987.

Young, Peter. *The Israeli Campaign 1967.* London: William Kimber, 1967.

Youngs, Tim. "The Middle East Crisis: Camp David, the 'Al-Aqsa Intifada' and the Prospects for the Peace Process." United Kingdom House of Commons Library, Research Paper 01/09, January 24, 2001.

Yuchtman-Yaar, Ephraim, and Tamar Herman. "Shas: The Haredi-Dovish Image in a Changing Reality." *Israel Studies* 5, no. 2 (2000): 32–77.

Zabih, Sepehr. *Iran since the Revolution.* Baltimore, MD: Johns Hopkins University Press, 1982.

————. *The Mossadegh Era: Roots of the Iranian Revolution.* Chicago: Lake View Press, 1982.

Zahlan, Rosemarie Said. *The Making of the Modern Gulf States: Kuwait, Bahrain, Qatar, the United Arab Emirates, and Oman.* London: Unwin Hyman, 1989.

Zakaria, Rafiq. *Muhammad and the Quran.* New York: Penguin Books, 1991.

Zureik, Elia. "Being Palestinian in Israel." *Journal of Palestine Studies* 30 (Spring 2001): 88–96.

Index

Abbas, Mahmoud, 253–54
Abbas, Shah (r. 1588–1629), 31–32
Abbasids, 21–25, 35
Abd al-Rahman I, 21
Abdel Aziz ibn Abd el-Rahman (Ibn Saud), 64–68, 317
Abdullah, Saudi Crown Prince/King, 253, 256
Abdullah, son of Sharif Hussein ibn Ali, 43–44, 48, 72, 85
Abdullah II (b. 1962), King Hussein's son, 317–18, 319, 320
Abdulmejid (1839–76), 28
abortion, 378
Abu Bakr (632–34), 20
Abu Dhabi, United Arab Emirates, 294
accommodationists: Palestinian-Israeli conflict, 239–41; state-*ulama*, 336
Achemenids, 12
Adelson, Roger, 39
Adl wal-Ihsan (Justice and Welfare Party) Morocco, 340, 362
Adonis (pen name for Ali Ahmad Said), 337
Afghanistan, 392; Ghalzai Afghans, 32; Mujahedeen guerrillas, 199, 200; Soviet invasion (1979), 160, 170, 199, 200; Taliban, 195, 200–201, 341; U.S. in, 195, 200–201, 208, 252, 355
Aflaq, Michel, 91, 108, 173
Africa: independent nations, 71; Jews from, 219; Mabuto's Zaire, 300; population data, 375, 378; rentierism, 271, 274; revolutions, 140; U.S. targets attacked in, 195, 200; water, 388. *See also* North Africa
age: marriage, 378; population by, 380, 382*table*. *See also* children
agriculture, 6, 13, 260, 265–67; Arab Israeli, 326; domesticated animals, 13; Egypt, 95–96, 265–67, 280, 388; Iran, 60, 62; irrigation, 14, 35, 385, 387, 388; Israeli-Occupied Territories, 238; Italians in Libya, 52; pollution from, 387; population and, 381; Saudi, 6, 65, 267; Turkey, 260
Aherdane, Mahjoub, 333
Ahmad, Imam (Yemen), 115
Ahmadinejad, Mahmoud, 166–69, 307, 348*fig*
Ahmad Shah (Qajar king), 33, 58–59
aid: Soviet, 57, 97, 123–24, 129–30; U.S., 112, 132, 145, 147, 186, 197, 255. *See also* loans
airline violence: hijackings, 125, 391; Iranian jetliner shot down (1988), 181; September 11, 2001, 172, 190, 194–96, 200–202, 204, 341, 391
air pollution, 375, 383–85
Ajami, Fouad, 1, 123, 196, 302, 336
Akkadians, 11
Albright, Madeleine, 248

Text:	10/13 Aldus
Display:	Franklin Gothic
Compositor:	BookMatters, Berkeley
Indexer:	Barbara Roos
Cartographer:	Bill Nelson
Printer and binder:	Sheridan Books, Inc.